Transplanting Commercial Law Reform

Developing a 'Rule of Law' in Vietnam

JOHN GILLESPIE
Monash University, Melbourne, Australia

Routledge
Taylor & Francis Group
LONDON AND NEW YORK

First published 2006 by Ashgate Publishing

2 Park Square, Milton Park, Abingdon, Oxfordshire OX14 4RN
52 Vanderbilt Avenue, New York, NY 10017

Routledge is an imprint of the Taylor & Francis Group, an informa business

First issued in paperback 2020

British Library Cataloguing in Publication Data
Gillespie, John (John Stanley)
Transplanting commercial law reform : developing a 'rule of law' in Vietnam
1. Commercial law - Vietnam 2. Law reform - Vietnam
I. Title
346.5'9707

Library of Congress Cataloging-in-Publication Data
Gillespie, John (John Stanley)
Transplanting commercial law reform : developing a "rule of law" in Vietnam / by John Stanley Gillespie.
p. cm.
Includes bibliographical references and index.
ISBN-13: 978-0-7546-4704-1
ISBN-10: 0-7546-4704-8
1. Rule of law--Vietnam. 2. Law reform--Vietnam. 3. Commercial law-Vietnam. I. Title.

KPV2020.G55 2007
340'.309597--dc22

2006018470

ISBN 978-0-7546-4704-1 (hbk)
ISBN 978-0-367-60389-2 (pbk)

TRANSPLANTING COMMERCIAL LAW REFORM

Contents

List of Tables

Acknowledgements

Writing this book was made possible by abundant institutional and personal support. I began reading and thinking about legal transplantation as a visiting fellow at the Research School of Pacific and Asian Studies at the Australian National University. During subsequent visits I benefited greatly from the many insightful comments made by Ben Kerkvliet and David Marr on early drafts of this book and from the superb Asian Studies collection. I presented many of the ideas in this book at conferences and workshops, where I received invaluable feedback from colleagues and the audience. Since my thesis challenges conventional understandings about the inevitable convergence of legal systems, reactions to my ideas ranged from enthusiastic agreement to outright disbelief. In all cases I benefited from comments, which forced me to recast some arguments, refine others and think through the overall purpose of the work.

I cannot begin to name all the people in Vietnam who have helped me research this book. But particular thanks are due to the many officials, academics, lawyers and entrepreneurs who generously gave their time to set me straight on how Vietnamese understand legal development. I am particularly grateful to the state officials and lawyers who patiently explained the complex and puzzling world of legal drafting and legislative enactment and to the judges and court officials who discussed the development of legal reasoning. I am also grateful to funding from the Australian Research Council that made the field studies in Vietnam possible.

Finally on a personal level, special thanks to Bui Thi Bich Lien and Nguyen Hung Quang for their friendship and support, and to Jo for her love, encouragement and lost weekends.

List of Abbreviations

ADB	Asian Development Bank
AFTA	ASEAN Free Trade Area
APEC	Asia Pacific Economic Cooperation
ASEAN	Association of Southeast Asian Nations
BTA	Bilateral Trade Agreement
CDL	Council of Democracy and Law
CIAC	Central Internal Affairs Commission
CIEM	Centre Institute for Economic Management
CPOC	Central Party Organising Committee
CPV	Communist Party of Vietnam
DRV	Democratic Republic of Vietnam
EL	Enterprise Law
EPF	Equipment Procurement Construction
FDI	foreign direct investment
GCOP	Government Committee on Organisation and Personnel
GTZ	Gesellschaft für Technische Zusammenarbeit
ICP	Indochinese Communist Party
IFC	International Finance Corporation
IP	intellectual property
JICA	Japan International Cooperation Agency
LAB	Legal Activities Board
LNA	Legal Needs Assessment
MPDF	Mekong Project Development Facility
MPI	Ministry of Planning and Investment
NA	National Assembly
ONA	Office of the National Assembly
OPE	Ordinance on Public Employees
PAR	Public Administration Reform
PSF	Public Sector Forum
RV	Republic of Vietnam
SOE	state-owned enterprises
TRIPS	Trade-related Aspects of Intellectual Property Rights
UCCP	Uniform Commercial Credit Practice
UK	United Kingdom
UN	United Nations
UNCDC	United Nations Capital Development Corporation
UNCTAD	United Nations Conference on Trade and Development

UNDP	United Nations Development Programme
UNESCAP	United Nations Economic and Social Commission for Asia and the Pacific
US	United States
USAID	US Agency for International Development
VAT	value-added tax
VBF	Vietnam Business Forum
VCCI	Vietnam Chamber of Commerce and Industry
VCGL	Vietnam General Confederation of Labour
VWP	Vietnamese Worker's Party
WTO	World Trade Organisation

Introduction

Law Reform by Legal Transplantation

Since the collapse of the Soviet bloc in the early 1990s, global social, economic and political interconnections have proliferated, stimulating renewed interest by large trading nations and international agencies in global legal harmonisation.[1] In the opinion of global lawmaking elites, financial and trading stability in developing countries require Western legal structures, such as rights-based commercial law, and above all else the 'rule of law'.[2] By attributing the East Asian financial crisis in 1997 to poor laws and governance procedures, the World Bank reinvigorated pressure for legal harmonisation in developing Asian states.[3]

Against this backdrop of legal globalisation, socialist transforming states in Asia (China and Vietnam) are attempting to use laws and institutions to engineer rapid economic development. Like Japan during the Meiji Restoration (1868), these states are trying to open up, industrialise and become world forces—in short, to catch up with their regional neighbours and the West.[4] Rather than waiting decades to distil commercial law from internal practices they have decided to borrow Western commercial law.[5]

---

1 See Gunther Teubner (1997), '"Global Bukowian": Legal Pluralism in the World Society' in Gunther Teubner (ed.), *Global Law Without a State,* Dartmouth, Aldershot, 1–11; William Twining (2000), *Globalisation and Legal Theory*, Butterworths, London, 1–10; Peter De Cruz (1999), *Comparative Law in a Changing World*, 2nd edn, Cavendish Publishing, London, 488–94.

2 See World Bank (1999), *Entering the 21st Century: World Development Report 1999/2000*, Oxford University Press, Oxford, 23. See generally Ugo Mattei (2003), 'A Theory of Imperial Law: A Study on US Hegemony and the Latin Resistance', 3 *Global Jurist Frontiers* (1), available at <www.bepress.com/gj/frontiers>.

3 The literature is vast but see generally Asian Crisis Home Page <www.stern.nyu/globalmacro/>; and Home Page Second Global Law and Justice Conference; <www4.worldbank.org/legal/ljro1/>.

4 See Masaji Chiba (1997), 'Japan', in Pho-Ling Tan (ed.), *Asian Legal Systems*, Butterworths, Sydney, 99–108.

5 The term Western legal systems is used to denote systems in Western European countries and former European colonies largely settled by Europeans, especially the United States, Australia and Canada. See Ugo Mattei (1997), 'Three Patterns of Law: Taxonomy and Change in the World's Legal Systems', 45 *American Journal of Comparative Law* (5), 12–40.

Most comparative theorists discussing the transfer of laws across national and cultural boundaries draw on North American and European experiences.[6] Working in 'rule of law' societies, they see law in state-centred terms as emanating from the state, uniform for everyone, exclusive of other legal sources and administered by state institutions. Laws consist of institutionalised rules, doctrines and epistemologies.[7] Transplantation theorists rarely consider comparative scholarship about functional equivalents to state-based law in non-Western legal systems. Instead, they assume that legal transfers will have an ordering, 'rule of law' effect in recipient countries. Even internal critics of this strand of comparative law such as Ewald and Legrand, for the most part, do not challenge these main assumptions.[8]

The legal, political and economic factors shaping legal transfers into socialist transforming Asia seem far removed from the conventional debates dominating much comparative discourse in Western industrial countries. The presumption that laws are central to economic and social stability does not readily correspond to elite, but especially non-elite, understandings of the 'role of law' in East Asian societies.

Legal transfers into Asia are under-researched and under-theorised. Most writings discuss Japan, and to a much lesser extent Southeast Asia and China.[9] In comparison, Vietnam has been largely ignored.[10] This is a missed opportunity because this country has absorbed an abundance of imported legal traditions. In successive historical periods—Chinese, French colonial, socialist, and Western commercial—legal ideas have created a layered legal architecture, the new overlaying the old. More significantly for this study, the commercial regulatory regime is growing increasingly complex and sophisticated, with many laws modelled on those from Western countries. Even more importantly, the theoretical basis of law seems to be

6 For a useful review of this literature, see David Nelken (2001), 'Towards a Sociology of Legal Adaptation', in David Nelken and Johannes Feest (eds), *Adapting Legal Cultures*, Hart Publishing, Oxford, 7–51.

7 See William Twining (2000), *supra*, 184–86. See generally Brian Tamanaha (1995), 'An Analytical Map of Social Scientific Approaches to the Concept of Law', 15 *Oxford Journal of Legal Studies*, 501.

8 See, for example, William Ewald (1999), 'What Was it Like to Try a Rat?', 143 *University of Pennsylvania Law Review*, 1889; Pierre Legrand (1995), 'Comparative Legal Studies and Commitment to Theory', 58 *Modern Law Review*, 262.

9 See, for example, Masaji Chiba (1986), 'Introduction', in Masaji Chiba (ed.), *Asian Indigenous Law: An Introduction to Received Law*, KPI, London, 4–6; Andrew Harding (2001), 'Comparative Law and Legal Transplantation in South East Asia: Making Sense of the "Nomic Din"', in Johannes Feest and David Nelken (eds), *Adapting Legal Cultures*, Hart Publishing, Oxford, 199–220; Jianfu Chen (1999), 'Market Economy and the Internationalisation of Civil and Commercial Law in the People's Republic of China', in Kanishka Jayasuriya (ed.), *Law, Capitalism and Power in Asia*, Routledge, London, 69, 76–86.

10 See generally Penelope Nicholson (2000), Borrowing Court Systems: The Experience of the Democratic Republic of Vietnam, 1945–1976, unpublished PhD Thesis, University of Melbourne (which discusses the court system); John Gillespie (2002), 'Transplanted Company Law: An Ideological and Cultural Analysis of Market-Entry in Vietnam', 51 *International Comparative Law Quarterly*, 641 (which discusses corporate governance).

changing as Vietnam cautiously moves away from a socialist-inspired instrumental approach to law towards a conception of the rule of law in which laws bind both citizens and state officials.

This study argues that we cannot easily recognise Vietnam in conventional theories of legal transplantation. They provide misleading criteria for understanding this phenomenon in developing East Asia. If we are to transcend current ways of thinking it is necessary to find better ways to understand how legal transfers interact with host-country systems. What is needed is a theoretical framework in which to describe and analyse the selection, adaptation and implementation of legal transfers in Vietnam.

This study will first attempt to make sense of Vietnam's extraordinary history of commercial legal development by devising a set of working postulates that bring us closer to the processes shaping legal transplantation. It will then apply these postulates to a series of case studies to develop a model that explains how legal transplants are adapted and implemented in Vietnamese (and other developing East Asian) legal and social systems.

What is Legal Transplantation?

Legal transplantation is generally understood as the transfer of laws and institutional structures across geopolitical or cultural borders. It can be imposed or voluntary, encompass entire legal systems or single legal principles and integrate similar or different cultures. Within host countries, legal transfers may permeate state and non-state social institutions, or in the case of many developing countries, reside in state law superimposed on indigenous legal structures. It is increasingly linked to international legal harmonisation projects sponsored by large trading nations and international donor agencies.

Legal Transfers are not New

For millennia, legal systems around the world have developed through legal transfers. Some of the best-documented transplantation occurred during the military expansion of the Roman Empire.[11] Roman jurists equated *ius gentium*, which applied to colonised people, with *ius naturale* (law that should be observed by humanity).[12] They considered 'universal laws of nature' capable of linguistic expression through universal legal codes. In the belief that differences between legal systems denied universal human attributes, natural law codes based on Roman morality were superimposed over indigenous cultural beliefs and practices.

11 See Ellen Goodman (1995), *The Origins of the Western Legal Tradition*, Federation Press, Sydney, 131–36.

12 See Barry Nicholas (1962), *An Introduction to Roman Law*, Clarendon Press, Oxford, 54–59; Ellen Goodman (1995), *The Origins of Western Legal Tradition: From Thales to Tudors*, Federation Press, Sydney, 131–39.

Later, until its displacement by rights-based law over the last two centuries, natural law legitimatised European colonisation of non-Christian peoples.[13] According to natural law doctrine, all humans had a right to salvation—and colonial laws were in theory not permitted to abrogate indigenous cultural practices and laws. French legal transplantation to Vietnam frequently ignored this tolerant formulation and invested central authorities with power to regulate or prohibit local customs (see Chapter 2).

Entire Systems Transfers

The substance of legal transfers varies enormously. At one extreme, the European conquest and colonisation of North America and Australia involved not only the displacement of indigenous populations and cultures, but also re-engineering the natural and built environments. The agricultural economy of northern Europe, including livestock, pasture, plant and tree species, displaced and supplanted indigenous species.[14] In addition to agriculture, colonists transplanted state institutions, religious orders, a mercantile economy and architectural preferences. For colonists surrounded by a facsimile of Europe, borrowing legal systems appeared both plausible and desirable.[15] Theoretical and moral objections to imposing foreign laws on indigenous populations were conveniently removed by the *terra nullius* doctrine that denied pre-existing legal entitlements. It was only after independence that a distance in legal perspective from the 'motherland' slowly emerged.[16]

More recently, extensive legal transplantation took place between West and East Germany following reunification.[17] Not only laws, but also legal personnel including judges, court officials and lawyers from western Germany were seconded to eastern Germany to administer the transplanted Western system.

Legal Transfers and Superpower Hegemony

Large-scale legal transfers are possible without colonisation or national reunification. During the 'Cold War', the USSR and United States used legal transfers as a weapon in their struggle for military and political supremacy. The nexus between political hegemony and law is well illustrated by legal transfers into the divided Vietnam from 1954 until 1975. As Chapter 2 discusses in more detail, Soviet legal ideas

---

13 See Michael Barry Hooker (1986), *The Laws of South East Asia*, Volume II, Butterworths, Singapore, 28–47. See generally H. McCoubrey (1987), *The Development of Naturalist Legal Theory*, Croom Helm, London.

14 See Tim Flannery (2001), *The Eternal Frontier*, Text Publishing, Melbourne, 312–48.

15 For a discussion linking Western law to colonization, see Peter Fitzpatrick (1992), *The Mythology of Modern Law*, Routledge, London, 107–11.

16 See Elizabeth Mensch (1982), 'The History of Mainstream Legal Thought', in David Kairys (ed.), *The Politics of Law: A Progressive Critique*, Pantheon Books, New York, 19–26.

17 Norbert Horn (1991), 'The Lawful German Revolution: Privatization and Market Economy in a Re-Unified Germany', 39 *American Journal of Comparative Law*, 725.

began influencing the early communist moment in Vietnam in the 1920s. Large-scale legal transplantation began after the nation was divided in 1954 and irreconcilable political fault lines emerged between the Democratic Republic of Vietnam (DRV) in the North and the Republic of Vietnam in the South.

In the North, the Soviet Union became both the institutional model and source of most law. Legal transplantation was comprehensive. The DRV imported an entire political-legal system including ideology, political and legal institutions, codes and procedures. Urban colonial capitalism and village subsistence agriculture were partially transformed into a Vietnamese version of a Soviet command economy. Thousands of Vietnamese were sent to Eastern Bloc countries from the 1960s until 1990 to learn the skills needed to manage and implement the imported system.

Although the Republic of Vietnam in the southern half retained much of the French colonial system, from 1954 to 1973 it increasingly succumbed to US legal influence. Inspired by US legal reforms in Japan, Latin America and elsewhere in the 'free world', Vietnamese scholars and jurists were sent to the United States for legal training and US academic institutions conducted training courses in Vietnam. Following reunification in 1975, Soviet law was transplanted by the victorious North to the South.

After the Soviet Union collapsed, US legal hegemony entered a new phase. Francis Fukuyama in his influential book *The End of History and the Last Man*, published in 1992, epitomised the euphoria that greeted the demise of Soviet communism and the perceived victory of Western liberal democracy. As he put it, 'for a very large part of the world, there is now no ideology with pretensions to universality that is in a position to challenge liberal democracy and universal principles of legitimacy other than the sovereignty of the people'.[18] A decade later his triumphalism seems premature. Chinese and Vietnamese communist regimes are still firmly entrenched and various orthodox Islamic organisations are mounting a radical challenge to liberal democratic values.

Undeterred by a growing literature showing the difficulties in transferring commercial legal models across cultural, political and economic borders, there is a largely US discourse that postulates an 'end of history' for competing legal systems.[19] For example, in discussing international corporate governance laws, some authors assert that 'over time, then, the standard [US] model is likely to win the competitive struggle ... because no important competitors to the standard model of corporate governance remain persuasive today'.[20] They dismiss longstanding European corporate governance regimes that privilege worker and stakeholder representation

18 Francis Fukuyama (1992), *The End of History and the Last Man*, H. Hamilton, London, 45.

19 See Brian Cheffins (1999), 'Current Trends in Corporate Governance: Going from London to Milan via Toronto', 10 *Duke Journal of Comparative and International Law*, 5; Henry Hansmann and Reinier Kraakman (2001), 'The End of History for Corporate Law', 89 *Georgetown Law Review*, 439.

20 Hansmann and Kraakman (2001), *supra*, 451, 454.

on boards of directors as less economically efficient than the deregulated US model. As a corollary, they assert that the US corporate governance model should become the international standard.

Commentators querying legal harmonisation point to evidence that corporate governance regimes in Britain, France and Germany, as well as in East Asia and Latin America, function effectively with different legal, political and economic logics.[21] They also show that attempts to transplant US corporate governance to the Russian Federation failed to induce corporate accountability and other anticipated benefits.[22] Further challenging the globalisation thesis, recent comparative studies suggest that, after an initial period of convergence, transplanted corporate regimes increasingly diverged from the original template.[23]

Some commentators attribute the trivialisation of regional economic, cultural and political differences found in much legal harmonisation literature to a conscious strategy to promote the laws and legal institutions required by liberal capitalism.[24] In discussing attempts by US agencies to influence legal development in Latin America, Yves Dezalay and Bryant Garth pondered why the 'law and development' movement in the 1960s is dismissed in US literature as a failure (discussed below), whereas more recent but equally uninformed projects are considered more successful.[25] They conclude that perceptions about the possibility and desirability of legal transplantation are inextricably bound up in broader contests for political and economic power.

Law and Development Reforms

Legal transplantation into developing East Asia has been profoundly influenced by 'law and development' movement. The early literature drew from Max Weber's causal links between industrial development and the 'rule of law'—one cannot proceed without the other.[26] Developing countries were urged to copy the 'modern'

21 See Curtis J. Milhaupt (1996), 'A Relational Theory of Japanese Corporate Governance: Contract Culture and Rule of Law', 37 *Harvard International Law Review* (1), 3; Katharina Pistor *et al.* (2002), 'The Evolution of Corporate Law: A Cross-Country Comparison', 23 *University of Pennsylvania Journal of International Economic Law*, 791.

22 See Bernard Black *et al.* (2000), 'Russian Privatisation and Corporate Governance: What Went Wrong?', 52 *Stanford Law Review*, 1731, 1752–57.

23 See Katharina Pistor *et al.* (2002), *supra*, 865–66.

24 See Douglas Branson (2001), 'The Very Uncertain Prospect of "Global" Convergence in Corporate Governance', 34 *Cornell International Law Journal*, 321.

25 See Yves Dezalay and Bryant Garth (2001), 'The Import and Export of Law and Legal Institutions: International Strategies in National Palace Wars' in Johannes Feest and David Nelken (eds), *Adapting Legal Cultures*, Hart Publishing, Oxford, 241–56.

26 For overviews of the law and development movement, see David Trubek (1985), 'Reconstructing Max Weber's Sociology of Law', 37 *Stanford Law Review*, 919, 920–26; Sally Ewing (1987), 'Formal Justice and the Spirit of Capitalism: Max Weber's Sociology of Law', 21 *Law Society Review* (3), 487, 487–500; Brian Tamanaha (1995), 'The Lessons of Law-and-Development Studies', 89 *American Journal of International Law*, 470.

institutional features of Western countries, such as judicial independence, legal education, the rule of law and especially the enactment of rights-based commercial laws. But law and development scholars conveniently ignored Weber's cautioning that law develops over time by interacting with local socioeconomic environments—processes that induce path-dependent development.[27]

Informed by 'Third World' development failures and a 'home-grown' US crisis of faith in the ability of Western law to induce political plurality, two leading 'law and development' exponents recanted. In a singularly influential article published in 1974, David Trubek and Marc Galanter accused Western legal assistance of 'ethnocentricity and naiveté' in assuming that transplanted Western law could be grafted onto host-country institutions and social conditions.[28] In their estimation these movements sought to impose a historically contingent legal system based on the rule of law and liberal democracy, values that were not easily received by other societies.

Debates about the crisis in the law and development movement were informed by a broader disenchantment among Western scholars with neoliberal economic prescriptions for reform. 'Basic Needs' theorists, for example, believed that neoliberal markets produced harsh outcomes because states did not redirect welfare income to the poor.[29] However, like neoliberal theorists, they urged states to make markets work for the poor by eliminating institutional blockages.

Transforming institutionalists presented a more radical challenge to neoliberalism.[30] Using neo-Marxist theory, they argued there were no 'natural' or 'free' markets and developing countries needed to address their dependency on globally dominant economic classes. From this perspective, legal harmonisation should be tightly controlled because it favours stronger nations.[31] Other theorists gave indigenous elites more credit for shaping their own destinies. What united these approaches was the belief that development theory must focus on the way the legal

---

27 See David Trubek (1972), 'Toward a Social Theory of Law: An Essay on the Study of Law and Development', 82 *Yale Law Journal* (1), 1 (distinguishes Weber's theories from the law and development movement).

28 See David Trubek and Marc Galanter (1974), 'Scholars in Self-Estrangement: Some Reflections on the Crisis in Law and Development Studies in the United States', *Wisconsin Law Review*, 1062, 1080–83; also see John Merryman (1977), 'Comparative Law and Social Change: On the Origins, Style, Decline and Revival of the Law and Development Movement', 25 *American Journal of Comparative Law*, 457.

29 Gunnar Myrdal (1968), *Asian Drama: An Inquiry into the Poverty of Nations*, Pantheon, New York.

30 See Dietrich Reuschemeyer and Peter Evens, 1985 'The State and Economic Transformation' in Peter Evens, Dietrich Reuschemeyer and Theodora Evens (eds), *Bring the State Back In*, Cambridge University Press, New York, 44.

31 See Mwangala Kamuwanga (1987), 'The Teaching of International Trade and Investment Law in a "Law and Development" Context': A View from Zambia', 5 *Third World Legal Studies*, 131.

order shapes institutions and fosters the emergence of elites who use markets for their own ends.

Undeterred by Western theoretical scepticism, interest in market-based legal systems increased in developing Asia (including Vietnam) during the 1990s, particularly after the East Asian financial crisis in 1997. This new wave of legal transplantation was supported by 'law and governance' and legal harmonisation projects backed by international agencies such as the World Bank, Asian Development Bank and bilateral donors (for example, USAID).[32]

Douglass North famously speculated that transplanted Western commercial laws require compatible dispute resolution forums, debt enforcement and bankruptcy mechanisms.[33] His reasoning persuaded legal assistance programs in socialist-transforming East Asia (including Vietnam) to concentrate resources to refashion (capacity building) institutions into a Western legal mould.[34] As we shall see in subsequent chapters, legal aid programs in Vietnam aim to perfect legislative drafting techniques and strengthen the courts and legal training.[35] Strong theoretical and empirical evidence that laws are not bare sets of prepositional rules and that legal transplants are most likely to produce desired outcomes in culturally compatible countries have not appreciably influenced the thinking of many foreign donors.[36]

Legal Evolution

Legal harmonisation projects are predicated on an evolutionary convergence theory. According to this thesis, legal change is a 'natural' Darwinian process in which less developed systems will evolve towards the more mature ones.[37] Since Western legal systems are more systematised than those in East Asia, the logical corollary

---

32 See Asian Development Bank, *Bulletin on Law and Policy Reform*, published from 1995 until 2002. Also see Katharina Pistor and Philip Wellons (1999), *The Role of Law and Legal Institutions in Asian Economic Development 1960–1995*, Oxford University Press, Oxford, 63–112.

33 New Institutional Economic theorists such as Douglass North and Joe Stiglitz have been especially influential in reshaping multilateral development projects. See Douglass North (1995), *The New Institutional Economics and Third World Development*, Routledge, London, 17–27; Joe Stiglitz (1999), Whither Reform? Ten Years of the Transition, unpublished paper presented at the Annual World Bank Conference on Development Economics, Washington, DC, 28–30 April. Also see W.W. Rostow (1990), *Stages of Economic Growth: A Non-Communist Manifesto*, Cambridge University Press, New York.

34 See Randall Peerenbom (2002), *China's Long March towards the Rule of Law*, Cambridge University Press, Cambridge, 150–53.

35 See Per Bergling (1997), 'Theory and Reality in Legal Co-operation: The Case of Vietnam', in Per Sevastik (ed.), *Legal Assistance to Developing Countries*, Kluwer Law International, Dordrecht, 64–66.

36 See Carol Rose (1998), 'The "New" Law and Development Movement in the Post-Cold War Era: A Vietnam Case Study', 32 *Law and Society Review* (1), 93, 126–35.

37 See Lawrence Friedman (1969), 'On Legal Development', 24 *Rutgers Law Review* (11), 26–64. For an evolutionary account of legal reform in post-communist Russia, see

is that East Asian systems will evolve or converge towards the West. This view has gained prominence with the emergence of globalised culture brought about by increased international communication, travel, education and entertainment. It is also hotly contested by those who point to the narrow range of elites participating in globalisation and the many examples of international cultural divergence.[38]

Legal evolution may occur when international treaties bind two or more nations to common (generally Western) legal rules.[39] Members of the World Trade Organisation (WTO), for example, are required to harmonise their domestic law with a wide range of customs, trading and intellectual property conventions and protocols. Much commercial legislation in developing East Asia, including Vietnam, is drafted with the objective of complying with WTO or other trade agreements. Legal harmonisation projects of this kind are often supported by international donor agencies.

Global business transactions are another potential catalyst for legal evolution.[40] According to Lawrence Friedman, businessmen and practising lawyers are the contemporary 'carriers of transnational law' and 'there is a tremendous amount of globalisation in businesses and the economy, and the law follows along'.[41] Globetrotting lawyers, financial advisers and related professions transfer laws to protect capitalist investors throughout the world. Western (primarily Anglo-American) commercial law is also globalised by 'offshore' dispute resolution centres.

Pressure for legal evolution is felt strongest in countries that are integrated into US and European global trading, investment and legal networks. Subsequent chapters consider whether Vietnam is receptive to this form of legal transfer.

Coming to Terms with Terms

Much confusion has been generated in the literature concerning legal transfers by the multiple terms and metaphors used to describe and explain this process.

Gianmaria Ajani (1995) 'By Chance and Prestige: Legal Transplants in Russia and Eastern Europe', 43 *American Journal of Comparative Law*, 93–99.

38 See David Nelken (2001), 'Towards a Sociology of Legal Adaptation', in Johannes Feest and David Nelken (eds), *Adapting Legal Cultures*, Hart Publishing, Oxford, 31–35.

39 See Lawrence Friedman (1996), 'On the Merging Sociology of Transnational Law', 32 *Stanford Journal of International Law*, 65, 70–72.

40 See David Trubek, Yves Dezalay, Robert Buchanan and John Davis (1993), *Global Restructuring and the Law: The Internationalisation of Legal Fields and the Creation of Transnational Arenas*, Working Paper on the Political Economy of Legal Change No. 1, University of Wisconsin, Madison, Wisconsin; John Merryman and David Clark (eds) (1978), *Comparative Law: Western European and Latin American Legal Systems: Cases and Materials*, Bobbs Merrill, Indianapolis, 285–342.

41 Lawrence Friedman (1996), 'Borders: On the Emerging Sociology of Transnational Law', 32 *Stanford Law Review*, 65, 67. Also see Yves Dezalay and Bryant Garth (1996), *Dealing in Virtue: International Commercial Arbitration and the Construction of a Transnational Legal Order*, University of Chicago Press, Chicago, 6.

Expressions such as legal harmonisation, unification, borrowing and convergence emphasise the compatibility and co-evolution of legal systems. Other terms, such as legal transplantation, are used to denote the transfer of law or legal systems into host countries.[42] When used by theorists such as Alan Watson, transplantation implies that legal ideas have taken root in foreign legal terrain.[43] But others use this metaphor with more circumspection.[44] They distinguish 'mechanical transplants', which transfer easily, from organic transplants, which require careful selection and maintenance to flourish in new legal environments. Either way, this term reminds us that transplant viability must refer in some way to legal behaviour in the recipient country. Otherwise there is no transplant, only an indigenous law containing foreign ideas.

Gunther Teubner used the term 'legal irritants' to avoid what he says is 'the false dichotomy' of repulsion or interaction that is the result of thinking with the legal transplant metaphor.[45] His term is useful in suggesting that once a law is transferred into a different system it does not automatically displace existing legal meanings and practices. Rather, it triggers a new set of unpredictable choices and outcomes.

Yet, as a metaphor, 'legal irritants' is limited by some conceptual shortcomings. It is suggestive about the processes that occur once law has transferred into a new system, but it says little about how, why and when foreign laws are selected for law reform. David Nelken goes further in suggesting that, as metaphors, 'legal transplantation' and 'legal irritants' share much in common, since they both 'direct our gaze mainly to the regulatory problems of trying to use law to change other legal and social orders'.[46]

It is suggested that some commentators pay too much attention to the metaphors describing legal transfers. Metaphors are after all only suggestive. Since there is little possibility of finding one term that describes all types of legal transfers, this study uses a variety of terms to denote particular stages in the transfer process.

---

42 See Alan Watson (1993), *Legal Transplants: An Approach to Comparative Law*, Second ed., University of Georgia Press, Athens, Georgia, 21.

43 See Alan Watson (1985), *The Evolution of Law*, John Hopkins University Press, Baltimore.

44 See, for example, Otto Kahn-Freund (1974), 'On the Uses and Misuses of Comparative Law', 37 *Modern Law Review*, 1–27.

45 Gunther Teubner (1998), 'Legal Irritants: Good Faith in British Law or How Unifying Law Ends up in New Divergences', 61 *Modern Law Review* (1), 11, 12.

46 See David Nelken (2001), 'Beyond the Metaphor of Legal Transplants? Consequences of Autopoietic Theory for the Study of Cross-Cultural Legal Adaptation' in Jiři Priban and David Nelken (eds), *Law's New Boundaries: The Consequences of Legal Autopoiesis*, Ashgate, Aldershot, 269–75.

Legal Transplantation into East Asia

Studies show that commercial legislation in contemporary East Asia has been drawn primarily from Western rather than indigenous legal sources.[47] Although the history of transplantation is as complex as the region, three basic patterns are discernable.

First, Myanmar, Malaysia, Hong Kong and Singapore received British commercial legislation and common law during the period of British colonial rule.[48] Similarly, the Dutch in Indonesia, French in Indochina, and Spanish and Americans in the Philippines imported civil law and jurisprudence. Following independence, colonial transplants were amended and substantially revised. For many decades after independence the Indonesian Constitution 1945, for example, retained colonial law provided it did not offend constitutional principles.[49] The former British colonies also retained many transplanted British law and legal institutions, although post-independence political and cultural imperatives have to varying degrees slowly changed both the substance and jurisprudential basis of law in these countries.[50]

Second, and contrasting with the colonial experience, legal transplantation elsewhere in the East was a matter of choice. Frequently motivated by a desire to 'catch up' with developed countries, independent East Asian states imitated, by importing, the substantive laws and legal institutions of more economically developed counties. Fearing economic isolation and political domination, the Japanese during the Meiji Restoration imported European, primarily Prussian, civil law and state institutions.[51] As a colonising power, the Japanese later transplanted their laws to Korea and Taiwan.[52] Both China and Thailand were never entirely colonised, but they too imported continental civil law systems.[53]

Third, following their Marxist-Leninist revolutions, China and the Indochinese states of Vietnam, Cambodia and Laos chose radically different paths to those taken elsewhere in the region. In China's case, Western commercial law was rejected in favour of a socialist legal system imported from the Soviet Union. It was not until

---

47 The Asian Development Bank commissioned the most comprehensive survey. See Pistor and Wellons (1999), *supra*, 36–52, 56–61.

48 See generally Andrew Harding (2001), *supra*, 199–219.

49 See Timothy Lindsey (1997), 'Paradigms, Paradoxes and Possibilities: Towards an Understandings of Indonesia's Legal System', in Veronica Taylor (ed.), *Asian Laws Through Australian Eyes*, Law Book Company, Sydney, 96–103; Charles Himawan (1997), 'Indonesia', in Pho-Ling Tan (ed.), *Asian Legal Systems*, Butterworths, Sydney, 223–33.

50 See, for example, Khoo Boo Teik (1999), 'Between Law and Politics: the Malaysian Judiciary since Independence', in Kanishkha Jayasuriya (ed.), *Law, Capitalism and Power in Asia*, Routledge, London, 205.

51 For Japanese legal history, see Masaji Chiba (1986), 'Three-Level Structure of Law in Contemporary Japan, The Shinto Society', in Masaji Chiba (ed.), *supra*, 301–13.

52 Dae-Kyu Yoon (1997), 'Korea', in Pho-Ling Tan (ed.), *Asian Legal Systems*, Butterworths, Sydney, 165; Taysheng Wang (1997), 'Taiwan', in Pho-Ling Tan (ed.), *Asian Legal Systems*, Butterworths, Sydney, 131–32.

53 See Jianfu Chen (1999), *Towards an Understanding of Chinese Law, Its Nature and Development*, Kluwer Law International, The Hague.

Deng Xiaoping's economic reforms in the late 1970s that the importation of Western commercial laws (sometimes via East Asian countries) resumed.[54]

Legal reforms in Indochina followed a similar trajectory. Following independence from France, colonial laws and legal institutions were gradually replaced with socialist laws and institutions largely derived from the former Soviet Union. With the demise of Soviet influence and subsequent dismantling of central command economic planning, lawmakers in these countries are now attempting to graft imported market legal principles onto administrative systems that retain high levels of state management.[55] Unlike transforming socialist counties in Eastern Europe, command institutions did not entirely collapse but rather are adapting to market conditions.

Large-scale commercial legal importation did not begin in Vietnam until the Sixth Party Congress in 1986 (see Chapter 2). Lawmakers initially looked to socialist countries for inspiration. They imported, with a few minor changes, non-commercial laws like the *Penal Code 1986* and *Family Law 1986* from the Soviet Union. Even the first wave of commercial laws, comprising the *Law on Foreign Investment 1987*, *Land Law 1988* and *Ordinance on Economic Contracts 1989* were primarily based on Chinese legal models. Only in areas where China lacked appropriate experience were laws imported from the capitalist West. For example, the *Law on Companies 1990* was based on French law.

The next reform period coincided with the formal recognition of a mixed-market economy in the 1992 Constitution. Lawmakers began to borrow directly from Western legal sources. As international economic integration gained momentum after the ratification of the US–Vietnam Bilateral Trade Agreement in 2001, both the pace and extent of commercial legal borrowing increased. Since most Western commercial law was transplanted after 1991, the period 1992–2005 forms the main focus of this study.

This brief overview reveals a legal history in Vietnam that is rich in legal transplants. Laws from the world's major legal families have been introduced through invasion, colonisation and, more recently, voluntary adoption. Just as importantly, Vietnam's experimentation with market-oriented laws is not yet two decades old. Contrasting with the multiple transfers, overlays and statutory amendments in some other East Asian countries, legal borrowing is still fresh in the minds of lawmakers and has not yet become clouded by decades of amendments, reforms and myth-making. As such, Vietnamese legal development offers many opportunities to study legal transplantation.

---

54 See Pitman Potter, 1999 'The Chinese Legal System: Continuing Commitment to the Primacy of State Power', *The China Quarterly* (159), 673, 674–78; Carol Jones (1994), 'Capitalism, Globalisation and Rule of Law: An Alternative Trajectory of Legal Change in China', 3 *Social and Legal Studies*, 195, 204–10.

55 See John Gillespie (1997), 'Bureaucratic Control of Business Regulation in Vietnam', in Veronica Taylor (ed.), *Asian Laws Through Australian Eyes*, Law Book Company, Sydney, 391–98.

The discussion so far raises numerous questions about the processes guiding legal transplantation into Vietnam. For example, with so many layers of legal borrowing, is there such a thing as indigenous Vietnamese legal thinking? Does Vietnam have a usable legal past? How are legal ideas from the past recycled and integrated with new legal thinking? These questions are not easily answered by conventional theories of legal transplantaion. If we are to transcend current ways of thinking we need to develop a theorectical framework in which to describe and analyse how legal transfers interact with legal and social systems in Vietnam.

Conceptualising Legal Transplantation

The way we understand law and legal change influences the way we understand and conceptualise legal transplantation. Most discussions about legal transplantation have polarised around convergence, divergence and legal evolutionary hypotheses.' Montesquieu captured the uncertain relationship between imported law and local environmental and social conditions when he opined that rules of law only coincidentally produce the same behavioural outcomes in different societies.[56] Underlying this view is the belief that laws change and respond to external forces, such as the workings of the market, political ideology, and cultural traits like individualism. Some theorists within this tradition caution that legal transplantation is just as likely to produce divergence as convergence in legal practice, because legal transfers do not transmit the 'whole law'.[57] Otto Kahn-Freund offered the valuable insight that 'there are degrees of transferability'.[58] Since all laws have 'de-coupled' to some extent from their social roots, he believed that legal transplantation across cultural boundaries was difficult but theoretically possible.[59]

Convergence theorists, on the other hand, contend that nation-states are enmeshed in an inevitable and accelerating shift towards internationalisation and globalisation. Ever-increasing telecommunications, urbanisation, international investment and trade are credited with collapsing regional differences that in the past inhibited legal transplantation.[60] For comparativists such as Rene de Groot, 'it is likely that the legal systems of the European States will form one great legal family with uniform

56 See Montesquieu (1970), *De L'Esprit des Lois* (The Spirit of Laws), reprint ed. J.P. Mayer & A.P. Kerr, Livre I Gallimard, Paris, chapter 3.

57 See Pierre Legrand (1997), 'The Impossibility of 'Legal Transplants', 4 *Maastricht Journal of European Comparative Law*, 111, 119.

58 See O. Kahn-Freund (1974), 'On Uses and Misuses of Comparative Law', 37 *Modern Law Review*1, 6, 7–11, 27; Otto Kahn-Freund (1978), 'Common Law and Civil Law-Imaginary and Real Obstacles to Assimilation', in Mauro Cappelletti (ed.), *New Perspectives for a Common Law Europe*, Sijhoff, Leyden, 160.

59 Ibid.

60 These views are summarised in K. Pistor and P. Wellons (1999), *The Role of Law and Legal Institutions in Asian Economic Development 1960–1995*, Oxford University Press, Oxford, 14, 36–40.

or strongly similar rules'.[61] Legal evolutionists believe that globalisation 'forces' legal systems to evolve towards the most 'efficient' solutions.[62] Still others, such as Gunther Teubner, claim that *lex mercatoria* has de-coupled from its cultural roots to create a stateless, globalised commercial law.[63]

The underlying disagreement is whether successful legal transfers need to reflect or comport with internal social forces—the 'felt needs of society'.[64] This debate is preoccupied with law's 'relative autonomy' from society and leaves unanswered many questions about how legal transplants interact with domestic laws and institutions and recipient countries. It also reflects historically conditioned state-centred approaches to law that may not necessarily pertain to other parts of the world.

Conventional transplantation theories do not adequately account for Vietnam's uneven history of legal borrowing. Given the importance of transplantation to legal development in Vietnam, there is a pressing need for theoretical alternatives that address local attitudes and approaches to law and institutional change. For example, alternative theories must assess the interaction between Western rights-based laws and institutions with Marxist-Leninist state ideology, polycentric political and legal power, network capitalism and cultural ambivalence towards law and legal processes.[65]

This study explores the usefulness of another analytical tradition that sees law in terms of patterns of behaviour or discourse.[66] Adherents, recognise that regulation, especially in non-Western societies, is frequently de-centred, having little or nothing to do with state rules and institutions. Contrasting with conventional comparative analysis, this tradition locates legal transfers in a much broader regulatory context that takes into account state and non-state regulation.

The Organisation of this Book

The theoretical discussion in Chapter 1 develops a methodological framework to guide research into legal transplantation into Vietnam. Three working postulates have been synthesised from the legal transplantation literature. According to the first working postulate, transplant viability increases where the ideological content

---

61 Rene de Groot (1992), 'European Education in the 21st Century', in Bruno de Witte and Caroline Forder (eds), *The Common Law of Europe and the Future of Legal Education*, Kluwer Law and Taxation Publishers, Maastricht, 54.

62 See Lawrence Friedman (1996), *supra*, 65.

63 See Gunther Teubner (1997), *supra*, 3–22.

64 See Ugo Mattei (1994), 'Efficiency in Legal Transplants: An Essay in Comparative Law and Economics', 14 *International Review of Law and Economics*, 3, 4.

65 Network capitalism is used to describe an economy that is predominately based on personal connections with state authorities as opposed to the atomistic market model presupposed in most Western legal theories.

66 This analytical tradition is derived from normative theorist such as Malinowski and Geertz, or systems theorists such as Luhmann (see Chapter 1).

of transplanted laws is compatible with the dominant ideology shaping legal and economic thinking in recipient countries. The second working postulate asserts that transplant viability increases where imported laws comport with power-distribution structures in recipient countries. Or, as Kahn-Freund put it, transplanted laws are sensitive to the ways legislators, bureaucrats and judges use state power to make and enforce law. The third working postulate suggests that non-state pressure groups influence the selection and implementation of foreign laws.

Chapter 2 describes Vietnam's long history of legal transplantation. It starts with the transfer of neo-Confucian notions of *li* (moral persuasion and adherence to rituals) and *fa* (rule through laws), which together with Chinese-inspired imperial statecraft formed the central organising principles for the pre-colonial legal system. It then explains why French colonial legality was so easily swept aside by Soviet-inspired revolutionary reforms. The chapter argues that pre-modern moral values were conflated with Marxist-Leninism to produce a revolutionary morality that guided state rule until more emphasis was placed on law-based governance during the 1980s. Imported Western commercial laws overlay institutional structures and epistemologies that are only slowly responding to right-based market reforms.

Chapter 3 applies the first working postulate to assess whether Marxist-Leninist state ideology in Vietnam impedes the transplantation of commercial laws. The discussion analyses changes in political-legal ideology in Vietnam and shows that new ideological thinking has flowered under the *nha nuoc phap quyen* (law-based state) doctrine introduced by the 1992 Constitution. It makes the significant finding that conflicting ideologies do not inevitably constrain legal borrowing. In fact, some degree of ideological confusion and discord may actually create space for imported ideas. This means that neoliberal ideals supporting property and contractual rights are not necessarily blocked by Marxist-Leninist ideology that privileges party power over law and state interests over private interests.

Chapter 4 uses the second working postulate to examine the interdependencies and competition between the party and state. More particularly, it explores whether communist party 'leadership' over state institutions creates a regulatory context that is inimical to the private rights embedded in imported commercial laws. The chapter concludes that, while party leadership has the capacity to destabilise imported private commercial rights, a limited rule of law in the commercial arena may advance party objectives.

Chapter 5 applies the second working postulate to determine how state lawmaking affects legal transplantation. Case studies contribute the insight that legislative drafters actively interpret and co-opt ideas in the official discourse to achieve strategic objectives. They further suggest the state's receptiveness to imported legal ideas depends on whether official epistemologies are closed and self-referential, or open and willing to engage imported ideas. In short, there is a powerful domestic political, epistemological and structural logic to legal borrowing.

In Chapter 6 the second working postulate is used again to assess how state agencies implement imported laws. Case studies show that imported commercial rights are negotiated in three-way contests between elite-level officials, local-level officials and businesses. They are also mediated in courtroom disputes between party, state and private interests. Evidence suggests that dialogical exchanges between legal officials and entrepreneurs and lawyers advocating commercial rights, are slowly making imported legal ideas the frame of reference for implementing the law.

Chapter 7 applies the third working postulate to evaluate how non-state pressure groups exercise leverage over the selection and implementation of foreign laws. Case studies show the 'whole' meaning of law is more likely to transfer intact when transplantation takes place between like-minded groups, such as foreign donors and the foreign educated lawmaking elite in Vietnam. They also reveal a strong correlation between socioeconomic status and influence over lawmaking. Evidence for this proposition is found in the increasing tendency for imported laws to reflect the interests of powerful pressure groups, leaving politically-unconnected entrepreneurs to self-regulate through hybridised relational transactions.

Chapter 8 considers the social demand for imported commercial laws. Drawing information from a survey of 60 private companies operating in five different industrial sectors, the discussion shows how self-regulation through private relational transactions is the most important mechanism controlling business behaviour. State laws and bureaucratic regulation primarily assumed importance when domestic entrepreneurs sought state privileges such as access to international markets or tenders. But there is some evidence that local entrepreneurs selectively used imported laws to augment shortcomings in the self-regulatory framework. The chapter asserts that foreign investors have the most to gain, at least in the short term, from imported commercial laws.

Chapter 9 concludes that it is not possible to model legal transplantation determinatively—there are simply too many variables to support testable propositions of cause and effect. Nevertheless it is possible to infer from case studies an analytical model to guide further research into legal transplantation. By analysing legal transplantation through state and non-state regulatory conversations, the model avoids the limiting confines of convergence, divergence theories, and globalisation paradigms.

Chapter 1

Developing a Legal Transplantation Theory

Introduction

We have seen that Vietnamese legal reformers aspire to 'catch up' with neighbouring countries by developing a modern legal system based on Western legal models. In borrowing Western commercial law, they have embarked on a social experiment first begun in Japan during the mid-nineteenth century and later copied by China and decolonising East Asian states. Attempts to understand legal transplantation into this region are profoundly influenced by the different ways socio-legal theories assess the relationship between law and society. Different theories give rise to different answers to basic questions, such as what is the connection between imported law and local culture? Can laws evolving in specific historical conditions transfer to different cultural settings? How is transplant viability determined? This chapter first critiques the theories explaining these issues. It then synthesises a series of working postulates that focus analysis in subsequent chapters on the ideology, state institutions and non-state pressure groups that interact with transplanted law.

Legal Transplantation: Convergence versus Cultural-essentialism

Much work has been done to document and explain the use of legal transplants among Western legal systems. Yet conventional legal theory offers little guidance on the present question—transferring laws from Western to East Asian legal systems. Despite a general consensus that legal transplantation in East Asia over the last 30 years has had a limited impact, few commentators agree on the reasons why borrowed laws have not easily moved from statutes into society.[1] Some argue it is too early to assess the effectiveness of reforms. Commercial legal reforms began in Vietnam more than 15 years ago; yet, as we will see, extensive legal borrowing has not produced a legal environment that remotely resembles regulatory systems in donor countries. Naturally it takes time for law to influence state institutions,

1 These views are summarised in K. Pistor and P. Wellons (1999), *The Role of Law and Legal Institutions in Asian Economic Development 1960–1995*, Oxford University Press, Oxford, 14, 36–40, 282–84. Also see Carol Rose (1998), 'The "New" Law and Development Movement in the Post-Cold War Era: A Vietnam Case Study', 32 *Law and Society Review* (1), 93.

households and firms. Moreover, there is a well-recognised gap between law in the 'books' and law in 'practice' in every jurisdiction. Nevertheless, an explanation for the legal fragmentation and hybridisation observed in Vietnam and elsewhere in developing East Asia requires theoretical alternatives to the unproductive state-centric, convergence and cultural-essentialist assumptions underlying most conventional analytical systems.

It is argued in this chapter that an effective transplantation theory needs to employ two sets of analytical tools. First, many transplantation studies focus on legislative adaptation—what happens in statute books—without considering integration with deeper sociopolitical legal structures. It is well to recall that scholars who stick to doctrinal analysis learn little, for in most cases questions about reception are not legal or doctrinal.[2] What is needed is an analytical approach that looks beyond law as legislative rules and addresses law-in-action—an entire systems analysis. A second theoretical approach needs to negotiate the extremes of legal convergence and cultural essentialism. It must account for legal fragmentation and hybridisation and guide research by identifying the points of resistance to, and reception of, legal transplants.

Mapping Transplantation Theories

Four main themes are discernable in the legal transplantation literature: legal evolution, limited legal autonomy, legal autonomy, and systems theory. There is not complete coherence within each approach, and most theorists argue elements from more than one approach. Despite these limitations, this conceptualisation is broadly illustrative of the main theoretical approaches to legal transplantation.

Legal Evolution

Evolutionary theory links laws to dynamic processes, and, most importantly for this discussion, with specific social configurations.[3] In an age of *laissez-faire* capitalism and colonial empires, early twentieth-century evolutionists like Sir Henry Main invoked Social Darwinist notions to explain why 'primitive' non-Western legal systems would evolve towards 'progressive' Western systems.[4] Darwinian survival

2 See Pierre Legrand (1996), 'European Legal Systems are not Converging', 45 *International Comparative Law Quarterly*, 52, 56; Mark Ramseyer (1990), 'Doctrine of Rents in Japan: A Comment on Professors Osaka and Nakamuru', 53 *Law and Contemporary Problems* (2), 29.

3 See Peter Stein (1980), *Legal Evolution: The Story of an Idea*, Cambridge University Press, Cambridge, 22–28; Ronald Lindley Meek (1976), *Social Science and the Ignoble Savage*, Cambridge University Press, Cambridge.

4 See Henry Maine (1917), *Ancient Law*, J.M. Dent, London.

of the fittest thinking persuaded colonial administrators to impose French legality in Vietnam.[5]

Later, Max Weber ascribed legal development to private wealth accumulation, freedom of labour, free movement of goods and a social need for calculable law and rational public administration.[6] He attributed development in Western legal systems to 'concrete political factors, which have only the remotest analogies elsewhere in the world'.[7] Weber's subtle theory recognised the possibility of co-evolution between different cultures. But in finding modern European law complete and rational, he inferred that what existed elsewhere was incomplete and irrational.

Building on Weber's 'calculable' and 'rational' legal ideal, some contemporary evolutionary theorists narrowly locate legal development in 'rational economic decisions'.[8] Applying neoliberal economic theory, these theorists contend that rational decision-making is a universal human characteristic that explains all human behaviour. Culture is marginalised in this calculus, because personal values are considered non-comparable. For example, Robert Cooter, a leading law and economics scholar, posits that 'economic competition changes products and techniques, which in turn creates new problems of coordination and cooperation. Communities of people solve these problems by developing norms of behaviour… The state raises some social norms to the level of law'.[9] In short, decision-makers everywhere reach similar conclusions when confronted with equivalent 'rational' economic problems.

Most evolutionary writing explains legal transplantation in terms of borrowing by less developed systems to catch up with more comprehensive systems. Drawing on these theories, multilateral and bilateral donors have encouraged developing East Asian states to discard irrational indigenous laws and adopt Western-modern law.

Limited Legal Autonomy

The relationship between law and underlying social forces is important to analysing legal transplantation. If laws are merely sets of bare propositional statements, as

5 See John De Francis (1977), *Colonialism and Language Policy in Viet-Nam*, Mouton, The Hague, 119–21.

6 See David M. Trubek (1972), 'Max Weber on Law and the Rise of Capitalism' *Wisconsin Law Review* (3), 720, 731–46; Sally Ewing (1987), 'Formal Justice and the Spirit of Capitalism: Max Weber's Sociology of Law', 21 *Law and Society Review*, 487, 488–93.

7 See Max Weber (1968), *Economy and Society*, Bedminster Press, New York, 695–99.

8 The term neo-liberal economics refers to a philosophy whose basic units are individuals that make rational decisions according to prevailing circumstances and available information. For a discussion of this philosophy in the context of legal development see Elizabeth Landes and Richard A. Posner (1978), 'The Economics of the Baby Shortage', 7 *Journal of Legal Studies*, 323; Robert Cooter (1996), 'The Theory of Market Modernization of Law', 16 *International Review of Law and Economics*, 141, 142–46.

9 Robert Cooter (1996), 'The Theory of Market Modernization of Law', 16 *International Review of Law and Economics*, 141.

some proponents of large-scale legal transplantation seem to believe, then legal transplantation is comparatively easily, because autonomous laws are not historically or culturally connected in any meaningful way. If, on the contrary, laws are socially embedded with limited autonomy, they cannot simply be de-coupled from their social moorings and require careful adaptation to fit the underlying social structures in recipient countries. Both approaches draw support from the uneven history of legal transplantation.

Montesquieu is credited with the belief that law is culturally embedded or coupled. He opined that 'the political and civil laws of each nation … must be so peculiar to the people for whom they are made; it is a very great accident should those of one Nation suit another'.[10] If laws mirror environmental forces, then legal change is path-dependent, oscillating with historical cycles.[11]

According to Pierre Legrand's contemporary formulation, legal rules may transfer, but legal cultures and meanings do not travel.[12] He thinks culture provides the wide framework giving meaning and sense to people's lives. If laws are culturally specific, 'a crucial element of the ruleness of the rule—its meaning—does not survive the journey from one legal culture to another'.[13] Legrand observed that, after transplantation, laws might look the same, be administered by similarly configured institutions, but be implemented by officials with radically different legal mentalities or epistemologies.[14] It follows that socially and environmentally untenable legal transplants are not only ineffective or short-lived, they may stimulate destabilising tensions that cause greater problems than those the transplants were intended to rectify.[15] For Legrand this comes about because the legal culture (or the mentalities) in recipient countries reads imported legal texts from new perspectives, reconstructing their original meaning. Compatible legal epistemologies are thus

10 Charles De Secondat Montesquieu, (1970), *De L'Espirt des Law* (The Spirit of Laws), Livre I Gallimard, Paris, reprint, ed. J. P. Mayer & A. P. Kerr, chapter three.

11 Montesquieu believed that history moves in cycles influenced by environmental considerations such as customs, geography and climate. See Charles De Secondat Montesquieu (1977), *The Political Theory of Montesquieu*, selected and translated by Melvin Richter, Cambridge University Press, New York.

12 See Pierre Legrand (1997a), 'The Impossibility of Legal Transplants', 4 *Maastricht Journal of European Comparative Law*, 111, 119; Pierre Legrand (1997b), 'Against a European Civil Code', 60 *Modern Law Review,* 44; Pierre Legrand (2001), 'What "Legal Transplants"', in David Nelken and Johannes Feest (eds), *Adapting Legal Culture*, Hart Publishing Oxford, 55–68.

13 Pierre Legrand (1997a), *supra*, 119.

14 Legal epistemologies are the historically conditioned, deeply rooted attitudes that influence the way officials use law to find reality. See Peter de Cruz (1999), *Comparative Law in a Changing World*, 2nd edn, Cavendish Publishing, London, 214–16.

15 See Tahirih V. Lee (1993), 'Risky Business: Courts Culture, and the Market Place', 47 *University of Miami Law Review*, 1335, 1338 (transplanted law has the capacity to create 'chaos'); M. Radetzki (1994), 'From Communism to Capitalism in Laos: The Legal Dimension', 34 *Asian Survey* (9), 802.

necessary for effective legal transfers. Donor and host country legal cultures must 'fit'.

Legrand's analysis contains the theoretical ingredients for a decentred approach to legal transplantation.[16] For example, in stressing that the *legal* cannot be analytically separated from the *non-legal*, he rejects Weber's linkage between formal rationality and legal certainty. In addition, he draws ideas about the underling cognitive structures or mentalities (the collective mental programme) that shape legal culture from theorists such as Claude Lévi-Strauss, and especially Clifford Geertz.[17] All this suggests that Legrand searches for the transplant effect beyond the rules, institutions and mentalities associated with the 'rule of law'. Yet his writings focus almost exclusively on the interaction between legal transplants and state institutions and mentalities in recipient countries. He speaks, for example, about civil and common law mentalities, legal reasoning and court culture without considering the pluralistic state and non-state regulatory systems that exist in both Western and East Asian societies. He does not consider what ordinary people engaging in self-regulation think about imported law.

Legrand's claim that legal cultural differences are unbridgeable fails to account for legal transplantation experiments that proceeded rapidly and smoothly.[18] He assumes that legal epistemologies are slow to change. Some research supports this view, but there are other examples where basic legal epistemologies changed relatively quickly, certainly within a generation. A study of legal reform between 1965 and 1995 in six Asian countries found a discernable shift from local discretionary rules to imported Western commercial legal norms, but concluded that legal imports did not always signal converging legal systems.[19] Legal rules, the study speculated, transplant more easily than culturally embedded institutions. At best it was concluded that 'throughout much of Asia's legal history, law preceded economic development, but economic development was an important condition for the acceptance and use of laws'.[20] This implies that some laws are less coupled to social processes than others and are thus more easily transplanted. Recognising the possibility of legal transferability allows law a limited autonomy.

Otto Kahn-Freund contributed the important insight that 'there are degrees of transferability'.[21] Like Legrand, he reasoned that because most laws are deeply embedded in their social and institutional matrices 'we cannot take for granted that rules or institutions are transplantable'.[22] But, unlike Legrand, he did not fully accept that laws are non-transferable.

---

16 See, for example, Pierre Legrand (1996), 'European Legal Systems are not Converging', 45 *International and Comparative Law Quarterly*, 58–64.

17 Clifford Geertz (1983), *Local Knowledge*, Basic Books, New York, 218.

18 See Tahirih V. Lee, 1993, *supra*, 1335–414.

19 Pistor and Wellons, *supra*, 280–84.

20 Ibid., 50.

21 Ibid., 6.

22 Otto Kahn-Freund (1974), 'On the Uses and Misuses of Comparative Law' 37 *Modern Law Review* 1-27.

In Kahn-Freund's estimation, transferability depends on the interconnectedness between transplanted laws and host-country political, legal, economic and cultural institutions.[23] At one end of a continuum, a 'flattening out of economic and cultural diversity' means that some laws have de-coupled from society and are relatively easy to transplant.[24] At the other end, laws 'designed to allocate power, rule-making, decision-making, above all, policymaking power' remained deeply embedded in social institutions, and are consequently unlikely to take root in foreign legal terrain.

Kahn-Freund claimed that the environmental, socioeconomic and cultural impediments to transferability posited by Montesquieu have lessened in importance over time, while political elements have gained significance.[25] He advised anyone contemplating transplanting Western commercial laws into communist systems to ascertain whether the legal imports owed their creation to Western legal and sociopolitical power structures and whether these or functionally equivalent structures existed in the communist country. This inquiry is especially pertinent to our study, because legal reforms in Vietnam are superimposing a Western legislative template over enduring socialist-inspired institutions.

Kahn-Freund's ideas about legal transferability are scattered in fragments throughout his writings. For the purposes of analytical clarity this study has condensed and synthesised them into three propositions.

- All laws have to some extent de-coupled from their sociopolitical moorings, making legal transplants across sociopolitical boundaries a theoretical possibility.
- Since laws de-couple to varying degrees, some are more likely to survive the journey across cultural borders than others.
- Sociopolitical factors determine the degree of coupling between law and society; these factors are the political role of law, the distribution of state power, and pressure from non-state institutions.

Legal Autonomy

Undoubtedly the most extreme articulation of legal autonomy is found in the works of Alan Watson.[26] His complex arguments are categorised by some commentators into

23 See Otto Kahn-Freund (1978), 'On the Uses and Misuses of Comparative Law', in Otto Kahn-Freund (ed.), *Selected Writings*, Stevens, London, 298–303.

24 Otto Kahn-Freund (1974), *supra*, 7–11.

25 He believed that industrialisation, urbanisation, and global communications had 'flattened' some of Mostesquieu's inhibiting factors. Kahn-Freund (1974), *supra*, 9.

26 Watson has authored over 50 books and hundreds of articles chronicling a rich history of legal transplants. See, for example, Alan Watson (1985), *The Evolution of Law*, Johns Hopkins University Press, Baltimore, 94; Alan Watson (1993), *Legal Transplants: An Approach to Comparative Law*, 2nd edn, University of Georgia Press, Athens, 95; Alan

'strong' and 'weak' propositions.[27] Watson maintains that transplants are determined by a small group of professional elites (composed of lawyers) who borrow laws without considering what the social context requires. Processes of change are endogenous, he believes, because 'to a large extent law possesses a life and vitality of its own; there is no extremely close, natural or inevitable relationship between law, legal structures, instruments and rules on the one hand and the needs and desires and political economy of the ruling elite or of members of the particular society on the other hand'.[28] Guided by lawyers, autonomous laws operating beyond the realm of social needs transfer freely across cultural barriers.

Watson's precise views on legal borrowing are difficult to ascertain. Some passages support the strong position that compatibility between donor and recipient legal systems is unnecessary for successful legal borrowing. Elsewhere, he expresses a weaker position where legal traditions and doctrines, rather than laws, are autonomous or insulated from society. Taken together, his diverse positions come down to three main propositions.

- The growth of law is primarily attributable to continuous legal recycling and borrowing. Most legal development has evolved through historical processes without reference to endogenous social, political or economic factors.[29]
- Social needs do not inevitably affect the transferability of borrowed laws. If laws ever reflected the spirit of peoples and nations, a long-term process of social differentiation and internationalisation has de-coupled this linkage, making law ever more remote as it becomes a sophisticated regulator of commerce. Distancing occurs every time lawmakers borrow legal principles from within their own legal system—by analogy—or from other systems.[30]
- The mechanisms regulating legal borrowing are controlled by legal professional elites such as legal drafters, judges and jurists. Lawyers borrow what seems comfortable, familiar and prestigious from the legal tradition in which they were trained.[31] Legal reasoning is highly abstract, remote in appearance from

---

Watson (1996), 'Aspects of the Reception of Law', 44 *American Journal of Comparative Law*, 335, 346–50.

27 Alan Watson's voluminous writings and shifting interpretations about the relationship between law and society make it difficult to state his position on legal transplanting confidently. For a good overview of Watson's protean utterances, see William Ewald (1995), 'Comparative Jurisprudence (II): The Logic of Legal Transplants', 43 *American Journal of Comparative Law*, 498–502. Also see Roger Cotterrell (1997), 'The Concept of Legal Culture', in David Nelken (ed.), *Comparing Legal Cultures*, Dartmouth, Aldershot, 70, 76–84.

28 Alan Watson (1978), 'Comparative Law and Legal Change', 37 *Cambridge Law Journal*, 313, 314–15.

29 Although Watson argues that there is no *inherent* correlation between law and society, this does not mean that there is *no* correlation.

30 See, generally, Alan Watson (1996), *supra*, 335.

31 For example, French speaking African countries do not borrow English law but former English colonies borrow from common law countries. See Alan Watson (1996), *supra*, 335;

social factors, and has a life of its own.[32]

Watson's theories only address one part of the legal transplantation puzzle. They examine why elites select foreign laws, but say little about how legal imports change recipient legal systems.[33]

Systems Theory

Gunther Teubner's theoretical approach to legal transfers provides a point of departure from the previously discussed state-centred theories.[34] His understanding of legal transplantation is based on 'Autopoiesis' theory, a complex cluster of ideas based on biological research into self-replicating organic sub-systems. Humberto Maturana generalised a systems theory to explain homeostasis, which is a natural biological state kept stable by complex systems of information and control, such as the chemical messages in cells.[35] He also raised the intriguing question whether the dynamics of human society are also determined by autopoiesis.[36]

Taking up this inquiry, Niklas Luhmann used autopoiesis to explain why people within institutions such as companies, political bodies or universities create their own kind of reality and meanings.[37] In his estimation, communication takes the place of metabolic pathways in creating autopoiesis within human social systems. Virtually the whole of society is fragmented into institutions that use language to communicate

---

Alan Watson (1985), *supra*, 95–96. Also see Gianmaria Ajani (1995), 'By Chance and Prestige: Legal Transplants in Russia and Eastern Europe', 43 *American Journal of Comparative Law*, 93, 115–16.

32 For Watson, 'Law develops by transplanting, not because some such rule was the inevitable consequence of the social structure and would have emerged even without a model to copy, but because the foreign rule was known to those with control over lawmaking and they observed the (apparent) benefits which could be derived from it. What is borrowed that is to say, is very often the idea'. Watson (1978), *supra*, 313, 315. Also see Kenneth Pennington (1997), 'The Spirit of Legal History', 64 *University of Chicago Law Review*, 1097, 1110–12.

33 Nelken points out that, when Watson's work is stripped of its anti-mirror theory polemic, it only differs from mirror theories by the ease with which he thinks laws can transplant. See David Nelken (2001a), *supra*, 12–15.

34 See Gunther Teubner (1998), *Autopoietic Law: A New Approach to Law and Society*, 218; Gunther Teubner (1998), 'Legal Irritants: Good Faith in British Law or How Unifying Law Ends up in New Divergences', 61 *Modern Law Review* 11–32; Gunther Teubner (1997), '"Global Bukowina": Legal Pluralism in the World Society', in Gunther Teubner (ed.), *Global Law Without States*, Dartmouth, Aldershot, 3–22; Gunther Teubner (1992), 'The Two Faces of Janus: Rethinking Legal Pluralism', 13 *Cardozo Law Review*, 1443, 1451.

35 See Humberto Maturana and Francisco Varela (1980), *Autopoiesis and Cognition*, D. Reidel, Dortrecht, 78–82.

36 Ibid., 118.

37 See Niklas Luhmann (1985), *A Sociological Theory of Law*, Routledge, London; Niklas Luhmann (1988), 'The Unity of Legal System', in Gunther Teubner (ed.), *Autopoietic Law: A New Approach to Law and Society*, Walter de Gruyter, Berlin, 21–35.

in their own way and perceive reality from their own perspective. Society is divided into functionally differentiated social systems with each subsystem undergoing autopoietic development. The legal sub-system is no exception. It too is constructed by particular sets of self-referential and self-reproducing discourses.

Teubner has taken from autopoiesis theory the notion that law is found in binary legal/illegal discourse. He believes 'the binary code legal/illegal is not peculiar to the law of the nation–state. This is in no way a view of "legal centralism". It refutes categorically any claim that the official law of the nation–states, of the United Nations or of international institutions enjoys any hierarchically superior position'.[38] By locating law in all discourse conducted in a legal/illegal mode, Teubner sensitises the analysis of legal transfers to transplantation effects occurring beyond the realm of state-based laws and legal mentalities.

Teubner is much more prepared then other theorists, such as Legrand, who also believe in a close connection between law and society, to accept that many laws have de-coupled from social sub-systems.[39] Laws transfer easily between legal sub-systems, because lawyers in different countries understand each other. But, in contrast to Watson's free-wheeling understanding of legal transplantation, Teubner thinks that legal sub-systems are influenced by external 'perturbations', which, if constantly repeated, will shape the way legal thinking evolves.[40] Legal transplants thus act like 'legal irritants' in host-country legal systems. They unleash an evolutionary dynamic in which the 'external rule's meaning will be reconstructed and the internal context will undergo fundamental change'.[41]

Comparing and Contrasting Legal Transfer Theories

Although portrayed as adversaries by some commentators, Legrand, Watson and Kahn-Freund occupy different positions on the same theoretical continuum.[42] Legrand is theoretically closest to Marx and Weber's deterministic link between law and the 'felt social needs', while Kahn-Freund and especially Watson lean towards

38 Teubner (1997), *supra*, 14.

39 As David Nelken points out, Teubner does not clearly explain how law that is closely couped to society can in some circumstances de-couple and transfer easily. See David Nelken (2001), 'Beyond the Metaphor of Legal Transplants? Consequences of Autopoietic Theory for the Study of Cross-Cultural Legal Adaptation', in Jirí Pribán and David Nelken (eds), *Law's New Boundaries: The Consequences of Legal Autopoiesis*, Ashgate, Aldershot, 285.

40 Gunther Teubner (1998), 'Legal Irritants: Good Faith in British Law or How Unifying Law Ends up in New Divergences', 61 *Modern Law Review* (1), 15–25.

41 Teubner (1998), *supra*, 12.

42 For a discussion that treats Watson and Kahn-Freund as adversaries see Steven J. Heim (1996), 'Predicting Legal Transplants: The Case of Servitudes in the Russian Federation', 6 *Transnational Law and Contemporary Problems*, 187, 190–92; William Ewald (1995), *supra*, 498–502; Lorraine McDonough (1992), 'The Transferability of Labor Law: Can an American Transplant Take Root in British Soil?', 13 *Comparative Labour Law Journal*, 504, 505–8.

legal autonomy. Their theoretical approaches to legal autonomy excite different analytical positions concerning legal transplantation.

In treating laws as cultural artefacts, Legrand attributes non-transferability to disjunctions between donor and host-country legal epistemologies, myths and narratives. Occupying the other end of the same theoretical continuum, Watson asserts that autonomous laws readily transfer between globalised legal elites, and only encounter resistance from organised pressure groups. Yet he admits 'some degree of correlation must exist between law and society ... [though] legal rules by no means accurately reflect the needs and desires of society…'.[43] Legrand and Watson disagree about the extent to which host-country culture affects legal transferability, but agree that congruence is important in some social spheres such as professional legal culture.

Teubner's autopoietic theory stands outside the state-centred socio-legal tradition in which Watson, Kahn-Freund and Legrand work. For this reason it has generated numerous fresh insights into legal transplantation that are not readily available using conventional analytical methods. For reasons outlined below, autopoietic theory is considered unsuited as a general theoretical framework. All the same, a version of discourse analysis that draws some notions from autopoietic theory and some from linguistic theory is used in this study to overcome shortcomings in conventional socio-legal analysis.

Kahn-Freund proposed a general theoretical architecture to guide research into legal transplantation. He considered Watson's analysis incomplete, because it did not fully account for resistance between donor and host-country political, economic and legal systems. Rectifying this oversight, he sought to identify the power structures and social groups within host countries that most commonly interact with imported law.

Rather than a fully realised analytical theory, Kahn-Freund's propositions resemble a collection of associated ideas. His analytical architecture is suggestive: transferability is affected by political structures, institutional cultures and organised pressure groups.

Synthesising Working Postulates

Three working postulates have been synthesised from the transplantation literature.

Political-legal Ideology

Transplantation theorists, especially Kahn-Freund, noted that politico-legal ideals radically alter the operation of otherwise similar institutional structures. For example, Marxist-Leninist and democratic liberal states both use legislative organs to crystallise state policy into law, but their different political orientations excite wildly

43 See Alan Watson (1978), *supra*, 313, 321.

divergent views regarding the role and substance of law.[44] One way of comparing the role of law in different countries is to consider the compatibility between politico-legal ideology in donor and recipient countries. Recent socio-legal research has shown that politico-legal ideology influences the adoption and implementation of borrowed laws.[45]

Gramscian ideological theory assists this inquiry in three ways. First, if state ideologies are comprised of competing precepts, legal transplants must comport with, or at least not be blocked by, the dominant ideological streams.[46] Second, legal transplants acquire contextual meaning where ideologies in host countries make them appear fair and acceptable to state officials and key social groups.[47] Third, and following from the second point, Gramsci's theory opens the discussion to the possibility that central elites and the public (or discrete communities) have competing ideological outlooks concerning the efficacy and desirability of transplanted law.[48]

---

44 For example, the politicisation of the state apparatus permitted in Marxist-Leninist legal systems is incompatible with Western liberal mythology that the 'rule of law' requires the separation of party and state. Kahn-Freund wrote that: 'problems such as those of housing, of town planning, of pollution may be no different in Russia or Spain or South Africa from what they are in this country [Britain] or the United States, but the procedure of arriving at a solution, the form of discussion, and the role of the individual in that discussion are different'. Otto Kahn-Freund (1974), *supra*, 11.

45 See Yves Dezalay and Bryant Garth (2001), 'The Import and Export of Law and Legal Institutions: International Strategies in National Palace Wars', in David Nelken (ed.), *Adapting Legal Cultures*, Hart Publishing, Oxford, 241, 246–57. Also see Mark Van Hoecke and Mark Warrington (1998), 'Legal Cultures, Legal Paradigms and Legal Doctrine: Towards a New Model for Comparative Law', 47 *International and Comparative Law Quarterly*, 495, 516–19.

46 Nicos Poulantzas hypothesised that certain ideals (which he termed 'regions') consistently influenced ruling elites, state institutions and economic behaviour more powerfully than others. See Nicos Poulantzas (1973), *Political Power and Social Classes*, trans. T. O'Hagan, NLB Sheed and Ward, London, 204–5.

47 Ideology has the 'capacity to persuade people that the world described in its images and categories is the only attainable world in which a sane person would want to live'. Robert Gordon (1984), 'Critical Legal Histories', 36 *Stanford Law Review*, 65, 108. Also see Muthiah Alagappa (1995), 'The Anatomy of Legitimacy', in M. Alagappa (ed.), *Political Legitimacy in South East Asia*, Stanford University Press, Stanford, 11–14; A. Sarat (1975), 'Support for the Legal System: An Analysis of Knowledge, Attitudes, and Behavior', 3 *American Politics Quarterly*, 3, 5–15.

48 As Gramsci demonstrated, elites use legal ideology to strengthen their hegemony over the public. See Antonio Gramsci (1971), *Selections from Prison Notebooks*, Q. Hoare and G. Nowell-Smith (eds), Lawrence and Wishart, London, 300–21; Maureen Cain (1983), 'Gramsci, The State and the Place of Law', in David Sugerman (ed.), *Legality, Ideology and the State*, Academic Press, London, 111–15; Alan Hunt (1985), 'The Ideology of Law: Advances and Problems in Recent Applications of Ideology to the Analysis of Law', 19 *Law and Society Review* (1), 11, 13–19.

Power-distribution

Another theme running through the transplantation literature is that legal transfers are sensitive to the ways legislators, bureaucrats and judges use state power to make and enforce law.[49] Macro-institutional frameworks ordering legislatures, courts and executive governments, say little about how internal power-distribution structures might influence legal borrowing. What makes state institutions distinctive are the rules, precepts and habits residing inside and outside the formal structures that guide the distribution of state power.[50] The mentalities and processes informing lawmakers and enforcers profoundly influence the meanings given to legal transplants.

Pressure Groups

Kahn-Freund and Allan Watson identified the pressure exerted by organised non-state groups as a potent force influencing the selection of, and meanings given to, imported laws.[51] Writing about the transplantation of labour laws from the United States to Britain, Kahn-Freund observed that dialogical agreements between employers and unions eventually develop normative codes that 'crystallise customs'.[52] Forces representing capital and labour decide whether to accept or resist borrowed labour law by reference to this body of 'crystallised customs'.

Stated in propositional form, pressure groups communicate local ideas and practices to state officials that shape the way imported laws are adapted and implemented. Pressure groups are more likely to communicate unconventional or controversial ideas to state officials in relatively unmediated discursive environments.

With the exception of the first postulate, which can draw on an extensive body of neo-Gramscian ideological theory, the other working postulates are too abstract to direct research on the forces influencing legal transplantation. What is needed is a methodology that not only encapsulates state power distribution and pressure forces, but also provides a means of assessing how these factors influence legal borrowing.

---

49 Once again this theme is most clearly seen in Kahn-Freund's writings. See Kahn-Freund (1974), *supra*, 12.

50 See generally Gianfranco Poggi (1978), *The Development of the Modern State: A Sociological Introduction*, Stanford, Stanford University Press, 1; also see James March and Johan Olsen (1989), *Rediscovering Institutions: The Organizational Basis of Politics*, Macmillan, New York, 17–22.

51 See Kahn-Freund (1974), *supra*, 12–14. Watson formulated a typology describing the social forces that influence legal borrowing. 'Pressure forces' promote the adoption of particular laws to realise 'felt needs'. 'Opposition forces' rally to block or amend imported laws. See Watson (1978), *supra*, 324.

52 Ibid., 3, 18. Otto Kahn-Freund (1948), 'Legislation through Adjudication', 11 *Modern Law Review*, 269. See also Lorraine McDonough (1992), *supra*, 507.

Discourse Analysis as a Comparative Methodology

An inference that can be drawn from the working postulates is that legal transfers are sensitive to variations in culture. Effective legal transplantation not only requires equivalent ideology and power-distribution structures, but also officials and pressure groups informed by a similar legal culture. Put another way, different legal cultures invest similar legal rules with different meanings.[53] Even where borrowed laws appear technically and contextually neutral, once assimilated into new legal cultures they adopt host-country characteristics.

A difficulty with using legal culture as a comparative methodology is its inherent vagueness.[54] It is so 'broad [that] it could encompass almost any phenomenon'.[55] Scholars have long debated a suitable universal definition with only marginal success. Friedman, himself an advocate of cultural analysis, conceded that legal culture is 'an abstraction and a slippery one'.[56] The underlying problem is that legal culture is a descriptive concept. It registers inconsistencies and incompatibilities between different legal cultures, but it has no way of assessing the interaction between cultures. In mature legal systems like the United States, which have well-defined legal doctrines and processes, legal culture makes limited sense. In cultures like Vietnam—where law is less socially defined—analysis does not progress far without also considering other sources of social ordering such as political and moral rule.

A related concern is that, within common borders, it is no longer as clear as it once seemed that central representations of culture universally reflect core cultural values.[57] Some theorists, such as Gunther Teubner, argue that it is no longer possible to talk about 'the totality of society', since wider cultures have 'fragmented [into a] multiplicity of discourses which "today" constitute society'.[58] Although he was describing social differentiation in Western countries, his general thesis resonates

53 See Pierre Legrand (2001), 'What "Legal Transplants"', in David Nelken and Johannes Feest (eds), *Adapting Legal Culture*, Hart Publishing, Oxford, 55–68.

54 The term 'legal culture' is used to mean the 'specific way in which values, practices, and concepts are integrated into the operation of legal institutions and the interpretation of legal texts'. John Bell (1995), 'English and French Law—Not So Different?', 48 *Current Legal Problems*, (2) 63; also see Susan Silbey (1992) 'Making a Place for a Cultural Analysis of Law', 17 *Law and Social Inquiry*, 41.

55 Lawrence M. Friedman (1997), 'The Concept of Legal Culture' in David Nelken (ed.), *Comparing Legal Cultures*, Dartmouth, Aldershot, 34–36; A. Sarat and T.R. Kearns (2001), 'The Cultural Lives of Law', in A. Sarat and T.R. Kearns (eds), *Law in the Domains of Culture*, University of Michigan Press, Ann Arbor, 1; C. Pennisi (2001), 'Sociological Uses of the Concept of Legal Culture', in D. Nelken (ed.), *Law in the Domains of Culture*, 107.

56 '"Culture" is a term that is repeatedly used without meaning much of anything at all, a vague gesture toward a dimly perceived ethos…'. S. Greenblatt (1997), 'Culture', in F. Lentricchia and T. McLaughlin (eds), *Critical Terms for Literary Study*, University of Chicago Press, Chicago, 225.

57 See generally, Oscar Schachter (1997), 'The Decline of the Nation–State and its Implications for International Law', 36 *Columbia Journal of Transnational Law*, 7, 8–15.

58 Teubner (1998), *supra*, 21.

in Vietnam, where highland–lowland and urban–rural divides fragment legal values (see Chapters 5 to 7). If core national values are difficult to ascertain, transnational cultural comparison becomes increasingly complex and demands an analytical approach that recognises cultural difference across cultural sub-systems in recipient countries.

One way to harness legal culture for our study is to focus on its capacity to shape world views. As Legrand noted, legal culture orders perceptions of reality, moulding the 'right way' to think and act.[59] Kahn-Freund made a similar observation when he asserted that civilian lawyers mainly argue from principle, while common law lawyers use precedent. Each tradition predisposes legal argument towards different realities.[60] In other words, it is in part the epistemological assumptions regarding rationality, efficiency and merit that make legal cultures distinctive.

We need a framework in which to place and compare different epistemological understandings about imported laws. Discourse analysis is promising because legal transplantation is largely (though not entirely) a discursive process.[61] Communication is vital to the selection, formulation and implementation of foreign laws. Understanding regulatory conversations has the potential to furnish insights into the epistemological settings and 'inner life' of those processes.[62] Discourse analysis provides a set of tools to analyse language and communication and assess whether those involved in legal borrowing are likely to learn from foreign ideas and each other.

Discourse analysis is a relatively recent theoretical development in legal studies.[63] The central propositions underpinning discourse analysis are that 'communicative interaction produces meaning, and that understanding is situated'.[64] Put differently, shared epistemological and tacit understandings used in conversations convey legal meaning. Meaning is inter-subjective, in the sense that shared understandings are largely generated within epistemologically compatible social or organisational groups.

---

59 See David Nelken (2001b), *supra*, 282–87.

60 See Pierre Legrand (1996), *supra*, 60–65.

61 Anthony Beck (1994), 'Is Law an Autopoietic System?', 14 Oxford Journal of Legal Studies (3), 401, 404–15; Gunther Teubner (1993), Law as an Autopoietic System, Blackwell, Oxford, 69; Niklas Luhmann (1987), A Sociological Theory of Law, trans. Elizabeth King and Martin Albrow, Routledge, London.

62 For a discussion showing the links between legal culture and regulations see E. Meidinger (1987), 'Regulatory Culture: A Theoretical Outline', 9 *Law and Policy*, 355.

63 It is beyond the purposes of this study to survey this highly contested area, rather, we shall focus on the principal claims made about the relationship between discourse and social practices and show how they illuminate legal transplantation. For a general review of law and communication see David Nelken (1996), 'Law as Communication: Constituting the Field' in David Nelken (ed.), *Law as Communication*, Dartmouth, Aldershot, 3–30.

64 Julia Black (2002), 'Regulatory Conversations', 29 *Journal of Law and Society* (1), 163, 174. Also see J. Paterson and G. Teubner (1998), 'Changing Maps: Empirical Legal Autopoiesis', 7 *Social and Legal Studies*, 451–86; T.A. van Dijk (1997), 'The Study of Discourse', in T.A. van Dijk (ed.), *Discourse as Structure and Process* Sage, London, 3–20.

Discourse analysis shares with Gramscian ideological theory the notion that there are no meta-ideologies (or meta-discourses). Ideological regions and discourses compete with each other. Their point of departure is that discourse analysis includes non-aspirational communication. According to discourse theorists, social behaviour can only be interpreted by exploring the meanings that give rise to action.[65] Meaning is not something that is discovered; rather, it is constructed through discourse and other forms of expression. For the purposes of this study, discourse is taken to mean 'all forms of spoken interaction, formal and informal, and written texts of all kinds', especially political, economic, moral, cultural and legal modes of communication.[66]

As previously mentioned, Teubner used autopoiesis theory to circumvent the state-centred assumptions underpinning conventional socio-legal approaches to legal transplantation. In formulating autopoiesis theory, Luhmann contributed the valuable insight that, through a process of functional differentiation, social discourse has fragmented into 'discrete discursive systems'.[67] He claims that legal, economic and ethical discourses have become so self-referential that they understand their environments from internal frames of reference.[68] This novel way of understanding law shows how epistemological assumptions in different discourses have fragmented the meaning of law and suggests reasons why laws transplant unevenly.

While agreeing with his central premise, many discourse theorists believe that Luhmann's 'discrete discursive systems' overstate epistemological divisions within society.[69] They argue that a limited role for human agency and a lack of space for social interaction constrains the capacity for Luhmann's theory to explore the conflicts and negotiations that shape laws. As a corrective, they propose a less divided world where regulatory discourse exists in 'semi-autonomous', rather than 'fully-discrete', sub-systems. For example, although Jürgen Habermas is clearly influenced by Luhmann's systems theory, he is careful to avoid a holistic analysis of society. For

---

65 See Arthur J. Jacobson (1989), 'Autopoietic Law: The New Science of Niklas Luhmann', 87 *Michigan Law Review*, 1647. Also see Gunther Teubner (1993), *Law as an Autopoietic System*, Blackwell, Oxford, 69.

66 See J. Potter and M. Wetherell (1987), *Discourse and Social Psychology*, Blackwell, London, 7.

67 See Niklas Luhmann (1987), 'The Unity of the Legal System' in Gunther Teubner (ed.), *Autopoietic Law: A New Approach to Law and Society*, W. de Gruyter, New York, 12.

68 See Anthony Beck (1994), *supra*, 404–15; Hugh Baxter (1998), 'Autopoiesis and the "Relative Autonomy" of Law', 19 *Cardozo Law Review*, 1987.

69 See Anthony Beck (1994), *supra*, 404–15; Hugh Baxter (1998), *supra*, 1987; Robert Post (1991), 'The Relatively Autonomous Discourse of Law', in Robert Post (ed.), *Law and the Order of Culture*, University of California Press, Berkeley, vii–ix; Alan Hunt (1993), *Exploration in Law and Society*, Routledge, London, 166–67, 320. Habermas also argues for relative autonomy by saying that 'ordinary language' holds together the disparate discursive threads that are specific to each subsystem. See James Bohman (1994), 'Complexity, Pluralism and the Constitutional State: On Habermas's Faktizitat und Geltung', 28 *Law and Society Review*, 897, 913–15.

him 'law is not a narcissistically self-enclosed system', but rather a non-generalised phenomenon that waxes and wanes in rhythm to changes in social discourse.[70]

There is another shortcoming with Teubner's use of autopoietic (discrete discursive systems) theory to analyse legal transplantation. David Nelken noted that in discrete discursive systems the 'legal mode' of thinking has reified from other social forces to the extent that it is primarily concerned with differences between legality and illegality.[71] Nelken believes that this narrow conceptualisation can hardly account for the rich and varied legal epistemologies that Legrand (and others) believe profoundly influence legal transplantation.

To some extent, Nelken's criticism presents a caricature of Luhmann and Teubner's understanding of autopoietic theory. Teubner in particular recognises that most regulatory conversations are conducted in more than one mode of thought.[72] The difficulty for Nelken is that 'autopoietic theory would seem to be unable to recognise differences between legal discourses in different cultures except as differences between law and other social communications'.[73] Analytical problems might arise where what is considered legal in one culture differs radically from what passes for legal discourse in another society.

The 'semi-autonomous' understanding of discourse analysis adopted in this study circumvents this problem. It acknowledges that a wider range of epistemological criteria shapes legal discourse than the legal–illegal criterion proposed by Teubner and Luhmann. If discourse analysis is to assist this study, it must be capable of contrasting and comparing differences in legal, and other kinds of thinking about legal, transplants. It needs to recognise that discourse modes are not entirely self-referential and that they communicate (albeit imperfectly) with one another. Otherwise, there

---

70 Habermas maintains that it is primarily through rational argument that members of society form the mutual understanding necessary to build the compromises that legitimise state enforcement of law. Legitimation is blocked when permitted forms of public debate are based on unqualified traditions, meta-physical beliefs, or ideology. Where discourse is less constrained, the contests and compromises needed to legitimise law collapse the gaps between state and societal values. See Jürgen Habermas (1996), *Between Fact and Norms: Contributions to a Discourse Theory of Law and Democracy*, Polity Press, Cambridge, 461. Also see Habermas (1987), *The Theory of Communicative Action*, vol. 2, trans. T. McCarthy, Beacon Press, Boston, 164–97.

71 See Nelken (2001b), *supra*, 282–86. Nelken discussed Teubner's article; see Teubner (1998), *supra*, 11. Also see Roger Cotterrell (2001), 'The Representation of Law's Autonomy in Autopoiesis Theory', in Jirí Pribán and David Nelken (eds), *Law's New Boundaries: The Consequences of Legal Autopoiesis*, Ashgate, Aldershot, 90–94.

72 See M. King (1993), 'The Truth about Autopoiesis', 20 *Journal of Law and Society*, 218, 224. Teubner's approach to discourse theory is influenced by Jürgen Habermas and Michel Foucault and he cannot be easily characterised as an autopoietic theorist.

73 Ibid., 285. Nelken's objection arises from a broader concern that, if legal subsystems are autonomous from other social processes, how do they adapt and change to reflect non-legal ideas and practices?

are few points of intersection between transplanted law and regulatory conversations in recipient countries.

'Semi-autonomous' Discourse Modes

Discourse analysis offers a promising technique to dissect conversations about legal transplantation into constituent modalities.[74] 'Semi-autonomous' discourse makes sense of law from internal frames of reference as well as from precepts that are selectively drawn from other discursive 'modes'.[75] Discourse is 'semi-autonomous' in the additional sense that it is not directly determined by social conditions (that is, mirror theory). What makes discourse modes distinctive is their orientation towards particular ways of ordering reality.[76] Each discourse mode has its own criteria or codes (epistemologies) for prioritising the relevance and value of external information. Groups simultaneously discussing the same law from different 'modes' may reach contradictory conclusions. For discourses to convey legal meanings effectively, they must share common or compatible criteria or modes of thinking. Foreign donors describing legal transplants in 'legal mode', for example, are unlikely to communicate Western liberal legal concepts successfully to Vietnamese regulators primarily thinking in 'political' mode. Effective transplantation requires compatible epistemological grammar.

Discourse analysis is used in this study, because it suggests reasons 'why different legal cultures (and epistemologies) invest similar legal rules with different meanings'.[77] For example, it is instructive to know whether lawmakers in recipient countries share common epistemological assumptions about the nature of regulatory problems and the appropriate legal responses.

Interpretive Communities

Major differences can exist in the distribution of knowledge in society. Peter Berger and Tomas Luckmann characterise this fragmentation as 'socially segregated subuniverses of meaning'.[78] Discourse analysis takes account of this fragmentation by describing attitudes to law from the standpoint of common responses on the part

74 See M. King (1993), *supra*, 223–24.

75 See Hugh Baxter (1998), 'Autopoiesis and the "Relative Autonomy" of Law', 19 *Cardozo Law Review*, 1987, 1993; also see Roger Cotterrell, 2001 'The Representation of Law's Autonomy in Autopoiesis Theory', in Jirí Pribán and David Nelken (eds), *Law's New Boundaries: The Consequences of Legal Autopoiesis*, Ashgate, Aldershot, 86–90.

76 See Angel R. Oquendo (2002), 'Deliberative Democracy in Habermas and Nino', 22 *Oxford Journal of Legal Studies* (2), 189, 205–6.

77 Pierre Legrand (1997a), *supra*, 119. Also see Susan Silbey (1992), *supra*, 41.

78 Peter Berger and Thomas Luckman (1966), *The Social Construction of Reality*, Anchor Books, New York, 75.

of institutions or groups.[79] A stock of knowledge and epistemologies is commonly available to groups, which collectively guides their responses.[80] Common responses to law suggest that certain groups function as interpretive or epistemological communities. This insight advances our study by suggesting that the uneven uptake of imported laws is partially attributable to differences in the way interpretive communities comprehend and respond to law.

There is no fixed definition about what constitutes an interpretive community.[81] Most theorists agree, however, that members of interpretive communities share common epistemological and tacit understandings about the meaning of law. According to Alfred Schutz, most assertions and propositions that constitute this knowledge are 'just taken for granted until further notice'.[82] Rather than identifying interpretive communities by their level of mutuality, theorists believe it makes more sense to mark out boundaries between communities. Factors that differentiate communities include different validity claims, epistemologies and tacit understandings.

Discursive Strategies

Interpretivist approaches to discourse analysis insist that the meaning of language is not fixed. It varies according to the context in which it is used.[83] If the meaning of legal ideas resides in their use, social actors can deploy language and interpretations in strategic ways. They may unknowingly or deliberately invest borrowed ideas with new meanings to secure particular advantages. This strategic dimension is highly relevant to legal transplantation, since it emphasises the role played by state

79 See Baxter (1998), *supra*, 2073–74. Also see George Herbert Mead (1934), *Mind, Self, and Society*, University of Chicago Press, Chicago, 21; Peter Berger and Thomas Luckman (1966), *supra*, 75; Gunther Teubner (1989), 'How the Law Thinks: Towards a Constructivist Epistemology of Law', 23 *Law and Society Review*, 727, 739.

80 As Alfred Schutz opined, 'we cannot understand an institution without understanding what it means for the individuals who orient their behavior with regard to its existence'. Alfred Schutz (1962), *The Problem of Social Reality*, Collected Papers Vol. II, Martinus Nijhoff, The Hague, 10–11.

81 See generally S. Fish (1989), *Doing What Comes Naturally: Change, Rhetoric and Practice in Literary and Legal Studies*, Duke University Press, Durham, North Carolina, 141–60; Brian Tamanaha (1998), *Realistic Socio-Legal Theory*, Clarendon Press, Oxford 170–72.

82 Alfred Schutz (1973), *Collected Papers I: The Problem of Social Reality*, Martinus Nijhoff, The Hague, 7.

83 See J. Potter and M. Wetherell (1987), *Discourse and Social Psychology: Beyond Attitudes and Behavior*, Sage Publications, London, 7; also see T.A. van Dijk (1997), 'The Study of Discourse', in T.A. van Dijk (ed.), *Discourse as Structure and Process*, Thousand Oaks, California. Also see Tamanaha (1998), *supra*, 170–72.

institutions, international organisations and domestic pressure groups in shaping the meaning of law.[84]

Communication is not passive, since it aims to achieve certain objectives. Yves Dezalay and Bryant Garth showed, for example, how Latin American elites used imported laws in 'palace wars' to advance their power bases.[85] Non-elite groups also organise to support or resist imported laws.

In using discourse analysis as an interpretive tool, cultural differences between Western and Vietnamese communication must be acknowledged. Without this adjustment, discourse analysis simply projects Western assumptions about 'rational' discourse onto a radically different socio-legal landscape. Cultural attribution is minimised (but not eliminated) by understanding law as whatever social actors themselves discuss in legal terms. This notion focuses attention on Vietnamese understandings about law. Applied flexibly and reflectively, discourse analysis will sensitise the study to the ways Vietnamese conceptualise transplanted law as something that does (or does not) or should (or should not) work.

Discourse analysis has the potential to assist our understanding of legal borrowing in three respects. First, it provides a methodology for assessing whether social actors discussing legal transfers understand and are likely to learn from each other. Second, it locates legal meanings in 'interpretive communities' that share common epistemological and tactical assumptions about the meaning and function of law. Third, it shows that legal meanings are never closed because they change to reflect the strategies of state and non-state parties. These interpretive tools are used to open the discussion to the possibility that foreign and local discourses may shape legal transplants in different ways.

Ascertaining the Viability of Legal Transfers

One of the main conceptual difficulties with assessing legal transplantation is determining the criteria for success. Is success measured by transferring a legal provision into a host-country's legislation? Must transplants induce behavioural change of the kind contemplated by donor or host-country lawmakers? Or is it sufficient for legal transplants to act as catalysts for change, stimulating behaviour modifications in ways unforeseen by lawmakers?

The idea of success assumes that laws have measurable goals. According to Watson, most legal transplants are viable, simply because legal borrowing is a major source of law reform around the world. Legrand, by contrast, argues

---

84 Dezalay and Garth claim the legal transfers show 'the triumph of personal connections'. Yves Dezalay and Bryant Garth (1997), 'Law, Lawyers and Social Capital: 'Rule of Law' versus Relational Capitalism', 6 *Social and Legal Studies*, 109–43.

85 See Yves Dezalay and Bryant Garth (2001), *supra*, 241, 246–57. Also see Mark Van Hoecke and Mark Warrington (1998), 'Legal Cultures, Legal Paradigms and Legal Doctrine: Towards a New Model for Comparative Law', 47 *International and Comparative Law Quarterly*, 495, 516–19.

against an instrumental understanding of legal transplants because it conveys the misapprehension that law is about social engineering. He argues that legal transfers should be treated as narratives rather than instruments. Although reaching different conclusions, both theoretical approaches agree that transplant viability must refer in some way to legal behaviour in the recipient country. Otherwise, by definition, there is no transplant, only an indigenous law with foreign provisions or an institution with a foreign name.

A related issue is determining from whose perspective transplant viably should be assessed. Conventional legal theory, exemplified by the work of H.L.A. Hart, presumes that laws exist as external propositions until internalised to inform the experience and perception of individuals.[86] By implication, legal transplants are ineffective until individuals choose to internalise them. A difficulty with focusing on individual choice is that consent need not be given to the norms embedded in rules, but rather to the processes and forms of legal power.[87] It is interesting to speculate, for example, to what extent elderly and poorly educated Vietnamese farmers—75% of the population—respond to borrowed law according to individual choice or habit, pragmatism and expediency. Studies conducted elsewhere have shown that respondents generally have meagre knowledge of the law they are supposed to have internalised.[88] What little they know is often derived through membership of organisations or groups.

Further complicating the inquiry, a legal import may appear viable for one social group but unviable from another perspective. By challenging established patterns of behaviour, imported laws have the capacity to create winners and losers. For Western foreign investors in East Asia, rights-based law appears authentic and useful, but for domestic entrepreneurs the same laws may appear inauthentic and imposed. As Roger Cotterrell observed, 'the way law is conceptualised ... colours the way that the success (indeed, the very possibility) of legal borrowing is judged'.[89]

It follows that legal transplantation cannot be assessed from an outside 'objective' position. What constitutes successful legal borrowing is contested and negotiated at many points and there will be multiple perspectives about transplant viability. In fact, what constitutes success is something that is fought over, since it determines whether foreign legal solutions can leave behind their sense of inauthenticity and become localised. Discourse analysis is well suited to this inquiry, because it focuses on the way legal transfers are interpreted and deployed within the receiving culture.

---

86 See H.L.A. Hart (1961), *The Concept of Law*, Clarendon Press, Oxford, 132–37.

87 See generally Roger Cotterrell (1994), 'Introduction: The Law and Society Tradition', in Roger Cotterrell (ed.), *Law and Society*, Dartmouth, Aldershot, England, xi, xi–xvi.

88 See Berl Kutchinsky (1973), 'The Legal Consciousness: A Survey of Research and Opinion about Law', in A. Podgorecki *et al.* (eds), *Knowledge and Opinion About Law*, M. Robertson, London, 105.

89 Roger Cotterrell (2001), *supra*, 79.

Methodological Problems with Assessing Transplant Viability

Most studies of transplant viability are positivist.[90] They treat knowledge about law as social facts to be discovered, rather than processes that adjust the meaning of imported law among state officials and the public. This positivist orientation makes empirically testable propositions about what matters in legal transplantation appear feasible and desirable.

Despite their reassuring empiricism, statistical studies frequently miss the richness of regulatory processes.[91] This is a critical failing if the working postulates are correct, and the meaning of law is largely (though not exclusively) found in ideological and communicative processes. Empirical studies at best inform observers that certain imported laws induce varying levels of compliance. On a more practical level, the statistical data required for this type of analysis is generally unavailable in Vietnam.

Compounding the problem, there is little critical analysis of legal reforms, especially legal transplantation, in the Vietnamese literature. As a consequence, this study has drawn information from the abundant descriptive literature in Vietnam about the interaction between law, state ideology and institutional/market structures. Despite tight government controls over legal research, the author has conducted hundreds of interviews and focus group sessions with Vietnamese officials, lawyers, academics and entrepreneurs. It has been possible to construct from social-survey research and archival material many richly textured, in-depth case studies that assess legal transplantation in Vietnam.

Conclusion

The working postulates offer promising ways to guide research towards the sites of interaction between imported laws and Vietnamese institutions, processes and discourses. Gramscian ideological theory sensitises our analysis to the political contests shaping legal reception. An examination of power structures opens the discussion to contests between elite and local attitudes to imported law. Finally, a

---

90 See, for example, Daniel Berkowitz *et al.* (2003), 'The Transplant Effect', 51 *American Journal of Comparative Law* 163, 180–88; Philip M. Nichols (1997), 'The Viability of Transplanted Law: Kazakhstani Reception of a Transplanted Foreign Investment Code', 18 *University of Pennsylvania Journal of International Law* (4), 1235, 1255–70.

91 For example, empirical studies usually assume equivalence in cultural responses to law. A recent study sought to rank the viability of legal transplants in over 40 countries by comparing 'legality'. This highly subjective notion was deduced from perceptional indexes about the 'rule of law', judicial effectiveness, low corruption, low risk of contract repudiation and low risk of government expropriation. What the perception indexes did not disclose is whether 'legality' is a product of cultural discord, political power struggles, administrative abuses, innovative adaptations of imported law, legal pluralism, or some combination thereof. See Daniel Berkowitz *et al.* (2003), *supra*, 180–88.

study of special interest groups directs analysis towards the dialogical exchanges between state and non-state groups that shape the meaning of imported laws.

The working postulates imply that comprehensive legal borrowing across political, economic and cultural boundaries is likely to excite fragmented and uneven legal compliance. This preliminary assessment presents a dilemma for Vietnamese lawmakers attempting to develop a market-oriented legal system. Either the entire sociopolitical structure must change to reflect the institutional environment in donor countries or, more plausibly, transplantation will induce layered or fragmented legal compliance.

The working postulates are flexibly applied in the following chapters to assess how Vietnamese ideologies, state institutions and special interest groups influence the meanings attributed to legal transplants. Since they act as heuristics, rather than rigid theoretical templates, some postulates are more relevant to particular case studies than others. Our inquiry begins in the next chapter by examining the history of legal transplantation to Vietnam.

Chapter 2

A Brief History of Legal Transplantation into Vietnam

Introduction

Before considering contemporary legal borrowing into Vietnam, it is necessary to understand the past. A theme underlying this chapter is that contemporary mental habits and perceptions are 'the end product of repeated action in the past, of prolonged behaviour in the past'.[1] Thus the historical patterns of legal transplantation have a bearing on the way contemporary lawmakers think about legal borrowing. The purpose here is not to attempt the impossible and present the legal history of Vietnam in a chapter, but rather to introduce the main ideas and processes that have contemporary relevance.

What little has been written about Vietnamese legal history suggests that legal transplantation into Vietnam is not a new phenomenon. Vietnamese lawmakers and citizens have been grappling for centuries with how to select, naturalise and implement foreign laws. A good starting point in understanding legal history is to map the who, when, how and why of legal change. Who imported law? What was the sequencing of legal borrowing? What were the sources of borrowed law? What institutions and practices were influenced? What part did ideology, state institutions and social structures play in these transformations?

In examining centuries of legal borrowing, the discussion considers the grand social forces shaping law, such as social movements, revolutions and significant individuals. Yet this chapter is primarily descriptive in nature. In subsequent chapters the focus shifts to finding explanations for the puzzles and anomalies in contemporary patterns of legal transfer.

---

1 See Owen Barfield (1979), *History, Guilt, and Habit*, Wesleyan University Press, Middletown, Connecticut, 74. See David Marr (2000), 'History and Memory in Vietnam Today: The Journal Xua & Nay', 31 *Journal of Southeast Asian Studies* (1), 1–25.

Legal Borrowing in the Pre-modern Legal System

The Period of Chinese Domination

The recorded history of legal borrowing in Vietnam begins with the Chinese domination in 111 BC. Small proto-states with differentiated state and social power structures emerged before this period,[2] but formal legal rules were undifferentiated from cultural precepts, state institutions were fused with personal rule, and specialised legal institutions and written laws were unknown.

More than any other external source, Chinese political-legal ideas influenced Vietnamese legal thinking and practices. Chinese ideas and practices came to Vietnam with the invading Han dynasty armies in 111 BC. For 1000 years (111 BC–938 AD), first under the Han dynasty (206 BC–220 AD) and later under the Tang dynasty (589–907 AD), Chinese scholarship, political theories, religious values, family structures and bureaucratic practices indoctrinated and moulded, though never entirely supplanted, indigenous Vietnamese outlooks.[3]

Commentators disagree about the extent to which Chinese political-legal thinking penetrated and transformed indigenous Vietnamese precepts and practices. Some contemporary nationalistic texts read history backwards to demonstrate an indigenous cultural core.[4] These writings implausibly maintain 'the regulations, customs and habits of Vietnam still prevailed, as they had existed long before' 1000 years of Chinese domination.[5] Some Western writers are more circumspect and believe fewer qualitative cultural differences survived Chinese annexation.[6]

During centuries of Chinese domination, several factors conspired to preserve local practices. The Chinese ruled urban centres leaving ethnic Vietnamese in

---

2 See Dinh Ngoc Vuong (1995), 'The State and Law in the Hung Kings Period', 1 *Vietnam Law and Legal Forum* (9), 31, 31–33; Nguyen Ngoc Huy and Ta Va Tai (1987), *The Le Code: Law in Traditional Vietnam*, Ohio University Press, Athens, Ohio, 4; cf. Charles Higham (1989), *The Archaeology of Mainland Southeast Asia: from 10,000 B.C. to the Fall of Angkor*, Cambridge University Press, Cambridge.

3 See Keith Taylor (1983), *The Birth of Vietnam*, University of California Press, Berkeley. Taylor modified some of his early views, see Keith Taylor (1998), 'Surface Orientations in Vietnam: Beyond Histories of Nations and Regions', 57 *Journal of Asian Studies* (4), 949.

4 See, for example, Phan Huy Le (1991), 'The Vietnamese Traditional Village: Historical Evolution and Socio-Economic Structure', *Vietnam Social Sciences* (1), 39, 40–43; Phan Huy Le (1994), 'The Problem of Democracy in Vietnam's Traditions', *Vietnam Social Sciences* (4), 3, 4–10; Dao Tri Uc and Le Minh Thong (1999), 'Su Tiep Nhan Cac Gia Tri Phap Ly Phuong Dong va Phuong Tay Doi Voi Su Phat Trien Cac Tu Tuong Phap Ly Viet Nam' (Reception of Oriental and Occidental Legal Values in the Development of Vietnamese Legal Ideology), *Nha Nuoc va Phap Luat* (5), 3, 3–15.

5 Pham Diem (1995), 'A Brief Look at the Rule by Feudal China (from 179 BC to the Xth Century)', 1 *Vietnam Law and Legal Forum* (10), 28–29.

6 See K.W. Taylor (1995), 'Preface', in K.W. Taylor and J.K. Whitmore (eds), *Essays Into Vietnamese Pasts*, Southeast Asia Program, Cornell University, Ithaca, 5.

control of villages and communes.[7] Language barriers prevented most villagers from gaining a deep understanding of Chinese culture and few Vietnamese completed the classical Confucian training required for social advancement.[8] Further limiting local access to Chinese culture, Chinese rulers evidently modified the transplanted Confucian canon to suit local conditions. Legalism (*fa*) rather than humanistic moral persuasion (*li*) was considered more appropriate for the resistive and morally unperfected indigenous population.[9]

Nevertheless, over 10 centuries of Chinese domination transplanted Confucian, Buddhist and Taoist religious values, transformed elite outlooks and indirectly influenced village thinking. That the early Vietnamese imperial regimes both resembled and differed from the Chinese template implies that sinic influence stimulated indigenous values, producing local political-legal adaptations.

Receiving Chinese Legal Thinking in Imperial Vietnam

Following independence from China in 939 the Ly dynasty (1009–1225) embarked on a period of national reconstruction in which Buddhism challenged the rather weak Confucian hierarchical structures.[10] Although Confucianism gained prestige during the Tran dynasty (1225–1400), it was not until the watershed Le (1428–1788) dynasty and later Nguyen (1802–1945) dynasty that rulers borrowed extensively from Chinese laws and bureaucratic processes. Chinese transplants eventually produced an elite political-legal culture more in line with the Tang and Ming dynasties than earlier Ly and Tran dynastic practices.

Confucianism was not the only political-legal thinking shaping indigenous approaches to law—far from it—but it exerted the most profound influence over political-legal thinking and practices. The following section traces the competing influences, both external and internal, that shaped Vietnamese dynasties' rule.

---

7 See K.W. Taylor (1980), 'An Evaluation of the Chinese Period in Vietnamese History', 23 *Journal of Asiatic Studies* (1), 146, 146–48; Pham Diem (1995), *supra*, 28–29; Alexander Woodside (1971), *A Comparative Study of Nguyen and Ch'ing Civil Government in the First Half of the Nineteenth Century*, Harvard University Press, Cambridge, Massachusetts, 7–8. Also see Pham Diem (1995), *supra*, 29.

8 See Woodside (1971), *supra*, 6–7.

9 See David Marr (1971), *Vietnamese Anticolonialism*, University of California Press, Berkeley, 10.

10 See Cuong Tu Nguyen (1995), 'Rethinking Vietnamese Buddhist History: Is the Thien Uyen Tap Anh a "Transmission of the Lamp" Text?', in K.W. Taylor and J.K. Whitmore (eds), *Essays into Vietnamese Pasts*, Southeast Asia Program, Cornell University, Ithaca, 81, 113–15; Ha Van Tan (1992), 'Buddhism from the Ngo to the Tran Dynasties', in Nguyen Tai Thu (ed.), *History of Buddhism in Vietnam*, Social Sciences Publishing House, Hanoi, 100–3,117–25.

Building a Political-legal System

After 1000 years of domination, Chinese knowledge was the natural cultural and legal reference point in the Ly and Tran dynasties.[11] The most important cultural import was the 'reduction of religions into the same source' (*tam giao dong nguyen*), which syncretistically blended Confucianism, Mahayana Buddhism and Taoism.[12]

Buddhist teachings that emphasised spiritual liberation through ethical conduct and discipline initially came to Vietnam from India, but Mahayana Buddhism (which arrived via China) came to dominate.[13] Taoism privileged the natural order, charting a passage to 'the way' through mysticism. It rapidly became interwoven with indigenous animist spirit cults and rituals. When combined with Confucian beliefs, the 'reduction of the religions into the same source' provided numerous ethical permutations and combinations to syncretically reinterpret and consolidate Chinese governance practices.[14]

In contrast with China, where the Confucian canon was treated as an all-encompassing source of political, social and moral authority, Ly and Tran officials in Vietnam used Confucian texts as persuasive precedents for guiding state policy. The moral and historical precepts that gave coherence and context to the canon were often ignored. As Wolters opined, 'they localised the Confucian corpus by fragmenting it and detaching passages, drained of their original contextual meaning, in order to appropriate fragments at their discretion and fit them into the context of their own statements'.[15]

Le and especially Nguyen emperors thought political-legal alternatives to neo-Confucianism, such as Buddhism, were incapable of managing a sophisticated

11 The literature dealing with the construction of a national identity following Chinese rule is extensive, see, for example, Ester Ungar (1986), 'From Myth to History: Imagined Polities in 14th Century Vietnam', in David Marr and A.C. Milner (eds), *Southeast Asia in the 9th and 14th Centuries*, Institute of Southeast Asian Studies, Singapore, 177–86; Keith K. Taylor (1988), 'Authority and Legitimacy in Eleventh-Century Vietnam', 12 *Vietnam Forum*, 20–59; Nguyen Ngoc Huy and Ta Van Tai (1986), 'The Vietnamese Texts' in M. B. Hooker (ed.), *The Laws of Southeast Asia: The Pre-Modern Texts*, Butterworths, Singapore, 449–51; Tran Thi Tuyet (1996), 'The State and the Law of the Tran dynasty', 2 *Vietnam Law and Legal Forum* (18), 28, 28–29.

12 See O. Wolters (1979a), 'Assertions of Cultural Well-being in Vietnam', 10 *Journal of Southeast Asian Studies*, 435, 442–43; L. Cadiere (1958), *Religious Beliefs and Practices of the Vietnamese*, Working Paper 60, trans. I. Mabbett, Centre for South East Asian Studies, Monash University, 11–20.

13 See Minh Chi (1992), 'Buddhism's Entry into Vietnam and Its Practice During Chinese Control', in Nguyen Tai Thu (ed.), *History of Buddhism in Vietnam*, Social Sciences Publishing House, Hanoi, 1–15.

14 See K.W. Taylor (1988), *supra*, 45–49; John K. Whitmore (1984), 'Social Organization and Confucian Thought in Vietnam', 15 *Journal of Southeast Asian Studies*, 294, 297–98.

15 O. Wolters (1979a), *supra*, 435, 437.

irrigated rice economy and resolving interminable imperial succession disputes.[16] Le rulers used Confucian social hierarchies backed by a Chinese-style bureaucratic legal system to centralise power over fractious aristocratic oligarchies.[17] In addition to the technical superiority of, and prestige commanded by, Chinese law, Nguyen emperors during the nineteenth century were attracted to sinic governance models as a means of counteracting increasing Western influence. Some high officials in the Nguyen court had fled the Ming dynasty. Their mixed Chinese-Vietnamese ancestry and their sinic cultural outlook facilitated highly sophisticated legal and institutional borrowing from China.[18]

Legal Borrowing

From the Le dynasty onwards, Vietnamese emperors applied a Sino-Vietnamese version of virtue-rule (*duc/nhan tri*) and legal rule (*phap tri*).[19] These principles rested on imported beliefs, such as the 'Heavenly Mandate' (*Thien Menh*), and the cultivation of virtuous conduct through the five cardinal relationships. As David Marr observed, 'Ethical cement for this structure was supplied by a set of cardinal virtues, the number eventually stabilising at five: "benevolence" (*nhan*), "righteousness" (*nghia*), "ritual" (*le*), "knowledge" (*tri*) and "sincerity" (*tin*)'.[20] Confucian scholars deduced moral principles from everyday life rather than from interpretations of

16 See Trung Anh (1995), 'Legal Thought of Vietnam Feudalist Class', 2 *Vietnam Law and Legal Forum* (13), 24, 24–25.

17 See Vu Van Vinh (1999), 'Development of Confucianism in the Tran dynasty and the Struggle of Confucian Scholars against Buddhism at the End of the XIV Century', *Vietnam Social Science* (2), 55, 57–60; J.K. Whitmore (1987), 'Foreign Influences and the Vietnamese Cultural Core: A Discussion of the Pre-modern Period', in Truong Buu Lam (ed.), *Borrowings and Adaptations in Vietnamese Culture*, Southeast Asia Paper No. 25, Center for Asian and Pacific Studies, University of Hawaii, 1, 8–10; R.B. Smith (1973), 'The Cycle of Confucianization in Vietnam,' in W.F. Vella (ed.), *Aspects of Vietnamese History*, University Press of Hawaii, Honolulu, 6–24.

18 See J.K. Whitmore (1977), 'Chiao-chih and Neo-Confucianism', 4 *Ming Studies*, 51, 51–91. Also see John R. Clammer (1981), 'French Studies on the Chinese in Indochina: A Bibliographical Survey', 12 *Journal of South East Asian Studies*, 15, 17–18.

19 Most contemporary accounts of the early Le dynasty rely on versions of the *Dai Viet Su Ky Toan Thu* (Complete Historical Records of the *Dai Viet*) that were revised during the Mac dynasties to emphasise the benefits of centralising and sinicising under Le Thanh Tong's regime. See J.K. Whitmore (1995), 'Chung-hsing and Cheng-t'-ung in Texts of and on Sixteenth-Century Viet Nam', in K.W. Taylor and J.K. Whitmore (eds), *Essays Into Vietnamese Pasts*, Studies on Southeast Asia No. 19, Cornell University Press, Ithaca, 116–36; Nola Cooke (1994), 'Nineteenth-Century Vietnamese Confucianisation in Historical Perceptive: Evidence from the Palace Examinations (1463–1883)', 25 *Journal of Southeast Asian Studies* (2), 277, 277–82, 303, 305.

20 See David Marr (1981), *Vietnamese Tradition on Trial 1920-1945*, University of California Press, Berkeley, 58. Also see Chuong Thau and Phan Ngoc (1994), 'Confucianism in Vietnam Seen from an Historical Tradition', *Vietnamese Studies* (1), 85.

sacred revealed texts.[21] They believed that if men were persuaded by education, social pressure and virtuous example to live morally, laws were unnecessary.

In practice legalist (*phap gia*) thinking intertwined with virtue-rule (*duc tri*) and played a prominent role in pre-modern governance.[22] Counterbalancing Confucian humanism, legalist thinking promoted by Chinese Confucian scholars such as Hsun-tzu saw state law as a means of codifying, though certainly never replacing, virtue-rule.[23] Imperial rulers in China and Vietnam saw no inconsistency in championing virtue-rule while controlling social behaviour with draconian penal laws (*phap tri*) and a strong administrative apparatus.

That legalist thinking influenced Le and Nguyen rulers is seen in the meticulous attention given to developing legal codes and administrative structures. Many provisions in the *Le Trieu Hinh Luat* (Le dynasty Penal Code), popularly called the *Bo Luat Hong Duc* (Hong Duc Code), were either borrowed directly from, or substantially influenced by, the Tang Code and Ming Codes.[24] Yet the Code contained many provisions that were not found in the Chinese legal texts. They included provisions compensating landowners for unauthorised government appropriation, private encroachment on land and fraudulent sales. In vitiating contracts for fraud and duress, and forbidding market manipulation and usury, the Code intervened in village commerce in ways never countenanced by Chinese law. Imperial interest in market regulation suggests that the Le dynasty in Vietnam was not as anti-mercantile as the Tang and Ming dynasties in China.[25]

Locally-developed legislative provisions were not confined to commerce and also reflected differences between Vietnamese and Chinese village and family structures. Unlike Chinese practice, in Vietnam it was the village officials, rather than family heads, who compiled the population registers used to assess taxation and corvée. The Code also adjusted gender rights to preserve the higher status women enjoyed

21 Randall Peerenboom (1998), 'Confucian Harmony and Freedom of Thought', in William Theodore de Barry and Tu Weiming (eds), *Confucianism and Human Rights*, Columbia University Press, New York, 234–60.

22 See Ta Van Tai (2001), 'The Rule of Law in the Traditional Law of Traditional China and Vietnam: Traditional East Asian Legal Practice in the Light of the Standards of the Modern Rule of Law', *Vietnamese Studies* (4), 128, 130–35.

23 See Hsun-tzu (1967), 'Human Nature is Evil', in B. Watson (trans. and ed.), *Basic Writings of Mo Tzu, Hsun Tzu and Han Fie Tzu*, Columbia University Press, New York, 162–63. Also see Randall Peerenboom (2002), *China's Long March to a Rule of Law*, Cambridge University Press, Cambridge, 28–36.

24 Of the Code's 722 articles, 200 were either directly borrowed from, or substantially influenced by, the Tang Code, and 17 were borrowed from the Ming Code. See Ta Van Tai (1982), 'Vietnam's Code of the Le dynasty (1428–1788)', 30 *American Journal of Comparative Law* (3), 523, 525. Also see Legal Research Institute (1999), *Mot So Van Ve Phap Luat Dan Su Viet Nam Tu The Ky 15 Den Thoi Phap Thuoc* (Some Issues about Civil Vietnamese Law From the 15th Century until French Colonisation), Vien Khoa Phap Ly (Legal Research Institute), Hanoi.

25 Whitmore (1984), *supra*, 304.

in Vietnamese society. Married women, for example, were entitled to reclaim their contributions to matrimonial estates after their husbands' death.[26]

Legal borrowing reached a zenith with the Nguyen dynasty. The *Hoang Viet Luat Le* (Laws and Decrees of Imperial Viet), completed by Emperor Nguyen Gia Long in 1815, slavishly copied the Ching Code.[27] Of its 398 articles, all but one were either identical to or closely based on Ching Code articles. It strengthened the criminalisation of neo-Confucian morality and removed most indigenous provisions found in the Le Code. Despite careful borrowing, subtle changes in meaning occurred during the translation of Chinese provisions into Vietnamese *nom* characters.

Insun Yu opined that 'Vietnamese law was basically concerned with the maintenance of the ruler's position, rather than with implementing the ultimate social ethics of Confucianism'.[28] Perhaps more than their Chinese contemporaries, Le and Nguyen rulers used criminal law as an instrument of state building.[29] Whether this implies qualitative differences between Vietnamese and Chinese political-legal thought is an open question.

There is little discussion in documents from the period about the practical implementation of law. Commentaries stress the merits of virtue-rule (*duc tri*) over legal rule (*phap tri*), but rulers used the law in tandem with virtue-rule to secure specific objectives. Mandarins were encouraged to base their decisions on written law.[30] The Nguyen Code, for example, required mandarins to cite the relevant legal sources when pronouncing a sentence.[31] In theory, even emperors could not change written laws without following amendment procedures.

The problem for mandarins was finding the penalty most suited to a case through either precedent or analogy. Problems arose in the numerous instances where provisions in the Codes and edicts did not directly relate to the facts in particular cases. In these circumstances, mandarins in the *Bo Hinh* (Justice Board) followed the Chinese practice and collected case commentaries to assist court decision-making. Case law was not binding and there was little attempt to categorise a system of

26 Le Code, articles 308, 322, 375, 388 and 391. See Tran Thi Tuyet (2000), 'Vietnam's Feudal Laws and the Protection of Women's Interests', 6 *Vietnam Law and Legal Forum* (65), 28, 28–30; Nguyen Viet Huong (1996), '*Quoc Trieu Hinh Luat* and the Personal and Property Relations in Feudal Families', 3 *Vietnam Law and Legal Forum* (25), 22, 22–25; David W. Haines (1984), 'Reflections of Kinship and Society under Vietnam's Le dynasty', 15 *Journal of South Eastern Studies*, 307, 309–13.

27 See Tran Thi Tuyet (1997), 'The Nguyen dynasty and its Legislation in the First Half of the 19th Century', 3 *Vietnam Law and Legal Forum* (32), 24, 24–25.

28 Insun Yu (1990), *Law and Society in 17th and 18th Century Vietnam*, Asiatic Research Center, Korea University, Seoul, 89–104.

29 See Nguyen Ngoc Huy and Ta Van Tai (1987), *supra*, 56–68; cf. Fu-mei Chang Chen (1970), 'On Analogy in Ching Law', 30 *Harvard Journal of Asiatic Studies*, 212.

30 See Pham Diem (2001), 'Judiciary Offences under Vietnam's Ancient Laws', 7 *Vietnam Law and Legal Forum* (82), 20–21, 32.

31 Nguyen Code article 380. See Ta Van Tai (2001), *supra*, 133.

doctrine and principles. Legalist jurisprudence had a rich 'case law', but no consistent means of drawing on accumulated experiences.

Where analogy failed, catchall provisions allowed mandarins to criminalise 'doing what should not be done', or those 'committing wicked acts'. It did not matter that such behaviour was not otherwise proscribed by statute.[32] Behind these provisions lay a concern to maintain moral order, notwithstanding gaps and contradictions in the written law. This practice gave considerable regulatory power to the Confucian literati. By setting the moral tone of virtuous behaviour, the literati infused written law with normative and contextual meaning. Later chapters find echoes of this system in contemporary judicial practices.

Written law was not intended to have autonomous authority. Indeed the people were not expected to know the law. As with China, no clear divisions separating legality and morality were thought possible or desirable. The Vietnamese term *thoa dang* describes the situational validity of law and morality.[33] *Thoa dang* encouraged decision-makers to syncretically select from moral and ethical sources (especially the 'reduction of religions into the same source') to find ethical solutions to specific problems. Exogenous normative sources such as laws were not considered absolute, universal or immutable, but rather alternate sources of guidance. Decision-making processes were expected to personalise rational rules. Outcome-orientated decision-making attempted to generate harmony by blending competing moral and social precepts. Legal rules were in the process subordinated to moral and pragmatic expediencies. Many Vietnamese proverbs highlight the transcendence of local norms and practices over generalised legal principles. For example, '*mot bo cai ly khong bang mot ty cai tinh*' (a granary of reason does not equal a little bit of feeling) and law is the lowest form of morality.

In sum, virtue-rule and legal rule coexisted and were intertwined. Legal rules and procedures were widely used to implement imperial policy and deliver justice to the people, but they were used instrumentally to secure particular outcomes. The normative content of law resided more in the writings of the Confucian literati than in legal codes. This meant that imperial rule relied on personal interaction and virtue-rule much more than abstract rules and processes. State-sponsored norms were situationally rather than universally relevant, their primary purpose being to make the punishment fit the crime and social status and to preserve Confucian social hierarchies.

---

32 'Whoever commits an act that should not be done shall be condemned to penal servitude or exiled for a major wrong and demoted or fined for a minor one.' Le Code, article 642; Nguyen Code, article 351.

33 These comments are based on interviews with Hoang Ngoc Hien, a Vietnamese sociologist and literary critic who specialises in state-village relations. Also see Nguyen Van Huyen (1995), *The Ancient Civilization of Vietnam*, (reprint) The Gioi Publishers, Hanoi, 277–48. Also see O. Wolters (1979a), *supra*, 442–43; L. Cadiere (1958), *supra*, 80–81.

Localising Chinese Political-legal Thinking

Imported Chinese political-legal thinking interacted differently with the imperial elite and villagers. It is possible that private writings may eventually reveal a diverse and even heterodox range of views among the literati that is largely missing from official accounts, but surviving records suggest that Chinese political-legal thought was imported with little recorded discussion and dissent. Even so, some discussion took place, because Confucian literati were expected to renew and reinvigorate neo-Confucian morality and political governance through discussion and criticism.[34]

Imported Chinese law not only interacted at an elite level, it also influenced village thinking. At the end of the fifteenth century, when the Le dynasty reached the peak of its power, court-appointed mandarins played an important role in administering villages.[35] When Gia Long tried to reassert central power over villages in the early nineteenth century, independently-minded local authorities resisted centralisation. Subsequent attempts by other members of the Nguyen dynasty to implement their vision for an orderly and morally homogeneous Confucian society conflicted with relatively flexible, loosely structured village organisations.[36] The familiar injunction *phep vua thua le lang* (the laws of the emperor give way to the customs of the village), which originated during this period, implies some degree of village resistance to imperial political-legal thinking. For example, central rules that restricted female inheritance never entered popular village practice.[37] At the same time, local religious and cultural precepts undoubtedly combined with, and moderated the penetration of, imported laws and institutions into villages.

Yet village autonomy was more a function of imperial forbearance than a formal legal doctrine; elite ideology influenced some local practices.[38] The Le dynasty and especially the Nguyen dynasty codes established a legal architecture that enmeshed village (*xa*) leaders and family heads into the state system. Emperors, for example, issued edicts regulating large provincial markets, and market chiefs (*trum cho*) were appointed by mandarins to maintain central laws.[39] The most substantial criminal penalties, which punished violations of the five-relationships (*ngu luan*), reached

34 See J.K. Whitmore (1972), 'Note: The Vietnamese Confucian Scholar's View of His County's Early History', in J.K. Whitmore and K. Hall (eds), *Explorations of Early Southeast Asian History*, Vol 1, Cornell University Press, Ithaca, 193–203. Also see Pham Duy Nghia (2003), 'Noi Doanh Nhan Tim Den Cong Ly' (Where do Entrepreneurs Go for Justice?), *Nghien Cuu Lap Phap* (3), 45–54.

35 See Martin Grossheim (2004), 'Village Government in Pre-Colonial Vietnam', in Benedict J. Tria Kerkvliet and David G. Marr (eds), *Beyond Hanoi: Local Government in Vietnam*, Institute of Southeast Asian Studies, Singapore, 55–58.

36 See Woodside (1971), *supra*, 60–66, 94–98.

37 See Nguyen Ngoc Huy and Ta Van Tai (1987), *supra*, 475–89; Nguyen Ngoc Huy and Ta Van Tai (1986), *supra*, 488–89.

38 See Marr (1981), *supra*, 58–61.

39 See David Marr (2004), *supra*, 30–32; Nguyen Thua Hy (2002), *Economic History of Hanoi*, National Political Publishing House, Hanoi, 285–86.

into village and family life. Crimes by wives against husbands and especially by children against parents (filial piety *hieu*) were considered more heinous than offences against social inferiors.[40]

As morally superior 'first knowers', mandarins were obliged to inculcate Confucian doctrines in those slower to understand.[41] They vetted village conventions (*huong uoc*) and rules (*huong le*) to ensure compliance with the neo-Confucian orthodoxy.[42] But in practice their influence was limited. Central-level mandarins rarely visited villages and the local literati practised non-orthodox versions of Confucianism. Contradictions in Confucianism between loyalty to ruler and family further compounded elite-village dichotomies.

In recognising practical limits to their power, Vietnamese rulers only extended control to larger centres, leaving village rituals and customs to regulate everyday commerce.[43] Conflicts arising from business deals and contracts were mediated by village elders, neighbourhood and merchant associations and families operating outside the state judicial hierarchy.[44] Official dispute resolution exposed disputants and, by extension, their families and village to loss of proper virtue and not infrequently to demands for bribes.[45]

Summary

For Alexander Woodside, 'Vietnamese borrowing from China exhibited the usual variegated patterns of acculturation in which some institutions and objects spread rapidly from one society to another, some spread more slowly, and some do not spread at all or are rejected'.[46] Nguyen rulers believed that effective neo-Confucian virtue-rule (*duc tri*) required the wholesale adoption of Chinese ideology,

---

40 See Pham Diem (1999), 'Criminal Offences under Ancient Laws of Vietnam', 5 *Vietnam Law and Legal Forum* (58), 27, 27–29.

41 See Alexander Woodside (1999), 'Exalting the Latecomer State', in Anita Chan *et al.* (eds), *Transforming Asian Socialism: China and Vietnam Compared*, Allen and Unwin, Sydney, 23–24.

42 See Le Hong Son (1995), 'Village Conventions and their Role in Rural Management in Vietnam', 1 *Vietnam Law and Legal Forum* (11), 21, 21–22; Bui Xuan Dinh (1985), *Le Lang Phep Nuoc*, (Customary Law and State Law), Law Publishing House, Hanoi, chapter three.

43 Ibid.

44 See Nguyen Duc Nginh (1993), 'Markets and Villages', in Phan Huy Le *et al.*, *The Traditional Village in Vietnam*, The Gioi Publishers, Hanoi, 352–55; Anthony Reid (1993), *Southeast Asia in the Age of Commerce 1450–1680*, Vol. 2, Silkworm Books, Chiang Mai, 136–38.

45 See Ta Van Tai (1988), *The Vietnamese Tradition on Human Rights*, Institute of East Asian Studies, Berkeley, 204; Pierre Poivre (1993), 'Journey to Cochinchina' in Li Tana and Anthony Reid (eds), *Southern Vietnam under the Nguyen: Documents on the Economic History of Cochinchina*, Data Paper Series, Institute of Southeast Asian Studies, Singapore, 68, 74–75.

46 Woodside (1971), *supra*, 81.

governmental organisations and political-legal culture, and eclectic borrowing risked organisational disunity. They thought that borrowing a complete system would minimise incompatibility between foreign and indigenous cultural precepts. The voluntary large-scale political-legal borrowing by Le and Nguyen rulers was unprecedented in other pre-colonial East Asian countries (with the possible exception of Korea) and foreshadowed the wholesale importation of the Soviet political-legal system centuries later.[47]

Through intense indoctrination over the centuries, imported neo-Confucian political-legal beliefs came to order many facets of elite and village life. What were once alien ideas and practices had, through a process of acculturation and hybridisation, become sino-Vietnamese virtue-rule, moral precepts and legal rules and practices. But imported ideas were not evenly adopted, and longstanding elite-village dichotomies persisted.

The French Colonial Period, 1862–1945

The shift from pre-modern to colonial rule in Vietnam demonstrates there are rarely clear lines marking the end of one era and the beginning of another. Colonial rule officially began when the Nguyen Emperor, Tu Duc, signed a treaty ceding three provinces to the French in 1862.[48] The French made Cochin China (Southern Vietnam) a colony in 1862, and Annam (Central Vietnam) and Tonkin (Northern Vietnam) became mandated territories in 1884 under the notional leadership of the Nguyen emperors.

Transplanting French Colonial Legal Thinking

French transplantation theories French colonial authorities used the pluralistic 'legal collaboration' policy to mould the interaction between French and neo-Confucian political-legal thought.[49] Legal collaboration permitted the metropolitan French legal system to coexist with a modified pre-colonial imperial and village administration in Annam and Tonkin. The metropolitan and indigenous systems were never equal because royal edicts were ineffective unless endorsed by the French

47 See Masaji Chiba (1986), 'Three-Level Structure of Law in Contemporary Japan—The Shinto Society', in Masaji Chiba (ed.), *Asian Indigenous Law: In Interaction with Received Law*, KPI, London, 304–7. Also see Dae-Kyu Yoon (1997), 'Korea' in Poh-Ling Tan (ed.), *Asian Legal Systems*, Butterworths, Sydney, 162–67.

48 Three more Vietnamese provinces were ceded to the French in 1867. See Nguyen The Anh (1985), 'The Vietnamese Monarchy Under the French Colonial Rule 1884–1945', 19 *Modern Asian Studies* 147–51; Michael Barry Hooker (1979), *A Concise Legal History of South East Asia*, Clarendon Press, Oxford, 175–85.

49 See Michael Barry Hooker (1975), *Legal Pluralism: An Introduction to Colonial and Neo-Colonial Law*, Clarendon Press, Oxford, 232–35; S.H. Roberts (1929), *The History of French Colonial Policy 1870–1925*, (new impression 1963) Frank Cass, London, 64–75.

Resident-Superieur.[50]

Contrasting with colonisation policies in *colonie de peuplement* (settlement colonies) like Algeria, where one legal system regulated everyone, a complex 'conflict of laws' regime existed in Vietnam. Collaboration policy permitted indigenous law to regulate village life provided it did not compromise public order. In theory, two different legal systems coexisted—one stacked upon the other—within the same geopolitical borders.[51]

French law governed disputes between French citizens and the indigenous population.[52] Vietnamese living in Cochin China and Tonkin (but not Annam) could voluntarily articulate disputes into the French system. The laws of France automatically extended to Cochin China and large urban centres (such as Hanoi, Hai Phong and Tourane), except where they conflicted with local administrative arrangements.

Elsewhere, the French preserved a modified version of pre-colonial governance.[53] Imperial cooperation was considered vital to colonial ambitions, since it confined local resistance within imperial and village organisational structures. Rule through local authorities was especially pronounced in Annam, where the Nguyen Emperors maintained imperial government structures staffed by court-appointed mandarins.[54] Mandarins enlisted sentimental loyalties—*trung quan* (loyalty to the king)—to legitimise neo-Confucian rule.

Implementing Colonial Rule

Over time, tensions emerged between the centralising aspirations of French colonial rulers and local indigenous practices.[55] In Cochin China, the French were forced to regulate villagers, because mandarins refused to collaborate with the colonial regime.[56] French-appointed village chiefs filtered administrative orders and central

---

50 See Nguyen The Anh (1985), *supra*, 153–54.

51 See Hooker (1975), *supra*, 247.

52 Ibid, 199–201, 230–37. Also see Pham Diem (1997), 'The State Structure in French-Ruled Vietnam (1858–1945)', 3 *Vietnam Law and Legal Forum* (33), 27; See Pham Diem (1999), 'Vietnamese Court System Under the French', 5 *Vietnam Law and Legal Forum* (54), 27, 27–30.

53 See Hooker (1975), *supra*, 232–33.

54 See Nola Cooke (1995), 'The Composition of the Nineteenth-Century Political Elite of Pre-Colonial Nguyen *Vietnam', 29 Modern Asian Studies (4), 741;* Nguyen The Anh (1985), 'The Vietnamese Monarchy under the French Colonial Rule 1884-1945' 19 *Modern Asian Studies*, 152–55; David Marr (1971), *supra*, 161–62.

55 See Hooker (1975), *supra*, 246–48 (French law cannot easily coexist with customary law).

56 See Milton Osborne (1969) *The French Presence in Cochin China and Cambodia: Rule and Response (1859-1905)*, Cornell University Press, Ithaca, New York, 78–79. Non-cooperation is also attributable to local resistance to the French assimilationist policies practised at this time.

edicts regulating the *état-civil* (registry system), tax collection and education programmes through neo-Confucian precepts.[57] It was not until the early 1920s in Tonkin and 1942 in Annam that French authorities attempted to strengthen control over village administrators with 'model' village conventions.[58] As Martin Grossheim noted, French attempts to democratise village authorities and reduce the corrupt power of village notables in Tonkin brought chaos to village administration.[59] Colonial authorities eventually acknowledged their failure to transplant democratic accountability and during the 1940s sought to restore the authority of village notables.

Implementing Transplanted Law

Colonial law could hardly have differed more from indigenous virtue-rule and asymmetric legal hierarchies. Revolutionary ideals infused French law with notions about 'mankind's natural, inalienable and sacred rights'.[60] These ideals translated into commercial rights governing sanctity of contract, private property, free enterprise and separate legal categories for administrative, criminal, commercial and civil law. French law also manifested liberal ideology promoting legal equality, positive liberty (only laws can remove liberty), religious freedom, public expression and, most importantly, the notion that private rights check public power.[61]

Like other colonising powers (for example, the Dutch in the East Indies), colonial authorities used law primarily to maintain social order and serve French commercial interests. They imported commercial laws (including contracts, land titling, security interests over land and company laws) required to regulate transplanted capitalist institutions.[62] Since imported commercial law only applied to Europeans and assimilated Vietnamese, incongruities with indigenous commercial practices were considered irrelevant.

In 1880, a committee, largely Vietnamese in composition, was convened to draft a civil code for Cochin China that reflected indigenous social and commercial practices. Drawing extensively from the Le and Nguyen Codes, the draft civil code contained legal principles embodying customary practices that were set in a legal framework recognisable to French legal theory. Even this modest reform offended colonial sensibilities, since aspects of Vietnamese legal culture were considered

57 See Osborne (1969), *supra*, 85–87.

58 See Martin Grossheim (2004), *supra* 55; Le Hong Son (1995), 'Village Conventions and their Role in Rural Management in Vietnam', 1 *Vietnam Law and Legal Forum* (11), 21, 21–22; Bui Xuan Dinh (1985), *Le Lang Phep Nuoc*, (Customary Law and State Law), Law Publishing House, Hanoi, chapter three.

59 Martin Grossheim (2004), *supra*, 70–73.

60 See J.H. Steart (1951), *A Documentary Survey of the French Revolution*, Free Press, New York, 113–15.

61 See generally F.H. Lawson *et al.* (1967), *Introduction to French Law*, 3rd edn, Clarendon Press, Oxford.

62 See Hooker (1979), *supra*, 157–54.

repugnant to 'civilised practice'. A compromise decree issued in October 1883 amalgamated French Civil Code provisions with indigenous provisions governing marriage, divorce, inheritance and patrimony.[63]

Colonial policy initially encouraged field officers to use the Nguyen Code to resolve village disputes. Without comprehending the role of legal codes in neo-Confucian governance, officials attempted to extract individual rights and obligations from penal provisions designed to sanction moral violations. Coming from a civil law tradition where legal codes contained generally applicable principles, colonial officials unsuccessfully searched the Nguyen Code for legal abstraction. For example, in the important area of land regulation, the French tried to use pre-colonial *dia bo* tax registers to create legally binding land boundary registers.[64] The policy of investing customary land boundaries with legal precision, failed to convert loose cultural assertions into abstract legal rights.

Officials eventually conceded that the Code lacked sufficient specificity to extend legal principles by analogy to case facts. French attitudes were discussed in a colonial report that concluded 'the Annamite legislator, in fact, instead of posing general principles and drawing deductions from them as required, foresees the various possible hypothetical situations and regulates these in a manner which is almost exclusive'.[65]

The replacement of an inferior translation of the Nguyen Code with Philastre's detailed commentaries did not solve the problem. The new draft also lacked jurisprudential guidelines. Efforts to apply the Nguyen Code to criminal behaviour were eventually abandoned and the French Penal Code replaced the Nguyen Code first in Cochin China, and later in Amman and Tonkin. Tentative steps to integrate French law into an indigenous framework continued in the 1930s with the translation of a simplified version of the French Civil Code into Vietnamese. A Vietnamese Commercial Code was eventually enacted in 1943.

Following the establishment of the Law College at the Hanoi University in 1933, Vietnamese bureaucrats, judicial officers and lawyers studied French law in greater numbers.[66] In Cochin China, French-trained Vietnamese assumed judicial posts in increasing numbers, and courts applied rules of procedure and evidence that gave lawyers an active role. Local courts in Tonkin, and especially Amman remained strongly influenced by pre-colonial procedures and attitudes that de-emphasised legal reasoning.[67] Legal study and research virtually discontinued under the Japanese occupation and during the subsequent independence struggle.

---

63 Similar laws were enacted in Tonkin (1931) and Annam (1936). See Dao Tri Uc and Le Minh Thong (1999), *supra*, 12–15.

64 See Nguyen Ngoc Huy and Ta Van Tai (1986), *supra*, 465–68.

65 G. Durrwell (1911), *Ma Chere Cochinchine: Trente Annees D'Impresions et de Souvenirs*, Fevrier 1881–1910, Paris, 269, reproduced in Osborne (1969), *supra*, 118.

66 See Stephen Young (1979), 'Vietnamese Marxism: Transition in Elite Ideology', 19 *Asian Survey*, 770.

67 See Pham Duy Nghia (2003), *supra*, 46–48.

In the decades following partition of the Vietnam in 1954, much French law and legal eduction continued in the South. For example, the *Cour d'Appelle Saigon* increasingly analysed and qualified traditional commercial practices.[68] The Republic of Vietnam repeatedly amended French colonial law to reconcile imported legality with local social and economic practices.[69] Following the adoption of Soviet law in the North during the 1960s, the influence of French law rapidly declined. A similar pattern emerged in the South after reunification in 1975.

Receiving Imported Law

Transplanted French commercial laws rarely touched the lives of most Vietnamese.[70] Only a small number of Vietnamese ever elected to submit property disputes to French law, and even then only for domestic, family or inheritance disputes.[71] Most Vietnamese remained remote from the colonial economy. As Jamieson observed, 'a mere handful of [French] men exerted near total influence over the entire financial and economic structure of Vietnam'.[72] The strong sense of community in villages meant that most commercial transactions, including disputes, were resolved without reference to colonial law.[73]

Not all Vietnamese, however, remained remote from imported rights-based law. A small merchant class acquired knowledge of French law, mainly to deal with colonial officials, French plantation owners and shipping companies. Especially in commercially oriented Saigon, anti-mercantile attitudes slowly gave way to commodity capitalism and rights-based law.[74] French legal ideals envisaged an orderly and predictable world in which some progressive Vietnamese wanted to live. Indeed, by the 1930s, French officials were complaining about the growing number of legal disputes initiated by Vietnamese in Cochin China.[75]

68 Cases appeared in the journal *Phap Ly Tap San* (Law Review) published in Vietnamese. Interview Quoc Manh, Former Chairman of the Bar Association Ho Chi Minh City, March 1991, April 1992.

69 Interviews Pham Duy Nghia, Lecturer, Law Faculty, National University, Hanoi September, 2000, March 2003; Interview Ngo Van Thau, Former Professor at the Judicial Training School, Hanoi March 2001.

70 See Hy V. Luong (1992), *Revolution in the Village*, University of Hawaii Press, Honolulu, 55–79.

71 See Stephen Young (1979), *supra*, 772.

72 See Jamieson (1993), *supra*, 91.

73 See Nguyen Ngoc Huy and Ta Van Tai (1986), *supra*, 493.

74 See Osborne (1969), *supra*, 276; Marr (1981), *supra*, 122–23.

75 David Marr (1981), *supra*, 96.

The Independence Movement

By the early twentieth century, the independence movement turned from neo-Confucianism to European intellectual sources for inspiration.[76] Prominent intellectuals such as Phan Boi Chau and Phan Chu Trinh borrowed French legal concepts to propose an independent Vietnamese state based on a constitutional monarchy.[77] Although organising their ideas around imported doctrines, they stressed that laws must suit local conditions.

For others, contradictions between the harsh implementation of colonial law and its lofty idealism (liberty, equality and fraternity) excited radical opposition to the imported political-legal system.[78] Examples abounded where French justice failed to match ideological principles. The lenient sentence given to a French plantation owner charged in 1930 with murdering a Vietnamese labourer convinced many that they could not trust colonial courts.[79] By questioning the impartiality of liberal legalism, revolutionaries and nationalists portrayed the colonial legal system as alien and imposed, serving foreign rather than indigenous interests.[80] Selectively appropriating neo-Confucian beliefs, revolutionary writers constructed ethical principles that stressed the moral superiority of the independence movement. This synthesis of neo-Confucian virtue-rule with Marxist-Leninism is considered in Chapter 3.

By the close of French rule, a layered pattern of legal borrowing had emerged. Imported political-legal ideas remained confined to small colonial enclaves, while neo-Confucian and village values dominated the rural landscape. French colonial policy institutionalised legal boundaries that separated those living in the colonial and indigenous worlds.

Transplanted political-legal ideas and practices functioned comparatively well where French-trained jurists applied them to the colonial world. But cultural misunderstandings and oppressive colonial rule impaired the application of colonial law to the indigenous population. By locating state power in normative rules, French law undermined the moral authority neo-Confucian literati exercised over village

---

76 See Marr (1971), *supra*, 185–211; Nguyen Khac Vien (1974), *Tradition and Revolution in Vietnam*, Indochina Resource Center, Berkeley, 42–43. Also see Dinh Xuan Lam (1990), 'Book Review', *Vietnam Social Sciences* (2), 89, 90–94.

77 See Dao Tri Uc and Le Minh Thong (1999), *supra*, 13–15. For a historical discussion of Phan Boi Chau and Phan Chu Trinh, see Marr (1981), *supra*, 15–23; Jamieson (1993), *supra*, 57–65.

78 See Nguyen Khac Vien (1994), 'Confucianism and Marxism', *Vietnam Studies* (1), 45, 54–55.

79 See Tran Tu Binh (1985), *The Red Earth: A Vietnamese Memoir of Life on a Colonial Rubber Plantation*, John Spragens and David G. Marr (trans and eds), Ohio University Press, Athens, Ohio, 42.

80 See Ho Chi Minh (1994), 'On Justice', in *Selected Works Volume II*, Foreign Languages Publishing House, Hanoi, 96–102.

officials and the rural population. Village regulation faltered because it increasingly lacked the moral authority required for virtue-rule.

Legal Borrowing following Independence

Just as pre-modern ideas continued under French rule, there was no clear line marking the end of the colonial era and the beginning of the socialist period. Vestiges of the colonial legal apparatus lingered for over a decade after the 1946 Constitution declared Vietnam independent of French rule. Such continuities caution against overly precise categorisations of legal change. Nevertheless, post-independence legal borrowing can be roughly divided into four periods that provide a framework for discussion.

The Early Independence Struggle (1920–45)

The shift to socialist thinking among many of Vietnam's anti-colonial leaders did not precisely coincide with the decline of neo-Confucian rule or disenchantment with Western philosophy and science. Its timing and origin are much more complex. By 1920, Ho Chi Minh was attracted to the Communist Third International, 'almost a decade before other Vietnamese had any reliable exposure to Marxist-Leninism'.[81] Other early Vietnamese independence leaders received their training in Moscow in the 1930s and were drawn more to Stalinist than Maoist ideology.[82] Revolutionary pamphlets circulating in colonial prisons prompted French authorities in the 1930s to complain that prisoners went into jails knowing nothing of Marxism, but emerged committed Marxist revolutionaries.

There was much more to the early independence struggle than the importation of Marxist–Leninist thinking. There was a rapid increase in Vietnamese writings exploring new ways of being Vietnamese. In 1933 alone, 27 permits for *quoc ngu* (the Romanised Vietnamese alphabet) newspapers and journals were granted.[83] Much of this writing sought to reconcile and naturalise colonial cultural and political thinking with local values and practices.

The intellectual leaders of the Indochinese Communist Party (ICP) (*Dong Duong Cong San Dang*), such as Pham Van Dong, Truong Chinh and Vo Nguyen Giap,

81 David Marr (1981), *supra*, 317.

82 See Robert F. Turner (1975), *Vietnamese Communism: Its Origins and Development*, Hoover Institution Press, Stanford University, Stanford, 290; William Duiker (1973), 'The Red Soviets of Nghe-Tinh: An Early Communist Rebellion in Vietnam', 4 *Journal of South East Asian Studies*, 186, 187–89; See Huynh Kim Khanh (1986), *Vietnamese Communism, 1925–1945*, Cornell University Press, Ithaca, New York, 272–74.

83 These publications joined the dozens of papers and journals already in publication. See Neil Jamieson (1993), *Understanding Vietnam*, University of California Press, Berkeley, 102.

dismissed this discourse as middle-class sentimentality.[84] For the communists the real social issues concerned the misery inflicted by colonisation and developing strategies to raise class-consciousness and mobilise resistance. The 'Political Thesis' promulgated by the ICP in 1930, for example, contained more Soviet anti-imperialist and anti-feudalistic sentiments than socialist theory.[85]

Like the incipient Chinese Communist Party, the ICP received literature and ideological support from the Soviet Comintern.[86] At least initially, Ho Chi Minh harboured doubts whether the road to socialism prescribed by the Comintern applied in Asian conditions.[87] By the 1940s, however, the ICP proclaimed that socialist-directed nationalism (path-dependent change) was a means to a socialist end, rather than an objective in its own right.[88] Soviet strategy emphasised the international revolutionary aspects of the anti-colonial struggle. During the 1950s the party moved closer to Chinese communism and its fixation on radical class-based land reform.

Creating an Independent State Apparatus (1945–59)

During this period, institution building assumed a secondary priority to prosecuting war against France. All the same, the incipient government enacted the 1946 Constitution and managed to establish the institutional trappings of a democratic state (president, legislature, executive and courts). The Constitution reflected the political heterogeneity of the ruling Vietnam National Alliance Front (*Lien Hiep Quoc Gia Viet Nam* or *Lien Viet*).[89] Western 'rule of law' notions promising inalienable, universal private rights and equality before the law were juxtaposed with Soviet 'people's power' imagery that invested in party leaders a duty to implement the 'will

84 Ibid., 156–59.

85 ICP (1930), 'Political Thesis of Indochinese Communist Party', October, partially reproduced in *Vietnam Documents and Research Notes*, (103), 1970, 58–91. Also see Bernard Fall (ed.) (1967), *Ho Chi Minh on Revolution*, Praeger, New York, 24; R.B. Smith (1978), 'The Work of the Provisional Government of Vietnam, August–December 1945', 12 *Modern Asian Studies*, 596–99.

86 See Truong Chinh (1994), *Truong Chinh Selected Writings*, The Gioi Publishers, Hanoi, 343–44; David Marr (1995), *Vietnam 1945: The Quest for Power*, University of California Press, Berkeley, 473–39.

87 See Ho Chi Minh (2000), *Ho Chi Minh's Collected Works*, National Politics Publishing House, Hanoi, 465–67.

88 See Huynh Kim Khanh (1982), *Vietnamese Communism, 1925–1945*, Cornell University Press, Ithaca, New York, 187–89; Pham Van Dong (1952), *May Van De Cot Yeu cua Chinh Quyen Dan Chu Nhan Dan Viet Nam* (Some Crucial Aspects of the People's Democratic Regime in Viet Nam), Ban Chap Hanh Trung Uong, (Party Central Committee Publishing), Hanoi, 7–19.

89 The Preamble borrowed from Abraham Lincoln's Gettysburg Address the famous recital 'for the people, by the people…'. See Constitution 1946, articles 22, 31, 43, 52, 63; also see Bernard B. Fall (1960), 'Constitution-Writing in a Communist State: The New Constitution of Vietnam', 6 *Howard Law Review*, 157, 158–59.

of the working classes'.[90] Further complicating the ideological mixture, Western democratic principles were interwoven with neo-Confucianism. For example, article 17 not only granted Vietnamese citizens universal suffrage, it also qualified participation in government affairs according to each person's 'abilities and virtues', a reference to neo-Confucian self-perfection.

The 1946 Constitution was drafted at a time of political compromise between communists and nationalists in the independence movement.[91] Communist leaders within the National Front for Independence (*Viet Minh*) were content to raise national reunification above class politics, provided 'state revolutionary power' remained under communist control.[92] This compact constrained the use of overtly revolutionary rhetoric in the 1946 Constitution.

Apart from raising expectations, the Constitution had little bearing on the way the Democratic Republic of Vietnam (DRV) functioned during the next decade. This story is revealed in decrees, circulars and party (*chu thi*) instructions. For more than a decade after independence, the DRV continued using French colonial civil laws, land registration and selected taxes.[93] Colonial laws that conformed to the 'principles of Vietnam's independence and democratic republican form of government' were used to fill the gaps in the embryonic legal system.

New administrative and judicial structures were established. A ministry of justice (*Bo Tu Phap*), for example, was established at the central level. People's Councils and their unelected executive arms, called Administrative Committees (*Uy Ban Hanh Chinh*), were formed by decree in November 1945 to regulate provinces (*tinh*), districts/communes (*huyen/xa*) and wards (*phuong*).[94] The provisional government of the DRV sought continuity in public administration and instructed

90 Writing in 1949, Ho Chi Minh placed constitutional rhetoric, such as 'for the people, by the people', in a socialist context. See Song Thanh (1995), 'President Ho Chi Minh Laid the Foundation for a Law-Governed State', 1 *Vietnam Law and Legal Forum* (9), 3, 6.

91 See Pham Van Dong (1952), *May Van De Cot Yeu cua Chinh Quyen Dan Chu Nhan Dan Viet Nam* (Some Crucial Aspects of the People's Democratic Regime in Viet Nam), Ban Chap Hanh Trung Uong, Hanoi, 7–19. Also see Bernard Fall (1956), *The Viet-Minh Regime Government and Administration in the Democratic Republic of Vietnam*, Greenwood Press, Westport, Connecticut, 39–41.

92 See Tran Thi Tuyet (1997), 'The Young State Prepares for the Anti-French Colonialist War of Resistance (1946–1954)', 4 *Vietnam Law and Legal Forum* (38), 25.

93 Order No. 97 22 May 1950, issued by Ho Chi Minh, declared the temporary retention of colonial laws, such as the Civil Land Law of Tonkin, Civil Code of Annam and an abridged version of the Civil Law in Cochinchina, except where they were inconsistent with the 'revolutionary spirit'. See Hoang The Lien (1994), 'On the Legal System of Vietnam', 1 *Vietnam Law and Legal* (1), 33, 34.

94 See A.G. Budanov (1958), *Gosudarstvennyi Stroi Demokraticheskoi Respubliki V'etnama* (State Structure of the Democratic Republic of Vietnam), Moscow, 29; quoted in George Ginsburgs (1962), 'Local Government and Administration in North Vietnam, 1945–1954 (Part I)', 12 *China Quarterly*, 211, 213.

state employees (*cong chuc*) to remain in their positions.[95] For example, despite sensitivities concerning colonial land practices, the Hanoi cadastral department continued to use French registration procedures under the new regime. Yet, as one staff member later reflected, 'as party members we knew what to do to preserve *loi ich cua nha nuoc* (state benefit)'.[96]

Many court procedural rules were initially based on modified French provisions.[97] Military courts (*toa an quan su*) and regional courts (*toa an khu vuc*) operating in liberated zones used simplified French court procedural rules and the Civil and Criminal Codes of Tonkin and Annam.[98] These courts were established as an interim measure to restore social order and try those accused of endangering national security. Courts were rearranged to reflect administrative divisions in the government structure (central, provincial and district levels), rather than the French system that was based on first instance, appeal and review courts.

In 1951 the communist party re-emerged into the open by forming the Vietnamese Workers' Party (VWP) (*Dang Lao Dong Viet Nam*).[99] Party cells mirrored and penetrated state and social organisations. By this time 'Party branches made all significant decisions and conveyed them to local government units, which in any event came to be composed largely of party members'.[100]

Imported Chinese thinking on land reform and socialist political consciousness was also gaining momentum.[101] DRV policy began to shift from preserving colonial legality and property rights towards state-owned industries, nationalisation and redistribution of land belonging to French 'imperialist aggressors' and 'reactionary' landlords. Special People's Courts (*Toa an nhan dan dac biet*) were established to administer the Land Reform Law 1953. Courts comprising one professional judge supported by lay advisers (middle and poor peasants (*trung ban co nong*))

95 See David Marr (2004), 'A Brief History of Local Government in Vietnam' in Benedict J. Tria Kerkvliet (eds), *Beyond Hanoi: Local Government in Vietnam*, Institute of Southeast Asian Studies, Singapore, 41.

96 Interview, Nguyen Thuc Bao, Former Legal Adviser to Ministry of Agriculture, Hanoi, September, 2000.

97 See Fall (1956), *supra*, 30.

98 Interviews Ngo Van Thoa, *supra*.

99 For discussions concerning Chinese assistance with land reform see Truong Chinh (1954), *Thuc Hien Cai Cach Ruong Dat* (Report to First Party Congress), Dang Lao Dong Viet Nam Xuat Ban (Vietnam Workers Party Publishers), Hanoi, 49–66; also see William J. Duiker (1977), 'Ideology and Nation-Building in Democratic Republic of Vietnam', 17 *Asian Survey*, 413, 414–19; Edwin Moise (1976), 'Land Reform and Land Reform Errors in North Vietnam', 49 *Pacific Affairs*, 70.

100 Marr (2004), *supra*, 47.

101 See Author Unknown (1951), *Cai Cach Ruong Dat O Cac Nuoc Dan Chu Nhan Dan*, (Agrarian Reform in Democratic Republic Countries), Truth Publishing, No 5, Liberated Territory; Author Unknown (1961), *Nhung Van De Co Ban ve Dan Phap Cua Nuoc Cong Hoa Nhan Dan Trung Hoa* (Major Issues in the Civil Code of the Peoples Republic of China), Tap III, Toa An Nhan Dan Toi Cao Xuat Ban, Hanoi.

implemented class-based land allocation policies.[102] According to popular accounts, courts were arbitrary and violent; their function was to further revolutionary reform rather than resolve disputes.[103] Legislative changes in 1950 encouraged defendants to select lay representatives over legally trained advocates. Writing about revolutionary justice, Fall concluded that 'trials, particularly those of enemies of the state, are held on a completely informal basis, with the public supplying most of the arguments as well as a good part of the final judgement'.[104]

The shift away from colonial legality accelerated when the Supreme Court prohibited the use of French colonial laws and practices in 1959.[105] This was followed in the early 1960s with the purge of French-trained legal personnel.[106] Most lawyers were viewed with suspicion because they were educated in the French legal system and had sworn allegiance to the French colonial government. Only a small number of French-trained lawyers proved their revolutionary loyalty and were permitted to work in the new government. The campaign against colonial legalism extended to a comprehensive purge of Sino-Vietnamese legal words that were tainted by their association with the colonial regime.[107] Even legal training was de-emphasised and tertiary level study did not resume until after reunification in 1976.[108]

With French legalism reviled as bourgeois and oppressive, the party and state ruled primarily through party resolutions, administrative edicts and virtue-rule (*duc tri*).[109] Inspired by Ho Chi Minh's teachings, legal writers of the period valued moral education (*giao duc*) more highly than laws and legal enforcement.[110] They believed

---

102 See Decree 264-TTg Regulating in Detail Order 149, 150 and 151 of 12 April 1953, 11 May 1953, article 1.

103 *Nhan Dan*, 13 August 1957, cited in J. Price Gittinger (1957), 'Communist Land Policy', 28 *Far Eastern Survey* (8), 118; Wifred Burchett (1955), *North of the 17th Parallel*, FLPH, Hanoi, 168–69.

104 Bernard Fall (1956), *supra*, 30.

105 See Circular, Ministry of Justice, 10 July 1959.

106 Interviews Le Kim Que, President Bar Association of Hanoi, Hanoi, June 1997, October, 1999; Nguyen Thuc Bao, Former Legal Adviser to Ministry of Agriculture, Hanoi, September 2000. Also see George Ginsburgs (1979), 'The Genesis of the People's Procuracy in the Democratic Republic of Vietnam', 5 *Review of Socialist Law*, 187, 191–92; Penelope Nicholson (2000), 'Borrowing Court Systems: The Experience of the Democratic Republic of Vietnam, 1945–1976', unpublished PhD Thesis, University of Melbourne, Melbourne, chapter 5.

107 Dinh Gia Trinh (1965), 'May Y Kien Ve Tinh Dan Toc va Tinh Khoa Hoc Cua Thuat Ngu Luat Hoc—Nhan Xet Phe Phan Ve Mot So Thuat Ngu Thong Dung' (Nationalistic and Scientific Use of Legal Terminology: Criticisms of Common Legal Terms), *Tap San Tu Phap* (3), 24–26.

108 See Mark Sidel (1993), 'Law Reform in Vietnam: The Complex Transition from Socialism and Soviet Models in Legal Scholarship and Training', 11 *UCLA Pacific Basin Law Journal* (2), 221, 224–25.

109 See Pham Duy Nghia (2003) *supra*, 49–50.

110 See Dinh Gia Trinh (1961), 'May Y Kien Dong Gop Ve Van De Bao Ve Phap Che' (Some Opinions on the Protection of Legality), Tap San Tu Phap (3), 20, 23–24.

that moral criticisms enabled violators to realise their mistakes and minimised recidivism. For them, the primary purpose of law was to educate officials to 'hate our enemies, love the working people and guide against waste and corruption'.[111] It did not matter whether party morality was formally legislated, since officials and the public were expected to follow party invocations as if they were law. As we shall see in Chapter 3, much of the new thinking came from the Soviet Union and China, but the domestic imperatives of war and revolution also shaped legal thought.

Some cadres, like Nguyen Huu Dang, lamented the decline of Western legalism during this period:

> Our contempt for bourgeois legality has reached such proportions that, for many of us, it has turned into contempt for legality in general. It is so because our long and arduous resistance has made us used to settling problems in a family atmosphere, according to our personal preferences. We have been used to replacing law with 'viewpoint' (*lap truong*).[112]

Outspoken criticism of this kind, which flourished during the brief publication of *Nhan Van- Giai Pham* in the mid 1950s, did not resurface. Instead, debates about legalism were confined to the Legal Studies Group (*To Luat Hoc*) under the auspices of the Social Sciences Division of the State Sciences Committee. Although this group included non-communist intellectuals and 'leading voices of legal reform' their concerns rarely appeared in published articles, much less party policy.

Building a Socialist Legal System (1959–86)

By the late 1950s, Soviet technical advisers were calling for the methodical substitution of ancient customary and colonial rules with 'rational, progressive socialist legislation'.[113] The Fourteenth Party Plenum in 1958 announced a three-year economic plan aimed at developing and transforming the economy along socialist lines.[114] Truong Chinh argued the need to 'strengthen proletarian ideology, fight all

---

111 Nguyen Duy Trinh (1956), 'Phat Trien Che Do Dan Chu Nhan Dan va Bao Dam Quyen Tu Do Dan Chu Cua Nhan Dan' (Developing the People's Democratic Regime and Ensuring People's Liberties and Democratic Rights), *Hoc Tap* (3), 23, 26–32

112 Nguyen Huu Dang (1956), 'It is Necessary to Have a More Regularised Society', *Nhan Van*, (4) 5 November, translated and reproduced in George Boudarel (1990), 'Intellectual Dissidence in the 1950s: The Nhan-Van Giai-Pham Affair', 13 *Vietnam Forum*, 154, 166. Also see Russell Heng Hiang-Khng (2000), 'Of the State, For the State, Yet Against the State', unpublished PhD Thesis, Australian National University, Canberra.

113 See George Ginsburgs (1979), *supra*, 191; Hoang The Lien (1994), 'On the Legal System of Vietnam', 1 *Vietnam Law and Legal Forum*, 33–34.

114 See Ho Chi Minh (1959), 'Report on the Draft Amended Constitution', December 18, 1959, reproduced in *Ho Chi Minh Selected Writings* (1920–1969), *supra*, 214, 221.

forms of bourgeois ideology, criticize petty-bourgeois ideology and do away with all vestiges of feudal and other erroneous ideologies'.[115]

The embrace of Marxist–Leninist orthodoxy required constitutional amendments to remove rhetorical references to liberal democracy in the 1946 Constitution. Ho Chi Minh played a leading role. He informed the National Assembly in 1959 that the new constitution should reflect the 'leadership of the working class over the people's democratic State'.[116] This organisational ideal required the importation of socialist political-legal doctrines and institutions designed to justify and maintain party supremacy.

Although the preamble of the VWP Statute identified the Soviet Union and China as the ideological and institutional models for the party and state, by the late 1950s Ho Chi Minh (among others) was urging the party to rely on Soviet support.[117] But this was a complex political period and, overall, the party tilted towards China, until moving closer to the Soviet Union in the mid-1960s.[118] This shift is reflected in the legal literature. Articles published in *Tap San Tu Phap* (Justice Review) from 1961 to 1970 regularly mentioned Marx, Engels, Lenin, Soviet legal scholars and occasionally Stalin, but never discussed Mao Zedong or other Chinese authorities. Conflict with China in 1979 further reduced the influence of the Maoist model and public support for sinic reforms. Nevertheless, the Party Institute for Research on Marxist-Leninism continued covertly collecting and analysing information on Chinese economic and legal reforms.

As the most developed socialist state, Soviet laws and legal institutions were preferred as a model to 'strengthen the role of law'.[119] The 1959 Constitution incorporated for the first time Soviet political-legal ideology such as *phap che xa hoi chu nghia* (socialist legality), *tap trung dan chu* (democratic centralism) and *lam chu tap the* (collective mastery) (discussed in Chapter 3). Legal officials active during

115 See Truong Chinh (1994), 'Forward Along the Path Charted by Karl Marx', in *Truong Chinh Selected Works*, The Gioi Publishers, Hanoi, 565.

116 Ho Chi Minh (1959), *supra*, 217.

117 See C. Brandt, B. Schwartz and J.K. Fairbank (1952), *A Documentary History of Chinese Communism*, Harvard University Press, Cambridge, Massachusetts, 422, 422–28; Ho Chi Minh (1954), 'Report to the 6th Plenum of the Viet Nam Workers' Party Central Committee', July 15, 1954, reproduced in *Ho Chi Minh Selected Writings* (1920–1969), *supra*, 181–82. Also see Woodside (1999), *supra*, 26–29; P.J. Honey (1962), 'The Position of the DRV Leadership and the Succession to Ho Chi Minh', 9 *The China Quarterly* (January–March), 24, 27–34.

118 See Russell Heng Hiang-Khng (2000), *supra*. Also see Dang Phong and Melanie Beresford (1998), *Authority Relations and Economic Decision-Making in Vietnam: An Historical Perspective*, Nordic Institute of Asian Studies, Copenhagen, 40–41.

119 See Nguyen Duy Trinh (1956), *supra*, 29–32. The First Party Congress in September 1951 instructed legal cadres to 'build up the law', but little was done until the Second and Third Party Congresses. See Hoang Quoc Viet (1962), 'Viec Xay Dung Phap Che Xa Hoi Chu Nghia va Giao Duc Moi Nguoi Ton Trong Phap Luat' (Building-Up Socialist Legality and Educating People to Respect Laws), *Hoc Tap* (6), 14, 14–15.

this time recall that Soviet legal theory and doctrines were preferred to the more radical Maoist approach to governance.

While retaining some of the French-inspired touches of the 1946 Constitution, the 1959 Constitution formalised the socialist political-legal structure. The 'leading role' (*vai tro lanh dao*) of the party was not as clearly articulated as in the later 1980 and 1992 Constitutions, nevertheless Soviet 'democratic centralism' was formally acknowledged as the main organisational principle.

A Supreme Court and procuracy were established along Soviet lines and the National Assembly was remodelled on the Supreme Soviet.[120] Eventually, as economic production was brought under centralised planning, the DRV imported from the Soviet Union an entire legal system based on socialist economic laws and legal institutions. Most contemporary party–state institutions remain largely unchanged from this period (see Chapter 4).

Following reunification in 1975, Northern laws and political-legal institutions were transplanted to the South.[121] They not only replaced the Southern, French-derived laws and institutions, but Northern officials were seconded to run the Southern legal apparatus. Most Southern and French-trained lawyers either fled the country or were incarcerated in 're-education camps'.[122] Either way, their knowledge of Western commercial law became redundant in the victor's socialist legal system.

Although most legal knowledge flowed south, there is evidence that the 1980 post-reunification Constitution took some account of Southern approaches to legality. For example, this Constitution, for the first time, provided for the establishment of a lawyer's organisation. Decree No 115-CP on Foreign Investment issued in 1977 was also drafted with Southern assistance.[123] Having defeated the United States and the Republic of Vietnam, the DRV's socialist legal system appeared entrenched for decades to come.

Post-1986 *Doi Moi* Reforms: Western Liberal Influences

Questions were raised during the Fifth National Congress of the Communist Party of Vietnam (CPV) (*Dang Cong San Vietnam*) in 1982 as to whether revolutionary

---

120 See Bernard Fall (1960), *supra*, 284.

121 See Editorial (1977), 'The Strength of the Socialist Legal System', *Nhan Dan*, 1 April, trans. 6 FBIS East Asian Daily Report (67), 7 April 1977, K7; *VNA* (1977), 'Legal Official Comments on Unified Enforcement of Laws', 8 April, trans. FBIS East Asian Daily Report (71), 13 April, K5–K6.

122 State documents pertaining to the treatment of Southern lawyers after 1975 are still classified. This information is based on anecdotal accounts gleaned from interviews with Ho Chi Minh City based lawyers.

123 See Tang Thi Thanh and Trai Le (1979), 'The Foreign Investment Code of the Socialist Republic of Vietnam', 13 *International Lawyer* 329; John Quigley (1980–81), 'Vietnam's Legal Regulation of Foreign Trade and Investment', 6 *International Trade Law*, 24.

ideology should continue dominating state institutions.[124] By this time it was becoming increasingly difficult to blame a stagnant domestic economy on external enemies. Reformers argued for a separation of the party from the day-to-day running of the government, and regulation through law, rather than party edict. The 'Party Report on Economic Guidelines and Tasks' stated that 'the power to rule the state must be reflected in the systems of laws. The law, as it is boiled down, is the institutionalisation of the party line and polices. But there must be no confusion among the line, policies and law'.[125]

Little was done, however, until the Sixth National Congress of the CPV in 1986. By this time, rampant inflation, falling production, a vibrant informal economy and the booming economies of Vietnam's capitalist neighbours could no longer be ignored.[126] Party leaders feared that unless Vietnam rapidly expanded its industrial and technological sectors the economy would fall further behind those of its neighbours, ultimately compromising CPV legitimacy and national sovereignty.[127] According to this narrative, the political impetus for change came from the internal failure of the command economy, the loss of Soviet aid and pressure to cooperate with multilateral agencies (that is, the United Nations Development Program (UNDP), World Bank, and Asian Development Bank) and to integrate with regional associations like ASEAN.[128]

Some Western commentators have posited that, in addition to pursuing 'catch-up' development, Vietnamese policymakers were struggling to control a vibrant entrepreneurial economy.[129] A spontaneous market coexisted and intertwined with the

124 See Adam Fforde (1999), 'From Plan to Market', in Anita Chan *et al.* (eds), *Transforming Asian Socialism: China and Vietnam Compared*, Allen and Unwin, Sydney 43, 44–63; Tu Tuan Anh (1994), *Vietnam's Economic Reform: Results and Problems*, Social Science Publishing House, Hanoi, 15–26.

125 See Circular No. 3831/TP on Some Immediate Work to be Done by the Judiciary Sector to Implement the 5th Party Congress Resolution, Ministry of Justice, first reproduced in *Phap Che Xa Hoi Chu Nghia* (Socialist Legality) (2), April 1982, 8–10, 15, trans. JPRS-1978, 25 January 1983, 90.

126 See Do Muoi (1994), 'Political Report to the Mid Term National Party Conference' 20 January, trans. FBIS East Asia Daily Report 94-015, 24 January 1994, 68, 69–70.

127 See Central Committee of the CPV (1994), 'Resolution on Industrialisation from the Central Committee Seventh Party Congress', *Voice of Vietnam*, 11 August, trans. *BBC Monitoring Service Asia-Pacific*, 19 August 1994.

128 See Le Hong Hanh (1998), *Giao Trinh Ly Luan Nha Nuoc va Phap Luat* (Textbook on State and Law), Nha Xuat Ban Cong An Nhan Dan (People's Police Publishing), Hanoi, 318–19; Author Unknown (1996), *Nhung Van De Ly Luan Co Ban Ve Nha Nuoc va Phap Luat* (Basic Theoretical Issues about State and Law), Nha Xuat Ban Chinh Tri Quoc Gia, (National Political Publishing House), Hanoi, 95–97; Vo Van Kiet (1997), 'A Look Back at the Guidance and Operation of the Government', *Vietnam Social Sciences* (5), 3, 6.

129 See Adam Fforde and Stefan de Vydler (1996), *From Plan to Market: The Economic Transition in Vietnam*, Westview, Boulder, 3–4; Carolyn Gates (1995), 'FDI, Institutional Change and Vietnam's Gradualist Approach to Reform', *Southeast Asian Affairs*, Institute of Southeast Asian Studies, Singapore, 382.

official state command economy. The commercial incentives for private production and distribution were extremely potent. In 1986, officials reported that less than 40 per cent of manufactured consumer goods passed through state-controlled trading networks.[130] According to this account, economic reforms were a gradual, pragmatic response to the 'spontaneous' market. A weak state struggled to maintain relevance by legally recognising 'bottom up' economic reforms.

By the early 1990s, *doi moi* (renovation) reforms were promoting three policy objectives:

- transforming Vietnam's highly centralised economy based on state ownership of the means of production, into a multi-sectored economy where the 'leading role' is reserved for State-Owned Enterprises (SOEs) regulated by 'socialist-oriented market mechanisms' (*co che thi truong theo dinh huong xa hoi chu nghia*);
- normalising social and economic transactions through legal, rather than ideological and moral apparatuses;
- pursuing an 'open door' (*mo cua*) policy that fosters cooperation and trading relationships between Vietnam and other countries.[131]

Economic Reforms

Doi moi reforms primarily concerned economic development. Abandoning decades of central economic planning, the state began devolving decision-making power to managers of SOEs and private enterprises.[132] In 1989, central economic planning had largely been replaced by a kind of state capitalism, euphemistically called the 'socialist oriented market economy' (*nen kinh te thi truong theo dinh huong xa hoi chu nghia*). Party leaders theorised that it had been a mistake to bypass capitalism, so 'state-guided market mechanisms' (*co che thi truong co su huong dan cua nha nuoc*) were a necessary, if temporary, diversion from socialism.[133]

Enacting market-oriented laws During the Sixth Party Congress in 1986 Truong Chinh argued that

130 See Vo Van Kiet (1986), 'Report to the National Assembly in the 1985 Socio-Economic Development Plan', *Hanoi Domestic Service*, 26 December, trans. FBIS Asia and Pacific Daily Report, 30 December, 9.

131 See Vo Dai Luoc (1996), *Vietnam's Industrialisation, Modernisation and Resources*, Social Sciences Publishing House, Hanoi, 15–47; Ngo Quang Xuan (1995), 'Vietnam: Potential Market and New Opportunities', 19 *Fordham International Law Journal*, 32–33. Until 1989, *mo cua* also encouraged a 'glasnost' style political opening.

132 See Nguyen Phu Trong (1994), 'In Vietnam Does the Market Economy Require the Party's Leadership?', *Tap Chi Cong San* (1), 29–33.

133 See Le Minh Tam (1998), 'Phap Che Xa Hoi Chu Nghia' (Socialist Legality), in *Giao Trinh Ly Luan Nha Nuoc va Phap Luat* (Textbook on State and Law), Nha Xuat Ban Cong An Nhan Dan (People's Police Publishing), Hanoi, 497, 511–12.

> [t]he management of the country should be performed through laws rather than moral concepts. The law is the institutionalisation of Party lines and policies and the manifestation of the people's will: and it must be applied uniformly throughout the country. To observe the law is to implement Party lines and policies. Management by law requires attention to be paid to lawmaking. It is necessary to supplement and perfect the legal system step by step so as to ensure that the State machinery can be organised and operated in accordance with the law.[134]

The state vigorously implemented this policy. In the first one-and-a-half decades following *doi moi*, more than double the number of laws and ordinances were enacted than in all the years from the declaration of independence in 1945 to the implementation of *doi moi*.[135] Most legislation has been commercial in nature, drafted to attract much-needed foreign investment and capital, comply with international treaties and control the domestic economy. Some indication of the size and complexity of the legislative program is conveyed by perusing *Cong Bao* (*Official Gazette*), the size of which increased fourfold from 1994 to 2004.

Borrowing Western liberal laws As the economy shifted from command to mixed-market principles, the state needed laws that regulated the horizontal commercial transactions between autonomous market players. The existing socialist economic laws were considered inappropriate legal models, since they privileged state and collective ownership. Meanwhile, law reform could not wait the decades needed to distil normative standards from domestic commercial practices, which lawmakers considered sub-optimal sources of legal norms. In the end, lawmakers were compelled to search for commercial law beyond Vietnam's borders.

China, having begun economic reforms earlier than the Soviet Union, was considered the more appropriate source. Chinese laws profoundly influenced the first wave of commercial legislation in Vietnam.[136] Although rarely mentioned publicly, the Foreign Investment Law 1987, Ordinance on Economic Contracts 1989, Land Law 1988, and other early post-*doi moi* statutes, borrowed extensively from sinic legal templates.

China was not the only legal source. In the late 1980s, for example, Vietnamese lawmakers turned to the French for assistance because the Chinese lacked a suitable company law model. More generally, however, Vietnamese lawmakers believed that similar cultural beliefs, economic structures and, above all else, political ideology

134 Truong Chinh (1986), 'Introduction to the Political Report', *Vietnam News Agency*, 15 December, Part 4.

135 From 1986 until 2001 the National Assembly passed 203 legal documents, including 5 codes (*bo luat*), 87 laws (*luat*) and 111 ordinances (*phap lenh*). From 1945 until 1985, no codes and only one law were passed.

136 Interviews Phan Huu Chi, Former adviser to the Minister of Justice (1986–92) Hanoi, March 1991, January and February 1992, February 1993; Interview Nguyen Chi Dung, Director International Department, Office of the National Assembly, Hanoi, 2000.

made China an appropriate legal source. Western liberal commercial laws borrowed via China were, they believed, already adapted for local conditions.

Western legal sources were not considered politically and constitutionally acceptable at the time. The 'open door' policy adopted under *doi moi* countenanced the importation of foreign investment and technology, but not social and legal systems. In addition, the long-standing tradition of national self-reliance, vindicated by victories in the French and American wars, crystallised into a conviction that legislative solutions lay in home-grown, or at a stretch in Chinese institutions and laws. The creed of self-reliance was reinforced by the perception that experimentation with Western political and legal institutions (especially a constitutional court) hastened the demise of communist power in the Soviet Union.

Some lawmakers believed a solution lay in selectively adopting the commercial laws of the former Republic of Vietnam (RV).[137] They argued that, like Eastern Europe, Vietnam should draw from pre-revolutionary rights-based civil law to draft a commercial legislative framework. Colonial laws, they noted, were translated into Vietnamese, taught in the Saigon Law School and applied in RV courts by generations of Southern judges and lawyers. The main proponents of this view were French-trained lawyers belonging to the *Hoi dong Dan chu va Phap Luat* (Council of Democracy and Law) (CDL), a Fatherland Front organisation.[138] They participated in drafting the 1992 Constitution, Civil Code 1995 and Criminal Code 1986, but their influence in shaping the commercial legal framework was constrained by professional and political factors. First, the CDL was primarily composed of criminal and administrative law specialists that lacked commercial expertise. The *Hoi Dong Kinh Te Xa Hoi* (Council on Economic and Social Affairs), another Fatherland Front organisation made up of Soviet-trained economists, advised the government on commercial law reform. Second, most CDL members were in their 70s and 80s, retired from public life, and had not been active members of the lawmaking community for years. Informants recall that comments sent to government draft committees were received as a courtesy to the Fatherland Front organisation, but were then mostly ignored.[139] Third, the adoption of RV and colonial legislation bestowed too much legitimacy on the discredited *ancien regimes* and undermined the authority of state–society relations based on socialist legality. Fourth, some legal drafters objected that French-based law arose out of, and was designed to regulate, capitalist economic relationships inimical to Vietnam's 'socialist-orientated market economy' (see Chapter 5). The CPV and state were, during the initial stages of reform, careful

137 Interviews with Luu Van Dat, Legal Advisor Minister of Trade, Hanoi, January 1990, March, April 1992; Phan Huu Chi, *supra* and Southern lawyers and advisors such as Nguyen Ngoc Bich, *supra* and Nguyen Xuan Oanh, *supra*.

138 The principal members of this group were Luu Van Dat, the former Director of the Law Department of the Ministry of Trade, Phan Huu Chi, the former Chief Advisor to the Minster of Justice, and Tran Cong Tuong, Head of the *Uy Ban Phap Che* (Legal Committee), the precursor of the Ministry of Justice.

139 Interview Lien Ngo Van Thau, Former Professor of Judicial Training School, Hanoi, October 2001.

to avoid importing laws that circumscribed state economic management (*quan ly nha nuoc ve kinh te*), a socialist organisational practice discussed in subsequent chapters.

As international economic integration gained political momentum, lawmakers increasingly borrowed laws directly from capitalist countries (see Chapter 5 for a detailed discussion). The Law on Business Bankruptcy 1993, Civil Code 1995, Commercial Law 1997 and Enterprise Law 1999, for example, were inspired by legal models supplied by bilateral (primarily Japan, France and Sweden) and multilateral donors (for example, the World Bank, Asian Development Bank and UNDP).[140]

Donors offered divergent, but by no means mutually exclusive, visions for legal change. They agreed that formalistic legal frameworks encouraged market predictability and regularity, but Japanese advisors in particular were more sympathetic to state-directed economic reform and bureaucratic regulatory powers.[141] Multilateral donors, on the contrary, championed neoliberal economic law as a means of keeping the government from interfering with the market (see Chapter 7).[142]

As subsequent chapters reveal, compliance rules under bilateral (for example, US–Vietnam Bilateral Trade Agreement (BTA)) and multilateral trade agreements (for example, AFTA, APEC and especially WTO) have profoundly influenced commercial reforms. For example, as a member of the AFTA free-trade zone Vietnam must reform its tariff regime; the US–Vietnam Bilateral Trade Agreement binds Vietnam to far-reaching legislative and institutional reforms. In addition foreign investors and lawyers are introducing new doctrines and procedures that assist bureaucrats and judges to implement imported rights-based law.

Conclusion

Vietnam's contemporary legal system is primarily constructed from local adaptations of laws derived from China, France, the former Soviet Bloc, and more recently from East Asian and Western countries. Together, these sources form a complex legal architecture that is based on different systems of knowledge, the new overlaying and interweaving the old. As the history of legal borrowing in Vietnam shows, the state legal system has always reflected the laws of conquerors, colonists and patron-states—national elites have superimposed their ideas on pre-existing habits and practices.

Successive borrowings from the Chinese and French legal systems generated layered reception patterns. Receptive elites rapidly adopted and combined new ideas

140 See Ministry of Justice (2002), 'Action Plan for Implementing Vietnam's Strategy for Development of its Legal System Until 2010', unpublished paper, 5 November, Hanoi.

141 Interviews JICA long-term legal representatives Kawazu Shinsuke, Legal Coordinator and Takeuchi Tsutomu, Judicial Expert, Hanoi, January 2002.

142 For a description of this neoliberal legal approach see John Bentley (1999), 'Completion of Viet Nam's Legal Framework for Economic Development', UNDP Discussion Paper 2, United Nations Development Programme, Hanoi, 1–8.

with notions recycled from the past. Mandarins in the neo-Confucian world and the indigenous elite in colonial society benefited materially and socially from imported political-legal thinking and practices. Similarly, Soviet political-legal ideas spread rapidly among some members of the independence movement. Within a few decades, imported socialism came to dominate legal thinking within the party and state.

Imported ideas faced more formidable barriers in entering village life, forcing elites to accommodate some village preferences. It took centuries for neo-Confucian political-legal ideas to infiltrate village practices, and even then distinct differences in elite-village thinking persisted. French colonists transplanted a facsimile of French society to provide the institutions and education required to recruit and train indigenous legal officials. Yet, even with the benefit of modern transportation and communication, the divide between imported legality and pre-colonial virtue-rule and relational practices proved difficult to traverse. Had Marxist–Leninist revolutionaries not cut it short, French colonial legality, like neo-Confucian rule, might eventually have moved out of urban enclaves into village life. The protracted uptake of colonial laws by indigenous elites has lessens for contemporary borrowing. Only those enmeshed in the transplanted colonial economy were remotely interested in rights-based property and contract laws designed for capitalist markets.

Marxist revolutionaries encountered difficulties in shifting imported socialist legality out of the statute books and into everyday life. But they were much more successful than the French in linking their political and legal ideas with familiar neo-Confucian and village ideas. It is nonsense to look for total continuities. Nevertheless, despite profound differences in the sociopolitical context, many commentators have observed a similarity in moral outlook and administrative style between pre-modern mandarins and contemporary socialist-trained officials.[143]

Historical borrowings are more than merely curiosities, because they generate insights into the mysterious processes conditioning contemporary legal transplantation. But glibly assuming that precepts and traditions continue overlooks the more difficult question considered in subsequent chapters: how do historical ideas influence contemporary thinking about legal borrowing? This inquiry is taken up in the next chapter. It applies the first working postulate discussed in Chapter 1 to search for reasons why Western liberal rights-based laws, which were comprehensively rejected by the pre-*doi moi* socialist elite, have in less then two decades become guiding principles in commercial laws.

143 Interviews Dao Tri Uc, Director, Institute of State and Law, Hanoi, July 1998 (Dao Tri Uc led a research team investigating ancient Vietnamese law). Also see Alexander Woodside (1999), *supra*, 23–24, 26–27.

Chapter 3

Transforming Socialist Legal Ideology

Introduction

Chapter 2 portrayed legal reform in Vietnam as a series of borrowings, with the new overlaying the old. During the most recent cycle, party leaders have superimposed Western commercial laws on socialist legal doctrines and institutions. Yet, when this process began, party writings denounced bourgeois laws as the political tools of capitalism.[1] This apparent contradiction between party ideals and legal imports raises questions about the role ideology plays in the selection and adoption of foreign law. The proliferation of multiple and sometimes contradictory ideals demands an analytical approach that can account for such diversity.

This chapter uses Gramscian ideological theory outlined in the first working postulate (discussed in Chapter 1) to examine the complex interaction between imported and local legal ideologies. Laws, according to this approach, are more likely to transfer between legal systems with compatible, or at least not incompatible, ideological outlooks. Ideological congruence is important, because legal transplants not only transmit ideology into recipient countries; they are also interpreted by local ideologies. This insight gives our study a way to assess the transferability of laws into Vietnam.

After first revisiting Gramscian ideology theory, this chapter outlines the different ideological themes underlying Western commercial laws imported into Vietnam. It next examines historical changes in the dominant ideological themes influencing legal thinking in Vietnam. The chapter then discusses the impact *nha nuoc phap quyen* (law-based state) ideals have had on longstanding socialist political-legal ideals. It concludes that tension between legal imports and Vietnamese ideology does not necessarily inhibit borrowing, provided the dominant ideologies do not actively block imports.

1 See Mid Term National Party Conference (1994), 'Sixth Installment of "Basic Contents" of the Hanoi 20–25 Mid Term National Party Conference Resolution', *Saigon Giai Phong*, 20 March, 2, trans. FBIS East Asia Daily Report 94-070, 75.

Comparing Legal Ideologies

When comparing ideologies it is vital to know which similarities and differences are central and which are peripheral to host countries' elites. Building on Gramsci's work, Nicos Poulantzas hypothesised that certain ideals (which he termed 'regions') consistently influenced ruling elites, state institutions and economic behaviour more powerfully than others.[2] For example, the conversion of feudal serfs into wage earners and the expansion and consolidation of national markets under capitalism required a shift from the religious ideology of feudalism to the politico-legal ideology of capitalism. The new dominant ideology of universal, normative law weakened communitarian values and constrained the monarch's (or central state's) prerogative or discretionary powers to appropriate property and disrupt the contractual relations required for investment and labour markets.[3] Dominant ideologies are thus reified from actual structures, activities and values to explain or represent the way societies function.[4]

Poulantzas's proposition suggests that legal ideologies transfer most easily where they agree or 'fit' with the dominant ideological 'regions' in host countries.[5] Incongruent domestic ideological signals may undermine the acceptance and credibility of borrowed laws. For example, we saw in chapter two that in the five years immediately following *doi moi*, Vietnamese socialist elites were reluctant to borrow models directly from the capitalist West.

Contemporary theorists differ from Gramsci in arguing that dominant ideologies are constructed not only from elite views, but also from the precepts governing the conduct of professional, occupational and even minority groups.[6] Local ideologies do not simply reflect the norms and precepts of the dominant ideology, they are constructed from an interaction between these values. Like dominant ideologies, local ideologies are comprised of interwoven strands of political, moral, religious and philosophical thoughts, which shape ethical perceptions. This observation raises the possibility that borrowed laws may interact differently with elites and other social groups in Vietnam, a prospect that is considered in Chapters 6 and 7.

---

2 Poulantzas subdivided state or dominant ideologies into 'moral, juridical and political, aesthetic, religious, economic, philosophical ideologies'. See Nicos Poulantzas (1973), *Political Power and Social Classes*, trans. T. O'Hagan, NLB Sheed and Ward, London, 204–5.

3 Ibid., 205.

4 See Colin Sumner (1979), *Reading Ideologies: An Investigation into the Marxist Theory of Ideology and Law*, Academic Press, London, 270–77. Also see Nicholas Abercombie, Steven Hill and Bryan Turner (1980), *The Dominant Ideology Thesis*, Allen and Unwin, London.

5 Many Western laws that did not directly contest Marxist–Leninist principles were transferred over several decades into communist Eastern European states. See G. Ajani (1995), 'By Chance and Prestige: Legal Transplants in Russia and Eastern Europe', 43 *American Journal of Comparative Law* 93, 99–101.

6 See Goran Therborn (1980) *The Ideology of Power and the Power of Ideology*, New Left Books, London.

Dominant and local ideologies differ not only in content, but also in function. As Gramsci demonstrated, elites use legal ideology to strengthen their hegemony over the public.[7] In manufacturing popular consent, ruling elites use 'ideological apparatus', such as the media, educational institutions and mass organisations, to inculcate a system of values, attitudes, beliefs and morals.[8] Hegemonic behaviour introduces human agency into ideology theory. It suggests that Vietnamese elites strategically use ideology to support or discredit foreign laws.

Finally, a direct comparison between donor and host country ideologies does not always measure ideological compatibility, because the ideology informing legal transfers may acquire new meanings during the transplantation process. For this reason, it is essential to investigate not only the ideology underlying imported commercial law, but more importantly the way it is represented within recipient countries. Before examining legal borrowing, it is necessary to outline briefly the legal ideology underlying commercial laws imported into Vietnam.

Western Legal Ideology

The 'rule of law' provides the background ideology for commercial laws. Like other important ideological concepts, such as justice and democracy, debates exist among and within Western countries about the proper form of the rule of law.[9] There is general agreement, however, that certain core ideas are common to most 'rule of law' ideologies. The centrepiece of the 'rule of law' in democratic liberal states has 'always been the idea that governmental action must be rendered calculable and restrained'.[10] There are three main elements to this conventional understanding.[11] One, the 'rule of law' is law of rules, designed to minimise arbitrary decisions by state officials and judges. This objective is achieved with transparent rules that are general, clear, specific, prospective, practicable and stable. Two, legal rules promote equality before the law and thus apply to everyone. Not even the highest officials and

---

7 See Antonio Gramsci (1971), *Selections from Prison Notebooks*, Q. Hoare and G. Nowell-Smith (eds), Lawrence and Wishart, London, 300–21; Maureen Cain (1983), 'Gramsci, The State and the Place of Law', in David Sugerman (ed.), *Legality, Ideology and the State*, Academic Press, London 111–15; Alan Hunt (1985), 'The Ideology of Law: Advances and Problems in Recent Applications of Ideology to the Analysis of Law', 19 *Law and Society Review* (1), 11, 13–19.

8 See Louis Althusser (1984), *Essays on Ideology*, Verso, London.

9 See J. Jowell (1994), 'The Rule of Law Today', in J. Jowell (ed.), *The Changing Constitution*, Clarendon Press, London, 57; Roger Cotterrell (1996), 'The Rule of Law in Transition: Revisiting Franz Neumann's Sociology of Legality', 5 *Social and Legal Studies* (4), 451–70; Thomas Carothers (1998), 'The Rule of Law Revival', 77 *Foreign Affairs* (2), 95–106.

10 W. Scheuerman (1994), *Between the Norm and the Exception: The Frankfurt School and the Rule of Law*, MIT Press, Cambridge, Massachusetts, 96.

11 See Phillip Selznick (1999), 'Legal Cultures and the Rule of Law', in M. Krygier and A. Czarnota (eds), *The Rule of Law after Communism*, Ashgate Dartmouth, Aldershot, 22–23.

politicians are exempt. Three, courts and some other institutions should remain free from political interference and have the power to check state action. This requires clear divisions separating political parties and state apparatus and laws that impose meaningful restraints on the state and individuals.

Although most theorists concede that these elements are never perfectly realised and sometimes exist in tension with each other, they also believe that Western rights-based capitalism could not function without the rule of law.[12] This raises the question, what is it about the rule of law that is vital to capitalism and capitalist laws?

Rule of Law Theories

Western 'rule of law' ideals are divided into procedural and substantive categories—a distinction that is not always clear.[13] Procedural rule of law means more than simply government through law, it also requires government under law. In democratic liberal societies, this means the rule of law has more to do with duties of governments than duties of citizens—general rules should control state power. This objective is generally realised by constitutional doctrines that have greater legal authority than political processes.

According to F.A. Hayek, transparent laws allow people, especially businesses, to plan. He opined:

> A government in all its actions is bound by rules fixed and announced beforehand – rules which make it possible to see with a fair degree of certainty how the authority will use its coercive powers in given circumstances, and to plan one's individual affairs on the basis of this knowledge.[14]

Calculability and predictability are the chief ideological objectives of Western commercial law systems.

Western substantive versions of the rule of law encompass notions of justice and social good. As such, they are much more deeply embedded in democratic liberal ideals than the procedural rule of law.[15] These ideals are also closely allied

---

12 See David Sugarman (1983), 'Law, Economy and The State in England, 1750–1914: Some Major Issues', in David Sugarman (ed.), *Legality, Ideology and the State*, Academic Press, London, 218–19; Oliver Williamson (1985), *The Economic Institutions of Capitalism: Firms, Markets, Relational Contracting*, Free Press, New York, 68–75, 273–98.

13 The literature is vast, but see Joseph Raz (1979), 'The Rule of Law and its Virtue', in Joseph Raz (ed.), *The Authority of Law*, Clarendon Press, Oxford; Robert Summers (1993), 'A Formal Theory of Rule of Law', 6 *Ratio Juris* (2), 127, 127–42; Randall Peerenboom (2001), 'Globalization, Path Dependency and the Limits of Law: Administrative Law Reform and Rule of Law in the People's Republic of China', 19 *Berkeley Journal of International Law* (2), 32.

14 F.A. Hayek (1944), *The Road to Serfdom*, University of Chicago Press, Chicago, 54.

15 See Joseph Raz (1994), *Ethics and the Public Domain,* Clarendon Press, Oxford, 210–37, 373–76.

with capitalism. They promote liberty together with the protection of core capitalist rights, property ownership, sanctity of contracts and the corporate veil.[16] Whether rule of law ideology preceded or was produced by capitalism is unclear, but it is widely believed that without state support for these ideals Western capitalism could not continue in its current form.[17]

Some contemporary theorists query the contemporary relevance of Hayekian representations of the 'rule of law'.[18] Jürgen Habermas, for example, argues that legal ideology in the West is fragmenting precisely because free-market ideals, which make capitalist laws appear natural and desirable to commercial players, say nothing to those (such as welfare recipients) who are excluded from the exchange values of capitalism.[19] Other theorists question the attachment in conventional representations of the rule of law to formal aspects of law.[20] They have relaxed this connection and find the rule of law operating in decentred self-regulation that is functionally, though not formally, equivalent to state law.

The conflicting ideological signals sent by the rule of law make ideological comparison between countries difficult. It is necessary to determine which ideological representations accompany transplanted laws.

Assessing Ideological Congruence

In order to determine the ideological content of imported law it is necessary to know how laws are represented to, and comprehended by, Vietnamese lawmakers. This complex task is greatly simplified because most commercial laws imported into Vietnam come pre-packaged in a Hayekian version of the rule of law. The rule of law is generally presented as an undifferentiated concept, but it encompasses a procedural rule of law, together with Western liberal substantive rights, especially contractual, property and corporate rights (see Chapter 7). Foreign donors sponsoring legal drafting projects spend millions of dollars on legal training courses and study tours so that Vietnamese lawmakers understand commercial laws according to this

16 See C.B. MacPherson (1975), 'Capitalism and the Changing Concept of Property', in E. Kamenka and R.S. Neale (eds), *Feudalism, Capitalism and Beyond*, Australian National University Press, Canberra, 105; Bernard Bailyn (1967), *The Ideological Origins of the American Revolution*, Belknap Press, Cambridge, Massachusetts, 34–93.

17 See David Sugarman, *supra*, 223–30.

18 This view is based on Max Weber's belief that Western legal legitimacy rests on 'consistent systems of abstract rules'. See Max Weber (1978), *Economy and Society*, G. Roth and R. Wittich (eds), University of California Press, Berkeley, 568–659; David Trubek (1972), 'Max Weber on Law and the Rise of Capitalism', *Wisconsin Law Review*, 720.

19 Jürgen Habermas (1976), *Legitimisation Crisis*, trans. T. McCarthy, Heinemann, London, 36–46; also see Yash Ghai (1986), 'The Rule of Law, Legitimacy and Governance', 14 *International Journal of the Sociology of Law*, 179, 179–84.

20 See Martin Krygier (2001), 'Transitional Questions About the Rule of Law: Why, What and How?', 28 *East Central Europe*, 1–34; Selznick (1999), *supra*.

ideological orientation.[21] Their principal concern is generating a stable and transparent environment in which businesses (especially foreign investors) can plan their affairs according to law. Donors rarely mention the intense political and economic contests in Western countries surrounding the meaning of the rule of law. Nor do they explain why commerce flourishes in highly bureaucratic states like Japan, Korea and Taiwan that are a long way from being paradigmatic democratic liberal systems.[22]

Extensive interviews with Vietnamese lawmakers suggest that there is as yet little awareness of the subtle and complex ideological debates in the West concerning alternatives to the Hayekian approach.[23] Perhaps, in time, overseas studies or research will widen Vietnamese lawmakers' understanding of these alternatives, leading to a more textured representation of the rule of law. For the moment, however, Hayekian rule of law ideology dominates imported commercial law.

Finally, domestic ruling elites and special interest groups selectively co-opt imported and local ideological beliefs to support particular positions (see Chapter 7).[24] They invest imported ideals with new meanings to advance rhetorical positions. Subsequent chapters place ideological discourse in a context that is sensitive to the contests between agents for change. The remainder of this chapter first maps the political-legal ideological landscape in Vietnam and then considers whether the dominant ideology is compatible with imported commercial laws.

Importing Socialist Political-legal Ideologies

The capacity of imported ideas to transform elite thinking in Vietnam is well documented. Chapter 2 showed that Vietnamese rulers during the nineteenth century (and before) borrowed widely from Chinese sources. Later, under French colonial rule, the Vietnamese elite rapidly assimilated European ideologies. From the 1920s, Vietnamese intellectuals were well read in Montesquieu, Rousseau and Herbert Spencer, and after the 1945 revolution in Marx and Lenin.[25] More recently, Alvin Toffler and other post-modernists have influenced policy makers.

Vietnamese leaders have for decades repeated Ho Chi Minh's aphorism that without ideology the party and state are 'like a person without wisdom or a ship

21 See Carol V. Rose (1998), 'The "New" Law and Development Movement in the Post-Cold War Era: A Vietnam Case Study', 32 *Law and Society Review*, 106.

22 See Richard Posner (1998), 'Creating a Legal Framework for Economic Development', 13 *World Bank Research Observer* (1), 1, 2–3.

23 After reviewing the scholarly literature about the rule of law and conducting hundreds of interviews with Vietnamese officials, lawyers and academics for over a decade, the author is unaware of any Vietnamese in a position to influence lawmaking who are familiar with Western ideological discourses that challenge Hayekian orthodoxies (see Chapters 5 and 7).

24 See Maureen Cain (1983), *supra*, 98–99; David Kairys (ed.) (1982), *The Politics of Law: A Progressive Critique*, Pantheon Books, New York.

25 See David Marr (1981), *Vietnamese Tradition on Trial 1920-1945*, University of California Press, Berkeley, 61.

without a compass'.[26] Economic progress and development is only considered possible by adhering to state-sponsored ideology.[27]

The term 'legal ideology' makes sense as a category in democratic liberal legal systems that broadly understand (if not universally approve) law's autonomy from other social spheres. It is less meaningful in Vietnam where, this study argues, law remains largely undifferentiated from political, social and family relations. For this reason, our discussion about legal borrowing in Vietnam links legal ideology with other sources of aspirational thinking such as political and moral ideology. The discussion first traces the origins of three Vietnamese political-legal ideologies—socialist legality (*phap che xa hoi chu nghia*), democratic centralism (*tap trung dan chu*) and collective mastery (*lam chu tap the*)—and then evaluates their contribution to the dominant legal ideology. It then examines the epistemological and moral factors shaping the importation of Soviet legal thinking.

Socialist Legality

It was not until the First Congress of the Vietnam Workers Party (*Dang Lao Dong Viet Nam*) in September 1951 that legal cadres were instructed to 'build up socialist law'.[28] The Third Party Congress in 1960 adopted as state ideology the Soviet *sotsialisticheskaia zakonnost'* (socialist legality) doctrine, which translated into Vietnamese as *phap che xa hoi chu nghia*.[29]

Prominent legal writers such as Dinh Gia Trinh considered economic conditions in people's democracies like the DRV insufficiently evolved to sustain Soviet-style socialist legality.[30] Eventually, the Soviet view that legality in people's democracies and socialist republics was equivalent prevailed, and by the 1970s Vietnamese writers uniformly accepted imported socialist legal thinking as their own.[31] Three doctrines constitute the 'core' socialist political-legal canon—socialist legality, democratic centralism and collective mastery.

---

26 Do Muoi (1995), 'Building and Perfecting the State', 1 *Vietnam Law and Legal Forum* (6), 3, 5. See generally Thaveeporn Vasavakul (1995), 'Vietnam: The Changing Models of Legitimization', in Muthiah Alagappa (ed.), *Political Legitimacy in Southeast Asia: The Quest for Moral Economy*, Stanford University Press, Stanford, 257–89.

27 See Marr (1981), *supra*, 320; Thaveeporn Vasavakul (1995), *supra*, 357–89.

28 See Hoang Quoc Viet (1962), 'Viec Xay Dung Phap Che Xa Hoi Chu Nghia va Giao Duc Moi Nguoi Ton Trong Phap Luat' (Building-Up Socialist Legality and Educating People to Respect Laws), *Hoc Tap* (*Study Review*) (6), 14, 14–15.

29 See Tran Hieu (1971), *25 Nam Xay Dung Nen Phap Che Viet Nam* (25 Years of Building Vietnamese Legality), Nha Xuat Ban Lao Dong, Hanoi, 108.

30 See Dinh Gia Trinh (1961), 'May Kien Dong Gop Ve Van De Bao Ve Phap Che' (Some Opinions on the Protection of Legality), *Tap San Tu Phap*, (3), 20, 20–21.

31 For Vietnamese translations of Soviet legal writings on socialist legality see V.M. Lesnoi (1961), 'Phap Che Xa Hoi Chu Nghia Xo Viet' (Soviet Socialist Legality), *Tap San Tu Phap*, (4), 30, 30–34; V.M. Lesnoi (1961), 'Viec Bao Dam Phap Che Xa Hoi Chu Nghia' (Implementing Socialist Legality), *Tap San Tu Phap*, (12), 32, 32–38.

Socialist legality (*phap che xa hoi chu nghia*) is the main legal doctrine. Vietnamese writings during the 1960s defined the doctrine as a tool of proletarian dictatorship (*chuyen chinh vo san*) to defeat enemies, protect the revolution and the collective democratic rights of people to organise, manage and develop a command economy.[32]

Vietnamese writers reasoned from Marxist theory that worker-controlled societies require legal systems that reflect proletarian aspirations.[33] The connection between law and class was explained by the familiar injunction that law is part of the 'superstructure', which reflects the 'will of the ruling class' (*y chi cua giai cap thong tri*) and their domination over the means of production.[34] As the executive committee of the ruling class, the party determined the content of law. The conflation of party policy and law enabled the party and state to use law as a 'management tool' (*cong cu quan ly*) to adjust or balance (*dieu chinh*) social relationships—a practice permitting the substitution of policy for law.

State plans (*ke hoach nha nuoc*) were also treated as legal instruments, further complicating socialist legality.[35] Inspired by Lenin's observation that 'politics is the mirror of the economy', theorists posited that the 'objectives and methods of economic activities must be based on the political task and must support this task'.[36] As mentioned in Chapter 2, the party and state during the 1950s began replacing market planning with administrative planning. Especially after the Fourth Vietnam Workers Party (VWP) Congress in 1976, state economic planning became the primary tool of 'state economic management' (*quan ly kinh te nha nuoc*).[37]

Devised in the Soviet Union to link state planning and economic production in command economies, 'state economic management' unified political and economic leadership in the state.[38] State economic management was also regarded as part of the class revolution to protect the working class from exploitative capitalism. Calls by

32 See Dinh Gia Trinh (1961), 'May Y Kien Dong Gop Ve Van De Bao Ve Phap Che' (Some Opinion on the Protection of Legality), *Tap San Tu Phap*, (3) 20–32.

33 Writing in the Vietnamese Court Review (*Tap San Tu Phap*), several Soviet law professors set out the basic principles of Soviet law. See, for example, V.M. Lets Noi (1961), 'Phap Che Xa Hoi Chu Nghia Xo Viet: Tinh Lich Su va Tinh Giai Cap Cua Phap Che' (Socialist Legality Historical and Class Features), *Tap San Tu Phap* (6), 36–41.

34 See Song Thanh (1995), 'President Ho Chi Minh Laid the Foundation for a Law-Governed State in Vietnam', 1 *Vietnam Law and Legal Forum* (9), 4–6.

35 See Hoang Quoc Viet (1974), *Strengthening Socialist Legality in Economic Management*, Truth Publishing, Hanoi, 42–43.

36 See Le Thanh Nghi (1975), *Mot So Van De Co Ban Trong Quan Ly Kinh Te Xa Hoi Chu Nhgia* (Several Basic Matters on Socialist Economic Management), Nhan Xuat Su That (Truth Publishing House), Hanoi, 15, 45.

37 See *Cong Tac Ke Hoach* (1976), 'Carrying Out Good National Economic Planning and Summarizing National Economic Planning Well', 9 April, 9–11, trans. JPRS 67923, 16–22.

38 See Nguyen Nien (1976), 'Several Legal Problems in the Leadership and Management of Industry under the Conditions of the Present Improvement of Economic Management in Our Country', *Luat Hoc* (Jurisprudence) (14), 33, 33–35, trans. JPRS, 30 September, 34–36.

legal commentators in the 1970s to legalise and systematise command planning with an economic code were rejected by party leaders, who argued that 'state economic management' was needed to fine tune the economy with prerogative powers.[39]

According to Nguyen Nhu Phat,

> planning was the main instrument used by the state to administer the national economy. Planning would always prevail over law. Any conflict between law and planning would be resolved in 'favour' of planning. Generally speaking the law was only a subsidiary instrument while the policy and resolutions passed by the party, administrative commands and planning documents were the main instruments in governing economic activities.[40]

Plans also possessed a 'party nature' (*tinh dang cong san*) that 'organically linked' the party's economic line with economic regulation.[41] Ultimately, state economic management was considered 'organically linked to the [party's] economic line, economic positions and economic plan'.

Democratic Centralism

Lenin conceived democratic centralism (*tap trung dan chu*) as an organisational ideal binding party and state.[42] A facsimile of the concept appeared in the political report delivered by President Ho Chi Minh to the Second National Congress of the Vietnamese Workers Party in 1951.[43] By the time it was formally adopted in the 1959 Constitution it had matured into a two-pronged doctrine linking popular participation in state activities with centralised party and state power.

Party documents indicate that democratic centralism was introduced to consolidate central party control over regional party cadres, state officials and the general public.[44] According to socialist strategic thinking, party power constituted the most potent

39 The term 'prerogative' is used because these powers often had no statutory basis. See generally Hoang Quoc Viet (1973), *Tang Cuong Phap Che Xa Hoi Chu Nghia Trong Cong Tac Quan Ly Xi Nghiep* (Strengthening Socialist Legality in Management Enterprises), Nha Xuat Ban Su That, Hanoi, 8–12; Pham Thanh Vinh (1964), 'Tinh Chat Phap Lenh Trong Ke Hoach 5 Nam Lan Thu Nhat (1961–1965)' (Command Nature of the First Five Year Plan (1961–1965)), in *Nghien Cuu Nha Nuoc va Phap Quyen* (Studies about State and Legality), Nha Xuat Ban Su Hoc (Historical Studies Publishing House) Hanoi, 120.

40 Nguyen Nhu Phat (1997), 'The Role of Law during the Formation of a Market-Driven Mechanism in Vietnam' in John Gillespie (ed.), *Commercial Legal Development in Vietnam: Vietnamese and Foreign Commentaries*, Butterworths, Singapore, 398.

41 See Nguyen Nien (1977), 'Several Legal Matters Concerning Planning in Our Country', *Luat Hoc* (2), 22, 22–28, trans. JPRS 70119, 24–26.

42 See Olympiad S. Ioffe (1985), *Soviet Law and Soviet Reality*, Martinus Nijhoff Publishers, Dordrecht, 21–45.

43 Ho Chi Minh (1994), 'Political Report at the Second National Congress of the Vietnam Workers Party', in *Selected Writings of Ho Chi Minh*, Gioi Publishers, Hanoi, 127.

44 See Le Van Luong (1960), 'Tang Cuong Che Do Tap Trung Dan Chu Trong Dang Ta' (Strengthening the Democratic Centralism in Our Party), *Hoc Tap* (6), 27, 27–30.

remedy for 'regionalism' (*dia phuong chu nghia*) and 'departmentalism'.[45] Only a hierarchically organised, disciplined party could deliver the social and bureaucratic unity required for command economic planning. Article 10(f) of the VWP Statute 1960 explained the meaning of 'centralism':

> Individual Party members must obey the Party organisations. The minority must obey the majority. Lower organisations must obey higher organisations. Party organisations throughout the country must obey the National Delegates' Congress and Central Executive Committee.[46]

The second arm of democratic centralism was based on Lenin's assertion that democracy is only possible where the working class 'centralise power in their hands'.[47] Socialist democracy (*dan chu xa chu nghia*) was conceived in two ways. Theorists argued that popularly elected legislatures (National Assembly and provincial legislative councils) should supervise state power on behalf of the people.

Socialist 'democracy' also encompassed Lenin's revolutionary view that bourgeois democracy transferred the peoples' democratic rights to elected representatives. He believed the working class had comparatively few opportunities to participate in government by influencing political decision-makers though 'lobbying' (*chay lo thu tuc*) and popular demonstrations. Democratic rights were better safeguarded by 'proletarian dictatorship' (*chuyen chinh vo san*) in which the 'ruling class' directly supervised state organs through their proxies—the communist party and mass organisations. Democratic centralism validated party leadership (*su lanh dao cua dang*) over state and society.

Collective Mastery

The ideas that eventually coalesced into the 'collective mastery' (*lam chu tap the*) doctrine appeared in party publications from the 1950s onwards.[48] Unlike socialist legality and democratic centralism, collective mastery was imagined through Soviet and revolutionary Chinese thinking. It drew from Lenin's assertion that true

---

45 See Nguyen The Phung (1960), *Nguyen Tac Tap Trung Dan Chu: Dam Bao Thuc Hien Tot Nhiem Vu Cach Mang Truoc Mat* (The Principle of Democratic Centralism: A Justification for Implementing the Revolutionary Task Before Us), Nha Xuat Ban Su That, Hanoi, 4–9.

46 Party writings encouraged local party committees and state organs to 'cooperate and show solidarity to the party–line'. Le Van Luong (1960), 'Tang Cuong Che Do Tap Trung Dan Chu Trong Dang Ta' (Strengthening the Democratic Centralism in Our Party), *Hoc Tap* (6), 27, 33; Le Duy Vau (1956), 'The Nao La Phat Huy Tap The va Dan Chu Dung Muc?' (How to Satisfactorily Expand Collectivism and Democracy?), *Hoc Tap* (2), 70, 70–72.

47 See Dinh Gia Trinh (1964), *Nghien Cuu Nha Nuoc va Phap Quyen* (Studies about State and Legality), Nha Xuat Ban Su Hoc (Historical Studies Publishing House) Hanoi, 90–92.

48 See generally Pham Van Dong (1952), *May Van De Cot Yeu Cua Chinh Quyen Dan Chu Nhan Dan Viet Nam* (Some Crucial Aspects of the People's Democratic Regime in Viet Nam), Ban Chap Hanh Trung Uong, Hanoi, 7–19.

democracy is only possible where workers exercise mastery over the economy and other social spheres. Vietnamese leaders were also captivated by radical Maoist mass-mobilisation theories, long after Stalinist jurists in the 1930s rejected public participation in state administration as 'the old twaddle about the mobilisation of socially active workers'.[49] This utopian vision enlisted law to 'fundamentally remake the conscience of the people'.[50]

Party General Secretary Le Duan discussed collective mastery during the 1960s and 1970s, but the doctrine did not take hold until the euphoria surrounding reunification in 1975 made radical social transformation seem possible.[51] At the Fourth VWP Congress in 1976, collective mastery was described as a system where 'the true and supreme masters are the social community, the organised collective of working people, with the worker-peasant alliance as the core'.[52] The slogan 'the party is the leader, the state is the manager and people are the masters' (*dang lanh dao, nha nuoc quan ly, nhan dan lam chu*) unified party, state and public relationships under collective mastery.

Theorists claimed that the path to collective mastery lay in eliminating opposition between the state and individuals.[53] This goal is evident in the party slogan 'the important target of the revolution is to strengthen the unification between politics and the spirit of the people' (*tang cuong su nhat tri ve chinh tri va tinh than cua toan dan*). In classless societies, collectivism replaced individualism, enabling socialist people to live harmoniously without the laziness, individualism, selfishness and corruption associated with the 'old society' (*xa hoi cu*). Collective mastery rejected civil society or individual space outside state and collective orbits as bourgeoisie individualism. As a corollary, the doctrine was hostile to private legal rights.

Taken together, socialist legality, democratic centralism and collective mastery constituted the core socialist legal ideals. First, as an extreme manifestation of legal positivism, there is no space in socialist legality for customary rules or natural rights. It invested the party and state with prerogative powers to substitute policy for law. Laws in Vietnam, as a corollary, were understood as 'management tools' (*cong cu quan ly*) to realise party policy. Law facilitated but never constrained state power. Second, the central 'party leads' (*su lanh dao cua dang*) the state and society. State

---

49 A. Vyshinski (1936), 'Raise the Red Banner of Socialist Legality', *Sotsial'naia Zakonnost'*, November, cited in F.J.M. Feldbrugge and William B. Smith (eds), *Perspectives on Soviet Law for the 1980s*, Martinus Nijhoff Publishers, The Hague, 81.

50 See I.T. Goliakov, quoted in Harold J. Berman (1963), *Justice in the U.S.S.R.*, Second edition, Harvard University Press, Cambridge, Massachusetts, 307.

51 Collective mastery is discussed in Le Duan's writings from the 1960s and 1970s. See Le Duan (1994), *Le Duan: Selected Writings*, The Gioi Publishers, Hanoi, 301–3, 352–53.

52 Le Duan (1976), 'Political Report to the Fourth VWP Congress 1976', FBIS East Asia Daily Service, (4), 29 June 1976, K1–K28.

53 See Le Thi (1977), 'Create a Correct Relationship between the Collective and the Individual in the Socialist System', *Tap Chi Cong San* (8), 54, 54–61; Ha Huy Giap (1977), 'The Inevitable Nature of the System of Socialist Collective Ownership', *Tap Chi Cong San* (10), 32, 32–38.

power is thus instrumental and top-down. Third, the people participate in government through their proxy, the communist party (and party dominated mass-organisations). Fourth, individual rights give way to the collective good.

Importing Socialist Political-legal Thought

Paradoxically, party leaders imported socialist law (Chinese and Soviet) with few concessions to local conditions. They ignored their own warnings against unreflective borrowing. Truong Chinh denounced 'gulping down raw other people's culture, parrot-fashion learning, or the mechanical introduction of a foreign culture into our own without taking into account the particularities and concrete conditions of the country and its people'.[54] Ho Chi Minh wrote that 'we are not like the Soviet Union; they have different habits and customs, history and geological conditions. We can take another road to socialism'.[55]

By the 1960s, Soviet legal ideology effectively displaced pre-socialist legal thinking from Vietnamese ideological discourse. First-hand observers such as George Ginsburgs noticed that party resolutions and scholarly writings presented Soviet legal ideology as official thinking. Officials involved in legal reforms during the 1960s and 1970s identified a duality in Vietnamese thinking. Socialist political-legal ideology was conceptually isolated from the domestic political morality espoused by Ho Chi Minh. At the same time, party leaders slavishly borrowed Soviet ideology; they 'endorsed the idea of a timeless Vietnamese spirit, and fashioned their own approved pantheon of immortal Vietnamese heroes'.[56]

It is important in the context of this study to understand why party leaders ignored their own advice and imported Soviet law with few concessions to local conditions. An understanding of the ideals, precepts and contingencies shaping borrowing from the Soviet Union offer glimpses into how ideology affects legal borrowing in contemporary Vietnam.

Adapting Socialist Legal Ideology

The party's reluctance to localise imported ideology is partially attributable to Marxist-Leninist hostility to the notion that culture plays a role in determining the characteristics of legal systems. Historical materialism emphasised economic influences over law, but did not incorporate an 'Asiatic' mode of production (East Asian rice-growing economies) into Marxist–Leninist theories about the legal

54 This statement referred to French colonial culture. Truong Chinh (1994), 'Marxism and Vietnamese Culture', Report delivered at the Second National Culture Conference, July 1948, reproduced in Truong Chinh (1994), *Truong Chinh Selected Writings*, The Gioi Publishers, Hanoi, 251.

55 Ibid., 23.

56 Marr (1981), *supra*, 362.

'superstructure'.[57] This left Vietnamese theorists with a choice: uncritically apply Marx's Eurocentric legal theory to Vietnam or comprehensively rethink Marxist theory in the context of 'Asiatic' production. Like the Chinese, they adopted a Maoist land reform programme, but applied the Soviet legal template to other social spheres.[58]

Marx also followed a well-established European intellectual tradition that depicted Asian societies in undifferentiated ways as 'barbarians' or 'semi-barbarians', portrayals that generated socialist antipathy to neo-Confucian and 'feudal' culture.[59] Truong Chinh evinced this orientalist thinking when he blamed the 'Asian mode of production' for backward economic and social conditions in Vietnam. He vilified traditional cultural precepts as 'unscientific', promoting 'superstition, idealism, mysticism, bungling, carelessness, all those habits that are irrational or retrograde'.[60] Vietnamese leaders sought a 'new-democracy culture' (*tan dan chu*) based on 'rational, progressive socialist legislation'.[61]

Party leaders considered the Soviet Union the most advanced socialist state and, as a corollary, the most appropriate development model. They thought the Soviet 'proletarian culture' should link the working classes in different countries. National cultural barriers based on 'Asiatic' and 'feudal' modes of production were supposed to dissolve in the face of this unifying force.[62]

The adaptation of imported ideology to local conditions was further constrained by ethnocentric Soviet jurists, who encouraged 'satellite' nations to 'build socialism' through imitation, rather than experimentation. In his exhaustive review of Soviet commentaries on Vietnamese legal development, George Ginsburgs attributed the reluctance to localise legal borrowings to political policy,[63] writing that

---

57 See Shlomo Avineri (1969), 'Introduction', in Shlomo Avineri (ed.), *Karl Marx on Colonialism and Modernization*, Doubleday, New York, 6–16.

58 See Truong Chinh (1948), 'Marxism and Vietnamese Culture', Report delivered at the Second National Cultural Conference, July 1948, reproduced in Truong Chinh (1994), *Selected Writings*, *supra*, 205–11, 220–21.

59 Karl Marx (1877), 'Otechestvenniye Zapiski', reproduced in Shlomo Avineri (1969), *supra*, 6. Marx adapted Hegel's idea that Asian development represents the beginning, and European history the end or pinnacle, of social development. See Georg Wilhelm Hegel (1956), *The Philosophy of History*, trans. J. Sibree, Dover Publications, London, 103.

60 Truong Chinh (1948), 'Marxism and Vietnamese Culture', Report delivered to the Second National Cultural Conference, July 1948, reproduced in Truong Chinh (1994), *Selected Writings*, *supra*, 251–52.

61 See George Ginsburgs (1979), 'The Genesis of the Peoples' Procuracy in the Democratic Republic of Vietnam', 5 *Review of Socialist Law*, 187, 191.

62 Truong Chinh (1948), 'Marxism and Vietnamese Culture', Report delivered at the Second National Cultural Conference, July 1948, reproduced in Truong Chinh (1994), *Selected Writings*, *supra*, 264–66.

63 George Ginsburgs (1973), 'Soviet Sources on the Law of North Vietnam', 7 *Asian Survey*, 659, 661–67.

> academic exploration of the distinctive attributes of socialist experimentation in the countries of the Soviet bloc became both safe and fashionable – as long, of course, as the main accent remained on the common heritage and the disparities were treated either as necessary tactical adoptions to 'objective conditions' or components in a pragmatic region-wide search for better solutions to existing socialist problems.[64]

Vietnamese officials working in the legal sector during the 1960s recalled that law reform aimed to transplant 'proletarian culture', and Soviet advisers discouraged local adaptation as 'extreme nationalism' (*chu nghia dan toc cuc doan*).[65] A reluctance to address local conditions and contemplate deviations from the Soviet legal template is revealed in a series of articles written by Soviet jurists about Vietnamese legal development.[66] They seldom acknowledged, much less analysed, incongruities between imported Soviet ideals and local institutional and cultural conditions.

Debates about the practical realities of introducing a foreign legal system were generally highly abstract and focused on technical issues such as procedural rules affecting Civil and Criminal Codes.[67] The Legal Studies Group (*To Luat Hoc*) debated and published articles about law reform in the *Luat Hoc* (Jurisprudence) journal.[68] Analysis took place within a Soviet jurisprudential framework that made few references to Vietnamese institutions and practices. As one participant recalled, discussions on technical matters were frequently conducted in Russian.[69] An extensive review of the Vietnamese legal literature over this period has failed to find a single article analysing local political, economic and cultural barriers to transplantation of Soviet (or Chinese) law and organisational practices.

Finally, Marxist-Leninism promised a socialist utopia built on an infallible scientific methodology. Party leaders promoted the belief that 'Marxist doctrine is

64 Ibid., 661.

65 Interviews Le Kim Que, President Bar Association of Hanoi, Hanoi, June 1997, October, 1999; Nguyen Thuc Bao, Former Legal Adviser to Ministry of Agriculture, Hanoi, 11 September, 2000.

66 See V.M. Lets Noi (1963), 'Nen Tu Phap Cua Nuoc Viet Nam Dan Chu Cong Hoa' (The Judiciary of the Democratic Republic of Vietnam), *Tap San Tu Phap* (11), 26, 26–28; Sarogoratisky (1961), 'Vai Tro va Quan He Giua Cuong Che va Thuyet Phuc Cua Phap Luat Trong Thoi Ky Xay Dung Chu Nghia Cong San Tren Quy Mo Rong Lon' (Roles and Relations between Enforcement and Legal Education in the Communist Period), *Tap San Tu Phap* (11), 41, 42–57.

67 See Ta Thu Khue (1963), 'Can Than Trong Trong Viec Ap Dung Kinh Nghiem Lien-Xo Vao Trinh Tu Phuc Tham' (We Need to be Cautious in Applying Soviet Experience in Appellate Procedures), *Tap San Tu Phap* (2), 12, 13–14.

68 A legal studies group (*to luat hoc*) under the auspices other State Science Committee formed to discuss legal reform during the 1960s and 1970s. See Mark Sidel (1997), 'Some Preliminary Thoughts in Contending Approaches to Law in Vietnam, 1954–1975', unpublished paper, Association for Asian Studies, Michigan, March, 14.

69 Interview Dao Tri Uc, Director Institute of State and Law, Hanoi, July 1998.

omnipotent because it is true. It is complete and harmonious'.[70] As an all-embracing philosophy, the doctrine could only accommodate other viewpoints from a Marxist perspective. Looking back on this period, a Vietnamese commentator observed, 'there was a scholastic manner in researching and applying Marxism in Vietnam... We always considered every position or argument of this doctrine as correct, regardless of practice in Vietnam. Therefore, there was a gap between theory and practice'.[71]

By adopting Marxist scientism—a comprehensive search for the fundamental guides to life—Vietnamese leaders created a doctrinaire intellectual environment. Since the party and state determined which class relationships gave rise to legal consequences, legal concepts were by definition limited to subjects approved by the state. Critical analysis of legal ideology challenged Marxist–Leninist infallibility and was politically unacceptable.

Various factors combined to constrain local discourses from reshaping Soviet legal ideology:

- The deterministic link between the economic base and the superstructure discouraged investigation into cultural links between Soviet law and Vietnamese society.
- Soviet legal thinking discredited East Asian economic and cultural practices.
- Socialism promoted a global workers' culture that de-emphasised regional differences.
- As a holistic ideology, Marxist-Leninism only permitted analysis from its own self-referential perspectives.
- Vietnamese were reluctant to offend Soviet providers of economic aid.
- Vietnamese lawmakers reconciled law and society through pragmatic experimentation (learning by doing) rather than theorising.

Forging a Vietnamese Political-legal Ideology

Vietnamese revolutionaries understood that ideology is an important arena for revolutionary practice. They were aware that ideals existing in the colonial and feudal regimes had maintained and reproduced those systems. For them, socialist change not only required new Marxist–Leninist ideas, it also called for the delegitimisation or reconfiguration of old ideas.

---

70 See Truong Chinh (1968), 'Forward Along the Path Charted by Karl Marx', in Truong Chinh (1994), *Selected Writings*, *supra*, 547; Le Duc Tho (1976), 'Report Summarizing Party Building Work and the Amended Party Statues', *Nhan Dan*, 20–23 December, 2, 3, trans. FBIS East Asia Daily Report, 14 January.

71 Nguyen Thi Doan and Do Minh Cuong (1999), *Triet Ly Kinh Doanh: Voi Quan Ly Doanh Nghiep* (The Business Philosophy of the Management of Enterprises), Nha Xuat Ban Chinh Tri Quoc Gia, Hanoi, 147.

Party leaders soon discovered that imported egalitarian socialist ideology could not easily displace neo-Confucian values and hierarchical practices.[72] Authorities struggled to apply Soviet law in everyday life and embraced neo-Confucian and traditional moral principles as a pragmatic way to bring authorities 'in touch with the people' (*duong loi quan chung*).[73] Since people responded to *tinh cam* (sentiment) more than abstract socialist law, moral leadership became a way to mobilise public support.[74]

Nguyen Khac Vien observed that the party conflated neo-Confucian and traditional moral principles with Marxist-Leninism.[75] He believed neo-Confucianism and Marxism shared similar frames of reference that transcended doctrinal differences. The party promoted shared communitarian values—people are 'a totality of their social relationships', 'collective discipline' and the 'fulfillment of social obligations'—to legitimise democratic centralism, collective mastery and ultimately 'party leadership' (*su lanh dao cua dang*). But they condemned heavenly mandates and feudal hierarchies that obstructed Leninist organisational principles.

According to Frances FitzGerald, government for the Vietnamese was not 'merely one organisation among others, but a complete enterprise that comprehends much of what Westerners would consign to personal life and private morality'.[76] Party leaders sought to present 'a picture of the "correct" way of life and show the people what had to be done'. For example, Ho Chi Minh frequently stressed the importance of moral leadership by the party. He opined that 'if one does not have morality, one can hardly lead the people however talented one can be'.[77] This approach differed from Soviet teachings that acknowledged the role moral teachings play in law enforcement, but rejected the notion that morals could substitute for law.[78]

The party manufactured revolutionary morals (*dao duc cach mang*) from traditional and Marxist–Leninist principles as a pragmatic way to bring itself and

72 See Hoang Quoc Viet (1964), 'Can Dam Bao Cho Phap Luat Duoc Ton Trong Trong Cong Tac Quan Ly Linh Te Cua Nha Nuoc' (We Must Ensure the Enforcement of Law in State Economic Management), in *Nghien cuu Nha Nuoc va phap quyen* (Studies about State and Law), Truth Publishing Hanoi, 35–36.

73 See Thanh Duy Thanh Duy (1997), 'Co So Khoa Hoc va Van Hoa Trong Tu Tuong Ho Chi Minh Ve Nha Nuoc va Phap Luat' (Scientific and Cultural Basis of Ho Chi Minh's Ideas of State and Law), *Tap Chi Cong San* (1), 26, 27–28.

74 Hoang Quoc Viet (1964), *supra*, 33–36.

75 See Nguyen Khac Vien (1974), *Tradition and Revolution in Vietnam*, Indochina Resource Centre, University of California, Berkeley.

76 Frances FitzGerald (1972), *Fire in the Lake*, Random House, New York, 35.

77 Ho Chi Minh (1995), *Complete Works*, Vol. 5, The National Political Publishing House, Hanoi, 338; reproduced in Nguyen Duy Quy (1997), 'Ho Chi Minh's Viewpoint on Socialism and the Path to Socialism in Vietnam', *Vietnam Social Sciences* (5), 15, 16.

78 Soviet legal commentaries emphasised the educative role of law and morals without mentioning moral perfection. See V.M. Lesnoi (1961), *supra*, 32–34.

the state closer to the people.[79] Ngo Van Thau, a professor teaching in the Judicial Training School from the 1960s until the 1980s, remembers that party and state officials were required to interpret laws from five moral perspectives: *can* (diligence), *kiem* (thrift), *liem* (honesty), *chinh* (loyalty) and *chi cong vo tu* (social needs first).[80] These 'traditional' values that 'everyone understood', assumed different shades of meaning according to their application. For example, diligence and thrift retained their everyday meaning when applied to work practices within the justice system, but honesty, loyalty and 'social needs first' transformed obedience to party policy into a moral virtue—'new wine in old bottles'. Revolutionary values were rarely discussed in the context of theory or ideology, rather they were expressed through what officials did (or did not do).[81]

The Bifurcation between Socialist Legality and Revolutionary Morality

The discussion so far implies that socialist legality and socialist organisational principles (that is, democratic centralism and collective mastery) followed different ideological trajectories. Soviet-trained Vietnamese lawyers imported socialist legality into a reified Soviet-influenced legal environment that rarely engaged the world outside elite legal institutions. This bifurcation is illustrated by the dual meanings given to the Sino-Vietnamese term *phap che*.[82] In scholarly legal discourse it retained its Soviet meaning—laws and processes that follow legally prescribed pathways. But in political discourse it came to mean 'ensuring legal compliance' through mass legal/moral education campaigns. In this guise *phap che* described a form of virtue-rule—a process that did not follow legally prescribed pathways.

Negotiating the potent political and epistemological constraints to naturalisation, some Soviet legal ideas slowly acquired Vietnamese nuances. Vietnamese legal personnel, for example, cautiously adjusted Soviet laws to suit Vietnamese legal institutions.[83] As previously mentioned, bureaucrats used party edicts and revolutionary morality to implement imported Soviet laws. In addition, certain

---

79 See Thanh Duy (1997), 'Co So Khoa Hoc va Van Hoa Trong Tu Tuong Ho Chi Minh Ve Nha Nuoc va Phap Luat' (Scientific and Cultural Basis of Ho Chi Minh's Ideas of State and Law), *Tap Chi Cong San* (1), 26, 27–28.

80 Interview Ngo Van Thau, Former Professor of Judicial Training School, Hanoi, March 2001.

81 'If we speak of ideology without speaking of organizations that is mere empty theorising and empty morality without any practical effect. That is the inherent defect of petty-bourgeois intellectuals and Confucian scholars'. Le Duan (1994), *supra*, 447.

82 Dinh Gia Trinh (1965), 'May Y Kien Ve Tinh Dan Toc va Tinh Khoa Hoc Cua Thuat Ngu Luat Hoc—Nhan Xet Phe Phan Ve Mot So Thuat Ngu Thong Dung' (Nationalistic and Scientific Use of Legal Terminology: Criticisms of Common Legal Terms), *Tap San Tu Phap* (3), 24, 28–29.

83 See Penelope Nicholson (2000), 'Borrowing Court Systems: The Experience of the Democratic Republic of Vietnam 1945–1976', unpublished PhD Thesis, The University of Melbourne, Melbourne, chapters four and five; See George Ginsburgs (1979), *supra*, 187.

Soviet procedures were changed to suit the Vietnamese court structure. Judges were also encouraged to 'use reason and sentiment in carrying out the law' (*ly va tinh trong viec chap hanh phap luat*) (see Chapter 6). This practice conflated laws, party edicts and local customary practices to produce highly contextualised solutions. In short, acculturation slowly took place through small-scale, localised and pragmatic adjustments, but officials did not meditatively theorise a distinctly Vietnamese legal ideology.

Various factors discouraged lawmakers from fundamentally reconfiguring socialist legality to suit local conditions. Marxist–Leninist theory disassociated law from cultural relationships. It also assumed that a global workers' culture would flatten out regional differences separating socialist countries. Most policymakers presupposed the infallibility of Soviet ideology and believed that society should resemble laws, rather than adjusting laws to resemble society. They attributed low levels of compliance with imported socialist laws to incomplete legislation, poorly trained legal cadres, low educational levels and a failure to follow party morality, but rarely considered inconsistencies between imported legal ideology and local social conditions. French-trained legal officials, who might have challenged Soviet ideals, were purged from influential positions by the 1960s (see Chapter 2). A general antipathy to legality can also be inferred from residual anti-colonial sentiment.

In contrast with socialist legality, democratic centralism and collective mastery ideals were deeply interwoven with local political and moral arguments that legitimised party 'leadership'.[84] These notions stressed hierarchies and communitarian sentiments that were analogous to, and easily blended with, revolutionary virtue-rule. As organisational principles, they influenced party and state institutional structures. Further entrenching their influence, these principles primarily addressed party and state cadres—the group controlling the levers of power.

Given their importance to party legitimacy, the leadership promoted ideals such as party paramountcy, virtue-rule and collective interests much more vigorously than Soviet notions of legality and procedural justice. Although efforts were made to introduce the institutional trappings of a law-based state, such as courts and procuracy, the notion that law should normalise state-society relationships did not gain ideological dominance until after *doi moi* reforms commenced.

Incompatibilities between laws and political/moral rule did not especially matter in the command economy, where the state mainly used prerogative powers to order society. But they assumed more importance when the Sixth Party Congress in 1986 formally agreed that 'management of the country should be performed through laws rather than moral concepts'. By this time, market forces were already undermining the administrative apparatus used to regulate the command economy. The next

84 See Nguyen Khanh Toan (1964), 'Nha Nuoc va Phap Quyen Xa Hoi Chu Nghia va Cong Tac Nghien Cuu Luat Hoc' (State and Law: Socialist State and Legal Research), in *Nghien Cuu Nha Nuoc va Phap Quyen* (Studies about State and Law), Truth Publishing, Hanoi, 14 –15.

section examines how Vietnamese ideological thinking has responded to post-*doi moi* discourses.

Renovating Socialist Legal Ideology

Importing nha nuoc phap quyen *(Law-based State)*

After decades of socialist orthodoxy, questions were raised during the Fifth National Congress of the Communist Party of Vietnam (CPV), held in 1982, whether revolutionary ideology should continue to dominate legal thinking.[85] Reformers argued for a separation of the party from the day-to-day running of the government, and regulation through law, rather than moral rule and administrative edict. Little was done until the Sixth National Congress of the CPV in 1986 when party leaders gradually accepted that command planning could no longer regulate the emerging mixed-market economy.

In searching for a new form of legal regulation, Vietnamese lawmakers turned once again to the Soviet Union for ideological inspiration.[86] During the mid-1980s, Mikhail Gorbachev introduced a series of constitutional changes designed to formalise economic and social liberalisations (*perestroika*), without fundamentally disrupting communist party power.[87] Soviet lawmakers developed a constitutional doctrine—*pravovoe gosudarstvo* (law-based state)—that proclaimed the supremacy of law and the constitution.[88]

Pravovoe gosudarstvo was based on German *Rechtsstaat* (state-law) principles.[89] Developed in autocratic nineteenth-century Prussia, *Rechtsstaat* promoted the implementation of state policy through legislation. It de-emphasised social customs and precedents derived from sources outside the state that were capable of checking political and bureaucratic power. Contrasting with Diceyan common law notions of the 'rule of law', there were no unwritten legal conventions that the state was

---

85 See Circular No. 3831/TP Concerning Some Immediate Work to be Done by the Judiciary Sector to Implement the 5th Party Congress Resolution, 11 June 1982, Minister of Justice.

86 See Hoc Vien Hanh Chinh Quoc Gia (The National Administrative Institute) (1991), Ve *Cai Cach Bo May Nha Nuoc* (On the Reform of the State Apparatus), The Truth Publishing House, Hanoi.

87 The literature is vast but see Robert Sharlet (1992), *Soviet Constitutional Crisis from De Stalinistion to Disintegration*, M.E. Sharpe, New York, 85–98; John N. Hazard (1992), 'The Evolution of the Soviet Constitution', in Donald Barry (ed.), *Towards the Rule of Law in Russia?*, M.E. Sharpe, New York, 103–11; M. Gorbachev (1987), *Perestroika*, Collins, London, 110.

88 See Harold J. Berman (1992), 'The Rule of Law and the Law-Based State (*Rechtsstaat*), in *Towards the 'Rule of Law' in Russia?*, M.E. Sharpe, New York, 50–52.

89 Ibid., 46–47.

powerless to change. Even so, *pravovoe gosudarstvo* radically departed from the emphasis in socialist legality on party supremacy and legal instrumentalism.[90]

In a speech delivered to the Seventh Congress of the CPV in 1991, the new General Secretary (Do Muoi) introduced *nha nuoc phap quyen* (law-based state), a Vietnamese adaptation of *pravovoe gosudarstvo*.[91] Like *pravovoe gosudarstvo, nha nuoc phap quyen* required stable, authoritative and compulsory law; equality before the law; and the use of law to constrain and supervise the enforcement and administration of law.[92] Yet as the following discussion reveals, *nha nuoc phap quyen* has acquired a diverse range of meanings. At one end of an ideological continuum, the term means little more than legal formalism in which the party and state rule through law. At the other end it approaches a procedural 'rule of law', where the party and state are bound by legal rules. *Nha nuoc phap quyen* also presupposed a functional separation of party and state. The party was supposed to formulate socioeconomic objectives, leaving the state apparatus to enact and implement the party line (see Chapter 4).

Unlike their Soviet mentors, Vietnamese legal theorists refused to abandon socialist legality and are endeavouring to create a 'socialist law-based state' (*nha nuoc phap quyen xa hoi chu nghia*). There are various explanations for the party's cautious adaptation of *nha nuoc phap quyen*. Some leaders considered the Soviet legal system more legalistic and rule-bound than the Vietnamese system, and believed that constitutionalism would not easily transfer. Whatever the reasons, by juxtaposing socialist legality and *nha nuoc phap quyen* principles, party leaders set in motion unresolved ideological contests.

Current Directions in nha nuoc phap quyen *Thinking*

More a conceptual label for new legal thinking than a coherent ideology, *nha nuoc phap quyen* is used by theorists as a convenient catch-all to smuggle new ideas into the political-legal ideology.[93] Five main ideals are discernible in *nha nuoc phap quyen* writings.

---

90 See H.J. Berman (1991), 'Some Jurisprudential Implications of the Codification of Soviet Law', in Richard M. Buxbaum *et al.* (eds), *The Soviet* Sobranie *of Laws: Problems of Codification and Non-Publication*, University of California Press, Berkeley, 173.

91 See Do Muoi (1992), *Sua Doi Hien Phap Xay Dung Nha Nuoc Phap Quyen Viet Nam, Day Manh Su Nghiep Doi Moi* (Amending the Constitution, Establishing a Law-Based-State and Promoting *doi moi* Achievements), Nha Xuat Ban Su That, Hanoi, 30–38.

92 See generally, Nguyen Van Tai (1996), 'On the State Ruled by Law and a Multipartisan Regime', *Vietnam Social Sciences* (1), 3, 7.

93 The literature concerning *nha nuoc phap quyen* is as confusing as it is large. Since writers rarely acknowledge sources, ideological precepts are frequently thrown together with little explanation, much less logical organisation. This summary of *nha nuoc phap quyen* attempts to distil the main points, leaving analysis to later sections in the text. See generally Le Honh Hanh (1998), *Giao Trinh Ly Luan Nha Nuoc va Phap Luat* (Themes of State and Law), Nha Xuat Ban Cong An Nhan Dan, (People's Police Publishing House), Hanoi, 322–

1. Law rather than morality must adjust basic social relationships. Calls for legal formalism periodically appeared in writings about socialist legality, but party paramountcy legitimised the substitution of policy for law. The section below dealing with party paramountcy ascertains whether party paramountcy is conceding ground to *nha nuoc phap quyen* ideals such as legal formalism or a procedural version of the 'rule of law'.
2. State power belongs to the people and is used to elect state bodies. This ideal is consistent with Lenin's assertion that democracy is only possible where the working class 'centralise power in their hands'.[94] Whether the new democratic symbolism associated with *nha nuoc phap quyen* reforms is changing longstanding democratic ideals is discussed elsewhere.[95]
3. State organs and citizens 'must respect and act within the law' (*phai ton trong va thuc hien phap luat*). This proposition is consistent with the extreme legal positivism in socialist legality—that is, legal rights emanate from the state. The discussion in the following section dealing with economic regulation considers whether *nha nuoc phap quyen* thinking has sensitised the dominant political-legal ideology to the notion that citizens enjoy inherent civil and commercial rights.
4. Legislative, executive and judicial powers are distributed among state bodies '*hoc thuyet tam quyen phan lap*' (division of powers doctrine). The 1992 Constitution rejected Montesquieu's separation of powers doctrine and retained the socialist organisational principle that unifies (*thong nhat*) and centralises (*tap trung*) state power in the National Assembly. Efforts by *nha nuoc phap quyen* reformers to clarify party and state powers are examined in Chapters 4 and 6.
5. Courts should operate independently of local government organs (people's committees) and should freely exercise judicial discretion in applying the law. Contemporary writers unambiguously call for courts to take centre stage in resolving social grievances, but are less clear about whether justice is done by realising party objectives or following due process. The interplay between socialist legality and *nha nuoc phap quyen* notions of justice is examined in Chapter 6.

25; Nguyen Duy Quy (1993), 'On the Problem of Building a Juridical State in Our Country', 3 *Vietnam Social Science* 10, 10–11; Anonymous (1996), *Nhung Van De Ly Luan Co Ban Ve Nha Nuoc va Phap Luat* (Basic Theoretical Issues about State and Law), Nha Xuat Ban Chinh Tri Quoc Gia (National Political Publishing House), Hanoi, 112–16.

94 Vietnamese writers cited V.I. Lenin in *Nha nuoc va Cach Mang* (State and Revolution) Chapters Two and Three. See, for example, Dinh Gia Trinh (1964), *supra,* 90–92.

95 See John Gillespie (2004), 'Concepts of Law in Vietnam: Transforming Statist Socialism', in Randall Peerenboom (ed.), *Asian Discourses of Rule of Law: Theories and Implementation of Rule of Law in Twelve Asian Countries, France and the U.S.*, Routledge, London, 146, 157–61.

The ideological contests between socialist legality, democratic centralism, collective mastery and *nha nuoc phap quyen* are discussed in the following sections about party paramountcy and economic regulation. But first it is necessary to briefly consider the role Ho Chi Minh thought has played in opening-up discussion about *nha nuoc phap quyen*.

Ho Chi Minh Thought and nha nuoc phap quyen

'Ho Chi Minh thought' (*Tu Tuong Ho Chi Minh*) was added to Marxist–Leninist doctrine (*chu nghia Mac-Lenin*) as a state ideology in 1991.[96] Some legal writers have enlisted Ho Chi Minh's vague and eclectic teachings to camouflage new political-legal ideology. Several ideological strategies are evident in this literature. Many writers argue that Ho Chi Minh imported 'rule of law' ideals into Vietnam decades before the introduction of *nha nuoc phap quyen* ideology. They assert that the *Revendication du Peuple Annamite* (Demands of the Annamese People), sent by Ho Chi Minh (and others) to the Versailles Peace Conference in 1919 to demand constitutional rule for colonised people, demonstrated the party's longstanding commitment to the principle that law should constrain political power.[97] Ho Chi Minh, they argued, synthesised 'traditional' neo-Confucian concepts of Vietnamese humanism—'love the country, love her people'—with imported notions of equality and liberty derived from French Enlightenment thinkers, such as Montesquieu and Rousseau.[98]

This narrative conveniently ignores Ho Chi Minh's previously discussed support for Lenin's proletariat dictatorship, which placed an 'alliance of the working class with the peasantry' under party leadership. It also overlooks the reality of governance under Ho Chi Minh (discussed in Chapter 2) where party edicts and revolutionary morality displaced colonial legalism.

Other writers inventively use Ho Chi Minh thought as a 'political umbrella' to smuggle democratic liberal precepts into *nha nuoc phap quyen* discourse without overtly challenging socialist legality.[99] Procedural rule of law concepts such as legal

96 See Pham Van Dong (1990), 'Ho Chi Minh: His Theory and Action', *Vietnam Social Sciences* (2), 3, 9–11; Hoang Trung (2002), 'Pham Tru Trung—Hieu Trong Triet Ly Phuong Dong va Tu Tuong Ho Chi Minh Voi Van De Giao Duc Dao Duc Cach Mang Hien Nay' (The Notion of Loyalty—Piety in the Oriental Philosophy and Ho Chi Minh's Ideas about the Current Problem of Morality Education), *Tap Chi Cong San* (9), 18.

97 See Tran Dinh Huynh (1999), 'Moi Quan He Giua Tri Luc—Dao Duc—Phap Luat Trong Quan Ly Dat Nuoc Cua Chu Tich Ho Chi Minh' (Relationship between Intelligence—Morality-Law in Ho Chi Minh Thoughts on Administration), *To Chuc Nha Nuoc* (5), 3, 3–5; Song Thanh (1995), *supra*, 3–6.

98 See, for example, Thanh Duy (1997), 'Co So Khoa Hoc va Van Hoa Trong Tu Tuong Ho Chi Minh ve Nha Nuoc Phap Luat' (Scientific and Cultural Basis for Ho Chi Minh's Ideas of State and Law), *Tap Chi Cong San* (504), 26–27.

99 See Dao Tri Uc (1999), 'The Principle of Legality and Its Presentation in the Criminal Code of Vietnam', *Tap Chi Cong San* (8), 40, 40–41; Nguyen Duy Quy (1993), *supra*, 10–11.

'transparency' (*ro rang*) are used to promote legal institutions that constrain state power with law.[100]

Several writers have bypassed Ho Chi Minh altogether and directly attribute rule of law ideals to European Enlightenment philosophers.[101] By appropriating the language and thinking of Kant, Locke and Montesquieu, they have taken the first tentative steps away from class-based explanations of law. Since it is not politically acceptable to compare *nha nuoc phap quyen* with Marxist-Leninism without acknowledging the latter's superiority, they juxtapose democratic liberal and socialist legal ideals, implicitly inviting readers to reach inferred conclusions.[102]

Party Paramountcy and nha nuoc phap quyen

There is an ongoing struggle in the dominant ideology in Vietnam between *nha nuoc phap quyen* ideology and party paramountcy. One way to ascertain which ideological strain dominates official thinking is to examine the ideals the party invokes to legitimise its paramountcy. A shift away from class or moral assertions of legitimacy towards legal imagery signifies changes in the official political-legal ideology.

For decades, the party legitimised its monopolisation of power through assertions of Marxist-Leninism and moral and intellectual leadership.[103] During the second half of the twentieth century the party gained considerable popular support by claiming responsibly for military successes over the French and Americans. As the victories fade, the party is searching for new sources of legitimacy.[104]

Class-based Ideology

In Marxist–Leninist ideology, party paramountcy arose from the party's role in defending the 'ruling-class' (*giai cap thong tri*). As the executive committee of the 'ruling class', the party decides which laws 'benefit the working people'—a formula that justifies party paramountcy.

---

100 Le Hong Hanh (1998), *supra*, 322–23.

101 See, for example, Nguyen Duy Quy (1994), 'The Question of Building a State of Law in Vietnam', 1 *Vietnam Law and Legal Forum* (2), 32, 33.

102 See, for example, Institute of State and Law (1998), *Giao Trinh Ly Luan Nha Nuoc va Phap Luat* (Textbook on State and Law), Nha Xuat Ban Cong An Nhan Dan, Hanoi; Author Unknown (1996), *Nhung Van De Ly Luan Co Ban Ve Nha Nuoc va Phap Luat* (Basic Theoretical Issues about State and Law), Nha Xuat Ban Chinh Tri Quoc Gia (National Political Publishing House), Hanoi.

103 Stephen Young argued that 'Vietnamese invest true authority with those who posses the quality of *uy tin* (moral legitimacy)'; Stephen Young (1977), 'Unpopular Socialism in United Vietnam', 22 *Orbis* (2), 227, 228.

104 See Barrett McCormick (1999), 'Political Change in China and Vietnam: Coping with the Consequences of Economic Reform', in Anita Chan, Benedict Kerkvliet and Jonathan Unger (eds), *Transforming Asian Socialism: China and Vietnam Compared*, Allen and Unwin, Sydney, 151, 164–70.

As private entrepreneurs and foreign investors acquire greater economic importance in the mixed-market economy, class-based imagery appears increasingly implausible. To meet this challenge, party leaders have been forced to expand the ranks of the 'working class-peasant' alliance. The 1992 Constitution initially added intellectuals to the ruling class to form the 'cooperation of workers, peasants and intellectuals' (*lien minh giua giai cap cong nhan voi giai cap nong dan va tang lop tri thuc*).[105] More recently, the ruling class was further enlarged to include the 'interests of the entire people' (*toan the quan chung nhan dan*), including entrepreneurs.[106] The final class barrier collapsed when the Party Central Committee in 2002 officially permitted party members to engage in private business. The recruitment of former class enemies into the 'ruling class' is undermining the ideological potency of class-based justifications for party paramountcy.

As revolutionary morality loses its legitimising power, there are mixed signals that the party and state are seeking legitimacy from domestic, and especially foreign, audiences by stressing the procedural 'rule of law' elements in *nha nuoc phap quyen* discourse. But since not all sectors of the economy have the same need for the 'rule of law', this claim for legitimacy has limited appeal. Foreign investors are the most vocal advocates for legal reforms.[107] Lacking the political and personal connections required to secure state privileges, foreign investors rely on legal rules for fair tax collection, regulation of market failures and credible dispute resolution. Yet for the vast majority of domestic entrepreneurs working at the periphery of state regulation, the 'rule of law' means more state interference with few compensating benefits (see Chapter 8). For them, 'rule of law' imagery is much less attractive than other sources of legitimacy such as nationalism and economic prosperity.

Efforts by the state to demonstrate its commitment to due process in high-profile criminal trials have been ineffectual, even counterproductive. In the Minh Phung corruption trial of 1998, for example, 200 witnesses were called during a

---

105 See Vo Khanh Vinh (2000), 'Ve Cac Dac Diem va Dieu Kien Cua Su Hinh Thanh Nha Nuoc Phap Quyen O Viet Nam' (The Characteristics and Conditions for the Establishment of a Law-Based State in Vietnam), unpublished paper presented at the 'Rule of Law and its Acceptance in Vietnam' Conference, 11 September, Hanoi, 3. Nguyen Huu Tho (1988), 'Phan Dinh Chuc Nang Giua To Chuc Dang va Nha Nuoc-Dieu Kien Dau Tien Thuc Hien Phap Luat' (Assignment of Functions between Party Organisations and the State—The Pre-Conditions for Observance of Laws), *Tap Chi Cong San* (5), 7–9.

106 Article one of the Constitution 1992 added intellectuals to the 'peasant and worker alliance'. Also see Pham Xuan Nam (2002), 'Some Preliminary Ideas on the Change of Social Structure and Classes in Viet Nam During the Transition to a Socialist-Oriented Market Economy', *Vietnam Social Sciences* (6), 31, 39–40.

107 The international donor and investment community in Vietnam periodically call for increased efforts to introduce a procedural rule of law. See The Vietnam Business Forum, which promotes neoliberal economic versions of the 'rule of law'. See, for example, Tony Foster (2002), 'Rule of Law—Benefits for Private Sector', unpublished paper, Vietnam Business Forum, Hanoi, May; see American Chamber of Commerce Position Papers available online at <http://www.amchamhanoi.com/adPositionPapers.htm>.

67-day trial.[108] More recently, in Nam Cam's corruption trial during 2003, 155 defendants faced 24 different types of criminal charge in a trial that lasted more than two months.[109] In both cases, carefully stage-managed images showing exhaustive investigations and rigorously tested evidence were subverted when party prerogative powers favoured high-ranking party and state officials. Due process was further compromised in the Nam Cam case when the procuracy and police attempted to intimidate Nam Cam's lawyers with criminal charges.

The party's continued support for democratic centralism further undermines their representations of a law-based state. Party leaders comprehensibly defeated an attempt by the former Prime Minister Vo Van Kiet in 1996 to reconfigure democratic centralism by extending more autonomy to executive and juridical agencies—a procedural 'rule of law'.[110] By retaining this doctrine, party leaders could continue to use prerogative powers that blur distinctions between political policy and law. Democratic centralism undermines the legal formalism promoted by *nha nuoc phap quyen* ideology.

The party has been more successful in generating legitimacy by appealing to developmentalist and nationalist sentiments. As Marxist-Leninism loses heuristic power, party writers portray the party as defender and definer of core social customs and values.[111] They have selectively plundered traditional customs based on essentialised *kinh* traditions to create *the* national culture (*van hoa dan toc*). Like articles of faith, certain Vietnamese cultural institutions, such as ancestral links to the mythical Lac Hong kings, Red River Delta villages and freedom from foreign domination, are placed within the traditional core.[112] Popular films such as *Thuong Nho Dong Que* (Our Beloved Countryside) reinforce certain cultural values by depicting serene village morals providing refuge from the 'whirlwind of the market

---

108 See John Gillespie (2001), 'Self-Interest and Ideology: Bureaucratic Corruption in Vietnam', 3 *Australian Journal of Asian Law* (1), 13–23.

109 See VNS (2003), 'Court Sentences Nam Cam, Five Henchmen to Death', *vietnamnews on-line*, 7 June <www.vietnamnewsagency.org.vn>; VNS (2003), 'Crime Boss Faces Court in Nation's Biggest Trial', *vietnamnews on-line*, 27 February, <www.vietnamnewsagency.org.vn>.

110 The letter was published in *Viet Luan*, No. 1053, 5 January 1996, 30–31, 58–60; trans. Vnnews website <www.vnnews.com.vn>.

111 There is extensive literature in this area, but see Le Thi (1999), *The Role of the Family in the Formation of the Vietnamese Personality*, The Gioi Publishers, Hanoi, 140–46.

112 See Le Kha Phieu (1998), 'Party Leader Addresses Cultural Officials', *Nhan Dan*, 9 October, 1, 5, trans. FBIS East Asia Daily Reports 98-289; Le Truyen, 'Ho Chi Minh's Thoughts on Unity', 9 *Vietnam Law and Legal Forum* (108), 10. National cultural values are used to create the 'Great Unity' (*dai doan ket*), which encompasses state-sanctioned thinking and values. Officially approved values include well-established historical values, especially patriotism, national independence, collective values that tie individuals, families, communities and the homeland, kindness, tolerance, appreciation of *nghia tinh dao ly* [Confucian values], diligence, creativeness, elegance and modesty.

economy'.[113] Other deeply embedded cultural traditions, particularly those derived from colonial and foreign sources, are relegated to the periphery of the imagined cultural identity.[114]

In sum, the party is seeking legitimisation from a manufactured set of 'traditional' values, Marxist-Leninism as well as economic prosperity. Legitimisation is a dynamic process, in which moral representations change, but not party paramountcy and the notion that only the party is morally and intellectually capable of determining the context and extent of legal rights.

The representations of legitimacy suggest ongoing tensions in the political-legal ideology between *nha nuoc phap luat* ideals, such as legal formalism and a procedural 'rule of law', and party paramountcy. Most party leaders have not yet accepted that party policy needs state legislation to acquire coercive force.[115] But, as the following discussion suggests, some party leaders are convinced that 'rule of law' ideals are needed to deliver modernisation, industrialisation and ultimately economic prosperity.

Economic Regulation

The mixed-market economy has changed political-legal ideology in Vietnam more than any other factor. Since *doi moi* reforms began in 1986, the state has increasingly borrowed foreign laws and procedures to regulate the mixed-market economy and secure entry into international trade agreements. Especially since the mid-1990s, the pace and depth of legal borrowing has increased as the state has struggled to harmonise domestic laws with market-access treaties such as the US–Vietnam Bilateral Trade Agreement (BTA) and the World Trade Organization (WTO).

Legal harmonisation poses an ideological dilemma for a party that does not countenance inherent civil rights, much less a democratic liberal substantive 'rule of law'. In order to attract foreign investment and benefit from market-access treaties, the party is under pressure to create a rights-based system that gives entrepreneurs legal weapons that might check party and state powers. This section explores the ideological struggles informing commercial law reforms.

The Ideological Transition to a 'Socialist-oriented Market Economy'

After more than a decade of economic reforms, party theorists still rather confusingly refer to a 'market economy following a socialist orientation' (*nen kinh te thi truong*

113 See Ngo Phoung Lan (1998), 'The Changing Face of Vietnamese Cinema During Ten Years of Renovation', in David Marr (ed.), *The Mass Media in Vietnam*, Political and Social Change Monograph 25, Australian National University, Canberra, 95–96.

114 See Le Kha Phieu (1998), *supra,* 289; Le Truyen (2003), 'Ho Chi Minh's Thoughts on Unity', *Nhan Dan*, reproduced in 9 *Vietnam Law and Legal Forum* (108), 10–11.

115 In 1996, party paramountcy was reaffirmed in the Party Statute—'The party rules and uses the state as a tool to manage society'. See Party Statute (1996), articles 41–43.

theo dinh huong xa hoi chu nghia).[116] Vague terminology accommodates different views about the appropriate role for 'state economic management' and ownership in the economy. It is beyond our purposes to explore this complex literature, but several ideological themes emerge in writings about the transitional period (*thoi ky qua do*) to a mixed-market economy.

Especially after *doi moi* reforms began in 1986, party ideology incrementally changed from outright hostility to qualified support for private entrepreneurs. Article 15 of the 1992 Constitution formally recognised a mixed-market economy and 'private capitalist' production but specified state ownership as the key form of economic activity. The Eighth Party Congress reaffirmed this formula in 1996 and publicly lauded the positive economic contributions made by the private sector.[117] By the Ninth Party Congress in 2001, party leaders 'encouraged the extensive development of the private capitalist economic sector'.[118] In 2003, the prime minister, Phan Van Khai, went one step further in raising the ideological status of the private sector by telling entrepreneurs that 'your success in the marketplace is no less glorious than a victory on the battlefield'.[119]

Yet support for private sector development does not necessarily signal movement away from socialist legality and 'state economic management'. Some commentators argue that imported property, contract and company law rights are permitted only insofar as they support party socioeconomic policies.[120] Viewed from this perspective, private economic rights are valued for stimulating private production and developing the national economy, but they have not altered key ideological preferences for state ownership and 'state economic management'.

---

116 See Luu Ha Vi (1997), 'Vietnam: Industrialization Viewed from the Interplay between Productive Forces and Relations of Production' *Economic Development Review* January, 1–4; Nguyen Phu Trong (1994b), 'Market Economy and the Leadership of Role of the Party', *Tap Chi Cong San* (1), 29–33.

117 See Do Muoi (1994), 'Build a Uniform Market Mechanisms Under State Management and in Accordance with Socialist Orientations', Political Report to the Seventh Central Party Committee, 20 January, trans. FBIS East Asia Daily Report 94–016, 25 January, 67–68. Also see Lewis Stern (1999), 'The Political Report to the 8th Congress of the Vietnamese Communist Party: An Anatomy of the Writing Process', 16 *Journal of Third World Studies* (1), 49, 65–66.

118 See Central Committee of the CPV (2001), The Communist Party of Vietnam Central Committee's Political Report to the 9th National Party Congress, Central Committee of the Communist Party of Vietnam, Hanoi, Chapter IX.

119 See Tu Giang (2003), 'The Nation's Corporate Spirit', *Vietnam Investment Review*, 12 September, <www.vietnam.investmentreview.com.vn>.

120 Viet Xuan (1998), 'Market Economy: Which Orientation?', *Vietnam Social Sciences* (4), 15–29; Vu Ngoc Nhung (1999), 'Role of the State in Market Economy with Socialist Orientation', *Vietnam Social Sciences* (6), 19–23; Luu Ha Vi (1997), *supra*, 1–4; Nguyen Phu Trong (1994b), *supra*, 29–33.

Three ideals are struggling to dominate ideological approaches to economic regulation. They are neoliberal economic regulation, international legal harmonisation and 'state economic management'.

Neo-liberal Legalism

Proponents of neoliberal legalism draw from Hayek the notion that markets require facilitative legislative frameworks administered by reactive state institutions such as courts.[121] This regulatory ideal limits state intervention to correcting market pathologies and deregulating state licensing. Neo-liberal legalism is clearly evident in legal reforms proposed by the Comprehensive Legal Needs Assessment Report published in 2002:

- citizens may do everything not expressly prohibited by law
- the 'state must not do anything, except that which is expressly permitted by law'
- citizens should have increased powers to 'know, discuss and check' state power.

There is little discernible support for neoliberal economic ideas in Vietnamese legal literature. A small number of legal academics contend that 'state economic management' compromises liberal market rights such as freedom to conduct authorised business activities.[122] Nevertheless, they are sceptical whether sweeping economic deregulation is an appropriate economic model for a poor country with increasing economic inequality. Many writers support a Marxist or Keynesian view that states should proactively redistribute wealth according to need.

Other commentators favour an East Asian developmental model.[123] They agree with neoliberal theorists that facilitative law encourages market stability and predictability, but believe that economic growth requires 'Rhine capitalism'

121 This view is most strongly advocated by some economists working in CIEM. Interviews Nguyen Dinh Cuong, Director of the Enterprise Department, CIEM, Hanoi, July 2002, March 2003; Also see Le Dang Doanh (1999) 'Enterprise Law—A Must for Further Development of Multi-Sectoral Economy', 5 *Vietnam Law and Legal Forum* (56), 11–13.

122 See Pham Duy Nghia (2002), 'Tiep Nhan Phap Luat Nuoc Ngoai—Thoi Co va Thach Thuc Moi Cho Nghien Cu Lap Phap' (Transplantation of Foreign Law—Chances and Challenges for Legislative Studies in Vietnam), *Tap Chi Nghien cuu Lap Phap* (5), 50, 53–56; Pham Duy Nghia (2000), 'Phap Luat Thuong Mai Viet Nam Truoc Thach Thuc Cua Qua Trinh Hoi Nhap Linh Te Quac Te', (Commercial Law Faces the Challenges of International Economic Integration), *Nha nuoc va phap luat*, (6), 9–18; Nguyen Nhu Phat (1993), 'Our Country's Economic Laws During the Transition to the Market Economy', *Nha Nuoc va Phap Luat* (2), 4.

123 Interviews Kawazu Shinsuke, JICA Long-Term Legal Representative, and Takeuchi Tsutomu, Judicial Expert, Hanoi, January 2002. See generally Lawrence Tshuma (1999), 'The Political Economy of the World Bank's Legal Framework for Economic Development', 8

combined with proactive state economic regulation.[124] A balance is struck between these conflicting regulatory ideals by giving 'state economic management' an ongoing role in controlling large state-owned enterprises and micro-managing the private sector, while at the same time promoting legal rights to protect entrepreneurs against state malfeasance. The unifying theme in these economic models is support for a procedural 'rule of law' that protects private commercial rights.

International Legal Harmonisation

International legal harmonisation has profoundly influenced legal thinking. By the mid-1980s, party leaders had concluded that central planning, trade with Eastern bloc countries and import replacement strategies could not produce the economic growth experienced by Vietnam's neighbours.[125] *Doi moi* reforms in 1986 adopted an 'open door' (*mo cua*) policy that cautiously opened the economy to foreign trade and investment from capitalist countries. Harmonisation gained momentum after the Politburo issued Resolution No. 7-NQ/TW on International Economic Integration 2001, which instructed the party and state to 'initiate international economic integration' to expand markets, import capital and technology and advance industrialisation and modernisation.[126]

We saw in Chapter 2 that legal borrowing from Western countries began soon after the Sixth Party Congress. But it was not until the Vietnamese government began preparing for WTO entry in 1995 that the initial caution gave way to large-scale importation.[127] Treaty accession rules place Vietnamese lawmakers under pressure not only to harmonise substantive law, but also develop a procedural 'rule of law' that makes private commercial rights credible.[128]

Social and Legal Studies (2), 75–96; Doan Duy Thanh (2000), 'Market Economy and the Operation of the Market Mechanism in Vietnam', *Vietnam Social Sciences* (2), 28, 32–33.

124 See generally Vu Tuan Anh (ed.) (1994), *The Role of the State in Economic Development: Experiences of the Asian Countries*, Social Sciences Publishing House, Hanoi, 283–354.

125 See Adam Fforde (1999), 'From Plan to Market', in Anita Chan *et al.* (eds), *Transforming Asian Socialism: China and Vietnam Compared*, Allen and Unwin, Sydney 43, 44–63; Tu Tuan Anh (1994), *Vietnam's Economic Reform: Results and Problems*, Social Science Publishing House, Hanoi, 15–26.

126 Also see Central Committee of the CPV (2001), '2001–2010 Socio-Economic Development Strategy', 9th National Party Congress, Central Committee of the CPV, chapter IV, part 4.

127 Tran Thu Hang (1999), 'Vietnam's Trade in the Course of International Integration', *Vietnamese Studies* (2), 121.

128 See Ministry of Justice (2002), 'Report on the Comprehensive Needs of Developing Law Making Bodies, Law Implementation and Enforcement, International Treaty Reception and Dispute Resolution', Ministry of Justice, Hanoi, August, 25.

Most government sources uncritically promote international economic integration.[129] Numerous studies purporting to show that integration has improved domestic economic growth and reduced poverty are used to argue that any loss of national sovereignty caused by legal harmonisation is more than offset by the economic benefits.[130] In tandem with this ideological campaign, some government leaders have used treaties to entrench domestic market liberalisations against those who continue to oppose market reforms.

Contradicting the government's legal harmonisation rhetoric, some party members attribute international integration to economic necessity rather than an ideological shift towards free trade or the 'rule of law'. Nguyen Tan Dung, a Politburo member, cautions that harmonisation and globalisation will erode national sovereignty.[131] Foreign competition may compromise the leading role of SOEs as 'an important managerial force and macro instrument for the state to orient and regulate the economy'.[132] Such views are heavily coloured by nationalism and deeply ingrained notions of 'self-sufficiency' (*phat huy noi luc*, literally to promote internal strengths). Those advocating self-reliance ultimately believe that the erosion of national sovereignty outweighs the putative benefits of international trade and investment.[133]

Those arguing from this nationalistic standpoint call for the state to reassert its sovereignty over legal harmonisation. They oppose attempts to introduce a procedural rule of law, because legal accountability may undermine the party's prerogative powers to adjust laws to reflect the Vietnamese 'national identity'. Party paramountcy, they believe, prevents the legal system from becoming a dependent variable in a globalised legal system (see Chapter 4).

Despite these broadly based concerns, international legal harmonisation has been a powerful force in overcoming ideological resistance to imported rights-based law.

---

129 See, for example, Nguyen Minh Tu (1999), 'Integration of Vietnam's Economy into the Regional and World Economy at Present', *Vietnam Social Sciences* (6), 91–96; Viet Nam News (2002), 'BTA a Gateway to Access the WTO', 25 December, <www.vietnamnews.vnagency.com.vn/2002-12/24htm>.

130 See, for example, Giang Chau (2003), 'Trade to Firm up After Solid Promotion During First Year', *Vietnam Investment Review* 10 February, 1; *Viet Nam News* (2002), 'BTA a Gateway to Access the WTO', 25 December, <www.vietnamnews.vnagency.com.vn/2002-12/24htm>.

131 Nguyen Tan Dung (2002), 'Building a Socialist-Oriented Independent and Sovereign Economy', *Quan Doi Nhan Dan*, 13 September, 3; reprinted in 9 *Vietnam Law and Legal Forum* (98), 18.

132 Ibid., 20.

133 See, for example, Pham Van Chuc (2002), 'Dang Co Chang Mot Toan Cau Hoa Cho Moi Nguoi' (Is There Now a Globalisation for all People?), *Tap Chi Cong San* (12), 33, 35–37; Nguyen Minh Hoan (1999), 'The Trend of Globalisation and Vietnam's Integration and Protection of National Interests', *Vietnam Social Sciences* (6), 88–91; Vu Quoc Huy (2002), 'Trade Liberalisation and Poverty in Vietnam', *Vietnam's Socio-Economic Development* (29), 37.

Qualified party support for legal harmonisation was put beyond doubt by the Legal Sector Development Strategy, which prioritised the legislative reforms required to comply with the BTA and WTO.[134]

State Economic Management

'State economic management' still dominates party ideology.[135] But it now stresses the compatibility between socialism and mixed-market economies—'commodity production is not the opposite of socialism'.[136] It has even moderated its antipathy to private entrepreneurs. Yet it has not entirely lost its original meaning. At the same time the Fifth Plenum of the Party Central Committee in 2002 endorsed private sector development, it also reconfirmed the need to place the 'socialist-oriented market economy under state management and senior state officials'.[137]

In ideological terms, this means that private commercial rights should remain 'under state management'.[138] According to party sources,

> [s]tate economic management' is needed to ensure that resource allocation complies with party socioeconomic objectives ... it ensures stable growth and efficiency for the economy, particularly social equality and progress. No one else but the state can reduce the gap between the rich and poor, the towns and the countryside, industry and agriculture and among regions in the country.[139]

In short, the party supports the use of extra-legal or prerogative powers countenanced by 'state economic management' to micromanage the economy to

---

134 See Politburo Resolution No 48 NQ/TW on Building and Perfecting the Socialist Orientated Economic System and *Nha Nuoc Phap Quyen* 24 May 2005. Also see Bach Quoc An and Lai Thi Anh (2002), 'BTA's Impacts on Vietnam's Current Legal System', 8 *Vietnam Law and Legal Forum* (91), 16, 16–18.

135 See Vu Ngoc Nhung (1999), *supra*, 21–24; Do Phuong (1995), 'Party–State–Law' 1 *Vietnam Law and Legal Forum* (5), 3–5; Do Muoi (1995a), *supra*, 6.

136 Vu Son Thuy (1997), 'Interview With Politburo Standing Board Member Nguyen Tan Dung, Head of the CPV Central Committee Economic Department: New Year Discussion on Economic Issues', *Hanoi Tuan Quoc Te*, 16 February, 1–2; Pham Xuan Nam (2002), *supra*, 32–34.

137 See Party Central Committee (2002), 'The Party on Further Development of Private Economy', 8 *Vietnam Law and Legal Forum* (93), 25, 20, 27; also see Central Committee of the CPV (2001), 'Central Committee Political Report, 9th Party Congress', Communist Party of Vietnam, Hanoi, chapter III.

138 See Vu Ngoc Nhung (1999), *supra*, 22–23; Mai Huu Thuc (2001), 'Characteristics of Market Economy with Socialist Orientation in Vietnam', *Vietnam Social Sciences* (1), 20, 22–24.

139 See Mai Huu Thuc (2001), *supra*, 24.

ensure the entrepreneurs cannot use legal rights to accumulate levels of wealth that pose a threat to party power.[140]

The Impact of Market Ideals on the Political-legal Ideology

Two antagonistic legal ideologies coexist within party discourse. Some party leaders support a narrow, procedural 'rule of law' that implicitly challenges the socialist instrumental thinking underlying 'state economic management'. However, so far, the notion that laws should circumscribe state power has not broadened into a general principle that constrains party paramountcy.

It is intriguing to speculate why some party leaders are prepared to countenance a limited procedural 'rule of law' in the economic arena, while remaining implacably opposed to substantive civil and democratic rights that could challenge party paramountcy.[141] Kanishka Jayasuriya labels this phenomena 'economic constitutionalism'.[142] He notes that elsewhere in South East Asia (e.g. Singapore and Malaysia) illiberal rule and a procedural rule of law are ideologically reconcilable—even symbiotically beneficial. The rule of law regularises commerce and centralises power in state bodies, while party prerogative powers de-politicise the commercial arena by limiting special interest groups hostile to economic producers (for example, consumer associations taking product liability actions).

Even 'economic constitutionalism' faces considerable hurdles in shaping the dominant ideology in Vietnam. It was not until 2005 that high-level party leaders accepted the 'rule of law' notion that entrepreneurs are permitted to do anything not expressly prohibited by law.[143] It is likely to take decades (if it happens at all) before party and state officials accept that laws have a genuinely autonomous role beyond party policy. In the meantime, imported commercial laws struggle to tame the prerogative powers underlying 'state economic management' and party paramountcy.

Contests between the 'rule of law' and 'state economic management' profoundly affect the way the party and state regulate the economy. For example, decades after commercial rights were introduced, it is still unclear in what circumstances private

140 Interview Vu Duy Thai, Vice Chairman & Secretary, The Hanoi Associations of Industry and Commerce (member of the Central Committee of the Fatherland Front), Hanoi, April 1999; September 2000.

141 Some commentators argue that party leaders stand to benefit from legal rights that protect property rights. Others suggest that party leaders are concerned that once 'rule of law' ideas are established for commercial transactions, they could migrate into the political arena. Interview officials from the Office of the National Assembly, Hanoi, November 2002, March 2004.

142 See Kanishka Jayasuriya (1999), 'The Rule of Law and Governance in the East Asian State', 1 *The Australian Journal of Asian Law* (2), 107, 119–21.

143 See Politburo Resolution No 48 NQ/TW on Building and Perfecting the Socialist Orientated Economic System and *Nha Nuoc Phap Quyen* 24 May 2005.

rights will prevail over the 'state benefit' (*loi ich cua nha nuoc*). This debate is taken up in subsequent chapters dealing with the selection and implementation of foreign commercial rights.

Mapping the Dominant Political-legal Ideology

Poulantzas's contention that different ideological regions compete to form the dominant ideology sits comfortably with Vietnam's contested ideological landscape.[144] Four ideological regions—socialist legality, *nha nuoc phap quyen*, democratic centralism and collective (or people's) mastery—strive for political and legal stability, but differ radically in the steps they prescribe to realise this common objective.

The shift in party imagery away from class theory towards developmentalism and international legal harmonisation opened ideological space for new legal concepts. Rather then directly confronting deeply entrenched socialist ideals, reform-minded party and state leaders smuggled 'rule of law' ideas into *nha nuoc phap quyen* ideology. They also strategically used legal harmonisation treaties to entrench private commercial rights and backed legal reforms needed to create institutions that could deliver legal transparency, equality before the law, and legal constraints to executive power. Under their guidance, a procedural 'rule of law' is slowly making inroads into socialist legality, which for decades legitimised a ritual observance of legal formalism. Public affirmations of the 'rule of law' are no doubt also intended to secure support from foreign and domestic investors.

The 'rule of law' is encountering strong ideological resistance from some central, and especially provincial, party and state officials. The central issue is whether *nha nuoc phap quyen* and neoliberal ideology can displace the 'state economic management' thinking being deployed to prevent deregulatory reforms (see Chapters 5 and 6). Rule of law ideas struggle against party paramountcy, nationalism and rent seeking in making private commercial rights appear plausible and desirable to state officials. This task is especially difficult where the legislative framework is largely constituted by imported rules that to many state officials appear alien and imposed.

An ancillary question is whether 'rule of law' ideals unleashed in the economic arena will eventually spill over to constrain party and state power in other social realms. This seems unlikely, since procedural versions of the rule of law promote transactional certainty but lack a transcendent political morality that is capable of ordering other social relationships. The Hayekian notion that contractual relationships generate human dignity is unlikely to resonate in Vietnam's communitarian society. Kanishka Jayasuriya's 'economic constitutionalism' suggests a more plausible ideological trajectory where illiberal rule and a procedural rule of law are ideologically compatible.

---

144 See Nicos Poulantzas (1973), *supra*, 206–8.

In contrast to rapid changes in economic legal thinking, there has been glacial progress towards a 'rule of law' in the organisational principles (collective mastery and especially democratic centralism) that underpin party paramountcy. One possible explanation for this uneven ideological change is that socialist legal thinking has been confined within a semi-autonomous discourse conducted behind the walls of academic institutions and superior courts. As a mere surface adaptation, it lacked political and institutional roots and could change relatively quickly when lawyers were exposed to 'rule of law' ideology.

Socialist organisational principles (democratic centralism and collective mastery), on the other hand, were woven into the fabric of revolutionary morality. As such, they were directly responsible for legitimising and organising party paramountcy. Unwavering support for party paramountcy has prevented 'rule of law' ideals from penetrating collective mastery and democratic centralism ideology. Further movement in this direction is blocked by constant official pronouncements that privilege political stability and economic growth over civil liberties and democratic rights.

Chapter 7 argues that, without support from special interest groups outside the party and state orbit, rule of law ideology lacks persuasive power. As Roberto Unger showed, law's relative autonomy from political morality was only possible because democratic liberal societies recognised the voluntary association of equal, rational individuals willing to confer minimum powers on states to preserve basic liberties.[145] Ideological hegemony is generated and reproduced by public discourse sponsored not only by the state, but also by professional associations, media, businesses, religious organisations and trade unions.[146] Vietnam does not necessarily require the same configuration of non-state interests to legitimise the 'rule of law', but it does require relatively unmediated forums in which non-state voices can make imported commercial laws appear plausible and natural.

Conclusion

Fifty years, ago party leaders began importing from the Soviet Union and China an all-encompassing ideology that was backed by complementary state institutions and economic objectives. Imported socialist legal ideals operated in a context that gave

145 See Roberto Unger (1976), *Law in Modern Society*, Free Press, New York, 166–92. Whether these conditions ever existed in reality is open to speculation. What matters, however, is that ruling elites believe they exist and order legal development accordingly. See generally Elizabeth Mensch (1982), 'The History of Mainstream Legal Thought', in David Kairys (ed.), *The Politics of Law: a Progressive Critique*, Pantheon Books, New York, 18–37.

146 Habermas maintains that it is primarily through rational argument that members of society form the mutual understanding necessary to consent to dominant ideologies. See Jürgen Habermas (1987), *The Theory of Communicative Action*, Beacon Press, Boston, Vol. 2, 164–97; Jürgen Habermas (1996), *Between Fact and Norms: Towards a Discourse of Law*, Polity Press, Cambridge, 426.

them meaning and legitimacy. The importation of Western commercial laws over the last two decades could hardly have been more different. Laws have been selectively borrowed with little thought to the ideology and institutional trappings that make them work in capitalist economies. To make matters worse, domestic socialist legality, democratic centralism and collective mastery ideals are antagonistic to imported commercial rights and the 'rule of law'.

The rapid entry of imported commercial laws into Vietnam suggests, however, that conflicting ideologies do not inevitably constrain legal borrowing. During the transitional period, the party is preserving ideals (such as party paramountcy, democratic centralism and 'state economic management') that give coherence and stability to existing institutional structures. At the same time, they are experimenting with *nha nuoc phap quyen* ideas to facilitate international legal harmonisation and to regulate the mixed-market economy. The resulting ideological tensions do not necessarily inhibit legal borrowing. In fact, some degree of ideological confusion and discord may actually create space for imported ideas. Provided the dominant ideological regions do not actively block imported ideas from entering institutional thinking, the lack of a congruent domestic ideology does not prevent legal borrowing.

Western liberal experience suggests that commercial laws perform best in a 'rule of law' environment that stabilises economic relations, makes officials accountable, and efficiently resolves disputes. Yet economic development in East Asia shows democratic liberal versions of the 'rule of law' are not necessarily the only, or even the best, ways to facilitate commercial development. Different versions of the rule of law are needed to support different variants of capitalism. Moreover, the rule of law is not an all-or-nothing concept and may eventually evolve into a more fully realised form in Vietnam. Subsequent chapters suggest that this process is strongly linked to social demand for laws and legal institutions.

It remains unclear to what extent 'rule of law' ideals remain mere ideas or have taken root in the discourses shaping institutional and social thinking. Put differently, does the dominant legal ideology make a procedural 'rule of law' (at least in the commercial arena) appear natural and desirable to party and state officials? A more textured understanding of legal thinking needs to look beyond surface ideas to consider the discourses that generate, maintain and transmit ideology. To this end, the next three chapters examine how party and state institutions select and implement foreign commercial laws.

Chapter 4

Party Leadership: The Separation of Party and State

Introduction

The discussion in Chapter 3 about the 'rule of law' and Vietnamese political-legal ideology assessed legal transferability from a reified perspective. Ideology comprehends law as a depersonalised 'thing' or 'it'. This approach is useful in comparing broad state and societal ideals (or aspirations), but conceals power structures and organisational practices shaping the formulation and implementation of law.

The second working postulate, discussed in Chapter 1, deepens our understanding of legal borrowing by suggesting that the ways legislators, bureaucrats and judges use state power influences the meanings given to legal transplants. As laws transfer among different power-distribution structures they acquire different meanings. For this reason, Kahn-Freund cautioned anyone transferring Western laws to communist regimes to search for functionally equivalent legal structures and processes.[1]

This chapter takes up his recommendation. It explores how 'party leadership' (*su lanh dao cua dang*) over state institutions in Vietnam affects legal transplantation. Subsequent chapters apply these findings by asking the vital questions: how (if at all) does 'party leadership' influence the importation of law? Is the separation of party and state a necessary precondition for commercial rights-based laws and a procedural rule of law? How does the substitution of party policy for legal norms change the meaning of imported laws?

This chapter begins by briefly outlining the interrelationship between party and state organs. It then contrasts state organisational ideals in Western liberal counties with the principle of party leadership in Vietnam. Bound up in this inquiry is the perplexing question of whether the party, more than the state, is the main location of lawmaking power in Vietnam. The discussion next evaluates progress towards separating the function and roles of party and state in Vietnam. It concludes that, where party policy is in sympathy with imported commercial norms, borrowed law is likely to move rapidly into the state system. But polycentric party power structures undermine legal certainty, transparency and movement towards a procedural 'rule of law' that could preserve imported commercial rights.

---

1 Otto Kahn-Freund (1978), 'On the Uses and Misuses of Comparative Law' in Otto Kahn-Freund (ed.), *Selected Writings* Stevens, London, 298–303.

Party and State Institutional Overview

Before considering how 'party leadership' affects legal borrowing, which is the central theme in this chapter, it is necessary to set the stage by briefly reviewing the structural machinery of the party and state.

Vietnam has a unitary state system comprising five arms: National Assembly (NA), President, Government (executive), People's Courts and People's Procuracy. The Communist Party of Vietnam (CPV) (*Dang Cong San Vietnam*) both overarches and infiltrates state institutions in the Vietnamese one-party state. Although the state is not autonomous from the party, as we shall see, the party is not monolithic and is itself influenced by state organs. This section briefly introduces the main party and state organs.

Any discussion about the state makes little sense without first discussing the role of the CPV, which is the 'force leading the state and society'.[2] The party is led by the Politburo, which functions like an executive committee deciding important policy and legal issues on a day-to-day basis. The Central Committee formulates long-term socio-economic plans during its two or three plenary meetings each year. In addition, the party has an extensive organisational network mirroring the four state levels: central, provincial/city, district and ward/village. As this chapter reveals, behind the facade of unanimity, polycentric power structures generate considerable dissent that must be contained within party organs.

Mass organisations have historically been the vehicles used by the party to mobilise public support for socioeconomic campaigns. The Fatherland Front (*Mat Tran To Quoc*), which acts as an umbrella for other mass organisations, was formed in 1955 to replace the Vietnam National United Front (*Mat Dan Toc Thong Nhat*).[3] Mass organisations are difficult to categorise according to conventional understandings of state power, since they are neither part of civil society, nor entirely under state control. They are described in the 1992 Constitution as 'the political base of the people's administration' and they 'encourage the people to exercise their rights as masters'.[4] Although some commentators believe mass organisations have traditionally existed as 'instruments of top-down control, despite playing lip service to being representative of group interests',[5] case studies presented later in this chapter suggest some mass organisations are changing their traditional Leninist functions and playing a more state corporatist role.

State power is divided in Vietnam according to the imported Soviet 'concentration-of-power' (*tap trung quyen luc*) doctrine that vests ultimate state power in the

2 Constitution 1992, article 4.

3 See *VNA*, 1995 'Do Muoi Addresses Meeting', *VNA*, trans. FBIS East Asia Daily Reports, 95-226, 60.

4 Constitution 1992, article 9. Also see Law No. 14 QH10 on Vietnam Fatherland Front 1999, articles 1–2.

5 Tran Thi Thu Trang (2004), 'Local Politics and Democracy in a Muong Ethnic Community', in Benedict J. Tria Kerkvliet and David Marr (eds), Beyond Hanoi: Local Government in Vietnam, Institute of Southeast Asian Studies, Singapore, 137–60.

National Assembly (*Quoc Hoi*), Vietnam's supreme legislature.[6] Its importance as a legislative body has undoubtedly increased over the last decade, although real power still resides with the government. The National Assembly shares certain powers with the president (*Chu Tich Nuoc*), who acts as the ceremonial head of state and exercises limited legislative and political powers.

The government (*Chinh Phu*) is constitutionally divided among central and local executive bodies—ministries at the centre; provincial/city, district and village people's committees at the local level. Central authorities devolve (*phan bo*) power through branch (*nganh*) and vertical (*doc*) power sharing arrangements.[7] Branches function as specialised departments attached to people's committees (*uy ban nhan dan*) at provincial/city and district/village levels. Some central agencies, such as the police and taxation department, bypass local governments and vertically control their own branch offices at the local level.

Courts are organised to reflect the three main levels of the unitary state. The Supreme People's Court (*Toa An Nhan Dan Toi Cao*) is responsible for judicial work (*cong tac xet xu*), hearing appeals and supervising and reviewing decisions made by provincial courts. It is led by a president and several vice presidents and consists of the Council of Judges (the highest adjudication body) and three Appeals Courts (*Toa Thuc Tham*). Judges are organised into chambers of courts that specialise in criminal, civil, economic, military and administrative law. At the second hierarchical level, provincial/city courts hear first instance and appellate cases. Over 600 district-level courts comprise the lowest level in the court system, hearing first instance cases in rural *huyen* districts or urban districts (*quan*).

The People's Procuracy (*vien kiem sat nhan dan*), an institution devised in the Soviet Union to implement democratic centralism, was imported in Vietnam in 1960. As the fifth arm of the state, the Supreme Procuracy vertically controls provincial/city and district/village level branches.[8] Blurring policing and juridical functions, procurators investigate and prosecute criminal violations in the courts while supervising the legality and enforcement of court decisions.

Comparing Power-distribution Patterns

A structural comparison between Western liberal and Vietnamese state institutions tells us little about differences in the formulation and implementation of law. Everywhere modern states have similar institutional configurations such as legislatures, executives and courts. What makes state institutions distinctive are the mentalities (or epistemologies) and habits residing inside and outside formal

6 'Concentration of power' (*tap trung quyen luc*) is more generally termed 'concentration of democracy' (*tap trung dan chu*) in contemporary legal literature. See Vietnamese Constitution 1992, articles 112, 118, 124.

7 Vietnamese Constitution 1992, articles 112, 118, 124.

8 See Vietnamese Constitution 1992, articles 137–140; Law on the Organization of the People's Procuracy 2002.

structures (see Chapter 1). Institutional epistemologies guide the distribution of state power.[9] They order organisational assumptions about the rationality, efficiency and merit of foreign laws.

Chapter 1 showed that discourse analysis offers a promising framework for evaluating epistemological assumptions. It has the potential to assist our understanding of legal borrowing in three respects. First, it provides a way of assessing whether communication conveys meaning. Second, it locates legal meanings in 'interpretive communities' that share common epistemological assumptions about the meaning and function of law. Three, it shows that legal meanings are never closed because they change to reflect the strategies of social actors. These interpretive tools are used in this, and subsequent, chapters to open the discussion to the different ways that foreign and local discourses shape legal transplants.

Much foreign writing assumes that imported commercial laws are most likely to bring order to business transactions in Vietnam if they are implemented by constitutionally determined relationships, such as popularly elected legislators, robust judiciaries, the 'separation of powers' and effective legal constraints to political power.[10] In short, effective legal transplantation requires democratic institutions and the 'rule of law'.

On most measures, constitutional configurations in Vietnam differ from the democratic liberal template.[11] As we shall see in subsequent chapters, citizens have little say over who stands for elections in the National Assembly, delegates rarely share sympathies with their constituents and only peripherally influence the way the country is run. Judicial enforcement of statutory rights is unpredictable and frequently compromised by extra-legal political interventions. Above all else, the CPV has only conditionally accepted constitutional constraints to its political power.

This critique implies that conditions in Vietnam do not support a democratic liberal 'rule of law'. It does not explain, however, whether borrowed Western commercial law requires a democratic liberal 'rule of law' to function. The wide range of constitutional configurations in Western and Asian countries implies that capitalism can function under many different versions of the 'rule of law'. Institutions and processes that are unrecognisable as democratic liberal structures may nonetheless support imported commercial legal rights. It is important not to

9 Gianfranco Poggi (1978), *The Development of the Modern State: A Sociological Introduction*, Stanford University Press, Stanford, 1; also see James March and Johan Olsen (1989), *Rediscovering Institutions: The Organizational Basis of Politics*, Macmillan, New York, 17–22.

10 See Carol Rose (1998), 'The "New" Law and Development Movement in the Post-Cold War Era: A Vietnam Case Study', 32 *Law and Society Review* (1), 93–140; Brian Quinn (2002), 'Legal Reform and its Context in Vietnam', 15 *Columbia Journal of Asian Law* (2), 219, 235–50.

11 See generally Robert M. Cover (1982), 'The Origins of Judicial Activism in the Protection of Minorities', 9 *Yale Law Journal*, 1287. Some argue that rules are not as important as general principles in mature constitutional environments. See Daryl J. Levinson (1999), 'Rights Essentialism and Remedial Equilibration', 99 *Columbia Law Review*, 857.

economic development development requires linear progress towards a paradigmatic democratic liberal state.[12]

This chapter explores whether 'party leadership' (*su lanh cua dang*) in Vietnam can accommodate a 'rule of law' that allows imported commercial laws to protect and maintain capitalist property rights. In a rapidly changing society like Vietnam's, we need to understand the transformative capacity for party and state institutions to regulate a rights-based commercial legal system. Discourse analysis assists our investigation by illuminating the different mentalities and approaches to institutional change.

Separating Party and State

In Kahn-Freund's estimation, political domination of state institutions in communist countries presents a formidable barrier to Western legal transplants (see Chapter 1). He thought that party 'leadership' over state institutions undermined the neutrality required for a 'rule of law' society. If political processes allowed one group to dominate, then the meaning of legal rules would invariably reinforce that group's interests.

This section examines the ways party leadership over the state (party paramountcy) in Vietnam influences transplanted commercial law. This investigation commences by contrasting the separation of party and state in Western countries with reforms in Vietnam designed to clarify party and state roles.

Democratic Liberalism and the Separation of Party and State

According to democratic liberal theory, the separation of party and state is a central pillar of the rule of law.[13] Depoliticised, neutral states are considered necessary to regulate different values and ways of life impartially. Naturally, democratic liberal assumptions about the separation of party and state are not always observed in societies that formally claim to uphold them. From the American Realist Movement in the 1930s onwards, the possibility—even desirability—of politically neutral states was subjected to considerable scepticism.[14] Critics showed that bureaucrats and judges, like everyone else, are socialised by prevailing political and moral views.

---

12 See Michael William Dowdle (2000), 'Preserving Indigenous Paradigms in an Age of Globalization: Pragmatic Strategies for the Development of Clinical Legal Aid in China', 24 *Fordham International Legal Journal*, 56.

13 See Geoffrey de Q. Walker (1988), *The Rule of Law: Foundation of Constitutional Democracy*, Melbourne University Press, Melbourne, 23–42; M.J.C. Vile (1967), *Constitutionalism and the Separation of Powers*, Clarendon Press, Oxford.

14 See R. Hale (1943), 'Bargaining, Duress and Economic Liberty', 43 *Columbia Law Review*, 603. Also see Elizabeth Mensch (1982), 'The History of Mainstream Legal Thought', in David Kairys (ed.), *The Politics of Law*, Pantheon Books, New York, 18, 26–36.

Most Western theorists agree, however, that a democratic liberal version of the 'rule of law' requires some laws (especially constitutions) to confine the way leaders exercise political power. Without a clear constitutional separation between party and state (constitutionalism), the roles of party leadership, political policy and law are blurred.

Party 'leadership' in Vietnam raises serious questions about the viability of commercial laws that have been borrowed from systems predicated upon the separation of party and state. Does party leadership displace or subvert the role of law in society? Can the party substitute political policy for legal meanings in borrowed law? Under what conditions will the party leave the formulation and implementation of law to constitutional institutions? Answers to these questions in Vietnam are bound up in administrative reforms aiming to clarify party and state functions.

The Evolving Meaning of Party 'Leadership' over the State

Public Administration Reforms (PAR) endorsed by the Seventh Party Congress in 1996 are the latest instalment in a cycle of reforms that for decades have sought clearer party and state relationships in Vietnam.[15] The Public Administration Reforms are attempting the Herculean task of retaining party 'leadership', while at the same time building a more accountable and transparent administrative system.[16]

Their overriding objective is taming the bureaucratic juggernaut with laws. Reforms have attempted to streamline administrative procedures, close licensing gateways and enhance accountability through citizen complaint procedures and administrative courts. In tandem with this Weberian agenda, PAR also reaffirms the importance of party leadership and democratic centralism.

What remains unclear from the official discourse is whether reforms are intended to limit party 'leadership' over the state with imported constitutional rules and organisational procedures. Vietnamese have described this approach as creating a 'neutral', 'universal', 'administrative' state, as opposed to a 'class' state.[17] Some foreign commentators have gone so far as to suggest that PAR will undermine the

---

15 See Doan Trong Truyen (1996), 'An Overview on Public Administration Reform in the Socialist Republic of Vietnam', in UNDP, *International Colloquium on Public Administration Reform*, UNDP, Hanoi, 92; UNDP (1995), 'Public Administration Reform Programme', UNDP Programme Support Document, VIE/92/002, UNDP, Hanoi, 9 June; Nguyen Khanh (1995), 'Administrative Reform in Action', 2 *Vietnam Law and Legal Forum* (3), 3–6.

16 See Government of Vietnam (1994), *National Programme on Public Administrative Reform*, 26 May 1994, 2–6; Doan Trong Truyen (1996), 'An Overview on Public Administrative Reform in the Socialist Republic of Vietnam', in UNDP (1995), *International Colloquium on Public Administration Reform*, UNDP, Hanoi, 84–93.

17 See Thaveeporn Vasavakul (1999), 'Rethinking the Philosophy of Central-Local Relations in Post-Central Planning Vietnam' in Mark Turner (ed.), *Central-Local Government Relations in the Asia-Pacific Region*, Macmillan, London, 176.

formal and informal authority of the party.[18] Others are more circumspect, suggesting instead that the party is using the PAR to regain central control over middle-level cadres that had been lost during previous experiments with decentralisation.[19]

For decades, two issues have dominated party and state relationships: does party 'leadership' substitute for law and to what extent does state law bind the party?

From the inception of the Democratic Republic of Vietnam (DRV), party control over state organs generated confusion. Nguyen Nhu Phat wrote:

> In the first years of the people's democratic system, the distinction between the leadership of the Party and the administration of the State was out of the question because the State could not be present everywhere in the country and secret Party cells had to play the role of the State.[20]

The introduction of Soviet laws and legal instructions during the 1960s reinvigorated attempts to formalise party and state functions.[21] Little, however, was done during the anti-American war (1961–75), provoking Party General Secretary Le Duan to lament in 1978 that the party was supposed to 'lead the state, but not replace the state'.[22] Appeals by party leaders for cadres 'not [to] step on the toes of state organs by interfering in their work' periodically reappeared in party writings.[23]

After decades 'building socialist law', party theorists in the 1970s were still debating whether 'the party-line and policies are enough and that building the laws will only set self-imposed limits that impede production and work'.[24] In other words, a decision had not been taken to limit party power within constitutional and legal parameters. Party reformers had first to consider whether the party or the legislature should make laws. At the time this distinction was not considered theoretically important, since the party-line, state laws and planning directives

18 See Adam McCarty (2002), 'The Policy-Making Process in Vietnam', unpublished paper, ADB Public Administration Reform Study, Mekong Economics Group, June, 60.

19 See Thaveeporn Vasavakul (2002), 'Rebuilding Authority Relations: Public Administration Reform in the Era of *Doi Moi*', unpublished paper, Asian Development Bank, Hanoi, 26–28, 54–55.

20 Nguyen Nhu Phat (1997) 'The Role of Law in Vietnam during the Formation of the Market-Driven Mechanism in Vietnam', in John Gillespie (ed.), *Commercial Legal Development in Vietnam: Vietnamese and Foreign Commentaries*, Butterworths Asia, Singapore, 398.

21 Vietnam Workers Party (1960), '1960 Statute of the Vietnam Workers Party', *Nhan Dan*, 15 September 1960, trans. Vietnam Documents and Research Notes No. 103, United States Mission in Vietnam, Saigon.

22 See Le Duan (1978), *Phat Huy Quyen Lam Chu Tap The Xay Dung Nha Nuoc Vung Manh* (Develop the Rights of Collective Mastery Build a Strong State), Nha Xuat Ban Su That, Hanoi, 91.

23 Le Duan (1981), *Ve Lam Chu Tap The Xa Hoi Chu Nghia* (Report on Socialist Collective Mastery), Nha Xuat Ban Su That (Truth Publishing House), Hanoi, 152–53.

24 Dam Van Hieu (1976), 'Some Ideas about Building a Unified Legal System in the SRV', *Luat Hoc* (4), 35, trans. JPRS, 69122, 19 May 1997, 20–21.

were interchangeable in socialist legal ideology (see Chapter 3). It also had little practical relevance—so few laws were passed by the National Assembly that one commentator opined that 'in such a situation even a semblance of legality became superfluous or just a formality'.[25] Finally, the question whether party committees or state administrators should run the country rarely arose in a regulatory system where party leadership was 'direct, unified and detailed'.[26]

Tentative reforms were evident in the Soviet-inspired constitution enacted in 1980, which for the first time required the party to operate 'within the framework of the Constitution'.[27] More profound questions were raised during the Fifth and Sixth Party Congresses (held in 1982 and 1986 respectively) such as whether party edicts should continue to dominate state power distribution. Reformers such as Truong Chinh argued for a separation of the party from the day-to-day running of the government. Administrative reforms were intended to 'overcome resolutely and definitely the longstanding confusion of functions between party and state organs'.[28] Party leaders pondered whether the party should obey laws and abandon rule through edict and virtue, whether party organs should transfer supremacy to the legislature, and finally whether the party should surrender control over government administration.

*Distancing the Party and State: post-*doi moi *discourse*

Reformers promoting *nha nuoc phap quyen* (law-based state) called for the party to formulate policy and for the state to legislate and implement law. Article 4 of the 1992 Constitution rather nebulously endorsed this ideal by requiring the party to operate 'within the framework of the Constitution and the law'. Yet, as we saw in Chapter 3, *nha nuoc phap quyen* ideals have not displaced support for party paramountcy.[29]

Tensions between political, moral and legal ways of conceptualising party power have recently resurfaced in discourse about the PAR program. Official pronouncements about PAR acknowledge that

25 Hoang The Lien (1994), 'On the Legal System of Vietnam', 1 *Vietnam Law and Legal Forum* (1), 33, 34.

26 See Gareth Porter (1993), *Vietnam: The Politics of Bureaucratic Socialism*, Cornell University Press, Ithaca, 84–85.

27 Constitution 1980, article 4.

28 Quoting Le Duc Tho at the Fifth Party Congress in 1982. Reproduced in Carlyle Thayer (1991), 'Renovation and Vietnamese Society: The Changing Role of Government and Administration', in Dean Forbes *et al.* (eds), *Doi Moi: Vietnam's Renovation Policies and Performance*, Political and Social Change Monograph No. 14, Australian National University, Canberra, 23.

29 See generally, Nguyen Van Tai (1996), 'On the State Ruled by Law and a Multipartisan Regime', *Vietnam Social Science* (1), 3, 7. Party paramountcy is affirmed in the Party Statute, which states, 'the Party rules and uses the State as a tool to manage society'. Party Statute 1996, articles 41–43.

> the state administrative apparatus in the new situation remains unclear and inconsistent; many theoretical and practical issues have not been clarified; many policies mapped out under the old mechanism of centralised and bureaucratic management with state subsidies have not been amended or replaced in time.[30]

However, they avoid discussing the historical links between party 'leadership' and the now discredited command economy. Official discourse instead focuses on improving the capacity of the state to manage the mixed-market economy, while leaving room for different views about party 'leadership'.

Some party leaders actively promote direct party involvement in running state organs.[31] They oppose legal constraints designed to clarify party 'leadership' over the state, believing this will 'weaken both the Party's leading role and the State's managerial role and the people's right to mastery'.[32] Do Muoi authoritatively argued that 'life is richer and more complicated than stipulations … it is not always possible to establish clear demarcation lines between the areas within the competence of the Party and those within the competence of the administration'.[33] Party leaders insist that 'the CPV is the political force leading the whole system … and reforms of the political system should absolutely not touch the decisive point that the CPV has the sole leading role'.[34] According to this narrative, party leadership or paramountcy constitutes an immutable political ideal.

Behind the high rhetoric of party paramountcy, party leadership was increasingly contested during the 1990s as the government began to acquire significant resources through its control over the burgeoning economy. Never far below the surface in party discourse is the strategic concern that party organisations will lose relevance and dominance if the party disengages from the state.

Others within the party believe that effective state administration is only possible if party and state responsibilities are constitutionally defined.[35] As previously mentioned, Vo Van Kiet in 1995 sent an internal letter to the Politburo complaining that party 'leadership' interfered with the flexible and decentralised state regulation needed in the mixed market.[36] Riedel and Turley summarised his concerns:

---

30 Decision No. 136/QD-TTg on the Overall Program on State Administrative Reform in the 2001–2010 Period, 2001, Chapter I, point 1.

31 Interview Tran Dai Hung, Vice-chairman, Central Party Committee of Internal Affairs, Hanoi, November 2002.

32 Do Muoi (1995), *Vietnam: New Challenges and New Opportunities*, The Gioi Publishers, Hanoi, 162.

33 Ibid.

34 See Hoc Vien Hanh Chinh Quoc Gia (The National Administrative School) (1991), *Ve Cai Cach Bo May Nha Nuo* (On the Reform of the State Apparatus), The Truth Publishing House, Hanoi, 11–19.

35 These views were gleaned from interviews with officials in the Office of Government, Hanoi, January 2000, November 2002, March 2003.

36 The letter was published in *Viet Luan*, No. 1053, 5 January 1996, 30–31, 58–60; trans. Vnnews website <www.vietnamnews.vnagency.com.vn/>.

> Party and state functions need to be separated more clearly. The party must cease passing its directives through party committee secretaries and instead pass them through the government chain of command, allowing government officials to take full responsibility for implementation.[37]

Party members calling for reform stop short of demanding an end to party leadership and the depoliticisation of state institutions. Instead, they favour formalised divisions of labour and jurisdictions between party and state organs. Some promote the imported organisational science (*khoa hoc to chuc*) principle that a reduction in the number of *trung gian* (intermediaries) between party and state improves the transmission of party policy to state functionaries. This approach is consistent with Western 'organisation and management' theories that promise efficient modern government through a legal-rational, politically neutral Weberian bureaucracy.[38]

Discourse of this kind maintains that the party's long-term interests are served by a clear delineation between political and state power, because differentiated states are more efficient resource allocators. It asserts that undifferentiated party and state structures transmit political uncertainties into state policies and laws. As a consequence, laws only have a limited autonomy from political policy and lose their potency as regulatory instruments. Attempts by reformers in 2001 to amend the Constitution to clearly 'separate state functions' (*hoc thuyet tam quyen phan lap*) from 'party functions' failed. Legal and economic arguments did not prevail against the political and moral defence of direct party 'leadership'.

Since much is learnt in Vietnam by observing what is done rather than said, it is useful next to consider how in practice party 'leadership' affects *nha nuoc phap quyen*.

Party 'Leadership' over State Institutions

Dang Phong and Melanie Beresford vividly portrayed the party from 1955 until *doi moi* reforms in the 1980s as simultaneously operating in parallel with and intertwining state organs.[39] Reforms in 1989 began unravelling these linkages by consolidating party supervision over the state into specialised committees (*uy ban*),

---

37 J. Riedel and S. Turley (1999), *The Politics and Economics of Transition to a Market Economy in Vietnam*, Technical Paper No. 152, Organisation for Economic Cooperation and Development, Paris, 37.

38 See Vinyu Vichit-Vadakan (1996), 'Reforming the Policy and Institutional Framework for a Market Orientated Economy', in *International Colloquium on Public Administration Reform*, UNDP, Hanoi, 124, 228–29.

39 See Dang Phong and Melanie Beresford (1998), *Authority Relations and Economic Decision-Making in Vietnam: An Historical Perspective*, NIAS Publications, Copenhagen, 92–94.

commissions (*ban*) and offices (*van phong*).[40] Economic policy formulation at the central level, for example, was consolidated into the Economic Commission (*Ban Kinh Te Trung Uong*) in the Central Party Committee.[41]

There are tentative signs that the PAR program has cautiously begun to untangle party and state roles. For example, the Central Party Organising Committee (*Ban To Chuc Trung Uong*), which is responsible for coordinating party and state organs, now only arranges certain state activities. Some commentators construe these reforms as the party refocusing supervision into selected areas and devolving more policymaking power to state organs.[42] Explanations for this transformation focus on the changing decision-making environment. It was thought infeasible for a small number of central party officials to discuss and decide every policy change in a mixed-market economy (if ever). Despite these reforms, most commentators agree that, when so inclined and sufficiently informed, party organs still actively 'lead' the state. The following discussion examines the mechanisms used to secure state compliance with party policy.

Both the constitution and theoretical writings avoid transparent distinctions between the roles and functions of the party and state in Vietnam.[43] Although the principle of party 'leadership' over the state is clearly articulated, the mechanisms used to realise this objective are rarely discussed. One method of assessing the extent and depth of party leadership is by examining power sharing between party and state. The party uses five principle mechanisms to lead the state: party lines and policies, the *nomenklatura*, 'party affairs sections' (*ban can su dang*), party moral leadership and mass organisations. But the starting point in this investigation is determining whether party officials are state personnel.

Who are State Employees?

Article 1 of the Ordinance on Public Employees 1998 (OPE) (as amended) describes state employees as 'Vietnamese citizens who are on the State payroll and get paid from the State budget'.[44] This expansive definition includes personnel working in the government (that is, ministries and people's committees), elected National Assembly delegates, judges, army, police and teachers. It does not mention party members directly, but describes 'people who are recruited, appointed or assigned regular tasks

---

40 Nguyen Huu Tho (1989), 'Renovation of Mechanism—Pressing Needs of the Renovation Process', *Tap Chi Cong San*, March, trans. FBIS, East Asia Daily Report, 086, 5 May 1989, 65.

41 See Mark Sidel (1997a), 'Generational and Institutional Transition in the Vietnamese Communist Party', 37 *Asian Survey*, (5), 483–84.

42 See, for example, Yeonsik Jeong (1997), 'The Rise of State Corporatism in Vietnam', 19 *Contemporary Southeast Asia* (2), 152, 160–65.

43 Both the Constitution 1992 and Party Statute 1996 describe separate organisational frameworks for the party and state. See Constitution 1992, articles 4, 6. Party Statute 1996, preamble.

44 Ordinance on Public Employees 1998 (as amended), article 1.

in political and sociopolitical organisations' as state employees. Since the party and mass organisations are the only political organisations permitted in Vietnam, it seems logical that party members paid from the state budget are state employees.

But there are many differences between party and state officials. Party officials are not accountable under the OPE as state officials. Although the state financially supports party organs, party personnel are not treated as state officials.

Party Lines and Policies

Major state decisions are made in conjunction with the Politburo.[45] Although the Law on Organisation of the Government makes no mention of party leadership, this omission has little practical relevance as the prime minister and some senior ministers are Politburo members. Below this level, the party 'leads' the state with resolutions and policy statements.

In contrast to political policy in democratic liberal countries, CPV policy has coercive force over party and state officials without being enacted into law. Socialist legality (*phap che xa hoi chu nghia*) invests party policy and resolutions with law-like characteristics (see Chapter 3). Article 1 of the Ordinance on Public Employees 1998, for example, requires state employees to obey state law and party resolutions. Article 4 places the work of state employees under the 'uniform leadership of the Communist Party of Vietnam', while article six requires state employees to 'strictly abide by the Party's lines and policies, and the State's policy and law…'. State employees, whether or not they are party members, face administrative and criminal sanctions for violating both party and state directives.[46]

Regulation by Party Directive

Party control over government decision-making is illustrated by the internal rules guiding the powers and functions of Market Management Authorities (*ban quan ly thi truong*).[47] Decree No. 10 on the Tasks and Powers of Market Management 1995 established market control authorities with powers to 'inspect and control' and 'manage' (*quan ly*) economic markets.[48] They are required to 'propagate party undertakings and lines as well as state policies and laws'.[49] The meaning of regulations

45 See Martin Painter (2002), 'Public Administration Reform', unpublished paper, Hong Kong, 9; Yeonsik Jeong (1997), 'The Rise of State Corporatism in Vietnam', 19 *Contemporary Southeast Asia* (2), 152, 160–70.

46 See Decree No. 97 ND-CP on the Disciplining and Material Responsibilities of Pubic Employees, 1998, article 3.

47 This case description is based on discussions with two employees of the Hanoi Market Control Board during April 1999 and September 2000.

48 Decree No. 10 1995 gave the Ministry of Trade central powers to direct market control authorities established at the city and provincial level.

49 See Decree No. 2 CP on the Development and Management of Marketplaces 2003, article 13.

and laws (*qui dinh phap luat*) is determined by internal sub-legal documents (that is, official letters and internal operational directives) based on 'policy regimes' (*che do chinh sach*) established by party committees. 'Policy regimes' contain definitions and standards that fine-tune the implementation of 'state power'.

Laws make it clear that the overriding purpose of market management is to 'organise the market ... to promote production development, expand goods circulation according to the law'.[50] Numerous sub-legal documents promote *thi truong lanh manh* (healthy markets) as a regulatory ideal, but provide few practical standards or principles to guide state officials. As a result, the precise meaning of healthy markets is never fixed and changes constantly to reflect nuances in party economic policy.

The rules governing inspection powers are similarly open-ended. Market control authorities are required to 'observe the law and the working statute on market management'.[51] General provisions concerning penalties for violating 'market management' rules are contained in the Ordinance on the Handling of Violations of Administrative Regulations 2002. Subordinate rules determine the type of identification and firearms carried, uniforms worn and documentation used by market control authorities. They do not convey practical guidelines determining the scope and nature of 'state power'.

To summarise, state officials derive policy guidance more from political, economic and legal discourse emanating from party sources than from norms and prescriptive rules codified in state legislation. Party communication is 'self-enacting' in the sense that it guides party members controlling the state apparatus without being formally enacted into state legislation. As discursive law, party communication has the capacity to change the meanings given to statutory norms regulating market behaviour in superior legislation such as the Competition Law 2004.

Party Leadership within State Institutions

Recruitment and promotion The *nomenklatura* (*to chuc can bo*) system, which was borrowed from the Soviet Union, ensures that party members occupy key lawmaking positions within state institutions.[52] It has no legislative basis.[53] Internal party rules

50 Decision No. 96 TTg Promulgating Regulations on the Responsibility and Relations of Coordination of Activities among State Management Agencies in the Management of the Market and the Fight Against Smuggling and Other Acts of Illicit Trade, 1995 (Prime Minister), article 7.

51 Decree No. 10 on the Organisation and Responsibilities of the Market Management Authorities, 23 January 1995, article 6.

52 See Melanie Beresford (1988), *Vietnam: Politics, Economics and Society*, Pinter Publishers, London, 105–8; Mark Sidel (1997b), 'Vietnam: The Ambiguities of State-Directed Legal Reform', in Poh-Ling Tan (ed.), *Asian Legal Systems: Law, Society and Pluralism in East Asia*, LBC, Sydney, 364.

53 The Party Statute entitles 'the party to recommend qualified cadres for state agencies ... for selection and employment'. Party Statute, article 41(2).

require party and state personnel departments to select appropriate candidates according to criteria established by central party organs. Before state institutions formally confirm appointments, *nomenklatura* lists are sent for approval to the Central Party Organising Committee (CPOC) (*Ban To Chuc Trung Uong*).

Informants describing recruitment and promotion procedures within the Ministry of Science and Technology maintain that the CPOC, in consultation with the party committee (*dang uy*) inside the ministry, selected senior personnel, including the minister.[54] The system was structured to enable party members to move easily in and out of senior state positions. Staff were promoted according to three criteria: political qualifications (*pham chat chinh tri*), moral qualifications (*pham chat dao duc*) and professional requirements (*yeu cau chuyen mon*).[55] These highly flexible standards stressed party loyalty, demonstrated by knowledge of party rules and policies, and active participation in party social activities, such as singing competitions.

The party is now stressing the importance of recruiting well-educated state officials, and some positions are reserved for those with prescribed professional qualifications.[56] In a transition they label 'statisation', Phong and Beresford argued that the *nomenklatura* system has declined in importance since *doi moi*.[57] The CPOC now shares some personnel functions with the Government Committee on Organisation and Personnel (GCOP). Reflecting the growing importance of meritorious recruitment, the GCOP was upgraded into a ministry in 2002.

Despite the trend towards meritorious recruitment, many party writers call for greater rather then less party control over state recruitment.[58] For example, informants in the Office of the National Assembly question Phong and Beresford's assertion that the National Assembly, rather than party organs, has the final say over the appointment of ministers. They maintain that National Assembly delegates are briefed about CPOC recommendations before voting to appoint state ministers. Others believe that the slogan '*hong hon chuyen*' (red is better than expert) still applies, especially for senior positions.

There are also few signs the *nomenklatura* system has weakened at the provincial level. A strong correlation exists between senior party membership and senior people's committee positions. For example, since 1975 most chairmen of the Ho Chi

---

54 Interviews four former officials from the Ministry of Science and Technology Hanoi, March 1999, April 1999.

55 Author Unknown (1996), 'Nhung Van De Ly Luan Co Ban Ve Nha Nuoc va Phap Luat' (Basic Theoretical Issues about State and Law), Nha Xuat Ban Chinh Tri Quoc Gia (National Political Publishing House), Hanoi, 147–48.

56 See Decision No. 136/QD-TTg on the Overall Program on State Administrative Reform in the 2001–2010 Period, 2001, Chapter III, point 3. Also see VNS (2003), 'Politburo Member Tells Party Official to Shape Up', *vietnamnews-online*, 24 January, <www.vietnamnews.vnagency.com.vn>.

57 See Phong and Beresford (1998), *supra*.

58 See Do Muoi (1995), *supra*, 177–78. Also see Mark Sidel (1997a), *supra*, 481, 485.

Minh City People's Committee have been Central Committee members.[59] This close nexus is replicated at the district level.[60] Sub-district (*phuong* and *xa*) officials are not considered public servants and are directly controlled by the next highest party organ.

The *ly lich* (dossier) system, comprising secret files that meticulously record details about all party members, also remains firmly in place. By selectively capturing information, this system gives senior party officials considerable control over junior officials' careers.

In short, PAR initiatives have introduced public service examinations and meritorious recruitment, but the *nomenklatura* system fills enough key state positions to ensure party leadership over the state. It does not, however, guarantee that the party elite is the state elite. Many party cadres work their entire lives inside one ministry, developing institutional attitudes and loyalties that are not easily explained if one assumes the party and state invariably share similar objectives and organisational logics.[61]

'Party affairs sections' (ban can su dang) Although the *nomenklatura* system places party members in state positions, 'the party exercises its rule through party organisations and not through individual members'.[62] 'Party affairs sections' (*ban can su dang*) operate at each hierarchical level within every state institution. They 'lead and motivate members in the organisation; to implement the party-line and policies'.[63] This system remains entrenched despite longstanding criticism that it confuses lines of authority and erodes the prestige of state managers.[64]

Central-level 'party affairs sections' generally comprise ministers, vice-ministers and senior department heads. They act as intermediaries between party and state, converting broad policy initiatives formulated by central committee commissions into sub-legal internal directives and *quan triet* (comprehensive) instructions.

---

59 See Martin Gainsborough (2004), 'Ho Chi Minh City's Post-1975 Elite: Continuity and Change in Background and Belief', in Benedict J. Tria Kerkvliet and David Marr (eds), *Beyond Hanoi: Local Government in Vietnam*, Institute of Southeast Asian Studies, Singapore, 259–72.

60 See Pham Quang Minh (2002), 'Caught between Tradition and Modernisation: Local Cadres in Hai Duong Province in the Renovation Period', in Benedict J. Tria Kerkvliet and David Marr (eds), *Beyond Hanoi: Local Government in Vietnam*, Institute of Southeast Asian Studies, Singapore, 90–102.

61 See Dang Phong and Melanie Beresford (1998), *supra*, 92–94.

62 See CPV (1996), 'Political Report Presented by the Seventh CPV Central Committee to the Eighth National Congress 28 June–1 July 1996', *Quan Doi Nhan Dan*, 30 June, 3, 6, trans. FBIS East Asia Daily Report 96-134, 98.

63 Party Statute, articles 42(3), 43(1).

64 See Le Quang Thuong (1996), 'Mot So Van De Ve Cong Tac Dan Van Trong Tinh Hinh Hien Nay' (Several Problems Concerning Cadre Work Under the Current Situation), *Tap Chi Cong San* (14), July, 18, 19.

They also report back to the Politburo and relevant Central Committee organs on government decisions and implementation policies.

For specifics, let us return to the Ministry of Trade case study. The 'party affairs section' in the ministry formulated the 'policy regimes' (*che do chinh sach*) that guided the implementation of 'state economic management' by city/provincial market control authorities. 'Party affairs sections' at city/provincial levels further refined 'policy regimes' to suit local conditions. In this way, the party mediated lawmaking discourse within state institutions.

Democratic centralism, as explained in Chapter 3, binds central party organs, 'party affairs sections' and party members.[65] Party members are enjoined to strictly obey central party resolutions and the 'monolithic thought and action' of the party and state.[66] 'Party affairs sections' are required to 'submit themselves to higher-echelon organisations'.[67] 'No party members should be allowed to distance themselves from the management of organisations'.[68] The ultimate objective is to ensure that party members remain loyal to party rather than state bodies. As previously noted, this objective is difficult to achieve where party cadres work for long periods within state institutions.

To conclude, 'party leadership' collapses the binary divisions between party and state contemplated by *nha nuoc phap quyen* reformers. Party paramountcy allows the party to lead the state through resolutions, internal policy directives and the *nomenklatura* system. The party leads from inside and outside the state.

The following discussion turns to the projection of party power through non-state agencies. It suggests that constitutional definitions of the state do not adequately account for the role party moral leadership and mass organisations play in implementing state power.

Party Moral Leadership

The party not only projects its power through state organs; it also leads by moral example. Chapter 3 argued that the party slavishly copied Soviet legal ideology and laws, but used 'revolutionary morality' to reconcile foreign borrowings with local conditions. By conflating neo-Confucian morals and Marxist-Leninism, the party manufactured a 'revolutionary morality' recognisable to a population that was unfamiliar with law-based rule. Morality rule emphasised (and continues to emphasise) ideological and moral homogeneity, strict organisational hierarchies (democratic centralism), advancement through party (*nomenkultura*) and personal contacts, government by example and intolerance towards non-elite opposition.

65 See Doan Khue (1998), 'Scrupulously Implementing the Party's Fundamental Organisational Principles in Military Party Organisations', *Tap Chi Quoc Phong Toan Dan*, January, 6–9, trans. FBIS East Asia Daily Report 98-061.

66 Ibid.

67 CPV Statute 1996, article 9.

68 See CPV (1996), 'Political Report of the Seventh CPV Central Committee', 97.

Although nominally configured as a Leninist organisation, the party functioned as a traditional-Leninist hybrid.[69]

Inculcating the Correct Viewpoint

The party could not rely on morals alone to induce change. It also needed cadres infused with the correct viewpoint (*quan diem dung dan*) and mass organisations to mobilise popular support. As 'superior men', party members were, and still are, expected to work at self-improvement. The Party Statute 1996 requires those in senior state positions to 'constantly study and steel oneself to improve one's knowledge, working ability, political quality and revolutionary ethics; adopt a wholesome lifestyle; struggle against individualism, opportunism, departmentalism, bureaucracy, corruption, wasteful spending and other negative phenomena'.[70]

Those aspiring to manage state institutions were (and still are) required to attend political education that instils the correct moral outlook.[71] Ethical standards are maintained by first vetting the political background of party applicants and three generations of their extended families, and second, by inculcating political theory.

Central Committee Resolution No. 210 on Teaching Political Theory and Ideology to Cadres and Party Members 1970 established party theoretical training schools at district, provincial, and central levels. This system continues today. As public employees climb the state hierarchy they must attend political training courses at middle-level party schools and eventually complete advanced degree courses at the Ho Chi Minh National Political Academy (*Hoc Vien Chinh Tri Quoc Gia Ho Chi Minh*).[72] In addition to teaching Marxist-Leninist theory and Ho Chi Minh thought, training courses familiarise cadres with the party viewpoint on state policies and laws. The overriding objective is to inculcate standardised moral and ideological principles that promote uniform interpretations.

Cadres equipped with a political education, possess the cognitive tools required to formulate, decode and implement complex and often convoluted party directives and policies. Shared epistemological outlooks and cognitive skills ensure that high-level cadres debate policies in a mutually comprehensible political and moral language. For example, members of legislative drafting committees, discussed in the next chapter, say that party representatives communicate in a symbolic language that contains signals, assumptions and messages that only the initiated can comprehend. Later chapters develop this notion that senior party and state officials belong to an

69 See Oskar Weggel (1986), 'The Vietnamese Communist Party and its Status under Law', in D. Loeber (ed.), *Ruling Communist Parties and their Status under Law*, Martinus Nijhoff, The Hague, 418–19.

70 Communist Party of Vietnam Statute 1996, article 2(2).

71 Vu Oanh (1994), 'Great National Unity in the New Situation and Tasks', *Nhan Dan*, 4 February, 3, trans. FBIS East Asia Daily Report 94-043, 69-72.

72 See Nguyen Phu Trong (1999), 'Effect a New Change in the Study of Political Theory of Cadres and Party Members', *Tap Chi Cong San*, November, 7–8, trans. FBIS East Asia Daily Report 1999-0707.

'interpretive community' based on common political and moral 'modes' of thought. The core assumptions shaping this 'interpretive community' share few points of reference with the epistemologies underlying imported rights-based legal discourses, especially the 'rule of law'.

Virtue-rule

Virtue-rule, backed by administrative directives, worked well enough in the command economy. But most Vietnamese lawmakers now realise that virtue-rule undermines legal formalism and the transactional certainty required to secure investments in industrialising economies. Nevertheless, some commentators believe 'vestiges of the Confucian conception of government by virtue (*duc tri*) make our cadres and people not fully conscious of socialist legality and lack a full understanding of the necessity to apply the law and this prevents the building of a socialist jurisdiction'.[73]

The PAR program is increasingly compelling state employees to behave like Weberian bureaucrats and base their decisions on formally enacted laws rather than moral pronouncements and political expedience. Important PAR initiatives such as regulatory streamlining presuppose an organisational logic in which state power is projected through constitutional institutions (legislature, executive and courts). The conflicting loyalties and values generated by the interplay between revolutionary morality, local political imperatives and imported Western organisational designs profoundly influence the meaning given to rights-based laws (see Chapter 6).[74]

PAR reforms aiming to separate party and state require immensely complex systemic changes to reconfigure constitutional and extra-constitutional party and state power-sharing arrangements. The transfer of power required to legally circumscribe party 'leadership' over the state would unravel constitutional and personalistic institutions built up over several generations. Each stage of reform is likely to excite political conflict over the direction and pace of change.

Party and Mass Organisations

The party uses political slogans to communicate its message to the 'masses'. Mass-mobilisation campaigns copied from China have been used since the early 1950s to rectify social wrongs. Early moral campaigns demanded 'selfless' commitment to resisting foreign reoccupation, purged residual French cultural influences (1946–52), reformed land ownership (1953–56) and attacked 'feudalistic property ethics and Confucian morals'.[75] Although mass-mobilisation campaigns peaked in the 1960s,

73 Vu Hoa (1994), 'The Ideological Heritage of Confucianism is Unimportant', *Vietnamese Studies* (1), 71, 74.

74 See John Gillespie (2002), 'The Political-Legal Culture of Anti-Corruption Reforms in Vietnam', in Timothy Lindsey and Howard Dick (eds), *Corruption in Asia: Rethinking the Governance Paradigm*, Federation Press, Sydney, 183–95.

75 Oskar Weggel (1986), *supra*, 415.

the party continued to use them during the 1970s and 1980s to 'revolutionise the whole of life' by remodelling society along state lines.[76]

Maoist 'mass line' theory infiltrated socialist democratic (*dan chu xa hoi chu nghia*) and collective mastery (*lam chu tap the*) ideology (see Chapter 3). Mass organisations were enlisted as two-way communication channels—from the lowest to the highest—to give citizens a forum to communicate with the government. The party took ideals distilled from the subtle processes of everyday life and transformed them into moral messages, which were then represented to the masses as if they were their own ideas. Neo-Confucian notions such as deference to moral authority invested social steering of this kind with cultural legitimacy.

Nguyen Khac Vien in 1981 wrote an open letter to the National Assembly exposing collective mastery through mass organisations as a fraud. Rather than furthering democratic participation, he argued, mass organisations maintained party control over social organisations in order to suppress potential political rivals.[77] The party only listened to its own members and was not interested in new and challenging views. As discussed more fully in Chapter 7, this depiction holds true today. For example, the party and state support Fatherland Front Buddhist mass organisations, but vigorously suppress the Unified Buddhist Church (*Giao Hoi Phat Giao Thong Nhat*) for refusing to promote the party line.[78] Protestant evangelical groups have also been banned from proselytising among ethnic minorities in highland provinces. In contrast with its stringent regulations of religious movements, the party has partially relaxed controls over the formation of entrepreneurial and other non-political 'associations' (*hiep hoi*), giving them a limited political space to communicate with lawmakers.

Mass organisations proved highly effective in mobilising popular support for party policies during times of crisis.[79] Peacetime apathy and the abolition of state subsidies have unquestionably reduced their contemporary social leverage. A rapidly aging membership signals their decline.

Numerous civic organisations (non-state, volunteer and non-profit) established as state research institutes, non-profit companies and professional associations have filled the void left by declining membership in Fatherland Front (*Mat Tran To Quoc Viet Nam*) organisations.[80] Attempts by the party's Commission for Mass

---

76 See Le Phuong (1994), 'Civil Society: From Annulment to Restoration', unpublished paper, 'Vietnam Update Conference: *Doi Moi*, The State and Civil Society', 10–11 November, 5.

77 The letter appeared in a French translation in George Boudarel *et al.* (eds) (1983), *Bureaucratie au Vietnam*, l'Harmattan, Paris, 115–19.

78 See Human Rights Watch (2002), 'World Report, Vietnam', Human Rights Watch, Washington, DC, <www.hre.org/wr2k2/asia11.html>.

79 See William S. Turley (1993), 'Party, State, and People: Political Structure and Economic Prospects', in William S. Turley and Mark Seldon (eds), *Reinventing Vietnamese Socialism: Doi Moi in Comparative Perspective*, Westview Press, Boulder, 260–62.

80 See Joerg Wischermann and Nguyen Quang Vinh (2003), 'The Relationship between Civic and Governmental Organisations in Vietnam: Selected Findings', in Ben J. Tria

Mobilisation to resurrect mass organisations as revolutionary apparatus have been unsuccessful.[81] There are tentative signs, however, that mass organisations are readjusting their social role.

State Corporatism

Research in Vietnam suggests that some mass organisations and quasi-state bodies are transforming from agents of mass mobilisation into members of state-corporatist alliances. If true, this shift foreshadows closer cooperation between the party, state and privileged non-state entities (see Chapter 7). It could invest local interest groups with strong voices to adjust imported law to suit their particular interests.

State corporatism is understood to mean a pattern of organising state-society interaction that grants representational monopolies to certain groups. It aims to generate social harmony by incorporating privileged groups into the decision-making structure of the state. Especially in continental Europe, the collaboration of state and non-state interests centralises and monopolises public policy and statutory formulation. Tripartite configurations of state, employer and labour bodies shape much commercial lawmaking.[82] If it functions effectively, state corporatism might give the Vietnamese party and state the means to implement policy without resorting to formal legal regulation.

State corporatism is not just a Western phenomenon; it has been identified in countries with widely varying political and economic structures, including China, Indonesia and Vietnam.[83] But the notion of a state-society compact requires rethinking when applied to socialist East Asia, where civil society organisations struggle to operate beyond the party and state orbit. Philippe Schmitter modified state corporatism to reflect socialist realities by investing social organisations with a limited autonomy to challenge state policy, but not party and state power.[84]

As mass organisations lose their potency there are reasons for believing that party leaders find state corporatism an attractive adjunct or alternative system of

---

Kerkvliet, Russell H.H. Heng and David W.H. Koh (eds), *Getting Organised in Vietnam: Moving in and Around the Socialist State*, Institute of Southeast Asian Studies, Singapore, 199–213.

81 See, for example, Vu Oanh (1994), 'Great National Unity in the New Situation', *Nhan Dan*, 1 February, 3, trans. FBIS East Asia Daily Report 94-043, 4 March 1994, 69–72.

82 See Goran Therborn (1992), 'Lessons from "Corporatist" Theorizations', in J. Pekkarinen *et al.* (eds), *Social Corporatism*, Clarendon Press, Oxford, 33–40.

83 See, for example, Yeonsik Jeong (1997), 'The Rise of State Corporatism in Vietnam', 19 *Contemporary Southeast Asia* (2), 152, 159–64; Jonathan Stromseth (1998), 'Reform and Response in Vietnam: State-Society Relations and the Changing Political Economy', unpublished PhD thesis, Columbia University, New York.

84 His definition includes quasi-state organisations that are 'recognised or licensed (if not created) by the state'. Philippe C. Schimtter (1974), 'Still the Century of Corporatism?', in Fredrick B. Pike and Thomas Stich (eds), *The New Corporatism: Social and Political Structures in the Iberian World*, University of Notre Dame Press, Notre Dame, 93–94.

social control. Party Resolution No. 10 on Renovating Mass-Proselytising Work and Truly Developing the People's Right to Mastery 1990 aimed to co-opt new forms of social organisation excited by the mixed-market economy. Pham Chi Lan, the former vice-president of the Vietnam Chamber of Commerce and Industry (VCCI), put this new approach in context. She described the relationship between the state and private entrepreneurial associations as a 'partnership' in which the state assists private firms to follow party and state socioeconomic policy.[85] In return for market information, training and access to state tendering systems, VCCI members are expected to comply with the extra-legal nuances of state socioeconomic policy (see Chapter 7).

It is plausible, given the structural similarities between Leninist mass organisations and state corporatist 'partnerships', that mass organisations may evolve into hybrid entities. They could give the party leverage over social groups and in return grant members access to state privileges and information. Both structures are designed to persuade specific social groups to follow state policies. Movement in this direction depends on whether new entrepreneurial elites have something to gain from party and state policies.

At first glance, the Vietnam General Confederation of Labour (VGCL) (*Tong Lien Doan Lao Dong Viet Nam*) seems to exhibit some state-corporatist characteristics.[86] Long privileged in Vietnamese political life as the protector of the 'working class and working people', in the command economy the VGCL acted as a mass organisation mobilising workers for party causes. It is still required to 'encourage workers to help build the State and Party'.[87]

The social dynamics that formed the VGCL are changing in the mixed-market economy. Behind the Marxist–Leninist rhetoric that privileges the working class, the CPV is in practice pursuing policies such as equitisation (privatisation) (*co phan hoa*) and socialisation (*xa hoi hoa*) (user-pay systems for health and education) that adversely affect worker interests.[88] In order to remain relevant to its members in the new economic environment, the VGCL is metamorphising into a labour advocate. It must balance worker interests with party policy that requires labour to moderate adversarial contests that threaten economic development.

The VGCL reconciles these conflicting objectives by organising strikes in foreign-owned enterprises, but rarely in state-owned enterprises.[89] Worker advocacy evaporates, however, where demands conflict with state-sponsored development.

85 Interview Pham Chi Lan, Vice-president VCCI, Hanoi, March 2003.

86 See Eva Hansson (2003), 'Authoritarian Governance and Labour: The VGCL and the Party-State in Economic Renovation', in Ben J. Tria Kerkvliet, Russell H.K. Heng and David W.H. Koh (eds) (2003), *Getting Organized in Vietnam: Moving in and Around the Socialist State*, Institute of Southeast Asian Studies, Singapore, 171–76.

87 See Editorial (1998), 'National Labor Congress Held in Hanoi', 5 *Vietnam Law and Legal Forum* (51), 5, 6.

88 See Decree No. 64 on the Equitisation of State Owned Enterprises 2002.

89 See, for example, Agence-France Presse (1995), 'Workers Strike at South Korean Shoe Factory', in FBIS East Asia Daily Report 95-244, 20 December, 77.

The VGCL, for instance, implemented the party directive commanding 'more active involvement in encouraging workers to participate in equitisation', even though the sale of SOEs invariably lowers worker benefits and increases unemployment.[90]

The party is also experimenting with using mass organisations to perform extra-legal regulatory functions. In Vu Oanh's opinion, 'the law alone cannot resolve all issues in daily life … mass organisations are needed to settle these social issues'.[91] Consider the role of the Vietnam Standards and Consumer Protection Association (Vinastas), a mass organisation affiliated with the Fatherland Front.[92] The Ministry of Science, Technology and Environment 'manages' Vinastas and associated consumer associations and clubs.[93] Vinastas encourages industry groups to raise production standards and provides one of the few authorised outlets for consumer concerns about product quality and safety. In another guise, it is responsible for guiding consumer consciousness into non-political and non-litigious areas of dissent.

Party leaders fear consumer groups will mobilise public opposition to SOEs that produce poor quality goods and services. Vinastas aims to channel spontaneous consumer resistance expressed through buyer boycotts and public demonstrations into media campaigns organised by consumer magazines such as *Nguoi Tieu Dung* (Consumer) and *Saigon Tiep Thi* (Saigon Marketing) and/or informal dispute resolution meetings with suppliers. It also uses the media to publicly rebuke recidivists. In this way, Vinastas provides a state-mediated replacement for civil action expressed in demonstrations and litigation.

Despite growing pluralism within Vietnamese civic organisations, mass organisations do not fit any description of civil society that stresses independence from the state and opposition to state ideology. Whether the VGCL or Vinastas are too closely bound to the party to qualify as independent social organisations under Schmitter's corporatist model is beyond the purposes of this discussion. What matters is that the party and state are attempting to reinvent mass organisations and quasi-state organisations as extra-legal mechanisms to inculcate official policies and lines. Since social steering of this kind functions in tandem with formal legal rules, it has the capacity to undermine the relevance and meaning of imported laws.

---

90 Le Kha Phieu (1998), 'Le Kha Phieu Addressees Labour Congress', *Quan Doi Nhan Dan*, 6 November, 1, 2, trans. FBIS East Asia Daily Report 98-331.

91 Vu Oanh (1994), *supra*, 3.

92 Interviews Hoang Manh Tuan, President, Vinastas, Hanoi, March 1992, November 1996; Do Gia Phan, Permanent Member, Vinastas, Hanoi, September 1994, June 1995, November 1996.

93 See Ordinance No. 13 PL-UBTVQH10 on the Protection of Consumer Interests 1999; Decree No. 69 CP Detailing the Implementation of the Ordinance on the Protection of Consumer Interests 2002.

Conceptualising the Party and State

Some commentators believe that party organs have penetrated state institutions to such an extent that the compound term 'party-state' accurately describes state power distribution.[94] Although a fused 'party-state' is conceptually convenient, it blurs power-sharing arrangements between party and state organs and conceals attempts by some party leaders to clarify party and state functions. It also infers that party and state interests coincide, obscuring the possibility that they have different substantive agendas and organisational logics.

We have seen that the party in some circumstances functions as a type of political bureaucracy that formulates policy for the state. Like democratic liberal political parties, in this manifestation the party is functionally separate from, and frequently competes with, state institutions. In revolutionary mode, the party functions like a mass organisation infiltrating, managing and controlling state institutions through resolutions, 'party affairs sections', the *nomenklatura* system and morality rule. In this guise, the party 'uses the state as a tool to manage society'.[95] Rather than fused entities, the party and state are better seen as separate but often intertwined and co-dependent bodies. Either way there are few analogues in Western constitutionally ordered societies for this type of party and state power-sharing.

Official images of party 'leadership' depict an orderly process in which party and state organs obediently follow top-down power structures. Commentators observing party and state machinations believe, on the contrary, that parallel systems of party paramountcy and state rule generate confusion and fragmentation. Many accounts have 'conservative' and 'reform-minded' groups locked in battle. But Gainsborough argues that these depictions over-emphasise idealised positions and conflicts more typically revolve around short-term political and economic imperatives.[96] Others believe that regional groupings are the main source of conflict.[97]

In rejecting monolithic explanations for party and state power sharing, Carlyle Thayer located party-power in clusters of interests that have developed in response to social and economic change.[98] According to this view, sectoral interests have coalesced around the party's ideological apparatus, the People's Army and state

94 See, for example, Gareth Porter (1993), *supra*; David Koh (2001), 'The Politics of a Divided Party and Parkinson's State in Vietnam', 23 *Contemporary Southeast Asia* (3), 533.

95 Nguyen Nham (1997), 'Why is the Management of the State by Law Still Weak?', *Quan Doi Nhan Dan* (Peoples Army), 13 June, 3, trans. FBIS East Asia Daily Report 97-203.

96 See Martin Gainsborough (2002), 'Beneath the Veneer of Reform: The Politics of Economic Liberalisation in Vietnam', 35 *Communist and Post-Communist Studies*, 353, 356–57.

97 See David Koh (2001), *supra*, 538.

98 See Carlyle Thayer (1995), 'Mono-Organizational Socialism and the State', in Benedict Tria Kerkvliet and Doug J. Porter (eds), *Vietnam's Rural Transformation*, Westview Press, Boulder, 60.

organs.[99] Personnel exchanges and *nomenklatura* appointments brokered by the Central Party Organising Committee reinforce many sectoral coalitions. Others describe formal and informal sectoral blocs (*khoi*) that link party and state at every level of government.[100] Sectoral blocs compete to place their members in positions of authority in the party and state. In order to manage conflict and present a united front, the party shrouds the entire politico-economic decision-making process in secrecy.[101]

Attempts by PAR reformers to constitutionalise party and state relationships are partly determined by how much decision-making power the central party is prepared to devolve to state agents. This in turn depends on whether the 'rules of the game' guiding constitutional processes are more effective (from the party's perspective) in resolving social problems than existing processes. But the party's room to manoeuvre is undoubtedly limited by what is politically possible, and by the epistemological assumptions guiding party decision-making.

As we saw in Chapter 3, party moral and political discourse is bound up in its own self-referential criteria. Party ideological units and the political education system inculcate this discourse. Together, they have created an 'interpretive community' that shares common epistemological assumptions about the nature of political and legal problems and the most effective solutions. Once party 'leadership' is conceived as a moral good or an essential source of political power, it is difficult for party leaders to accommodate or learn from imported PAR notions that argue for the separation of party and state. For example, much party discourse uses *a priori* notions of good and bad that portray party leadership as an immutable moral good. By implication, legal ideas aiming to separate party and state are morally bad. The ideal, much less the institutional reality of constitutionalism, is unlikely to take hold until legal modes of thinking that privilege the 'rule of law' over political policy gain more credence in party and state discourse. The following chapters argue that legally-binding obligations under international trading treaties, in concert with *nha nuoc phap quyen* discourse, are gradually making a procedural 'rule of law' that governs economic (but not political) relations appear socially useful, even desirable.

Party Leadership and Legal Borrowing

The second working postulate, discussed in Chapter 1, speculated that if political parties monopolise state power, laws will invariably reflect their interests. This observation raises two questions that pertain to Vietnam: how does party 'leadership'

99 See Carlyle A. Thayer (2000), 'The Economic and Commercial Roles of the Vietnam People's Army', 24 *Asian Perspective* (2), 87, 88–120.

100 See Nguyen Kim Dinh (1995), 'The Bloc Party Organisation in the Party Organizational System', *Tap Chi Cong San*, August 57–58, 66, trans. FBIS East Asian Daily Report 96-019, 67–70.

101 See Quan Xuan Dinh (2000), 'The Political Economy of Vietnam's Transformation Process', 22 *Contemporary Southeast Asia* (2), 360, 364.

influence legal borrowing; and would the constitutionalisation of political power stabilise the meaning of imported commercial laws?

Party leadership has the potential to produce highly contextual outcomes for borrowed law. Party political and moral discourse fine-tunes the meaning given to open-ended rights-based laws. For example, in determining the meaning of 'healthy market' competition, party 'policy regimes' (*che do chinh sach*) control the utility of imported contractual and property rights. In some circumstances, party policy may support legal harmonisation projects and shield lawmakers from public opposition. In other circumstances, party policies may generate highly fragmented and protean interpretations of legal imports that undermine contractual and property rights.

We saw in Chapter 3 that an influential group of senior party leaders has come to believe that a robust economy requires a productive private sector. Policy choices within the party are also increasingly shaped by the pressing need to sustain economic growth, attract foreign capital and comply with international treaty conditions. All this suggests that party ideology, projected through 'party leadership', is less likely in the future to oppose private contractual and property rights actively.

Although ideological opposition to private commerce has diminished, structural impediments to a procedural 'rule of law' remain. Party leadership creates parallel systems of governance in which legal meaning resides in both party resolutions and state laws. This fragmentation of authority exposes imported laws to uncertainty. If 'party leadership' were stable and transparent, perhaps it could coexist with, or even augment, private commercial rights. But in Vietnam's polycentric power structures, party organs produce guidelines that excite wildly divergent interpretations across factional lines and between central and local authorities. This uncertainty undermines a procedural 'rule of law' and, as we shall see in subsequent chapters, destabilises imported private commercial rights.

A final question remains: can commercial legal transplants flourish in a society 'led' by the party? The point is often made that commercial legal systems have effectively transplanted to illiberal party-dominated countries such as Singapore and Malaysia,[102] but there are substantive differences between these regimes and Vietnam. They have no functional equivalent of the dual governance mechanism that projects party power into Vietnamese state institutions. More importantly, these countries have well-developed judiciaries and legal professions, backed by comparatively depoliticised and professionalised state institutions that can support private commercial rights with a procedural 'rule of law'. Subsequent chapters explore what changes are required to 'party leadership' in Vietnam for rights-based laws to flourish.

---

102 See Surain Subramaniam (2001), 'The Dual Narrative of "Good Governance": Lessons for Understanding Political and Cultural Change in Malaysia and Singapore', 23 *Contemporary Southeast Asia* (1), 65, 72–79.

Conclusion

The discussion commenced with the observation that anyone transferring Western laws to communist regimes should search for functionally equivalent legal structures and processes. Although Vietnam has the institutional trappings of a constitutional state, 'party leadership' guides, directs and occasionally displaces the state. Party discourse is antagonistic or at best ambivalent to imported PAR arguments that effective governance requires a separation of party and state. Even as party leaders enthusiastically use law to as a tool to implement policies, they are unwilling to accept a 'rule of law' that checks their power.

Despite this reluctance, party and state officials are increasingly required to comply with the law, especially compared to the scant regard for legality before *doi moi* reforms. Although party leaders still openly intervene in politically sensitive areas, direct day-to-day party involvement in state operations is increasingly uncommon. As the party disengages from direct involvement in state affairs, opportunities for conflict between party policy and law will slowly diminish. This shift towards a law-based state is most evident in the economic arena, where the party is cautiously devolving lawmaking power to the state. Subsequent chapters develop this discussion by considering how far this process has proceeded and whether (if at all) the transformation affects legal borrowing.

The next chapter examines how foreign and local discourses shape the selection and meanings given to imported commercial laws. Chapter 6 investigates how central and local discourses guide the way state institutions interpret and apply imported property and contract rights. Chapter 7 explores whether those outside the party and state have a voice in influencing imported laws and progress towards a 'rule of law'.

Chapter 5

Discursive and Strategic Lawmaking

Introduction

Chapter 1 argued that the mentalities and processes informing lawmaking profoundly influence the selection and adoption of legal transplants. The meanings ascribed to imported laws may change when lawmakers in recipient countries do not fully comprehend the norms and tacit assumptions underlying these laws or the processes in which they operate. Even when the foreign regulatory context is well understood, lawmakers may borrow laws for strategic reasons based on political expedience, familiarity, prestige or legal fashion, rather than compatibility with the recipient legal system.

Commercial law reform in Vietnam is a fertile ground to test this proposition, because lawmakers steeped in the Soviet legal tradition are importing rights-based legal norms to regulate the mixed-market economy. Our inquiry needs an analytical framework in which to explore the epistemological assumptions and strategies influencing the selection and adoption of foreign laws in Vietnam.[1] Discourse analysis seems promising, since lawmaking largely (although not exclusively) relies on communicative processes. By imagining lawmaking as the 'contact zone' between different modes of exchange, discourse analysis offers insights into the ways lawmakers transform political, economic and moral discourse into legislative questions of legality and validity.[2]

This study uses 'official' party and state discourses to assess how local meanings, processes and strategies influence the selection and adaptation of foreign law. Distinctions between 'official' and 'unofficial' discourse are somewhat artificial in Vietnam, since mass organisations and state corporatism blur the boundaries between state and society. For our purposes, 'official' discourse is taken to mean ideas generated by party cadres and state employees that are communicated through party and state organisational channels and publications. Although highly influential, 'official' discourse is not the only source of ideas shaping lawmaking. Chapters

---

1 The term lawmaking is used broadly to denote any processes that transform regulatory knowledge into state laws, rules and processes.

2 See Hugh Baxter (1998), 'Autopoiesis and the "Relative Autonomy" of Law', 19 *Cardozo Law Review*, 1987, 2041–44.

6 and, especially, 7 explore how local-level officials and entrepreneurs influence drafting committees and legislative deliberations in the National Assembly.

This chapter begins by examining the different discursive narratives informing legal borrowing. After mapping the ideas and epistemological assumptions guiding lawmakers, the chapter then uses a series of case studies to examine how legislative drafters and National Assembly delegates strategically use the 'official' discourse to understand and adapt the meanings of borrowed laws. It asks the question: what factors make some foreign ideas appear more appropriate than others? The discussion concludes that lawmakers rarely passively follow discursive ideas, but rather they strategically use borrowed ideas to advance institutional interests.

Legal Borrowing Discourse

Chapter 3 showed that cultural and legal compatibility seemed relatively unimportant to lawmakers during the 1960s and 1970s, because they were convinced that Vietnamese society was evolving into a transcultural socialist utopia. Unreflective borrowing of this kind is not a viable option for contemporary lawmakers importing Western rights-based law into a socialist-inspired political-legal system. Yet, as the following section suggests, most discourse informing contemporary lawmakers de-emphasises the need to reconcile imported commercial norms and practices with local conditions.

Four analytical threads run through contemporary discourse about legal borrowing. First, party writers depict a national culture (*van hoa dan toc*) based on essentialised *kinh* traditions, surrounded by layers of received external influences.[3] Like articles of faith, certain Vietnamese cultural institutions—such as ancestral links to the mythical Au Lac kings, Red River Delta villages and independence from foreign invaders—are placed within the traditional core.[4] Other deeply embedded cultural traditions, particularly those derived from colonial and foreign sources, are relegated to the periphery of the imagined cultural identity.

This politically constructed identity is rarely explicitly invoked, though it exerts a strong influence over attitudes towards legal imports. For example, the Legal Research Institute (*Vien Nghien Cuu Khoa Hoc Phap Ly*), a body attached to the Ministry of Justice, conducted extensive research to identify 'core' Vietnamese socio-legal norms.[5] This project was strongly influenced by the belief that Vietnam has a usable legal past that could be codified into contemporary laws. It also recalled

3 See Le Truyen (2003), 'Ho Chi Minh's Thoughts on Unity', *Nhan Dan*, reproduced in 9 *Vietnam Law and Legal Forum* (108), 10–11. Also see Do Huy (2003), 'Achievements of Building and Developing a New Culture in Vietnam in the 20th Century', *Vietnam Social Sciences* (3), 14–15.

4 See Le Kha Phieu (1998), 'Party Leader Addresses Cultural Officials', *Nhan Dan*, 9 October, 1, 5, trans. FBIS East Asia Daily Reports 98-289; Le Truyen (2003), *supra*, 10.

5 Interviews, Duong Thi Thanh Mai, Deputy Director of the Institute of Law Research, Ministry of Justice, Hanoi, March 1999.

the 'Asian values' thesis that nation-states can withstand 'negative' global pressures, maintain social stability and preserve elite power by asserting core 'traditional', mainly Confucian, moral values.[6]

Researchers failed to find meaningful ways of importing traditional norms (*duc tri*) and laws (*phap tri*) based on pre-industrial village life into a legal system serving an educated, internationally integrated mixed-market society. The project provided legislative drafters with insufficient contextual information to ascertain whether pre-modern Vietnamese norms and laws could regulate contemporary life. It nevertheless created a general impression that laws in East Asian countries are more compatible with Vietnamese conditions than Western laws.

Second, most commentaries use a narrow technical legal analysis that avoids assessing the relevance of foreign laws to local conditions.[7] They treat legal imports as technical fragments that can be reassembled without reference to underlying institutions and practices. Frequently resembling medieval scholasticism in its use of elaborate arguments about minutiae, writings of this kind protect core political ideas in the 'official' discourse from scrutiny.

There are undoubtedly practical reasons for basing legal analysis on 'black letter law', such as poorly developed comparative law and research skills. But never far below the surface is the concern that since law reflects party policy, contextual analysis may offend the party-line and policies. Political constraints are enforced by administrative penalties that prohibit state employees from criticising party and state policy (see Chapter 4).

Third, some writers have reconfigured Marxist-Leninism to make legal borrowing from capitalist countries a theoretical possibility. Dao Tri Uc, for example, is strongly influenced by Chinese Marxist theorists, who insist that 'laws have their relative independence and influence on the economic system'.[8] By abandoning orthodox class-based theory that insists on causal links between working class interests and law, he concluded that progressive and counter-progressive laws are determined not necessarily by their class origins, but rather by whether they eventually become generally acceptable and promote the national interest. This reformulation gives

6 The party actively promotes the idea that certain indigenous 'cultural' values promote economic development. See Philip Taylor (2001), 'Apocalypse Now? Hoa Hao Buddhism Emerging from the Shadows of War', 12 *The Australian Journal of Anthropology* (3), 339, 350.

7 Most Vietnamese legal writings fall within this category. See, for example, Hoang The Lien (1996), 'Subject System in Vietnam's Civil Code', 2 *Vietnam Law and Legal Forum* (18), 22, 22–24; Vu Mao (1996), 'The Civil Code—A Great Achievement in the 5-Year History of Legislation of the National Assembly of Vietnam', 2 *Vietnam Law and Legal Forum* (17), 17.

8 See Dao Tri Uc (1995), 'The Study of Vietnam's State History and Law', 1 *Vietnam Law and Legal Forum* (8), 38, 38–40; Dao Tri Uc (2002), 'Tac Dong Cua Toan Cau Hoa Doi Voi Su Phat Trien va Doi Moi Cua Phap Luat Viet Nam' (Effect of Globalisation Towards the Development and Renovation of Vietnam's Laws), *Tap Chi Cong San* (12), 22, 24–26.

lawmakers a theoretical licence to borrow laws from capitalist countries without modifying core Marxist–Leninist axioms such as party paramountcy.

Le Minh Thong, another prominent legal commentator has filtered Kahn-Freund's (or *Kalm Jreund* in Vietnamese) ideas through a Marxist prism to devise three factors that should be taken into account when importing foreign laws:[9]

- ensuring the spirit of the imported law is similar to the dominant (*thong tri*) legal ideology in the recipient country,
- determining whether the imported law comes from a legal system that is similar in structure to the way state power is organised in the recipient country,
- ensuring the imported legal system comports with the dominant production mode in the recipient country.

Unfortunately, Le Minh Thong did not further elaborate his ideas. But it is instructive to note that Kahn-Freund's neo-Marxist ideas, such as ideology, power structures and production modes, were highlighted in this narrative, whereas his socio-legal notions that link law to autonomous social processes were de-emphasised.

Fourth, a few commentators have quietly replaced Marxist-Leninism with Western sociological theory that embeds borrowed law in a broad discursive context. Pham Duy Nghia, for example, took from Weber the notion that imported laws should correspond to social conditions in recipient countries. He argues that 'mechanical copies' (*sao chep may moc*) of Western law are generally incompatible with domestic economic and cultural conditions and are thus difficult to 'bring into effectiveness' (*dom hoa ket trai*).[10] However, since legal borrowing is the only way to develop a commercial legal system rapidly, he concludes that lawmakers should devote more resources to reconciling foreign laws with local conditions.

These variegated narratives suggest continuity and change in contemporary attitudes to legal borrowing. In some areas, legal discourse has borrowed and assimilated rights-based thinking; in others, it has recycled decades-old Soviet ideas. The receptiveness of these narratives to imported ideas seems to depend on whether they are influenced by epistemological criteria that are closed and self-referential, or

9 Le Minh Thong is a researcher at the Institute of State and Law. See Le Minh Thong (2003), 'Mot So Van De Phap Ly Cua Qua Trinh Toan Cau Hoa' (Some Legal Issues on Globalisation), *Tap Chi Nghien Cuu Lap* (1), 65–75.

10 See Pham Duy Nghia (2002), 'Tiep Nhan Phap Luat Nuoc Ngoai—Thoi Co va Thach Thuc Moi Cho Nghien Cu Lap Phap' (Transplantation of Foreign Law-Chances and Challenges for Legislative Studies in Vietnam) *Tap Chi Nghien cuu Lap Phap* (Legislative Studies) (5), 50–54. Also see Pham Duy Nghia (2001), 'Mot So Anh Huong Truc Tiep Cua Qua Trinh Hoi Nhap Kinh Te Khu Vuc va The Gioi Doi Voi Phap Luat Viet Nam' (Some Direct Influences of the World's and Regional Economic Integration into Vietnamese Law), *Tap Chi Nghien cuu Lap Phap*, 2, 3–7; Nguyen Nhu Phat (2005), 'Minh Bach Hoa Phap Luat va Yeu Cau Dat Ru Doi Voi He Thong Phap Luat Trong Qua Trinh Hoi Nhap Kinh Te Quoc Te' (Transparent Laws and their Requirement for the Legal System During International Economic Integration), *Nha Nuoc va Phap Luat*, 16–20.

are open and willing to engage imported ideas. Epistemologies determine the types of imported ideas that seem familiar and acceptable to legal commentators.

The epistemologies regulating the entry of new knowledge into political discourse about party paramountcy have undergone the least change. Most commentators present Marxist-Leninism and the thoughts of Ho Chi Minh as infallible and eternal truths, creating a self-referential discursive environment that conditions lawmakers to search for laws from similar 'political systems' (*he thong chinh tri*).

But even sacrosanct political epistemologies are not immune to change. Some commentators have selectively drawn ideas from Ho Chi Minh's eclectic thoughts and '*nha nuoc phap quyen*' (law-based state) discourse to reinvent attitudes to non-socialist ideas.[11] Dao Tri Uc, for example, replaced 'working class' interests with the national interest, a reformulation that enables lawmakers to bypass class theory and select laws from capitalist countries.[12] This change in the epistemological settings is eroding many of the conceptual barriers that prevented pre-*doi moi* lawmakers from borrowing laws from non-socialist systems.

Marxist–Leninist 'scientific' infallibility is also being worn down by the infiltration of Weberian socio-legal thinking that places law in a social matrix. Some commentators have smuggled 'rule of law' ideas into legal discourse to challenge the instrumental view that law exists to implement party policy. This new thinking not only has the potential to open legal thinking to borrowed ideas, it may also encourage lawmakers to examine the compatibility of legal transplants with local cultural and political 'realities'.

As we saw in Chapter 3, economic ideas are also mounting a powerful challenge to closed political thinking. Longstanding prohibitions against trading with capitalist economies have given way to international economic integration policies that encourage lawmakers to harmonise domestic commercial law with international trade agreements. Imported neoliberal legalism, which underpins international commercial law, openly challenges socialist 'state economic management' principles.

Finally, lawmaking discourse is not conducted in a hermetically sealed intellectual environment. Law reform everywhere comprises a set of conscious strategies by competing social agents to structure state power. Consequently, our analysis needs to consider the context of lawmaking.[13] Are imported legal ideas systematically filtered through party ideals? Do legal drafters enlist imported ideas to support particular institutional priorities in 'palace wars'? How relevant are theoretical approaches to legal borrowing compared to familiarity with, and the prestige of, imported ideas?

11 See Dao Tri Uc (2002), *supra*, 24–26.

12 See Dao Tri Uc and Le Minh Thong (1999), 'Su Tiep Nhan Cac Gia Tri Phap Ly Phuong Dong va Phuong Tay Doi Voi Su Phat Trien Cac Tu Tuong Phap Ly Viet Nam' (Reception of Oriental and Occidental Legal Values in the Development of Vietnamese Legal Ideology), *Nha Nuoc va Phap Luat* (5), 3–10.

13 See Yves Dezalay and Bryant G. Garth (2002), *The Internationalization of Palace Wars*, University of Chicago Press, Chicago, 246–50.

The next section uses a series of case studies to examine how specific institutional contexts mediate the discursive influence over legislative drafting committees.

A Contextual Analysis of Lawmaking

So far, the discussion has depicted lawmaking as an orderly process where lawmakers filter imported ideas through the dominant themes in the 'official' discourse. This portrayal underestimates human agency. To acquire the force of law someone must enact borrowed ideas into domestic legislation.

Brian Tamanaha and others advocating 'interpretivist' approaches to discourse analysis argue that application and context also shape legal meaning.[14] As Clifford Geertz reminds us, 'law is local knowledge not placeless principle'.[15] In other words, the meaning of words is never fixed, and varies according to the context in which the words are used. The meaning of legal ideas resides in their discursive representation and their strategic use.

To understand how legislative drafting changes the meaning of legal imports it is thus necessary to consider the strategies and interpretive positions adopted by lawmakers. Alan Watson brought human agency into the lawmaking calculus by considering strategic reasons for adopting foreign laws. He used the term 'transplant bias' 'to denote a system's receptivity to a particular question outside law, which is distinct from an acceptance based on a thorough examination of possible alternatives'.[16] The acceptability of law is determined by the prestige commanded by particular legal systems, together with linguistic and other accessibility factors. He also believed the 'inertia' or 'the general absence of a sustained interest on the part of society and its ruling elite to struggle to adopt the most satisfactory rule', inhibits transferability.[17] Cost and potential political instability generated by legal change sometimes discourage legal elites from borrowing foreign laws.

This study examines the proposition that legal ideas are adopted not just because they are good, but also because they are effectively communicated across cultural boundaries and possess authority and prestige. A series of case studies is used to examine how institutional contexts shape the selection and adaptation of borrowed laws.

---

14 See Brian Tamanaha (1998), *Realistic Socio-Legal Theory*, Clarendon Press, Oxford, 144, 170–72; M. Wetherell (2001), 'Introduction', in M. Wetherell, S. Taylor and S. Yates (eds), *Discourse Theory and Practice: A Reader*, Sage, London, 4; David Nelken (1996), 'Law as Communication: Constituting the Field' in D. Nelken (ed.), *Law as Communication*, Dartmouth, Aldershot.

15 Clifford Geertz (1983), *Local Knowledge*, Basic Books, New York, 218.

16 See Alan Watson (1978), 'Comparative Law and Legal Change', 37 *Cambridge Law Journal*, 313, 327.

17 See Watson (1978), *supra*, 331.

Translating Foreign Legal Terminology

Before turning to legislative drafting, it is useful to consider the role terminology plays in legal borrowing. Borrowed laws are not just ideas; they come encoded in foreign (to Vietnamese legal drafters) languages. Ideally, drafters must not only understand foreign legal terminology, they must also find Vietnamese words or phrases that import legal meanings without stripping away and/or adding too many new normative concepts. Studies about legal terminology provide insights into the contribution words make to building legal identities and outlooks.[18]

The reception of foreign legal terminology into Vietnamese is not a recent phenomenon. Ta Van Tai asserts that most governmental and legal terms used during imperial times were borrowed from Chinese sources.[19] Widespread familiarity with imported Chinese legal thinking was restricted by the use of Chinese and *nom* (modified Chinese) characters in official discourse.[20] Although literacy levels in pre-modern Vietnam were high by regional standards, less than 60,000 literati could read official laws and proclamations written in these characters.[21] Many legal terms were eventually translated into the more widely understood *quoc ngu* (Romanised script). Nevertheless, after the revolution, few lawmakers understood Chinese and *nom* characters with sufficient fluency to acquire a deep knowledge of pre-modern legal thinking.

Linguistic barriers also impeded the naturalisation of French colonial laws. With the exception of the Code de Annamite 1922, which mixed French law with an abridged Nguyen Code, French colonial authorities made little effort to translate French legal documents into *quoc ngu* (see Chapter 2). French was not only the legislative language, legal training was also conducted in French and superior courts enforced the law in French.[22]

In order to establish a socialist legal system, the DRV in 1959 forbade the use of French legal terminology and purged French-trained officials with questionable loyalties.[23] Ho Chi Minh next led a campaign to transpose complex Chinese-

---

18 For a general discussion about how Vietnamese words assume meanings through context see Hy V. Luong (1990), *Discursive Practices and Linguistic Meanings: The Vietnamese System of Person Reference*, John Benjamins Publishing Company, Amsterdam, 30–35, 166–71.

19 See Ta Van Tai (1982), 'Vietnam's Code of the Le Dynasty (1428-1788)', 30 *American Journal of Comparative Law* (3), 523.

20 Many, though not all, Chinese legal terms were translated into *nom* for official writings. Interview Tran Thi Tuyet, Institute of State and Law, Hanoi, March, 2001.

21 See Alexander Woodside (1971), *Vietnam and the Chinese Model*, Harvard University Press, Cambridge, Mass., 194–223.

22 See Michael Barry Hooker (1975), *Legal Pluralism: An Introduction to Colonial and Neo-Colonial Law*, Clarendon Press, Oxford, 175–235.

23 Circular, Ministry of Justice, 1959. See George Ginsburgs (1979), 'The Genesis of the People's Procuracy in the DRV', 5 *Review of Socialist Law* (2), 187, 192–94.

Vietnamese legal words into everyday Vietnamese terms familiar to the masses.[24] Cadres working in villages found that Chinese-Vietnamese words used to translate Soviet legal terms caused confusion among the people, because this terminology was associated with mandarins and feudal regimes.

Establishing a Vietnamese legal lexicon proved difficult. Chinese-Vietnamese words described many basic legal notions, such as *luat* (law), *phap che* (legality), *quyen* (right), *lam don thinh xin* (petition) and *hinh phat* (penalty). Legal terms of Vietnamese origin, on the other hand, lacked precision and were treated more like aphorisms than technical terms. Legal officials gradually reverted to using Chinese-Vietnamese terms. For example they changed *nghia vu*, the Vietnamese term for obligation, back to the original Chinese-Vietnamese term *trai vu*.[25] Other Vietnamese terms such as *phat vit* (punishment) appeared in official legal documents, while legal officials continued to use the Chinese-Vietnamese word *che tai* in regulatory conversations. Adding to the confusion, some terms acquired different meanings in different discourses. The Sino-Vietnamese term *phap che*, for example, was used in legal discourse to translate the Soviet concept of legality, but in political discourse it reverted to its pre-modern meaning—to 'ensure legal compliance' through mass moral education campaigns.

By the 1980s, most Chinese-Vietnamese legal terms had acquired Soviet legal meanings. This process took place through the association of Chinese-Vietnamese terms with Soviet legal ideas expressed in party policies and resolutions, legal education and organisational language. Over time, party leaders also came to accept that legal officials needed their own technical language containing terms that were not in everyday use.

Soviet-inspired legal meanings were soon disrupted by a new wave of post-*doi moi* legal borrowing. Rather than importing foreign legal words directly into the local language—a practice adopted in some other Southeast Asian countries—Vietnamese legal officials preferred local adaptations. Four processes are underway.

First, terms with Soviet legal meanings are gradually acquiring a new significance from their association with market transactions. The changing meanings of *luat* and *phap che* have already been discussed. Superior legislation frequently uses technical Chinese-Vietnamese terms to import foreign legal ideas, whereas subordinate legislation enacted by ministries to implement the law contain more non-technical Vietnamese words. This discrepancy is attributable to a general lack of precise legal

---

24 See Dinh Gia Trinh (1965), 'May Y Kien Ve Tinh Dan Toc va Tinh Khoa Hoc Cua Thuat Ngu Luat Hoc—Nhan Xet Phe Phan Ve Mot So Thuat Ngu Thong Dung' (Nationalistic and Scientific Use of Legal Terminology: Criticisms of Common Legal Terms), *Tap San Tu Phap* (3), 24–26.

25 The following conversions were unsuccessful: replacing the Chinese-Vietnamese term *thu dac* (to acquire) with the Vietnamese *lau duoc* (which had a similar meaning); replacing the Chinese-Vietnamese *thu ly* with the Vietnamese *nhan xu ly* (to accept a case); and replacing the Chinese-Vietnamese *khang cao* (to appeal) with the Vietnamese *chong an* (to protest a judgment).

terms and a conscious decision to use simple terms that are understood by low-level administrative officials.

Informants connected to foreign donor projects say that the Ministry of Justice has resisted attempts to compile an 'official' legal lexicon.[26] They ascribe this reluctance to internal struggles between the National Assembly, Ministry of Justice and Supreme People's Court to control the meanings given to legal terms. As discussed below, these institutional contests have amplified the fragmentation of legal discourses.

Second, some Chinese-Vietnamese legal terms that were discredited because of their association with capitalism in the Republic of Vietnam have been rehabilitated. For example, the word *khe uoc* is now commonly used to describe commercial agreements. The Civil Code also uses many Chinese-Vietnamese legal terms to describe complex contractual and civil obligations, such as *vat dac dinh* (distinctive object) in article 186 and *nghia vu lien doi* (joint obligation) in article 304. Other legal terms have become unfashionable because they are considered too closely associated with Soviet legal thinking. The Hanoi Law University, for instance, changed its name from *Dai Hoc Phap Ly* to *Dai Hoc Phap Luat*, because *phap ly* was used to describe legal processes in the command economy.

Third, where there are no equivalent local terms, drafters have literally translated imported foreign terms into Vietnamese. For example, *cong ty me-con*, which translates as mother-child company, was coined to describe holding-subsidiary companies for the amended Law on State-Owned Enterprises 2003.[27]

Fourth, foreign grammar and syntax are also influencing the way the Vietnamese language is used to discuss legal issues. Consider the UNDP-sponsored Legislative Framework Report drafted by the Law Department at the Ho Chi Minh National Political Academy and Ministry of Justice in 1998. The Vietnamese version of the report was translated into English by a Canadian-trained official working for the Ministry of Justice. Ministry officials decided that the English version more clearly expressed the intentions of the original authors and translated the English version back into Vietnamese. Not only were the legal terms more precise in English, but the English syntactical structures linked legal ideas more clearly in logical patterns. This practice further distances legal discourse from the everyday language.

In showing that recycled words retain traces of their original meaning, etymological studies imply that legal thinking lags behind legal transplantation. Chinese-Vietnamese legal idioms, for example, retained Mandarin overtones long after they had been redeployed to serve socialist legality. Decades later, socialist meanings are still evident in legal terms recycled in rights-based legislation. The following discussion examines how lawmaking changes the meaning of legal imports.

---

26 Interviews, officials of the Ministry of Justice, Hanoi, November 2002.

27 Drafters writing the Competition Law have invented many new Vietnamese words to import complex Anglo-American anti-trust doctrines into the bill. For example, the word *ban hang da cap* is used to describe multi-level marketing (sales into networked industries).

Legislative Drafting

In order to understand how context influences legal borrowing it is useful to identify the institutional agents that select and adapt foreign laws, and ascertain whether particular lawmaking practices privilege certain types of ideas.

Soviet Lawmaking

Once social relations had stabilised in the DRV during the 1960s, more importance was attached to developing technically proficient legislation. Soviet law professors teaching at the Hanoi Judicial Training School introduced drafting techniques.[28] But most legislation was imported, with few concessions to local conditions, from Soviet bloc countries.[29] Even statutes regulating areas such as crime, where a rich body of local law already existed, closely followed Soviet templates.[30]

If suitable socialist models were unavailable, lawmakers codified party resolutions. Legislation of this kind retained much of the original political language and syntactical structure. For specifics, Decree No. 182 on Socialist Collective Mastery Rights of Workers and State Officials in State-Owned Enterprises 1979 codified Resolution No. 10 on Collective Mastery issued by the Central Committee of the CPV in 1979, by copying most of the original language, headings and organisational structure. There was no attempt to change the hortative political language into legal norms and prescriptive rules.[31]

Similar political language appeared in the Statute on Higher-Level Agricultural Producer Cooperatives, an extremely important regulatory instrument.[32] It consolidated a series of party resolutions and subordinate regulations, but did not convert political passages exhorting farmers to comply with *khau hieu* (political slogans) into legal standards prescribing legitimate forms of behaviour. In short, Vietnamese laws either recycled Soviet legal ideas or codified party resolutions and state reports. It did not occur to lawmakers that they should transform broad political exhortations and pragmatic solutions into the legal language of norms and rules.

---

28 A series of articles appearing in the journal of the Supreme Court (*Tap San Tu Phap*) during the 1960s introduced Soviet legal drafting techniques to Vietnam. See, for example, Pachakop (1964), 'Van De Xay Dung Bo Luat Dan Su O Lien Xo' (Drafting the Civil Code in the Soviet Union), *Tap San Tu Phap* (2), 20, 20–24.

29 Interviews Le Kim Que, President Bar Association of Hanoi, July 1998, September 1999.

30 See Phuong-Khanh T. Nguyen (1987), 'The Criminal Code of the Socialist Republic of Vietnam', 13 *Review of Socialist Law* (2), 103–20.

31 See Author Unknown (1981), *Phap Che va Quyen Lam Chu Tap The* (Legality and Collective Mastery Rights), Jointly Published by Department of Legality and Department of Cultural Information in Binh Tri Thien Province, 3–7, 30–61.

32 See generally Adam Fforde (1984), 'Law and Socialist Agricultural Development in Vietnam: The Statute for Agricultural Producer Cooperatives', 10 *Review of Socialist Law*, 315, 315–17.

Contemporary Lawmaking

Following *doi moi* reforms in 1986, lawmakers began searching for legal sources beyond the socialist world. Drafting laws for the new economic conditions proved difficult, because lawmakers could no longer assume that borrowed law complied with domestic political imperatives. Since Soviet lawmaking techniques did not show lawmakers how to turn party resolutions into law, the Ministry of Justice drafted the Law on the Promulgation of Legal Documents 1996 to clarify and standardise this complex process.

The law aimed to 'improve the quality and effectiveness of legislation work, institutionalise in time party-lines and policies, meet the requirements of social management by law and build the law-governed state'. As a first step, it established a lawmaking hierarchy. At the apex, the National Assembly enacted superior legislation (codes, laws and resolutions), while arms of the state (government, Supreme People's Court and Supreme People's Procuracy) were given powers to promulgate subordinate, implementing legislation. As a second step it clarified which bodies were permitted to propose draft legislation to the National Assembly.[33]

Superior legislation is initiated in two main ways. Most commonly, ministries propose bills to the Standing Committee of the National Assembly.[34] Occasionally, party and Fatherland Front organisations propose bills. For example, the *Hoi Dong Kinh Te Xa Hoi* (Council on Economic and Social Affairs), a Fatherland Front organisation made up of Soviet-trained economists, proposed some commercial laws (for example, Company Law) to the government during the initial stages of law reform. Drafting cannot commence until the Politburo or the Party Central Internal Affairs Commission (CIAC) (*Ban Noi Chinh Trung Uong*) issues a resolution appointing a drafting agency.

Until recently party leaders did not permit National Assembly bodies to both draft and enact superior law.[35] Party leaders believe that National Assembly delegates lack the 'professionalism' (*chuyen nghiep*) required to transform party policy into law, while others are concerned that drafting powers might transform the National Assembly into a rival political organ.[36] The party currently entrusts most drafting to

33 State bodies (including some National Assembly committees), the Fatherland Front and its member organisations and National Assembly delegates. See the Law on the Promulgation of Legal Documents 1996, article 3; Constitution 1992, article 87. A National Assembly delegate unsuccessfully introduced a bill on religious freedom. Interview Nguyen Si Dung, Director Center for Information, Library, and Research, Office of National Assembly, Hanoi, February 2000.

34 See Law on the Promulgation of Legal Documents 2002, article 22.

35 In 2004, the Politburo directed the National Assembly Committee on Science, Technology and Environment to draft an Electronic Transactions Law. See VN Law Find (2005), *Legal Newsletter*, NH Quang & Associates, Hanoi, March, 4.

36 See Nguyen Duc Lam (2002), 'De Tien Toi Chuyen Nghiep' (Towards Professionalism in the National Assembly), *Nghien Cuu Lap Phap* (6), 23, 25–30. Nguyen Duc Lam (2002),

specialised committees attached to government agencies.[37] Other state bodies, such as the Supreme People's Court and Procuracy occasionally draft bills.[38] Finally, the National Assembly Law Committee, in association with other National Assembly bodies, prioritises the enactment of bills in the lawmaking agenda.

Legal drafters are constantly reminded 'the most important point is to ensure that processes followed in drafting laws and statutes and preparing the State's plans and policies correctly expresses the Party's ideology and viewpoint'.[39] Yet this fundamental injunction is difficult to put into practice because party resolutions authorising legislation are generally hortative and contain few substantive instructions. One commentator equated the process to building a house, where policymakers specify the cost of construction and general size and function, but provide no architectural vision.[40] For example, the Party Central Committee instructed the Central Institute of Economic Management (CIEM), a research organisation attached to the Ministry of Planning and Investment, to draft the Law on Business Bankruptcy and the Enterprise Law.[41] Party resolutions authorised the drafting committees to import laws to meet foreign loan conditionalities, without indicating how drafters should reconcile imported rights-based law with underlying 'state economic management' practices.

Drafting committees usually comprise personnel drawn from the lead ministry and officials seconded from the Ministry of Justice, other relevant ministries, CIAC and Fatherland Front organisations.[42] They are required to 'review [sic] the institution of law enforcement: evaluate the current legal documents relating to the draft document: conduct surveys to assess the actual situation of the social relations related to its main contents'.[43] Lead agencies decide who to consult and whether (and how) their comments are incorporated into drafts.[44] Information and opinions are collected from interested state agencies, mass organisations and other relevant bodies, but prime ministerial approval is required to use foreign expertise. Working groups of legal experts may provide additional advice where bills contain complex technical issues. Non-state participation in legislative drafting is considered in Chapter 7.

'Suy Nghi Hau Ky Hop Cung Lo' (Some Thoughts on a National Assembly Session), *Tap Chi Nghien Cuu Lap Phap* (9), 8, 10–12.

37 Law on the Promulgation of Legal Documents 2002, article 25(1).

38 Law on the Promulgation of Legal Documents 2002, articles 25–28.

39 Do Muoi (1995), *Vietnam: New Challenges and New Opportunities*, The Gioi Publishers, Hanoi, 174.

40 Interview, Official of National Assembly, Hanoi, March 1999.

41 See Le Dang Doanh (1999), 'Enterprise Law – A Must for Further Development of Multi-Sectorial Economy' *Vietnam L. Legal Forum*, (56), 11–13.

42 Law on the Promulgation of Legal Documents 2002, article 29(3).

43 Ibid., article 26(1).

44 See Decision No. 280 QD-BTP on the Evaluation of Bills and Draft Legal Documents 1999, articles 3, 5, 10.

Once completed, bills are next submitted to the government for consideration.[45] As meetings occur only two or three days a month, government working agendas are extremely crowded, leaving little time to consider the policy ramifications of draft laws.[46] Drafting committees, moreover, are rarely asked to justify their selection of imported and local legal ideas. Memoranda accompanying drafts generally lack detailed research and assert more than argue the appropriateness of legislative provisions.[47] This means the selection of foreign legal ideas takes place during the initial drafting stage and borrowing rarely occurs during the final stages before bills are presented to the National Assembly.

Party organs make legislative decisions before, during and after drafting committees complete their work.[48] But different allegiances and organisational logics sometimes generate sharp distinctions in the interpretation of official policy by officials from the CIAC, other central party agencies and internal party groups within ministries (see Chapter 4). Adding to the conceptual confusion, as we saw in Chapter 3, party organs and state agencies do not always agree about the pace and direction of legal reform. Informants report that CIAC nominees frequently adopted the narrowest and most cautious interpretation of the party's drafting instructions and try to limit reforms needed for international legal harmonisation.

Long delays and numerous drafts generally signal protracted internal party and state consultation and conferral. Informants report that party officials routinely request changes to bills once they realise that imported legal rights might transfer decision-making power from state officials to private entrepreneurs. Although these opaque interventions are rarely discussed, much less documented, the case studies considered below should be interpreted in the context of active party involvement in legal drafting.

As we have seen, there are numerous, sometimes conflicting, themes in the 'official' discourse concerning legal borrowing. Five legislative drafting case studies have been selected to identify how lawmaking processes mediate the 'official' discourse in ways that influence the selection and adoption of borrowed laws.

45 Ibid., articles 7–10.

46 See Ngo Duc Manh (1994), 'Some Thoughts on the Legislation by the National Assembly', *Nha Nuoc va Phap Luat* (4), 8, 13–14.

47 See Office of Government (2003), 'Study Report to Improve the Quality of Law and Ordinances Drafted by the Government to be Submitted to the NA and NA Standing Committee', unpublished report, Working Delegation No. 804, Hanoi.

48 Nominees from the Central Internal Affairs Commission (*Ban Noi Chinh Trung Uong*) sit on most drafting committees, and controversial provisions are referred to the Politburo for approval before bills are passed to the National Assembly. Interview Tran Dai Hung, Vice Chairman, Central Party Internal Affairs Committee, Hanoi, November 2002.

Case Study One: Ordinance on the Transfer of Foreign Technology

The capacity of party-sponsored discourses to influence legal transplantation is well illustrated by the draft Ordinance on the Transfer of Foreign Technology 1988. A member of the drafting committee recalls that the party Central Committee directed the Ministry of Science and Technology to draft an ordinance regulating foreign 'intellectual property' (IP) in Vietnam.[49] The Minister appointed Professor Luu Van Dat to head the drafting committee, which comprised representatives from the Ministries of Science and Technology, Finance, Planning and Justice and the CIAC. As with most commercial drafting committees, academic lawyers and Fatherland Front members were not represented.

Drafters were directed by the party to use 'state economic management' licensing to regulate technology transfers by foreigners to Vietnamese parties. Research reports prepared by the drafting committee were written in a highly ideological and discursive language consciously designed to validate the political objectives set out in party resolutions. Drafters did not evaluate the proposed reforms from economic, moral and legal perspectives, because these lines of inquiry might have contradicted the drafting directive. For example, drafters realised that foreign intellectual property regimes were based on market valuations, but were reluctant to assess the impact of commodified intellectual property rights on the domestic market.

Using information provided by UN agencies, drafters based the ordinance on three legal sources.[50] First, Chapter Four of the UNCTAD Draft International Code of Conduct on the Transfer of Technology was imported to regulate mutual obligations, while Chapter Five of the Code provided the rules governing improvements in licensed technology.[51] Second, provisions were also borrowed from the technology transfer laws in China, the Republic of Korea, Malaysia and the Philippines, since these countries were considered culturally similar and economically successful. Third, drafters formed the view that technology transfer laws in some South American countries demonstrated high levels of state control that would facilitate 'state economic management'.

Unable to research local conditions, drafters selected foreign intellectual property laws largely because they appeared to agree with 'state economic management'. Vague notions of cultural compatibility were also considered. Without a fully realised drafting methodology, the completed bill consisted of conceptually incompatible imported ideas patched together with 'state economic management' licensing powers. Consistency between legal styles and substantive content was considered relatively

49 This case study is based on interviews with a former official from the Ministry of Science and Technology, Hanoi, March–April 1999, March 2000.

50 ESCAP, UNDP and UNCDC provided legal texts, but little contextual material, from a variety of Western, East Asian and South American countries.

51 See Vu Khac Trai (1996), 'Legislative Framework for Intellectual Property Rights in Vietnam' in M. Blakeney and P. Sinden (eds), *Proceedings of the National Symposium on the Role of Intellectual Property Rights in International Trade and Business*, Asia Pacific Intellectual Property Law Institute, Hanoi, 23.

unimportant compared with the political directive to preserve 'state economic management'. Drafters were relatively unconcerned about adjusting imported legal ideas with local precepts and practices. They primarily aimed to ensure that state officials possessed discretionary powers to reconcile imported private rights to the state interest.

Ministry of Science and Technology officials dominated committee meetings. The views of other committee members were only heard on technical issues directly concerning their respective areas of expertise. For example, Ministry of Justice officials were asked to ascertain whether drafts complied with superior legislation, especially the Law on Foreign Investment 1987. The Ministry of Science and Technology, in consultation with party representatives, decided major policy issues, such as the role of 'state economic management' in regulating private intellectual property transfers and the criteria used to select foreign regulatory models.

After several drafts, the ordinance was circulated within the government for discussion. This was the first time Ministry of Science and Technology drafters encountered competing visions for regulating technology transfers. Most comments proposed procedural changes designed to advance the regulatory powers of competing ministries, and raised few normative issues. The Ministry of Trade, for example, unsuccessfully complained that the draft did not give regulatory authorities sufficient 'state economic management' powers—an argument aiming to secure control over lucrative intellectual property registration processes. Non-state interest groups, such as foreign and domestic entrepreneurs, were not consulted before the draft ordinance was submitted to the Standing Committee of the National Assembly for promulgation.

Lawmakers drafted the ordinance in a highly regulated economy soon after *doi moi* reforms commenced. At this time, the preservation of 'state economic management' and the protection of state-owned enterprises from foreign investors dominated lawmaking discourse. Concerns that restrictive transfer provisions reduced economic efficiency and that propriety rights over intellectual property were culturally inappropriate were glossed over.

Later, when the ordinance was redrafted in the mid-1990s, drafters paid more attention to harmonising domestic regulations with international standards.[52] Several factors contributed to this change in thinking. Gradual economic liberalisation after the ordinance was enacted in 1988 made redundant the restrictions preventing foreign entities from appointing private sales agents. The Company Law 1990, for example, permitted entrepreneurs to deal with licensed intellectual property. In addition, government leaders stressed that foreign direct investment (FDI) was a

52 Foreign investors pressed Vietnamese lawmakers to harmonise the FDI laws with FDI regimes in neighbouring countries that had liberalised investment rules to attract foreign direct investment. Pressure for change also came from bilateral and multilateral trade agreements (ASEAN, US-Vietnam Bilateral Trade Agreement and negotiations to enter the WTO).

critical source of development capital and expressed concerns that overly restrictive technology transfer rules would reduce FDI flows.[53]

In 1993, a member of the drafting committee received a telephone call from Nguyen Dinh Loc (then the Minister of Justice). During a subsequent meeting, the minister revealed that the Politburo wanted to convert the redrafted ordinance into a chapter in the Civil Code. The party thought this would raise the profile of intellectual property law and assuage foreign criticism that Vietnam was not doing enough to protect property rights. Officials from the National Office of Intellectual Property unsuccessfully opposed this initiative by advancing legal arguments that public law provisions in the ordinance were inappropriate for a private law Civil Code.

After the government applied for WTO membership in 1995, drafters at the ministry were directed to codify the Treaty on Trade Related Aspects of Intellectual Property Rights (TRIPS) into domestic law.[54] Gradually, starting with Decree No. 63 on Procedures for Establishing Property Rights in 1996, and most recently with Decree No. 11 ND-CP on Technology Transfer 2005, drafters have imported most of the provisions required for WTO accession.[55]

The debate about the appropriate location for technology transfer rules resurfaced in discussions in 2005 about the draft law on technology transfers.[56] This time, legal arguments that specific civil relationships (such as technology transfers) should not be included in the Civil Code were taken more seriously. Contemporary discourse invokes 'rule of law' ideas, such as legal transparency and doctrinal certainty, to back the need for a discrete law on technology transfers. In other words, legal arguments are beginning to assume a more prominent role in shaping legislative drafting.

To sum up, the Ministry of Science and Technology used its control over the drafting committee to exclude conflicting views from the lawmaking processes. Although the ministry-dominated drafting committee presented decisions to the outside world as *nhat tri* (consensus), informants suggest that processes more closely resembled *chap thuan*, an expression that connotes a diversity of opinion cajoled and bullied into unanimous outcomes by those exercising hierarchical and personal power. Rather than manufacturing personal harmony, the main function of collective decision-making was to disseminate information and build inter-ministerial cooperation. A recent report compiled by the Office of Government supports this

53 See generally Vo Dai Luoc (1996), *Vietnam's Industralisation and Modernisation and Resources*, Social Sciences Publishing House, Hanoi, 24–26.

54 Under the US–Vietnam Bilateral Trade Agreement, ratified in 2001, Vietnam agreed to accede to the WTO and become fully TRIPS compliant on patent, trademark, copyright and trade secret protection by 2005. See US Commercial Service website <www.ustr.gov/regions/asia-pacific/text.html>.

55 See Vietnamnet (2005), 'Technology Transfer Decree Draws Flak', *Development Vietnam*, Intellasia News Service, 23 February, 15–16.

56 See VNS (2004), 'Do IP Rights Belong in the Civil Code?', *Vietnam News*, 29 December, <www.vietnamnews.vnagency.com.vn>.

analysis, as it demonstrated that lead drafting agencies routinely use their control over drafting committees to advance sectorial interests.[57]

Drafters initially filtered Western laws through political directives to retain state economic management. As party support for international economic integration gained momentum following the adoption of the US–Vietnam Bilateral Trade Agreement (BTA) in 2001, drafters began to de-emphasise state economic management over IP transfers. Discretionary controls have been incrementally replaced by property rights and procedural protocols stipulated in international conventions. As a corollary, 'rule of law'. ideas have slowly penetrated the lawmaking calculus.

Case Study Two: Ordinance on Economic Contracts

Discussions about reforming the Ordinance on Economic Contracts 1989 reveal ongoing tensions between 'state economic management' and international legal harmonisation. During the early stages of *doi moi* reforms in 1987, the Ministry of Trade appointed a drafting committee (again led by Luu Van Dat) to prepare an ordinance regulating contracts governing commercial activities.[58]

Drafting commenced at a time when the Council of Ministers was still undecided about the role of state planning. Marxist–Leninist antipathy to private ownership of the 'means of production' was also evident in provisions in the Constitution 1980 and Penal Code 1986, still in force at that time, which criminalised private commercial activity.[59]

The party Central Committee instructed ministry officials to draft an ordinance with three goals:

- Preserve 'state economic management' over the economy.
- Establish contract rules to facilitate autonomous business transactions among state and private businesses.
- Provide contractual guidance to inexperienced business players.

Drafters realised these objectives by drafting an ordinance that juxtaposed imported (primarily French) rights-based provisions with 'state economic

57 See Office of Government (2003), 'Study Report to Improve the Quality of Laws and Ordinances Drafted by the Government to be Submitted to the NA and NA Standing Committee', unpublished report, Working Delegation No. 804, Hanoi. Also see Pham Tuan Khai (2004), 'Nang Cao Chat Luong Xay Dung Cac Du An Luat Phap Lenh Do Chinh Phu Soan Thao' (The Quality of Laws Drafted by Government Bodies), *Tap Chi Nghien Cuu Lap Phap* (3), 20–28.

58 Information concerning the initial drafting of the Ordinance on Economic Contracts 1989 was gleaned from interviews with two members of the drafting committee: Luu Van Dat, Legal Adviser to the Minister of Trade, Hanoi, January 1990; and Phan Huu Chi, Legal Advisor to Minister of Justice, Hanoi, April 1992.

59 Constitution 1980, articles 24, 26; Penal Code 1986, article 168.

management' provisions recycled from the Soviet-inspired Decree No. ND 54 CP Regulations on Economic Contracts 1975. Reflecting the distinction in the command economy between contracts for profit and personal consumption, only commercial entities with business registration (SOEs, private firms and cooperatives) were permitted to enter economic contracts.[60] Violators were punished with administrative and criminal penalties.[61]

The distinction between civil and economic contracts reflected administrative divisions in the command economy between contracts regulating production and distribution under Decree No. 217 CD 1987 and civil contracts regulating personal consumption. Drafters preserved this division in the belief that it would be difficult to apply 'state economic management' to transactions for both profit and consumption.

Command economic thinking was also evident in provisions that based economic contracts on the 'state plan' (article 10) and gave state economic arbitrators powers to intervene and adjust contractual rights (article 8). Highly prescriptive provisions governed the formal requirements for making economic contracts and intruded into commercial bargains by regulating provisions governing price, quality and delivery. Luu Van Dat formed the opinion that, during the initial stages of economic reforms, Vietnamese businessmen were inexperienced and required detailed guidance. Above all else, he insisted that discretionary 'state economic management' powers should moderate contractual rights to preserve the 'state benefit' (*loi ich cua nha nuoc*).[62]

Despite their misgivings about Vietnamese entrepreneurs, drafters also adopted provisions that championed autonomous contractual rights. Article 4 of the ordinance protected signatories from duress; article 5 introduced the concept of voluntary commercial relationships, and article 6 guaranteed state protection for contractual promises.

In 1999, the party Central Committee directed the Supreme People's Court to redraft the ordinance. The party selected the Court over the Ministry of Trade (the first drafting agency) to take advantage of the Court's accumulated experience in implementing the earlier version. Contrasting with the clear instructions given to the original drafting committee, the Court was ordered to make the ordinance more relevant to current economic conditions. Behind this cryptic directive lay an unresolved dispute about the role of 'state economic management' in Vietnam's mixed-market economy.

---

60 See Ordinance on Economic Contracts 1989, articles 2, 4, 6, 7, 8, 42-43. See generally Duong Dang Hue (1994), 'Phap Luat ve Viec Cap Giay Phep Thanh Lap Doanh Nghiep Dang Ky Kinh Doanh o Viet Nam: Thuc Trang va Mot Vai Kien Nghi' (Legal Regulations in Relation to Issuance of Permits to Establish Enterprises and Business Registration in Vietnam: The Present Situation and Some Recommendations), 4 *Nha Nuoc va Phap Luat*, 20.

61 See Ordinance on Handling of Administrative Violations 2002.

62 See Nguyen Thi Khe (1996), 'Cac Bien Phap Bao Dam Thuc Hien Hop Dong Kinh Te Trong Nen Kinh Te Thi Truong O Vietnam' (Measures to Ensure the Implementation of Economic Contracts in the Market Economy in Vietnam), *Nha Nuoc va Phap Luat* (9), 17, 23–24.

Members of the drafting committee agreed about the need to amend the ordinance to clarify technical rules governing contractual termination, to remove references to state planning (article 10) and add provisions regulating new business practices, such as electronic commerce. They disagreed on two fundamental issues: should the conceptual distinction between economic and civil contracts be abolished, and should unregistered household entrepreneurs be permitted to enter economic contracts? At issue was the state's power to determine proactively the type of entrepreneurs permitted to form economic contracts and engage in large-scale commerce.[63]

The Ministry of Justice led the opposition to fundamental change. According to Hoang The Lien, a senior ministry official, 'parties to economic contracts should be business persons (i.e. individuals or units that the government has allowed to carry out business). Not all people are allowed to participate in business processes and conduct business activities'.[64] In other words, divisions between economic and civil contracts are necessary to manage proactively the type of entrepreneurs entering business transactions.

Duong Dang Hue, the Ministry of Justice representative on the drafting committee, used class-based arguments to block reforms.[65] He opined that businesses are operated by 'rich people' who enjoy many privileges over 'ordinary citizens'. Breaches of economic contracts have the potential to generate wide-ranging social harm by causing business failure and unemployment. Civil contracts, in contrast, produce highly particularised harm to consumers and families. In short, 'state economic management' over market entry is needed to protect the economy and 'working class' interests. His views were interesting not only for retaining deterministic links between regulation and class, but also for showing that new economic thinking that has compressively discredited orthodox socialist determinism in some other ministries, has not penetrated the Department of Economic and Civil Law at the Ministry of Justice.

Other members of the committee thought that separate economic and civil contractual regimes had outlived the economic conditions in which they arose, but concluded that this legal distinction was too deeply entrenched in the legal system to remove. Only judges on the drafting committee argued for a unified economic and civil contract system. While not opposing 'state economic management' as an

---

63 See the arguments made by the Duong Dang Hue (2000), 'Nhung Co So Cua Viec Xay Dung Phap Lenh Hop Dong Kinh Te (Sua Doi)' (Foundation for Building Up Ordinance on Economic Contracts (Amendment)), *Kien Nghi Ve Xay Dung Phap Luat Hop Dong Kinh Te Tai Viet Nam* (Recommendations in Building up the Economic Contract Legislation in Vietnam), VIE/95/017, Ministry of Justice-UNDP, Hanoi, 14–19.

64 Hoang The Lien (2000), 'Xac Dinh Doi Tuong va Pham Vi Dieu Chinh Cua Phap Lenh Hop Dong Kinh Te (Amendment)' (Identification of Governing Objectives and Governing Scope of the Ordinance on Economic Contracts (Amendment)) Kien Nghi Ve Xay Dung Phap Luat Hop Dong Kinh Te Tai Viet Nam, (Recommendations in Building up the Economic Contract Legislation in Vietnam), Ministry of Justice-UNDP VIE/95/017, Hanoi, 21.

65 See Duong Dang Hue (2000), *supra*, 14–18.

ideal, they argued that the dual contract system was conceptually confusing.[66] The Supreme Court Annual Report in 2000, for example, showed that most contractual cases reviewed by higher courts involved procedural irregularities, such as filing actions in the wrong court division. Judges attributed these irregularities to the dual contract system.[67]

Judges also found the dual system troublesome, because it prevented them from using provisions from the comprehensive Civil Code to cover the numerous regulatory omissions and ambiguities in the ordinance and Commercial Law. They maintained that a comprehensive legal framework is required to replace the discretionary provisions in the ordinance that give government agencies powers to 'manage' market entry proactively.

As a comparatively weak institution, the Supreme Court struggled to leverage its leadership over the drafting committee and mobilise support for a unified contractual system. Representatives from the Ministries of Justice and Public Security were instrumental in blocking reforms. Tran Huu Huyen, the director of the VCCI Legal Department, summarised the dilemma faced by the Supreme Court lawmakers: 'drafting committees are limited or affected not only by practical concerns and real life experience, but also by the self-defense psychology of the "guardians" who always want to "maximise" the safety of society'.[68] This is a clear reference to the use of 'state economic management' to control private commercial rights.

Pressure for Vietnam to harmonise its commercial laws with international standards and remove regulatory barriers to preventing small traders from forming economic contracts increased after accession to the BTA in 2001 and the lead-up to WTO accession in 2006.[69] In order to circumvent the stand-off in the drafting committee and formulate an ordinance that complied with treaty conditionalities, the party transferred control over the committee to the Ministry of Trade in early 2004.[70] By March 2004, the third draft of the new Commercial Law proposed the repeal of

66 See Tran Van Su (2000), 'Nhung Vuong Mac Trong Che Do Hop Dong Kinh Te Hien Hanh' (Problems in the Current Economic Contract Regime), *Kien Nghi Ve Xay Dung Phap Luat Hop Dong Kinh Te Tai Viet Nam* (Recommendations in Building up the Economic Contract Legislation in Vietnam), VIE/95/017, Ministry of Justice-UNDP, Hanoi, 9–13.

67 See *Cong Tac Toa An Nam* (2000), *Bao Cao Tong Ket 2000* (Supreme Court Annual Report 2000), Hanoi, 34, 40

68 See Tran Huu Huynh (2002), 'Roles Played by the Chamber of Commerce and Industry of Vietnam on the Participation in the Formulation and Implementation of the Legal Normative Documents on the Economy', unpublished paper, Workshop on Amending, Supplementing the 1996 Law on the Promulgation of Legal Normative Documents, Hanoi, 22–24 August, 2.

69 The Minister of Trade indicated that changes to the contractual rules were needed to comply with APEC, ASEAN, BTA and WTO conditions. See VNS (2003), 'Fast Reform for Commercial Law', *Vietnamnews-online*, <www.vietnamnews.vnagency.com.vn/2003-11/06/Stories/04.htm>.

70 Interview Nguyen Thanh Hung, Vice Director Legal Department, Ministry of Trade, Hanoi, 2 March 2004.

the ordinance and the integration of economic contract provisions into the redrafted law.[71] In compliance with treaty conditionalities, the draft law abolished distinctions between types of entrepreneurs and permitted anyone with legal capacity to enter contracts for commercial purposes. But much to the consternation of Supreme Court drafters, the longstanding and confusing distinctions between economic and civil contracts were retained. The new Commercial Law was enacted in 2005.

It is possible to infer from this case study that political arguments for 'state economic management' no longer automatically dominate lawmaking debates. A reform-minded group from the Ministry of Trade used the legal argument that Vietnam was bound by international treaty to give entrepreneurs equal contractual rights. Their position was, however, ultimately secured by the party's political support for international economic integration.

Compliance with treaty conditionalities does not necessarily signify that most members of the drafting committee supported the neoliberal ideas underlying facilitative regulation. On the contrary, neoliberal legal arguments were unable to persuade the committee to abolish the Soviet distinctions between civil and economic contracts and further deregulate 'state economic management' powers over entrepreneurs. All the same, the Ministry of Trade drafters were prepared to deploy neoliberal legal arguments to obtain a more deregulated contractual regime.

Most members of this drafting group were Western educated and had acquired an understanding of, even sympathy for, neoliberal legalism through prolonged treaty negotiations (especially the BTA and WTO) and participation in numerous foreign donor-sponsored study tours and workshops. Although they are not as cohesive and openly identified with neoliberal ideas as some ministry research institutes (discussed below), as a group they are more prepared than previous Ministry of Trade drafters to use abstract neoliberal legal thinking to re-engineer domestic commercial regulation.

This case study also demonstrated that politically weak state institutions, such as the Supreme People's Court, struggle to influence the law reform agenda. Yet, as the following case studies show, raw political power is not the only factor shaping lawmaking. Well-researched and argued ideas sometimes prevail.

Case Study Three: Drafting the Company Law

The Politburo in 1988 issued a resolution instructing the Central Institute for Economic Management (CIEM), a research organisation attached to the State Planning Commission, to draft laws regulating private commercial organisations.[72] The resolution stressed the need to order private business activities with 'state

71 Nguyen Thi Thu Ha (2004), 'Weak Commercial Law Gets Extra Muscle', *Vietnam Investment Review*, 24 May, sourced from <www.asia.proquestrefercne.info/pqrasia>.

72 Communist Party of Vietnam Resolution No. 16 of 1988.

economic management' discretionary controls.[73] Like the Ordinances on Technology Transfer and Economic Contracts, the Companies Law was drafted during the early stages of economic reform before private commerce had received constitutional approval. Drafters once again resolved tensions between business freedoms and 'state economic management' by protecting the state interest.

Company laws based on the French *droit des sociétés* existed in the North before partition in 1954. By the 1960s, the legal system did not countenance a role for private commercial organisations and only recognised SOEs and cooperatives.[74] When drafters commenced work on the Companies Law the official discourse regarded companies as colonial and capitalistic artefacts standing outside indigenous experience. There were few domestic laws or institutional practices to guide the drafters.

Articles 4 and 5 of the Companies Law recited provisions in Politburo Resolution No. 16 of 1988 that recognised legal equality for all economic sectors, freedom for private enterprises to conduct business activities and the right to own and bequeath 'the means of production'. After first legally recognising private business organisations, the drafters set about importing a corporate legal framework. Professor Luu Van Dat (an experienced legal drafter from the Ministry of Trade), backed by French legal advisers, dominated the drafting committee.

The committee first proposed borrowing the company law from the former Republic of Vietnam.[75] Members of the Standing Committee of the National Assembly rejected this initiative. Since the law contained over 300 articles, it was considered too complex for the embryonic market conditions. Perhaps more importantly, the adoption of law from the Republic of Vietnam conveyed too much legitimacy on the discredited 'Sai Gon regime'.

Instead, the committee based the Companies Law on the French Law No. 66-537 on Commercial Companies 1966. Chapter II of the law followed the French system of authorising the establishment of companies and specifying chartered capital for different industries and services. Chapter III established shareholding companies (*cong ty co phan* or *société anonyme*) and Chapter IV created limited-liability companies (*cong ty trach nhiem huu han* or *société à responsabilité limitée*).[76] With a mere 46 articles, the Companies Law was a skeletal facsimile of the 509 provisions in the French Law. Despite its brevity, however, the law contained most elements of modern company law. For instance, company members shared profits and losses in proportion to their capital contributions and were not personally liable for company

73 Information about the draft Company Law was primarily derived from interviews with officials supporting the drafting committee, especially Nguyen Dinh Cung, Dang Duc Dam, and Le Dang Doanh.

74 See Pham Thanh Vinh (1966), 'The Obligatory Nature of Planning Targets', 12 *Review of Contemporary Law*, 89–97.

75 See Le Dang Doanh (2004), 'The Enterprise law and the Development of the Domestic Private Business Sector in Vietnam', *Vietnam's Socio-Economic Development* (38), 6–7.

76 See John Gillespie (1999), 'Corporations in Vietnam', in Roman Tomasic (ed.), *Company Law in East Asia*, Ashgate, Aldershot, 297–330.

debts (Companies Law, article 2). Companies were entitled to own property and enter legally binding transactions (Companies Law, article 12). The law rather indeterminately separated the functions and powers of members, company officials and employees. Shareholding companies were authorised to issue shares and raise capital from the public and rules-governed company mergers and liquidations. In short, the drafters imported the legal rules that enabled entrepreneurs in the Western world to create wealth from the 'surplus value' of employees while protecting personal assets from business losses.

Since companies had few roots in domestic trading culture and socialist theory, the 'official' discourse had little to say about corporate theory and practice. Contrasting with the vigorous academic debates on corporate law reform in China, Vietnamese reforms passed virtually unchronicled.[77] Most scholarly legal literature was preoccupied with narrow doctrinal issues such as company law terminology, the efficacy of licensing procedures and inconsistencies between corporate and commercial laws.[78]

The few changes made to the French legal template are mainly attributable to the drafters' familiarity with Soviet law. For example, drafters varied the French law by giving limited-liability companies (with fewer than 12 members) the right to appoint only one director to act on behalf of the company (Companies Law, article 27(3)). In Soviet law, there was no need for executive directors and boards of directors to represent SOEs, because supervising authorities (Ministries and People's Committees for SOEs) ran SOEs like administrative agencies.

In another example, drafters took from French Law a general duty requiring directors and boards of management to account to members for 'shortcomings in the management of the company including breaches of the charter or the law' (Companies Law, article 39). But they thought it was unnecessary to enact interpretive guidelines that would assist members to sue malfeasant directors. In the command economy, supervising authorities used discretionary administrative penalties to discipline wayward SOE directors. In both instances, drafters recycled notions from the Soviet administrative model without considering their relevance to autonomous legal persons.

Interviews suggest that drafters did not fully comprehend the jurisprudential notions of legal personality underpinning the imported law. Drafters perceived legal personality in a highly state-centred context as institutions created by law.[79] Natural and legal persons were differentiated along functional lines by highlighting the independence of the latter from the former. Indeed, the struggle in Western legal theory to attribute personal authority to abstract legal bodies did not enter the

77 For an overview of the vernacular literature see Fu Tingmei (1993), 'Legal Person in China: Essence and Limits', 41 *American Journal of Comparative Law*, 261.

78 See generally Duong Dang Hue (1994), *supra*, 20.

79 See Nguyen Ngoc Tuan (1993), 'Renovating the Enterprise Model in Our Country', *Tap Chi Cong San* (12), 29–33; Nguyen Nhu Phat (1993), 'Conceptions on the Legal Status of Entrepreneurs in the Market Economy', *Nha Nuoc va Phap Luat* (2), 25–27.

lawmaking discourse. Without a tradition of natural rights theory and individualism (*chu nghia ca nhan*), it did not occur to drafters that corporate rights require a source of legitimacy outside legislative and bureaucratic power. Western legal theory investing companies with natural or human legal capacity to conduct businesses did not transplant with the imported French law.

The concessionary licensing of companies persisted in Europe until the doctrine of freedom of contract attempted to extend law over the privileged and corrupt power relationships entrenched in late 18th-century England.[80] Liberal ideology extolled entrepreneurs as the engines of capitalism and promoted market liberalisation that transformed corporations into vehicles for harnessing capital and risk-taking. Concessionary business licences used by the state to control corporate activities were replaced in England during the middle of the 19th century, and later in continental Europe, with registration systems that made incorporation inexpensive and freely available to anyone fulfilling routine registration procedures.

Most Vietnamese drafters opposed the liberal, free market ideology underlying the French corporate law, because it contradicted Marxist tenets that companies are the preserve of the capitalist class. Some drafters were familiar, through Soviet literature, with Berle and Means's classic study '*The Modern Corporation and Private Property*'.[81] They found Marx's warnings about corporate capitalism echoed in the passage: 'the corporate system has done more than evolve a norm by which business is carried on. Within it exists a centripetal attraction which draws wealth together into the hands of fewer and fewer men'.[82] Analogous views occasionally appeared in newspaper articles.[83]

Drafters learnt from Chinese legislative experiments conducted in Shenzhen and Shanghai during the 1980s that 'state economic management' could minimise the exploitation and social harm caused by private companies.[84] Adopting this approach, they used business licensing controls to limit the economic sectors in which private companies could operate (Companies Law, article 11). Local authorities (People's Committees) were directed to use capitalisation, education and health permits to guide private capital proactively into state-sanctioned areas (see Chapter 6).

80 See David Sugarman (1983), 'Law, Economy and The State in England, 1750–1914: Some Major Issues', in David Sugarman (ed.), *Legality, Ideology and the State*, Academic Press, London, 240–42.

81 Interviews Nguyen Nhu Phat, *supra*, February 1997, June, July 1998.

82 Adolf Berle and Gardiner Means (1968), *The Modern Corporation and Private Property*, Harcourt, New York, 18.

83 See, for example, Huy Duc (1997), 'Bi An Minh Phung' (Minh Phung Mystery), *Thoi Bao Kinh Te Sai Gon* (Saigon Economic Times), 24 April, 36; 38; Author Unknown (1997), 'More Arrested as Size of Fraud Case Hits $700 Million', *Vietnam Economic Review*, 13 October, 4.

84 See generally Roman Tomasic and Jian Fu (1999), 'Company Law in China', in Roman Tomasic (ed.), *Company Law in East Asia*, Dartmouth Press, Aldershot, 137–38.

Once companies were established, drafters imposed further operational restrictions by strictly interpreting the legal doctrine of *ultra vires*.[85] The legal capacity of companies to conduct business was determined by the 'rights and obligations' set out in company licences. Operational objectives were prescribed with considerable precision by licensing authorities. General powers to pursue authorised objectives appeared in the Companies Law (article 12), but companies were not permitted to expand their business capacity by adopting a 'shopping list' of associated and tangential objectives. Administrative and criminal penalties applied to company officials who strayed beyond the authorised parameters (Companies Law, article 44).

Rigorous state management of companies was justified to minimise social harm caused by exploiting workers' 'surplus value'. Small-scale household businesses employing family members were, on the contrary, considered non-exploitative and consequently were trusted to pursue business opportunities unshackled from business licences.

In summary, Vietnamese lawmakers used Marxist critiques of capitalism to filter and adapt the imported French corporate law principles. By the mid-1990s, procedural shortcomings in the Companies Law began to constrain domestic investment.[86] Lawmakers began to look beyond Marxist-Leninism for solutions to corporate regulation.

Case Study Four: Drafting the Enterprise Law

In 1995 the Eighth Plenum of the party Central Committee instructed CIEM to draft a new company law to implement three main reforms: legal equality, market reforms and legal harmonisation.[87] CIEM studied corporate regulation for several years before forming a drafting committee in 1998 headed by Le Dang Doanh, then the director of CIEM. Departing from previous practice, the drafting committee included a representative from the Vietnam Chamber of Commerce and Industry (VCCI), an association representing state and private business (discussed in Chapter 7). It was not until the ninth draft in July 1998 that the name of the law changed from Company to Enterprise Law (EL). This amendment reflected the draft's expanded jurisdiction, which by this stage included partnerships and possibly SOEs and FDI joint ventures.

---

85 Literally meaning 'beyond power', the doctrine implies that companies only have the capacity to form legal relationships in areas expressly permitted in incorporation documents. For the treatment of the *ultra vires* doctrine in French law, see J. Le Galland and P. Morel (1992), *French Company Law*, Second edition, Longman, London, 68–73.

86 See Nguyen Trinh Binh (1995), 'It is Time to Amend the Law on Companies', *Saigon Giai Phong*, 3 July, 3.

87 See Le Dang Doanh (1999), 'Enterprise Law – A Must for Further Development of Multi-Sectorial Economy', *Vietnam Law Legal Forum* (56), 11–13.

Legal Equality

The party rather nebulously directed CIEM to draft an enterprise law that formalised legal equality among business sectors. Drafters concluded that a uniform company law regulating foreign, state and privately owned entities was the most effective way to achieve this objective.[88] Members of the CIAC monitoring the Enterprise Law project rejected this legal argument on the basis that a universal company law would compromise the leading role of SOEs. They also supported the proposal that problems with the Enterprise Law were best rectified before extending the law to foreign investors.[89] By insisting on separate legislation for private and publicly owned companies, the party could bring into play dual policy regimes to ensure that the state-owned sector remained the 'foundation of the economy'.

In 2004, the party instructed CIEM to commence drafting a unified enterprise law that regulated both private and state-owned companies.[90] Rather than a shift towards neoliberal thinking, this change in policy is more likely to reflect the party's drive for international economic integration. Anti-discrimination rules in the WTO require uniform corporate rules governing private and state sectors.

Market Reforms

The party also wanted the drafting committee to bring the Companies Law more in line with market reforms. This vague directive was subject to many possible interpretations. By the mid-1990s, the official discourse recognised that private sector investment generated most of the new jobs needed to absorb the rapidly growing population.[91] Government policy had initially favoured foreign investment, since it strengthened the politically favoured SOE sector.[92] However, FDI flows concentrated in the main cities and, being relatively capital intensive, failed to increase employment opportunities significantly. By 1998, foreign direct investment had dramatically declined in importance following the investment slump triggered by the East Asian economic crisis. In addition, concerns that the Companies Law might excite a domestic capitalist class opposed to party paramountcy were seen by

---

88 Ministry of Justice (1997), 'General Report: Law of Enterprises of Different Forms in Vietnam', UNDP Program VIE/94/003, 14–18.

89 See Dang Duc Dam (1997), 'Administrative Reform – Changes to Meet the Requirements of the Market-Orientated Economy', in John Gillespie (ed.), *Commercial Legal Development in Vietnam: Vietnamese and Foreign Commentaries*, Butterworths, Singapore, 483–91.

90 See VNS (2005), 'New Enterprise Law: Playing on a Level Field', *Vietnam News*, 26 January, <www.vietnamesenews.vnagency.com.vn>.

91 See Dang Duc Dam (1997), *Vietnam's Macroeconomy and Types of Companies*, The Gioi Publishers, Hanoi, 49–82.

92 See Le Dang Doanh (1997), 'Foreign Investment and the Macro-Economy in Vietnam' in V.H. Tran (ed.), *Economic Development and Prospects in the ASEAN–Foreign Investment and Growth in Vietnam, Thailand, Indonesia and Malaysia*, Macmillan, Basingstoke, 44–86.

members of the CIAC to have been exaggerated. The economic contribution made by private companies was also beginning to erode Marxist antipathy towards the private sector.

Some economic researchers from the CIEM believed that considerable scope existed to mobilise domestic investment by liberalising 'state economic management' provisions in the Companies Law. They thought that the 'corporate law shirt' (*ao so mi luat cong ty*) had not kept up with the 'economic body' (*co the kinh te*) and deregulating market access for companies would increase business investment.[93] Informed by neoliberal economic theory, they decided to enact an Enterprise Law that removed investment barriers as an alternative to offering further investment incentives to private business.

CIEM officials working for the drafting committee prepared a report that contained a sustained legal commentary.[94] They collaborated with the VCCI in compiling case studies that exposed the economic costs caused by administrative barriers to market access (see Chapter 7). Arbitrary licensing rules governing education, health and capital requirements, which were designed to exclude unwanted investment, were criticised for failing to distinguish good investments from poor ones. CIEM officials used the accumulated evidence to demonstrate that business licences increased the time and cost of incorporation and stifled business investment.

The report concluded:

> there is a common opinion in the business community and among [Vietnamese] scholars that the current state management has no clear objective; it is implemented arbitrarily with severe violation of business freedom; it becomes an obstacle for expansion, diversification and improvement of business activities and efficiency on one hand, and provides opportunities for bribery and corruption on the other hand.[95]

In contrast to the empirical research underpinning market-entry reforms, researchers primarily based other corporate reforms on foreign advice and research.[96] It is often difficult to demonstrate causal links between foreign advice and legal change, because the drafting process involves considerable internal (and some external) conferral and consensus. Articles in the Enterprise Law concerning minority shareholders' and directors' duties, however, were clearly imported from foreign sources with few concessions to local interests and conditions. Drafters

---

93 See Phan Van Tan (1998), 'Laws Should Predict New Economic Forms', *Kinh Doanh va Phap Luat* (Law and Enterprises), 27 May, 3.

94 Vien Nghien Cuu Quan Ly Kinh Te Trung Uong (Central Institute of Economic Management (CIEM)) (1998), *Danh Gia Tong Ket: Luat Cong Ty va Kien Nghi Nhung Dinh Huong Sua Doi Chu Yeu* (Review of the Current Company Law and Key Recommendations for its Revision), CIEM, Hanoi, April.

95 CIEM (1998), *supra*, 103.

96 David Goddard and Reinier Kraakman were perhaps the most influential foreign advisors to CIEM. See Reinier Kraakman (1997), 'Comments on the Draft General Report: Law of Enterprises of Different Forms in Vietnam', unpublished paper, UNDP Program VIE/94/003, Hanoi.

sought guidance about the civil and common law approaches to corporate regulation, but were eventually persuaded to draw heavily from Canadian and New Zealand corporate models. Above all else, CIEM officials sought to shift the regulatory focus in the Enterprise Law from concessionary 'state economic management' to a facilitative approach that allowed capitalism a much freer hand.

Legal Harmonisation

Arguments favouring international economic integration were gaining momentum by the mid-1990s. Party instructions to the drafting committee reflected concerns by foreign investors and multilateral organisations, such as ASEAN and APEC, that Vietnam should harmonise the Companies Law with international protocols. Uncertainties surrounding corporate governance rules (directors' duties and the rights of minority shareholders) and winding-up provisions were targeted for reform. The Companies Law also lacked rules governing partnerships, shareholding in limited-liability companies and the conversion of limited-liability companies into shareholding companies. More fundamentally, foreigners complained that the Companies Law did not treat foreign investment entities like domestic companies. Separate legal regimes had the effect of quarantining foreigners from the domestic market. Investors also thought that legal distinctions between foreign and domestic companies unnecessarily complicated business transactions and arbitrarily inhibited novel and adaptive ownership structures.

The first tranche of a US$100 million Financial Sector Development and Capital Market Loan advanced by the Asian Development Bank (ADB) included conditions that sought to tie the government to a set of harmonisation reforms. The loan stipulated five substantive company law reforms:[97]

- Abolish market-entry rules and allow companies to enter any lawful area of business.
- Abolish distinctions between domestic, state and foreign enterprises to enable foreigners to incorporate as, and own shares in, domestic companies.
- Clarify the division of responsibilities between corporate managers and members. Specific reforms promoted by foreign consultants included rules governing the division of powers between directors and members, protection of minority shareholders, and more clearly delineated directors' duties.
- Regulate dividend payments, mergers and winding up with prescriptive regulation.
- Compel companies to provide accurate and timely information concerning

97 See Chapman Tripp Sheffield Young (1998), 'Enterprise Law Reform – Some Issues and Some Suggestions', unpublished paper, Hanoi. Also see Research Report (1999), 'Improving Macroeconomic Policy and Reforming Administrative Procedures to Promote Development of Small and Medium Enterprises in Vietnam', MPI-UNIDO Project (US/VIE/95/004), Hanoi, 99–101.

directors, share registries and financial records to a central registrar.

Raymond Mallon, a foreign economic adviser closely connected with the Enterprise Law project, put the pressures for legal harmonisation in perspective: 'because of the strong national ownership of reform, policy-based lending was only effective when it was supporting reform measures for which there was already a broad national support'.[98] The Enterprise Law, which was eventually enacted in 1999, complied with all the conditionalities imposed by the ADB, save for extending the law to cover foreign investment entities.

In contrast to the Companies Law, which drew heavily from French law, the Enterprise Law reflects the influence of Anglo-American legal advisers (discussed in Chapter 7). CIEM drafters retained the civil law (French) statutory framework of the Companies Law, while borrowing normative standards from common law countries (primarily Canada and New Zealand). In 134 articles it regulates directors' duties, disclosure, members' rights (especially those of minority shareholders), boards of management, inspection boards, dividend payments, conversion among corporate entities, dissolution merger and liquidation. By permitting enterprises 'to select an industry, line [of business], area and form of investment and take the initiative to broaden the scope and line of business', article 7(2) of the Enterprise Law gives entrepreneurs a right 'to choose forms of production'.[99]

Drafters assessed the utility of foreign corporate laws by comparing what the rule purported to do against local requirements. This methodology involved considerable guesswork about the interaction between law and society in donor countries, as well as local demand for corporate regulation. Drafters, as a consequence, relied extensively on foreign advisers. They were persuaded that common law norms are less 'theoretically embedded' than civil law provisions and figure more prominently in global trading protocols. Change occurred not only in the selection of legal norms, but also in the use of theory to evaluate the regulatory impact of the Enterprise Law. CIEM drafters consciously used neoliberal economic theory to challenge longstanding Marxist political and moral attitudes to entrepreneurs.

Rather than passively following the advice given by foreign advisers, the drafters actively debated and selectively used imported ideas to realise institutional and broader objectives. For example, they rejected foreign legal advice to give companies the legal rights of natural persons, a position also opposed by the party. As a compromise, they prescribed a list of corporate rights in section 7 that falls well short of international standards.[100] CIEM drafters were careful to use foreign knowledge and skills in ways that did not offend the hierarchies and policies in their host institution (Ministry of Planning and Investment). Le Dang Duong

98 Raymond Mallon (2002), 'Approaches to Support the Development of an Enabling Environment for Small Enterprises: Viet Nam Case Study', GTZ Report to the Committee of Donor Agencies for Small Enterprise, Turin, 26.

99 Constitution 1992, article 21.

100 See Reinier Kraakman (1997), *supra*, 3.

was especially skilled in emphasising different aspects of the Enterprise Law for different audiences. In an address to a conference of donors in 2000 he described the Enterprise Law as a weapon to roll back state economic regulation, whereas, to ministry officials, he stressed nationalist arguments about the competitive advantages the law gave domestic investors. Over time, however, the perceived success of the Enterprise Law increased the drafters' prestige and influence, allowing their ideas to spread further into the organisational hierarchy.

As discussed in more detail in Chapter 7, it is possible to discern a loosely constituted interpretive community encompassing CIEM drafters, foreign donors and local consultants and lawyers involved in the drafting project. They shared common understandings about the nature of the problems with the Companies Law and the need to introduce neoliberal economic solutions to deregulate market entry. Drafters and advisers worked closely together and spoke a mutually comprehensible neoliberal legal language. This common approach to legal reforms assisted the rapid transfer of complex corporate law doctrines between foreign advisers and local drafters.

Mediating Lawmaking Discourses

Although CIEM drafters favoured a deregulated approach to market entry, as members of a research institution, they lacked the political power to exclude 'state economic management' views from entering lawmaking discussions. CIEM drafters speculated that forces supporting 'state economic management', such as the Party Economic Commission, Ministry of Trade and Ministry of Industry would have undermined reforms if their views had been stifled.

Drafters from the Ministry of Industry, for example, argued that licensing provisions were necessary to prevent private transport companies from exploiting the 'working class'. Rigorous 'state economic management' favoured state ownership and worker entitlements. Ministry representatives also offered the political argument that market liberalisations compromised party paramountcy. CIEM drafters believed these notions were raised as a pretext to preserve regulatory (frequently corrupt) powers over market entry.

Unable to exclude contrary views from lawmaking discussions, CIEM drafters encouraged consultation that exposed other members of the drafting committee to neoliberal ideas about the economic benefits of market deregulation. Although CIEM drafters did not directly challenge Marxist–Leninist underpinnings of 'state economic management', they used empirical evidence to show that deregulation would stimulate economic development.[101] In the end, well-researched economic and (to a much lesser extent) legal arguments defeated political and moral arguments.

101 See CIEM (1998), *supra*, 100–1.

Case Study Five: Civil Code

Work commenced on the Civil Code in 1980.[102] As the lead agency, the Ministry of Justice formed seven drafting subcommittees, one for each chapter in the code.[103] The first draft was primarily based on provisions borrowed from civil codes in the Eastern bloc (principally the Soviet Union). Following *doi moi* reforms, drafters began looking elsewhere for legal sources. Where existing legislation was considered inappropriate for mixed-market conditions, sub-committees were instructed to select provisions from non-socialist sources. Nguyen Dinh Loc (the former Minister of Justice) and other senior government lawyers in the principal drafting committee prepared the final drafts that were sent to the prime minister and Politburo for comment.

Drafters were given vague political instructions to preserve *quan ly nha nuoc ve phap luat* (state management of law), but little guidance regarding the appropriate sources of foreign law. Interviews with members of the drafting committee suggest two factors influenced the selection of foreign laws: the range of laws provided by foreign donor agencies and the drafters' familiarity with particular types of laws.[104] These factors influenced the selection and adaptation of future property rights provisions in the Civil Code.

Japanese legal consultants advised the property law sub-committee that market economies require future property rights that give creditors interests over property acquired after the creation of security interests.[105] They recommended provisions in the Japanese Civil Code as a suitable model. Most members of the property law sub-committee were trained in the German Democratic Republic and understood future property rights from the pre-communist German Civil Code. Future property rights in both the Japanese and German Civil Code 1900 were inspired by provisions in the 19th-century Prussian Civil Code.

For senior members of the principal drafting committee trained in the Soviet legal tradition, future property rights seemed artificial and alien. They replaced the Japanese provisions with a conceptually confusing article that repeated the Soviet

---

102 See Decision No. 350 November 1980. Also see Pham Diem (2004), 'Civil Law Making in Vietnam During the 1945-1995 Period', 11 *Vietnam Law and Legal Forum* (122), 20; Dao Tri Uc (1995), 'Some Basic Issues Concerning the Civil Code of Vietnam', *Nhan Dan*, 6 October, 6, trans. FBIS East Asia Daily Report EAS-95-233, 86–89.

103 Most information used in this case study was derived from a series of roundtable discussions conducted with members of the Civil Code drafting committee in March and September 1999 and August and September 2000.

104 Interviews Bui Thi Mai Lan, Civil Law Department, Ministry of Justice, Hanoi, March, April 1999; Tran Huyen Nga, Civil Law Department, Ministry of Justice, March 1999.

105 Interviews Muto Shiro, JICA Legal Advocate to the Ministry of Justice, Hanoi, February 1998. See Phan Huu Chi (1994), 'Explanation on the Civil Code Sixth Draft', (unpublished Paper), Hanoi, 14.

formula that 'benefits are the natural products of property', whereas 'income is the gain derived from the exploitation of property'.[106]

The public law emphasis in Soviet legal education failed to acquaint senior drafters with the institutional structures and jurisprudential doctrines needed to comprehend and accept future property rights. Senior drafters were more familiar with public law principles that made the state an active commercial player. They used Russian to discuss complex technical considerations and felt politically secure in borrowing from the Soviet Civil Code. Future property rights were suspect, since they carried the risk of conveying an advantage to foreign investors and bankers.

The principal drafters also selected foreign ideas for their perceived cultural compatibility. They borrowed provisions from the Chinese Civil Code to give the heads of households legal status, in the belief that Chinese morals and family practices were analogous to conditions in contemporary Vietnam.[107] For similar reasons, they recycled some pre-modern Vietnamese practices such as '*bao lanh bang tin chap*' (preserving prestige or reputation) and leases for '*thue khoan*' (aggregate) assets.[108] Many provisions governing private contracts, property rights and civil obligations were taken from the French Colonial Code de Annamite 1922 and Republic of Vietnam Civil Code on the understanding that these notions had become localised.[109] Other provisions were borrowed from the French and Japanese Civil Codes. Informants estimate, however, that approximately 70 per cent of the articles in the Civil Code were derived directly or indirectly (via Vietnamese re-enactments) from the Soviet Civil Code.

Finally, education played a significant role in shaping legal borrowing. It not only conveyed interpretive skills that facilitated legal borrowing, it also inculcated proclivities and biases that made some legal traditions appear more prestigious than others. Even so, legal education only seemed to operate in circumstances where political instructions gave drafters the latitude to select laws from a diverse range of sources. The important role foreign donors play in promoting particular legal educations, ideas and practices is explored in more depth in Chapter 7.

This case study also confirms earlier findings that drafters may contemplate the cultural relevance of foreign laws, but lack the methodological tools to assess whether legal imports are compatible with local conditions.

---

106 See Civil Code, article 182.

107 See Civil Code, articles 116–119.

108 Article 614 of the Civil Code creates a civil right to protect *bao lanh bang tin chap*. This is a neo-Confucian moral concept that conveys rights that go well beyond the English notions of 'honour, dignity and reputation'. Articles 503–514 regulate *thue khoan* assets, which are collections or aggregations of different types of property bundled into common lease agreements. There is no equivalent Western concept.

109 For example, provisions dealing with civil obligations were borrowed from the Republic of Vietnam Civil Code 1972 and provisions governing mortgages, pledges and suretyship were adopted from the Code de Annamite 1922.

Summary

The case studies show the importance of political, moral and economic concepts in shaping the selection and adaptation of foreign laws. As international legal harmonisation gained momentum, drafters placed less emphasis on 'state economic management' and moved towards (without fully embracing) a facilitative approach to economic regulation. Case studies suggest that, although lawmakers are still constrained by party-sponsored discourse, the range of views permitted is rapidly expanding.

Given the dominant instrumental view of law, it is unsurprising that most drafters treated legal discourse as the handmaiden of political, moral and economic considerations. A fragmented legal grammar and contested legal meanings, themselves symptoms of law's subordination, also impeded legal conversations. There is a growing awareness among some lawmakers, however, that neoliberal economic reforms require a procedural 'rule of law'. The sociological notion that imported laws should correspond to domestic political, economic and social conditions is also slowly entering the lawmaking calculus.

The case studies further demonstrate there is more to legal borrowing than discursive ideas and meanings. The Enterprise Law drafting project showed that alliances between domestic entrepreneurs and institutions such as CIEM and VCCI legitimised deregulatory arguments. Strong ministries (such as Science and Technology, and Trade) used their powers to exclude or discredit arguments from rival government agencies. Less powerful institutions, like the Supreme Court, required party intervention to prevail. The strategic use of power mediates the 'official' discourse according to institutional imperatives.

These findings suggest that drafting agencies draw on ideas from the 'official' discourse to select and adapt foreign law. They further demonstrate that the meanings given to imported laws partially reflect the strategic objectives of the dominant drafting agencies. Yet, despite their close nexus, the discursive meaning of law is not entirely subordinate to state power and institutional objectives, each works on the other.[110]

In addition, the case studies intimate that imported ideas acquire different meanings within different 'interpretive communities'. For example, CIEM drafters used empirical research, informed by neoliberal economic views, to wear down political resistance to market-entry deregulation. Similarly, different sub-committees drafting the Civil Code reached entirely different conclusions about the suitability and utility of borrowed laws according to their respective educational backgrounds and interpretive positions. Chapter 7 explores in more depth the notion that laws transfer more readily among members of 'interpretive communities'.

110 This study contests the arguments of some post-Marxists and Foucauldians that there is no distinction between discourse and power relations in a social context.

Lawmaking Discourse in the National Assembly

Once completed, draft laws are submitted to the National Assembly for approval. National Assembly deliberations provide another opportunity for official discourses to influence the selection and adaptation of foreign laws. Much depends, however, on the discursive space available to delegates to examine, debate and change draft laws.

There is some evidence that delegates are increasingly behaving more like legislators. Debates in the National Assembly have forced amendments to some draft bills (for example, Press, Labour and Land Laws),[111] deliberations have increased in length, there are more full-time delegates, and the budget and economics committee has acquired more oversight powers.[112]

Discourse analysis provides a nuanced way to understand how National Assembly delegates draw on ideas to deliberate and naturalise imported legal provisions.

Decision-making Procedures in the National Assembly

Before National Assembly delegates are given an opportunity to discuss draft legislation, three policy filters focus their deliberations. First, as noted above, government drafting agencies privilege their own interests in draft bills and explanatory memoranda. If the Standing Committee, which has constitutional powers to guide the passage of bills through the National Assembly, agrees with drafting agencies, the range of issues presented for deliberation is highly circumscribed. The Standing Committee is nominated by, and ultimately acts as, the agent of the Politburo in the National Assembly.[113]

Second, the National Assembly Law Committee, in association with other National Assembly bodies, decides which bills to send to National Assembly delegates for deliberation and which bills to refer to the Standing Committee for promulgation as ordinances. The Law Committee uses this power to refer politically sensitive issues to the Standing Committee for resolution, before, sometimes years later, they are given to National Assembly delegates to enact into law (*luat*).[114] For specifics, legislation governing economic contracts, minerals, technology transfers, labour contracts and banking were first issued by the Standing Committee as ordinances.

---

111 See, for example, VNS (2003), 'Draft Land Law Leads to Lively NA Debates', *Vietnamnews-online*, 4 June, <www.vietnamnews.vnagency.com.vn>.

112 The Press Law was amended 27 times. See Russell Heng Hiang Khng (1993), 'Leadership in Vietnam: Pressure for Reform and Their Limits', 15 *Contemporary Southeast Asia* (1), 102.

113 See generally Lam Nguyen (2002), 'Procedures-Observations from a National Assembly Session', *Legislative Studies Journal* (8), 12, 12–13.

114 Speech Nguyen Chi Dung, editor of *Tap Chi Nghien Cuu Lap Phap* (Legislative Studies), at the 'Law and Governance: Socialist Transforming Vietnam Conference', Deakin University and Melbourne University, Melbourne, 12–13 June 2003.

Third, the Legislative Activities Board (LAB) (*Ban Cong Tac Lap Phap*), established in 2003, scrutinises draft bills before they are presented to National Assembly delegates. It decides which legislative issues are 'technical' (*ky thuat*) and require further clarification by professional drafters, and which issues concern policy and should be resolved by delegates.

Mediating National Assembly Discourse

The Law on the Promulgation of Legal Documents 2002 divides the deliberation of bills into two National Assembly sessions (article 45b). During the first plenary (*hoi truong*) session, delegates consider the main policy issues, as determined by the Standing Committee and LAB. The chairman of the National Assembly may refer complex matters to smaller group (*thao luan o to*) sessions for consideration. The secretariat of each session summarises the delegates' opinions, and bills are then amended by the drafting committee to reflect these concerns. But the Standing Committee ultimately decides which opinions should be codified into law. For example, the Standing Committee rejected concerns expressed by many delegates deliberating the Land Law in November 2003 that the expression 'land is owned by the people but managed by the state' should be replaced by the more accurate designation the 'state owns the land'.[115] Overruling objections raised by many delegates, it also accepted the drafting committee's recommendation that, for the purposes of taxation and compensation, land should be valued close to market rates.

At the second plenary session, the Standing Committee reports whether revised bills have incorporated opinions raised during the first session. Delegates then vote by simple majority to pass bills into law. Even controversial bills like the BTA (64 per cent) and the Land Law 2003 (85 per cent) were passed by large majorities.

The protocols governing National Assembly deliberations are based on unwritten rules originally derived from the Soviet Presidium. They have changed over several decades to reflect consensus-generating practices and power structures designed to induce policy conformity. According to informants, attempts to codify these rules have failed, because informal and flexible procedures facilitate centralised leadership over deliberations.

The National Assembly chairman opens sessions by restating deliberative parameters established by the Standing Committee. Consider the opening address delivered by the Chairman, Nguyen Van An, to the National Assembly session discussing constitutional amendments in November 2001. After summarising institutional reforms proposed by the Constitutional Drafting Committee (*Uy Ban Soan Thao Hien Phap*), he instructed delegates to confine discussions to increasing

115 See VNS (2003), 'NA Passes Much-Awaited Amendments to Land Law', *Vietnam News Agency*, 8 November, <www.vietnamnews.vnagency.com.vn>.

inferior courts' powers and reducing procuratorial investigation powers.[116] He expressly ruled out broader changes to clarify the relationship between party and state and National Assembly supervision of other state organs.

The chairman also imposed deliberative constraints during the National Assembly session considering the draft Law on the Promulgation of Legal Documents in December 2002. He informed delegates that the party Central Committee required certain amendments to improve legislative 'results (*hieu qua*) so as to increase the productivity of the NA'.[117]

Delegates wishing to speak at plenary sessions must give the chairman a written summary before sessions commence. The chairman also mediates policy debates by prearranging the order in which delegates speak and limiting speaking time for those presenting unwelcome opinions. For example, less than half of the 32 delegates registered to discuss important amendments to the Land Law in 2003 were given time to speak.[118] Only 20–30 of almost 500 delegates address the twice-yearly National Assembly sessions. Fewer than 10 speakers, mainly from National Assembly committees (especially the Standing Committee), dominate most sessions.

Well-known delegates command enough popular prestige to enter debates without waiting for approval. During the April 2002 National Assembly sessions, Professor Nguyen Lan Dung, a prominent intellectual, questioned the prime minister on the government's failure to enforce a decree requiring state officials to declare their assets. The National Assembly chairman quickly moved to protect the prime minister by referring the questions to the next plenary session. When the delegates voted against this proposal, the prime minister informed the session that the matter was politically sensitive and under review by the Politburo. This intervention signalled an end to further discussion.

Procedures designed to limit individual discourse in plenary sessions are not as rigorously enforced during smaller group (*thao luan o to*) sessions.[119] Senior party and state members leading 'party affairs sections' (*ban can su dang*), nevertheless, promote the party's viewpoint during these sessions.[120] Group reports about draft laws are compiled by the session secretary into 'forms for requesting delegates' opinions' (*phieu xin y kien dai bieu*).

116 See Author Unknown (2001), 'Quoc Hoi Nghe To Trinh Ve Viec Sua Doi Bo Sung Mot So Dieu Cua Hien Phap Nam 1992 va Mot So Thuyet Trinh Bao Cao Bao', *Nhan Dan*, 21 November, 3.

117 See Ministry of Justice (2002), 'Program on Reforms of Drafting, Promulgating and Enhancing the Quality of Legal Normative Documents', Ministry of Justice, Hanoi, 1.

118 See VNS (2003), 'NA Passes Much Awaited Amendments to the Land Law', *Vietnam News Agency*, 8 November, <www.vietnamnews.vnagency.com.vn>.

119 See Legis (2001), 'The National Assembly in a Nutshell', *Tap Chi Nghien Cuu Lap Phap*, English edition, (1), 60.

120 See Tran Ngoc Duong (2005), 'Noi Dung va Phuong Thuc Lanh Dao Cua Dang Doi Voi Quoc Hoi O Nuoc Ta Hien Nay' (Leadership of the Communist Party Over the National Assembly in Vietnam – Content and Method), *Tap Chi Nghien Cuu Lap Phap* (2), 17–23.

Party leaders quickly and publicly rebuke delegates who express views outside parameters sanctioned by the Politburo. On the rare occasions when significant numbers of National Assembly delegates disagree with central party policy, the Standing Committee holds an 'internal party vote' (*dang doan quoc noi*) to resolve differences. If agreement is not reached, the Politburo makes a determination, which is then communicated to the National Assembly plenary session. The Politburo infrequently exercises its extra-constitutional prerogative to amend legislation already passed by the National Assembly. This informal process is euphemistically referred to as *hoan thieu* (perfecting) legislation.

Constitutional Discourse

Lawmaking deliberations in the National Assembly are not solely controlled with procedures. Party-mediated discourse lacks the 'rules of the game' or 'secondary coding' that enables legislators in constitutionally mature societies to transform political, economic and moral concepts into statutory language.[121] These 'codes' are contained in formal constitutional doctrines and informal, but still binding, conventions derived from parliamentary and judicial sources. Constitutional texts establish the broad rules governing power-sharing among state agencies and between state and society. Informal constitutional rules and precedents guide legislators in selecting and rejecting legal, economic, political and moral concepts for codification into law. The process of commercial codification, which condenses a large number of particular cases into general principles governing business transactions, is achieved at the expense of relational nuance and richness. Without generally agreed 'rules of the game', legislators struggle to agree on which commercial networks and interpersonal relationships are worth preserving and which should be rejected. Western constitutional rules provide 'ground rules' that enable legislators to agree about the criteria for selecting and adapting commercial laws.[122]

The Vietnamese Constitution does not perform this function. Vietnamese constitutions have changed over time to announce and legitimise party policy (see Chapter 2). Current constitutional settings were developed to organise political power during the early stages of market reforms in the late 1980s. Subsequent amendments have adjusted power-sharing arrangements among state organs to reflect the gathering momentum of the mixed-market economy.

Constitutional reform debates suggest the 1992 Constitution has not yet acquired an independent (from the party) and determining legal role. Analysing articles in *Tap Chi Cong San* (Communist Review), Mark Sidel showed that contests over state

121 Louis Fisher (1988), *Constitutional Dialogues: Interpretation as Political Process*, Princeton University Press, Princeton, 11.

122 See Hugh Baxter (1998), 'Autopoiesis and the "Relative Autonomy" of Law', 19 *Cardozo Law Review*, 1987, 2041–44.

power-sharing arrangements used political and constitutional language.[123] One group argued that the Constitution operates as a political text for realising party policy. It legitimises and formalises power-sharing arrangements decided by party organs, but it does not function as a legal text that guides delegates in codifying political, economic and moral arguments.[124] Put differently, the Constitution's meaning is strictly confined to the text. Party leaders insist that constitutional debates take place within a predetermined political context that restricts interaction with public discourses.[125] Despite these strictures, some discussion about politically sensitive issues is permitted under the constitutional 'umbrella'.

A small group (consisting mainly of academic lawyers) advocate radical constitutional change. They argue that the Constitution should evolve beyond its instrumental role and provide legally enforceable standards controlling the exercise of political and state power.[126] For this to happen, they believe that constitutional rules should include not only the Constitution and state laws, but also encompass judgements from a constitutional court, constitutional customs and even natural law (*luat tu nhien*) principles.[127] In advocating unwritten legal conventions that the state is powerless to change, reformers recognise that effective 'rules of the game' must reflect the actual ways delegates negotiate power, not just the structures imposed by the party in legal texts.

There are a few tentative signs discussed in Chapter 7 that the party is prepared to loosen its monopoly over legal codification and devolve more lawmaking power to the National Assembly. Meanwhile, delegates lack the constitutional 'ground rules' to agree among themselves which business networks and interpersonal relationships to privilege with codification and which ones to reject.

---

123 See Mark Sidel (2002), 'Analytical Models for Understanding Constitutions and Constitutional Dialogue in Socialist Transitional States: Re-Interpreting Constitutional Dialogue in Vietnam', 6 *Singapore Journal of International and Comparative Law*, 42.

124 Constitutions should conform to 'realities of life'. Dao Tri Uc (2001), 'Ve Nhu Cau, Muc Do Sua Doi Hien Phap Nam 1992 va Quan Diem Xay Dung Nha Nuoc Phap Quyen' (The Needs, the Scope of Revising the 1992 Constitution and the Concept of Law-Based State), *Tap Chi Cong San* (10), 21–29.

125 See Dao Tri Uc (2001), 'Mot So Quan Diem Co Ban Ve Sua Doi Bo Sung Mot So Dieu Cua Hien Phap 1992' (Key Points of View on Amendment, Addition to the 1992 Constitution), *Nha Nuoc va Phap Luat* (9), 6, 6–10.

126 See Ngo Huy Cuong (2001), 'Luat Hien Phap va Van Hoa Chinh Tri' (Constitutional Law and Political Culture) *Tap Chi Nghien Cuu Lap Phap* (1), 29, 30–34.

127 See Le Cam (2002), 'Cai Cach He Thong Toa An Trong Giai Doan Xay Dung Nha Nuoc Phap Quyen Viet Nam' (Reform the Court System to Build Up a Law Based State in Vietnam), *Tap Chi Nghien Cuu Lap Phap* (4), 21, 27; Nguyen Manh Cuong (2002), 'Yeu Cau Cua Viec Xay Dung Nha Nuoc Phap Quyen Doi Voi Doi Moi To Chuc va Hoat Dong Cua Cac Co Quan Tu Phap' (How to Reform Judicial Authorities to Build up a Law-Based-State), *Tap Chi Nghien Cuu Lap Phap* (10), 30, 35.

Legislative Discourse

Working within the party-sponsored epistemological framework, it is unsurprising that delegates devote hours of debate to politically safe technical issues such as the meaning of words used in draft provisions. Occasionally, however, debates erupt in National Assembly sessions when issue-oriented coalitions invoke (usually without success) political rhetoric to block imported laws. For example, 36 per cent of delegates voted unsuccessfully to oppose the ratification of the BTA. Equally large minorities could not stop the Enterprise Law from stripping away local discretionary powers and introducing overly complex corporate governance provisions.[128]

In some cases, minority votes have successfully blocked imported legislative provisions. Take for example amendments in 2002 to the Law on the Promulgation of Normative Documents. Ministry of Justice drafters imported the 'incorporation doctrine' into the bill, making treaties ratified by heads of state automatically binding in domestic law. The bill submitted to the National Assembly stated 'it is necessary to ensure that issued legal normative documents accord with relevant international treaties to which the Socialist Republic of Vietnam is a signatory or party to the extent of its undertakings'.[129]

Some delegates were concerned the 'incorporation doctrine could compromise national sovereignty'.[130] Rather than addressing the legal arguments presented by Ministry of Justice drafters that civil law countries observe the doctrine, they recited passages from the constitutional preamble about Vietnam's independence struggle, aiming to excite nationalistic sentiment against the 'doctrine'. Soviet international law principles used in Vietnam provided little guidance because they assess the supremacy of international law on a case-by-case basis according to the 'economic, sociopolitical development and interests of the nation'.

Once the issue was conceived as a matter of national sovereignty, it was difficult to persuade delegates to think about treaty obligations in a legal way as binding international agreement. In political mode, delegates understood the treaty 'incorporation' doctrine as a way for foreigners to increase their power in Vietnam. Without constitutional 'secondary codes' or precedents to guide them, delegates could not easily convert political arguments about power contests into legal rules that provided orderly ways to resolve conflicts between international and domestic law.

---

128 See VNS (2001), 'Constitutional Debate Heats Up', *Vietnam News Agency*, 21 September 2001, <www.vietnamnews.vnagency.com.vn/2001-09-20/Stories/01.htm>.

129 The new article 1(2)(a) appeared in the draft Law on Amending and Adding to Certain Articles of the 1996 Law on Issuing Legal Normative Documents, dated 30 November 2002. This provision was inserted to comply with provisions in the BTA.

130 See Dinh Ngoc Vuong (2001), 'Van De Sua Doi Bo Sung Quy Dinh Cua Hien Phap 1992 Ve Ky Ket Quyet Dinh Viec Phe Chuan Gia Nhap Bai Bo Dieu Uoc Quoc Te' (Problem of Amending and Adding Stipulations to the 1992 Constitution on Signing, and Deciding to Ratify and Abrogate International Treaties), *Nha Nuoc va Phap Luat* (9), 43, 44–47.

More recently, NA delegates deliberating the Commercial Law in 2005 successfully weakened imported rules that sought to open services provided by SOEs to foreign competition. Again their argument relied on political and moral issues of sovereignty and economic self-reliance. Without constitutional 'secondary codes', delegates could not agree on how to codify domestic concerns into the law.

In the cases considered, delegates occasionally surprised party leaders by using political and moral arguments circulating in the 'official' discourse to challenge imported law. But lawmaking deliberations lacked the sustained and relatively unmediated discourse required for preference convergence. As a consequence, lawmaking rarely progresses from blocking imported rules to proposing amendments that adapt imports to underlying social practices. Discursive problems are exacerbated by a general lack of practical experience in debating and formulating legal policy as well as an onerous legislative workload. By default, most decisions taken to naturalise legal imports take place (if at all) in government drafting committees. We will consider the transformative potential for the National Assembly to behave more like a legislature in Chapter 7.

Conclusions

This chapter commenced by posing the question: what factors make some foreign legal ideas appear more appropriate than others? Three interrelated factors, deduced from the case studies, influence the way legislative drafters select and adapt borrowed law.

In the first place, the epistemological settings guiding the 'official' discourse have expanded and now permit drafters to borrow laws from a diverse range of sources. Care should be taken not to overstate the importance of socialist ideas—Vietnam in the 21st century is different from that in the 1950s, or 1970s, or even the 1990s. Yet each case study showed that, although international legal harmonisation has eroded many political objections to capitalist laws, core socialist ideas still strongly orientate lawmaking discourse. The studies also showed that drafters are not indifferent to incompatibilities between legal imports and local conditions. Rather, localisation is hindered by a general reluctance to research issues that may implicitly contradict party directives and socialist tenets, compounded by inadequate comparative methodologies and a poor understanding of how laws function in donor countries.

To make matter worse, most drafters take an instrumental approach to lawmaking that de-couples imported laws from their social contexts. From this reified perspective, legal borrowing appears as uncomplicated as making a series of technical adjustments between legal systems. The distancing of law from reality does not in itself produce poor laws, since laws everywhere function as highly edited maps of reality. Lawmakers produce poor laws because they are reluctant or unable to imagine innovative adaptations of borrowed laws that create new legal solutions for Vietnam's commercial problems. Lawmakers drafting the Enterprise Law imaginatively borrowed deregulatory ideas to open markets to private entrepreneurs, but they missed an opportunity to refashion imported corporate governance provisions to provide solutions to organisational problems emerging in family-based enterprises (see Chapter 8).

The second factor influencing legal borrowing is the tactical use of ideas in the official discourse to achieve strategic objectives. Powerful state agencies use drafting committees to encode and inculcate certain perspectives or orthodoxies in legislation to secure advantage in 'palace wars' with other agencies. Perceptions of legal prestige and fashion, instilled through education and workplace relations, also predispose drafters toward certain legal sources and styles.

All this indicates there is a powerful domestic political and organisational logic to legal borrowing. However, in an important finding, the case studies suggest that, in pursing their institutional interests, Vietnamese drafters generally use ideas that conform to the epistemological settings that order 'official' discourse. For example, CIEM drafters could not have used neoliberal economic ideas to wear down 'state economic management' arguments, unless 'official' epistemological conventions permitted such thinking. Legal drafters cannot simply assert raw political power; they must play by the 'rules of the game' and camouflage self-interest with ideas drawn from the official discourse. CIEM drafters succeeded because they worked assiduously over several years to inveigle neoliberal legal ideas into the official discourse. In brief, although institutional imperatives shape legal borrowing, they are largely conceived and realised within the range of ideas permitted by the 'official discourse'.

The third factor shaping legal borrowing is the lack of a shared legal grammar. Chinese-Vietnamese terms eventually acquired new and commonly agreed meanings because Vietnamese lawmakers trained in the Eastern bloc invested them with Soviet legal consequences. The case studies show that a new meta-legal language is yet to emerge among contemporary legal drafters. Instead, legal drafters use a syncretic mixture of pre-modern, Soviet, East Asian and Western ideas that endow imported laws with fragmented meanings. This conceptual variation undermines the certainty and transparency necessary for a procedural 'rule of law'.

Movement towards shared legal understandings is discernable in the groups or communities of like-minded lawmakers that are coalescing around certain key institutions. For example, some researchers at CIEM share common epistemological assumptions, tacit understandings and even educational backgrounds with certain foreign donors, domestic lawyers and consultants. The possibility that 'interpretive communities' linking drafters and foreign donors are promoting a 'rule of law' is considered in Chapter 7.

The first and second factors considered above also apply to lawmaking in the National Assembly. Further research is required to ascertain whether 'interpretive communities' are forming in the National Assembly, but the case studies suggest two additional factors influence legal borrowing in the Assembly. First, delegates lack the constitutional 'ground rules' to agree among themselves how to localise imported legal ideas. Instead, they use political, economic and moral discourse to oppose particular imported laws. This discourse engages with the policy behind the law, but lacks the legal precision required to imaginatively reconfigure imported legal ideas to solve local problems. The fine-tuning that localises legal imports primarily takes place in the administrative and judicial processes discussed in the next chapter.

Second, the party uses procedural rules to mediate National Assembly discussions. These processes limit the interaction between imported ideas and 'official' discourse, further constraining the opportunities for preference convergence and innovative adaptations of borrowed laws.

Taken together, the case studies imply that the epistemological criteria guiding official discourse establish the ground rules governing legal borrowing. Within these broad parameters, lawmakers pursue institutional and personal objectives and converse in a disjunctive legal discourse that produces fragmented legal meanings. But under the impact of international legal harmonisation, external ideas—including a procedural 'rule of law'—are increasingly taken as the frame of reference for change. The following chapter explores how bureaucrats and judges change the meanings that drafters and legislators invest in borrowed commercial laws.

Chapter 6

Implementing Imported Laws

Introduction

The preceding chapters have shown that Western rights-based laws are imported into Vietnam with few concessions to the needs and aspirations of domestic entrepreneurs. This chapter investigates how 'official' and 'unofficial' discourses influence the way state institutions interpret and apply borrowed commercial rights. This investigation subsumes a number of more specific inquiries, which are considered sequentially in this chapter. The first inquiry assesses how Vietnamese regulators use discretionary powers to manage (*quan ly*) imported rights-based laws. The second investigation examines how tensions between central and local discourses allow officials to overcome rigidities in imported legal rights and flexibly respond to local business norms and practices. The third inquiry unravels the meaning of judicial independence and determines whether judges are sufficiently autonomous from external influences to develop a 'rule of law' discourse that supports imported commercial rights. The chapter concludes that different interpretive structures and conflicting strategic agendas fragment the implementation of imported laws.

Western Commercial Regulation

In order to grasp how Vietnamese regulators may change the meaning of imported laws, it is necessary first to understand the regulatory environment shaping Western commercial law. Most commentators trace the genesis of property and contractual rights to the codification of mercantile practices in nineteenth-century Europe.[1] Codification aimed to condense vast amounts of information governing transactions into discretionary criteria that regulators could process. It achieved this objective by only officially recognising certain types of commercial rights and obligations.[2] By the second half of the nineteenth century the process had reified to the stage where legal discourse used internal doctrinal rules to distinguish legally recognised

1 See R.J. Ross (1998), 'The Commoning of the Common Law: The Renaissance Debate over Printing English Law, 1520–1640', 146 *University of Pennsylvania Law Review*, 323.

2 See generally Max H. Boisot (1995), *Information Space: A Framework for Learning in Organisations, Institutions and Culture*, Routledge, London.

and unrecognised commercial transactions. Mature commercial rights emerged when most Western countries moved from comprehensive discretionary regulation towards normative rights-based regulation.[3] As Weber observed, this transformation involved a shift from regulatory particularism to facilitative regulation based on universal legal rights.

According to Weber, stable commercial rights required regulatory systems in which bureaucrats based their determinations on written rules and organisational practices. This decision-making calculus assumed perfect information, high degrees of trust and communication and stable property rights. Scientific managers from the 1930s argued that correct decisions required clear legal rules to circumscribe bureaucratic discretion and minimise government interference with private commercial rights and freedoms.[4] Even so, Western regulators to greater or lesser degrees still intervened to correct 'market failures'.

'Public-choice' theories developed in the United States during the 1960s devised behavioural models that equated bureaucratic decision-making with entrepreneurial wealth maximisation.[5] They conceded that in real life situations officials work in a 'bounded rationality' where some decisions were not based on rules. Deviations from central rules are caused, they thought, by unstable policy settings, organisational pressures, and incomplete or misunderstood information.[6] To remedy the problem, administrative reforms sought to quarantine bureaucrats not only from political patronage, familial and societal influences, but also from the market place. This prescription for deregulating bureaucratic controls fitted comfortably with neoliberal economic attempts to minimise state interference in the market place.

As we saw in Chapter 4, public choice deregulatory ideas profoundly influenced Public Administrative Reforms (PAR) adopted in Vietnam during the mid 1990s. More recently, both the US–Vietnam Bilateral Trade Agreement (BTA) and WTO presuppose a facilitative regulatory regime that follows a public choice blueprint. For example, they envisage politically neutral state institutions that implement treaty-based norms and a 'rule of law' that enables entrepreneurs to use private legal rights to shape their transactional environment.[7] Regulators are only supposed to

3 This transformation is by no means complete. After decades of neo-classical economic deregulation, administrative rules are still the primary economic regulator in the United States, and especially in Continental Europe. See E. Rubin (1989), 'Law and Legislation in the Administrative State', 89 *Columbia Law Review*, 369.

4 See generally Dennis Mueller (1989), *Public Choice II*, Cambridge University Press, Cambridge.

5 See D.A. Farber and P.P. Frickey (1991), *Law and Public Choice: A Critical Introduction*, University of Chicago Press, Chicago, 5–10; Jonathan R. Macey (1988), 'Public Choice: The Theory of the Firm and the Theory of Market Exchange', 74 *Cornell Law Review* 45, 46–52.

6 See H.A. Simon (1976), *Administrative Behavior*, Free Press, New York.

7 See, for example, Mark Manyin (2001), 'The Vietnam-US Bilateral Trade Agreement, CRS Report for Congress'; available online at <www.ustc.org/BTA/CRS%20Vietnam %20BTA.21jun01.pdf>.

intervene in market decisions when applying uniform legal principles that apply to everyone.

The following section examines 'official' and 'unofficial' Vietnamese narratives to better understand why imported commercial laws seldom perform the neoliberal legal function of preserving private property and contractual rights. In the process it reflects on why imported deregulatory reforms are struggling to reconfigure Vietnamese institutions.

Changing the Meaning of Imported Law with 'State Economic Management'

Mapping the Vietnamese Discretionary Legal Framework

Prior to *doi moi* reforms in 1986, most economic production was generated by state and collectively owned entities.[8] Following Soviet central-planning, production contracts conformed to planning orders issued by line-ministries and people's committees, only technical decisions such as packaging and delivery were devolved to production managers.[9] By 1989, central-planning mechanisms had been effectively dismantled and the state began enacting laws that formally devolved decision-making powers to state-owned enterprises (SOEs) and then eventually to private households and entrepreneurs.[10] But reforms did not fundamentally disturb the longstanding belief in the principle of 'state economic management' (*quan ly kinh te nha nuoc*) discussed in earlier chapters.

The introduction of the mixed-market economy created a dilemma for central regulators. They could no longer simply suppress private markets, but they thought imported rights-based law gave market players too much discretionary control over resource allocation. Regulators needed a rights-based legal framework that attracted foreign investors, conformed to international trade agreements, but in addition conveyed discretionary powers that enabled government officials to 'manage' (*quan ly*) the economy.

Commercial regulation everywhere uses state discretionary power to control and guide private legal rights. This study argues that 'state economic management' powers in Vietnam achieve this objective in ways rarely experienced in Western 'rule of law' societies. Lawmakers have created a regulatory system that is far removed from the facilitative rights-based system contemplated by neoliberal deregulatory reforms and international trade treaties. This observation brings us to a central inquiry in this

8 See *Cong Tac Ke Hoach* (1976), 'Carrying Out Good National Economic Planning and Summarizing National Economic Planning Well', *Cong Tac Ke Hoach*, 9 April, 9–11, JPRS 67923.

9 See Wladimir Andreff, 1993 'The Double Transition from Underdevelopment and from Socialism in Vietnam', 23 *Journal of Contemporary Asia* (4), 515–31.

10 See generally Adam Fforde and Stefan de Vylder (1996) *From Plan to Market: The Economic transition in Vietnam*, Westview Press, Boulder, 30–32; Brian Van Arkadie and Raymond Mallon (2003), *Viet Nam: A Transition Tiger?*, Asia Pacific Press, Canberra.

chapter: how do Vietnamese regulatory practices change the meaning of imported commercial rights? Regulators use four mechanisms to 'manage' imported legal rights.

- *Subordinate legislation.* As we saw in Chapter 5, most commercial laws passed by the National Assembly lack normative detail. Open-ended drafting techniques used to strip laws of controversial detail in National Assembly debates devolve responsibility for formulating much commercial policy to government agencies.[11] Inferior legislation coexists with, and frequently contradicts, superior laws in a complicated network of overlapping and criss-crossing similarities and differences. This regulatory confusion gives government agencies wide latitude to use subordinate rules to influence the meaning and utility of private legal rights.
- *Discretionary licensing.* Government agencies at the central level, but especially at the local level, use discretionary licences and permits to circumscribe the permitted range of business transactions and to control the use property rights.
- *Official inspections.* Local-level state agencies use inspections not only to monitor legal compliance, but also as a method of 'state economic management'.
- *Criminalising private rights.* Administrative and criminal laws give officials powers to transform commercial transactions into administrative or criminal infractions.

Before exploring these regulatory techniques, which officials use to 'manage' private rights, it is instructive briefly to consider the mentality guiding the interpretation of private legal rights.

The Mentality of State Economic Management

There is a well-documented disdain among state officials (especially at the local level) towards entrepreneurs that goes back to pre-modern Vietnam.[12] Encapsulated by the Confucian saying, 'emphasise agriculture, commerce is peripheral' (*trong nong mat thuong*), imperial policy prohibited large-scale commercial organisations independent of royal patronage.[13] After independence, Confucian anti-mercantilism

---

11 See Ngo Duc Manh (2003), 'Legislative Work for Implementation of Vietnam-US Bilateral Trade Agreement', 10 *Vietnam Law and Legal Forum* (110), 21–22.

12 See Pham Duy Nghia (2005), 'Confucianism and the Conception of the Law in Vietnam' in John Gillespie and Pip Nicholson (eds), *Asian Socialisms and Legal Change: The Dynamics of Vietnamese and Chinese Reforms*, Asia-Pacific Press, Canberra, 76–88.

13 See generally Nguyen Thua Hy (2002), *Economic History of Hanoi in the 17th, 18th and 19th Centuries*, National Political Publishing House, Hanoi, 221–70.

fused with Soviet regulatory practices and class theory to reshape bureaucratic thinking profoundly.

Economic production in the command economy resided in dual, but interwoven, systems. One system operated as a facsimile of Soviet central-planning.[14] Line-ministries and people's committees regulated production through administrative directives that allocated raw materials according to quantitative planning targets. The other economic system produced spontaneous markets that coexisted with, and infiltrated, state distribution networks. Commercial incentives for unauthorised private production and distribution were extremely potent. Officials estimate that by 1986 less than 40 per cent of manufactured consumer goods passed through state-trade networks.[15]

Economic duality deeply influenced bureaucratic perceptions of socialist regulation. Class-based morality tolerated small-scale household producers, but demonised large-scale private producers, imbuing bureaucrats with an antipathy to private traders and respect for the state economic sector.[16] The state also used incentives—like housing and consumer goods—to reward loyalty to class ideology. Yet at the same time bureaucrats were encouraged to believe that socialist ideology expressed reality, they lived in a world where family and friends profited from private markets. The ensuing ideological ambivalence and cynicism were exacerbated by *doi moi* reforms that required the guardian of socialism (the state) to defend—even create—markets.

In the command economy, bureaucrats used concessionary licences and permits based on state plans to control business activities tightly. After *doi moi*, the state began importing rights-based laws that purported to give entrepreneurs broad commercial freedom to conduct business transactions. In practice, however, the internal architecture of most commercial legislation reflected the tension in the 'official' discourse between private rights and proactive concessionary regulation. As we saw in Chapter 5, lawmakers reconciled these competing objectives by grafting 'state economic management' discretionary powers onto imported rights-based laws. The following section uses a series of case studies to ascertain how regulatory authorities use 'state economic management' powers to guide imported legal commercial rights.

---

14 For a comprehensive description of this system see Dang Phong and Melanie Beresford (1998), *Authority Relations and Economic Decision-Making in Vietnam: An Historical Perspective*, NIAS Publications, Copenhagen, 58–71.

15 Vo Van Kiet (1986), 'Report to the National Assembly on the 1987 Socio-Economic Development Plan', Hanoi Domestic Service, 26 December, trans. FBIS Asia and Pacific Daily Report, 30 December, 9.

16 See Pham Duy Nghia (2005) *supra*; Dang Phong (1999), 'The Private Sector: In Vietnamese Industry from 1945 to the Present', in *Vietnam's Undersized Engine: A Survey of 95 Larger Private Manufacturers*, MPDF Discussion Paper No. 9, Mekong Project Development Facility, Hanoi, 78–80.

State Economic Management and Subordinate Legislation

The Law on the Promulgation of Legal Documents 2002 explains that National Assembly legislation determines basic social issues, while the government issues subordinate legislation to implement and concretise superior law. The astoundingly high level of inconsistency between higher and lower-level legislation presents a significant challenge to the introduction of a procedural 'rule of law'.[17]

In some cases government authorities delay the enactment of implementing regulations that direct officials to follow superior laws. This practice persists even though there is no legal impediment to making superior laws self-executing. For example, it took eight years after the Civil Code 1995 took effect before state agencies passed implementing rules that gave citizens rights to enforce 'civil obligations' (tortious actions) for non-contractual loss.[18] Citizens aggrieved by trespass to land and damage caused by pollution still rely on sympathetic state authorities to remedy violations. This reluctance to activate civil rights with implementing legislation is attributed to concerns among some party leaders that state officials are better equipped to solve social problems then courts.

Adding to the regulatory confusion, some subordinate rules alter the meaning of National Assembly legislation. As one commentator put it, 'the main legal documents are the raw materials used to produce a series of subsequent regulations, but the guiding regulations have "covered" all these decisions and "replaced" the role of the main documents.'[19] For example, the General Department of Land Management (now part of the Ministry of Natural Resources and Environment) issued a circular in 2000 that permitted SOEs to mortgage land. This contravened the Civil Code, which provides that mortgages should only attach to registered land-use rights.[20] When questioned about this anomaly, officials explained that the rule only applied where SOEs intended to apply for land-use right certificates, 'so the spirit of the law was satisfied'.[21]

A directive issued by the prime minister in 2004 to implement the Enterprise Law clearly illustrates the use of subordinate legislation to infuse private rights with socioeconomic policy.[22] Not only did the directive require entrepreneurs to 'raise

---

17 Ministry of Justice (2002), 'Final Report Legal Needs Assessment', Ministry of Justice, Hanoi, point 2.3.2.

18 See Civil Code 1995, articles 308–314.

19 Truong Thanh Duc (1999), 'Nhung Bat Cap Trong Viec Xay Dung va Ban Hanh Van Ban Quy Pham Phap Luat' (Defects in Building and Promulgating Legal Instruments), *Nha Nuoc va Phap Luat* (2), 22, 29.

20 Article 728 of the Civil Code 1995 and Decree No. 178 1999 provided that only houses with land use rights are able to be mortgaged.

21 Interview Dang Trung Chinh, Legal Expert, General Department of Land Administration, Hanoi, June 2001.

22 See Directive No. 27 CT-TTg On Further Stepping Up the Implementation of the Enterprise Law, Encouraging the Development of Small and Medium-Sized Enterprises 2004, article 16.

their legal understanding and sense of law observance', they were also instructed to increase 'efficiency, productivity and competitiveness' and adopt advanced technologies and market information to exploit foreign markets. As a legally binding instrument, the directive sought to enlist private capital to further the state's international economic integration policies—a project that is not contemplated in the Enterprise Law.

A report written by officials in the Office of Government also found that government agencies use open-textured and opaque drafting techniques to increase their discretionary powers.[23] Ministries routinely regulate sensitive issues in superior legislation with sub-legal, but highly persuasive, administrative rulings such as guidance letters (*thong tu huong dan*) or dispatches (*cong van*) (literally, official correspondence).Vague and inconsistent rules increase the discretionary latitude of government agencies to 'manage' (*quan ly*) business entities. They also undermine the normative authority of superior law by changing the meanings ascribed to imported contract and property rights.

State bodies responsible for legislative consistency, such as the Ministry of Justice, lack the resources to evaluate the thousands of subordinate statutes passed by government agencies every year. Statutory requirements compelling enacting bodies to lodge copies of legislation with a central database and repeal inconsistent laws may eventually induce more consistent legislation. Progress is hampered, however, by the perception among some government agencies that legislative conformity constitutes a political constraint on policy implementation. As we shall see, there is little commitment, especially at the provincial level, to the notion that legislation in unitary states has a 'single mind'.

State Economic Management and Licensing Powers

In the years following *doi moi* reforms, government agencies used strict licensing powers to control private commercial rights. It will be recalled from Chapter 5 that heavy-handed concessionary (asking-giving) licensing under the Company Law 1990 tightly regulated market entry and business activities. Consider, for example, an application in 1998 to incorporate a musical promotion company by a group of famous artists. The Hanoi People's Committee rejected the application on the grounds that Decree No. 222-HDBT 1992 did not specify the legal capital required for music promotion companies. Adopting a concessionary approach to market entry, the officials contended that 'since the law does not specifically provide a legal framework for such business activities, it means that people are not allowed to do such business'.

The struggle between private commercial rights and 'state economic management' is illustrated by deregulatory procedures leading up to the enactment of the Enterprise

---

23 Office of Government (2003), 'Study Report to Improve the Quality of Laws and Ordinances Drafted by the Government to be Submitted to the NA and the NA Standing Committee', unpublished report, Working Delegation No. 804, Hanoi, December.

Law. The first tentative step towards market-entry deregulation came in a circular issued by the Ministry of Justice, which abolished discretionary powers to determine health and educational standards for company promoters.[24] This reform aimed to minimise rent-seeking and other administrative abuses, without fundamentally dismantling concessionary powers.

The Enterprise Law introduced more far-reaching liberalisations by notionally replacing some business licences with a simple registration system.[25] It permitted private investors to engage in any type of business activity that is not prohibited or licensed by the state. Decree No. 2 ND-CP 2000 implementing the Enterprise Law, unequivocally provided that 'to establish an enterprise and to carry out business registration in accordance with the law is the right of the people and of organisations, which shall be protected by the state'.[26]

By abolishing more than 150 licences and/or certificates (*giay phep kinh doanh*), the Enterprise Law stimulated impressive growth in new company registrations.[27] Studies show that in some localities deregulatory reforms have induced a 'strong commitment to simple, transparent and abridged transactions between public officials and businesses'.[28] Reforms have systematised legal rights and given entrepreneurs the freedom to select their own business activities. Entrepreneurs report that licensing procedures have by varying degrees reduced the time required to incorporate, and have streamlined the 'work culture' (*van hoa lao dong*). The simplified procedures have reduced the discretionary space in which officials can infuse private rights with local imperatives.

Despite impressive changes, a series of studies indicate that Enterprise Law reforms have only just begun to transform the deeply ingrained concessionary and anti-mercantile mentality among state officials. An investigation conducted by CIEM six months after the Enterprise Law was enacted found that most corporate regulators were still applying the repealed procedures.[29] Twelve months later, the Enterprise Enforcement Mission Group (*Nhom Nhiem Vu Cuong Che Doanh Nghiep*), which the prime minister convened to prevent re-regulation under the Enterprise Law, reported that 'many local authorities still hold on to their powers to issue sub-licences and continue to employ the "ask-favour system" (*co che xin cho*) without regard for the consequences for the business community.'[30]

---

24 Circular No. 5, 10 July 1998, Ministry of Justice and Ministry of Planning.

25 Not all business licences were abolished. Licences remain in key manufacturing, mining, tourism and various import/export sectors. See Enterprise Law, article 6(1).

26 Decree No. 02-2000 ND-CP, on Business Registration, 2000, article 2(1).

27 Company registrations increased to 11,121, but had reached a plateau in 2002–04. Interview Trang Nguyen, Manager, MPDF, Hanoi, August 2004.

28 See CIEM (2003), 'Comparative Provincial Performance in Private Business Development', VIE01/025, November, Hanoi, 23.

29 See Quy Hoa (2001), 'Dung Lam Kho Doanh Nghiep: Nhin Lai Mot Nam Thi Hanh Luat' (Do Not Make it Difficult for Business: Reviewing a Year's Enforcement of the Enterprise Law), *Hoi Khoa Hoc Kinh Te Viet Nam* (43), 9 April, 2.

30 Lan Phuong Nguyen (2000), 'Local News', *Reuters*, Hanoi, 1 November.

A UNDP field study conducted in 2003 discovered that some provincial people's committees used 'one-door' registration procedures to establish services companies.[31] These fee-for-service companies used personal links with people's committee officials to give applicants access to the unpublished nuances of municipal policy. Information of this kind is required to negotiate cryptic business regulations successfully.

Other officials used technically illegal sub-licences to re-regulate market entry.[32] Before deregulation, food safety inspectors routinely incorporated food hygiene standards into business licences. The abolition of business licences embodying these standards exposed consumers to unhygienic services. In response, officials in Ho Chi Minh City began inventing health permits to control standards in food processing firms.[33]

Employing another strategy, some city-level officials used discretionary powers over public resources to discourage unwanted business activities.[34] For example, they delayed processing documents, charged excessively for utility tariffs and imposed arbitrary environmental, fire and building controls. Other officials used access to land to 'manage' private investment. Le Quang Chien, a prominent ceramics manufacturer complained 'my company and thousands of other private businesses are unable to develop or expand their operations simply because they are not given the land to do so'.[35] Officials used their regulatory powers to negate or 'manage' market entry rights conferred by the Enterprise Law.

Deregulatory reforms are only gradually changing deeply ingrained concessionary attitudes that discretionary power should proactively regulate company formation. CIEM investigators concluded that an institutional culture that held officials morally, if not legally, responsible for corporate criminality and business failures, perpetuated state economic management thinking. In 2005, the Politburo for the first time endorsed the 'rule of law' notion that entrepreneurs can carry out any business that is not prohibited by law. To what extent this important ideological change will filter down to local officials is debateable, because CIEM officials unofficially concede that re-regulation has much to do with rent-seeking.

State Economic Management and Supervisory Powers

In addition to licensing powers, officials use supervisory powers to control private commercial rights.[36] According to an authoritative CIEM report, 'entrepreneurs feel that the difficulties they face in Vietnam is [sic] not to find ways of producing

31 See CIEM (2003), *supra*, 22.

32 See Author Unknown (2002), 'Enterprise Law Ups and Downs', *Vietnam Investment Review*, 18 February, 3; Quy Hoa (2001), *supra*, 2.

33 See Nguyen Van Cam (2000), 'Business Beat', *Vietnam News* 2, February, 2.

34 See Quy Hoa (2001), *supra*, 2–3.

35 Duc Hung (2002), 'Enterprise Law Ups and Downs, *Vietnam Investment Review*, 18 February, 4.

36 See Law on Inspection 2004, articles 2–29, 60–63.

cheap and good products, but coping with inspection agencies and satisfying their requirements'.[37]

A variety of city/provincial agencies, including market management authorities (*chi cuc quan ly thi truong thanh pho*),[38] economic police (*canh sat kinh te*) and economic security police (*an ninh kinh te*) supervise compliance with the Enterprise Law and associated commercial legislation. Adding to the regulatory web, some ministries and people's committees conduct specialised inspections. For example, the Ministry of Labour monitors compliance with the Labour Code, the Ministry of Transport inspects company vehicles, traffic police control road safety and the Taxation Department collects and monitors taxation.

Entrepreneurs complain that inspectors do not confine themselves to supervising compliance with standards or practices stipulated in laws, but in addition use their powers to 'manage' business activities.[39] As discussed in Chapter 4, market management authorities use discretionary powers to promote *thi truong lanh manh* (healthy markets). The types of activities that constitute healthy markets are continuously changing to reflect nuances in party and state policy. Policy settings are explained to officials in internal sub-legal documents (that is, official letters and internal operational directives) that reflect 'policy regimes' (*che do chinh sach*) established by party committees. For example, officials in Ba Dinh district market-management group (*doi quan ly thi truong*) in Hanoi were instructed to encourage firms engaged in similar businesses to group together in the same locality to make policing easier. This practice contravenes provisions in the Enterprise Law allowing entrepreneurs to select their place of business.

Regulators also 'manage' entrepreneurs using *lam luat* (make law), a popular expression describing the misuse of discretion to extract bribes. Consider the attempts by a company in Ngo Thi Nham *Phuong* (ward) in Hanoi to purchase a receipt book (*hoa don*) from the General Department of Taxation.[40] Before agreeing to certify that the company was trading legally, a precondition for the sale of receipt books, the Phuong People's Committee required a notarised copy of the company's business lease. Public notaries claimed they lacked the powers to certify leases. Officials then refused to accept the lease without a copy of the lessor's civil registration and identity card. Without the receipt book, the company was not legally permitted to trade.

Other entrepreneurs reported that numerous (five to ten) visits to tax authorities are needed to convince officials to sell receipt books. In one case, it took six meetings

---

37 See Vien Nghien Cuu Quan Ly Kinh Te Trung Uong (Central Institute of Economic Management) (1998), *Danh Gia Tong Ket Luat Cong Ty va Kien Nghi Nhung Dinh Huong Sua Doi Chu Yeu* (Review of the Current Company Law and Key Recommendations for its Revision), Hanoi, January, 104.

38 Decree No 1 on Administrative Punishment for Economic Actions 1996.

39 See, for example, Cao Cuong (1998), 'No More Harassment', *Saigon Times*, 11 July, 28–29.

40 See Manh Quan (2003), 'Doan Truong Hau Dang Ky Kinh Doanh' (The Painful Process of Post-Registration), *Thanh Nien*, 7 August, 5.

to persuade a tax official that vice-chairmen, in addition to chairmen of local people's committees, are permitted to certify lease agreements.

Many commentators believe that officials use supervision to extract bribes from entrepreneurs.[41] According to an investigative journalist, 'all difficulties that local authorities or tax officials create for businesses aim to make money. To clear the bureaucracy, businesses often agree to pay bribes. For example, a company reported paying approximately one million *dong* (US$70) for one meeting with a tax official to thank them for their hard work'.[42] Inspections and rent-seeking evidently reaches a climax immediately before *Tet* (lunar new year).

Administrative Penalties

Government agencies use a comprehensive system of administrative penalties to sanction violations of subordinate legislation.[43] Penalties range from fines to custodial sentences for repeat offences. For example, fines of 500,000 dong sanction company officials providing false information to business registration departments. Officials from people's committees can order administrative penalties and custodial sentences without first seeking permission from judges. As discussed below, there are few opportunities for entrepreneurs to appeal administrative decisions to the courts.

Criminalising (*hinh su hoa*) Commercial Activities

Entrepreneurs regard the blurred distinction between administrative and criminal penalties, which is used to criminalise (*hinh su hoa*) commerce, the most potent weapon in the 'state economic management' arsenal.[44] Criminal penalties not only apply to offences described in the Criminal Code 1999, they also extend to administrative violations of commercial regulations. Recidivism and quantitative thresholds transform relatively minor administrative infractions into criminal offences. It is a crime, for example, to intentionally conduct a business without business registration.[45]

Criminalisation occurs in two situations: where government agencies (and courts) use criminal powers to resolve commercial problems, and where the regulatory

41 See CIEM (2003), *supra*; Nguyen Phuong Quynh Trang (2001), 'Doing Business Under the New Enterprise Law: A Survey of Newly Registered Companies', MPDF, Private Sector Discussions 12, 20–21.

42 See Manh Quan (2003), *supra*, 5.

43 See Ordinance on Handling Administrative Violations 2003; Decree No. 37 ND-CP On Sanctioning Administrative Violations in Business Registration 2003.

44 See Tan Duc (1999), 'Bo Dieu 164 Cho Doanh Nhan Yen Tam Lam An' (Revoke Article 164 to Make Businessman Feel Assured in Doing Their Business), *Thoi Bao Kinh Te Sai Gon* (*Saigon Economic Times*), 20 May, 10, 11.

45 Criminal Code 1999, article 159 (penalties range from one to seven years imprisonment).

regime is so vague that businesses cannot trade profitably without infringing subordinate regulations.

Officials have broad powers to criminalise commercial activities. It is a criminal offence to 'act against' (*hanh dong nguoc lai*), though not necessarily breach legislative rules, unpublished ministerial dispatches (*cong van*), and even oral directives given by officials.[46]

Criminalisation of commercial decision-making routinely takes place under Decree No. 324 QD-NHNN Promulgating Regulations on Loans for Credit Institutions 1998. The decree makes bank officials criminally liable for 'lack of responsibility' (*thieu trach nhiem*) (or negligence) in processing loans. Liability extends not only to fraudulent lending, but also to failing to predict credit risks.[47]

The decree was enacted after state bank officials lost approximately US$280 million in loans to the Minh Phung group of companies in 1997.[48] Although bank officials in that case were charged with misappropriating 'socialist property' (*tai san xa hoi chu nghia*), many commentators believe the officials merely made poor commercial decisions.[49] By allowing the state to prosecute bank officials for making commercial decisions, the new provisions have frustrated banking liberalisation designed to increase the availability of loan capital for the private sector.

Officials also use vague and contradictory subordinate rules to criminalise commercial activities. For example, many regulations governing trade promotion (*xuc tien thuong mai*) do not clearly delineate the boundaries between acceptable and unacceptable advertising and promotion. Entrepreneurs using advertising to increase their market share risk violating discretionary powers that criminalise 'unhealthy market' (*thi truong phi lanh manh*) activities. Market control officials know that many rules are not obeyed and in fact cannot be obeyed if businesses are to remain viable. Opaque rules are useful precisely because they give officials discretionary powers to prevent entrepreneurs from competing with state-owned enterprises, extract bribes and retaliate against political adversaries.[50]

Nguyen Thi Nghia, a Ho Chi Minh City-based company director, encapsulated the uncertainty surrounding criminalisation when she said:

---

46 Criminal Code 1999, article 174 (penalties range from three and 12 years imprisonment).

47 See Criminal Code 1999, articles 144 and 179.

48 See Dang Hong Nga (1999), 'Code of the New Period', *Vietnam Economic Times* (24), 39.

49 Nguyen Nhu Phong and Vu Cao (1998), 'Minh Phung Lam Giau va Sup Do The Noa' (Minh Phung—How did It Get Rich? How did It Collapse?), *Anh Ninh The Gioi* (World Security Magazine) 13 February, 1–3. Also see John Gillespie (2001), 'Self-Interest and Ideology: Bureaucratic Corruption in Vietnam', 3 *Australian Journal of Asian Law* (1), 1, 13–23.

50 See Pham Duy Nghia (2000), 'Hinh Su Hoa Cac Giao Dich Dan Su Kinh Te: Quan Niem Bieu Hien va Mot So Giai Phap Khac Phuc' (The Process of Criminalisation of Civil and Economic Transactions: Ideas, Manifestations and Some Solutions), *Tap Chi Nghien Cuu Lap Phap* (6), 30, 36.

> In principle, 'intentional contravention' breaches the law, however, it is very difficult to apply the relevant law in practice. *Boi duong* (feeding up) customs officers, for example, is obviously an intentional contravention, but we cannot help doing it while operating our businesses. It is very difficult to do business in a vague legal environment that is full of unclear and general provisions. In fact, enterprises cannot exist without 'intentional contravention'.[51]

In another manifestation of 'state economic management', trade competitors use public security officials to criminalise the activities of their competitors. The public security police in Hai Phong, for example, began investigating 19/8 Hai Phong Fertiliser Company in 2001 for manufacturing and selling counterfeit fertiliser.[52] The security police alleged the company used a red additive to make the fertiliser resemble a product imported by fertiliser companies owned by the Hai Phong People's Committee. According to newspaper accounts, several independent state agencies tested the additive and concluded that it contained trace elements required for plant growth. Further, the product was clearly labelled to avoid confusion with the more expensive imported product. Despite this certification, the People's Committee in 2002 sent 50 police to close down the factory and arrest the company director. Commentators speculate that the action was taken to protect the state-owned fertiliser companies from private competition.

In another example, Thai Thang Long, the chairman of a construction company, was arrested by police in 2001 for allegedly offering bribes and violating the Enterprise Law.[53] According to lawyers acting for the accused, the charges were manufactured by the Vinh Long People's Committee to bankrupt a highly successful private sector company. Police charged Thai Thang Long with establishing a company for the purposes of 'swindling and misappropriation' without producing evidence supporting their accusation. He was also charged with bribing a state official to award construction contracts unlawfully. Further investigations revealed, however, that the alleged bribe-taker lacked the official power to confer such benefits. Eventually police charged him with sub-contracting under a tender agreement, an activity that is not prohibited by the law. Appeals by the accused to authorities to review his case were unsuccessful.

Officials in these cases used criminalisation as a market 'management' tool when private commercial rights did not produce locally acceptable outcomes. Criminalisation is a potent instrument because it induces a psychology of compliance. Politically unconnected entrepreneurs are never certain when commercial activities will offend vague 'state economic management' principles and policies.[54] The mere threat of prosecution transforms calculable commercial risk into incalculable criminal

---

51 Tan Duc (1999), *supra*, 10, 11.

52 KT-PL (2001), 'Hinh Su Hoa De Lam Gi?' (What is Criminalisation For?), *Thoi Bao Kinh Te Viet Nam*, 16 April, 12.

53 See Theo Duong Day Nong (2001), 'Day Dut Lon Tu Vu An Nho' (Deep Concern Over a Small Case), *Dau Tu*, 18 September, 6.

54 See Pham Duy Nghia (2000), *supra*, 30–42; Tan Duc (1999), *supra*, 10, 11.

risk, which in turn limits the utility of private contractual and property rights. Despite efforts to reduce criminalisation, the National Assembly Legal Committee estimated that over 30 per cent of commercial violations were criminalised (*hinh su hoa*) by state officials.[55]

To summarise, regulators everywhere combine statutory and discretionary powers to control economic activities. Vietnam differs from the Western regulatory approach in the extensive powers given to officials to 'manage' statutory commercial rights. The problem for rights-based regulatory reforms is threefold. First, as in any modern state, it is impossible for the central government in Vietnam to exercise complete supervision over all subordinate authorities. Officials at every level must exercise some discretion to implement central laws and policies, but central control over local discretion is frustrated by unclear boundaries between the jurisdictions of different levels of government and between the state and party.

Second, the guidelines giving meaning and utility to imported private rights primarily reside in internal 'policy regimes' and instructions. For entrepreneurs to understand the limits of private rights, they need to form personal (frequently corrupt) relationships with state officials. This process undermines formal legal rules' capacity to control policy flexibility.

Third, it is never clear whether officials exercising 'state economic management' are grounding their decisions on 'official' socioeconomic policies. Uncertainty exists because officials are tacitly permitted in some circumstances to arrogate discretion to regulate, even criminalise, otherwise lawful behaviour. In other situations the arrogation of power is considered corrupt. The conundrum facing entrepreneurs is knowing in what circumstances 'state economic management' follows 'official' or 'unofficial' discourses.

Interaction between Central and Local 'Official' Discourses

Not only is it sometimes unclear whether officials interpreting private rights are legitimately following 'official' discourse or acting contrary to conferred authority (*uy quyen*) by following 'unofficial' discourse, boundaries distinguishing 'official' and 'unofficial' discourses are also blurred. This section examines evidence that central and local levels of government operate in different discursive environments and sometimes reach contrary conclusions about the correct interpretation of imported law.

Elite-level Discourse

Studies considered below intimate that some elite-level state officials are in sympathy with the rights-based, neoliberal legal practices advocated by most foreign donors

---

55 See Author Unknown (1999), 'Chong Hinh Su Hoa: Moi Dung O Chi Thi Hoi Thao' (Fighting Against Criminalisation is only Conducted in Directives and Workshops), *Thoi Bao Kinh Te Sai Gon*, 27 May, 14.

and lawyers. Even officials who are unfamiliar with rights-based discourse may, through dialogue with foreign donors, investors and lawyers, come to accept that private commercial rights play a valid role in ordering economic activity. Chapter 7 builds on this discussion by considering whether similar (mutually constituted) neoliberal-oriented interpretive communities are forming between foreign donors and some elite-level lawmakers.

Lawyers acting for large foreign companies routinely form personal relationships to secure relatively unmediated access to high-level state officials.[56] They use imported legal doctrines to explain how tersely worded statutory provisions function in Western or East Asian (typically Singapore or Hong Kong) legal systems. Training courses and study trips are conducted to clarify international practices and show officials how regulators in other systems use laws to balance private and state interests. Lawyers also help officials codify legal principles and practices into subordinate legislation. Incrementally, these interventions are beginning to weave a protective web around the private legal rights that secure the interests of capitalist enterprises.

Consider the negotiations about the appropriate levels of corporate income tax levied against a large foreign-funded construction project in Phu My Hung near Ho Chi Minh City.[57] A Taiwanese construction firm formed a joint venture in 1993 with a Vietnamese SOE to engage in civil construction (*cong trinh dan dung*) projects. When the joint venture commenced work on the Phu My Hung apartment project in 2003, the Ministry of Planning and Investment (MPI) increased the tax rate from 10 to 25 per cent per annum, claiming that residential construction attracted a higher tax rate.

The joint venture successfully persuaded the Ministry of Justice to issue an Official Letter stating that 'civil construction' projects include residential apartments.[58] When MPI refused to follow the Official Letter and reduce the tax, the Office of Government ordered the Ministry of Finance, MPI and the Ho Chi Minh City People's Committee to resolve the impasse. Lawyers acting for the Taiwanese investors say that over the course of many meetings they convinced key state officials that article 121 of Decree No. 24 Implementing the Foreign Investment Law 2000 gives foreign investors legal protection against future adverse change. In practice, this meant profits generated from construction activities authorised by the investment licence were legally exempt from future tax increases.

For six months it seemed that this legalistic interpretation of Decree No. 24 of 2000 would prevail against political arguments used by the MPI to support the tax

56 These observations are based on over 100 interviews and focus group discussions with lawyers from leading domestic Vietnamese law firms, Investconsult, Leadco, Vilaf, and I&L Associates from 2000–05.

57 Hoang Hai Van (2004), 'Bo Tu Phap, UBND TPHCM de Nghi: Giu Nguyen Muc Thue Thu Nhap Doanh Nghiep 10% Cho Lien Doanh Phu My Hung' (Ministry of Justice and Ho Chi Minh City People's Committee Propose that Corporate Income Tax Rate Remain at 10% for Phu My Hung Joint Venture), *Thanh Nien-Online*, 17 February, 3.

58 See Official Letter No. 5, TP PL QT, 5 November 2003, Ministry of Justice.

increase. But in August 2004 the prime minister intervened in the dispute by issuing a decision that forced the Phu My Hung Corporation to pay the 25 per cent tax.[59] Phu My Hung Corporation was also pressured to drop an administrative court action against MPI when the Ho Chi Minh City People's Committee began investigations for alleged Land Law violations. This study shows that legal arguments have the capacity to persuade technically trained bureaucrats, but party and state leaders do not hesitate to subordinate private rights when important questions of political and economic policy such as tax revenue are threatened.

More generally, private lawyers form *quan he tot dep* (good relationships) with state officials, often secured with bribes, to access the 'official' discourse that gives meaning to statutory rules. The quality of information received depends on the strength of the relationship. For example, officials only reveal the intricate policy nuances required to exploit private commercial rights to close associates; less well-connected lawyers receive basic procedural information. Officials believe that relationships based on trust and *tinh cam* (sentiment) reduce the risk that lawyers will use 'official' information in damaging ways.

Overtures by lawyers are, nevertheless, rarely welcomed. Officials prefer direct contact with entrepreneurs. They generally perceive lawyers as meddlesome *nguoi moi gioi* (middlemen) who interfere with the personal relationships officials use to 'manage' entrepreneurs. Lawyers also believe that officials fear the intervention of legal professionals, who are capable of systematically analysing and challenging the legal authority underpinning state economic management. Corruption is also an important part of the problem. It is less profitable for officials to solicit bribes from entrepreneurs when lawyers are present.

Rights-based discourse is usually limited to exchanges between lawyers acting for foreign investors and state officials. It aims to protect private rights from political, economic and moral precepts that are hostile towards private enterprise. Lacking the relational connections that privilege SOEs and domestic companies, foreign investors rely heavily on contractual and property rights to secure business transactions against interference from the state and competitors.

Lawyers acting for SOEs regularly use political, economic and moral arguments to counter private rights asserted by entrepreneurs. For example, lawyers acting for SOEs involved in the Phu My Hung project convinced the Tax Department that foreign investors, rather than domestic companies, should pay withholding tax. They employed moral arguments that the tax burden was huge and beyond the resources of Vietnamese companies and political arguments that officials should favour state companies.

Lawyers occasionally use legal rights to protect SOEs. Lawyers acting for a consortium of state banks participating in a syndicated loan, for instance, framed the transaction with rights-based provisions imported from a standard foreign loan

59 See Author Unknown (2004), 'Cloudy Reasoning in Phu My Hung Tax Row', *Sai Gon Giai Phong*, 21 August, 3, trans. *Development Vietnam*, Intellasia News Services, 25 August, 14–15.

agreement. The state banks shared the same state supervising authority and could not rely on administrative measures to protect their respective interests.

In general, lawyers believe their interaction with some elite-level officials is slowly generating common perspectives about legal meanings and the regulatory responses required to protect legal rights. They discern more willingness by certain officials to imagine a decision-making environment in which commercial rights are protected by politically neutral state regulators. Yet this consensus evaporates every time lawyers reach working arrangements with officials to change or ignore sub-laws that impede their clients' interests. State intervention in the Phu My Hung case also sends a message that the 'rule of law' is struggling to make private rights seem credible alternatives to forming personal relationships with state authorities.

Local-level Discourse

Far removed from the neoliberal legal ideas circulating in elite-level discourse, a more localised set of norms and mentalities informs officials working in people's committees. As we saw in Chapter 2, there are historical divides between centre and periphery in Vietnam. Commentators have observed that ancient regionalisms have been amplified by recent cycles of centralisation and decentralisation.[60] Following the dismantling of central-planning in the late 1980s, middle-level officials in line-ministries (*bo chu quan*), SOEs and city/provincial people's committees gradually assumed control over resource allocation. As Thaveeporn Vasavakul observed,

> [p]olitics during the period of transition from central-planning was characterised by high local autonomy devolving on middle-level cadres, the expansion of horizontal connections, and the bypassing of existing rules and regulations imposed by the central government.[61]

Habits learnt over decades have persisted and studies suggest that officials in ministry branch offices and people's committees routinely use 'state economic management' powers to reinterpret and occasionally sabotage central legislation.[62]

Further intensifying centre-local differences, most local officials have not been exposed to rights-based discourses. Research indicates that market liberalisation is only gradually changing an underlying antipathy to the private sector.[63] It further suggests that many local-level bureaucrats are convinced that most companies

60 See, for example, David Marr (2004), 'A Brief History of Local Government in Vietnam', in Benedict J. Tria Kerkvliet and David Marr (eds), *Beyond Hanoi: Local Government in Vietnam*, Institute of Southeast Asian Studies, Singapore, 40–49.

61 Thaveeporn Vasavakul (1996), 'Reform of State Institutions in the Post-Socialist Era', in Suiwah Leung (ed.), *Vietnam Assessment: Creating a Sound Investment Climate*, Institute of Southeast Asian Eastern Studies, Singapore, 46–47.

62 See Bao Tram (1997), 'Phap Luat Ve Dat Dai: Cuon Chi Can Go Roi' (Law on Land: A Coil of Thread to be Rearranged), *Phap Luat*, July, 6, 7.

63 See MPDF (1999), 'Private Companies in Vietnam: A Survey of Public Perceptions', Private Sector Discussion No. 9, MPDF, Hanoi, 15–16.

are engaged in illegal activity, such as tax evasion or forming *cong ty ma* (ghost companies) to fraudulently raise capital from state banks.[64] According to a widely held logic, the private sector is responsible for endemic corruption that has overtaken the transitional market. Robust 'state economic management' is seen as a way to promote a 'healthy' market and reduce corruption.

Local bureaucrats were primarily recruited for 'morality and talent', rather than technical proficiency. Their training in universities or ministry-based programs provides a sound grounding in public law concepts underpinning bureaucratic law, especially the central importance of 'state economic management', but few of the theoretical tenets of neoliberal legalism. Soviet-style education that places the state at the centre of society, inculcates state officials with an unqualified confidence in their ability and moral mission to manage society and protect the 'state benefit' (*loi ich cua nha nuoc*) against the private sector. A practice termed 'manage in order to manage' (*quan ly de quan ly*) has emerged whereby 'state economic management' is treated as an objective in its own right, independent from central socioeconomic or legal imperatives. The criminalisation of otherwise lawful activities is justified by the need to 'manage' the economy.

Like their central-level counterparts, local-level officials are also deeply influenced by dialogue, especially negotiations with members of the public. But in contrast to the rights-based discourse promoted by foreign investors and lawyers, local-level discussions (especially at the district and lower levels) revolve around political, economic and moral precepts that blur and de-emphasise commercial rights.

Local-level discourse is typified by the negotiations supporting applications to convert informal land tenure into legal titles.[65] Following the enactment of the Land Law 1993, the state began a campaign to convert informal occupancy into formal land-use rights. It has been remarkably unsuccessful. At current conversion rates it will take decades to legalise urban land.

A distinguishing feature of land management in Vietnam is the extent to which housing has developed 'informally'—without full conformity to legislative standards. Surveys speculate that more than 85 per cent of urban households live in informal or 'popular housing' (*nha khong phep*) (literally houses lacking authorisation) and 75 per cent of land transactions are informal.[66] Informal housing covers most types of accommodation, from luxury villas to squatter settlements, and often coexists in the same geographical space as formal housing. It is used for mixed residential and commercial purposes, and approximately 75–80 per cent of private entrepreneurs

64 See Luu Quang Dinh (2001) 'Dung Do Loi Cho Luat Doanh Nghiep' (Do Not Blame the Enterprise Law), *Lao Dong*, 30 July, 3.

65 See Hoang Hai Van (2001), 'Ky 2: Dan "Tien" Nha Nuoc "Lui"' (Number 2: People 'Marching Forward' State 'Stepping Backwards'), *Tuoi Tre*, 6 August, 3; Hoang Hai Van (2001), 'Ky 3: Giu Dat va Dieu Khien Thi Truong' (Number 3: Land 'Keeping' and Market Control), *Tuoi Tre*, 10 August, 3.

66 See David Koh (2000), 'Wards of Hanoi and State-Society Relations in the Socialist Republic of Vietnam', unpublished PhD, The Australian National University, chapter five.

have located their place of business on informal land. In order to gain access to bank loans or lease business premises, entrepreneurs must convert informal land tenure into formal land-use rights recognised by the state.

Local urban and regional land officials interviewed during a World Bank mission in 2001 openly opposed central land conversion rules and policies. Centrally enacted land conversion rules were considered unnecessarily restrictive and infused with a highly legalistic approach to property rights. This view is echoed in government reports that blame state policy for the large numbers of 'unofficial' land transactions.[67] Officials also thought the procedural rules contained numerous evidential requirements that were vague and onerous. And, in addition, conversion procedures were costly, time consuming and imposed an unrealistically high tax burden. They concluded that informal and formal land is distinguishable in a legal sense only, because formal land has legal titles.

Legal classifications lack authority, because statutes and discretionary powers regulate both informal and formal housing. For example, *phuong* officials certify informal housing sales and levy land taxes, and district officials routinely legalise land occupancy that is unsupported by documents required by statute. In addition, police (*canh sat*) give informal households residency permits, and construction departments 'legalise' unlawfully constructed houses and additions with fines.

Local officials struggle to bring order to urban development with rules that appear to make arbitrary legal distinctions between informal and formal housing and land. In order to reconcile statutory property rights with local conditions, officials mediate with applicants in a personal and highly contextual language. Arguments concerning legality rarely surface in these negotiations. Even the terminology used by local officials to describe the discretionary processes is infused with contextual subjectivity. A popular term for discretion (*niem tin noi tam*) literally means 'believe in one's self', but it conveys the impression that appropriate decisions are made with 'good heart' (*tam*), compassion (*thong cam*), sentiment (*tinh cam*) and social understanding. Officials are also expected to respect reciprocal obligations and intervene on behalf of family, friends and neighbours.

Local decision-making is also portrayed as *lam luat* (literally 'make law'). This term has the positive connotation of finding flexible solutions to rigid centrally imposed law and the previously discussed negative implication of inventing laws to extract rents. A morality of good neighbourliness or *tinh cam lang gieng* (sentiment among neighbours) enures that community interests are balanced against legal interests. Correct official behaviour is assessed in terms of 'being right and compassionate (*co ly co tinh*).

This case study describes two main discourses shaping local decision-making. Operating in legal mode, central authorities emphasise contract and property rights as defined by law. This is an ambiguous position, since the central state recognises that some discretion is needed to adjust impractical central dictates to local conditions.

67 See Hoang Hai Van (2001), 'Nha Nuoc Co Chay Theo Thi Truong? (Is the State Running After the Market?), *Tuoi Tre*, 6 August, 3.

Legal authority is further undermined because central leaders have not fully accepted that law is autonomous from, and guides the implementation of, state socioeconomic policy.

Working at the shadowy interface between official and personal obligations, local officials risk losing local authority and trust unless they apply the law flexibly. From a local perspective, informality and formality describe regulatory styles rather than binary legal/illegal cleavages between property rights and unlawful occupation. Local regulation generates shades of informality, and each degree of informality attracts different levels of official toleration and 'legality'. Informal and formal understandings of land tenure function as different facets of the same system. But each discourse sends particular messages to officials about the meaning and relevance of private property rights. Without a strong system of legal accountably, many local officials feel more responsible to the people in their locality than to higher-level authorities and rules. They are consequently reluctant to enforce laws that are locally unpopular.

Improved systems of accountability are only a partial solution to uneven legal enforcement, because local officials live in a different discursive environment to the one informing many elite-level officials. Most local-level officials were domestically educated, have few contacts with foreigners and have little knowledge of Western legal epistemologies. Foreign knowledge and expertise is not the only difference distancing elites from local officials. The benefits of globalisation appear remote to local officials, especially when international economic integration comes at the cost of deregulatory reforms that strip away opportunities (frequently corrupt) to generate living wages. It is difficult methodologically to distinguish rhetoric from conviction, but most local-level officials interviewed by the author over a ten-year period appeared to believe sincerely in their mission to 'manage' entrepreneurs and genuinely worried that reforms aiming to minimise discretionary powers were unworkable in a society unused to private legal rights.

The Transformative Potential for Rights-based Discourse

The case studies intimate that imported commercial rights do not constitute simple binary alternatives between state and private interests. Rights are negotiated in three-way interactions between elite-level officials, local-level officials and entrepreneurs. In an important development, some elite officials have acquired an understanding, even sympathy for neo-liberal legality. Their fluency in English, Western education and regular association with lawyers and international agencies, give them access to neo-liberal legal ideas and practices. They are prevented from overtly identifying with the neo-liberal position, because such beliefs are too closely associated with foreigners. Nevertheless, they strategically apply neo-liberal interpretive positions in implementing commercial laws.

Despite progress in this direction, not all central-level officials are persuaded by rights-based discourse (see Chapter 5). Negotiations at the local level, which are predominately conducted in political or moral modes, produce rights that are strongly oriented towards personal relationships and family and community interests. As a consequence, imported legal rights are implemented in a highly fragmented legal space in which small 'rule of law' islands are surrounded by an ocean of legal instrumentalism, communitarianism and corrupt personal relationships.

There is also a strategic dimension to rights formation. From a central perspective, local discretionary regulation is both a hindrance and an advantage. By 'softening law' (*luat mem*) to conform to local ideas and practices, local officials sometimes obstruct central policies and undermine uniform rights-based definitions. Discretionary regulation also forces entrepreneurs to transact in the shadow of bureaucratic rule, a regulatory matrix that produces corrupt alliances and blurred distinctions between public and private rights.

In other circumstances, it suits all levels of government to invest local officials with discretionary powers that technically exceed their statutory authority. Officials are required in some circumstances to arrogate discretion in overcoming rigidities in code-based definitions of commercial rights. Strict adherence to statutory rules reduces dialogue between local officials and small-scale businesses, constraining the creative processes that invest imported rights with locally appropriate meanings. From this regulatory perspective, both codified rights and bureaucratic discretion are used as state management tools—interchangeable mechanisms for producing contextually appropriate market outcomes.

Changing the Meaning of Legal Rights in the Courts

Bureaucrats are not the only officials who reinterpret the meaning of imported commercial laws. In 'rule of law' states, courts are supposed to be the primary sites of normative change, because they find the most 'efficient' legal solutions to social problems.[68] Even theorists who believe that the social importance of judicial pronouncements is exaggerated concede that the 'rule of law' requires a transfer of discretionary power from bureaucrats to judges. Courts need decision-making power to enforce contracts and property rights fairly and impartially.[69] A fully functioning court system standardises legal meanings and tames the wild growth of normative projections in society. Yet experience elsewhere shows that courts are the last state institution to gain power over political decision-making.[70]

---

68 See, for example, Ronald Dworkin (1986), *Law's Empire*, Belknap Press, Cambridge, Massachusetts, 12–14; Richard Posner (1986), *The Economic Analysis of Law*, Little and Brown, Boston.

69 See Michael Kammen (1986), *A Machine that Would Go of Itself: The Constitution in American Culture*, Knoft, New York, 31. Also see Alec Stone (1990), 'The Birth and Development of Abstract Review: Constitutional Courts and Policymaking in Western Europe', 19 *Policy Studies Journal*, 81.

70 See Laurent Pech (2004), 'Rule of Law in France', in Randell Peerenboom (ed.), *Asian Discourses of Rule of Law*, Routledge, London, 89–98.

In order to perform this 'rule of law' function, courts require jurisdiction over commercial disputes and, more fundamentally, the authority to make autonomous decisions. Finally, courts require the power to make their decisions binding. This discussion first explores jurisdictional issues before assessing whether courts have the decision-making authority to make imported commercial rights appear credible and desirable.

Court Access

Courts can only make legal rulings on matters before them. Contrasting with the broad discretionary powers used by government officials to creatively re-imagine imported laws, courts are supposed to confine their judgements to facts raised by litigants. Public access to the courts thus has a critical bearing on the types of imported laws that are influenced by judicial rulings. Two factors limit access to courts in Vietnam: one, a social preference for mediation and conciliation minimises adversarial litigation and, two, narrow jurisdictional powers restrict the range of issues referred to courts.

Perceptional factors limit court access in Vietnam. Although French colonisation and Soviet legality left their imprint on the collective legal consciousness, some commentators believe that pre-modern values still profoundly influence attitudes to litigation.[71] They contend the people were conditioned into treating law as a punitive instrument, rather than a means of ordering horizontal social transactions. Judicial intervention also signalled a personal moral failing and a loss of status, factors that induced a social preference for non-adversarial mediation (*hoa giai*) (see Chapter 2).

A recent survey suggests that these values remain potent in contemporary Vietnam. More than 41 per cent of respondents cited loss of face and harmony as reasons for avoiding adversarial litigation.[72] Judges and lawyers interviewed also discern a continuing social preference for mediation over litigation.[73] Aversion to litigation is also implied by the extremely low rates of court usage in Vietnam. For example, economic cases in the entire country have averaged approximately 600 per annum from 2000–2004—a period of unparalleled commercial development.[74]

71 See Pham Duy Nghia (2005), *supra*; Pham Duy Nghia (2003), 'Noi Doanh Nhan Tim Den Cong Ly' (Where do Entrepreneurs Go for Justice?), *Tap Chi Nghien Cuu Lap Phap* (3), 45–54.

72 See UNDP (2004), 'Access to Justice: Survey from the People's Perspective', unpublished paper, UNDP, Hanoi, 12–13.

73 The views in this section are based on more than 50 interviews with Vietnamese judges from the Supreme Court, Hanoi; Ho Chi Minh City Provincial Court; and district court judges in Hanoi, Ho Chi Minh City, Nam Dinh and Yen Phu provinces between 1999 and 2005 [hereafter called 'Interviews with Judges'].

74 See Toa An Nhan Dan Toi Cao (2000), *Bao Cao Tong Ket Cong Tac Nganh Toa An Nam 2001 va Phuong Huong Nhiem Vu Cong Tac Toa An Nam 2001* (Report on 2000 and the Plan for 2001 Supreme People's Court), Hanoi, 1–15; and Toa An Nhan Dan Toi Cao (2004), *Bao Cao Tong Ket Cong Tac Nganh Toa An Nam 2001 va Phuong Huong Nhiem Vu Cong Tac*

This aversion is not unique to Vietnam. Entrepreneurs everywhere are unwilling to jeopardise trading relationships and incur legal expenses in court actions.[75] The difference lies in the social significance attached to court rulings. In the West, courts set commercial standards that influence pre-court negotiations. The general indifference among most Vietnamese entrepreneurs towards legal rights (discussed in Chapter 8) induces a low social demand for law-based dispute resolution.

A well-justified public scepticism about the professional competency and impartiality of judges further reinforces litigation aversion.[76] Surveys rate dishonest and unfair judges (74 per cent) and unclear legal rules (65 per cent) as the most important reasons for avoiding litigation.[77] Judges are considered unsympathetic towards the private sector, basing decisions on status as well as bribes, and treating legal rules as convenient, but optional, ways of getting things done. The perception of systemic bias, incompetence and corruption influenced more than 90 per cent of private sector respondents surveyed to conclude that courts would not satisfactorily resolve commercial disputes.[78]

Litigation in Vietnam generates justifiable anxiety that courts will use legal rules to interfere with family and patron-based trading networks. Making matters worse, there is ample evidence that contractual enforcement is difficult in Vietnam. According to the World Development Indicators, in 2005 it took on average 404 days to enforce a contract in Vietnam, compared to 241 days in China and 69 days in Singapore.[79] On a rational calculation of their interests, most businesses prefer to use comparatively effective extra-judicial, particularistic routes and means to resolve business disputes. Reflecting the strong preference for consensual rather than winner-take-all outcomes, respondents surveyed in 2004 showed high-levels of satisfaction with dispute resolution by 'grassroots' mediation boards comprised of members of neighbourhood councils (*to dan pho*), people's committee officials and members of the Fatherland Front.[80]

Toa An Nam 2005 (Report on 2004 and the Plan for 2005 Supreme People's Court), Supreme People's Court, Hanoi.

75 See generally John O. Haley (1978), 'The Myth of the Reluctant Litigant', 4 *Journal of Japanese Studies* (2), 366–89.

76 Interviews with lawyers from Investconsult, Vilaf and Leadco, Hanoi, and IMAC, Ho Chi Minh City, between 2000–2005, as well as Interviews with Judges, *supra*.

77 See UNDP (2004), 'Access to Justice: Survey from the People's Perspective', unpublished paper, Hanoi, 22–23.

78 John McMillan and Christopher Woodruff (1999), 'Interfirm Relationships and Informal Credit in Vietnam', 114 *Quarterly Journal of Economics* (4), 1285–86. A more recent study of courts in general found that only 35 per cent of respondents thought that courts would fairly and impartially resolve disputes. See UNDP (2004), *supra*, 14–15.

79 World Development Indicators, World Bank 2005 <www.devdata.worldbank.org/wdi2005/Table5 3.htm>.

80 Approximately 68 per cent of respondents who had used grassroots mediation were satisfied. See UNDP (2004), *supra*, 16.

Jurisdictional powers are the second major factor that affects court access. Economic courts have a broad jurisdiction over most types of disputes that are likely to arise from imported commercial rights. Low litigation rates are partially attributable to the narrow range of commercial entities entitled to bring actions in these courts. Until 2005, unregistered household businesses, which comprise by far the largest economic sector, were only permitted to litigate a small range of contractual and leasehold disputes in civil courts. Now that amendments to the Commercial Law have abolished the jurisdictional distinction between registered and unregistered entities, it is possible that more disputes will be litigated in economic courts.

In contrast to the relatively broad jurisdiction enjoyed by economic courts, administrative courts have limited powers to resolve the cases that matter most to entrepreneurs. As previously discussed, administrative licences and state inspections, more than any other factor, constrain the profitable exploitation of private commercial rights. Administrative courts have wide powers to review illegal or *ultra vires* administrative decisions such as licensing, taxation, housing permits and land-use charges that affect commercial activities.[81] Unfortunately for entrepreneurs, administrative review is ineffectual.[82] A government report estimated that in a five-year period from 1999 until 2003 approximately 41 per cent of administrative claims were legitimate, but only 800 cases from over 10,000 complaints were filed in administrative courts.[83]

One reason for low review rates is that judges avoid hearing cases by exploiting inconsistencies between the Law on Complaints and Denunciations 1998 (amended 2004) and the Ordinance on Procedures for Settling Administrative Cases 1996 (as amended).[84] Citizens must first complain internally to administrative agencies before bringing complaints to administrative courts. Although it is no longer necessary to exhaust all internal appeals before transferring complaints to the courts, initial administrative processes filter out many cases. For example, a private businessman seeking compensation from local authorities who expropriated his business during the 1980s eventually sought political intervention by the prime minister to convince the Hanoi Administrative Court to accept his case.[85]

81 See Resolution No. 3 NQ-HDTP Guiding the Implementation of a Number of Provisions of the Ordinance on Procedures for Handling Administrative Cases 2003, articles 3 and 4.

82 Of the 728 administrative cased submitted in 2002, less than 20 were resolved by court orders. Interviews with Judges, *supra*.

83 See Author Unknown (2004), 'Public Complaints Understated by Government', *Nguoi Lao Dong*, 21 May, 3, trans. *Development Vietnam*, Intellasia News Service, 26 May, 26–27.

84 Ordinance on the Procedures for the Settlement of Administrative Cases 1996 (as amended), article 11. Also see 'Bao Cao Cua Chanh An Toa An Nhan Dan Toi Cao Tai Ky Hop Thu 6 Quoc Hoi Khoa 10 Ve Cong Tac Toa An' (Report of the Chief Judge of the Supreme People's Court at the Sixth Meeting of the Tenth Session of the National Assembly Regarding the Work of Court), No. 67 BC/VP, 22 October, 1999.

85 See Author Unknown (2001), 'Hanoi People's Committee Sued', *Phu Nu*, Ho Chi Minh City, 14 July, 1.

Further constraining their powers, administrative courts are only permitted to consider decisions that violate or exceed legal authority. They are not authorised to review *intra vires* administrative bias against the private sector or question the constitutionality of laws. Making matters worse, judges lack powers to enforce their judgments against officials.

Compared with the moribund administrative and economic jurisdictions, civil litigation has risen from approximately 25,000 cases in 1994 to over 50,000 in 2004. Civil courts have jurisdiction over some areas that concern businesses, such as leases and civil debts. But over 80 per cent of cases pertain to non-commercial matters such as inheritance, civil obligations (tortious actions) and housing disputes. Most of the growth in civil action has been in this area.

In conclusion, a social aversion to adversarial dispute resolution more than jurisdictional powers limits the numbers of commercial cases reaching the courts. Empirical research shows that litigation aversion is grounded as much in pragmatic concerns about the quality of judicial decision-making as it is informed by traditional values. These concerns touch the fundamental problem that courts lack both independence and authority.

Judicial Decision-making

A central requirement for a procedural 'rule of law' is a judiciary that enjoys sufficient powers to resolve disputes fairly and impartially. There are two aspects to judicial power. Judges must not only have the discretion within their jurisdiction to make significant choices, but in addition they require independence from outside interference. Decision-making power requires secondary legal sources, such as doctrines and jurisprudence, that enable judges to transform everyday disputes into legal disputes. It is also relies on resources such as legal training, court support staff and other facilities.

Judicial independence refers to the mechanisms that shield judges from internal and external pressures that may compromise the fairness and impartiality of their decisions.[86] Although power and independence are separate factors, they can intersect and influence each other. For example, judicial power is partially conferred by legislation and in part depends on the ability of judges to decide cases independently in accordance with the law and jurisprudential rules and without interference from other parties. It also depends in practice on the degree to which judges are protected from improper influence. Judicial power and decisional independence are so tightly intertwined in Vietnam that it makes little sense to consider them separately.

Discourse analysis suggests that a primary function of judicial reasoning is to subsume particular cases under general legal rules.[87] Legal reasoning transposes

86 See Shimon Shetreet and Jules Deschenes (1985), *Judicial Independence: The Contemporary Debate*, Martinus Nijhof Publishers, Boston.

87 Gunther Teubner (2001), 'Alienating Justice: On the Surplus Value of the Twelfth Camel' in Jiří Pribán and David Nelken (eds), *Law's New Boundaries: The Consequences of*

social problems into a legal framework. To understand how judges construe imported commercial rights, it is thus necessary to examine the arguments and procedures that shape courtroom discourse.

Western judges use secondary legal sources, such as jurisprudence, parliamentary debates and academic commentary, to resolve conflicts between competing legal rights. Legal arguments first seek reasons or grounds for why legal authority applies to disputes.[88] This generally includes the application of pre-existing principles or doctrines to case facts. Legal arguments next search for redundancies, or reasons why some contextual elements pertaining to the case are irrelevant. They selectively establish connections with past legal findings to ascertain whether it is appropriate to extend protection to the legal rights before the court.

Vietnamese judges face two major difficulties in moving from a Soviet-inspired instrumental legalism to legal reasoning that transposes commercial disputes into rights-based contests. First, most commentators agree that judicial independence from political interference, together with adherence to some form of separation of powers, is a precondition for rights-based legal reasoning.[89] Legal reasoning establishes autonomous (from external inference) epistemological rules that filter non-legal ideas that might disrupt the legal meanings attached to private rights. It also creates a closed epistemology with its own rules and regulations that generate conceptual stability by discouraging judges from using non-legal arguments to rethink established legal meanings.

Second, judges in developing legal systems like Vietnam must creatively interpret imported commercial laws to find legal solutions to local problems. But Vietnamese judges lack secondary legal sources to guide the interpretation of vaguely worded imported rights.

This discussion explores the extent to which autonomy from state and social forces is necessary for Vietnamese courts to acquire more power to make significant decisions. It also examines the transformative potential for more judicial power and what this might mean for the implementation of imported commercial laws.

Revolutionary Notions of Judicial Independence

Lenin's observation that under capitalism 'judicial powers are an exploitation machine for the bourgeoisie', combined with the Vietnamese experience of colonial criminal justice to profoundly shape revolutionary courts.[90] After independence,

Legal Autopoiesis, Ashgate, Dartmouth, 28–29.

88 See Hugh Baxter (1998), 'Autopoiesis and the "Relative Autonomy" of Law', 19 *Cardozo Law Review*, 1987, 2027–28; Martin Shapiro (1972), 'Toward a Theory of *Stare Decisis*', 1 *Journal of Legal Studies*, 125.

89 See, for example, Michael H. Davis (1986), 'The Law/Politics Distinction: The French Conseil Constitutionnel and the US Supreme Court', 34 *American Journal of Comparative Law*, 45.

90 Cited in Dinh Gia Trinh, 1964, *Nghien Cuu Nha Nuoc va Phap Quyen*, (Studies about State and Legality), Nha Xuat Ban Su Hoc, 39. For a comprehensive account about

communist leaders replaced colonial law-based dispute resolution within socialist institutions. From 1954 both military courts and the Supreme Court were established as 'people's courts to serve as tools (*cong cu*) employed by the people to implement the proletarian dictatorship'.[91] Vietnamese courts were expected to: (1) 'repress counter-revolutionaries and the enemies of the people and socialist regime'; (2) 'protect public property ... ensure the socialist reform of non-socialist economic sectors'; (3) 'guarantee order and socialist security'; (4) 'peacefully settle petty quarrels, conflicts and law suits among the people'; and (5) educate citizens to show loyalty to the Fatherland, observe the law, respect social regulations and fight crime.[92] Pham Van Bach, the Chief Judge, instructed court personnel during the 1960s that the primary role of the courts was to implement party and state policy.[93] Courts were accordingly treated as instruments of state rule, and Western notions of judicial independence were dismissed as 'bourgeois' propaganda.[94]

The 1992 Constitution appeared to end decades of instrumentalism by requiring judges to determine cases according to the law. It also expected judges to protect the 'collective rights and the lives, property, freedom, honour and dignity of citizens'.[95] Although these reforms took tentative steps towards rights-based decision-making, they were qualified by a duty to protect 'socialist' legality, the state and the people's right to mastery.[96]

More generally, '*nha nuoc phap quyen*' (law-based state) reforms, discussed in Chapter 3, have encouraged a shift from strict legal instrumentalism to a situation where law is given a relative autonomy from party and state policy. But can the reforms give judges more decision-making power in a political environment where courts are required by 'socialist' legality to protect party and state interests? In the context of 'party leadership', what does judicial independence mean—from what, or whom, are courts independent? Our inquiry conflates these questions by asking whether courts possess sufficient decision-making power and autonomy to

---

the pre-*doi moi* Vietnamese court system, see Penelope Nicholson (2000), 'Borrowing Court Systems: The Experience of the Democratic Republic of Vietnam 1945–1976', unpublished PhD Thesis, The University of Melbourne, Melbourne, chapters four and five.

91 Editors (1961), 'To Understand Clearly the Functions and Characteristics of People's Courts in Order to Implement the New Philosophy of the Spring Rectification Campaign', *Tap San Tu Phap* (4), 1, 2.

92 Circular Letter No 556-TT issued by the Prime Minster on 24 December 1958, preamble.

93 See Pham Van Bach (1970), 'Le Nin Voi Van De Phap Che Xa Hoi Chu Nghia', (Lenin and Socialist Legality), *Tap San Tu Phap* (3), 9–16.

94 For a discussion of the role of courts in a socialist system see Le Trung Ha (1965), 'Chuyen Huong To Chuc Cua Cac Toa An Nhan Dan Dia Phuong De Dap Ung Voi Tinh Hinh va Nhiem Vu Moi' (Changes in Local Court to Meet the Requirements of the New Conditions and Requirements), *Tap San Tu Phap* (8), 1, 2.

95 Law on the Organisation of People's Courts 1992, article 1; also see Vietnamese Constitution 1992, article 126.

96 See Constitution 1992, article 126.

interpret imported commercial rights according to legal doctrines, rather than party socioeconomic policies.

Post-Doi Moi *Judicial Reforms*

Legal reforms in 1992 aimed to reconfigure courts geared for a command economy to resolve rights-based disputes in the mixed-market economy.[97] Attempts were made to centralise court administration by relocating powers to appoint judges from local government to the president. Programs were introduced to professionalise the judiciary through higher education and specialised legal training courses. Reforms also sought to reduce government authority over local courts and give superior courts greater powers to promote law-based decision-making throughout the court system.

Despite better standards of judicial reasoning and an improved social status for judges, press articles during the 1990s increasingly reported false prosecutions, judicial corruption and the criminalising of civil and economic cases.[98] Accusations of corruption within the judicial sector reached a zenith with the arrest of Truong Van Cam (Nam Cam) in December 2001. The indictment alleged complicity between Nam Cam's criminal gang and high-level officials in the courts and procuracy.

Adding their voice to the demands for reform, the international donor community also agitated for judicial reform. Their campaign gained momentum following the ratification of the US–Vietnam Bilateral Trade Agreement, which required Vietnamese courts to extend US companies' and citizens' rights to protect treaty privileges (see Chapter 7). Some state officials sympathetic to neoliberal legalism advocated judicial reforms to attract more foreign investment and make rights-based adjudication available to domestic entrepreneurs.[99]

Responding to public and donor pressure, a political report prepared by the party identified a need to restructure courts and further improve the professional capacity of judges.[100] The Politburo incorporated the report's finding into Resolution No. 8 NQ-TW on Forthcoming Principal Judicial Tasks in 2002.[101] Resolution No. 8 first criticised aspects of judicial work (*cong tac tu phap*) and called for strong and stable

97 See Le Cam (2002), 'Cai Cach He Thong Toa An Trong Giai Doan Xay Dung Nha Nuoc Phap Quyen Viet Nam' (Reform the Court System to Build Up a Law Based State in Vietnam), *Tap Chi Nghien Cuu Lap Phap* (4), 21.

98 See Author Unknown (2002), 'Vietnam Da Xuat Hien Toi Pham Co To Chuc o Trinh Do Cao' (High-Level Organised Crime Makes Its Appearance in Vietnam), *Vnexpress*, 15 June.

99 See Khanh Van (2003), 'Cai Cach Tu Phap: Nhin Tu Nhieu Goc Do' (Judicial Reform: From Different Angles), *Tap Chi Nghien Cuu Lap Phap* (4), 3–8.

100 See Communist Party of Vietnam (2001), *Vietnamese Party Congress Political Report*, 19 April, 35.

101 See Vo Chi Cong (2002), 'Thay Gi Ve Cong Tac To Chuc va Quan Ly Can Bo Qua Vu An Truong Van Cam' (What Can be Seen About Organising and Managing Cadres Through the Truong Van Cam Affair?), *Tap Chi Cong San* (9), available online at <www.tapchicongsan.org.vn>.

judicial personnel, clearer organisational structures that minimised inefficiencies and overlapping responsibilities and more systemic analysis and management of problems. It then established four objectives for judicial work:

- strictly follow party policies and lines,
- efficiently resolve criminal offences,
- allow the people to participate in judicial work,
- build strong judicial institutions that defend the party and state.

The Law on the Organisation of the People's Courts 2002, which implements Resolution No. 8, sends mixed signals about judicial independence. It encourages centralisation of judicial authority by placing inferior courts under the direct administration of the Supreme Court and it protects judicial processes from 'all acts obstructing judges and/or people's assessors from performing their tasks'.[102] At the same time, it recycled longstanding instrumental notions that judges should 'resolutely struggle against persons and acts harmful to the party, the Fatherland and people'.[103] The long awaited Resolution No 49 NQ/TW on the Judicial Reform Strategy to 2020, issued by the Politburo in May 2005, did not change the fundamental direction or substance of earlier reforms.

Some of the reforms, such as financial and organisational autonomy, comply with the preconditions for judicial autonomy identified by the International Bar Association.[104] Other factors, such as party leadership, fixed term appointments, poor remuneration and unclear rules governing judicial appointment, are at variance to an independent judiciary. The next section examines what is meant by judicial independence in Vietnam and how external and internal controls constrain the emergence of decision-making power.

Party Leadership over the Courts

Courtroom discourse in Vietnam is poorly researched. But one issue is clear: judicial decision-making is not 'independent' (*doc lap*) from 'party leadership' (*su lanh dao cua dang*). The scope for party involvement in court affairs was outlined in Resolution No. 8: 'The party shall lead judicial agencies closely in political organisation and personnel matters and ensure that the judicial activities really follow the viewpoints of the party and the law of the state'. According to party sources, judges should act impartially (*khong thien vi*), though not independently of party leadership.

---

102 Law on the Organisation of People's Courts 2002, articles 17, 38, 45 and 46.

103 This injunction was enacted in the Joint Circular No 1/2003/TTLT/TANDTC-BQP-BNV-UBTWMTTQVN Guiding the Implementation of a Number of Provisions of the Ordinance on Judges and Jurors of the People's Courts 1993, article 2(c).

104 See full text of the International Bar Association standards, online at <www.ibanet.org/pdf/HRIMinimumStandards.pdf>.

The party uses many mechanisms to 'lead' judicial decision-making. Like other public employees, judges are required to 'strictly abide by the party's lines and policies'. The Supreme People's Court Annual Report in 2001 placed party resolutions ahead of National Assembly resolutions and laws in the hierarchy of sources judges must follow in resolving cases.[105] For example, economic court judges hearing bankruptcy cases are required to follow internal party rulings not to evict debtors until creditors provide alternate accommodation. These internal rulings qualify with a social obligation creditors' statutory rights to enforce debt securities.

Recruitment and selection procedures sensitise judges to the party-line. First, the *nomenklatura* system (discussed in Chapter 4) ensures that over 90 per cent of judges are party members.[106] Second, judges are reappointed (every five years) according to selection criteria that stress 'loyalty to the motherland', good moral character, especially honesty and truthfulness, legal knowledge and support for socialist legality.[107] Selection committees generally interpret these highly subjective criteria by assessing whether judges have complied with party policies. Judges aspiring to high judicial positions are inculcated with the finer points of party ideology and policies at the Ho Chi Minh Political Academy.

Party groups (*dang bo* and *chi bo*) operating in every court are instructed to raise ideological and political awareness and ensure that judges adhere to the party line.[108] Judges and court officials attend regular 'party group' meetings to discuss party resolutions pertaining to court work. Senior party cadres lead discussions by repeatedly sensitising judges to the political and social implications of their decisions. Loyalty is assessed during monthly self-criticism (*phe binh tu phe binh*) meetings.

Finally, judicial panels in important cases comprise one judge sitting with two people's assessors. Decisions are made by majority vote. Assessors are non-professional lay representatives appointed by people's councils on the basis of political loyalty and personal reliability.[109] Some commentators believe the party uses people's assessors to implement the party-line in the unlikely event that a judge acquires a predilection for independent decision-making.[110]

105 See Supreme Court (2001), 'Bao Cao Cong Tac Nganh Toa An Nam 2000 va Phuong Huong Nhiem Vu Cong Tac Toa An Nam 2001' (Report on Court Sector in 2000 and Operational Direction in 2001), 9 February, 2.

106 See generally Pip Nicholson and Nguyen Hung Quang (2005), 'The Vietnamese Judiciary: The Politics of Appointment and Promotion', 14 *Pacific Rim Law and Policy Journal* 1, 14–22.

107 See Law on Organisation of the People's Courts 2002, articles 37, 40, 41.

108 See Party Central Directive No. 29/CT-TW on the Enhancement of Party Leadership over Law Enforcement Agencies 1993.

109 Law on People's Courts 2002, article 41.

110 See Brian J. Quinn (2002), *supra*, 245–46.

Party Interference

Judges interviewed by the author seemed genuinely unclear what the Constitution means by judicial independence.[111] When asked what is more important, the party-line or law, most responded that in principle there is no conflict since law implements party policy. Although, on reflection, many judges added that the party leads courts in understanding the meaning of law.

They understood judicial independence to mean freedom from party 'interference' (*su can thiep*), but conceded the distinction between party leadership and interference is unclear. The difference is significant because, as state officials, judges are required to follow party resolutions and lines (leadership), but they are supposed to disregard the direction of individual party members. Unsurprisingly, judges expressed confusion whether informal party directives pertaining to particular cases constituted party leadership or interference.

Take, for example, the party instructions given to the trial judge in the Tang Minh Phung corruption trial in 1998.[112] Procurators alleged that Tang Minh Phung and business associates fraudulently misappropriated socialist property by using misleading property valuations to borrow approximately US$200 million from state banks.

Lawyers defending Tang Minh Phung claimed the party instructed the presiding judge to use 'legal analogy' (*ap dung phap luat tuong tu*) to overcome evidentiary inconsistencies in the indictment. The crime of fraudulently misappropriating socialist property required the prosecution to prove that Tang Minh Phung acquired loans by fraudulently overvaluing his collateral. Rebutting these allegations, the defence counsel demonstrated that bank officials investigated and confirmed the accuracy of collateral valuations. Even more damaging to the state's case, the prosecution commenced before a legal obligation to repay the loans arose. If the defence counsel was correct no misappropriation occurred.[113]

When it became apparent that the defendants might escape conviction if the judge applied rights-based reasoning, the party instructed the judge to overcome evidentiary deficiencies by applying the doctrine of legal analogy. Under the direction of 'higher authorities' (a euphemism for the party), the doctrine permits courts to criminalise (*hinh su hoa*) otherwise legal behaviour that seriously damages state interests.[114] According to the defence counsel, the party regarded the economic harm caused by the 'misuse' of 'socialist property' as sufficiently serious to invoke the doctrine. This case shows that, in addition to formal resolutions, party leadership extends to informal directions that privilege political expediency over statutory rights. Recent

111 Interviews with Judges, *supra*.

112 See John Gillespie (2001), 'Self-Interest and Ideology: Bureaucratic Corruption in Vietnam', 3 *The Australian Journal of Asian Law* (1), 1, 15–18.

113 Interview, Nguyen Thi Loan, Lawyer, Ho Chi Minh City, October 1999.

114 See Dinh Van Que (1999), *Phap Luat Thuc Tien va An Le* (Legal Practice and Precedent), Da Nang Publishing House, 181–87.

cases suggest that Resolution No. 8 has not diminished active party leadership in sensitive criminal cases.[115]

One would expect to find party leadership in sensitive criminal trials, but lawyers report its use in commercial contests between private (especially foreign) and state interests. It is difficult to evaluate this perception empirically since court cases are not published. Nevertheless most judges interviewed thought that improper interference occurs where party organs or officials circumvent party decision-making processes and directly pressure judicial officials. This is most likely to happen where assets belonging to the party or party members are in dispute or personal favours are required.

Consider, for example, the Vong Thi Landscape Architectural Village (*Lang Kien Truc-Phong Canh Vong Thi*) case. The Hanoi People's Committee in 1999 allotted ten hectares of land in the salubrious West Lake suburb in Hanoi to Madam Thuy. According to the allotment conditions, Madam Thuy was supposed to construct a traditional display village for international tourists. Instead, she built a few traditional houses and illegally sold land worth several million US dollars to private residential developers. Like Tran Minh Phung, she was charged with fraudulently misappropriating socialist property.[116] Despite a strong prosecution case that included a confession, Madame Thuy was sentenced to a short period of house detention. Lawyers reported seeing the private secretary of Le Kha Phieu, at that time the Party General Secretary, sitting in on the trial. They believe that the presence of a senior party official 'influenced' the sentence. Tang Minh Phung, in contrast, received the death penalty from a much weaker prosecution case.[117]

It is clear that courts are not independent from party leadership. Leadership operates both inside and outside courts. What is less clear is how party leadership affects the decision-making power of judges.

Party leadership is primarily concerned with setting the political and moral tone for judgements.[118] It inculcates general principles that favour the state benefit over private interests and national interests over foreign interests. How these principles apply to the facts in specific cases is not always clear to court officials. For example, in an action taken by an SOE in the Hanoi Economic Court in 2003, the judge decided the state benefit was served by allowing the SOE to recover unlawfully transferred foreign currency. Confiscating the money would have compromised the company's competitiveness against private competitors. Taking a different approach, the procurator argued it was to the state's benefit to confiscate and turn the currency over to the state.

---

115 A similar outcome was recorded in Case No. 57, First Instance Criminal Court, Thai Binh Provincial People's Court, 8 March 2004. Interview with the Defence Counsel, Hanoi, March 2005.

116 Penal Code 1986, article 134.

117 See Author Unknown (1999), 'The Court of First Instance of Minh Phung – Epco Finished on August 4, 1999, after Three Months of Trial', *Saigon Giai Phong* 5 August, 1.

118 See Tran Dai Hung (2005), 'Improving Party Leadership over Judicial Work', 11 *Vietnam Law and Legal Forum* (128), 2.

In sensitive political trials, general political and moral notions about the state benefit are too vague to guarantee desired outcomes. In these cases, the party 'leads' by giving judges detailed instructions on how to conduct the trials. The extent to which 'improper' party interference frustrates judges' ability to decide cases according to private commercial rights is difficult to gauge,[119] but as an informal and covert form of communication it lacks the sustained influence party 'leadership' exerts over judicial discourse.

Government Interference in Court Decisions

The notion of judicial independence from the state needs rethinking in Vietnam's polity, where state power is divided according to the Soviet 'concentration-of-power' (*tap trung quyen luc*) doctrine.[120] 'Concentration-of-power' is best understood as specialisation, rather than separation, of powers. Both the government and Supreme Court can, for example, pass legislation and exercise judicial power. Further blurring the distinction between the executive and courts, government agencies have historically funded and managed inferior courts.

In the command economy, State Economic Arbitrators used administrative rulings to adjust economic contracts among SOEs.[121] With the introduction of private commercial rights following *doi moi* reforms, adjudicators could no longer use administrative measures to resolve disputes. They needed deliberative independence from the government apparatus.

The first round of post-*doi moi* reforms sought to untangle the government from the courts by removing the power of local governments to elect judges. They next abolished the economic arbitration and established economic courts in 1994.[122] The National Assembly was given constitutional powers to appoint the Chief Justice of the Supreme Court, while the President appointed other judges.[123] In practice, however, the President lacked the resources and the political will to perform this function and by default local governments arrogated authority to select and appoint judges.[124] This meant that lower-level judges owed their primary loyalties to local government officials, rather than to the Supreme Court.

119 See Le Tho Binh and Vu Thuong (1997), 'Fighting Corruption: In Addition to Energy, Courage is Needed', *Tuoi Tre*, 8 April, 3.

120 'Unity of power' (*tap trung quyen luc*) or literally 'concentration of power' is more generally termed 'unity of democracy' (*tap trung dan chu*) in contemporary legal literature.

121 See Hoang The Lien (1993), 'On the Model of an Economic Court in Vietnam', *Nha Nuoc va Phap Luat* (2), 19, 19–25.

122 See Constitution 1992, article 103; Law on the Organisation of People's Courts 1992, article 38.

123 Constitution 1992 articles 84, 103.

124 See Ba Tuan (2002), 'De Chanh An TANDTC Co Dieu Kien Bo Nhiem Tham Phan Duoc Xac Thuc Hon' (Allowing the Chief Justice of the Supreme People's Court the Ability to Nominate Judges Will Be More Realisti), *Phap Luat*, 19 March, 2.

The second round of court reforms in 2002 sought to centralise power over local courts into the hands of the Supreme Court.[125] Administrative control over court budgets has been transferred from local government authorities and the Ministry of Justice to the Supreme Court. Further strengthening the Supreme Court's power, the Chief Justice, rather than the President now appoints judges. But central control is qualified by the requirement that the Chief Justice must confer with local people's councils when appointing and dismissing the chief and deputy chief judges of local courts.[126]

An insight into the way local government perceives judicial autonomy is provided by the debates surrounding the 2002 judicial reforms.[127] Local governments argued that Supreme Court control would compromise judicial autonomy. Re-centralisation, they argued, would result in unjust decisions if the Supreme Court had an improper understanding of the law. For government agencies, judicial autonomy meant freedom from central legal rulings that frustrated local imperatives. Their arguments not only reveal centre-local tensions, but also indifference towards uniform legal doctrines that generate predicable judicial outcomes.

Senior judges countered these arguments by asserting that government bodies are reluctant to transfer discretionary power to 'manage' commercial transactions to the courts. The next case demonstrates the profound influence government directives have over the discretionary power of judges.

Government Directives to Courts

There is compelling evidence that local government authorities guide many court decisions. The action by New World Cong Ty against the Nghia Tan People's Committee illustrates this process.[128] A dispute arose in 2002 between Nghia Tan People's Committee (a *phuong* in Cau Giay district, Hanoi) and New World over a joint venture agreement for an amusement park. Under the joint venture the People's Committee provided land in return for a fixed profit set at 7 million dong per month (approximately US$430). The joint venture did not perform to expectations and after a year the People's Committee accepted a reduced profit share of 1 million dong per month.

When the joint venture terminated in 2001, the People's Committee demanded payment of the profit foregone over the five-year term of the contract. In response, New World petitioned the economic division of the Hanoi Provincial Court to declare the contract invalid. It claimed that the People's Committee had waived its contractual

125 See Law on the Organisation of People's Courts 2002, articles 45, 46.

126 Law on the Organisation of People's Courts 2002, article 40.

127 Ba Tuan (2002), 'Sua Luat Lieu Co Giam Oan Sai?' (Will Changing the Law Reduce Problems, Mistakes?), *Phap Luat*, 20 March, 2; D. Hoc (2002), 'Phai Dam Bao Tinh Doc Lap Xet Xu Cua Toa An' (We Must Guarantee the Independence of the Court), *Nguoi Lao Dong*, 20 March, 2.

128 Interviews with lawyers working for Leadco Attorneys, Hanoi during March 2003, July 2004.

right to the profit and the joint-venture agreement was void and unenforceable. In the alternative, it argued that the People's Committee was forbidden by the Ordinance on Economic Contracts 1989 from entering economic contracts and thus lacked the authority under the Land Law 1993 to lease land.

Disregarding these statutory limitations to the People's Committee's contractual authority, Hoang Huu But (the trial judge) decided that the joint venture agreement was enforceable. The judge relied on a letter from the Cau Giay District People's Committee confirming that the Nghia Tan People's Committee was authorised to enter the joint-venture agreement. He reasoned that, once instructed to lease the land, the Nghia Tan People's Committee was legally compelled to 'obey a higher level' (*tuan theo menh lenh cap tren*). In essence, the judge decided that a letter from a district People's Committee overruled central laws governing the formation of contracts.

Lawyers acting for New World believe that local officials pressured (*suc ep*) the judge to disregard the law and find in favour of the local government agency. From comments made in court, they speculated that the judge sympathised with *phuong* officials, who maintained they would lose 'face' (*be mat*) and authority if the government lost the case. The judge also followed general party principles by protecting the state benefit against contractual rights asserted by the private sector.

New World's lawyers convinced the procuracy that the judge erred in law and the Supreme Court agreed to review the case in 2003. In the meantime, the Supreme Court Judicial Council issued Professional Guidance No. 4, which provides that state agencies, such as the Phuong People's Committee, can legally form economic contracts. Lawyers did not proceed with the review because they were uncertain whether Supreme Court professional guidelines (which are a sub-legal instrument) are governed by the principle that laws are not retroactive.

Courts Rely on Government Agencies for Evidence

Modest adversarial reforms introduced by the Civil Procedure Code 2004 have given lawyers more opportunities to submit evidence in court.[129] But judges in Vietnam's civilian legal system still assume the main burden of finding evidence. Litigants also lack interlocutory and freedom of information powers to compel other parties and state authorities to produce evidence.

Functioning essentially as local government offshoots, courts have for decades relied on government officials to investigate litigants, gather evidence and in many cases determine liability. For specifics, consider the action by Nguyen Kim-Manh against Pham Loc (Director) and Hang Phim Truyen VN (Film Production

---

129 See Nguyen Phu Son (2004), 'Bo Luat To Tung Dan Su Can The Hien Thin Than Cai Cach Tu Phap' (Civil Procedure Code Should Express the Spirit of Judicial Reform), *Tap Chi Nghien Cuu Lap Phap* (4), 24–31.

Studio VN) for breach of copyright (*ban quyen*).[130] Nguyen Kim-Manh alleged the defendants had infringed his copyright in a novel entitled *Hon Nhan Khong Gia Thu* (literally 'Marriage without Registration') by changing key elements of the story during the adaptation of the novel into a film script. The protagonist in the novel was depicted as an ace fighter pilot, war hero and a complex man struggling against his moral imperfections. Among his many moral transgressions, the protagonist refused to recognise his illegitimate son. Glossing over the moral contradictions between national loyalty and personal betrayal, the film script presented a one-dimensional war story depicting *tinh yeu thuong mai* (commercial love) relationships.

Nguyen Thi Loi, the presiding judge in the Hanoi People's Court, was asked to determine whether the producer's obligation to comply with censorship directions overruled the author's property rights under article 751(e) of the Civil Code.[131] Censors from the Ministry of Culture and Information requested script changes without specifying which elements of the story were unsuitable for public viewing. The author, Nguyen Kim-Manh, contended that the producers breached copyright by making unnecessary changes.

After establishing that the contract gave the complainant copyright over the film script, the judge called on officials from the Political Bureau of the Airforce and the Censorship Committee from the Ministry of Culture and Information to ascertain whether the script modifications exceeded the changes demanded by the censors. In effect, she allowed government officials to decide the core evidentiary question of whether the producers breached copyright by making unnecessary script changes. Lawyers acting for the author were not permitted to challenge the veracity of evidence submitted or conclusions based on the evidence by submitting their own evidence and cross-examining government officials.

The notion that state officials possess the expertise and knowledge required to assess liability is deeply embedded in judicial thinking. Judges generally confine themselves to ensuring that procedural rules are followed and determining the appropriate remedies. Their deference to higher authorities (*cap tren*) allows government agencies to dominate courtroom discourse and take over judicial functions. By assessing commercial rights according to state socioeconomic policies, they transform judicial reasoning into an extension of 'state economic management'. This dependency undermines the judges' capacity to interpret imported legal rights according to 'secondary legal rules' and doctrines. As a consequence, lower-level judges lack the discretionary power and autonomy to make significant decisions.

---

130 This case study is based on interviews with Nguyen Thi Loi, Deputy Chief Judge, Civil Division, Hanoi People's Court, Hanoi, April 1999 and September 1999, and the transcript of the first instance judgment Case No. 41, 16–19 October 1998.

131 Article 751(e) of the Civil Code gives authors rights to 'protect the integrity of their work and permit or not permit other persons to alter the content of the work'.

Judicial Interference in Court Decisions

Judicial power requires autonomy from both external and internal interference. Autonomy from internal interference requires a decision-making environment in which judges are not compelled to follow instructions from other judges.

Collegial decision-making Historically, judicial committees (*Uy Ban Tham Phan*) comprising superior judges reviewed all inferior court cases before decisions were announced.[132] The chief judge also reviewed provincial court decisions in closed sessions (*xin y kien lanh dao*, literally 'request leadership's opinions'). In principle, majority decisions prevailed, but in practice chief judges dictated most outcomes.[133] Although there is no legislative basis for the practice, lawyers interviewed believe collegial decision-making is still widely practised as a means of inducing consistency and minimising corruption. Yet by encouraging a culture of 'first decide then try' (*quyet dinh truoc khi xet xu*), collegial decision-making compromises independent decision-making by inferior court judges.

Supreme Court professional guidance (chi dao chuyen mon) 'Professional guidance' by the Supreme Court constitutes another type of internal interference. The practice was borrowed from China in the 1950s to unify the application of law by lower-level judges possessing little or no legal training. Professional guidance comprises individual rulings made by chief judges in provincial courts or the Judicial Council (*Uy ban tham phan*) in the Supreme Court to resolve legal questions referred by inferior courts. Senior judges justify this practice as a way to further the democratic centralist objective of moderating local improvisation and inducing uniformity in decision-making across the country. It is considered necessary to correct wild improvisation by under-trained and inexperienced lower-level court judges.

Lower-level judges seek professional guidance to avoid making politically risky decisions about new normative practices, disputes involving foreigners and sensitive claims against the party and state. Consider the proceedings taken by foreign companies against Vietnamese state-owned banks for failing to honour letters of credit. Hyosus Hong Kong Ltd sued the Vietnam Commercial Joint Stock Bank (issuing bank) in the Hanoi Economic Court for allegedly breaching Uniform Commercial Credit Practice (UCCP) rules incorporated into the contract of sale. After receiving shipping documents (namely, the bill of lading and manufacturing certificates) stipulated in the contract of sale, the bank refused to honour the irrevocable letter of credit. Lawyers acting for the complainant believed that the Vietnamese buyer, a large SOE owned by the Hanoi People's Committee, persuaded Hanoi provincial authorities to issue an official letter stating that the SOE and Hyosus

132 This practice was entrenched by judicial reforms after the 1959 Constitution that aimed to bring democratic centralism into the court system. Interview with Judges, *supra*.

133 See Bui Ngoc Son (2003), 'Su Doc Lap Cua Toa An Trong Nha Nuoc Phap Quyen' (Independence of the Court and the Rule of Law), *Tap Chi Nghien Cuu Lap Phap* (4), 43, 48.

Hong Kong Ltd were in dispute and instructing the issuing bank to dishonour the letter of credit. According to UCCP rules, issuing banks are only lawfully entitled to dishonour letters of credit when courts have found the seller guilty of fraud.

The complainant lodged a petition with the Hanoi Provincial Court in 1998. Under Vietnamese law, the UCCP rules were incorporated into the economic contract binding the litigants.[134] Rather than applying the law, the court immediately sought guidance from the Supreme Court 'Judicial Council' (*Uy ban tham phan*). The Judicial Council issued Professional Guidance (*chi dao chuyen mon*) No. 37/TKT on 18 May 1998, ordering proceedings to stop not only in this case, but also in letter of credit actions pending in other provincial courts.[135] The Professional Guidance made the narrow and technically incorrect argument that letters of credit are not economic contracts and as such are not justiciable by economic courts. Lawyers for the complainants speculated that the Professional Guidance was used to protect the state benefit by shielding state-owned banks from foreign creditors.

The Judicial Council sought an administrative ruling from the State Bank to determine whether state banks should honour the letters of credit. Rather than examining secondary legal sources, such as National Assembly debates and academic commentary, the Judicial Council relied on a government agency to determine the detailed rules that guided the application of laws.[136]

Some professional guidance supports private commercial rights by clarifying legal texts, but many others privilege the state benefit. Judges regularly follow guidelines given by superior courts, which in the court system have a higher legal value than constitutionally superior laws. Since litigants are seldom given 'professional guidance' rulings, these instruments only implicitly inform courtroom discourse.

To recapitulate, in stressing broad political and ethical principles, party leadership contrasts with government and judicial influence, which is more tightly focused and case specific. In some circumstances, such as the letter of credit cases, government rulings reflect central party directives designed to protect the state benefit. More typically, however, these rulings aim to secure local political or economic imperatives. Either way, government discourse infuses imported commercial rights with state socioeconomic objectives. Professional guidance from the superior courts often has a similar purpose.

Moral and Sentimental Discourse in the Courtroom

We have seen that judicial decision-making is guided more by political and economic arguments than by legal reasoning. Judges first attempt to order and evaluate claims from a statutory perspective. But as this section shows, where primary legal texts do

134 Ordinance on Economic Contracts 1989.

135 See Kim Chi (1998), 'Potential Quicksand', *Vietnam Economic News* (33), 18–19.

136 The State Bank (Vietnam's central bank) promulgated Decision No. 711, 25 May 2001, and Decision No. 1233, 26 September 2001, outlining the circumstances in which state owned banks can issue deferred letters of credit.

not fit the facts, judges not only seek solutions from professional guidance, but also from non-legal social orderings.

In civil cases observed by the author, judges used 'reason and sentiment in carrying out the law' (*ly va tinh trong viec chap hanh phap luat*), a practice that developed during the pre-*doi moi* era. They encouraged litigants to argue their case using moral and sentimental language. In disputes over house ownership, for example, claimants based their cases on principles of fairness (*cong bang*) and reasonableness (*hop ly*). A war widow claimed she had a greater 'social need' (*nhu cau xa hoi*) for a house than a farmer defending his ownership rights. A local government official invoked the sentiment of *co long tot voi dan* (good heartedness towards the people) to support his claim for possession of a house owned by another villager. A district court judge hearing a housing dispute evaluated evidence according to what was 'reasonable' in the circumstances. It was reasonable, even constitutional, he decided, for some clan elders to allow landless relatives to occupy a clan house.

District court judges interviewed believe the legal consciousness of the people is low and judgements based entirely on legal argument lack popular legitimacy.[137] Like local-level bureaucrats discussed above, judges draw from common experiences—moral and sentimental practices—to produce socially acceptable outcomes. Even central authorities recognise a judicial duty to 'protect the *gia tri chung* (common values) of human beings',[138] although judges are encouraged to model their understanding of 'common values' on party-lines and policies. In the end, morality and sentiment often substitute for legal doctrines and other 'secondary legal' sources that might support rights-based outcomes.

Legal argument based on universal standards of legality is more common in superior courts. Judges in the economic divisions in the Supreme and provincial courts sometimes argue from analogy to extend legal principles to the facts of cases. For example, lawyers acting in the previously discussed clan house case on appeal convinced the Hanoi Provincial Court to overturn the district court decision on the grounds that the Land Law 1993 did not recognise social obligations to relatives.[139]

But legal argument by no means dominates discourse in superior courts. In cases observed by the author, provincial court judges used political and moral arguments to resolve cases according to the social status of litigants. They pointedly extolled the war records and party and community affiliations of socially prominent litigants to pressure less well-connected parties to settle.

The situationally valid decision-making (*thoa dang*) applied by many lower-level (and some superior) courts further de-emphasises uniform rights-based outcomes. Tracing its origins to pre-colonial dispute resolution practices discussed in Chapter 2, *thoa dang* encourages judges to balance competing claims for redemptive justice

137 Interviews with Judges, *supra*.

138 Nguyen Manh Cuong (2002), 'Yeu Cau Cua Viec Xay Dung Nha Nuoc Phap Quyen Doi Voi Doi Moi To Chuc va Hoat Dong Cua Cac Co Quan Tu Phap' (How to Reform Judicial Authorities to Build up a Law-Based-State), *Tap Chi Nghien Cuu Lap Phap* (10), 31.

139 Hanoi People's Court, Case No. 20-PTDS, 31 January 1996.

against broader considerations derived from 'reality processes' (*qua trinh thuc tai*). Judgements are valued for the skill shown in selectively applying a wide range of local and imported political, economic, moral and legal values to resolve social problems. They take into consideration the interests and feelings of interested parties, especially the party and state. Compromises reached to avoid winner-take-all outcomes are much more highly valued than rights-based solutions that apply universal codified legal norms and procedures.

Consider the action by Arteh Tonh Long (an SOE) against a private company in the Hanoi Provincial Court in 2003. Arteh advanced a foreign currency loan to the private company for the purposes of establishing a wig export business. When the enterprise failed, the private company reneged on repaying the loan, arguing that since the agreement violated State Bank regulations, it was unlawful and unenforceable.

The trial judge (Tuan Anh) ordered the private company to repay the loan in an out-of-court settlement. If the case had proceeded to trial, the director of Arteh would have been charged with the serious criminal offence of causing losses to socialist property and the foreign currency would have been confiscated. The judge was persuaded by the moral argument that Arteh's director made one innocent mistake in his otherwise unblemished trading record. By ignoring statutory contractual rules that clearly showed the loan agreement was unlawful, the judge saved the director from a custodial sentence. By returning working capital to an SOE, the judge preserved the state benefit.

In this case, imported commercial rights were not considered absolute, universal or immutable, but merely situationally relevant sources of guidance. *Thoa dang* solutions generated contextual rather than universal truths required for legal doctrines.

The case studies considered so far suggest that government and judicial officials remain unconvinced that courts should resolve cases according to autonomous legal reasoning. Yet there are signs that the Supreme Court is cautiously formulating secondary legal sources to give lower-level courts more autonomy to use legal reasoning in deciding commercial disputes.

Developing Secondary Legal Sources

The decision-making power of courts is not only weakened by its institutional dependence on the party and government, it is also weakened by limited access to legal sources. As in other civil law countries, courts in Vietnam do not have the power to make law, but they are allowed to interpret the law pertaining to particular cases. If this is to happen, judges need 'secondary legal sources' to guide their interpretation of primary laws.

For decades, courts were discouraged from making even the most rudimentary interpretations. Over the last decade, however, the Supreme Court has been slowly developing a body of secondary legal sources to assist judges in interpreting rights-based commercial law. The Court publishes similar fact case judgments (*nghi quyet hoi dong tham phan*) that show lower-level court judges how laws should be applied in particular circumstances. It also produces an annual report that contains detailed guidelines giving legal solutions to commonly encountered substantive and procedural issues. In addition, the court is slowly changing professional guidance from top-down instructions given to specific courts, into more generalised rulings applicable to every court.

Annual reports give judges procedural guidelines about examining witnesses and collecting evidence. For example, the Annual Report in 2000 directed administrative court judges to decide cases cautiously in consultation with state bodies.[140] Lawyers interviewed believe that prescriptive rules of this kind can be used to remind judges to follow predetermined procedures. Evidently, most judges lack the skills required to extend the doctrines contained in similar fact cases to particular cases. Applying legal principles from case summaries requires analytical skills that are in short supply in a judiciary that was trained to follow the party-line and narrow prescriptive rules strictly.

To augment these reforms, the Supreme Court is preparing a judicial handbook that will give inferior court judges broad ethical and procedural advice regarding court cases. It is also publishing and distributing, for the first time, selected economic decisions from superior-level economic courts. Written decisions have in the past been brief recitals of facts and determinations, without reference to the reasoning of the court. The new Civil Procedures Code now expects judges to include legal analysis and reasoning in their opinions, making written opinions a more useful source of guidance.

Although not legally binding in a civil law country, these secondary sources could become highly persuasive, since they set standards that superior courts may use to review appeals from lower-level courts. Like 'party leadership', government directives and judicial guidance, Supreme Court secondary rulings promote party and/or government policies. Where they differ is that secondary rulings have the potential to form legal doctrines that will enable judges to convert political, economic and moral ideas into legal arguments. In time, these reforms may generate a more autonomous decision-making environment in which appropriately trained judges have the discretionary power to use legal reasoning creatively to interpret imported commercial rights.

---

140 See Toa An Nhan Dan Toi Cao (Supreme People's Court) (2000), 'Giai Dap Mot So Van De Ve Hinh Su, Dan Su, Kinh Te, Lao Dong, Hanh Chinh va To Tung, (Annual Report on Criminal, Civil, Economic, Labour, Administrative and Procedural Laws), Supreme People's Court, Hanoi, 1 February, 60–61.

The Role of Lawyers in Courtroom Discourse

A competent and independent legal profession is widely regarded as a fundamental component of the 'rule of law'.[141] Lawyers are essential for drafting clear and transparent legislation, as well as interpreting and implementing the law. In addition to providing technical expertise, lawyers have been agents for change, promoting adherence to the 'rule of law' in legal drafting, litigation and public advocacy for law-based governance. Although an independent legal profession is still emerging in Vietnam, there are signs that lawyers are playing an active role in establishing a procedural 'rule of law'.

Before *doi moi*, lawyers were peripheral players in Vietnam's judicial system.[142] State authorities appointed lawyers in serious criminal trials, but litigants in civil cases were generally unrepresented. While fewer than 10 per cent of litigants in post-*doi moi* Vietnam retain legal representation, approximately 50–60 per cent are represented in economic cases.[143] Lawyers interviewed believe they are beginning to play a more significant role in promoting legal discourse in economic courts.[144] This development is important to our discussion because economic courts deal more directly with imported private commercial rights than other courts.

It is essential to understand the limitations the judicial system places on the role of lawyer. Lawyers report that, even in economic courts, legal reasoning is rudimentary. We have seen that judges prefer legal arguments based on highly prescriptive legislation to discourse grounded in legal principles extracted from superior laws. In fact, judges find sub-legal 'official letters' highly persuasive because they convert the party's and state's socioeconomic objects into detailed rules.

Where prescriptive rules are vague or irrelevant, judges occasionally listen to arguments based on general legal principles derived from superior-level legislation. For example, some judges are sympathetic to imaginative legal reasoning that extends principles extracted from the Civil Code to the facts in economic cases. More commonly, however, judges are unmoved by doctrinal arguments and prefer 'professional guidance' to clarify the law.

Lawyers representing foreign clients regularly use foreign legal protocols and doctrines to challenge political modes of thinking. This tactic is most effective

141 See, for example, Geoffrey Walker (1988), *The Rule of Law*, Melbourne University Press, Melbourne, 36–37; Richard Abel (1995), *Politics by Other Means: Law in the Struggle against Apartheid, 1980–1994*, Routledge, New York, 20–22.

142 Interviews Le Kim Que, President Bar Association of Hanoi. Also see Pham Duy Nghia (2003), *supra*, 49–52.

143 Fewer then 2500 lawyers (*luat su*) are available to appear in over 230,000 cases per annum. See Pham Hong Hai (2002), 'Vai Tro Cua Luat Su Trong Hoat Dong To Tung—Thuc Trang va Phuong Huong Doi Moi' (The Role of Lawyers in Procedures—A Look at Realty and Recommendations for Change), *Tap Chi Hghien Cuu Lap* (4), 110–16.

144 These comments are based on interviews with lawyers from six Hanoi based law firms (Investconsult, Vision & Associates, Vilaf, N. H. Quang & Associates, Leadco and Pham Hong Hai & Associates) from 2000–2005.

where lawyers can point to an international protocol in a trade agreement that binds Vietnam. Foreign legal ideas also enter courtroom discourse when judges are required to construe the meaning of foreign legal documents. It is common practice for judges to request private *ex parte* meetings with lawyers to discuss new legal ideas such as electronic commerce or international banking law principles. In some cases legal argument serves an educational function to acquaint judges with the ideas and doctrines used by the lawyers.

When it is strategically advantageous, lawyers selectively use political arguments derived from party pronouncements and the Constitution. In the lead up to WTO accession, for example, lawyers have used party support for international economic integration to argue for domestic application of international treaty obligations. As an alternate strategy, lawyers sometimes enlist political support from foreign embassies to lobby superior courts to respect legal rights conferred by treaties (especially the BTA) and to resist external pressure to favour the state benefit.[145]

For most of the post-*doi moi* period, strict procedural rules have constrained legal discourse in the courtroom. Modest procedural reforms giving lawyers more opportunities to protect their clients, foreshadowed in Resolution No. 8, were primarily aimed at criminal trials.[146] Nevertheless, the Civil Procedure Code 2004 extended limited adversarial rights to lawyers in economic and civil cases to examine witnesses, test evidence and present legal arguments. Some commentators have questioned the scope and depth of these reforms, arguing the code has failed to integrate adversarial reforms into procedural rules and merely consolidated existing rules favouring the inquisitorial system.[147] However, Resolution No. 49 confirms the party's commitment to these reforms.

Structural changes to judicial practice cannot be achieved quickly. In the inquisitorial tradition, judges were responsible for framing outcomes that reconciled litigants' claims to the state benefit and sent ideologically correct educational messages to the people.[148] Reforms that give lawyers rights to advocate their clients' interests, even if this means opposing state interests, run into obstacles set up by recalcitrant judges who, by training, habit and temperament, are not disposed to arguments predicated on private legal rights. It is too early to assess accurately whether procedural changes will overcome deeply ingrained attitudes, but a party resolution in 2005 urging judges to take legal arguments into account when writing

---

145 Ambassadors from the United States have been particularly active in petitioning superior courts to give US litigants equal treatment to domestic litigants, as required in the US–Vietnam BTA. The irony in lobbying courts to make politically independent decisions is apparently unrecognised by the foreign business community.

146 See Opinions (2004), 'Judicial Reform Steps in 2004', *Doi Song va Phap Luat*, trans. 10 *Vietnam Law and Legal Forum* (114), 30.

147 Nguyen Phu Son (2004), 'Bo Luat To Tung Dan Su Can The Hien Tinh Than Cai Cach Tu Phap' (Civil Procedure Code Should Express the Spirit of Judicial Reform), *Tap Chi Nghien Cuu Lap Phap* (4), 24–31.

148 Le Trung Ha (1965), *supra*, 1, 2.

decisions, if rigorously implemented, may go some way towards convincing judges the state is serous about 'rule of law' reforms.[149]

While they wait for procedural reforms to take hold, lawyers continue to use informal processes to increase their leverage in the courtroom. For example, lawyers in the Hero Cong Ty case discussed earlier were prevented by the trial judge (Nguyen Thi Hoai Linh) from challenging the court's flagrant misapplication of the law. In order to encourage the judge to apply the law correctly, the lawyers approached journalists to publish a series of stories exposing the legal irregularities. Recent surveys show that 64 per cent of respondents believe that the press plays a vital role in securing just court decisions.[150]

The Role of Procurators in Economic Court Cases

As well as prescribing modest adversarial processes, Resolution No. 8, followed by Resolution No. 49, sought to clarify the investigation, prosecution and supervisory functions of the procuracy. The Ministry of Justice argued the government should assume responsibility for prosecutions to avoid possible conflicts of interest with the procuracy's other functions. Rejecting broad reforms, the Law on the Organisation of the People's Procurators 2002 instead refocused the procuracy on prosecuting criminal actions and supervising court proceedings (including economic and civil actions).[151] But it retained the socialist-inspection functions that require procurators to appear in non-criminal cases (including economic and civil cases) as a third party to preserve the state benefit (article 2). According to lawyers interviewed, procurators take this statutory duty seriously and routinely support the state interests over private commercial rights in economic and civil cases.

The dual function performed by procurators compromises the ability of lawyers to produce evidence and raise legal arguments. In addition to representing the state's interest, which frequently conflicts with private commercial rights, procurators supervise legal compliance within the courtroom and prosecute judges found deviating from the law. Lawyers are convinced that judges are unlikely to treat the arguments raised by procurators and lawyers impartially given the procurators' power to supervise legality in the courtroom.

Courtroom Corruption

The extent to which corruption influences court decisions is difficult to gauge. Lawyers interviewed, however, believe it is a significant problem.[152] Their anecdotal

149 Party Resolution No 48 NQ/TW 24 May 2005 on Perfecting the Socialist Oriented Economy and *Nha Nuoc Phap Quyen* (Law-based State).

150 UNDP (2004), *supra*, 18.

151 See Law on the Organisation of the People's Procuracy 2002, articles 12–22.

152 See generally Pip Nicholson (2000), *supra*, 215–17.

accounts suggest that at one level corruption is formalised in a range of extra fees charged to process court documents. These small bribes rarely determine outcomes, although they may reduce access to courts by increasing costs.

At another level, bribes routinely modify the way judges assess liability and/or allocate remedies. Bribes persuade judges to interpret 'party leadership', government directives, 'professional guidance' and superior legislation in ways that advance particular personal interests. Corruption flourishes where subordinate rules implementing rights-based laws are vague and contradictory. Judges are more reluctant to accept bribes where government regulation is clear or the Supreme Court has issued professional guidance specifying particular outcomes. In these circumstances, corrupt deviation from the 'official' line is more difficult to disguise.

Lawyers were uncertain whether corruption supports or hinders imported commercial rights, since bribes are used both to support and oppose legal rights. What is certain is that corruption constitutes yet another extra-legal variable that compromises legal reasoning. By undermining the predictability and enforceability of imported private commercial rights, corruption corrodes the 'rule of law'.

Judicial Implementation of Imported Commercial Laws

Three main factors appear to shape judicial implementation of imported commercial legal rights. The first factor is the epistemological rules judges use to decipher imported laws. 'Party leadership', which generates the most hierarchically important epistemological settings, persuades judges to privilege the party and state benefit over private interests and to elevate domestic interests above foreign interests (except where they conflict with international economic integration). These historically conditioned orientations deeply influence the way judges interpret private commercial rights.

Since the party-line is generally vague and non-specific (except in politically sensitive cases), judges look to subordinate legislation issued by government agencies for prescriptive rules that specify how party and state socioeconomic policies should be implemented. Further clarification is provided by 'professional guidance'. This epistemological hierarchy discourages judges from using legal reasoning to resolve commercial disputes.

The second factor is that the narrow categories of 'legal sources' (*thua nhan luat*) impede the development of judicial reasoning.[153] As we saw in Chapter 3, for decades socialist legal thinking discouraged legal officials, including judges, from bringing 'official' legal discourse into conversation with local moral and economic norms and practices. This closed epistemology prevented knowledge gained by judges applying Soviet law from percolating up to inform Vietnamese lawmakers.

Contemporary judges are similarly constrained by the 'official' legal discourse from drawing ideas from local precepts and practices that could generate creative

153 Judges are required to rely narrowly on party guidelines and *ban hanh luat* (issued law). Interviews with Judges, *supra*.

adaptations of imported commercial laws. Without access to 'secondary legal' sources of the kind that inform Western legal doctrines, such as parliamentary debates, sustained academic commentary and legal cases, Vietnamese judges struggle to develop home-grown legal doctrines that naturalise imported commercial rights.

Many judges (especially in lower-level courts) routinely use *thoa dang* (situational) reasoning to create solutions to commercial problems that did not exist in rights-based law. This practice produces socially acceptable outcomes because it selectively draws ideas from 'official' and 'unofficial' local discourses to produce contextually relevant outcomes. Even if higher-level authorities were prepared to learn from *thoa dang* reasoning, a possibility currently discouraged by democratic centralist thinking, this form of reasoning does not contemplate generalised normative solutions that are easily transformed into universal legal principles.

The third factor shaping judicial interpretations are the procedural reforms governing courtroom discourse. Even before the Civil Procedure Code introduced modest adversarial reforms, lawyers acting in economic cases were using legal arguments to bring judicial deliberations closer to the law. Most lawyers support legal discourse because it provides a set of rules that in some circumstances enables them to protect their clients' property and contractual rights against private interference, though much less frequently against state encroachment. They also promote law-based decision-making because legal processes generate demand for their professional skills.

Even as some lawyers are promoting a procedural 'rule of law', competitive pressures, low professional standards and a lack of professional role models have excited many unethical practices. Lawyers routinely pay introduction fees and kickbacks to secure new clients and use a broad range of extra-legal tactics, including moral and political appeals, press campaigns and even bribery to secure an advantage. By strategically substituting legal reasoning with political and moral arguments, lawyers can erode the uniform and predictable legal meanings that make imported rights-based laws credible alternatives to clientism and relational transactions.

To conclude, judges currently base most decisions on a combination of party and government directives and corrupt incentives. As a result, the meanings ascribed to imported commercial rights reflect the protean nuances of state policy and personal imperatives more than law-based reasoning. For this to change, judges need to develop secondary legal sources that draw inspiration from domestic commercial precepts and practices. Supreme Court case guidelines and annual reports are tentatively moving in this direction. But reforms that give judges the power to make significant decisions, require a more fundamental change that places legal reasoning at the apex of the epistemological hierarchy.

Assessing the Potential for Courts to Base Decisions on Legal Reasoning

Chapter 3 argued that courts during the revolutionary period performed a largely instrumental role in furthering party and state rule. Courts are now required to follow both party leadership and laws to resolve commercial disputes. What remains unclear is how they will reconcile these sometimes competing sources of authority. There are two questions to consider: what messages do laws and 'secondary legal' sources send to judges about imported commercial rights, and will courts be given (or arrogate) the epistemological independence to use legal reasoning to filter party and government directives?

Several factors militate against the emergence of autonomous judicial decision-making. According to an influential Supreme Court judge, the leadership worries that legal reasoning might disrupt the strict hierarchies encouraged by democratic centralism and 'party leadership'.[154] This concern recalls the historical suspicion in socialist legal thinking that jurisprudence stimulates autonomous judicial decisions that reinterpret the official line. The emergence of legal reasoning is further impeded by *thoa dang* or situational judicial decision-making.

It is interesting to speculate in what circumstances the party and government might contemplate a judiciary with epistemological autonomy. As previously mentioned, in times of rapid change, party institutions may search for more effective ways of resolving social problems. Judicial independence may, for example, distance the party from sensitive commercial struggles between foreign and local enterprises and intractable civil disputes over housing and personal debt. It may also reinforce the party's ideological depiction of Vietnam as a law-based state.

Consider the action by two founders of Hero Cong Ty against the company's manager.[155] They alleged the manager, in contravention of the Company Law 1990 and Law on Enterprises 1999, used his control over the company seals and records to exclude them from making management decisions and participating in dividend declarations.

The main struggle took place outside the courtroom. Both the founders and manager were well-connected party members and used their influence to manipulate decisions made by district-level party units and city-level people's committee departments. According to lawyers acting for the founders, the manager used his more powerful party connections to block these initiatives. The people's committee refused to act, but sent a letter to the Chief Judge of the Hanoi Provincial Court ordering the Economic Court to resolve the dispute. This case is significant in showing that, when political processes were unable to resolve a commercial dispute, some party and state authorities sought a judicial solution.

Even if the party supports judicial autonomy, it does not automatically follow that judges will protect imported commercial rights. Like other state officials, judges are immersed in 'official' discourses that convey mixed messages about the sanctity of private rights. Some arguments favour the 'state benefit' over private rights,

---

154 Interviews Dang Quang Phuong, Director, Institute for Judicial Science, Supreme Court, Hanoi.

155 This case study is based on information provided in interviews with lawyers with Leadco, the law firm acting for the company founders, during March 2003.

others promote international legal harmonisation and the preservation of private commercial rights.

Changes to adversarial processes will also give lawyers more opportunities to use rights-based discourse in the courtroom. A few lawyers already employ imported doctrinal arguments to show judges how private legal rights function in market economies. As lawyers gain more procedural power it will become more difficult for judges to ignore legal arguments and base their decisions on political, moral and pecuniary considerations. Scrutiny by the international press and foreign donor community is also increasingly pressuring judges to reach rights-based outcomes.

Current reforms suggest a potential for legal reasoning to develop in commercial and possibly civil cases. There is a precedent in the illiberal regimes in Singapore and Malaysia for well-developed commercial courts that promote trade and investment to coexist with tight executive control over politically sensitive cases. The procedural reforms instigated by Politburo Resolution No. 8, and now confirmed by Resolution No. 49, suggest that party leaders in Vietnam are sensitive to popular perceptions about judicial impartiality, competence and legal certainty. But there are few signs the party countenances a form of judicial independence that gives courts power over political decision-making. As previously noted, courts are generally the last state institution to gain this type of power.

Conclusion

The previous chapter showed that party leaders have opened lawmaking discourse to international legal harmonisation and foreign legal imports. For legal drafters informed by these narratives, law reforms based on legal borrowing appear both desirable and technically feasible. Case studies explored in this chapter suggest, on the contrary, that efforts to move law out of the statute books into everyday life are more complicated than legal harmonisation theories admit.

Two main factors account for the complexity in implementing imported laws. The first level of complexity is generated by differences in the way central and local officials interpret imported laws. Studies showed that regulatory conversations between elite-level government officials and foreign investors and lawyers are changing official attitudes to rights-based laws. These exchanges inform central regulators about how legal rights function in facilitative legal systems and aim to create a regulatory network that supports capitalist contractual and property rights.

Just as neoliberal oriented interpretive communities are coalescing around certain central-level drafting committees, some central-level regulators are beginning to think through neoliberal legalism.[156] Although the case studies show that regulators converse in a rather heterogeneous assortment of ideas, some generally support the deregulation of state economic management powers and private commercial rights. Within these loosely constituted neo-liberal oriented interpretive communities,

156 In some ministries, such as the Ministry of Planing and Investment and the Ministry of Trade, the same officials are involved in both legal drafting and regulation.

borrowed ideas are increasingly becoming the frame of reference for implementing the law.

Just as some legal drafters resisted neo-liberal legalism, some central regulators (especially from the Ministry of Transport and Ministry of Culture and Information) show little sympathy for imported facilitative regulation and search for ways to limit private rights with state economic management.

Many local-level officials, principally at the district and *phuong* (ward) levels, are either isolated from or reject foreign discourses. Steeped in pre-colonial and socialist anti-mercantilism, communitarianism and nationalism, they hardly need reminding to privilege the state benefit over private, particularly foreign, commercial rights.

Since courts function differently from other state bureaucracies, judges have been comparatively isolated from foreign-influenced interpretive communities.[157] Judges alone are supposed to interpret private rights according to legal rules. They are discouraged from seeking ideas outside laws and authorised 'secondary legal' sources such as internal party and state guidelines. Courtroom discourse and foreign donor-funded training courses are among the few arenas where judges are exposed to detailed explanations about how imported rights laws function in market economies. The penetration of rights-based discourse into judicial decision-making is further constrained by epistemological rules that privilege party leadership and government policies over law and by *thoa dang* (situational validity) decision-making that treats imported commercial rights as one of many contextually relevant sources of authority. Together, these factors have limited the capacity for judges to create new legal fictions from imported laws that provide solutions to commercial problems—solutions that are unavailable in local precepts and practices. Put differently, epistemological constraints coupled with limited resources (especially legal skills) have limited the judiciary's power to make significant decisions that imaginatively adapt imported laws to local conditions.

The second main factor that complicates the implementation of imported laws is the power struggles within and among state agencies. A difficulty with examining legal borrowing solely from a discursive perspective is that key state agencies use ideas strategically to pursue self-interests. For example, central regulators promoting facilitative regulation may benefit through family and friends from rights-based laws.[158] Meanwhile some line-ministers use state economic management ideas to camouflage institutional rent-seeking. Here the debate is not so much between

157 With the exception of one provincial level judge in Ho Chi Minh City, no senior economic court judges read English with sufficient fluency to absorb Western legal ideas without the support of foreign-educated junior staff.

158 Some party leaders oppose market law reforms that may increase competition and damage family businesses, while others see commercial opportunities in international integration. See Quan Xuan Dinh (2000), 'The Political Economy of Vietnam's Transformation Process', 22 *Contemporary Southeast Asia* (2), 360–88; Martin Gainsborough (2003), *Changing Political Economy of Vietnam: The Case of Ho Chi Minh*, RoutledgeCurzon, London, 98–110.

rival ideas about how best to import legal reforms, but rather between conflicting institutional and personal interests.

Some of the confusion about deregulating entrepreneurial activity is attributable to conflicting political agendas. Although some central policymakers are unquestionably moving to deregulate business licences and inspections, as a matter of political strategy it suits others to retain 'state economic management' powers to ensure that private commercial rights support state socioeconomic policies. For example, the prime minister used state inspection powers over land to force Phu My Hung Corporation to abandon court action that challenged the state's right to increase taxes levied over foreign investors. Discretionary powers enable party and state leaders to import commercial legal rights secure in the knowledge that state officials possess the prerogative powers to minimise harm to state interests.

Power-sharing contests between local government agencies and the Supreme Court are likewise changing the way legal rights are implemented. As the Supreme Court gains control over lower-level courts, the interpretation of private legal rights may increasingly follow judicial guidelines rather than government directives. But it is still unclear whether the strict epistemological hierarchies governing legal reasoning will enable courts to develop the legal doctrines required to naturalise imported legal rights. This shift also requires a judiciary that is willing and sufficiently well-trained to use legal doctrines to guide the application of rights-based law to commercial disputes. Although still peripheral players, lawyers are bringing judges into contact with foreign legal discourse and neoliberal legalism in ways that may eventually stimulate local innovation and adaptation.

Finally, the implementation of imported laws highlights conceptual and institutional impediments to the introduction of a procedural 'rule of law'. Most state officials are far removed from the lawmaking discourse promoted by foreign donor and some elite-level government agencies that make the 'rule of law' seem both desirable and inevitable. Even some elite-level regulators acknowledge the premium placed on legal stability by the 'rule of law' is not necessarily desirable in a transitional environment in which imported commercial rights require creative localisation to resolve local business disputes. Even more troubling, a procedural 'rule of law' that protects commercial legal rights from administrative action might undermine the ability of party leaders to use prerogative powers to ameliorate the damaging impact of international economic integration.

Chapters 4 to 6 examine how commercial laws transplant into state power structures. The next chapter expands this inquiry by considering how social demand for law influences legal transplantation. This discussion focuses on the ways organised pressure groups influence the importation and adaptation of commercial laws.

Chapter 7

Non-state Pressure Groups and Legal Borrowing

Introduction

Studies in democratic liberal societies show that law does not just happen when there is a social need, someone or some group generally presses for statutory reform. Pressure groups lobby drafting committees and use electoral leverage to correct or ameliorate social and economic problems.[1] As the third working postulate (discussed in Chapter one) intimates, the way lawmakers interact with pressure groups strongly influences the selection and adaptation of borrowed laws. It is possible, for example, that state-owned enterprises and foreign investors in Vietnam may use their political connections to influence lawmakers and regulators to the detriment of politically unconnected domestic entrepreneurs.[2] This chapter assesses how entrepreneurial pressure groups influence the meanings given to commercial laws imported into Vietnam.

Discourse analysis assists our inquiry by suggesting that pressure groups are most likely to influence the 'official' discourse informing lawmakers where communicative channels are relatively unmediated by party and state instigation and coercion. Open discursive environments enable pressure groups to communicate unconventional or controversial ideas and models (unofficial discourse) to lawmakers. This interaction produces the preference convergence required to adapt and localise imported law. Conversely, laws drafted in secret, without public consultation, are less likely to reflect local contextual concerns.

Much literature concerning public participation in lawmaking presupposes a political space (civil society) in which non-state pressure groups can organise and influence lawmakers through unmediated discursive exchanges (deliberative democracy) and elections.[3] But civil society concepts do not readily extend to

1 See Alan Watson (1978), 'Comparative Law and Legal Change', 37 *Cambridge Law Journal* 313, 324.

2 See Martin Gainsborough (2003), *Changing Political Economy of Vietnam: The Case of Ho Chi Minh City*, RoutledgeCurzon, London, 16–39.

3 Some writings treat civil society as a metaphor for uncoerced political space that can confront the state. See Michael Walzer (1992), 'The Civil Society Argument', in Chantal Mouffe (ed.), *Dimensions of Radical Democracy: Pluralism, Citizenship, Community*, Verso, London, 89–91. This thinking has been applied to Vietnam; see, for example, Joe Hannah (2005), 'Civil-Society Actors and Action in Vietnam: Preliminary Empirical Results and

Vietnam, because, as discussed in Chapter 4, the party and state possess extensive powers to co-opt and suppress 'unofficial' discourse. This study takes the position that, although public discourse and political space in Vietnam differ significantly from Western conditions, we can derive a conceptual language from civil society analysis that is useful for understanding non-state influence over Vietnamese lawmaking.[4]

The first part of this chapter uses discourse analysis to ascertain whether entrepreneurs (foreign and domestic) can influence legislative drafters through formal and informal organisational structures. In the second part, the discussion explores whether voters (including entrepreneurs) can harness representative processes to influence lawmaking in the National Assembly (NA).

Influencing Legislative Drafters

Habermas, to some extent, initiated thought about discursive lawmaking that takes place outside constitutional processes with the publication in 1962 of his book *Structural Transformation of the Public Sphere*.[5] He considered representative government more as an ideal than a practical reality and explored ways the public can use deliberative pathways to influence lawmakers.[6] Laws (and ultimately democracy) are shaped, he argued, by morals, ethics and pragmatic matters synthesised from exchanges and contests between lawmakers and society—a process he termed 'communicative rationality'.[7] These deliberative exchanges presupposed a political space (civil society) in which pressure groups can organise and lobby lawmakers.

Habermas imagined preference convergence taking place in state-societal interactions that are particular to Western Europe. Nevertheless, research suggests that his 'communicative rationality' has heuristic value in Vietnam's tightly controlled political space. Scholars studying agricultural reforms in Vietnam during the 1960s and 1970s observed that dialogical exchanges between state officials and farmers influenced lawmaking.[8] A quiet, sometimes covert, process of negotiation

---

Sketches from an Evolving Debate', in Heinrich Böll Foundation (ed.), *Towards Good Society: Civil Society Actors, The State, and The Business Class in Southeast Asia—Facilitators of or Impediments to a Strong, Democratic, and Fair Society?*, Heinrich Böll Stiftung, Berlin, 101–10.

4 It is important not to conflate the descriptive and normative aspects of civil society.

5 Jürgen Habermas (1991), *Structural Transformation of the Public Sphere: An Inquiry into a Category of Bourgeois Society*, trans. Thomas Burger, MIT Press, Cambridge, Massachusetts.

6 Jürgen Habermas (1999), 'Between Facts and Norms: An Author's Reflections', 76 *Denver University Law Review*, 938.

7 See Jürgen Habermas (1984), *The Theory of Communicative Rationality*, trans. T. McCarthy, Beacon Press, Boston, 261.

8 See Adam Fforde (1984), 'Law and Socialist Agricultural Development in Vietnam: The Statute for Agricultural Producer Cooperatives', 10 *Review of Socialist Law* 315, 317–19; Melanie Beresford (1989), *Vietnam: Politics, Economics and Society*, Pinter, London, 116–18.

and compromise adjusted party policy with notions proposed by groups operating outside constitutional and party mechanisms. 'Dialogical lawmaking' is significant because it occurred at a time when the party and state vigorously suppressed unauthorised associations and autonomous political space.

Ben Kerkvliet characterised these exchanges as 'dialogue in the broadest sense of the word, which incorporates communication of contentious ideas and preferences in ways that, in Vietnam, are often indirect and non-verbal'.[9] He showed that party and state lawmakers were unable to cope with widespread resistance to cooperative farming practices. An effective response to this pressure was to find alternative sources of institutional order—'discursive sources of order'—comprising ideology, epistemologies, organisational practices and other communicative acts that allowed the state to converse with recalcitrant social groups. 'Dialogical lawmaking' enabled state authorities to secure cooperation from farmers in return for limited participation in the lawmaking process.

Farmers could not use constitutional or party mechanisms to express their views, because the 'official' discourse prohibited private farm production.[10] During a decade of 'dialogical lawmaking' state officials and farmers reached shared understandings (or preference convergence) about the appropriate balance between state and private farm production. Principles extracted from these exchanges slowly gained party consent and eventually crystallised into new regulatory approaches to agriculture.

Kerkvliet questioned whether the depiction of Vietnam as a 'dominating' or 'state-corporatist' state adequately explained the dialogical exchanges occurring at the periphery of state power.[11] If the state formulates policies and laws entirely within the party and state orbit and channels public voices through party-controlled mass organisations, how does it respond to ideas that challenge the official discourse? Dialogical studies show that sustained communication between state and society generates the preference convergence required to codify unorthodox or dissenting norms ('unofficial' discourse) into law. This chapter extends this investigation by using discourse analysis to assess how dialogical exchanges between non-state entrepreneurs and lawmakers change the meanings of imported commercial laws.

The Emerging Influence of Pressure Groups in Vietnam

Discourse analysis informs us that the communication of unorthodox or dissenting ideas to lawmakers is most likely to succeed in exchanges that are relatively

---

9 Benedict J. Tria Kerkvliet (2001), 'An Approach for Analyzing State–Society Relations in Vietnam', 16 *Sojourn* (2), 1, 2–3; also see Benedict J. Tria Kerkvliet (2005), *The Power of Everyday Politics: How Vietnamese Peasants Transformed National Policy*, Cornell University Press, Ithaca, New York.

10 See the Statute on Higher-Level Agricultural Producer Cooperatives, discussed by Adam Fforde (1984), 'Law and Socialist Agricultural Development in Vietnam: The Statute for Agricultural Producer Cooperatives', 10 *Review of Socialist Law* 315, 315–17.

11 See Kerkvliet (2001), *supra*, 2–3.

unmediated by the party and state. In some cases (discussed below) individuals communicate directly with lawmakers in unmediated exchanges. But more generally, pressure groups must organise to make their views known. Since lawmakers cannot consult 'the masses', the state encourages entrepreneurs to express their views through 'authorised' associations. The following discussion considers whether business associations operate with sufficient autonomy from the state to contest state policy and convey unconventional ideas and practices to lawmakers.

State Recognition of Popular Participation in Lawmaking

Official attitudes to popular participation in lawmaking were influenced by collective mastery (*lam chu tap the*) and socialist democracy (*dan chu xa hoi chu nghia*), principles that stressed the need to 'make the people part of the process' (*duong loi quan chung*).[12] Collective mastery rejected civil society (*xa hoi dan su*) or individual space outside state and collective orbits as bourgeoisie individualism.[13] In pre-*doi moi* society the party insisted that the views of 'the masses' should be transmitted through party and mass organisations to lawmakers.

The 1992 Constitution reconfigured socialist democracy by stipulating that the 'people must know, discuss, act and examine' (*dan biet, dan ban, dan lam, dan kiem tra*). Drawing on notions of people's power that underlie collective mastery principles, the party began to emphasise the need for 'direct democracy' (*dan chu truc tiep*) to encourage the public to become involved in lawmaking. Increased public participation was justified on the basis that it would make laws more efficient by 'bringing the law into real life' (*dua phap luat vao cuoc song*).[14] Various scholars argued that direct democracy would induce 'people's sovereignty' (*chu quyen nhan dan*) and make 'laws reflect the common will of society' (*phap luat la y chi chung cua xa hoi*).[15] But they also insisted the party should lead public participation by stimulating 'legal consciousness' (*y thuc phap luat*) and discrediting 'false' opinions and ideologies.

In tandem with 'direct democracy' reforms, the party is cautiously granting social actors, including entrepreneurs, more autonomy from party organisations. Carlyle Thayer wrote in 1995,

---

12 See Dinh Gia Trinh (1961), 'May Y Kien Dong Gop Ve Van De Bao Ve Phap Che' (Some Opinions on the Protection of Legality), *Tap San Tu Phap* (3), 20, 23.

13 See Nguyen Vinh (1977), 'Building the System of Socialist Collective Ownership' *Tap Chi Cong San* (4), trans. JPRS 69283, 20 June 1977, 28; Do Sang and Duc Hanh (1986), *Ve van De: Lam Chu Xa Hoi Chu Nhgia bang Nha Nuoc* (On the Use of the State to Realise Socialist Collective Mastery), Nha Xuat Ban Phap Ly (Law Publishing House), 11–12.

14 See *Lay Y Kien Cac Van Ban Quy Pham Pham Luat* (Obtaining Comments on Legal Documents), Official Letter No. 2012/VPCP-PC, 27 May 1998.

15 See Nguyen Dang Dung (2001), 'Phap Luat Khong Chi La Cong Cu Cua Nha Nuoc' (Law is Not Only the Instrument of the State), *Tap Chi Nghien Cuu Lap Phap* (11), 53–57.

> Vietnam's market reforms have not only given birth to a legalised private sector, but have led to the revitalisation of groups and associations formed as a result of local initiatives. With the exception of groups which have attempted to engage in overtly political activity, state authority has generally tolerated—if not encouraged—the activities of revitalised organisations and newly formed associations.[16]

By the late 1990s the proliferating number of associations began to concern party leaders and the Politburo called on state agencies to ensure that associations closely followed party policies.[17] After years of debate and numerous redrafts, Decree No. 88 ND-CP Providing for the Organisation, Operation and Management of Associations was passed in 2003. It attempts to reconcile the party's desire for associations that promote economic and social development with concerns that non-state organisations may oppose party and state policies.

Article 4 of the Decree rather nebulously instructs state agencies to 'make favourable conditions enabling associations to operate efficiently in accordance with their character'. A government directive encourages business associations to gather their members' views on laws and state management and make proposals to responsible authorities. But other provisions in the Decree signal the state's intention to retain tight control over associations. The Interior Ministry, for example, has discretionary 'state management' (*quan ly nha nuoc*) powers to license associations, change association charters, guide *nghiep vu* (operating skills), evaluate office bearers and control funding sources (articles 15, 34, 35).

Recent studies suggest that the state exercises its extensive powers over associations selectively.[18] Associations supporting state development objectives such as poverty reduction, education and the economy are flourishing. World Values Survey data showed that Vietnamese in 2001 were more likely to belong to mass organisations and associations (2.33 groups), than Chinese (0.91 groups) and Japanese (1.41 groups).[19] Although the state tolerates some spontaneous gatherings and demonstrations, it vigorously suppresses organised pressure for political and civil rights that challenge party and state policies.

---

16 Carlyle A. Thayer (1995), 'Mono-Organizational Socialism and the State', in Benedict J. Tria Kerkvliet and Doug J. Porter (eds), *Vietnam's Rural Transformation*, Westview Press, Boulder, 52.

17 See Chi Thi so 42/CT-TW Cua Bo Chinh Tri ve Viec Tang Cuong Su Lanh Dao Cua Dang Doi Voi To Chuc va Hoat Dong Cua Cac Hoi Quan Chung, Ngay 6-10-1998, Directive No. 42/CT-TW on the Strengthening of the Party Leadership in the Organisation and Activities of Popular Associations, issued by the Politburo on 6 October 1998.

18 See generally Ben J. Tria Kerkvliet, Russell H. H. Heng and David W. H. Koh (eds) (2003), *Getting Organised in Vietnam: Moving in and Around the Socialist State*, Institute of Southeast Asian Studies, Singapore.

19 R. Dalton and N. Ong (2001), *The Vietnamese Public in Transition: The World Values Survey – Vietnam 2001*, Center for the Study of Democracy, University of California, Irvine. Available online at <www.uci.edu/csd> (hereafter referred to as World Values Survey Vietnam 2001).

It is beyond our purposes to speculate whether the liberalisation of popular associations constitutes a 'creeping pluralism' that will eventually create a civil society or that changes in state regulation are better explained as pragmatic political responses to social pressure. Evidence supports both contentions.[20] This discussion focuses instead on whether the state permits business associations to negotiate with lawmakers about the selection and adaptation of imported commercial laws.

Entrepreneurial Associations

The government stresses the need to 'cooperate and listen closely to the opinions of the business community'.[21] The Law on the Promulgation of Legal Normative Documents 2002 formalised this policy by giving entrepreneurs a right to *tham gia* (participate) in lawmaking. Although article 3 requires drafting agencies to 'organise public comment' from those affected by draft bills, they retain the discretion whether, and with whom, they should consult.[22]

Selected entrepreneurs are invited to express their views about business laws to the prime minister during annual meetings; although, for more sustained dialogue with lawmakers, entrepreneurs must join business associations (*hiep hoi kinh doanh*) or clubs (*cau lac bo*).[23]

There are no reliable records of the number of business associations, but estimates range from 100 to 200 in 2002.[24] The proliferating number of business associations conveys the erroneous impression that entrepreneurs interact with lawmakers through many deliberative channels. A study conducted by the Mekong Project Development Facility in 2001 challenged this view by showing that entrepreneurs predominately direct their concerns through one umbrella organisation—the Vietnam Chamber of

20 See generally Ben J. Tria Kerkvliet *et al.* (2003), *supra*.

21 Phan Van Khai (1997), 'Pho Thu Tuong Phan Van Khai: Chinh Phu Thong Qua Phong Thuong Mai va Cong Nghiep Viet Nam De Cac Doanh Nghiep Hop Tac Voi Chinh Phu Nham Day Nhanh Tien Trinh Doi Moi' (Deputy Prime Minister Phan Van Khai: The Government Approves the Chamber of Commerce and Industry of Vietnam to Cooperate with the Government to Speed up the Process of Renovation), *Dien Dan Doanh Nghiep* 4 April, 2.

22 Law on the Promulgation of Legal Documents 2002, article 3.

23 See Directive No.27 CT-TTg Prime Minister, 2003, article 14. In addition to formal associations, many groups have formed clubs, research centres and social service centres. For example, the 'High Quality Vietnamese Products Club' was formed in 2001 to (among other objectives) collect and forward opinions to state authorities. See Phung Long (2004), 'The High Quality Vietnamese Product Club', *Vietnam Economic News* (29), 34. See generally Michael Gray (1999), 'Creating Civil Society? The Emergence of NGOs in Vietnam', 30 *Development and Change* (4), 693.

24 See Nguyen Phuong Quynh Trang and Jonathan Stromseth (2002), 'Business Associations in Vietnam: Status, Roles and Performance', MPDF No. 13 Private Sector Discussions, Hanoi, 21. Also see Jonathan Stromseth (1998), 'Reform and Response in Vietnam: State-Society Relations and the Changing Political Economy', unpublished PhD thesis, Columbia University, 137–39.

Commerce and Industry (VCCI).[25] Participation in lawmaking is further limited by the small number of entrepreneurs that belong to business associations.[26] Membership is especially meagre in rural provinces.

VCCI (originally called the Vietcochamber) was established in 1963 primarily to represent the interests of SOEs trading with socialist bloc countries.[27] Following market liberalisations in the late 1980s, it was reconfigured as 'an independent, non-government organisation' to represent state and private enterprises. During the 1993 National Congress, Pham Chi Lan, then the vice-president, committed VCCI to represent the business community and develop 'an independent and reliable voice of its own'.[28]

Although describing itself as an 'independent' (*doc lap*) body, VCCI is expected to operate 'with the support and under the supervision of the Vietnamese state'. It retains strong formal and informal linkages with the state. For example, the current chairman is the former Minister of Trade and party Central Committee member, while many staff members have worked with government bodies and are party members.[29] Vu Oanh, the Politburo member responsible for mass-mobilisation, confirmed this close relationship when he described VCCI as the 'highest representative of the business community and the appropriate instrument for the party and state to gather and guide the business community for all economic sectors of the country in the cause of building the economy'.[30] More recently, the government directed VCCI to act as a conduit between government agencies and other business associations.

In some respects VCCI resembles Schmitter's model of socialist state-corporatism (discussed in Chapter 4). Its management is closely connected with the party and state, and 30 per cent of its revenue is contributed by the state. It is positioned at the apex of a hierarchical structure that controls regional branches and industry-specific employer organisations. Associations representing entrepreneurs may join

---

25 See MPDF, *supra*, 20–25.

26 See CIEM (2003), 'Comparative Provincial Performance in Private Business Development: Some Preliminary Observations from Nine Provincial Case Studies', UNDP VIE01/025, Hanoi, November, 37–38.

27 Decree No. 58 CP, 26 April 1963.

28 VCCI (1993), 'Strengthening the Organization and Activities of the Chamber of Commerce', unpublished paper 11, VCCI, Hanoi, 3.

29 Interviews Pham Chi Lan, Vice President VCCI and Pham Thi Thu Hang, Deputy General Director, VCCI (Small and Medium Enterprise Promotion Center) Hanoi, 2001–03.

30 Vu Oanh (1995), 'Phong Thuong Mai da Tro Thanh Mot To Chuc Tin Cay de Tap Hop, Van Dong, Giup Do Ho Tro va Bao Ve Loi Ich cac Doanh Nghiep Trong Su Nghiep Kinh Doanh: Bai Phat Bieu cua Dong Chi Vu Oanh Uy Vien Bo Chinh Tri Ban Chap Hanh Trung Uong Dang Cong San Viet Nam tai Hoi Nghi Hoi Dong Quan Tri Phong Thuong Mai va Cong Nghiep Viet Nam Lan Thu VI' (The Chamber of Commerce has Become a Reliable Organisation for Gathering, Mobilising, Assisting and Protecting the Interests of Enterprises in Business Affairs: Speech by Vu Oanh, Meeting of the Politburo of the Communist Party of Vietnam at the Sixth Meeting of the Executive Committee of the Chamber of Commerce and Industry of Vietnam), *Dien Dan Doanh Nghiep*, 22 September, 12.

as full voting members, although membership is still overwhelmingly dominated by SOEs. Members are directed to transmit concerns through VCCI or Fatherland Front organisations such as the Hanoi Association of Industry of Commerce and are discouraged from dealing directly with state organisations.[31] For example, when the Union of Associations of Industry and Commerce (UAIC) (*Hiep Hoi Cong Thuong Thanh Pho Ho Chi Minh*) in Ho Chi Minh City began to influence local policymaking, its leadership was replaced by party appointees. Finally, government drafting committees are required to consult VCCI and (some Fatherland Front business associations) when preparing commercial legislation.[32]

Although VCCI's structure resembles a state-corporatist body, doubt remains whether it performs the state-corporatist function of recognising and legitimising the interests of entrepreneurs, while preventing these interests from disrupting state policy. What remains unclear is whether VCCI is sufficiently independent from the party and state to advocate views that challenge the government's legal harmonisation agenda.

The Participation of Entrepreneurs in Legislative Drafting

Detailed consultation between VCCI's executive and its members about draft legislation primarily takes place within the Advisory Board and Executive Committee. Representatives on this body are drawn from the leadership of VCCI's main constituents such as SOEs, Fatherland Front organisations and other business associations. Yet even this select group complains that consultation periods of two weeks or less are too short to solicit comments from members.[33] Although most draft legislation is now posted on VCCI's website for comment, this initiative has done little to broaden participation in lawmaking. Individual entrepreneurs generally lack the time, skills and resources required to formulate detailed comments. Responses tend to be highly contextualised and based on personal opinion rather than a sustained

31 These views are based on interviews with private entrepreneur associations in Hanoi and Ho Chi Minh City (hereafter refereed to as the 'Associations Interviews'). Vu Duy Thai, Vice Chairman and Secretary The Hanoi Associations of Industry and Commerce (member of the Central Committee of the Fatherland Front), Hanoi, April 1999, February 2000; Nguyen Trung Tuc, Chairman, Vietnam German Entrepreneurs' Club, Hanoi, 1999, 2000; Pham Thi Thu Hang, Deputy General Director, VCCI (Small and Medium Enterprise Promotion Center) Hanoi, 1998, 1999, 2002; Nguyen Hoang Luu, General Secretary, Hiep Hoi Cac Doanh Nghiep Vua Va Nho Ha Noi (Hanoi Small and Medium Enterprises Council), Hanoi, 1999, 2000; Cao Thi Kim Dung, Information Service Manager, Union of Associations of Industry and Commerce (Hiep Hoi Cong Thuong Thanh Pho Ho Chi Minh), Ho Chi Minh City, 1998, 1999.

32 See Directive No. 16 CT-TTg on Solving Recommendations of Enterprises 1998; Official Letter No. 2012/VPCP-PC Obtaining Comments on Legal Documents May 1998, issued by the Office of Government.

33 Interviews Vu Duy Thai, Vice Chairman and Secretary, The Hanoi Associations of Industry and Commerce, Hanoi, March 1999, January 2000, March 2003.

analysis. As such, they lack persuasive power compared with comments prepared by the Advisory Board and Executive Committee.

VCCI's involvement in drafting the Enterprise Law (EL) exemplifies its role in representing entrepreneurial voices to lawmakers (see Chapter 5). It had direct access to the drafting committee. The vice-president sat on the steering committee, and the head of the legal department was appointed as a member of the drafting committee.

A great deal of the information that eventually convinced the drafters to partially deregulate market entry for corporations came from research reports prepared by VCCI and CIEM. CIEM officials needed to cooperate with VCCI to counter arguments made by other members of the drafting committee that proactive market-entry controls were necessary to manage the economy. VCCI organised a series of workshops to collect evidence from its members showing how proactive market-entry controls generated high compliance costs. As anticipated, case studies revealed that business licensing was costly, inefficient and produced some absurd market distortions. CIEM synthesised these findings into an especially influential report that was presented in 1998 to the government and members of the drafting committee.[34]

Some entrepreneurs that took part in the workshops revealed in interviews that VCCI's staff tightly managed interaction with the drafting committee.[35] Participation in the workshops was by invitation only. VCCI officials used pre-determined agendas to control the topics discussed. They also vetted written comments prepared by entrepreneurs. Face-to-face discussion with drafters was equally constrained. Entrepreneurs were given few opportunities to conduct the prolonged discussions needed to convey a nuanced understanding of their views. Most business associations lacked the resources to prepare their own submissions and relied on VCCI to portray their views accurately.

Although entrepreneurs supported market-entry deregulation, they were much less enthusiastic about imported corporate governance rules that prescribed complex internal management, statutory reporting, minority shareholder and merger and acquisition rights and obligations. They worried that elaborate, rights-based corporate governance provisions were remote from everyday family-based business organisations (see Chapter 8). For example, some entrepreneurs thought that increased rights for minority shareholders would disrupt family-based management hierarchies and discourage the practice of granting employees shares. Most entrepreneurs actively opposed new provisions that increased reporting requirements, fearing that disclosure would give the state and business competitors access to sensitive business information and impose additional compliance costs. They reasoned that a complex

34 See Vien Nghien Cuu Quan Ly Kinh Te Trung Uong, (Central Institute of Economic Management) (1998), 'Danh Gia Tong Ket: Luat Cong Ty va Kien Nghi Nhung Dinh Huong Sua Doi Chu Yeu' (Review of the Current Company Law and Key Recommendations for Its Revision), unpublished paper, Hanoi, 25–39.

35 These views are based on the Associations Interviews.

law would further isolate entrepreneurs from the legal system and confuse poorly trained regulators and judges.

VCCI ignored opposition from its members and supported complex corporate governance rules. Entrepreneurs interviewed were unsurprised by this lack of consultation, because they did not expect VCCI to function as a member-directed organisation. Surveys corroborate this view. Entrepreneurs responding to a Mekong Project Development Facility questionnaire in 2002 indicated they were much more likely to join VCCI and other business associations to network with other businesses (67 per cent), gain market information and access technical training (41 per cent) than rely on the association to lobby lawmakers (15 per cent).[36]

A senior VCCI official involved in drafting the Enterprise Law conceded that 'the collection of opinions from entrepreneurs is not conducted regularly and scientifically' while 'opinions contributed by enterprises are not always considered and accepted strictly by drafting committees'.[37] More generally, a report prepared by the Office of Government about public participation in legal drafting accused drafting committees of 'being conservative, refusing to accept comments, generally compartmentalising their thinking and favouring the states' interests over private interests'.[38]

It is possible to interpret the Enterprise Law case study as showing that the VCCI, together with its government allies, took on powerful adversaries to champion greater market access for its private sector members.[39] What this account fails to show is that economic arguments favouring private sector development were deeply entrenched in the 'official discourse' well before the Enterprise Law. Starting in 1993 with the draft Law on the Promotion of Domestic Investment, VCCI and CIEM worked together to convince party and state leaders that domestic entrepreneurs supported the national economy. They claimed that entrepreneurs would only mobilise domestic capital if they were extended the same privileges as those given to the state sector and foreign investors.

Rather than fearlessly championing the interests of their members, VCCI joined with CIEM and like-minded government agencies drafting the Enterprise Law in a 'palace war' against ministries struggling to retain 'state economic management' powers (see Chapter 5). They selectively represented (*dai dien*) entrepreneurial

36 Nguyen Phuong Quynh Trang and Jonathan Stromseth, 2002, *supra*, 31.

37 See Tran Huu Huynh (2002), 'Roles Played by the Chamber of Commerce and Industry of Vietnam on the Participation in the Formulation and Implementation of the Legal Normative Documents on the Economy', unpublished paper, Workshop on Amending, Supplementing the 1996 Law on the Promulgation of Legal Normative Documents, Hanoi, 6.

38 Office of Government (2003), 'Study Report to Improve the Quality of Laws and Ordinances Drafted by the Government to be Submitted to the NA and the NA Standing Committee', unpublished report, Working Delegation No. 804, Hanoi, December, 5.

39 See Jonathon Stromseth (2003), 'Business Associations and Policy-Making in Vietnam' in Ben J. Tria Kerkvliet, Russell Heng and David Koh eds., *Getting Organized in Vietnam: Moving In and Around the Socialist State,* Institute of Southeast Asian Studies, Singapore, 88-92.

views that supported market liberalisation, while ignoring opposition to complex corporate governance provisions. CIEM, the lead drafting agency, was persuaded by foreign legal advisers to apply uniform corporate governance rules to both large and small companies.

The preceding discussion suggests VCCI has the capacity to convey entrepreneurial concerns to lawmakers during regular meetings with lawmakers, yet it is unlikely to communicate unorthodox or controversial ideas without the support of powerful allies in the government.[40] Rather than promoting 'unofficial' discourse, it takes positions in debates within the 'official discourse'. These findings are consistent with Jonathan Stromseth's evaluation of VCCI as 'a hybrid system the combines residual aspects of Leninism with emerging elements of corporatism'.[41] Without strong government support, VCCI lacks the political authority to advocate views from its members that challenge party and state policies.

This position has not appreciably changed. Public consultations for the draft Unified Enterprise Law conducted during 2004 and 2005 suggest that six years after the Enterprise Law was enacted, domestic entrepreneurs still remain outside the lawmaking calculus. The party appointed CIEM to draft a law that, in compliance with the US–Vietnam Bilateral Trade Agreement (BTA), abolished distinctions between foreign and domestic investment.[42] Public consultations have overwhelming focused on concerns raised by foreign investors, donors and law firms.[43] Vietnamese entrepreneurs were provided few opportunities to express their opposition to legal reforms that will give foreign competitors greater access to domestic markets. Throughout the drafting process, VCCI has remained remarkably silent about the growing unease among its domestic members about increased foreign competition that will arise from the Uniform Enterprise Law and other legal harmonisation projects.

Business Discussion Fora

Contrasting with the highly structured and mediated exchanges organised by VCCI, for a brief period from 1998 until 2001, the Private Sector Forum (PSF) (*Dien Dan Khu Vuc Tu Nhan*) promoted open dialogue among government officials, foreign donors and foreign and domestic investors.[44] The PSF was established to 'improve investment and the business environment for the private sector in Vietnam in order

---

40 See Tran Huu Huynh (2002), *supra*, 4.

41 Stromseth (1998), *supra*, 234.

42 See Duong Dang Hue, (2005) 'Unified Enterprise Bill and the Fulfillment of Investment Relation Development Commitments in the BTA' 11 *Vietnam Law and Legal Forum* (132), 2-6.

43 Workshops were arranged by the Starr project, funded by USAID, and by GTZ, funded by the German government. See generally VNS (2005), 'Unified Enterprise Law Coming Soon', *Viet Nam News*, 18 March, 16, 18.

44 The Private Sector Forum was jointly organised by the Ministry of Planning and Investment (MPI), the International Finance Corporation and World Bank.

to stimulate economic development, increase employment and improve people's lives'.[45]

During monthly meetings, government officials and legal drafters discussed policy in informal and relatively unmediated exchanges with domestic and foreign entrepreneurs.[46] Domestic entrepreneurs often criticised state policy and advocated reforms to bring commercial laws more in line with local normative practices. Eventually the press began reporting PSF communiqués in which domestic and foreign entrepreneurs joined forces to criticise government policy.

Although domestic and foreign entrepreneurs were united in their opposition to 'state economic management' (*quan ly kinh te nha nuoc*), they often disagreed about legal reforms aiming to give foreign investors increased market penetration, such as market liberalisations and fair trade laws. Domestic entrepreneurs pressed lawmakers to incorporate local business practices into law and not merely rely on imported models.

In July 2001, the government symbolically renamed the Private Sector Forum the Vietnam Business Forum (VBF) (*Dien Dan Doanh Nghiep Viet Nam*) and limited membership to business associations.[47] Domestic firms that critically challenged government policy in the PSF were excluded under the VBF rules. In their place, quiescent domestic business organisations, such as the Hanoi Business Association (formerly the Young Entrepreneurs' Club) and Hanoi Association of Small and Medium Enterprises Trade Association, adopted a more conciliatory, even collaborative, approach to state policy. Business associations presented a range of views within established policy settings (official discourse). Foreign business associations, however, continued to advocate neoliberal legal views that contested many official positions.[48]

Each year, VBF members appoint a different foreign law firm to chair Consultative Group Meetings and coordinate working groups to critique particular aspects of state regulation.[49] VBF members, especially foreign law firms, work closely with the foreign donor community to promote neoliberal legal reforms (discussed below).[50] Discussions between the VBF and the government about the draft Ordinance on

45 See Nguyen Hong (2002), 'Policies Given Modest Thumbs up at Forum', *Vietnam Investment Review*, 27 May, 4.

46 Comments about the Private Sector Forum are primarily based on interviews with Vietnamese lawyers working in Investconsult, Vilaf and Vietbid law firms during February and August 2000, January and March 2001, March 2003 and March 2005.

47 Ibid.

48 American investors and law firms, for example, are grouped together in the American Chamber of Commerce. See AmCham position papers available at <http://www.amcham hanoi.com/adPositionPapers.htm>.

49 In 2004, 25 foreign law firms were licensed to practice in Vietnam.

50 The Vietnam Business Forum promotes neoliberal economic versions of the 'rule of law'. See Tony Foster (2002), 'Rule of Law – Benefits for Private Sector', unpublished paper, Vietnam Business Forum, Hanoi, May.

Arbitration demonstrate the comparatively unmediated interaction between foreign law firms and drafting committees.

A UNDP report in 1999 identified the lack of commercial arbitration independent from the courts as a major impediment to foreign investment.[51] Two years later, in 2001, the government began drafting a new arbitration ordinance to comply with the BTA. VBF members and foreign donors funded workshops to discuss the bill with the drafting committee. Some government lawyers were taken on study tours to familiarise themselves with regional practices and legal and economic arguments for non-government arbitration.

Deliberations were conducted in a mutually comprehensible legal and economic language, which minimised political arguments that might otherwise have transformed discussions into power contests between local and foreign interests. For example, in overcoming government resistance to foreign-appointed arbitrators, foreign advisers reminded the drafting committee about Vietnam's legal obligations under the BTA to provide an 'international best practice' arbitration system. Using a similar logic, they also informed drafters that international arbitration rules give domestic courts limited opportunities to review arbitration wards. The original Decree No. 116 CP on the Organisation and Operation of Economic Arbitration 1994 allowed litigants to refer arbitral awards to domestic courts for review (article 31). Finally, foreign advisors stressed the nexus between independent arbitration and flourishing foreign investment in highly successful economies such as Singapore. Most reforms advocated by the VBF were incorporated into the Ordinance on Commercial Arbitration 2003.

In comparison to domestic entrepreneurs, foreign investors enjoy sustained and relatively unmediated contact with lawmakers. Despite periodic complaints by the VBF that neoliberal legal reforms have not gone far enough, the incremental deregulation and liberalisation of the economy, coupled with the massive importation of rights-based law suggests that foreign pressure groups have introduced new, and often controversial, ideals into the lawmaking discourse.

Foreign Donor Influence over Vietnamese Legal Discourse

Following *doi moi* reforms, lawmakers could no longer rely on Soviet discourse for solutions and began looking for new sources of inspiration. Few possessed the linguistic skills required to comprehend Chinese legal theory and practice, and at least initially they considered Chinese thinking unrealised and derivative.[52] Especially

---

51 See UNDP (1999), 'Completion of Viet Nam's Legal Framework for Economic Development', UNDP Discussion Paper No. 2, United Nations Development Programme, Hanoi, 52–55.

52 Vietnamese legal journals (especially Tap Chi Nghien Cuu Lap Phap) and newspapers such as Phap Luat have since 2002–03 increasingly published accounts about Chinese legal reforms. See generally Mark Sidel (1995), 'The Re-emergence of China Studies in Vietnam', *The China Quarterly* (142), 521–40.

since the mid-1990s, however, Chinese legal experience has become increasingly influential.

From the Law on Foreign Investment 1987 onwards, every major commercial law has been drafted with foreign donor support.[53] A matrix prepared by the Ministry of Justice (MOJ) for the Legal Needs Assessment (LNA) shows that bilateral and multilateral donors have agreed to provide legal advisers to support the government in drafting every commercial bill and most of the non-commercial bills until 2010.[54] The collective effort of foreign donors rivals, and perhaps exceeds, the legal assistance provided by the Soviet Union during the 1960s and 1970s.

Despite the considerable resources devoted to legal drafting, the ideas communicated by donors are more fragmented and diverse than was the case under Soviet tutelage. Another obvious difference is that contemporary legal advice must negotiate a political culture that still strongly influenced by Soviet legal thinking (see Chapters 3 and 4). Yet another difference is the existence of a donor hierarchy—some donors are listened to more closely then others.

Donor Assistance Projects

The French were among the earliest Western donors to provide legal assistance. Given the antipathy many Vietnamese feel towards the French and their colonial legal system (discussed in Chapter 2), the decision to borrow law from France for the Company Law 1990 warrants closer scrutiny. One explanation is that Professor Luu Van Dat, the senior legal drafter, was trained in French law at the Faculty of Law, Hanoi University, during the French colonial period.[55] He understood French legal documents and could discuss complex contractual and corporate law principles in French with foreign legal advisers. Few members of the drafting committee understood English or Anglo-American corporate legal principles. As English language proficiency among state officials increased during the 1990s, the French policy of uncompromisingly linking legal assistance to French language training limited their influence.[56]

The Japanese, whose legal assistance is funded by the Japanese Bank for International Cooperation and JICA, have closely targeted reforms identified under

53 See 'Bulletin on Law and Policy Reform' from 1995 until 2002, published by the Asian Development Bank.

54 See Ministry of Justice (2002), 'Summary Matrix in Order of Priority: The Action Plan for Implementing Vietnam's Strategy for Development of its Legal System until 2010', unpublished paper, Ministry of Justice, Hanoi.

55 These comments are based on numerous interviews with Phan Huu Chi, former Legal Advisor to the Minster of Justice, Hanoi, April 1992, February 1993; Luu Van Dat, Legal Advisor to the Minster of Trade, September 1994, March 1999.

56 Interview Line Petitclerc, Maison de Droit, Hanoi, November 2002.

the 'New Miyazawa Initiative'.[57] The current cycle of assistance aims to support the 'Investment and Protection Agreement' signed by Vietnam and Japan in 2003.[58] A distinctive feature of the agreement is the conditional linkages between aid and investment plans for specific industries such as the automobile and electronics industries. While the reform program supports neoliberal legal concerns such as transparent property rights and effective enforcement regimes, it also encourages state institutions to use import tariffs and other government imposts to stimulate industrial development. The Japanese legal model is appealing to the Vietnamese, since it offers a compromise between state-directed socioeconomic planning and the neoliberal legal model advocated by other donors.

Japanese legal assistance is also highly regarded by Vietnamese recipients. In the first place, the Japanese are the largest bilateral source of funds. But, more importantly, their legal system commands prestige because it shows how to adapt Western rights-based law to an East Asian system. In practice, however, there is little evidence that Japanese projects encourage sensitive localisation of transplanted norms and practices. On the contrary, Vietnamese informants note that Japanese advisers frequently promote legal models based on Japanese laws and legal practices. Finally, generous legal education scholarships make Japanese legal assistance attractive to government agencies.

Other foreign legal projects share a common interest in promoting variations of neoliberal legal reforms.[59] As the leading donor in the legal sector, the UNDP's approach to legal development epitomises the neoliberal legal agenda.[60] US-trained lawyers acted as the resident advisers for two of the most important legal projects in Vietnam.[61] They took their inspiration from Hayek's proposition that transparent, universal and predictable legal rules (a procedural rule of law) provide the optimal regulatory environment for entrepreneurs to maximise their self-interest (see Chapter 3). Hayekian entrepreneurs seek out profit-making opportunities through spontaneous

---

57 Japan is the largest bilateral donor in Vietnam. See Hiroshi Suzuki (2002), 'Vietnam Private Promotion and Business Environment', unpublished paper, Vietnam Business Forum, May.

58 See Interview (2003), 'Japanese Ambassador, Hattori Noroi and Pham Van Dung, Head of the Government's Negotiating Team', *Vietnam Economic Times*, May, 16–17.

59 See UNDP (2002), 'Legal System Development, Past Ongoing, and Planned Donor Programmes', unpublished paper, United Nations Development Programme, Hanoi <www.undp.org.vn/themes/governance/matrix.html>.

60 See John Bentley (1999), 'Completion of Viet Nam's Legal Framework for Economic Development', UNDP Discussion Paper 2, United Nations Development Programme, Hanoi, 1–8. For similar views see Asian Development Bank (2004), 'Report on Asian Development Bank's Law and Policy Activities in Support of Poverty Reduction', Asian Development Bank, Manila, <www.adb.org/Documents>.

61 For eight years, John Bentley was the senior UNDP legal resident advisor. Theodore Parnell, also a US-trained lawyer, led a Danish-funded UNDP project through 1996–99, providing technical assistance to the Supreme People's Court, Supreme People's Procuracy and Office of the National Assembly.

individual action that is primarily (though not exclusively) guided by external state rules. Non-state relational norms and ethno-religious and sentimental factors that regulate Vietnamese businesses, by implication, are considered unbounded, inefficient and potentially anarchic. Other influential multilateral donors such as the World Bank, Asian Development Bank and most bilateral donors treat this neoliberal version of the rule of law as the *a priori* model that should guide legal interventions in Vietnam.[62]

Promoting Neoliberal Economic Ideology

To some extent, the ascendancy of neoliberal legal thinking over other legal models (such as the Japanese approach) mirrors a broader hegemony propelled by US political, economic and military supremacy.[63] Conditions attached to loans for structural development under the Comprehensive Poverty and Growth Strategy prepared by the World Bank aimed to promote the neoliberal legal agenda.[64] Studies considered in preceding chapters show that foreign donors have used Vietnam's commitment to international market-access treaties (especially the BTA and the WTO) to promote the neoliberal legal agenda. These ideas were incorporated into the previously discussed Legal Needs Assessment prepared by the Ministry of Justice.

Some donors use legal drafting projects to advance neo-liberal legal ideas. Take for example the International Finance Corporation's (IFC) support for the draft Decree No. 165 Implementing Articles of the Civil Code Concerning Secured Transactions. From the outset, informants reported deep divisions in the approaches advocated by the State Bank, the lead drafting agency, and the IFC. The State Bank made the political argument that foreign creditors should not gain control over 'land-use rights' (*quyen su dung dat*) by foreclosing mortgages. If foreign banks were to use foreclosure procedures to secure property rights (*quyen so huu*), the State Bank worried they could bypass 'state economic management' controls over land transfers.[65] In promoting the neoliberal ideal that property rights should be freely transferable, the IFC challenged the state's political commitment to state management as a means of safeguarding public assets against foreign domination.

Legal consultants acting for the IFC used economic arguments to support the deregulation of property transfers. In most foreign joint-venture agreements the Vietnamese party (usually SOEs) contributes capital in the form of land-use rights.

---

62 See generally Tom Ginsburg (2000), 'Review Essay: Does Law Matter for Economic Development? Evidence from East Asia', 34 *Law and Society Review* 829, 847–50.

63 See generally Ugo Mattei (2003), 'A Theory of Imperial Law: A Study on U.S. Hegemony and the Latin Resistance', 3 *Global Jurist Frontier* (1). Available at <www.bepress.com/gj/frontiers>.

64 See Irene Norland, Tran Ngoc and Nguyen Dinh Tuyen (2003), *Dealing with Donors: The Politics of Vietnam's Comprehensive Poverty Reduction and Growth Strategy*, Policy Paper 4, Institute of Development Studies, University of Helsinki, Helsinki, 6–9, 21–28.

65 Land is treated as a special commodity (*hang hoa dac biet*) or public good and its transfer requires state approval.

If foreign banks were permitted to use land-use rights as collateral, the country-risk premium charged on loans would drop, thereby encouraging more investment. Consultants also argued that the preamble to the Civil Code, which proclaims the principle of legal equality, guides the interpretation of civil relations, such as mortgages. Since article 349 of the Civil Code allows mortgagees to secure land-use rights, by implication this right should extend to foreign bank branches, which are considered Vietnamese entities.

Informants reported that a pattern emerged in which the drafting committee liberalised property rights during workshop meetings, but 'higher authorities' reinserted state management powers when the draft bill was circulated among state agencies for comment. Attempting to break the deadlock, the IFC sent the entire drafting committee to Singapore to prepare a final draft in an environment 'free from external distractions'. As expected, the final draft reflected the IFC position and Decree No. 165 on Security Transactions 1999 granted foreign creditors rights to secure land. The victory was short-lived because the State Bank subsequently issued a series of interagency circulars restricting the rights of foreign banks to secure land-use rights.[66] This position was entrenched in the Land Law 2003.

Emerging Interpretive Communities

Previous chapters have intimated that certain legal drafters, donors and consultants are forming discrete interpretive communities. Before considering evidence for this important development, it is worth considering why interpretive communities have the potential to influence legal borrowing. Discourse analysis informs us that communication is influenced by interpretive knowledge and skills.[67]

> Members of regulatory communities have ongoing relationships with each other. In those relationships, they both pursue their own, often inconsistent, interests and struggle to define a shared vision of the collective good. Because they live significant parts of their lives with each other, members of the community frequently influence each other, act with reference to each other, and desire each other's respect. Therefore, as well as being arenas for the pursuit of pre-existent interests, regulatory communities appear to have the capacity to be 'constitutive'—that is, to be forums in which appropriate individual and collective behaviour (and interests) are defined and redefined.[68]

66 See Joint Circular No. 1417 TT-TCDEC Outlining Procedures on Mortgaging Land Use Rights 1999; Joint Circular No. 3 TTLT-BTP-BCA BTC-TCDC Providing Guidelines on the Realisation of Security Property for Loans to Recover Debts Owing to Credit Institutions, 23 April, 2001.

67 See Christine Parker (1999), 'Compliance Professionalism and Regulatory Community: The Australian Trade Practices Regime', 26 *Journal of Law and Society* (2), 215–40.

68 E. Meidinger (1987), 'Regulatory Culture: Theoretical Outline', 9 *Law and Policy* 355, 365.

This observation suggests that members of 'regulatory' or 'interpretive' communities are likely to have similar views about the meaning and social function of particular laws. It further suggests that the meanings underlying imported laws are much more likely to be transferred intact between members of the same 'interpretive' community than between members of different interpretive communities.

Research suggests one of the key constituting factors binding 'interpretive' communities is a shared language and similar education. The difficulty in understanding foreign ideas transposed into Vietnamese idioms is not unique to law. But legal language differs from ordinary usage, since it requires specific training to understand the doctrinal meanings invested in words. Western linguistic studies draw attention to the lexicality of law (its use of unique words), the high occurrence of mononyms (using words with only one accepted meaning) and the greater incidence of 'restricted connotations' (changing the meaning of ordinary words when used in legal conversations).[69] These internal meanings are revealed through education and interpretive communities that generate shared understandings.

Foreign donors and investors involved in legislative drafting projects recognise the importance of language and devote considerable resources to 'capacity building' projects that inculcate neoliberal legal ideas through English language training. A review of legal projects in the ADB's *Bulletin on Law and Policy Reform*, published in 2001, revealed that most included sub-programs giving Vietnamese officials English language training, followed by detailed instruction in neoliberal 'rule of law' concepts.[70] This pattern continues. Most projects back-up short-term in-country courses by strategically selecting Vietnamese officials for masters and PhD training, primarily at Australian, US and UK universities.

It is difficult to estimate the precise number of Vietnamese exposed to neoliberal legal discourse, but donors suggest that virtually every legal official at the central level of government has received some foreign training.[71] Hundreds of officials and privately funded students are now returning to Vietnam with Anglo-American post-graduate legal training.

It is implausible to infer a direct correspondence between legal training and the inculcation of neoliberal legal ideas. Foreign legal ideas are difficult to translate and explain in short-term training programs and they do not enter Vietnamese legal thinking unopposed. As we have seen, there are many discursive streams within

69 See B. Jackson (1988), *Law, Fact and Narrative Coherence*, Deborah Charles, Roby, Merseyside, England, 29–31.

70 Twenty-one of the 28 legal projects listed for Vietnam involved some form of training for 'rule of law' ideas. See Asian Development Bank (2001), *Bulletin on Law and Policy Reform*, ADB, Manila, 62–68.

71 It is possible to infer from information gleaned by the author in interviews with donor agencies from 2000–2004 that thousands of state officials have received English language training, hundreds have participated in specialised legal English courses, and about 100 receive scholarships to study law in the United States, Australia and United Kingdom each year.

Vietnamese legal thinking that actively block or change the meaning of neoliberal legal ideas.

There is stronger evidence that long-term training, especially if it is conducted in Anglo-American (neoliberal legal) countries, influences legal thinking. Foreign-trained officials act as conduits between foreign advisers and legal drafting committees. They possess the linguistic and interpretive knowledge needed to present neoliberal legal ideas in modes of thought that appeal to Vietnamese legal drafters. Officials from CIEM who participated in the Enterprise Law drafting committee, for example, were trained at Australian and UK universities in neoliberal economic and legal theory.

Even long-term legal and economic training does not automatically change legal thinking. Many state officials returning with foreign qualifications discover their superiors are indifferent, even hostile, towards new legal ideas. It might take them years to gain enough status to introduce new ideas into state institutions. Moreover, foreign qualifications are now seen by many as a means of securing political advancement. What seems to matter most is whether the interpretive traditions in the workplace encourage, or at least do not obstruct, new thinking.

Rather than converting to neoliberal legalism *en masse*, the law making elite develops small but influential cliques sympathetic to this thinking. The strongest evidence for the emergence of neoliberal interpretive communities is found in the collaborative structures formed between foreign donors/lawyers and certain Vietnamese consultants and state officials. Legal projects inculcate neoliberal legalism by bringing foreign advisors into a close working environment with a growing number of local legal consultants, who either enjoy close connections with, or are still employed as, state officials.[72] Consultants are frequently foreign-educated and well-acquainted with neoliberal legalism. They also share stylistic similarities with foreign donors. Information in reports prepared by local consultants, for example, is ordered, analysed and presented according to standard donor formulas. Even report-writing styles and structures reflect predetermined templates. The stylistic similarities suggest the professionalisation of domestic consultants, where the rhetorical assertion of neoliberal legal objectives is the substance and stylistic presentations are the output.

The incentive to conform is provided by access to donor-funded projects, foreign travel and education. Tendering rules reinforce the stylistic requirements, while friendships and networking with members of the foreign donor/investment community provide access to the unwritten 'rules of the game'. Projects are awarded to consultants who have learnt how to analyse problems and prescribe solutions from neoliberal legal perspectives.

72 Investment consultant firms such as Investconsult, Galaxy, Leadco, Vietbid, and Concetti work closely with foreign investors and donors in providing research and strategic advice promoting law reform.

A small but influential clique within the lawmaking elite are also becoming enmeshed in neoliberal-oriented interpretive communities.[73] These technocrats work in central ministries or central research institutions and are responsible for adapting foreign laws to Vietnamese conditions. Collaborating closely with foreign legal advisers, they treat legal ideas as technical fragments unconstrained by cultural borders, and evince an unwavering conviction in the capacity of the 'rule of law' to induce economic development.

All this suggests that foreign and domestic economists and lawyers involved in drafting commercial laws are forming interpretive communities. These lawmaking clusters should not be thought of as communities in a physical sense, but rather as abstract bonds with the potential to generate cooperation and shared responses to legal borrowing. Government technocrats, donor staff and locally based foreign and domestic consultants know each other, work on the same projects, and increasingly share similar educational backgrounds and worldviews. Common social interests and professional ideas encourage an enclave-like and self-referential approach to policy alternatives. This in turn generates a propensity for foreign-funded projects to exclude or minimise critical legal and political perspectives.

Members of these interpretive communities are rather heterogeneous in their use of the language and ideas. This is explained by the need to reconcile neo-liberal ideas with the epistemological traditions governing the foundational interpretive communities (such as party, state and family) to which they first belonged. In order to function within multiple interpretive environments, they need to use neo-liberal ideas strategically. But in working closely with foreign donors, they are constantly exposed to particular story-lines or narratives about the correct approach to regulatory problems. In providing detailed explanations for solving economic problems, neoliberal legalism frequently gives these technocrats an edge over lawmakers struggling to make 'state management' apply to market conditions.

The extent to which neoliberal legalism has infiltrated Vietnamese state institutions is probably underestimated. It often suits both foreign and local interests to downplay the extent of foreign influence, because the spectre of foreign influence is easily used to discredit legal change. Donors also frequently miscalculate the extent of their influence. They conflate legal reforms that are amenable to resolution in the short to medium term with reforms that address transactional practices that are so deeply rooted that they are only likely to respond to long-term historical changes. This leads them to underestimate their influence in changing attitudes to imported law.

73 See Irene Norland, Tran Ngoc and Nguyen Dinh Tuyen (2003), *Dealing with Donors: The Politics of Vietnam's Comprehensive Poverty Reduction and Growth Strategy*, Policy Paper 4, Institute of Development Studies, University of Helsinki, Helsinki, 149.

Informal Deliberative Exchanges

Personal Exchanges

As Kerkvliet reminds us, local voices reach the ears of lawmakers through informal dialogical exchanges. Well-connected local and foreign entrepreneurs bypass formal deliberative fora and communicate directly with lawmakers. Secretive informal pathways to state power are naturally difficult to research. Informants describe two types of exchanges. Some wealthy entrepreneurs have formed clubs in major cities to press claims in regular meetings with state officials. Discussions are unmediated and generally concern requests for regulatory reforms that secure specific competitive advantages.

Consider the regulation of private banking in Ho Chi Minh City.[74] Regulators 'manage' bankers by ensuring that the boundaries separating lawful and unlawful activities are never clearly understood.[75] Contradictory and poorly disseminated State Bank lending provisions and vague bank licensing conditions make it virtually impossible to predict the limits of regulatory power. Compounding the problem, provincial and even central bank officials cannot provide accurate advice, because only ministers and/or deputy prime ministers decide high-level banking policy.

Lacking the political networks available to state-owned banks, private banks are forced to form personalistic relationships with officials in order to navigate the dangerous legal landscape. Bankers approach ministerial advisers or other senior bureaucrats obliquely through 'clubs' or professional mediators. They lobby ministers to issue official letters that clarify lending practices and convey privileged information that confers a competitive advantage over rivals. Inside information and 'umbrella' (*o du*) protection against interference by provincial/city officials enables select banks to expand their businesses into new profitable areas.

Economically powerful multinational entrepreneurs also negotiate directly with lawmakers. For example, legal advisers acting for BHP Petroleum, a large investor in offshore gas production during the early 1990s, worked directly with lawmakers in PetroVietnam to import international profit-sharing and profit-repatriation principles into Vietnamese law. Foreigner advisers persuaded lawmakers to base profit-repatriation rules on normative practices in the international oil and gas industry.[76] More recently, in 2003, Japanese motorcycle manufacturers directly negotiated with the Ministry of Trade to reduce tariffs that had been increased to encourage foreign investors to source more components from local producers.

74 This case study was gleaned from interviews with officials from the Asian Commercial Bank, Ho Chi Minh City, June 2001.

75 See Duong Xuan Minh (2001), 'Viec Hinh Su Hoa Quan Le Giua Ngan Hang va Doanh Nghiep Rat Nang Ne' (Heavy Criminalisation of Relationships between Banks and Businesses), *Dau Tu*, September, 18, 1–2 (banks are reluctant to loan money to private sector clients because they fear criminalisation of loan agreements by state inspection authorities).

76 Interviews Noel Fabri, Senior Legal Advisor, BHP Petroleum, May 1992, June 1993.

State officials drafting laws are also exposed to domestic conversations with family and friends. Raymond Mallon observed that contacts between entrepreneurs and lawmakers developed during the initial periods of regulatory change.[77] Many state and party officials had family and friends in businesses and through these connections were personally acquainted with the difficulties faced by entrepreneurs in a legal system run by socialist-trained bureaucrats.

Communicating with Lawmakers through Popular Resistance to Laws

Even those without political connections find ways to influence lawmaking. Take, for example, the prolonged social campaign for market-compensation (*boi thuong*) for land compulsorily acquired by the state. In Marxist–Leninist theory land has no market value because it is owned by the people and managed by the state. As a 'special' (*dac biet*) commodity (public good), land lacks *gia tri* (value) and *gia tri su dung* (consumption value).[78] State compensation formulas attempted to replicate market prices 'scientifically' using indicators such as location and building quality.

Intense competition for housing in Vietnamese cities excited rapid price rises during the 1990s that outstripped compensation paid to residents and entrepreneurs relocated for road and infrastructure development projects.[79] Compensation paid under government valuation formulas was insufficient to purchase properties with equivalent income-generating potential.[80] Community dissatisfaction with compensation was expressed in numerous public demonstrations throughout urban and rural Vietnam. Demonstrations slowed infrastructure projects considered vital for economic development. Villagers living in An Tho village, in Ha Tay Province, for example, opposed the compulsory acquisition of 30 hectares of land to construct the An Khanh Industrial Park.[81] During 2001 and 2002 villagers damaged construction equipment and prevented local security forces from levelling the site. Development was delayed for three years while residents pressed claims for increased compensation

77 See Ray Mallon (2002), 'Approaches to Support the Development of an Enabling Environment for Small Enterprises', unpublished report, GTZ Country Report, Hanoi, 16.

78 See Tran Quang Huy (2001), *Giao Trinh Luat Dat Dai* (Land Law Text Book), Nha Xuat Ban Cong An Nhan Dan, Hanoi, 12–14.

79 See Author Unknown (2001), 'Co Phai Nha Nuoc Chay Theo Thi Truong?' (Is the State Running after the Market?), *Tuoi Tre*, 2 August, 4; Author Unknown (2001), 'Tangle Solving Land Law Enforcement: People Marching Forward, State Stepping Backward', *Tuoi Tre*, 6 August, 3, 4.

80 See Anh Thu (2001), 'Tu "Khuc Xuong" Giai Phong Mat Bang' (Site Clearance 'A Hard Nut to Crack'), *Dau Tu*, 14 August, 6; VNS (2002), 'City Needs New Plan to Soothe Disgruntled Resettled Residents', Vietnam News Agency, 1 November. Available at <www.vietnamnews.vnagency.com.vn>.

81 See Nguyen Hung Quang (2003), 'Provincial Case Study: Ha Tay', unpublished paper, Hanoi.

payments. Similarly, in 2004, 170 households in Ho Chi Minh City refused to accept compensation and delayed the construction of a tunnel under the Saigon River.[82]

In challenging compensation laws, some press articles raised the moral argument that 'it is unfair for the state to keep asking the people to sacrifice themselves for development' to criticise government compensation policies.[83] Public confidence in state compensation has been further eroded by persistent rumours that party and state officials used convoluted pricing formulas to compensate preferentially their families and friends.

A foreign adviser to the Ministry of Finance committee reviewing state compensation in 2002 surmised that public demonstrations coupled with unfavourable media reporting convinced members of the Party Central Committee to reconsider long-established socialist pricing formulas. The Seventh Plenum of the Party Central Committee in 2003 recommended amendments to the Land Law that required the government either to compensate land occupants with equivalent land or to provide financial compensation at or near market valuation rates. The reforms were enacted in 2004.

Underlying this reform is a fundamental shift in the way the party conceptualised land. Although the 1980 Constitution nationalised land ownership, it did not extinguish an informal real-estate market that has flourished in Vietnamese cities since colonial times. Along with title-by-registration and cadastral mapping, the French introduced the quintessential capitalist principle that land is a tradable property right (see Chapter 2). In giving land a market value, the party discarded the socialist notion that land is a 'special commodity' and moved one step closer to recognising land-ownership practices followed by urban residents.[84] The Land Law 2003 entrenched these reforms by formally sanctioning a real-estate market (articles 42–43, 61).

It can be inferred from this case study that popular resistance to socialist-inspired pricing formulas eventually convinced lawmakers to accept land as a commodity. Other factors, such as the state's desire to capture more revenue from land transfers and auctions were also influential. These findings show that even in highly mediated public settings popular demands can directly challenge the most sacred tenets in the 'official discourse'. But changing deeply entrenched preferences takes decades, making popular resistance an inefficient method of localising imported legal norms.

---

82 See Author Unknown (2004), 'Recalcitrant Residents Delay Start to Saigon River Tunnel', *Saigon Daily Times*, 5 February, trans. *Development Vietnam*, 11 February, 22.

83 See Hoang Van Minh (2001), 'Giai Phong Mat Bang, Di Doi Dan o Da Nang—Mot Cach Lam Dang De Tham Khao' (Site-Clearance and Population Relocation in Da Nang—A Worthy Measure to be Consulted), *Lao Dong* (Labourer), 15 August, 3.

84 Phung Minh (1998), *40 Nam Quan Ly Nha Cua O Ha Noi* (40 Years of Housing Management in Hanoi), unpublished monograph, Hanoi, 1–9.

Sentimental Communication

Besides reasoning with each other, pressure groups and lawmakers exchange unpleasantries, invoke sentimental imagery and assert their status. Many exchanges are influenced by emotions such as offence, resentment, shame (loss of face), loyalty, respect and self-esteem.[85] In short, public sentiment can influence lawmakers without (or in addition to) reflective discourse.

Emotional and other non-analytical influences on lawmaking are under-theorised and under-researched in every jurisdiction.[86] There are reasons for believing, however, that emotive or sub-verbal communication influences lawmaking in Vietnam. Chapter two informed us that during imperial times written laws and legal discourse were only thought necessary for the morally unperfected. There is a long history of using sub-verbal communication, such as leadership through moral example and civil resistance, to influence regulatory decision-making.

Kerkvliet depicted exchanges between authorities and farmers in the 1960s and 1970s as a 'nearly imperceptible dialogical give-and-take between what the state stipulated and what villagers did'.[87] Silent or emotive communication is discernable in current exchanges between the government and urban land users. Fewer than 20 per cent of householders in some major urban centres possess registered land-use rights (*quyen su dung dat*).[88] The other householders assert informal occupancy rights based on long-term usage or titles issued by French Colonial, Republic of Vietnam and provisional revolutionary authorities.[89]

Chapter 6 discussed the negotiations between local officials and residents securing access to urban land-use rights. Interviews with residents in Hanoi and Ho Chi Minh City reveal an analogous rejection of state land registration procedures that is communicated sub-verbally through mass popular resistance.[90]

Many residents choose not to legalise their land by applying for land-use right certificates. Residents interviewed invoked moral credibility (*uy tin*) to justify 'informal' claims to land. For example, they said it was wrong for the state to take

85 For a review of the literature supporting theories of normative development through non-deliberative processes, see Richard McAdams (1997), 'The Origin, Development and Regulation of Norms', 96 *Michigan Law Review* 338, 356–60.

86 See Cass Sunstein (1996), 'On the Expressive Function of Law', 144 *University of Pennsylvania Law Review*, 2021.

87 Benedict J. Tria Kerkvliet (1999), 'Dialogical Law Making and Implementation in Vietnam' in Alice Tay (ed.), *East Asia—Human Rights, Nation-Building, Trade*, Nomos, Baden-Baden, 373.

88 Approximately 80 per cent of residents in Hanoi and 60 per cent in Ho Chi Minh City lack formal land titles. See Duc Tho (2001), 'Secret Market Rankles Property Officials', *Vietnam Investment Review*, 8 October, 5.

89 Information about urban land conversion was gleaned from a series of interviews with land officials in Hanoi, Ho Chi Minh City, Hai Phong and Nam Dinh from 2001–2004.

90 Five focus group interviews with Hanoi and Ho Chi Minh City residents were conducted under the auspices of a World Bank Urban Infrastructure Project in June 2001.

away ownership rights conferred by French land titles. Or, more commonly, they asserted that since their grandfather owned their house it was wrong for the state to interfere in family inheritance by taking away ownership rights. Underlying these concerns is the fear that Soviet-inspired land-use rights based on state ownership will extinguish or diminish 'informal' rights.

Most residents thought that informal occupancy already conveyed the advantages of formal titles, such as transfer and security rights, without the disadvantages of transfer fees and land tax.[91] They sell their houses through land brokers, real-estate centres and in real-estate sections in newspapers.[92] The informal market is so well established that many residents had formed the view that eventually the state would abandon unpopular conversion policies and formally recognise land ownership.

Most residents had no intention of expressly communicating their concerns to authorities. Although some local authorities were sympathetic to 'informal' land use, they discouraged residents from lodging formal complaints that directly challenged state ownership over land. Residents also found their subtle, sentimental and moral attachments to land difficult to express in the formal language of petitions. Silent resistance to land titling communicated a message to lawmakers that land laws are morally incompatible with ownership rights claimed under informal land tenure.

Lawmakers responded to large-scale resistance by incrementally changing legislation to make land conversion more attractive. The state initially expanded the types of land tenures that could be legalised into a formal title. It then reduced the taxes imposed on land conversion from 20 per cent to 2 per cent.

Despite these concessions to local resistance, the official discourse continues to dismiss moral attachments to popular housing as superstitious or irrational with no place in a modern law-based society. From a legal perspective, land rights are privileges bestowed by the state and customary or moral land claims have no legitimacy until they are legalised. This strict instrumentalism gives lawmakers little discretionary space to reconcile state laws to moral claims. Paradoxically, the same lawmakers who unwaveringly advocate strict legal positivism in public admit in private that they and their families live in popular housing. In moral mode, they agree with the public that popular housing is an appropriate way to recognise land entitlements.

This case study demonstrates that, through silent resistance, residents changed the state's approach to land registration. Residents used ideas about property ownership imported during the colonial period to influence socialist precepts in the 'official' discourse. Silent resistance continues, however, because law reforms have addressed

91 A Ministry of Finance study has shown that in 2004 only 30 per cent of land transactions were registered with state authorities. See Author Unknown (2004), 'Two-Thirds of Property Informally Sold', *Lao Dong*, 1, trans. *Development Vietnam*, Intellasia News Service, 3 November, 15.

92 See Annette Kim (2004), 'A Market Without the "Right" Property Rights: Ho Chi Minh City, Vietnam's Newly Emerged Private Real Estate Market', 12 *Economics of Transition* (2) 275, 281–87.

economic concerns about the cost of title conversion, rather than the conviction that informal tenure has moral credibility (*uy tin*).

Entrepreneurial Voices in the Media

Our discussion would be incomplete without mentioning the role of the media in communicating entrepreneurial ideas to lawmakers. Habermas stressed the importance of the press in stimulating public discourse and making lawmakers accountable to popular concerns. Russell Heng has convincingly shown that, since *doi moi* reforms began, the volume, diversity and quality of media coverage in Vietnam has dramatically increased.[93] By 2003, there were over 500 accredited media agencies, with more than 600 publications, 20 online newspapers and over 10,000 media officials.[94]

There are approximately 10 newspapers specialising in business reporting and many more in-house publications produced by ministries, mass organisations and business associations. Some newspapers give entrepreneurs a public voice by carrying 'letters to the editor' sections and *Dien Dan* (Forum) sections in which selected topics are discussed and editorialised.

It is beyond our purposes to survey comprehensively the contribution the media make to communicating entrepreneurial concerns to lawmakers. It is sufficient to observe that the party and state control the media. Only state or Fatherland Front organisations are permitted to own media outlets. The Law on Press 2004 gives the party's *Ban Van Hoa Tu Tuong* (Culture and Ideology Commission) and the *Bo Van Hoa Thong Tin* (Ministry of Culture and Information) comprehensive powers to manage media content.

In practice, internal policy contradictions and uneven enforcement allow adventurous media editors to explore the boundaries of public expression and publish unorthodox or even dissenting views. For example, the press published many of the arguments that challenged core Marxist–Leninist axioms discussed in Chapter 3.

Party and state agencies use the press in campaigns against rivals. In drafting the Enterprise Law, for example, CIEM and VCCI initiated a series of articles in *Dau Tu* (Investment) and *Dien Dan Doanh Nghiep* (Business Forum) lauding the contribution domestic investors make to the economy. Stories in other journals focused on technical reforms to company law or criticised the complex 'state economic management' provisions that allowed administrative discretion to restrict business investment.[95]

---

93 See Russell Heng Hiang Khng (2000), 'Of the State, For the State, Yet Against the State', unpublished PhD thesis, The Australian National University, Canberra. Also see Russell Heng Hiang Khng (2001), 'Media Negotiating the State: In the Name of the Law in Anticipation', 16 *Sojourn* (2), 213.

94 See Ha Dang (2003), 'Improvement of the Party's Media Work in the Light of Ho Chi Minh Thought', *Tap Chi Cong San* (11). Available online at <www.tapchicongsan.org.vn>.

95 See, for example, Tran Huu Hiep (1996), 'Thuat Ngu Phap Ly Trong Cac Van Ban Phap Luat Kinh Te' (Legal Terminology in Economic Legal Instruments), *Tap Chi Toa An*

The diversity of views expressed in the media highlights a difficulty with conceptually distinguishing 'official' and 'unofficial' discourse. In some areas, the 'official' discourse in the media reflects a broad range of unorthodox and dissenting views. According to Russell Heng, certain editors and journalists use their personal initiative to introduce controversial views into the public domain. However, without support from party or state factions, media outlets are unlikely to run a sustained campaign promoting controversial views from entrepreneurs. It will be recalled that the media did not report entrepreneurial concerns that imported corporate governance provisions were overly complex and unsuited to local management practices.

Summary

The case studies show that politically-unconnected private entrepreneurs struggle to communicate unorthodox or controversial concerns to legal drafting committees. Their attempts to localise imported rights-based laws are filtered through imperatives and priorities determined by business associations. They also lack the resources to buy access to lawmakers. Politically well-connected entrepreneurs, on the other hand, benefit from personal (frequently corrupt) unmediated exchanges with lawmakers. The brief flowering of the PSF demonstrates both the demand by entrepreneurs for unmediated access to lawmakers and the unwillingness of the party and state to contemplate open public discussion.

Giving politically-unconnected entrepreneurs greater access to lawmakers is only one step towards more inclusive public participation in lawmaking. In addition, entrepreneurs need to distil their highly contextualised transactional practices into the abstract, codified standards understood by lawmakers. Legal drafters discussed in Chapter 5 lacked the skills, willingness and resources to subsume large amounts of local contextual detail under a general coding scheme. It is much easier for lawmakers to import and recycle legal norms and procedures than codify rules from the 'unofficial' discourse.

Foreign entrepreneurs, in contrast, have significantly more opportunities to influence drafting committees than their small-scale domestic competitors. Together with foreign donors, they have created interpretive communities that spread the neoliberal legal message into lawmaking institutions. Rather than codifying masses of local detail into legal texts—a process requiring politically sensitive decisions about which transactions deserve codification—many legislative drafters prefer to borrow well-prepared and prestigious foreign legal solutions. This approach is becoming increasingly attractive as market-entry treaties (especially the BTA and WTO) require neoliberal legal changes to the domestic legal system.

Despite their strong position, foreign entrepreneurs lack the close political connections enjoyed by SOEs. Yet, as Adam Fforde has demonstrated, SOEs do not

Nhan Dan, March, 7.

invariably oppose market deregulation and private rights.[96] In some circumstances it suits SOEs and their supervising agencies to support property rights that formalise the *de facto* privatisation of state assets. SOEs engaged in international trade appreciate well-conceived contract and property law regimes. However, in industries where SOEs retain monopolies or compete with foreign investors, they have vigorously opposed neoliberal legalism. For example, after years of intensive pressure, foreign banks have been unable to remove the SOEs' monopoly over lending for land. Foreign investors also ascribe the weak anti-monopoly rules adopted in the Competition Law 2004 to pressure exerted by SOEs and their supervising agencies.[97]

Lacking access to political power, residents used popular resistance to compel lawmakers to reconcile Soviet-inspired land laws with local land use practices. They communicated highly unorthodox views in a public arena that would not have been tolerated in constitutional forums. Over a decade, the combined weight of local-level negotiations and resistance to formal process compelled the state to accept market principles that substantially increased private rights over land. Nevertheless, the years required to convince lawmakers to change the law makes popular resistance an inefficient mode of legislative change.

Evidence that the state in some circumstances responds to social pressure does not necessarily signify movement towards deliberative democracy. Progress in this direction requires a profound change in state tolerance of 'lobbying' (*chay lo thu tuc*), demonstrations and ultimately political pluralism. It is instructive in this regard to contrast the tolerance shown to entrepreneurs and land users with the repression faced by those publicly agitating for democratic and civil rights.[98]

Since some communicative sites are more effective than others, politically connected local entrepreneurs and foreign investors are the most legally represented groups. One possible outcome is that imported commercial laws may come to reflect elite normative preferences, unless domestic entrepreneurs find other avenues to influence lawmaking.

Influencing National Assembly Delegates

We have seen that domestic entrepreneurs generally lack the connections needed to influence legislative drafters. If they are to raise their concerns with National Assembly delegates, several factors must be considered. Can entrepreneurs use

---

96 See Adam Fforde (2005), 'SOEs, Law and a Decade of Market-Orientated Socialist Development', in John Gillespie and Pip Nicholson (eds), *Asian Socialism and Legal Change: The Dynamics of Vietnamese Renewal and Chinese Reform*, Asia Pacific Press, Canberra, 242–53.

97 See Author Unknown (2004), 'Draft Competition Law Flawed: Professor Thanh Nien', 9 November, 3, trans. *Development Vietnam*, Intellasia New Service, 10 November, 7–8.

98 See Human Rights Watch (2001), 'Vietnam 2001', *Human Rights Watch World Report*, Human Rights Watch, New York. Available online at <www.hrw.org/wr2k1/asia/vietnam.html>.

representative processes to communicate with National Assembly delegates? Do entrepreneurs have opportunities to influence outcomes when draft laws are circulated by the National Assembly for public comment? Do National Assembly lawmakers listen to public voices?

Democratic Representation

Chapter 3 argued that Vietnamese 'socialist democracy' sharply contradicts democratic liberal notions of representative government. It draws from Lenin the conviction that popular elections, public hearings, referendums and civil society do not adequately secure the people's control over the state. Lenin rejected Lockean mythology that attributed legislative legitimacy to popular participation or authorship over lawmaking.[99] He thought that democratic rights were better safeguarded by 'proletarian dictatorship' (*chuyen chinh vo san*) in which the 'ruling class' directly supervised state organs through their proxy—the Communist Party. This Soviet doctrine that genuine democracy is only possible under socialist ownership and party leadership forms a consistent theme in Vietnamese legal writings.[100]

Influenced by Soviet *perestroika* reforms, Vietnamese leaders in the mid-1980s began critically reassessing the National Assembly's lawmaking.[101] They reasoned that orthodox socialist democracy had failed to alert the party adequately to economic and social problems. The National Assembly historically performed a largely passive, ceremonial function, approving and passing laws drafted by the party and state executive. For example, from 1945 until the 'Five-Year Plan for Legislation' (1981–85) the National Assembly only passed one law (*luat*).[102]

In order to reinvigorate the National Assembly, Nguyen Huu Tho, a former National Assembly chairman, declared in 1987 that the party would lead the National Assembly through persuasion, and unanimous votes would no longer be required

99 See Rainer Grote (1999), 'Rule of Law, *Etate de Droit* and *Rechtsstaat*—The Origins of the Different National Traditions and the Prospects for their Convergence in the Light of Recent Constitutional Developments', in Christian Starck (ed.), *Constitutionalism, Universalism and Democracy: A Comparative Analysis*, Nomos, Baden-Baden; David Held (1993), 'From City-States to a Cosmopolitan Order?', in David Held (ed.), *Prospects for Democracy*, Polity Press, Blackwell, Oxford, 20–22.

100 See, for example, Nguyen Duy Trinh (1956), 'Phat Trien Che Do Dan Chu Nhan Dan va Bao Quyen Tu Do Dan Chu Cua Nhan Dan' (Developing the People's Democratic Regime and Ensuring People's Liberties and Democratic Rights), *Hoc Tap* (3), 23, 24.

101 See Nguyen Dang Quang (1989), 'What is Socialism?', *Tap Chi Cong San*, (1), trans. FIBIS East Asia Daily Report, 12 May, 54; VNA, 30 December, 1989, trans. FBIS East Asia Daily Report, 2 January 1990, 70.

102 See Oskar Weggel (1986), 'The Vietnamese Communist Party and Its Status Under Law', in D. Loeber (ed.), *Ruling Communist Parties and their Status Under Law*, Martinus Nijhoff, The Hague, 411, 412.

on some substantive issues.[103] Reforms aimed to give National Assembly delegates more say over legislation. But the Politburo warned delegates not to 'take advantage of democracy and openness to distort the truth, to negate revolutionary gains, and to attack the party leadership and state management'.[104]

Constitutional changes in 1992 reflected these reforms by juxtaposing democratic symbolism borrowed from the United States, such as the 'state is of the people, by the people, for the people' with Leninist notions of democratic centralism (*tap trung dan chu*). In practice the party continued to 'manage' democratic rights by controlling the selection of candidates.[105] The Fatherland Front selects candidates to fill predetermined class and ethnic-minority quotas. Party loyalty is rarely an issue, since only 'politically dependable' (*co the phu thuoc ve mat chinh tri*) citizens are permitted to run as candidates.[106] Few studies have closely examined what actually happens during elections.[107] There is strong evidence, however, that selection is more important than election.

Currently, over 90 per cent of delegates are party members, and most are state officials or members of Fatherland Front organisations.[108] Only 25 delegates, or 5 per cent of the total number of delegates, work in businesses and just five delegates (1 per cent) are private sector entrepreneurs. A proposal to establish an 'enterprise club' (*cau lac bo doanh nghiep*) to advocate entrepreneurial concerns has not proceeded. Some entrepreneurs were concerned that any signs of mobilisation might incite much larger groups hostile to their interests (such as veterans) to form their own voting caucuses.[109]

Official policy now stresses the procedural trappings of electoral representation. Reforms have increased the number of full-time delegates (from 10 to 25 per cent). Candidates can self-nominate, and there are proposals to increase the number of

---

103 See Nguyen Huu Tho (1987), 'The Eighth National Assembly: Some Problems of Renovation', *Tap Chi Cong San*, March, 4–6, trans. FBIS East Asia Daily Report, 18 May, K/6-7.

104 See Political Bureau (1989), 'Conclusions on Ideological Work', Hanoi Domestic Service, 8 December, trans. FBIS East Asia Daily Report, 9 December, 63.

105 See Pham Van Hung (2001), 'Tu Tuong Ho Chi Minh Ve Viec To Chuc va Xay Dung Quoc Hoi Thuc Hien Quyen Luc Cua Nhan Dan' (Ho Chi Minh's thoughts on the National Assembly as an Institution to Perform People's Power), *Tap Chi Nghien Cuu Luat Phap* (4), 65, 66–69; cf. Vo Tri and Vo Vi (2003), 'Ve Bai Dan Chu va Viec Thuc Hien Quyen Dan Chu' (Democracy and Improving Democratic Rights), *Tap Chi Nghien Cuu Luat Phap* (3), 21–24.

106 See Report (2002), 'Newly Elected National Assembly Holds its First Session', 8 *Vietnam Law and Legal Forum* (95), 6, 7.

107 Most recent studies have examined provincial and district elections. See, for example, Tran Thi Thu Trang (2004), 'Local Politics and Democracy in a Muong Ethnic Community', in Benedict J. Tria Kerkvliet and David Marr (eds), *Beyond Hanoi: Local Government in Vietnam*, Institute of Southeast Asian Studies, Singapore, 142–43.

108 See Author Unknown (2002), 'Rights to Vote and Stand for National Assembly Election', *Nhan Dan*, 14 September. Available online at <www.nhandan.org.vn>.

109 See generally Minh Duc (2002), 'Tieng Noi Doanh Nhan Trong Quoc Hoi' (Entrepreneurs' Voice in the National Assembly), *Tap Chi Nghien Cuu Lap Phap* (12), 14, 15.

non-party candidates standing for election. Movement towards some version of electoral representation is evident in party efforts to encourage delegates to maintain close contact with their constituents and respond to voters' concerns.[110] Reforms are underway to give delegates access to electoral offices in their electorates. Media scrutiny of National Assembly plenary debates since 1998 has also undoubtedly increased public awareness of the National Assembly as a policymaking body.

Public Access to National Assembly Delegates

Before considering whether delegates listen to voters' concerns, it is necessary to know whether entrepreneurs can communicate issues to delegates. Even when they are in sympathy with their constituents, delegates do not have adequate resources and staff to investigate and respond to complaints. Recently appointed full-time delegates have more time to correspond, but they are located in Hanoi—in most cases far from their constituents.

The rules governing voter interaction with National Assembly delegates are unclear. Delegates meet constituents in gatherings organised by the Fatherland Front during and after elections. Organisers use agendas to control the issues discussed. Individual voters are rarely permitted to debate concrete issues, much less voice concerns outside those contemplated in the agenda. Reports prepared by organisers that summarise proceedings are distributed to interested mass organisations and authorised non-government organisations. It is necessary to 'read in' the complex party-state networks discussed in Chapter 4 to understand the ways politically connected groups influence delegates.

Frustrated by tightly controlled and infrequent meetings with delegates, voters express their concerns in petitions. Approximately 20,000 petitions are sent to the ONA People's Will Department annually.[111] Specialised committees deal with about 45 per cent of petitions, and the Standing Committee of the National Assembly deals with the remainder. Rather than sharing information with delegates, the committees forward complaints directly to government agencies for action. Committees then synthesise key issues into reports presented to the National Assembly. Voter concerns are thus filtered many times before they are presented in summary form to delegates.

Discourse theory informs us that effective communication is most likely to occur during sustained discussions (contact zones). In ideal conditions, unmediated and balanced (co-equal) communication over prolonged periods induces mutual comprehension and stimulates the transfer of unorthodox and contradictory ideas

110 See Dao Xuan Tien (2005), 'Responsibilities of Elected Deputies in Dealing with Citizens Complaints and Denunciations', *Tap Chi Nghien Cuu Lap Phap* (Legislative Studies Review) (2), 33–37.

111 About 40 per cent of complaints concern land and housing and 25 per cent concern court cases. See Goran Andersson *et al.* (2002), *Strengthening the Capacity of the Office of the Vietnam National Assembly*, SIDA Evaluation 12/12, Stockholm, 28, 25.

('unofficial discourse'). The highly mediated exchanges between voters and National Assembly delegates lack the sustained and unmediated contact zones considered necessary for effective communication. Evidence suggests that entrepreneurs rarely use these channels to influence imported commercial laws.

Do Lawmakers Listen to 'Unofficial' Discourse?

In promoting 'direct democracy', the National Assembly distributes draft legislation for public comment.[112] A central question in determining the effectiveness of public consultation is whether lawmakers believe they have an obligation not only to solicit, but also to reflect, 'people's opinions' (*lay y kien nhan dan*) in laws.[113] An early draft of the Law Amending the Law on the Promulgation of Legal Documents required drafting agencies to 'learn from comments to formulate legal normative documents'. In the final draft, this positive duty to take community concerns into account was weakened to read 'studying comments so as to revise the drafts'.[114]

The law further provides that drafting authorities have discretion to consult to 'an appropriate extent and in an appropriate manner'.[115] It does not specify whom lawmakers should consult, using instead the ambiguous word '*nhan dan*' (literally the 'people'). Some commentators interpreted this term as referring to individuals, while others, invoking its socialist meaning, believe it refers to collective comments gathered by mass organisations and associations.[116] Finally, the law does not require authorities to report back to interlocutors to explain whether their comments have been codified.

A report compiled by the ONA in 2002 concluded that National Assembly committees and government drafting committees were more interested in inculcating state policy than learning from the public.[117] During the survey period from 1996 until 2002, National Assembly committees always consulted state agencies, occasionally discussed bills with Fatherland Front organisations, but rarely with

112 See Author Unknown (2004), 'Direct Democracy for Public Issues', *Thanh Nien*, 19 August, 3, trans. *Development Vietnam*, Intellasia News Service, 19.

113 See Do Muoi (1992), 'Xay Dung Nha Nuoc Phap Quyen Thuc Su Cua Dan, Do Dan Va Vi Dan' (Building up a Law-based State that is Of the People, By the People and For the People), *Tap Chi Cong San* (10), 3, 5–6.

114 Law on the Promulgation of Legal Documents 1996 (amended 2002), article 62(3).

115 Law on the Promulgation of Legal Documents 2002, article 3.

116 See Nguyen Quang Minh (2002), 'Nhan Dan Voi Viec Tham Gia Y Kien Xay Dung Phap Luat' (People and their Participation in the Law Making Process), unpublished paper presented to the Workshop on Perfecting the System to Facilitate People's Participation in Forming and Implementing Law, Hanoi, November.

117 See Office of National Assembly (2002), 'Viec To Chuc Tap Hop, Tong Hop Y Kien, Viec Tiep Thu, Chinh Ly Du An Luat' (On the Collection and Synthesis of Public Comments and Revisions of Draft Bills), unpublished paper presented at the Workshop on Perfecting the System to Facilitate People's Participation in Forming and Implementing Law, Hanoi, November.

business associations (for example, VCCI). They sought opinions from SOEs on three occasions and did not consult private entrepreneurs at all. More recently, the draft Civil Procedure Code, which proposed adversarial reforms to commercial litigation, was only circulated to government agencies and state-funded research organisations for comment.[118]

In the first ten years of *doi moi* (1986–96), six draft laws were published in *Nhan Dan* (a national newspaper) for public comment. Although more draft laws are published in newspapers and on websites today, they are rarely accompanied by explanatory memorandums showing how the legal rules are supposed to function in everyday situations. Without this contextual information, members of the public (including small-scale entrepreneurs) lack a frame of reference in which to assess and comment on the draft legislation. This task is left to state authorities, mass organisations and large business associations with the resources and expertise needed to understand how a few terse words of legal prescription will affect regulatory practices.

For example, a Civil Code draft was published in *Nhan Dan* in 1995 and over a period of several months comments were invited from provincial authorities, mass organisations and foreign law firms.[119] Members of the Civil Code drafting committee reported that discussions organised by mass organisations were highly mediated, while less than 100 comments were received from the public. They concluded that provisions in the Civil Code were too far removed from everyday life to elicit meaningful comments from the public. In any event, drafters largely disregarded public comments. Boxes containing submissions sent to the drafting committee remained untouched long after the Civil Code was passed by the National Assembly.

In a society where decisions have been guided for decades by democratic centralism, lawmakers unsurprisingly confuse consultation for comment with consultation for approval. Behind the rhetoric promoting direct democracy, some lawmakers disparage the public's capacity to contribute. This means that public consultation is generally *ad hoc* and falls far short of the sustained and unmediated dialogue required to convey unorthodox or controversial views to lawmakers.

Assessing the Transformative Potential for the National Assembly to Become a Representative Body

For entrepreneurs to be able to voice their concerns about imported law more effectively, the National Assembly must evolve into a more representative body.

118 See Law Committee National Assembly (2004), 'Draft Report Synthesising People's Opinions on the Draft Civil Procedure Code', unpublished report, National Assembly, Hanoi, March.

119 See generally Nguyen Dinh Loc (1995), 'Bo Luat Dan Su Co Vai Tro To Lon Trong Viec To Chuc Cuoc Song Cong Dong' (The Civil Code Plays an Important Role in Organising Community Life), *Nhan Dan*, 13 February, 1.

To evaluate the potential for this transformation, we need to understand in what circumstances the party may voluntarily transfer lawmaking power. Discourse analysis provides an explanation for institutional transformation. In times of rapid change, party institutions will search for more effective ways of resolving social problems. For example, faced with falling rural production the party was forced to devolve planing power to peasants during the 1960s and 1970s.

Informants in the ONA speculate that as the pace and complexity of lawmaking increases, the party is struggling to predict the social impact of new laws.[120] The longstanding view that delegates should give legislation the 'people's' consent, without fundamentally revisiting policy, is giving way in the party to an appreciation that delegates should evaluate the social acceptability of legislation. Further progress in this direction depends on party leaders recognising that laws function best when they reflect local concerns. This adjustment is difficult for a party that for decades has equated *the phat* (spontaneous) debate with losing control and has used democratic centralism to subordinate local discourse.

Even though the National Assembly is overwhelmingly composed of party members, delegates have different views on laws. Divided loyalties to the central party, regional authorities, workplace relations and family commitments generate fresh insights into social problems. Delegates represent a spectrum of regional and professional interests that are arguably broader (or at least different) from views within party agencies. Delegates show the central party *du luan* (public opinion) without the political filtering that attenuates information transmitted by party and mass organisations.

Other informants believe the party lacks the internal deliberative processes needed to resolve turf battles between state organs. They suggest that the party tends to paper over internal differences in order to present a united front. This delays confrontation and the distribution of spoils, making conflict management more difficult. According to this view, it suits the party to give the National Assembly powers to resolve certain intractable problems.

Consider the resolution of urban housing disputes. During the late 1950s, state authorities commandeered and sub-divided large villas in northern cities to house party and state cadres.[121] Houses were confiscated (*tich thu*) from party enemies and requisitioned (*trung thu*) or acquired (*trung mua*) from those considered sympathetic to the party.[122] Wealthy but non-exploitative owners 'voluntarily' relinquished occupation, but not ownership rights, in return for a nominal rent.

120 Interviews with officials from the Office of the National Assembly, January, June and November 2002, March 2004.

121 See Anne Koperdraar (1998), 'Hanoi's Colonial Villas in Transition', unpublished thesis, University of Amsterdam, 52–53.

122 Articles 25 to 30 of the Decree on Agrarian Policy, 30 April 1953, and the preamble and article 3 of the Law on Land Reform 1953, authorised confiscation and redistribution of land to peasants. See Bernard B. Fall (1956), *The Viet-Minh Regime Government and Administration in the Democratic Republic of Vietnam*, Greenwood Press, Westport, Connecticut, 125–26.

Following *doi moi* reforms, the state recognised private ownership of houses.[123] This reform excited claims by owners who had 'voluntarily' transferred occupation rights to the state. By the mid-1990s, courts throughout the country were clogged with hundreds of politically sensitive cases seeking orders to evict party and state officials living in privately owned villas. Although legislation clearly supported the owners' claims, the courts sought a ruling from government ministries to take action against party and state officials. When government agencies refused to act, the Chief Justice sought direction from the Standing Committee.[124] Party leaders decided that housing issues 'can only be legally decided by authorities such as the National Assembly and the Standing Committee of the National Assembly, judicial organs themselves cannot determine civil relationships over residential housing'.[125]

Informants believe a dispute arose between the government and city people's committees over the appropriate formula for balancing ownership and occupation rights.[126] Rather than using party organs to resolve the impasse, the Politburo agreed to transfer the problem to the Standing Committee. Informants say that competing party factions agreed that the Standing Committee provided a 'neutral' forum for reconciling central and provincial interests. Unlike the party, the National Assembly's legitimacy does not depend on presenting a unified front. On the contrary, conflict resolution enhances the National Assembly's democratic credentials.

In 1998, the Standing Committee issued a resolution ordering ministries, provincial authorities and the courts to recognise certain types of ownership claims. After five years of intense lobbying by party and state officials, the National Assembly in 2003 changed its policy and issued a new resolution that disallowed private claims against land currently used by state agencies.[127] If this analysis is correct, the party voluntarily transferred policymaking power to the National Assembly because constitutional rules allowed delegates to discuss complex issues in a comparatively unmediated forum.

Whatever the party's motives in transferring authority, it is always possible that delegates may arrogate more power for themselves. It is too early in the reform cycle to ascertain whether delegates have accumulated enough policymaking power to compel party leaders to change contentious policies. More plausibly, delegates will expose deficiencies and sensitivities in imported laws that may or may not move party leaders. The transformative pressures discussed may increase the powers of

---

123 See Ordinance on Residential Housing 1991.

124 See Resolution of the National Assembly on the Implementation of the Civil Code 1996, article 4.

125 See Dinh Van Que (1997), 'Temporary Suspension of Dealing with Disputes over Residential House Transactions Established Before 1991', *Nha Nuoc va Phap Luat* (10), 12.

126 Interviews with senior officials at the Office of National Assembly, Hanoi January 2000 and March 2004.

127 Resolution No. 23/QH11 on Houses and Land Managed or Arranged by the State for Use in the Course of Implementation of House and Land Management Policies and Socialist Transformation Policies before 1 July, 1991, 2003.

delegates to adjust imported laws to suit local conditions without necessarily making delegates more democratically sensitive to voters.

Conclusion

Case studies considered in this chapter show non-state pressure groups influencing the selection and adaptation of foreign laws into Vietnam. This finding is consistent with the third working postulate. Case studies further suggest that access and influence correspond to social and economic status—leading to the conclusion that imported laws will eventually come to resemble elite interests. This supposition has ramifications for the development of a uniform commercial legal system governed by the 'rule of law'.

Foreign investors benefit from sustained and relatively unmediated access to legislative drafting committees. They have cultivated elite groups of lawmakers and consultants who are broadly in sympathy with the imported neoliberal legal agenda. The influence exerted by these interpretive communities is evident in the numerous foreign (especially US) rights-based principles that have successfully passed through the many deliberative processes *en route* from drafting committees to the National Assembly.

Politically connected local entrepreneurs and state-owned enterprises also enjoy close institutional and personal relationships with lawmakers. Although these interpretive communities are less ideas-oriented than the neoliberal legal alliances, they have successfully invoked socialist principles to preserve many monopolistic privileges for SOEs and domestic entrepreneurs in the face of imported free market ideals.

Small-scale domestic players, on the other hand, possess few personal networks with lawmakers and are not permitted to form member-directed business associations. Entrepreneurs promoting local ideas or norms that contradict the 'official' discourse must convey their message through public demonstrations and silent communication—communicative channels that are highly mediated and thus inefficient long-term modes of influence.

As the brief flowering of the Private Business Forum demonstrated, some entrepreneurs have an active interest in promoting the local norms underpinning most business transactions. More local participation in lawmaking will generate the preference convergence required to convince lawmakers to codify normative practices that reflect community, rather than elite, interests.

Exchanges between National Assembly delegates and entrepreneurs are highly mediated and do not constitute an alternative way to influence the adaptation of imported laws. Chapter 5 showed that, although some National Assembly delegates are prepared to oppose imported trade liberalisation laws, they were responding to the concerns of SOEs rather than those of private entrepreneurs. Only a tiny number of National Assembly delegates represent private entrepreneurial interests. Moreover, the devolution of policymaking powers needed for delegates to codify local norms and change the meaning of imported provisions is taking place only slowly (if at all).

There is some government support for the view that effective laws must comport with local conditions. But it seems unlikely the government will relax tight controls over the formation of independent business associations and allow entrepreneurs to oppose legal harmonisation projects and possibly jeopardise international trade agreements. Highly mediated state-society exchanges are attractive precisely because they quarantine lawmakers from social forces that might oppose socioeconomic goals. By limiting participatory democracy and channelling social dissent though state-corporatist business associations and mass organisations, factions within the state can selectively promote or reject local norms that challenge the rights-based rules favoured by foreign investors and some local elites.

The influence exerted by pressure groups also partially corresponds to their respective needs for law-based regulation (see Chapter 8). Foreign investors want a procedural 'rule of law' to preserve property and contractual rights against state intrusion. They are generally better organised and resourced and more focused on change than broadly dispersed local entrepreneurial groups, which are ambivalent towards law-based reforms. For example, foreign pressure groups successfully overcame weak domestic opposition to complex corporate governance provisions in the Enterprise Law. Weak anti-monopoly provisions in the Competition Law 2004 suggest, however, that foreign pressure groups lost the struggle with the Ministry of Trade to limit the market domination of politically connected SOEs.

Chapter 8 takes this discussion further, by considering the reasons for the uneven domestic demand for imported commercial laws and a procedural 'rule of law'.

Chapter 8

The Rule of Law and Vietnamese Relational Transactions

Introduction

In Chapter 7 a link was made between domestic commercial practices and local demand for the 'rule of law'. The selective support shown by domestic entrepreneurs towards the Enterprise Law (EL) suggested that some imported rights and processes were more relevant to local conditions than others. This chapter explores in more depth the capacity and willingness for domestic entrepreneurs to learn from imported rights-based laws.

This inquiry draws on recent research that has identified a correlation between viable legal transfers and domestic demand for particular types of regulation. A survey of law reform in six Asian economies showed that imported commercial laws only moved from statutes into everyday life when the local economies developed a need for property and contractual rights.[1] This research concluded that 'for law to be effective, a demand for law must exist so that the law on the books will actually be used in practice'.[2] For example in Vietnam, a low demand for external rules that regulate business organisations suggests reasons why domestic entrepreneurs supported market access provisions in the Enterprise Law, but were less enthusiastic about complex internal management rules.

This chapter begins by considering reasons why a 'rule of law' may not necessarily advantage domestic entrepreneurs and promote economic development. It then turns to a series of case studies that examine the interaction between state-based commercial regulation and self-regulation by domestic entrepreneurs. The chapter concludes that imported commercial laws are creating a layered and fragmented regulatory system.

---

1 See Katharina Pistor and Philip Wellons (1999), *The Role of Law and Legal Institutions in Asian Economic Development 1960–1995*, Oxford University Press, Hong Kong, 263–86.

2 Daniel Berkowitz, Katharina Pistor and Jean-Francois Richard (2003), 'The Transplant Effect', 51 *American Journal of Comparative Law*, 163, 167.

Is the 'Rule of Law' Necessary for Economic Development?

It is worth briefly speculating whether a 'rule of law' is necessary for economic development in Vietnam.[3] As previous chapters have shown, some Western scholars and development agencies have consistently maintained that a 'rule of law' is a precondition for economic development. Inspired by Rostow's modernisation thesis that Western legal systems will lead to economic growth, many legal development projects have set about replacing traditional economic, social and legal practices in the developing world with Western institutions and laws.[4] Various quantitative studies also purport to show causal links between economic development and the 'rule of law'.[5]

Contradicting the dominant assumption that economic growth requires the rule of law, some commentators are sceptical about finding operational linkages between law and economic development.[6] Some suggest rule of law may erode as economies grow, because there are increased opportunities for rent seeking and capture of government policy making, Others are doubtful whether quantitive research measures enough social detail to demonstrate meaningfully that individual laws have induced particular types of social change, much less predict broad social phenomena like the 'rule of law'.[7] After decades of legislation, 'implementation studies', researchers surmised that social change is governed by so many variables and competing interests that it is never clear whether behaviour that appears to comply with a particular rule is brought about by legal rules. Even the World Bank is now careful to emphasise the diversity and complexity of the factors that induce economic development.[8]

Other scholars argue that discretionary market management, flexible and decentralised market institutions and relational networks, more than laws, have stimulated private economic development in Vietnam.[9] The social norms that

3 See generally Randall Peerenboom (2002), *China's Long March toward Rule of Law*, Cambridge University Press, Cambridge, 450–62.

4 See W.W. Rostow (1960), *Stages of Economic Growth*, Cambridge University Press, Cambridge.

5 See, for example, Robert Barro (1997), *Determinants of Economic Growth*, MIT Press, Cambridge Massachusetts, 28

6 See, for example, Donald Clarke (2003), 'Economic Development and the Rights Hypothesis: The China Problem' 51 *American Journal of Comparative Law*, 89, 97–100; Patrick McAuslan (1997), 'Law, Governance and the Development of the Market: Practical Problems and Possible Solutions' in Julio Faundez (ed.), *Good Government and Law*, St Martin's Press, New York, 25–44.

7 See William H. Clune and R.E. Lindquist (1981), 'What "Implementation" Isn't: Towards a General Framework for Implementation of Research', *Wisconsin Law Review*, 1044, 1045–51.

8 See The World Bank (1999), *Entering the 21st Century: World Development Report 1999/2000*, Oxford University Press, New York, 17–23.

9 See A. Fforde and W. de Vylder (1996), *From Plan to Market: The Economic Transition in Vietnam*, Westview Press, Boulder, Colorado; Martin Gainsborough (2002), 'Understanding Communist Transition: Property Rights in Ho Chi Minh City in the Late

generate trust, self-enforcing market mechanisms and informal dispute resolution practices provide the necessary predictability and certainty required for commercial transactions, without the cost of formal rules and processes.[10] In discussing the apparently anomalous coexistence of rapid economic development and a poorly developed legal system in China, Carol Jones opined that 'informal alternatives to legal regulation may be more efficient than competitive markets based on law'.[11] More recently Donald Clarke has shown that rapid economic growth in China is entirely possible without a formal legal system securing contractual rights, provided the state protects property against interference and confiscation.[12] In fact, East Asian states have produced much of the world's economic growth over the last 30 years using state-guided regulatory systems, rather than rights-based laws and a 'rule of law'.

One of the main reasons why the Vietnamese state is cautiously supporting a procedural rule of law is the promise of economic dividends. To be sure there are other motivating forces, such as WTO membership and appeals to social legitimacy. All the same, if relational transacting is effective and efficient, then at the very least the state should rethink the way it integrates 'rule of law' reforms with underlying self-regulatory practices.

Relational Transactions and Production Regimes

Kahn-Freund speculated that both economic and non-economic pressure groups, such as unions, employer associations, religious organisations, political parties and family structures, influence and/or contribute to the existence of law.[13] He went on to hypothesise that laws are more likely to be transplanted successfully where they are supported by pressure groups in the recipient country. The third working postulate goes further in speculating that imported laws are strongly conditioned by the institutional and normative structures ordering pressure groups (Chapter 1).

Support for this view is found in research coming out of the former communist countries in East Europe. In discussing the failure of a transplanted 'rule of law' to take root in Russia, Carol Rose observed 'capitalist property has a kind of moral and cultural infrastructure that we may have mistakenly thought was simply natural,

---

1990s', 14 *Post-Communist Studies* (2), 227–43. See generally Tom Ginsburg (2000), 'Does Law Matter for Economic Development? Evidence from East Asia', 34 *Law and Society Review*, 701.

10 See Michael Dowdle (1999), 'Heretical Laments: China and the Fallacies of "Rule of Law"', 11 *Cultural Dynamics*, 285.

11 Carol Jones (1994), 'Capitalism, Globalisation and Rule of Law: an Alternative Trajectory of Legal Change in China', 3 *Social and Legal Studies*, 195.

12 Donald Clarke (2003), 'Economic Development and the Rights Hypothesis: The China Problem', 51 *American Journal of Comparative Law*, 89, 100–11.

13 See Otto Kahn-Freund (1974), 'On Uses and Misuses of Comparative Law', 37 *Modern Law Review* 1, 12.

whereas in fact it is learnt through sustained commercial practice'.[14] In other words, Western statutory norms regulating market institutions such as property, contracts and corporations are historically conditioned and do not necessarily comport with relational practices in socialist transforming economies.

Anthropologists and normative theorists for decades have recognised dual state and non-state regulatory systems in both Western and East Asian settings.[15] In her influential normative study of Chinese business practices, Janet T. Landa demonstrated that ethnically homogeneous Chinese communities used family and relational affiliations as alternatives to 'rule of law' property and contractual rights.[16] By focusing on non-state substitutes for the rule of law, she recognised the importance of business practices that displayed law-like characteristics. She found that without credible contractual rights, entrepreneurs based simple 'one-shot' transactions with strangers on 'cash on delivery' or other terms that transferred risk to the purchaser. Long-term transactions, on the contrary, needed sustained organisational cooperation made possible by relational networks.

Research throughout East Asia shows that relational networks are a potent regulatory force.[17] For example, in explaining the divergent forces shaping production in Japanese and American companies, Aoki identified a matrix of market institutions governing information systems, financial arrangements, corporate governance, industrial relations, contracting networks and cross-shareholding.[18] Comparative research examining the adoption of Japanese production methods in Europe has also demonstrated that, in addition to external laws,

14 Carol Rose (1996), 'Propter Honoris Respectum: Property As the Keystone Right?', 71 *Notre Dame Law Review* 329, 354.

15 See Stuart Macaulay, 1963 'Non-Contractual Relations in Business: A Preliminary Study', 28 *American Sociology Review* 55; Ian R. Macneil (1978), 'Contracts: Adjustment of Long term Economic Relations Under Classical, Neoclassical and Relational Contract Law', 72 *North Western University Law Review*, 854, 890–900; and Kauffman Winn (1994), 'Relational Practices and Marginalization of Law: Informal Financial Practices of Small Business in Taiwan', 28 *Law and Society Review* (2), 193–232.

16 Janet Landa (1981), 'A Theory of the Ethnically Homogeneous Middleman Group: An Institutional Alternative to Contract Law', 10 *Journal of Legal Studies*, 349.

17 See, for example, Jane Kaufman Winn (1994), 'Relational Practices and the Marginalization of Law: A Study of the Informal Financial Practices of Small Businesses in Taiwan', 28 *Law and Society Review* 193, 194–204; Harry Williams (1998), 'Property Reform and Legitimacy', 28 *Journal of Contemporary Asia* (16), 159; Robert Cooter and Janet T. Landa (1984), 'Personal Versus Impersonal Trade: The Size of Trading Groups and Contract Law', 4 *International Review of Law and Economics* 15, 16–19; Phillip Lawton (1996), 'Berle and Means, Corporate Governance and the Chinese Firm', 16 *Australian Journal of Corporate Law* (3), 348, 348–50; John O. Haley (1997), 'Relational Contracting: Does Community Count?', in Harold Baum (ed.), *Japan: Economic Success and Legal System*, de Gruyter, Berlin, 167, 167–80.

18 See Masahiko Aoki (1994), 'The Japanese Firm as a System of Attributes: A Survey and Research Agenda', in Masahiko Aoki and Ronald Dore (eds), *The Japanese Firm: The Sources of Competitive Strength*, Oxford University Press, Oxford, 12–22, 27–28; also see

'internal coalitions' of forces such as ideology, bureaucratic control, information/skills, labour controls and political autonomy hold companies together more than state rules.[19] These relational configurations were considered just responsible for determining the rules of the game as transplanted US company laws and legal institutions.

Research also shows that relational transactions also play a significant regulatory role in Vietnam. John McMillan and Christopher Woodruff found that relational connections provide the 'rules of the game' for many domestic business transactions in Vietnam.[20] They concluded that 'Vietnamese private firms do not yet have a formal legal system to fall back on' and rely on community norms, trade associations and market intermediaries in place of state-based rules.[21]

Many of the disparate threads of relational theory are brought together in the notion of 'production regimes'. The sociologist Michael Burawoy coined the term to explain how manufacturing processes influence workplace ideology and politics.[22] His central argument is that production relationships are more than economic acts that shape material products, they also influence subjective perceptions of economic and legal institutions. By organising production through markets, they determine incentives and constraints, in other words the 'rules of the game'.

According to Burawoy, production regimes are comprised of three main components: the role of the state, labour processes and the operation of market organisations.[23] States play both an external regulatory and internal participatory role in production. In addition to using command and control laws, states use an array of non-legal regulatory instruments. For example, prior to the introduction of formal regulations in the early 1990s, informal meetings between City of London financiers and government officials pursuant to the *London City Code on Takeovers and Mergers* controlled corporate mergers and acquisitions in London. Evidence

---

Veronica L. Taylor (1993), 'Continuing Transactions and Persistent Myths: Contracts in Contemporary Japan', 19 *Melbourne University Law Review*, 352, 270–76.

See C.J. Milhaupt (1996), 'A Relational Theory of Japanese Corporate Governance: Contract Culture and Rule of Law', 37 *Harvard International Law Review* (1), 3; Hideki Kanda and Curtis Milhaupt (2003), 'Re-Examining Legal Transplants: The Director's Fiduciary Duty in Japanese Corporate Law', 51 *American Journal of Comparative Law*, 887, 897–901.

19 See Alan Jenkins (1994), 'Just-in-Time "Regimes" and Reductionism', 28 *Sociology* (1), 21, 22–24.

20 See John McMillan, and Christopher Woodruff (1999), 'Interfirm Relationships and Informal Credit in Vietnam', 114 *Quarterly Journal of. Economics* (4), 1285.

21 McMillan and Woodruff (2000), 'Private Order under Dysfunctional Public Order' 98 *Michigan Law Review*, 2421–58. Only 9 per cent of Vietnamese entrepreneurs trusted courts to enforce contracts, against 87 per cent in Romania and 56 per cent in Russia.

22 See Michael Burawoy (1985), *The Politics of Production: Factory Regimes under Capitalism and Socialism*, Verso, London, 5–20.

23 Ibid. Also see Peter Hall and David Soskice (2000), *Varieties of Capitalism: The Changes Facing Contemporary Political Economics*, Cambridge University Press, Cambridge.

suggests that as the voluntary self-regulatory nature of the Code was progressively eroded by legislation, corporate practices began to conform outwardly to the new statutory provisions. An inference drawn from this experience is that

> modes of regulation—corporatist, market or bureaucratic—never exist in pure form in the real world. The practice of regulation is conditioned by a complex range of forces: the object of the activity, the administrative culture in which it occurs, the characteristic of the regulated… Actual modes of regulation are therefore hybrids.[24]

Burawoy argues that the composition and operation of market support organisations in capitalist economies, such as advertising, insurance and real estate brokers, accountants and lawyers shape production regimes by reducing costs, supplying specialised skills and market information and supporting financial management. Although these institutions are rarely directly mentioned in market laws, their support is vital to the effective operation of property, contract and company laws. Laws designed to operate in specific 'market frameworks', it follows, will not necessarily induce similar economic behaviour in new markets governed by different 'rules of the game'.[25]

Western 'production regimes' support commercial laws because they are market and rule-oriented. The remainder of this chapter explores what happens when market-oriented laws are imported into a 'production regime' that is largely compromised of trading networks that use relational connections to order and cement commercial transactions. Case studies of Vietnamese 'production regimes' are used to understand how domestic entrepreneurs interact with each other and with imported rights-based laws.

Vietnamese Production Regimes

Empirically, this chapter draws on qualitative interviews with 60 private companies in Vietnam (the survey) conduced between 2004 and 2005.[26] Companies working

---

24 M. Moran (1988), 'Politics and Law in Financial Regulation', in Cosmo Graham and Tony Prosser (eds), Waiving the Rules, Open University Press, Milton Keynes, 70.

25 Personalistic relationships regulate commerce in every society, what distinguishes societies is the composition of such relationships. See Milhaupt (1996), *supra*, 4–5; Boaventura de Sousa Santos (1985), 'On Modes of Production of Law and Social Theory', 13 *Journal of Sociology and Law*, 299, 320–39.

26 Some of the interviews were conducted with the assistance of Vietnamese lawyers (N. H. Quang and Associates and Investconsult), others were conducted with the help of research assistants. The company managers were interviewed at least twice, and in some cases many times. Companies working in five industry sectors were selected (construction, wood-processing, commodity trading (copper wire), retail sales (car batteries), computers (sales and service)). Studies concerning the construction and wood-processing industries were conducted in Hanoi and surrounding provinces. The term 'company' refers to enterprises under the Enterprise Law: sole proprietorships (doanh nghiep tu nhan), partnership companies

in five industry sectors were selected (construction, wood-processing, copper-wire trading, car battery sales and computer sales and service). Studies concerning the construction industry and wood-processing industries were conducted in Hanoi and surrounding provinces.

This section first summarises the research findings. It then examines in more detail the interplay between imported commercial laws, especially the Enterprise Law, and domestic production regimes.

Limited Liability

Limited liability is considered the cornerstone of Western corporate law and an essential ingredient for capitalist production regimes.[27] Yet research considered in this section suggests that limited liability (*trach nhiem huu han*) conveys few benefits to most Vietnamese entrepreneurs. The main reason why limited liability provisions in the Enterprise Law are not commercial significant is that creditors in Vietnam rarely use legal processes to recover debts. In Chapter 6 we saw that few private companies initiate court actions to recover business debts. On the rare occasions where this happens, judges regularly manufacture reasons to lift the 'corporate veil' and make company officials and their relatives personally liable for company debts.[28]

(cong ty hop danh), limited liability companies (cong ty trach nghiem huu han), and joint-stock companies (cong ty co phan).

27 See F.H. Easterbrook and Daniel Fischel (1995), 'Limited Liability and the Corporation', 52 *Chicago Law Review*, 89, 90–109.

28 Interviews with lawyers from Vilaf, Vision and Associates and Investconsult in Hanoi and Ho Chi Minh City August 2000, March 2001, March 2004 and January 2005. Also see Duong Dan Hue and Nguyen Minh Man (1993), 'Some Issues on the Draft Bankruptcy Law', *Nha Nuoc va Phat Luat* (State and Law) (2), 39; John Gillespie (2003), 'Receiving Bankruptcy Law into Vietnam', 11 *Asia Pacific Law Review* (1), 81, 102–5.

Table 8.1. Summary of company survey

Industry sector	Reasons for incorporating	Internal management	Trading relationships	Self-regulation
Construction	Required under state tendering rules.	Primarily reflects family structures and relational connections with SOEs involved in tendering transactions.	Personal connections and bribes to secure tendering information and connections with SOEs and tendering authorities.	The industry forms bidding groups to allocate work under construction tenders. The industry is too tightly linked with the state to benefit from independent associations.
Wood-processing	Required by local state officials. Reduces predatory inspections by district level authorities.	Primarily reflects family structures.	Mutual benefit and sentimental connections. Price and quality were secondary.	Well developed associations are used to regulate market prices and control dealings with state authorities.
Copper-wire traders	Required by state authorities, but uncommon in this sector.	Primarily reflects family structures.	Mutual benefit to secure markets with SOEs. But in a competitive urban market prices and quality are paramount.	Limited informal cooperation to control prices at the provincial level and to control dealings with state authorities.
Battery traders	Required to obtain VAT receipts.	Primarily reflects family structures.	Price and territorial cartels strictly control trading relationships.	A highly organised and cohesive association maintains a trading cartel and resolves disputes.
Computer traders	Required to import computers and obtain VAT receipts.	Primarily reflects family structures, but about half the companies surveyed had technical specialists in managerial positions.	Price controls loosely regulate tendering transactions with SOEs. Retail sector is highly competitive based on price and quality.	Commercial associations are formed to secure large tenders with SOEs, otherwise loosely structured associations control prices.

Company laws that insulate personal assets from corporate losses are neither intuitively appealing nor obvious to judges. This is especially true where debtors are state authorities or employees. The Western liberal presumption that the social cost of limited liability is counterbalanced by the 'utility' of entrepreneurial investment does not inform judicial thinking. The corporate veil consequentially lacks the legal and moral authority to quarantine shareholder and company officials from creditors.

Discretionary powers exercised by bankruptcy authorities overseeing creditors' petitions also severely limit the usefulness of creditor petitions as a debt recovery vehicle. The *Bankruptcy Law 2004* has removed some, but not all, of these discretionary powers.

Finally, limited liability does not protect investors against relational debt collection. Interviews with entrepreneurs suggest that, where intermediaries are unable to secure compliance, creditors use social pressure to shame debtors and their relatives into paying. In well-organised industries, such as the copper-wire, battery and computer trading sectors, creditors requested other suppliers to withhold sales until outstanding accounts are settled. As a last resort, police are paid by creditors to criminalise commercial debts and arrest debtors on fabricated charges. Evidently, quasi-criminal organisations (snakehead gangs) are taking over this business as central authorities encourage police to stay out of commercial transactions.

Internal Management Rules

Ever since the publication of Berle and Means' influential study about public corporation management, neoclassical scholars have postulated that the modern corporation is the optimal business organisation.[29] Confidence in corporations has endured structural changes where a managerial elite running large public companies displaced individualist, entrepreneurial capitalists as the dominant economic decision-makers.[30] Although some commentators point to discrepancies between neoclassical corporation theory and economic reality, few doubt that the separation of ownership from professional managers is a central feature of Western corporate organisation.[31]

29 See Adolf Berle and Gardiner Means, (1968), *The Modern Corporation and Private Property*, Harcourt, New York, 36. Also see Jensen and Mecklin (1996), 'Theory of the Firm: Managerial Behavior, Agency Costs and Ownership Structure', 4 *Journal Financial Economics*, 305; Fama and Jensen (1983), 'Separation of Ownership and Control', 26 *Journal of Law and Economy*, 301.

30 See generally W.J. Samuels (1985), 'A Critique of Capitalism, Socialism and Democracy', in R.D. Coe and C.K. Wilber (eds), *Capitalism and Democracy: Schumpeter Revisited*, University of Notre Dame Press, Chicago.

31 See, for example, Michael Barzelay and Rogers M. Smith (1987), 'The One Best System? A Political Analysis of Neoclassical Institutionalist Perspectives on the Modern Corporation', in Warren J. Samuels and Arthur S. Miller (eds), *Corporations and Society: Power and Responsibility*, Greenwood Press, New York, 81–84.

The separation of management from capital was unknown in pre-colonial Vietnamese society.[32] Case studies of early 20th-century companies show little change from traditional organisational structures. Vietnamese-owned ceramic manufacturers during the 1930s, for instance, exhibited few of the long-term (non-family) integrative relationships found in Western corporate structures.[33] With the exception of seasonal subcontractors, firms were structured entirely along familial lines. Village relatives were hired in preference to strangers (non-relatives) and daughters were forbidden from marrying outside the village to protect technical knowledge and business secrets. Hierarchical kinship rules arose out of, and defined, interlocking mutual obligations (family sentiment, secrecy and paternalism) that formed the building blocks of commercial organisations.[34]

This study indicates that kinship structures have endured socialist and, more recently, market forces and continue to order private business organisations. Survey respondents used proverbs like *gia dinh la trien het* (family first, others second) to invoke a social ordering where close family connections formed the bonds generating dependable and trustworthy management structures. When external skills were required, managers turned first to family and then friends from the same home village, or to those with longstanding personal ties developed in workplaces, universities or military units. In each case, attempts were made to find sentimental attachments that replicated *trung thanh* (loyalty), *tinh cam* (sentiment towards others) and *tin* (trust) binding family members.

Recruitment practices varied among the industries. The wood-processing sector, for example, relied the most on family members, perhaps reflecting the provincial location of much production. Computer traders were, on the other hand, more prepared to hire non-family members for technically skilled jobs. Positions within

---

32 See Nguyen Thi Doan and Do Minh Cuong (1999), *Triet Ly Kinh Doanh: Voi Quan Ly Doanh Nghiep* (The Business Philosophy of the Management of Enterprises), Nha Xuat Ban Chinh Tri Quoc Gia, Hanoi, 127–42; Anthony Reid (1993), *Southeast Asia in the Age of Commerce 1450–1680*, vol. II, Silkworm Press, Changmai, 62–77.

33 See Hy V. Luong (1997), 'Capitalism and Non-Capitalist Ideologies in the Structure of Northern Vietnamese Ceramics Enterprises', in Timothy Brook and Hy V. Luong (eds), *Culture and Economy: The Shaping of Capitalism in Eastern Asia*, The University of Michigan Press, Ann Arbor, 191–93, 198–200; Hy Van Luong and Diep Dinh Hoa (1991), 'Culture and Capitalism in the Pottery Enterprises of Bien Hoa, South Vietnam (1878–1975)', 22 *Journal Southeast Asian Studies*, 23–24, 26–28.

34 The family structure in Vietnam embodied elements blended from neo-Confucian, Buddhist, Taoist and animistic spirit cults. Although Buddhism and spirit cults ameliorated rigid neo-Confucianism, kinship power structures followed imported Confucian patterns. *Hieu* (filial piety) bound children to their parents through *on* (moral debt) and *de* (the relationship between brothers), required the eldest to 'teach, nurture and protect', and the younger brother to 'respect, support and obey' their elder sibling(s). See Neil L. Jamieson (1993), *Understanding Vietnam*, University of California Press, Berkeley, 16–18; Hy Van Luong (1989), 'Vietnamese Kinship: Structural Principles and the Socialist Transformation in Northern Vietnam', 48 *Journal of Asian Studies* (4), 742, 748–49, 753–54.

these companies involving money and business decision-making, such as sales and management, were, however, invariably given to family members or trusted friends.

The recruitment practices in the construction industry differed the most from other sectors surveyed. Large privately-owned construction firms were closely linked to the state sector, not only through covert cross-ownership patterns (discussed below), but also because management and most staff had previously worked together in the state sector. Smaller private companies, which formed the sub-contracting sub-stratum in the industry, more closely reflected family recruitment models observed in other industries.

Research further suggested that domestic management structures differed from the bifurcated ownership and management structures stipulated in the Enterprise Law. Most internal company structures resembled family hierarchies, with the senior male family member assuming most managerial functions. Less than 15 per cent of firms surveyed were led by women.

Management practices varied among the sectors. For example, wood-processing firms most closely resembled family hierarchies, while companies in the computer sales and service sector were closer to the professional corporate ideal. Respondents explained this difference in terms of labour specialisation. There are few skilled workers in the information technology sector, and company owners are compelled to recruit non-family members to fill management positions. However, even in this sector, respondents said that they were training family members to replace non-family managers.

In most cases, owners monopolised the management positions. This finding is consistent with small firms throughout the world where family members own and operate businesses. Yet, even on the rare occasions Vietnamese companies employed professional managers, the owners tightly controlled most management activities. In a representative example, the owner of a large wood and textile processing firm located in Nam Dinh province, which employed over 100 staff, treated her professional manager like a personal assistant. The owner made every major management decision and only delegated authority for low-value and repetitive transactions. In another manufacturing company with over 200 employees, the owners strictly controlled professional managers with internal company rules. These regulations were unrelated to the internal management guidelines stipulated in the Enterprise Law and the company's registered charter. The managers deliberately left the rules unwritten so that staff were never certain what activities were authorised and had to ask managers for permission. Far removed from the 'rule of law' notion that internal management rules generate efficiency by creating transparency and certainty, the studies suggested that owners place a high premium on direct control and deliberately created an 'ask-favour system' (*co che xin cho*) to control staff initiatives.

In the industries most dependent on state-tenders, such as construction and computer trading, some private companies appointed retired state officials into management positions. This practice gave the firm credibility with the state, without transferring decision-making power. In other cases, owners sought to avoid any formal association with their companies by appointing trusted family or friends to hold official positions. Similarly, some small family companies were managed by senior family members that did not hold an official company position.

These findings are corroborated by research conducted by CIEM.[35] Researchers found that entrepreneurs considered corporate rules separating family and corporate assets an impediment to effective commercial organisation. They concluded there were few benefits and numerous disadvantages to legally differentiating family and company assets. Entrepreneurs admitted to withdrawing invested capital to repay personal loans and passing assets among themselves and their companies without regard for legal doctrines. Creative accounting designed to avoid taxation further blurred distinctions between family and company assets. Discrepancies between the way families internally manage their companies and imported corporate rules have been observed elsewhere in East Asia.[36]

Few entrepreneurs interviewed were familiar with the Enterprise Law and company charters establishing the internal workings of their own companies. Even fewer had sought legal advice to understand their legal obligations. For most entrepreneurs, internal management is a matter for personal relationships guided by morality and sentiment and the state law should not intrude. Incorporation does not necessarily denote a shift towards organisational formality or compliance with the internal management rules in the Enterprise Law. In order to understand why so many companies function as if they were unincorporated it is necessary to look at the reasons why firms incorporate in the first instance.

Institutional Factors Influencing Incorporation

The Psychology of Incorporation

The Companies Law 1990 was enacted during the early stages of *doi moi* reforms, when Western consumer products, services and corporate structures appeared novel, progressive and exciting. The research showed that some firms were attracted by the mystique of the corporate (*cong ty*) entity. At this time, corporations derived a competitive advantage by being associated in the popular imagination with

35 See Vien Nghien Cuu Quan Ly Kinh Te Trung Uong (Central Institute of Economic Management; hereinafter called CIEM) (1998), *Danh Gia Tong Ket: Luat Cong Ty va Kien Nghi Nhung Dinh Huong Sua Doi Chu Yeu* (Review of the Current Company Law and Key Recommendations for Its Revision), CIEM, Hanoi, April, 69–70. Also see Hoang Kim Giao and Nguyen Dac Thang (1995), 'A Profile of Vietnamese Owners of Private Enterprise', *Vietnam Economic Review* (4), 29–30.

36 See, for example, Roman Tomasic and Jian Fu (1999), 'Company Law in China', in Roman Tomasic (ed.), *Company Law in East Asia*, Dartmouth, Aldershot 137–38, 143–44; Chuan Roger Peng (1996), 'Limited Liability in China: A Partial Reading of China's Company Law of 1994', 10 *Columbia Journal of Asian Law*, 264–69.

modernity and Western consumer society. Ironically, business licences designed to subordinate private corporate rights to state economic management, in the public's estimation, conveyed an impression of financial solidity and prestige. Close state supervision of companies enabled entrepreneurs to achieve hitherto unobtainable levels of commercial and social legitimacy.

State Economic Management of Companies

Years of press vilification and numerous scandals tarnished the corporate mystique.[37] Access to state quotas and incentives has now replaced public prestige as the primary reason for incorporating. Only companies are given access to state import/export quotas and permitted to operate in some economic sectors (such as tourism and construction). Respondents in each sector claimed that they were compelled to incorporate in order to gain access to government contracts, import licences and VAT receipts. Some entrepreneurs were instructed by local officials to incorporate because they were considered too large to continue operating as household enterprises. As discussed in Chapter 6, many officials still consider capitalist firms exploitative if the owners derive profits that exceed an average salary from the invested capital. Since 2004 it has been compulsory for firms with more then 10 employees to incorporate.[38]

For many small-scale entrepreneurs, incorporation is a strategy of last resort where trading as an unincorporated commercial entity is no longer officially permitted.[39] Consider wholesalers in the copper-wire business. Most preferred to remain unincorporated entities. They thought it was easier to maintain stable and harmonious relationships with district-level officials in the local neighbourhood than incorporate and deal with city and provincial officials. Sympathetic local officials minimise state interference as manifested in over-inspection and criminalisation.

Wherever possible, businesses disguise capital and employment levels to avoid the dubious privileges of corporate taxes and strict labour regulation that accompany incorporation. Unincorporated firms are permitted to negotiate taxes with local officials, a process that generally results in levies well below those imposed on comparable companies.

The Land Law 2003 has partially addressed the unequal distribution of land use rights (*quyen su dung dat*) across economic and social sectors. Both companies and unregistered businesses are now entitled to receive land allocations or land leases. However, the Land Law 2003 continues to favour unincorporated household

37 For an account of media treatment of the private sector see Leila Webster (1999), *SMEs in Vietnam: On the Road to Prosperity*, MPDF Private Sector Discussions No. 10, Mekong Project Development Facility, Hanoi 14–15, 17.

38 See Decree No. 109 Guiding Company Registration 2004.

39 See Hoang Kim Giao and Nguyen Dac Thang (1995), *supra*, 27–31. Overseas Chinese working through relatives accounted for 27.9 per cent of all medium to large enterprises in Ho Chi Minh City in 1995.

businesses by allocating (*giao*) land on a long-term basis. Allotted land is available for an unspecified duration (in perpetuity), is freely transferable, and in most other respects differs little from Western freehold estates.[40]

In contrast, companies are only permitted to lease (*thue*) land. These land-use rights cannot be transferred without state approval, subsist for a limited duration (usually the length of the investment license), cannot be mortgaged (except by Vietnamese banks) and on termination revert to the state. In short, the Land Law 2003 conveys considerable commercial advantages to unincorporated firms, providing another disincentive to incorporate.

Table 8.2. Summary of reasons for company incorporation

Benefits	Disadvantages
• Right to legally access broader markets (that is, trade beyond district) • Right to legally employ more than 10 workers • Stamp (*chop*) for officiating transactions • Access to VAT receipts • Right to set up branch establishments • Some companies report a more predictable relationship with government authorities • Ability to access equity and debt capital	• Greater registration costs • Annual registration fee (*thue mon bai*) • Requirement to have certified chief accountant • Increased restrictions due to labour contracts • Some companies report an increased level of discretionary 'management' by local authorities. Potential for increased taxes (with move from negotiated to standard tax calculations) • Increased state reporting requirements • Conversion of long-term allocated land-use rights into short-term leasehold rights.

To sum up, domestic entrepreneurs incorporate primarily to gain state benefits that are only available to corporate entities. The legal benefits conferred by incorporation, such as limited liability and separation of ownership and management, were seldom considered important. Nevertheless, a study commissioned by the Asian Development Bank found a loose correlation between incorporation and the perception of regulatory stability and predictability.[41] This finding is attributed to a directive from the prime minister calling for state officials not to harass private companies. More generally, however, incorporation confers few of the benefits enjoyed by companies in 'rule of law' societies.

40 Law on Land 2003, articles 31–35, 66–67.

41 See Markus Taussig and Pham Thi Thu Hang (2004), 'Private Enterprise Formality and the Role of Local Government', unpublished paper, Asian Development Bank, Hanoi.

Strategic Responses to State Regulation

Vietnamese commentators acknowledge that the command economy profoundly shaped attitudes 'that resulted in anti-business philosophies in production and consumption, such as "do whatever you want, the state will be responsible" (*cu lam da co nha nuoc chiu*)'.[42] State domination of the economy inculcated state regulators with a moral mission to micro-'manage' private entrepreneurs (see Chapter 6). It also imbued entrepreneurs with the notion that the state is central to economic well-being. The state was seen as the natural reference point for most business activities, and entrepreneurs devoted considerable time and resources to cultivating 'mutually beneficial' relationships with state officials.

As the private sector grows in size and economic importance, entrepreneurs are gradually losing their psychological, but not their economic, dependence on the state sector.[43] Entrepreneurs in every sector, but especially those working in the construction, computer and copper-wire industries, could not profitably operate without forming relationships with state officials. The strategies adopted by entrepreneurs to form collaborative arrangements with state regulators varied among the industries surveyed.

The construction industry, for example, is more ordered by state laws and tendering procedures than other sectors surveyed. Most construction work is commissioned by state authorities, who issue tender documents for general construction projects, or appoint Equipment Procurement Construction (EPC) contractors to construct large and/or complex projects. According to the law, two levels of contractors participate in construction transactions: general tenderers or EPC companies and their sub-contractors.[44] In practice, three levels exist. The first level comprises general tenderers or EPC companies, the second level includes large SOEs and private companies that have formed close personal (and frequently corrupt) relationships with the principal companies. Together these companies form construction 'groups' (*thau con*) that are bound together with interlocking ownership, management and profit and loss sharing arrangements. The third level consists of small private construction companies that are outside the 'group'. They lack the relational connections required to participate directly in tenders and as peripheral players survive on subcontracts allocated on a project-by-project basis. Informants reported that the 'external' subcontractors routinely pay illegal commissions of 10–15 per cent of the subcontract value in order to secure work.

---

42 Nguyen Thi Doan and Do Minh Cuong (1999), *supra*, 99.

43 The private sector grew from 20 per cent of national industrial output in 1999 to 27 per cent in 2003; see Le Dang Doanh (2004), 'The Enterprise Law and the Development of the Domestic Private Business Sector in Vietnam', *Vietnam's Socio-Economic Development* (39), 3, 12.

44 See Decree No. 88-1999-ND-CP on Tendering 1999 (as amended); Decree No. 66 ND-CP on Tendering 2003.

Computer traders operated in an economic sector that was more sensitive to conventional market signals such as price, supply and demand. Nevertheless they adopted various strategies to avoid detection from economic police and market control inspectors. They operate in a highly competitive industry in which large state and private firms use exclusive import licences and predatory pricing to squeeze smaller competitors out of wholesale markets in brand-named computer parts. In order to complete with these cartels, the medium-scale traders in the survey avoid import taxes by dealing in smuggled and fake components. Traders estimate that approximately 70–80 per cent of computer parts are smuggled and/or fake.

Traders used three strategies to avoid prosecution. The first is to negotiate a 'relationship friendship' (*quan he*) with state officials. Long-term stable relationships are much preferred to short-term bribes (*dut lot*). Traders encourage feelings of reciprocity and 'mutual obligations' by infusing relationships with *tinh cam* (sentiment). Networks based on family and friends are used to provide 'good introductions' (*gioi thieu tot*) and cement relationships with state officials. Officials are then invited to social occasions such as karaoke, weddings and birthdays and plied with goodwill-payments (*khoan thien chi*) and gifts on special occasions such as birthdays and *Tet*.

Computer retailers in some localities have negotiated standard payments for local officials. Payment formulas are loosely based on business turnover and aim to moderate excessive claims by officials and socially disruptive preferential deals. They also give entrepreneurs leverage over new market entrants, who must agree to follow local trading rules in return for receiving the payment formula. Officials tacitly support this type of market network by only negotiating payment relationships with traders familiar with the formula.

The second strategy is to sell smuggled goods with VAT invoices purchased on the black-market. VAT invoices not only provide a cloak of legality, because only components that have been certified by customs authorities are issued with official VAT invoices, purchasers also need them in order to claim tax deductions. Since VAT invoices purchased on the black-market are expensive, as a third strategy, traders form distribution networks with small retail outlets that do not require VAT invoices. Such networks are designed to distribute smuggled goods in ways that minimise payments to state inspectors. Wholesale distributors sacrifice market share to remain close to *phuong* (ward) officials who evidently are more easily persuaded than higher-level officials to tolerate businesses that sell fake or smuggled components priced for the domestic market.

Self-regulation through Business Cooperation

Traders in some sectors have formed trading networks to deal collectively with market problems. For specifics, consider the copper-wire traders in Hanoi. Most wholesale businesses dealing with copper wire emerged from the informal privatisation of *hop tac xa tieu thu cong ng hiep* (small industrial cooperatives) in the mid 1980s. They are primarily located in Hang Bong street and rely on mutual assistance (*tuong tro lan nhau*) to underpin a trade network. Business collaboration began as an extension of social engagements for weddings, funerals and other special occasions. Although business meetings are now much more frequent then social functions, traders do not distinguish between *tinh cam* (sentimental relationships) for business and non-businesses purposes.

There are two circles of cooperation. The inner group consists of wholesalers located in Hang Bong Street. They cooperate closely, meeting regularly at early morning tea clubs to share market information and negotiate deals. They not only share information about prices and supply, but also about appropriate ways to regulate the market. For example, they formulate retaliatory responses to predatory pricing practices used by competitors to gain market share. Members are not expected to attend tea club meetings regularly, but they are excluded for supplying misleading or inaccurate information.

Some of the business norms and tacit assumptions that guide business transactions in this industry are generated by this inner group. During meetings, members discuss appropriate business practices. The complex rules governing wholesale transactions, which may exceed US$100,000 in value, are embedded in personal relationships developed over decades. A set of explicit and tacit understandings are used to balance competition and cooperation. Members, for example, are expected not only to share commercially sensitive market information, but also to 'loan' each other copper-wire if necessary to fill large orders. They cooperate with each other to collect debts by sharing information about the creditworthiness of purchasers and by withholding supply to repeat offenders. They have attempted, without much success, to standardise product standards, prices, delivery terms and credit conditions. Sharp trading practices such as predatory pricing, misleading advertising, poaching customers by paying high commissions (kickbacks) and selling fake goods are discouraged. Members are encouraged to promote the image of copper-wire traders and avoid aggressive competition that disrupts trading relationships.

Members also cooperate to prevent competitors from entering the northern market. High levels of mutual cooperation are required for members to endure short-term losses to price competitors out of the market and secure the long-term objective of market dominance. Far from the Hayekian ideal of competitive and transparent markets, traders attempt to reduce risk through monopolistic and collusive practices.

Occasionally, members join together to combat state interference such as excessive demands for bribes or delayed payments by SOEs—a common problem for all entrepreneurs. Typically, a leading member of the group uses political connections and the collective voice of the group as social leverage in negotiations with officials. This strategy sends the message that officials cannot interfere with one member without dealing with all the members. Group mediation is most effective at the local level—central regulators apparently have less to gain from maintaining good relationships with traders. Tactics used against higher authorities include threatening to use the media to expose malfeasance.

The outer circle includes both wholesalers and retailers. Cooperation among this group is loose and rarely extends beyond sharing market information and advancing short-term credit. Attempts to build a more cohesive association have been frustrated by the limited means available to control opportunistic behaviour among group members. There are too many copper-wire suppliers and customers for the group to formulate sanctions that discourage members from undercutting each other to gain market volume.

Much higher levels of cooperation have been achieved by the *Hiep Hoi Cac Cua Hang Ac Qui Khu Vuc Phia Bac* (Northern Areas Battery Shops Group). This association was formed in 1997 by battery traders in Hanoi to share information, control market territory and settle internal grievances. Although it originally developed from *tinh cam* social engagements, the association is now formalised with a written charter, fee structure and office bearers. Like the copper-wire traders' association, it is not legally constituted in order to avoid the strict controls the state exerts over non-government organisations (see Chapter 7).

The main function of the Association is to implement a market distribution cartel. It is assisted by battery suppliers who, in the interest of a tightly managed and orderly market, cooperate with the Association in using supply as a lever to control market territories and pricing structures. The Association has developed effective mechanisms to control opportunistic behaviour. For example, when one member began selling batteries into other member's territory, the Association convened a meeting at a restaurant to persuade the wrongdoer that his business would suffer unless he followed the Association rules. Sanctions available to the Association include asking the battery manufacturers to withhold or ration supply, withdrawing market support and encouraging members to take over the wrongdoer's territory through predatory pricing.

The Association also promotes certain business norms and practices. Members are discouraged from using sharp trading practices to undercut other members or damage the reputation of battery suppliers and traders. For example, members are expected to supply goods that comply with basic contractual warrantees regarding quality, fitness for purpose and product service. The Association supplies a standard sales contract to its members. Although the provisions in the contact were borrowed from state laws, contracts are intended to function more like sales brochures than legally binding agreements. They promote battery sales by listing the after-sales services provided by Association members. Neither seller nor buyer contemplates the formation of a legally binding arrangement.

Both the copper-wire wholesalers and battery association function like interpretive communities. Members are constantly exposed to particular story-lines or narratives about the correct approach to regulatory problems. In providing detailed explanations for solving economic problems, the associations give their members a competitive edge over rivals operating in an unstructured environment. Although the associations exhibited certain differences, for example the battery traders were more formally structured than the copper-wire traders, they shared many common attributes. Not only did the associations largely ignore the commercial legislative framework regulating their industries, they actively developed cooperative practices to circumvent company and competition laws. Both associations co-opted and transmogrified state contractual rules to augment self-regulatory practices. 'Rule of law' institutions such as courts and lawyers were rarely used. Association members could not ignore state officials and 'state economic management' and they (and their associations) devoted considerable resources to controlling these interactions.

The study suggests that urban entrepreneurs inhabit three regulatory orbits—the state, family and trading networks. The facilitative legal system comprising commercial legislation exerted the least influence over the domestic entrepreneurs surveyed. Bureaucratic regulation, on the other hand, touched virtually every business activity. In some sectors it blurred distinctions between public and private order, while in other sectors it left entrepreneurs space to develop self-regulatory networks. Interaction between state regulators and entrepreneurs was characterised by power differentials and rent seeking. In the construction industry, for example, access to state tenders depended not only on kickbacks and commissions, but also on hierarchical positions within party and state organs.

Family structures dominated the internal organisation of most companies surveyed, but they were not a significant factor in ordering inter-firm relationships. Self-regulatory communities were a feature of each industrial sector. But entrepreneurs in the copper-wire and battery trading sectors displayed the highest levels of cooperation. Members of these communities had ongoing personal relationships with each other. In those relationships, they some times pursued their own inconsistent economic objectives, but more generally they struggled to define a shared vision of the collective good. Because they lived significant parts of their lives with each other, members influenced each other through personal and sentimental bonds to act for collective interests. Therefore, as well as being arenas for the pursuit of pre-existent interests, these communities appear to have the capacity to be constitutive forums in which appropriate individual and collective behaviour (and interests) are defined and redefined.

They generated a common stock of knowledge and tacit understandings about appropriate business practices. Over time, particular storylines about the nature of business problems and the correct regulatory solution gathered authority. The degree of cohesion varied among the networks surveyed. Copper-wire traders were rather heterogeneous in their use of language and ideas to construct regulatory meanings, while battery traders had formalised particular story-lines to construct a more unified identity.

Selective Demand for the 'Rule of Law'

Another important finding from the research was that not all sectors of the economy benefit equally from a 'rule of law'. The discussion so far suggests that the demand for the 'rule of law' is influenced by many factors such as normative and tacit understandings about commercial regulation, the viability of non-state self-regulation, the perceived relevance of legal institutions such as lawyers and courts, market complexity and exposure to foreign traders.

Foreign Direct Investors

Large-scale businesses (especial foreign investors) have been among the strongest advocates for a rule of law in Vietnam (see Chapter 7). According to most accounts they have struggled to take advantage of existing relational networks and need laws to protect their interests.[45] Yet this generalisation needs closer scrutiny because there are different attitudes about the utility of the 'rule of law' within this heterogeneous group. Large domestic companies, for example, frequently enjoy strong relational contacts with the state and are less reliant on laws to protect their interests than foreign direct investors. Even among foreign direct investors different attitudes prevail about the utility of the 'rule of law'. Western, and to a lesser extent Japanese multinational investors, are familiar with well-developed legal systems. Their internal bureaucracies are staffed with lawyers, and accountants who plan and organise business activities according to external policies and laws. As we saw in Chapter 7, these investors have the capacity to shape their own transactional environment through high-level negotiations with state officials.[46]

This group of foreign direct investors supports the domestic enactment of international protocols (WTO and BTA). Above all else, they argue that greater legal transparency and policy stability are needed to stabilise the transactional environment. Yet clearer commercial rights and greater market access mean little without an effective dispute resolution system that enforces agreements Currently foreign investors investors refer disputes to arbitration centres in neighbouring countries. This strategy is effective where the defaulting party owns assets outside Vietnam, but it has proved difficult to enforce foreign arbitral awards inside Vietnam.

In short, this group of foreign direct investors prefer an operational environment governed by legal transparency, codified legal standards and judicially defined boundaries between state and private interests—the objectives of the 'rule of law'. Many projects funded by the foreign donor community in Vietnam are devoted to creating a legal landscape that serves the needs of this highly influential group of investors.

Contrasting with Western and Japanese foreign direct investors, investors from East Asia and especially overseas Vietnamese find the lack of a well-developed legal environment less of an obstacle. Even large investments made in complex

45 These views are based on numerous interviews conducted between 2000–2005 with lawyers from Investconsult, Vilaf, Baker and McKenzie, Vision and Associates and Leadco practising in Hanoi and Ho Chi Minh City.

46 Since foreign direct investment contributes significantly to the economy and accounts for over 60 per cent of income tax payments, state policymakers are often prepared to act on investor complaints. See VIR (2005), 'Foreign Firms Pay 60% of Income Tax', *Vietnam Investment Review*, 30 May, 9.

manufacturing plants and hotels are largely based on personal connections and informal dispute resolution structures. Such investors routinely approach lawyers to 'legalise' these transactions retrospectively when their domestic counterparts come under investigation for corrupt practices. Most investments by overseas Vietnamese are small and family oriented and usually bypass formal investment channels. Funds are transferred to family members residing in Vietnam who establish businesses in their name.

The Regulatory Needs of Small-scale Domestic Businesses

The preceding discussion suggests numerous substantive differences in the way foreign and small domestic businesses perceive the 'rule of law'. Research findings have shown that small-scale domestic firms have a low demand for 'rule of law' regulatory mechanisms. Laws are only considered relevant when they regulate access to state benefits and natural resources. Firms primarily incorporate to gain state benefits. They are generally unconcerned with the legal status of land under the Land Law 2003, unless they are seeking a bank loan and need formal land-use rights as collateral. Current estimates suggest that 75–80 per cent of small-scale domestic firms occupy informal unregistered land.[47]

Small-scale entrepreneurs rarely look to contract law as a source of normative guidance.[48] Personalised relational processes provide the standards and processes that govern most transactions. Even high-value transactions in the copper-wire, battery and computer trading industries are either undocumented or simply recorded in *so giao hang* (commodity delivery books). In some industries, such as battery trading, well-organised associations function like interpretive communities that inculcate and constitute standardised businesses practices. Some entrepreneurs, it is true, strategically used standard form contracts in one-off retail transactions and dealings with state authorities. Yet in these circumstances contracts were considered statements of intent rather than legally binding covenants. They were used to exert moral and social pressure against a partner to comply with the terms of a deal. Only the entrepreneurs in the construction industry regularly used complex contracts, because state tending processes stipulate standard form contractual regimes.

Entrepreneurs' preference for relational transactions is strongly influenced by their interaction with state regulators. There are well-founded reasons why domestic entrepreneurs evince low levels of legal consciousness (*y thuc phap che*) and are reluctant to trust laws to order their business affairs. Commercial laws are contradictory, changeable and poorly disseminated. Compounding the problem,

---

47 See H. Dang and G. Palmkvist (2001), *Sweden-Vietnam Cooperation on Land Administration Reform in Vietnam*, SIDA, Hanoi. The MPDF/IFC study was reported in Stoyan Tenev *et al.* (2003), *Informality and the Playing Field in Vietnam's Business Sector*, IFC, Washington, 68–69.

48 See J. Gillespie, 'Transplanted Company Law: An Ideological and Cultural Analysis of Market-Entry in Vietnam', 51 *International and Comparative Law Quarterly* (1), 641–72.

local-level officials routinely use their discretionary powers to undermine the commercial rights conferred by superior-level laws. In addition, research conducted by McMillan and Woodruff shows that unprofessional and corrupt courts and debt enforcement agencies erode the authority and prestige of contractual, property and corporate rights in the eyes of domestic entrepreneurs.[49] According to the World Development Indicators, in 2005 it took on average 404 days to enforce a contract in Vietnam, 241 days in China and 69 days in Singapore.[50]

These findings suggest that the imported procedural 'rule of law' favours some entrepreneurs more than others. This is not an argument against 'rule of law' reforms, but rather it suggests that policymakers should more actively build bridges between imported commercial laws and domestic self-regulatory regimes.

Transformative Potential for Corporate Change

It is perhaps too early in the reform cycle to assess accurately whether domestic relational structures can complement, even compete with an imported 'rule of law' legal system. As the economy grows and domestic firms transact more frequently with foreigners (especially those requiring formal contracts), statutory contract and property norms may increasingly supplement personal sentimental bonds in commercial exchanges. But this transformation is by no means an inevitable and universal process. Only a small number of enterprises dealing with foreign entities need to harmonise the legal context for their transactions, leaving the vast majority of domestic business deeply embedded in relational practices. As studies in South Korea and Taiwan demonstrate, even after many decades of 'rule of law' reforms, the legal needs of domestic firms are still very different from those of foreign investors.[51]

Neoclassical company theory predicts that, as firms increase in size and market competition increases, separate management and ownership structures become more desirable. There were too few large companies (over 100 employees) in the study to determine conclusively whether internal management rules became more useful when companies outgrow family structures. Yet in seven large companies surveyed none conformed to neoclassical predictions. In each case the family-based owners sought eventually to replace professional managers with relatives who had been sent overseas for managerial training.

Larger-scale empirical studies in Vietnam also reveal few differences in the attitudes of large and small companies to legal rules. For example, approximately

---

49 See McMillan and Woodruff (1999), *supra*, 1285, 1286. Although differences between Western and Eastern approaches to law are presumably important constraining factors, company law flourishes in other East Asian states with sub-optimal legal systems. See Pistor and Wellons (1999), *supra*, 125–30.

50 World Development Indicators, World Bank 2005 <www.devdata.worldbank.org/wdi2005/Table5 3.htm>.

51 See Jane Kauffman Winn (1994), *supra*, 193–232.

two-thirds of large companies employing more than 100 workers are family owned and managed.[52] Like small companies, they borrow capital from family and friends; less than 10 per cent is derived from long-term bank loans.[53] Again, like small companies, they based business partnerships around family or trading networks located in the same city, and frequently in the same neighbourhood.[54] Taken together, these factors imply that even large companies are constructed from, and primarily rely upon, relational connections.

Lawyers report that separate legal personality is occasionally used as a moral, if not a legal means of quarantining family assets from non-family company managers. This occurs on the rare occasions where companies conduct business in provinces where family-owners lack personal contacts, or where founders commercialising scientific or technical knowledge require non-family business managers.

At first glance, these cases appear to support neo-classical theory, but deeper analysis discloses countervailing trends. Even as markets expand and local technology is commercialised, improved general educational levels (especially in finance and management) have reduced the need for non-family managers in manufacturing companies and, as a corollary, the need to separate management from capital ownership.[55] More significantly, in some economic sectors incorporation has become less important as the market-economy matures.

Consider the clothing industry in Ho Chi Minh City. During the years immediately following the introduction of the Companies Law, many family-based clothing manufacturers were incorporated. By 1998, the trend had reversed and reliance on company structures, both in terms of new incorporations and formal separation of capital and management, had declined.[56] Informants believe that, as the textile market grew in size and competitiveness, the capacity of state officials to influence commercial decision-making decreased. This, in turn, meant that retired officials and others hired to constrain state economic management became less useful and were

52 From a total of approximately 26,000 companies, each employing on average 19 workers, only 450 employ more than 100 workers. See Dang Phong (1999), 'The Private Sector: In Vietnamese Industry from 1945 to the Present', in *Vietnam's Undersized Engine: A Survey of 95 Larger Private Manufacturers*, MPDF Discussion Paper No. 9, Mekong Project Development Facility, Hanoi, 47.

53 Ibid., 50–51. A CIEM survey of private companies found that 54 per cent borrowed from friends and relatives, the others borrowed from trading partners (informal business associations), employees, veterans' and women's associations and '*huo ho*' credit circles. See Nguyen Dinh Tai (2002), 'Entrepreneurship in Vietnam and Promotion of the Private Sector: Some Judgements from a Survey' *Vietnam Socio-Economic Development* (29), 25, 26–30.

54 McMillan and Woodruff (1999), *supra*, 1295–96.

55 See Per Ronnas (1998), The Transformation of the Private Manufacturing Sector in Vietnam in the 1990s, unpublished paper, Stockholm Institute for Economics, University of Stockholm, 14–15.

56 In 1994, there were 383 licensed garment makers; after five years of unprecedented growth in the garment industry there were 241 companies. See Liesbet Steer (2000), The Private Sector in Vietnam, unpublished paper, Centre of International Economics, Hanoi, 8.

eventually jettisoned. Without the need to protect capital from non-family managers, corporate structures became less beneficial.

To summarise, Vietnamese entrepreneurs only use laws to gain access to state monopolies and resources, such as export quotas and construction tenders. There is little demand for the law to protect contracts, property rights and limited liability. Although there is little evidence for a domestic demand for the 'rule of law', it cannot be ruled out. To grow, some private companies will eventually need to access capital markets and secure protection for their intellectual property rights. Formal legal rights and functional state institutions are required for this type of business transaction.

In the meantime, most domestic entrepreneurs will continue to use clientist relational connections provided they offer an efficient and secure way to transact business. Currently there is little competition from the legal system. Many local-level officials and judges steeped in state economic management ideology are unprepared to defend private rights and support the vital transformation that makes contract, property and company laws attractive to entrepreneurs. A bare procedural 'rule of law' stripped of substantive commercial norms is also unappealing without administrative courts capable of checking state power. In addition, the special interest groups (such as lawyers, accountants, bankers, and insurers) that provide the services needed to support the uniform, transparent markets presupposed by the 'rule of law' have not yet fully developed in Vietnam. As market services develop and reforms further entrench a procedural 'rule of law', it is possible that entrepreneurs will increasingly orientate their activities around state-based law. So far, the point has not been reached where demand from domestic entrepreneurs is propelling 'rule of law' reforms.

Conclusion

The demand for the 'rule of law' among businesses in Vietnam is growing. But it is unevenly distributed between business sectors, industries and geographic localities. Foreign investors strongly support a neoliberal 'rule of law' that delivers private commercial rights. They are assisted in this endeavour by foreign donors and government officials in sympathy with neoliberal agenda.

Most domestic entrepreneurs, on the other hand, are more interested in a basic procedural 'rule of law' that controls predatory state activity, than in complex commercial rights. Yet as a group they lack the member-directed organisations and connections required to influence law reform (see Chapter 7).

State and large privately owned companies are the group least likely to support any form of the 'rule of law'. They generally rely on government connections for trading privileges and capital and will be worse off under a 'rule of law' regime that gives their competitors access to state institutions (especially courts) that protect private commercial rights.[57] In brief there are sharp divisions within the Vietnamese business community not only about what type of 'rule of law' is preferable, but also whether movement in this direction is desirable.

Despite their different attitudes to the 'rule of law', there are some unifying similarities within the business communities. They all want an orderly and predictable trading environment, but have radically different visions for achieving this objective. More research is required to ascertain to what extent the preferences for neoliberal legalism, relational networks and state sponsorship are pragmatic economic choices or are linked to deep-seated preferences for particular kinds of social organisation. For example, do entrepreneurs prefer relational networks for pragmatic reasons such as cost and efficiency or because of a psychological and cultural preference for communal forms of organisation?

What is clear is that the 'rule of law' and relational regulation are not parallel and separate systems. They are mutually constituted. The 'rule of law' does not always provide the most effective business solutions. As in the West, relational practices are likely to continue long after legal reforms have improved legal transparency and institutional accountability. What is needed is a legal system that makes imported 'rule of law' solutions more relevant to domestic self-regulatory practices. Laws are most effective when they compliment underlying ways of doing business.

Rather than a state-initiated, command and control 'rule of law', research suggests that effective regulation requires a more pluralistic approach where the state is only one of several actors. This is not neoliberal deregulation in disguise. Especially in Vietnam, where self-regulation is sometimes defensive, collusive and corrupt, the state is crucial in ensuring that decentred regulation furthers broad public purposes. Legal development needs to recognise that the background values of the 'rule of law' can be realised in ways that are functionally, though not necessarily formally, equivalent to state centred regulation. Lawmakers need to reconcile an imported 'rule of law' with the decentred self-regulation practised by domestic entrepreneurs.

---

57 Naturally there are differences within this large group. Some SOEs, for example, receive most of their income from joint ventures with foreign companies and would be well served by a neoliberal version of the 'rule of law'.

Chapter 9

Conclusion

Looking back on Vietnamese legal development since *doi moi*, it is difficult to deny that fundamental change has occurred. While socialist instrumentalism remains a potent force, imported Western 'rule of law' notions have profoundly changed statutory norms, and, more recently, institutional thought and practices. Although it is premature to proclaim a procedural 'rule of law', since the courts lack the capacity to check the bureaucracy meaningfully, some movement in this direction is unmistakable.

Progress towards a 'rule of law' has so far been largely (although not exclusively) confined to the commercial arena. Although most legislative activity and procedural reforms are directed at securing compliance with international treaties, the purpose of law reforms is not merely to enter international markets and placate anxious foreign investors. Reforms to the criminal justice system, land and housing regimes and civil law have a clear domestic focus. Despite these reforms, there is little evidence that a 'rule of law' will encompass civil, democratic and political rights. All this suggests that the 'rule of law' in Vietnam is likely to take a highly path-dependent trajectory that only remotely resembles liberal democratic 'rule of law'.

This study has used three working postulates to understand the processes shaping the importation and adoption of the 'rule of law'. We have seen that laws transfer into Vietnam much like other cultural artefacts, with the exception that as instruments of state power laws are highly sensitive to state ideologies and state power-distribution structures. The study has further shown that legal transplantation takes place as much through local invention and mediation as through centrally directed legal reform. By allowing us to think about legal transplantation outside the confines of conventional convergence and globalisation theories, the analysis used in this study provides a fuller explanation of the contests, negotiations and hybridisations shaping borrowed laws.

This chapter reviews the findings in this study and goes on to address three issues not discussed at length earlier: why conventional theories misdiagnose legal transplantation in Vietnam; whether it is possible to devise an explanatory model for legal transplantation; and whether a decentralised concept of law is likely to attract support from key government and foreign law reformers in Vietnam?

Analysing Legal Transplantation through the Three Working Postulates

This study synthesised three working postulates from the writings of Kahn-Freund and other legal theorists to direct research towards the primary sites of interaction between legal transplants and domestic political, social and economic conditions in Vietnam. They are political-legal ideology, the distribution of state power, and pressure from non-state organisations. This section assesses the utility of these postulates by examining their success in bringing the analysis closer to the processes shaping legal transplantation into Vietnam.

The Ideological Role of Law

The discussion in Chapter 3 used the first working postulate to assess ideological resistance to legal transplants. It found that laws transfer easily where they comport with the dominant ideology in recipient countries. During the 1960s and 1970s, socialist laws and practices were transferred *en masse* into Vietnam. The dominant Marxist–Leninist state ideology shielded these ideals from competing beliefs and opinions and, as a consequence, legal thinking barely changed in decades. Imported socialist organisational ideals, on the other hand, were more directly concerned with state power. Democratic centralism and collective mastery principles were woven into the fabric of government and used to discredit or revamp old ideas to prevent the re-emergence of pre-revolutionary practices. In the process, they interacted with local political, economic and social conditions, inducing long-lasting changes.

The importation of Western rights-based laws after *doi moi* presented an ideological dilemma for party leaders. Private property and contractual rights were incompatible with socialist ideology and had the potential to undermine party paramountcy. Party leaders attempted to paper over this conflict by importing *nha nuoc phap quyen* (law-based state) principles and recycling an eclectic assortment of ideas presented as Ho Chi Minh thought. The new thinking opened ideological space for neoliberal legalism without discarding socialist orthodoxies.

By juxtaposing socialist and neoliberal legalism, party leaders set in motion ongoing ideological contests. Unlike the socialist legality adopted decades earlier, neoliberal legal ideas were imported into a hostile political, economic and legal environment. Rights-based thinking initially struggled against deeply ingrained socialist and traditional modes of thought. More recently, international legal harmonisation policies have invested neoliberal legalism and a procedural rule of law with a qualified legitimacy. For example, the idea that entrepreneurs are free to form transactions unless they are specifically prohibited by law has gained ground in some elite circles.[1] Outside the commercial arena neoliberal legalism has so far made little impact on the socialist axioms that legitimise party paramountcy.

1 The notion was recently endorsed by Politburo Resolution No 48 NQ/TW on Building and Perfecting the Socialist Orientated Economic System and *Nha Nuoc Phap Quyen*, 24 May 2005.

A significant finding is that conflicting ideologies do not inevitably constrain legal borrowing. In fact, some degree of ideological confusion and discord may actually create space for imported ideas. The party is preserving democratic centralism, 'state economic management' and collective mastery and associated ideals that give coherence and stability to existing institutional structures. But this does not prevent experimentation with imported legal ideals that facilitate international legal harmonisation and economic development. Provided the dominant ideology does not actively block imported legal ideals, foreign ideals can enter the official ideology.

Ideological theory has helped this study understand changes in the state's receptiveness to imported ideas. Yet an ideological framework predicated on binary opposition between dominant and dominated ideas does not adequately account for the creative negotiation, hybridisation and metamorphisation of imported ideas in Vietnam. Imported legal ideas do not function just as binary alternatives to local thinking, but instead resemble changeable and self-transforming social catalysts. Variations in the official ideology do not automatically produce corresponding institutional and social change, because human agents functioning within the constraints of their institutional mentalities and self-interest choose how they respond to ideology. For example, state officials invoke rule of law imagery to convince investors that the state protects private commercial rights and, simultaneously, to justify religious and criminal laws that subordinate individual interests to the public interest.

In short, ideology operates at too high a level of abstraction to explain fully the transplantation of law. We need another analytical approach that considers the negotiations and contests that generate the preference conversion required to localise imported laws.

State Power Distribution

The second working postulate, discussed in Chapters 4 to 6, showed that legal transplants are sensitive to the ways legislators, bureaucrats and judges use state power to make and enforce law. Attitudes, debates and processes profoundly influenced the way lawmakers and regulators selected, adapted and implemented foreign laws. Discourse analysis provided a way to access and understand these regulatory conversations.

Case studies showed how powerful state agencies use imported legal ideas strategically to encode and inculcate certain perspectives or orthodoxies to secure advantage in 'palace wars'. Lawmaking debates not only concerned altruistic concerns such as the pace and direction of law reform, but also reflected institutional and personal interests. Lawmaking resembles an elite-centred model of decision-making, in which the selection and implementation of legal imports is influenced by struggles within political and bureaucratic elites. More importantly, the studies demonstrated that self-interest is partially constrained by the epistemological conventions that influence official discourse. For example, as international legal harmonisation gained momentum, powerful ministries involved in redrafting the

Ordinance on Economic Contracts could no longer use state economic management arguments to preserve their prerogative powers over entrepreneurs. Regulatory discourse plays a vital role in establishing limits to institutional and personal interests and plays a key role in determining the adaptation of imported laws. Reform is not simply a function of self-interest—ideas matter.

Another important finding indicates that some elite-level legal drafters and regulators are becoming enmeshed in neoliberal-oriented interpretive communities. These groupings should not be thought of as geographic communities. They are more accurately understood as formal and informal social relationships that have the potential to generate cooperation and shared responses to borrowed law and regulatory practices.

Highly visible communities associated with certain central-level research institutes and ministries connect elite-level legal drafters with foreign donors and consultants. Members diagnose regulatory problems from neoliberal perspectives and draw legal solutions to problems from neoliberal ideas. Complex legal doctrines transfer rapidly among members, who share similar educational backgrounds and epistemological assumptions about the proper direction for legal reforms. Constantly repeated principles, doctrines and strategies for reform play a central role in constituting and directing the way members select, adapt and implement foreign laws. Within these communities, borrowed ideas are increasingly becoming the frame of reference for drafting and implementing laws.

Since members must operate within local political contexts, they use neoliberal ideas strategically, and selectively follow foreign advice in order to work around political and institutional agendas. Although they never entirely extricate themselves from their foundational interpretive communities (based on party, state and family beliefs), over time their epistemological settings move closer to neoliberal legalism. Within the parameters set by political and institutional constraints, they work closely with foreign donors to guide imported neoliberal laws through the numerous conferral and consensus processes *en route* to the National Assembly. In the process, they must isolate or discredit the assumptions (principally 'state economic management') used by other interpretive communities to diagnose problems and formulate regulatory solutions.

Notwithstanding the increasing professionalism and specialisation within the National Assembly, delegates still lack the skills and constitutional 'ground rules' needed to localise imported legal ideas. Since they cannot agree among themselves which local precepts and practices should supplement or replace imported norms, their interventions tend to block specific imported rules without proposing innovative home-grown solutions. Adding to the problem, deliberations in the National Assembly are orchestrated by party organs, inhibiting the sustained and relatively unmediated debates that discourse analysis suggests are required for preference convergence and codification.

If the party devolves more deliberative power and/or delegates arrogate power for themselves, the National Assembly may become more responsive to local norms and practices. A more proactive legislative body could creatively combine imported legal ideas with general legal principles distilled from local business transactions. There is potential with hybrid laws to find new solutions to domestic problems.

In the meantime, the fine-tuning that localises legal imports largely takes place in judicial, and especially administrative, processes. At an elite-level dialogue between state officials and lawyers representing large-scale investors is increasingly investing imported commercial rights with law-like consequences. Lawyers show officials how commercial rights function in a market economy. Some officials learn from these exchanges and have changed the content and style of regulation to replicate neoliberal legal practices. Support for a robust procedural 'rule of law' that is capable of checking state discretion over commercial rights has now spread beyond officials directly influenced by neoliberal interpretive communities.

Local officials remain largely (though not entirely) beyond the reach of neoliberal legal discourse. They use ideas and practices derived from unofficial discourses to overcome rigidities in central code-based definitions of commercial rights. These highly creative, but frequently unstable and contextual solutions orient rights towards particularistic family and community interests. Norms generated from these accommodations occasionally influence subordinate legislation that requires less discretion to implement. However, more generally, there is little evidence that the negotiations and compromises made at this level are intended to produce anything more then one-off solutions to highly contexualised problems.

Courts currently play a peripheral role in adapting imported laws to local conditions. Legal reforms that have invested courts with greater jurisdictional powers and the capacity to develop legal doctrines may encourage judges to use legal rules to adjudicate commercial disputes. Movement in this direction is evident in the secondary legal sources such as similar fact cases, guidance letters (*thong tu huong dan*) and judgements developed by the Supreme Court. These doctrines are beginning to give superior court judges more 'room to manoeuvre' to combine imported legal ideas creatively with insights gleaned from cases.

Different narratives influence local courts. Judges routinely subordinate the rights-based intent of imported laws to regional political and economic imperatives, as well as to the corrupt interests of litigants. Although these *ad hoc* negotiations overcome rigidities in codified private rights, they produce hybrid legal-social solutions that are highly contextual and rarely generate broadly applicable legal solutions. Even though its progress appears glacial, centrally formulated legal doctrines are, according to the studies, gradually taming local-level improvisation.

Domestic entrepreneurs are unlikely to litigate until they trust courts to make decisions about what is right and wrong. Judicial legitimacy depends on the emergence of 'secondary rules' and independence from party and state. It also requires well-trained, impartial judges and mechanisms that efficiently enforce court decisions.

Discourse analysis has assisted this study by showing that imported laws come packaged in a neoliberal legal narrative that communicates effectively with some domestic interpretive communities, but not with others. The types of discourse modes used to discuss imported law differed little among the interpretive communities, since these groups at different times considered laws from political, legal, moral and economic perspectives. What differed was the importance each group attached to particular modes of thinking about law and the receptiveness of these dominant modes to borrowed legal ideas. Sharp differences between these dominant modes fragment legal interpretations and prevent imported laws from acquiring uniform state-sponsored meanings.

Research findings also highlight the capacity for interpretive communities to be constitutive; that is, to function as forums in which individual and collective attitudes and behaviour towards imported laws are defined and redefined. In suggesting that interpretive communities consolidate and standardise legal meanings, discourse analysis also provides glimpses into the processes that naturalise legal imports. Since interpretive communities comprise state and non-state entities, a fuller explanation of legal transplantation needs to take into account the lack of interaction between these groups.

Non-state Pressure Groups

According to the third working postulate, non-state pressure groups influence the selection and implementation of foreign laws. Discourse analysis supports this inquiry by focusing attention on the dialogical exchanges that give meaning to imported law. It suggests that non-state pressure groups are more likely to effectively communicate unconventional or controversial ideas that influence imported laws in relatively unmediated and sustained discursive channels. By assessing pressure for reform, the third postulate also provides glimpses into the social need for particular imported laws.

Case studies imply that preference conversion is most likely to occur when discourse takes place within interpretive communities. For example, legal reforms proposed by foreign donors and investors are given a sympathetic hearing by lawmakers associated with neoliberal-oriented interpretive communities. In a similar vein, SOE directors have successfully lobbied regulators steeped in 'state economic management' thinking for protection against imported rights-based laws that promote competition. However, politically-unconnected entrepreneurs standing outside elite interpretive communities struggle to have their interests codified into law.

In Vietnam's highly mediated public space, politically-unconnected entrepreneurs cannot form member-directed associations and engage lawmakers in the sustained debates required to change preferences towards imported laws. Further limiting their influence, they communicate in a political, economic and moral language that is not easily converted into the highly abstract, codified preferences understood by lawmakers.

Preference conversion is possible without formal organisations. Large numbers of people sharing similar 'interpretive' attitudes towards land ownership, for example, succeeded in forcing the state to change the land valuation and transfer systems. Public resistance to unpopular laws sends messages to lawmakers that are not easily communicated through state-managed communicative channels. It conveys unorthodox and controversial ideas derived from 'unofficial' discourses that directly challenge the epistemological assumptions guiding 'official' discourse. However, sub-verbal communication is an inefficient and long-term path to preference convergence. That it succeeds at all in influencing Vietnamese lawmaking is partially explained by the low social regard for 'rule of law'. Ironically, as the 'rule of law' gains greater legitimacy, authorities may more easily discredit popular resistance to established laws as socially disruptive and deviant behaviour. As it stands, mass-regarding ideology (such as collective mastery), which conditions the state to respond to the people, makes the Vietnamese party and state more attuned to popular dissent then many neighbouring developing states.

Evidence considered in Chapter 8 suggests that legal borrowing is producing a fragmented legal landscape. Commercial laws that reflect the interests of an entrepreneurial elite, frequently appear complex, alien and irrelevant to politically-unconnected entrepreneurs. A state-centred legal system that disregards local self-regulatory practices risks being circumvented, subverted and ignored.

Discourse analysis reveals the importance of unmediated dialogue between state and social groups to adjust imported laws to local conditions. Without a social space that facilitates public debate by pressure groups, imported laws will resemble the interests and epistemological preferences of those wielding the most influence over drafting committees, state regulators and courts. Reforms are needed to amplify the voice of politically-unconnected entrepreneurs so that imported commercial laws take into account self-regulatory regimes.

It is perhaps too early in the reform cycle to assess whether self-regulatory structures can compete with, or even complement, imported rights-based law. As the economy grows and domestic firms transact more frequently with foreigners (especially those requiring formal contracts), imported contract and property norms may increasingly supplement relational bonds in commercial exchanges. Demand for substantive legal rights is likely to stimulate more interest in a procedural rule of law that checks bureaucratic power and promotes powerful and efficient courts. Progress towards a 'rule of law' in the commercial arena also depends on the legal fictions derived from imported laws providing more innovative and efficient solutions than discretionary compromises and relational practices. But these adaptations are improbable without more dialogical engagement between lawmakers and a broad cross-section of domestic entrepreneurs.

Imported commercial reforms are unlikely to translate into a 'rule of law' society unless the state adopts a more pluralistic approach to regulation. Policymakers need to recognise that contractual and property rights can be preserved by self-regulatory systems in ways that are functionally, although not formally, equivalent to state centred regulation. A de-centred 'rule of law' requires the state to establish a more effective structure to prevent arbitrary confiscation (either directly or through excessive fees, arbitrary taxes, demands for bribes, and so forth) and regulatory groups need to adjust their norms and practices to conform with minimum state requirements.

Rethinking Legal Transplantation Theories

This study began with three possible explanations for legal transplantation. Proponents of legal convergence argued that laws have been de-coupled from society and can easily transfer across cultural borders. Those arguing for legal divergence focused instead on linkages between laws and their social context and stressed that successful transplants require compatible socio-political structures, precepts and practices. From an evolutionary perspective, global interaction between countries induces an inexorable convergence towards the most technically efficient system.[2] Taken together these critiques fail to account adequately for Vietnam's (and perhaps developing East Asia's) history of fragmented legal borrowing.

State-law Monist Theories

The way law is conceptualised affects our thinking about legal transplantation. Convergence theories come from a Western liberal legal tradition in which laws are supposed to operate independently from religion, political morality and other social norms.[3] They substitute an external perspective that sees law's social connections for an internal perspective that only sees legal rules. This positivist belief that laws are only recognisable according to legal criteria forms the philosophical basis of the neoliberal legal tradition. Some within this tradition have formed the view that laws have de-coupled from society and can, as autonomous technical instruments, transfer easily across cultural boundaries.

'Law in context' theorists, on the other hand, emphasise the linkages between legal transplants and underlying social values and practices. By focusing attention on how legal transplants are received and implemented by state officials, their methods illuminate the official ideals, epistemologies and practices that shape the way laws are imported.[4] The numerous inconsistencies between legal imports and local institutional conditions lead these theorists to caution against cross-cultural borrowing.

---

2 See, for example, Lawrence Friedman (1975), *The Law System: A Social Science Perspective*, Russell Sage Foundation, New York; Ugo Mattei (1994), 'Efficiency in Legal Transplants: An Essay in Comparative Law and Economics', 14 *International Review of Law and Economics*, 3.

3 The initial tentative separation of law from morality and religion took place in the Roman legal system. See Alan Watson (1970), *The Law of the Ancient Romans*, Southern Methodist University Press, Dallas, 5–7: Ugo Mattei, (1997), 'Three Patterns of Law: Taxonomy and Change in the World's Legal Systems', 45 *American Journal of Comparative Law*, 5, 19–40.

4 See, for example, Masaji Chiba (1986), 'Introduction', in Masaji Chiba (ed.), *Asian Indigenous Law: An Introduction to Received Law*, KPI, London, 4–6; Pierre Legrand (1995), 'Comparative Legal Studies and Commitment to Theory', 58 *Modern Law Review*, March, 262, 263–73.

Despite their different points of inquiry, both theoretical traditions perceive legal transplantation as the impact of foreign law on society. They share a historically determined monistic outlook that assesses legal transplantation from state perspectives: do transplants induce uniform state-sponsored meanings and are they implemented by epistemologically compatible state institutions? Their main disagreement regards the impact of transplanted laws on local social conditions. Convergence theorists see few points of interaction between law and society, making transplantation socially easy, whereas 'law in context' theorists see so much interaction that legal transplantation generates too many variables and too much uncertainty to succeed readily.

A major problem in applying state-centred legal theories in Vietnam is uncertainty regarding the boundaries of state power. Case studies not only reveal blurred distinctions between the party and state, but also between central and local authorities. It is frequently unclear whether laws derive meaning from party, state or hybrid state-societal authorities. These vague and protean distinctions problematise a state-centred analysis of legal transplantation.

An additional problem is that the myriad perspectives shaping legal borrowing resist categorisation in narrow ways as imported legal instruments impacting on state and society. The case studies suggest that legal borrowing is as much about bottom-up processes as top-down state-directed legal solutions. Exogenous or endogenous change presents a false dichotomy. Legal transplantation is highly negotiated, involving 'dialogical' lawmaking between central leaders, provincial authorities, the foreign donor community and local entrepreneurs. Transplantation is more likely to be guided by like-minded state and non-state individuals clustered together in 'interpretive communities' than by state officials championing reform from the top. It is also guided by alliances (frequently corrupt) between party, state and social forces.

Rather than indicating the failure of transplantation, as state-centred analysis suggests, incoherence, fragmentation and negotiation may be essential components of the transplantation process. However, conventional analysis misunderstands the negotiations underlying legal transplantation. A concept of legal borrowing that recognises the central importance of contests and alliances between state and societal forces suggests the need for a new way to conceptualise legal borrowing.

Legal Evolution

Some case studies supported the contention in legal evolutionary theory that, as societies grow more alike, legal systems will converge. For example, Chapter 6 showed that foreign and domestic law firms are guiding central-level officials towards international (primarily US) approaches to commercial regulation. Foreign donor agencies sponsor numerous law-reform projects that largely aim to engineer a Western-style rights-based legal system. And above all else, Vietnam's desire to secure foreign markets has led it to join international treaties that require legal harmonisation with foreign standards and procedures.

Nevertheless, by directing attention towards international legal transfers, legal evolution underestimates the extent to which legal reforms are propelled by domestic legal recycling and transfers within the legal system.[5] Since the global and local coexist, analysis should also consider bottom-up processes that assist or resist international harmonisation.[6]

Another difficulty with evolution theory is the observed degree of differentiation within the Vietnamese legal system. Some parts show convergence and other parts are taking a more idiosyncratic path. There are strong signs of convergence in the shift towards rights-based legislation, yet this change is largely confined to the commercial arena. Even within this arena there is differentiation. Procedural rules governing regulatory processes are far more resistant to foreign influence than commercial normative rules.

The desire for legal efficiency, which in evolutionary theory propels convergence, does not adequately account for the observed degree of legal differentiation and path-dependent development in Vietnam. We need a fuller explanation that considers the factors that shape local understandings about what constitutes an optimal regulatory system. It needs to explain why substantive laws transfer rapidly among like-minded lawmaking elites, but encounter resistance in local-level state and social institutions. Legal evolution overlooks the communicative barriers to legal transplantation and the strategic use of imported ideas for institutional and personal advantage. These are serious shortcomings for a predictive theory.

Modelling Legal Transplantation

Evidence considered in this study suggests it is not possible to model legal transplantation deterministically. From a scientific perspective, the transplantation phenomenon is unknowable because the causal links explaining human responses to borrowed laws are (if at all) only cognisable for the simplest transactions. There are simply too many variables to support testable propositions of cause and effect.

Yet it has been possible to gain valuable insights by examining indirect processes such as ideology and communicative action. These processes influence thinking, which in turn shapes approaches to legal transfers. This is causation in heavy disguise.

Of the three working postulates, state power distribution and pressure groups proved the most useful in guiding research towards the sites of interaction between

---

5 See generally Wolf Heydebrand (2001), 'From Globalisation of Law to Law under Globalisation', in Johannes Feest and David Nelken (eds), *Adapting Legal Cultures*, Hart Publishing Oxford, 129–32; Gunther Teubner (1997), '"Global Bukowian": Legal Pluralism in the World Society' in Gunther Teubner (ed.), *Global Law Without a State,* Dartmouth, Aldershot, 3–38.

6 See generally B. de Sousa Santos (1995), *Towards a New Common Sense*, Routledge, London; W.E. Scheuerman (1999), 'Globalisation and the Fate of Law', in D. Dyzenhaus (ed.), *Recrafting the Rule of Law*, Hart Publishing, Oxford, 243–66.

legal imports and local precepts and practices. But this conceptual architecture lacks the tools to analyse the regulatory conversations shaping legal transplantation. Our thinking on this problem has been greatly assisted by discourse analysis. It provides a methodology for analysing regulatory conversations that avoids the limitations associated with state-centred analysis. It makes us ask: who conducts these conversations, what are they about, and how do they advance the regulatory objectives of key players? It suggests that the transfer of laws and ideas has similar effects, because discourse analysis collapses distinctions between legal prescription and legal description. Further, it allows us to assess what types of conversations are most likely to generate preference convergence and the adoption of imported legal ideas. Discourse analysis also acknowledges the role played by human agency and reminds us that the story of legal borrowing is inextricably bound up with legal development strategies.

Above all else, this study has revealed the complexity of legal transplantation. There are simply too many processes and perspectives for one unified theory. The interpretive model proposed in this study is intended to complement and refocus, rather than supplant other theoretical approaches through which transplantation can be observed. In this way, it can guide researchers towards the processes and exchanges that shape and adapt legal imports into socialist-transforming East Asia (especially Vietnam). For example, there are complementary perspectives in Bourdieu's 'legal fields', legal pluralism's 'semi-autonomous social fields', the functionally complementary 'estates' of anthropological plural society models, relational transactions discussed by normative theorists and new institutional theory.[7] An exploration of the compatibility or otherwise of these theories with the proposed model is beyond the scope of this study, although it is one that is needed to advance research in this area.

In developing the interpretive model, it has been necessary to abstract from the rich detail of case studies. Each part of the model covers a narrow subset of the facts and situations governing legal transfers. They have been constructed not only to explain, but also to propose some hypotheses about the integration of legal transfers into recipient regulatory systems. There are five parts to the model: dialogical negotiations, effective communication, interpretive communities, strategic agendas and power relationships.

---

7 See, respectively, Pierre Bourdieu (1987), 'The Force of Law: Towards a Sociology of the Juridical Field', 38 *Hastings Law Journal*, 814; Sally R. Moore (1973), 'Law and Social Change in the Semi-Autonomous, Social Field as an Appropriate Subject of Study', 7 *Law and Society Review*, 719; Raymond Smith (1995), The Matrifocal Family: Power, Pluralism, and Politics, Routledge, New York; Stewart Macaulay (2000), 'Relational Contract Theory: Unanswered Questions a Symposium in Honor of Ian R. MacNeil: Relational Contracts Floating on a Sea of Custom? Thoughts about the Ideas of Ian MacNeil and Lisa Berstein', 94 *Northwestern University Law Review*, 775; Douglass North (1990), *Institutions, Institutional Change and Economic Performance*, Cambridge University Press, Cambridge, 118–21.

One: Contests and Negotiations

A consistent theme in this study is that contests and negotiations localise imported legal ideas. As previously suggested, rather than signalling transplant failure, mediation is the process through which preference convergence takes place. Dialogue and discord are necessary for legal transfers to enter and influence local regulatory mentalities and practices. In some circumstances these exchanges have creatively used imported ideas to imagine legal solutions to domestic problems that could not be resolved by local precepts and practices. But this proposition tells us little about the types of contests and negotiations that are most likely to generate preference convergence. We need a nuanced way to ascertain what kinds of dialogical exchanges effectively communicate foreign ideas into local contexts.

Two: Discursive and Non-discursive Communication

Discourse analysis has assisted this study by suggesting that not all communication produces preference convergence and the localisation of legal transfers. It shows that discussions conducted in mutually comprehensible communicative modes (or epistemologies) are more likely to prioritise and value similar aspects of imported laws and generate preference convergence. It will be recalled from Chapter 1 that a semi-autonomous approach to discourse analysis is used in this study to avoid the limitations imposed by systems theory's narrow legal–illegal characterisation of legal discourse.

Groups discussing the same law from different modes communicate with difficulty. For regulatory conversations to convey the deep epistemological meanings underlying borrowed law effectively, they must be conducted between interlocutors who share common or compatible criteria or modes of thinking. Supporting this proposition, case studies showed that laws transferred rapidly between foreign donors and Vietnamese lawmakers who shared similar legal grammar, educational background and epistemological assumptions.

Case studies also showed that lawmakers did not rigidly apply just one discourse mode in regulatory conversations. For example, legal drafters conversed in legal and economic modes with foreign legal advisors, but deployed political, even nationalistic arguments to persuade state and party leaders. All this suggests that lawmakers deliberated on laws from multiple perspectives, sometimes simultaneously. What shaped their ultimate view was the importance they attached to particular modes of thinking about law and the receptiveness of these dominant modes to borrowed legal ideas.

A shortcoming with discourse analysis is its search for legal meanings exclusively in regulatory conversations. This constitutes a limitation in societies such as Vietnam where the state strongly mediates public discourse. Case studies showed the importance of sub-verbal discourse and tacit understandings in communicating views across highly asymmetric state–society relationships. For example, silent resistance eventually forced lawmakers to adjust imported land laws incrementally to suit local conditions. Further research is required to assess the capacity for non-discursive factors such as ritual and symbolism as well as empathetic and sensory communication to influence legal transplantation.[8]

Three: Interpretive Communities

A key component of the model is the notion of interpretive communities. The term 'community' does not necessarily signify a spatial location or a specific place where particular interpretive positions are followed. Rather, interpretive communities form abstract social relationships that have the potential to generate cooperation and shared responses to borrowed law and regulatory practices. Some interpretive communities cluster around certain state institutions such as CIEM. Others are more dispersed and coalesce around loosely constituted entrepreneurial associations.

Research shows that commercial legal ideas transplant rapidly among members of neoliberal oriented interpretive communities, but are resisted by other state and non-state communities. What seems to matter is whether members share common epistemological and tacit assumptions about the nature of regulatory problems and the appropriate responses. For example, interpretive communities linking foreign donors and Vietnamese lawmakers are rather heterogeneous in their use of language and ideas. Yet they generate sympathy for neoliberal legal reforms by repeating story-lines that emphasise the importance of the 'rule and law' to solving particular regulatory problems. Self-regulatory communities, on the other hand, promote their own regulatory solutions that engage only marginally (if at all) with imported legal idea and processes.

Rather than identifying interpretive communities by their level of mutuality, it makes more sense to mark out boundaries between communities. Factors that differentiate communities include different criteria for validating imported ideas and different story-lines to inculcate similar views about the optimal forms of regulation. This is a negative definition that assesses differences in the dominant 'modes' of thinking and tacit understandings between those inside and outside interpretive communities.

Four: Strategic Discourse

Members of interpretive communities use discourse strategically to secure regulatory objectives. They co-opt and modify imported and local statutory norms, epistemologies and tacit assumptions to redefine internal regulatory boundaries and orient interactions with other interpretive communities. Most importantly, the

8 Philip Taylor has shown, for example, that some regulatory conversations in Vietnam are primarily ordered by religious, communal and emotional idioms that are communicated through symbolic, empathic and sensory means more readily than through written and oral messages. See Philip Taylor (2004), *Goddess on the Rise: Pilgrimage and Popular Religion in Vietnam*, University of Hawaii Press, Honolulu.

strategic use of discourse shows that meaning and behaviour, as they influence legal borrowing, are inseparably connected. This integrated understanding avoids the artificial separation in systems theory between communication about law and the action associated with law.

In some circumstances social actors use imported ideas to secure a blueprint for reform. CIEM legal drafters, for example, enlisted support from domestic entrepreneurs to promote market deregulation in the Enterprise Law. In other cases, interpretive communities use ideas to camouflage institutional or personal interests. Line-ministries and provincial people's committees, for example, used 'state economic management' ideas to preserve discretionary and frequently corrupt controls over market entry. In still other cases, self-regulatory communities may support imported deregulatory reforms, but reject alien normative rules. In each case, shared epistemologies and tacit understandings shaped the way the interpretive community perceived the world, defined its own interests and devised strategies to realise those interests.[9]

Five: Power Relationships Order Regulatory Conversations

A central problem with state-centred explanations for legal transplantation is their preoccupation with top-down reforms that locate power over law exclusively in the state. Research has revealed the diffuse and polycentric nature of state power. Far from being monolithic, state power is not unidirectional and responds to social forces seeking to influence the importation of law. Power-sharing arrangements influence whether interpretive communities control the selection, codification and regulation of imported laws. For example, interpretive communities involved in drafting committees use state power to promote their ideas and modify or suppress opposing views.

Power does not emanate from the state alone. Some entrepreneurial pressure groups use financial and political power to procure support from acquiescent state regulators. Small-scale entrepreneurs and urban residents, on the other hand, lack the resources to access state power and, as a consequence, struggle to influence the selection and implementation of imported laws. Their primary compensating strategy is self-regulation. Restated in propositional form, there is a loose correlation between access to power and the social and economic interests that imported laws come to reflect.

---

9 This finding contradicts Gainsborough's assertion that ideas are not especially important in securing self-interest. See M. Gainsborough (2002), 'Beneath the Veneer of Reform: The Politics of Economic Liberalisation in Vietnam', 35 *Communist and Post-Communist Studies*, 353, 357.

Applying the Interpretive Model in Vietnam

The search for a new way to understand legal transplantation raises another equally intriguing question; does the interpretive model provide a more contextually relevant understanding of law in Vietnam than state-centred theories? The central difference between these approaches is the reliance in the model on a decentred understanding of law. Rather than treating laws as universal instruments, the model locates law in state and non-state regulatory conversations. It also jettisons essentialist notions that laws have substantive meanings such as private rights, rule of law or procedural justice. 'Law is whatever people identify and treat their social practices as "law" (or *recht*, or *droit*, and so on)'.[10]

Rather than treating law as social fact, the model is more concerned with conceptualising social patterns as law. It rests on two notions. The first is that state regulation acquires social force through preference convergence and consensus. This notion ties in with the role interpretive communities play in constituting and reproducing common understandings about the meaning and role of imported and domestic rules. When enough key actors share common understandings, certain legal meanings become the authoritative or legitimate way of understanding rules. This requirement for some consensus or critical mass regarding what constitutes law prevents the model from sliding to the conclusion that all forms of social control are law. Sally Merry stated the problem with open-ended social-science depictions of law, 'Where do we stop speaking of law and find ourselves simply describing social life?'[11]

The second notion is that the usefulness of law is determined by its capacity to communicate meaning effectively.[12] Since law is what people say it is, law is only useful if it is understood. Thus, the main criterion for evaluating the effectiveness of legal transfers is whether they are maintained and reproduced in legal discourse. The content and quality of outcomes generated by the discourse, such as 'rule of

---

10 In this quotation, Brian Tamanaha was describing his non-essentialist conception of law, but it also aptly describes discursive law. See Brian Tamanaha (2000), 'A Non-Essentialist Version of Legal Pluralism', 27 Journal of Law and Society (2), 296, 313. Also see Niklas Luhmann (1982), The Differentiation of Society, Columbia University Press, New York, 122. There is a longstanding debate in Western legal theory about the definition of law. In many respects, the ideas raised in support of positivist and discursive interpretations mirror wider philosophical arguments about absolute and relative notions of truth. See Peter Fitzpatrick (1992), The Mythology of Modern Law, Routledge, London, 184–201; B.D. Santos (1987), 'Law: A Map of Misreading. Towards a Postmodern Conception of Law', 14 Journal of Law and Society (3), 279, 282–86. Also see Richard Rorty (1979), Philosophy and the Mirror of Nature, Princeton University Press, Princeton; J. McDowell (2000), 'Towards Rehabilitating Objectivity', in Robert B. Brandom (ed.), Rorty and His Critics, Blackwell, Malden, Massachusetts.

11 Sally Engle Merry (1988), 'Legal Pluralism', 22 *Law and Society Review*, 869, 870.

12 See E.W. Lehman (1992), *The Viable Polity*, Temple University Press, Philadelphia, Pennsylvania.

law' and social justice, are only secondary considerations that have meaning to those participating in specific interpretive communities.[13] The model understands laws as comprising pluralistic understandings where the most forceful and compelling narrative determines legal meaning. This notion differs radically from the assumptions underpinning state-centred analysis that invests law with 'rule of law' characteristics such as immutability, universality and some connection with organisational structures, such as legislatures, courts and lawyers.

Everything is left open in the model to empirical investigation and the analysis of legal transplantation following such investigation. It allows researchers to go beyond the effects legal transplants have on state notions of law to examine non-state or decentred regulation that appears to have little or no connection to state rules and institutions.

The conceptual shift in the model from state law to decentred legal discourses will encounter some formidable hurdles if it is to attract support from key government agencies and foreign legal reformers operating in Vietnam. The model could hardly differ more from the extreme positivism that informs official Vietnamese legal thinking. By investing non-state regulation with legal consequences, it challenges longstanding assumptions that the party and state should lead society. It also exposes shortcomings in current legal reforms, such as the facile distinctions between legal instrumentalism and deregulation. But if the state is prepared to relinquish its regulatory monopoly, the model suggests ways to decentre and extend a 'rule of law' to self-regulatory practices.

Foreign donors and investors are also unlikely to embrace a decentred understanding of law that recognises and validates non-state regulatory practices. Informed by the Hayekian proposition that productive capitalism needs a 'rule of law', many donor projects aim to create a stable and transparent legal environment that promotes transactional certainty and stability. Projects support formal adjudication in courts, judicially enforced contracts and inviolable property rights. Donors and investors view domestic regulatory practices based on relational, ethno-religious and sentimental factors as unbounded, inefficient and potentially anarchic.

By ignoring domestic precepts and practices, reforms produce laws that largely satisfy international treaties and foreign investors, rather than the vast majority of entrepreneurs. Too often, donors have sought to quarantine legal imports from local processes that would 'jeopardise the fragile momentum for reform'. However, donors struggle to insulate legal reforms from politically-connected SOEs and entrepreneurs. As a result, after two decades of 'rule of law' reforms, the legal system does not come close to producing the transactional certainty promised by Hayekian theory.

The model offers donors a way to imagine coexisting regulatory systems where imported laws and commercial arbitration provide formal arrangements for preserving contractual and property rights, while self-regulation provides transactional norms

13 See Tim Murphy (2001), 'Modernising Justice Inside 'UK PLC': Minesis, De-differentiation and Colonisation,' in Jiři Priban and David Nelken (eds), *Law's New Boundaries: The Consequences of Legal Autopoiesis*, Ashgate, Aldershot, 218.

and conflict resolution for small-scale entrepreneurs. Rather than a state-initiated, command and control 'rule of law', the model suggests that effective regulation requires a more pluralistic approach where the state is only one of several actors. The background values of the 'rule of law' can be realised in ways that are functionally, though not formally, equivalent to state-centred regulation. Finally, foreign human rights groups and local dissidents may worry that the model devalues universal standards of procedural and substantive justice against which government action is held accountable.

As a descriptor, the model comes close to depicting the way many Vietnamese understand and interact with imported law. It challenges the notion that law is exclusively from the state and recognises that laws may have little connection to the state. It drains laws of intrinsic and immutable normative characteristics. Instead, it treats laws as being inseparable from everyday discussions with their own particular histories and logics. Decentred laws can be syncretically applied to suit particular contexts. They have situational rather than universal meanings, and deviations from rules remake the rule.

Most importantly for our study, the model offers a way to understand how an imported 'rule of law' may function in Vietnam. If legal meaning is primarily located in regulatory conversations, a 'rule of law' does not have to be strongly attached to formal aspects of law—such as rules and legal institutions. From a decentred perspective, the development of a 'rule of law' in Vietnam is measured by assessing the extent to which imported ideas have stimulated new thinking in state and non-state discourse about uniform, transparent and predictable ways to regulate commercial relationships.

The prognosis for Vietnam is that domestic understandings about a 'rule of law' will dissolve into a myriad of regulatory conversations that re-imagine Western liberal meanings in highly localised contexts. In this fragmented legal landscape, successful commercial regulation will require a combination of state rules with other approaches that are not exclusively, or even apparently, legal. A unifying 'rule of law' is unlikely to emerge until the state relaxes controls over social discourse, opens lawmaking forums to a broad range of views and gives citizens effective recourse against abuses of state power.

Bibliography

Abel, R., *Politics by Other Means: Law in the Struggle against Apartheid*, 1980–1994 (New York: Routledge, 1995).

Abercombie, N., Hill, S., and Turner, B., *The Dominant Ideology Thesis* (London: Allen and Unwin, 1980).

Ajani, G., 'By Chance and Prestige: Legal Transplants in Russia and Eastern Europe', *American Journal of Comparative Law* 43(1)(1995): 93–118.

Alagappa, M., 'The Anatomy of Legitimacy', in M. Alagappa (ed.), *Political Legitimacy in South East Asia* (Stanford: Stanford University Press, 1995), pp. 11–65.

Althusser, L., *Essays on Ideology* (London: Verso, 1984).

Andersson, G., *et al.*, *Strengthening the Capacity of the Office of the Vietnam National Assembly*, SIDA Evaluation 12/12 (Stockholm: SIDA, 2002).

Andreff, W., 'The Double Transition from Underdevelopment and from Socialism in Vietnam', *Journal of Contemporary Asia* 23(4)(1993): 515–31.

Anh Thu, 'Tu "Khuc Xuong" Giai Phong Mat Bang' (Site Clearance 'A Hard Nut to Crack'), *Dau Tu*, 14 August (2001), 6

Anh, Trung, 'Legal Thought of Vietnam Feudalist Class', *Vietnam Law and Legal Forum* 2(13)(1995): 24–28.

Aoki, M., 'The Japanese Firm as a System of Attributes: A Survey and Research Agenda', in M. Aoki and R. Dore (eds), *The Japanese Firm: The Sources of Competitive Strength* (Oxford: Oxford University Press, 1994), pp. 11–40.

Asian Development Bank, *Bulletin on Law and Policy Reform* (Manila: Asian Development Bank, (2001).

——, *Report on Asian Development Bank's Law and Policy Activities in Support of Poverty Reduction* (Manila: Asian Development Bank, 2004). Available at <www.adb.org/Documents>.

Avineri, S., 'Introduction', in S. Avineri (ed.), *Karl Marx on Colonialism and Modernization* (New York: Doubleday, 1969), pp. 6–16.

Ba Tuan, 'De Chanh An TANDTC Co Dieu Kien Bo Nhiem Tham Phan Duoc Xac Thuc Hon' (Allowing the Chief Justice of the Supreme People's Court the Ability to Nominate Judges Will Be More Realistic), *Phap Luat* 19 March 2002: 2.

——, 'Sua Luat Lieu Co Giam Oan Sai?' (Will Changing the Law Reduce Problems, Mistakes?), *Phap Luat* 20 March 2002: 2.

Bach Quoc An and Lai Thi Anh, 'BTA's Impacts on Vietnam's Current Legal System' 8 *Vietnam Law and Legal Forum* (91)(2002): 16–18.

Bailyn, B., *The Ideological Origins of the American Revolution* (Cambridge, Massachusetts: Belknap Press, 1967).

Bao Tram, 'Phap Luat Ve Dat Dai: Cuon Chi Can Go Roi' (Law on Land: A Coil of

Thread to be Rearranged), *Phap Luat*, July (1997), pp. 6–7.

Barfield, O., *History, Guilt, and Habit* (Middletown, Connecticutt: Wesleyan University Press, 1979).

Barro, R., *Determinants of Economic Growth* (Cambridge, Massachusetts: MIT Press, 1997).

Barzelay, M. and Smith, R.M., 'The One Best System? A Political Analysis of Neoclassical Institutionalist Perspectives on the Modern Corporation', in W.J. Samuels and A.S. Miller (eds), *Corporations and Society: Power and Responsibility* (New York: Greenwood Press, 1987), pp. 81–110.

Baxter, Hugh, 'Autopoiesis and the "Relative Autonomy" of Law', *Cardozo Law Review* 19(1998): 1987–2090.

Beck, A., 'Is Law an Autopoietic System?', *Oxford Journal of Legal Studies* 14(3)(1994): 389–401.

Bell, J., 'English and French Law—Not So Different?' *Current Legal Problems* 48(1995): 63–102.

Bentley, J., *Completion of Viet Nam's Legal Framework for Economic Development*, UNDP Discussion Paper 2 (Hanoi: United Nations Development Programme, 1999).

Beresford, M., *Vietnam: Politics, Economics and Society* (London: Pinter, 1989).

Berger, P. and Luckman, T., *The Social Construction of Reality* (New York: Anchor Books, 1966).

Berkowitz, D., Pistor, K. and Richard, J., 'The Transplant Effect', *American Journal of Comparative Law* 51(1)(2003): 163–204.

Berle, A. and Means, G., *The Modern Corporation and Private Property* (New York: Harcourt, 1968).

Berman, H.J., *Justice in the USSR*, 2nd edn (Cambridge, Massachusetts: Harvard University Press, 1963).

———, 'Some Jurisprudential Implications of the Codification of Soviet Law', in R.M. Buxbaum and K. Hendley (eds), *The Soviet Sobranie of Laws: Problems of Codification and Non-Publication* (Berkeley: University of California Press, 1991), pp. 173–83.

———, 'The Rule of Law and the Law-Based State (*Rechtsstaat*)', in D. Barry (ed.), *Towards the 'Rule of Law' in Russia?* (New York: M. E. Sharpe, 1992), pp. 43–59..

Black, B., Kraakman, R. and Tarassova, A., 'Russian Privatisation and Corporate Governance: What Went Wrong?', *Stanford Law Review* 52(2000): 1731–1808.

Black, J., 'Regulatory Conversations', *Journal of Law and Society* 29(1)(2002): 163–96.

Boaventura de Sousa Santos, 'On Modes of Production of Law and Social Theory', *Journal of Sociology and Law* 13(1985): 299–339.

Bohman, J., 'Complexity, Pluralism and the Constitutional State: On Habermas's Faktizitat und Geltung', *Law and Society Review* 28(4)(1994): 897–930.

Boisot, M.H., *Information Space: A Framework for Learning in Organisations,*

Institutions and Culture (London: Routledge, 1995).
Bourdieu, P., 'The Force of Law: Towards a Sociology of the Juridical Field', *Hastings Law Journal* 38(5)(1987): 805–54.
Brandt, C., Schwartz, B. and Fairbank, J.K., *A Documentary History of Chinese Communism* (Cambridge, Massachusetts: Harvard University Press, 1952).
Branson, D., 'The Very Uncertain Prospect of "Global" Convergence in Corporate Governance', *Cornell International Law Journal* 34(2)(2001): 321–62.
Budanov, A.G., *Gosudarstvennyi Stroi Demokraticheskoi Respubliki Vietnam* (State Structure of the Democratic Republic of Vietnam), (Moscow: Gosudarstvennoe Izdatel'stvo Iuridicheskiy Literatury, 1958).
Bui Ngoc Son, 'Su Doc Lap Cua Toa An Trong Nha Nuoc Phap Quyen' (Independence of the Court and the Rule of Law), *Tap Chi Nghien Cuu Lap Phap* (4)(2003): 43, 48.
Bui Xuan Dinh, *Le Lang Phep Nuoc* (Customary Law and State Law), (Hanoi: Law Publishing House, 1985).
Burawoy, M., *The Politics of Production: Factory Regimes under Capitalism and Socialism* (London: Verso, 1985).
Burchett, W., *North of the 17th Parallel* (Hanoi: FLPH, 1955).
Cadiere, L., *Religious Beliefs and Practices of the Vietnamese*, trans. I. Mabbett, Centre for South East Asian Studies Working Paper 60 (Melbourne: Monash University, 1958).
Cain, M., 'Gramsci, The State and the Place of Law', in D. Sugarman (ed.), *Legality, Ideology and the State* (London: Academic Press, 1983), pp. 95–115.
Cao Cuong, 'No More Harassment', *Saigon Times* 11 July (1998): 28–29.
Carother, T., 'The Rule of Law Revival' *Foreign Affairs* 77(2)(1998): 95–106.
Central Committee of the CPV 'Resolution on Industrialisation from the Central Committee Seventh Party Congress', *Voice of Vietnam* 11 August 1994, trans. BBC Monitoring Service Asia-Pacific, 19 August 1994.
———, The Communist Party of Vietnam Central Committee's Political Report to the 9th National Party Congress (Hanoi: Central Committee of the Communist Party of Vietnam, 2001), Chapter IX.
———, 2001–2010 Socio-Economic Development Strategy, 9th National Party Congress (Hanoi: Central Committee of the Communist Party of Vietnam, 2001), chapter IV, part 4.
Chapman Tripp Sheffield Young, Enterprise Law Reform – Some Issues and Some Suggestions, unpublished paper (Hanoi: UNDP-CIEM Enterprise Law Project, 1998).
Cheffins, B., 'Current Trends in Corporate Governance: Going from London to Milan via Toronto', *Duke Journal of Comparative and International Law* 10(1)(1999): 5–42.
Chiba, M., 'Introduction', in M. Chiba (ed.), *Asian Indigenous Law: An Introduction to Received Law* (London: KPI, 1986), pp. 1–10.
———, 'Three-Level Structure of Law in Contemporary Japan – The Shinto Society', in M. Chiba (ed.), *Asian Indigenous Law: In Interaction with Received*

Law (London: KPI, 1986), pp. 301–58.

Chiba, M., 'Japan', in Pho-Ling Tan (ed.), *Asian Legal Systems* (Sydney: Butterworths, 1997), pp. 99–108.

Chuan Roger Peng, 'Limited Liability in China: A Partial Reading of China's Company Law of 1994', *Columbia Journal of Asian Law* 10(1)(1996): 263–80.

Chuong Thau and Phan Ngoc 'Confucianism in Vietnam Seen from an Historical Tradition', *Vietnamese Studies* (1)(1994): 85–91.

CIEM, *Comparative Provincial Performance in Private Business Development: Some Preliminary Observations from Nine Provincial Case Studies*, UNDP VIE01/025, (Hanoi: United Nations Development Programme, 2003).

Clammer, J.R., 'French Studies on the Chinese in Indochina: A Bibliographical Survey', *Journal of Southeast Asian Studies* 12(1)(1981): 15–26.

Clarke, D., 'Economic Development and the Rights Hypothesis: The China Problem', *American Journal of Comparative Law* 51(1)(2003): 89–112.

Clune, W.H. and Lindquist, R.E., 'What "Implementation" Isn't: Towards a General Framework for Implementation of Research', *Wisconsin Law Review* 5(1981): 1044–116.

Communist Party of Vietnam, *Vietnamese Party Congress Political Report* (Hanoi: Communist Party of Vietnam, 2001).

Cong Tac Ke Hoach, 'Carrying Out Good National Economic Planning and Summarizing National Economic Planning Well', *Cong Tac Ke Hoach*, JPRS 67923, 9 April (Hanoi: Supreme Court of Vietnam, 1976).

Cong Tac Toa An Nam, *Bao Cao Tong Ket 2000* (Supreme Court Annual Report 2000), (Hanoi: Supreme Court of Vietnam, 2000).

Cooke, N., 'Nineteenth-Century Vietnamese Confucianisation in Historical Perceptive: Evidence from the Palace Examinations (1463-1883)', *Journal of Southeast Asian Studies* 25(2)(1994): 270–312.

———, 'The Composition of the Nineteenth-Century Political Elite of Pre-Colonial Nguyen Vietnam', *Modern Asian Studies* 29(4)(1995): 737–56.

Cooter, R., 'The Theory of Market Modernization of Law', *International Review of Law and Economics* 16(2)(1996): 142–72.

——— ,and Landa, J.T., 'Personal Versus Impersonal Trade: The Size of Trading Groups and Contract Law', *International Review of Law and Economics* 4(1)(1984): 15–22.

Cotterell, R., 'Introduction: The Law and Society Tradition', in R. Cotterell (ed.), *Law and Society* (Aldershot: Dartmouth 1994), xii–xxii.

———, 'The Rule of Law in Transition: Revisiting Franz Neumann's Sociology of Legality', *Social and Legal Studies* 5(4)(1996): 451–70.

———, 'The Concept of Legal Culture' in D. Nelken (ed.), *Comparing Legal Cultures* (Aldershot: Dartmouth, 1997), pp. 13–32.

———, 'The Representation of Law's Autonomy in Autopoiesis Theory' in J. Přibáň and D. Nelken (eds), *Law's New Boundaries: The Consequences of Legal Autopoiesis* (Aldershot: Ashgate, 2001), pp. 84–104.

Cuong Tu Nguyen 'Rethinking Vietnamese Buddhist History: Is the *Thien Uyen Tap*

Anh a "Transmission of the Lamp" Text?', in K.W. Taylor and J.K. Whitmore (eds), *Essays into Vietnamese Pasts* (Ithaca: Southeast Asia Program, Cornell University, 1995), pp. 81–115.

D. Hoc, 'Phai Dam Bao Tinh Doc Lap Xet Xu Cua Toa An' (We Must Guarantee the Independence of the Court), *Nguoi Lao Dong* 20 March (2002), 2.

Dae-Kyu Yoon, 'Korea' in Poh-Ling Tan (ed.), *Asian Legal Systems* (Sydney: Butterworths, 1997), pp. 162–95.

Dalton, R. and Ong, N., *The Vietnamese Public in Transition: The World Values Survey – Vietnam 2001* (Irvine: Center for the Study of Democracy, University of California, 2001). Available online at <www.uci.edu/csd>.

Dang Duc Dam, 'Administrative Reform – Changes to Meet the Requirements of the Market-Orientated Economy', in J. Gillespie (ed.), *Commercial Legal Development in Vietnam: Vietnamese and Foreign Commentaries* (Singapore: Butterworths, 1997), pp. 477–98.

———, *Vietnam's Macroeconomy and Types of Companies* (Hanoi: The Gioi Publishers, 1997).

Dang Hong Nga, 'Code of the New Period', *Vietnam Economic Times* (24)(1999): 39.

Dang Phong, 'The Private Sector: In Vietnamese Industry from 1945 to the Present', in Mekong Project Development Facility (ed.), *Vietnam's Undersized Engine: A Survey of 95 Larger Private Manufacturers*, MPDF Discussion Paper No. 9 (Hanoi: Mekong Project Development Facility, 1999), pp. 47–80.

——— and Beresford, M., *Authority Relations and Economic Decision-Making in Vietnam: An Historical Perspective* (Copenhagen: NIAS Publications, 1998).

Dang, H. and Palmkvist, G., *Sweden-Vietnam Cooperation on Land Administration Reform in Vietnam* (Hanoi: SIDA, 2001).

Dao Tri Uc, 'Some Basic Issues Concerning the Civil Code of Vietnam', *Nhan Dan*, 6 October 1995, 6, trans. FBIS East Asia Daily Report EAS-95-233, 86–89.

———, 'The Study of Vietnam's State History and Law', *Vietnam Law and Legal Forum* 1(8)(1995): 38–40.

———, 'The Principle of Legality and Its Presentation in the Criminal Code of Vietnam', *Tap Chi Cong San* (8)(1999): 40–41.

———, 'Mot So Quan Diem Co Ban Ve Sua Doi Bo Sung Mot So Dieu Cua Hien Phap 1992' (Key Points of View on Amendment, Addition to the 1992 Constitution), *Nha Nuoc va Phap Luat* (9)(2001): 6–10.

———, 'Ve Nhu Cau, Muc Do Sua Doi Hien Phap Nam 1992 va Quan Diem Xay Dung Nha Nuoc Phap Quyen' (The Needs, the Scope of Revising the 1992 Constitution and the Concept of Law-Based State), *Tap Chi Cong San* (10)(2001): 21–29.

———, 'Tac Dong Cua Toan Cau Hoa Doi Voi Su Phat Trien va Doi Moi Cua Phap Luat Viet Nam' (Effect of Globalisation Towards the Development and Renovation of Vietnam's Laws), *Tap Chi Cong San* (12)(2002): 22–26.

——— and Le Minh Thong, 'Su Tiep Nhan Cac Gia Tri Phap Ly Phuong Dong va Phuong Tay Doi Voi Su Phat Trien Cac Tu Tuong Phap Ly Viet Nam' (Reception of Oriental and Occidental Legal Values in the Development of Vietnamese Legal Ideology), *Nha Nuoc va Phap Luat* (5)(1999): 3–15.

Dao Xuan Tien, 'Responsibilities of Elected Deputies in Dealing with Citizens Complaints and Denunciations', *Tap Chi Nghien Cuu Lap Phap* (Legislative Studies Review) (2)(2005), 33–37.

Davis, M.H., 'The Law/Politics Distinction: The French Conseil Constitutionnel and the US Supreme Court', *American Journal of Comparative Law* 34(1)(1986): 45–92.

de Cruz, P., *Comparative Law in a Changing World*, 2nd edn (London: Cavendish Publishing, 1999).

De Francis, J., *Colonialism and Language Policy in Viet-Nam* (The Hague: Mouton, 1977).

de Groot, R., 'European Education in the 21st Century', in B. de Witte and C. Forder (eds), *The Common Law of Europe and the Future of Legal Education* (Maastricht: Kluwer Law and Taxation Publishers, 1992).

de Sousa Santos B.D. 'Law: A Map of Misreading. Towards a Postmodern Conception of Law', *Journal of Law and Society* 14(3)(1987): 279–86.

———, *Towards a New Common Sense* (London: Routledge, 1995).

Dezalay, Y. and Garth, B., *Dealing in Virtue: International Commercial Arbitration and the Construction of a Transnational Legal Order* (Chicago: University of Chicago Press, 1996).

——, 'Law, Lawyers and Social Capital: "Rule of Law" versus Relational Capitalism' *Social and Legal Studies* 6(1997): 109–43.

———, 'The Import and Export of Law and Legal Institutions: International Strategies in National Palace Wars', in D. Nelken and J. Feest (eds), *Adapting Legal Culture* (Oxford: Hart Publishing, 2001), pp. 241–56.

———, *The Internationalization of Palace Wars* (Chicago: University of Chicago Press, 2002).

Dinh Gia Trinh, 'May Y Kien Dong Gop Ve Van De Bao Ve Phap Che' (Some Opinions on the Protection of Legality), *Tap San Tu Phap* (3)(1961): 20–24.

———, *Nghien Cuu Nha Nuoc va Phap Quyen* (Studies about State and Legality) (Hanoi: Nha Xuat Ban Su Hoc (Historical Studies Publishing House), 1964).

———, 'May Y Kien Ve Tinh Dan Toc va Tinh Khoa Hoc Cua Thuat Ngu Luat Hoc – Nhan Xet Phe Phan Ve Mot So Thuat Ngu Thong Dung' (Nationalistic and Scientific Use of Legal Terminology: Criticisms of Common Legal Terms), *Tap San Tu Phap* (3)(1965): 24–29.

Dinh Ngoc Vuong, 'The State and Law in the Hung Kings Period', *Vietnam Law and Legal Forum* 1(9)(1995): 31–33.

———, 'Van De Sua Doi Bo Sung Quy Dinh Cua Hien Phap 1992 Ve Ky Ket Quyet Dinh Viec Phe Chuan Gia Nhap Bai Bo Dieu Uoc Quoc Te' (Problem of Amending and Adding Stipulations to the 1992 Constitution on Signing, and Deciding to Ratify and Abrogate International Treaties), *Nha Nuoc va Phap Luat* (9)(2001): 43–47.

Dinh Van Que, 'Temporary Suspension of Dealing with Disputes over Residential

House Transactions Established Before 1991', *Nha Nuoc va Phap Luat* (10)(1997): 12.

———, *Phap Luat Thuc Tien va An Le* (Legal Practice and Precedent), (Da Nang: Da Nang Publishing House, 1999), pp. 181–87.

Dinh Xuan Lam, 'Book Review', *Vietnam Social Sciences* (2)(1990): 89–94.

Do Huy, 'Achievements of Building and Developing a New Culture in Vietnam in the 20th Century', *Social Sciences* (3)(2003): 14–15.

Do Muoi, 'Xay Dung Nha Nuoc Phap Quyen Thuc Su Cua Dan, Do Dan Va Vi Dan' (Building up a Law-based State that is Of the People, By the People and For the People), *Tap Chi Cong San* (10)(1992): 3–6.

———, *Sua Doi Hien Phap Xay Dung Nha Nuoc Phap Quyen Viet Nam, Day Manh Su Nghiep Doi Moi* (Amending the Constitution, Establishing a Law-Based-State and Promoting *Doi Moi* Achievements) (Hanoi: Nha Xuat Ban Su That, 1992).

———, 'Build a Uniform Market Mechanisms Under State Management and in Accordance with Socialist Orientations', Political Report of the Seventh Central Party Committee, 20 January 1994, trans. FBIS East Asia Daily Report 94–016, 25 January 1994.

———, 'Political Report to the Mid Term National Party Conference', 20 January 1994, trans. FBIS East Asia Daily Report 94-015, 24 January 1994.

———, 'Building and Perfecting the State' *Vietnam Law and Legal Forum* 1(6)(1995): 3–5.

———, *Vietnam: New Challenges and New Opportunities* (Hanoi: The Gioi Publishers, 1995).

Do Sang and Duc Hanh, *Ve van De: Lam Chu Xa Hoi Chu Nhgia bang Nha Nuoc* (On the Use of the State to Realise Socialist Collective Mastery), (Hanoi: Nha Xuat Ban Phap Ly (Law Publishing House), 1986).

Doan Duy Thanh, 'Market Economy and the Operation of the Market Mechanism in Vietnam', *Vietnam Social Sciences* (2)(2000): 28–33.

Dowdle, M., 'Heretical Laments: China and the Fallacies of "Rule of Law", *Cultural Dynamics* 11(3)(1999): 285–314.

Duc Hung, 'Enterprise Law Ups and Downs, *Vietnam Investment Review* 18 February 2002: 4.

Duc Tho, 'Secret Market Rankles Property Officials', *Vietnam Investment Review* 8 October 2001: 5.

Duiker, W., 'The Red Soviets of Nghe-Tinh: An Early Communist Rebellion in Vietnam', *Journal of Southeast Asian Studies* 4(1973): 186–98.

———, 'Ideology and Nation-Building in Democratic Republic of Vietnam', *Asian Survey* 17(5)(1977): 413–31.

Duong Dan Hue and Nguyen Minh Man, 'Some Issues on the Draft Bankruptcy Law', *Nha Nuoc va Phat Luat* (State and Law) (2)(1993): 39–42.

Duong Dang Hue, 'Phap Luat ve Viec Cap Giay Phep Thanh Lap Doanh Nghiep Dang Ky Kinh Doanh o Viet Nam: Thuc Trang va Mot Vai Kien Nghi' (Legal Regulations in Relation to Issuance of Permits to Establish Enterprises and Business Registration in Vietnam: The Present Situation and Some Recommendations), *Nha*

Nuoc va Phap Luat 4(1994): 20–24.

———, 'Nhung Co So Cua Viec Xay Dung Phap Lenh Hop Dong Kinh Te (Sua Doi)' (Foundation for Building Up Ordinance on Economic Contracts (Amendment)), in *Kien Nghi Ve Xay Dung Phap Luat Hop Dong Kinh Te Tai Viet Nam* (Recommendations in Building up the Economic Contract Legislation in Vietnam), VIE/95/017 (Hanoi: Ministry of Justice-UNDP, 2000).

———, 'Unified Enterprise Bill and he Fulfillment of Investment Relation Development Commitments in the BTA', *Vietnam Law and Legal Forum* 11(132)(2005): 2–6.

Duong Xuan Minh, 'Viec Hinh Su Hoa Quan Le Giua Ngan Hang va Doanh Nghiep Rat Nang Ne' (Heavy Criminalisation of Relationships between Banks and Businesses), *Dau Tu* 18 September 2001: 1–2.

Dworkin, R., *Law's Empire* (Cambridge, Massachusetts: Belknap Press, 1986).

Easterbrook, F.H. and Fischel, D., 'Limited Liability and the Corporation', *Chicago Law Review* 52(1995): 89–117.

Engle Merry, S., 'Legal Pluralism', *Law and Society Review* 22(5)(1988): 869–96.

Ewald, W., 'Comparative Jurisprudence (II): The Logic of Legal Transplants', *American Journal of Comparative Law* 43(1995):498–502.

——, 'What Was it Like to Try a Rat?', *University of Pennsylvania Law Review* 143(6)(1999): 1889–2150.

Ewing, S., 'Formal Justice and the Spirit of Capitalism: Max Weber's Sociology of Law', *Law and Society Review* 21(3)(1987): 487–512.

Fall, B.B., *The Viet-Minh Regime Government and Administration in the Democratic Republic of Vietnam* (Westport, Connecticut: Greenwood Press, 1956).

———, 'Constitution-Writing in a Communist State: The New Constitution of Vietnam', *Howard Law Review* 6(1960): 157–68.

——— (ed.), *Ho Chi Minh on Revolution* (New York: Praeger, 1967).

Fama, E.F. and Jensen, M.C., 'Separation of Ownership and Control', *Journal of Law and Economics* 26(2)(1983): 301–25.

Farber, D.A. and Frickey, P.P., *Law and Public Choice: A Critical Introduction* (Chicago: University of Chicago Press 1991).

Feldbrugge, F.J.M. and Smith, W.B. (eds), *Perspectives on Soviet Law for the 1980s* (The Hague: Martinus Nijhoff Publishers, 1982).

Fforde, A., 'Law and Socialist Agricultural Development in Vietnam: The Statute for Agricultural Producer Cooperatives', *Review of Socialist Law* 10(1984): 315–336.

———, 'From Plan to Market', in A. Chan, B.J.T. Kerkvliet and J. Unger (eds), *Transforming Asian Socialism: China and Vietnam Compared* (Sydney: Allen and Unwin, 1999), pp. 43–72.

———, 'SOEs, Law and a Decade of Market-Orientated Socialist Development', in J. Gillespie and P. Nicholson (eds), *Asian Socialism and Legal Change: The Dynamics of Vietnamese Renewal and Chinese Reform* (Canberra: Asia Pacific Press, 2005), pp. 242–53.

——— and de Vylder, S. *From Plan to Market: The Economic Transition in Vietnam*

(Boulder: Westview Press, 1996).

Fish, S., *Doing What Comes Naturally: Change, Rhetoric and Practice in Literary and Legal Studies* (Durham, North Carolina: Duke University Press, 1989).

Fisher, L., *Constitutional Dialogues: Interpretation as Political Process* (Princeton: Princeton University Press, 1988).

FitzGerald, F., *Fire in the Lake* (New York: Random House, 1972).

Fitzpatrick, P., *The Mythology of Modern Law* (London: Routledge, 1992).

Flannery, T., *The Eternal Frontier* (Melbourne: Text Publishing, 2001).

Foster, T., Rule of Law – Benefits for Private Sector, unpublished paper (Hanoi: Vietnam Business Forum, 2002).

Friedman, L., 'On Legal Development', *Rutgers Law Review* 24(11)(1969): 26–64.

———, *The Law System: A Social Science Perspective* (New York: Russell Sage Foundation, 1975).

———, 'Borders: On the Emerging Sociology of Transnational Law', *Stanford Law Review* 32(1996): 65, 67.

———, 'On the Merging Sociology of Transnational Law', *Stanford Journal of International Law* 32(1)(1996): 65–90.

———, 'The Concept of Legal Culture' in D. Nelken (ed.), *Comparing Legal Cultures* (Aldershot: Dartmouth, 1997), pp. 33–41.

Fukuyama, F., *The End of History and the Last Man* (London: H. Hamilton, 1992).

Fu-mei Chang Chen, 'On Analogy in Ching Law', *Harvard Journal of Asiatic Studies* 30(1970): 212–24.

Gainsborough, M., 'Beneath the Veneer of Reform: The Politics of Economic Liberalisation in Vietnam', *Communist and Post-Communist Studies* 35(1)(2002): 353–68.

———, 'Understanding Communist Transition: Property Rights in Ho Chi Minh City in the Late 1990s', *Communist and Post-Communist Studies* 14(2)(2002): 227–43.

———, *Changing Political Economy of Vietnam: The Case of Ho Chi Minh* (London: RoutledgeCurzon, 2003).

Gates, C., 'Foreign Direct Investment, Institutional Change, and Vietnam's Gradualist Approach to Reform', *Southeast Asian Affairs* 22(1995): 382–400.

Geertz, C., *Local Knowledge* (New York: Basic Books, 1983).

Ghai, Y., 'The Rule of Law, Legitimacy and Governance', *International Journal of the Sociology of Law* 14(2)(1986): 179–208.

Giang Chau, 'Trade to Firm up After Solid Promotion During First Year', *Vietnam Investment Review* 10 February 2003: 1.

Gillespie, J., 'Bureaucratic Control of Business Regulation in Vietnam', in V. Taylor (ed.), *Asian Laws Through Australian Eyes* (Sydney: Law Book Company, 1997), pp. 367–400.

———, 'Corporations in Vietnam', in R. Tomasic (ed.), *Company Law in East Asia* (Aldershot: Ashgate, 1999), pp. 297–330.

———, 'Self-Interest and Ideology: Bureaucratic Corruption in Vietnam', *Australian*

Journal of Asian Law 3(1)(2001): 1–36.

———, 'Transplanted Company Law: An Ideological and Cultural Analysis of Market-Entry in Vietnam', *International and Comparative Law Quarterly* 51(1)(2002): 641–72.

———, 'Receiving Bankruptcy Law into Vietnam', *Asia Pacific Law Review* 11(1)(2003): 81–110.

———, 'Concepts of Law in Vietnam: Transforming Statist Socialism' in R. Peerenboom (ed.), *Asian Discourses of Rule of Law: Theories and Implementation of Rule of Law in Twelve Asian Countries, France and the U.S.* (London: Routledge, 2004), pp. 146–82.

Ginsburg, T., 'Review Essay: Does Law Matter for Economic Development? Evidence From East Asia', *Law and Society Review* 34(3)(2000): 829–56.

Ginsburgs, G., 'Local Government and Administration in North Vietnam, 1945-1954 (Part I)', *China Quarterly* 12(10)(1962): 174–204.

———, 'Soviet Sources on the Law of North Vietnam', *Asian Survey* 13(7)(1973): 659–76.

———, 'The Genesis of the People's Procuracy in the DRV', *Review of Socialist Law* 5(2)(1979): 187–201.

Gittinger, J.P., 'Communist Land Policy in North Viet Nam', *Far Eastern Survey* 28(8)(1959): 113–26.

Goodman, E., *The Origins of the Western Legal Tradition: From Thales to Tudors* (Sydney: Federation Press, 1995).

Gorbachev, M., *Perestroika* (London: Collins, 1987).

Gordon, R., 'Critical Legal Histories', *Stanford Law Review* 36(1–2)(1984): 57–126.

Gramsci, A., *Selections from Prison Notebooks*, Q. Hoare and G. Nowell-Smith (eds) (London: Lawrence and Wishart, 1971.

Gray, M., 'Creating Civil Society? The Emergence of NGOs in Vietnam', *Development and Change* 30(4)(1999): 693–714.

Greenblatt, S., 'Culture' in F. Lentricchia and T. McLaughlin (eds), *Critical Terms for Literary Study* (Chicago: University of Chicago Press, 1997), pp. 225–32.

Grossheim, M., 'Village Government in Pre-Colonial Vietnam' in Benedict J. Tria Kerkvliet and D.G. Marr (eds), *Beyond Hanoi: Local Government in Vietnam* (Singapore: Institute of Southeast Asian Studies, 2004), pp. 54–89.

Grote, R., 'Rule of Law, *Etate de Droit* and *Rechtsstaat* – The Origins of the Different National Traditions and the Prospects for their Convergence in the Light of Recent Constitutional Developments', in C. Starck (ed.), *Constitutionalism, Universalism and Democracy: A Comparative Analysis* (Baden-Baden: Nomos, 1999), pp. 120–55.

Ha Dang, 'Improvement of the Party's Media Work in the Light of Ho Chi Minh Thought', *Tap Chi Cong San* (11)(2003): 1–9. Available online at <www.tapchicongsan.org.vn>.

Ha Huy Giap, 'The Inevitable Nature of the System of Socialist Collective

Ownership', *Tap Chi Cong San* (10)(1977): 32–38.

Ha Van Tan, 'Buddhism from the Ngo to the Tran Dynasties', in Nguyen Tai Thu (ed.), *History of Buddhism in Vietnam* (Hanoi: Social Sciences Publishing House, 1992), pp. 97–117.

Habermas, J., *Legitimisation Crisis*, trans. T. McCarthy (London: Heinemann, 1976).

———, *The Theory of Communicative Rationality*, trans. T. McCarthy (Boston: Beacon Press, 1984).

———, *The Theory of Communicative Action*, vol. 2, trans. T. McCathy (Boston: Beacon Press, 1987).

———, *Structural Transformation of the Public Sphere: An Inquiry into a Category of Bourgeois Society*, trans. Thomas Burger (Cambridge, Massachusetts: MIT Press, 1991).

———, *Between Fact and Norms: Contributions to a Discourse Theory of Law and Democracy* (Cambridge: Polity Press, 1996).

———, 'Between Facts and Norms: An Author's Reflections', *Denver University Law Review* 76(4)(1999): 937–42.

Haines, D.W., 'Reflections of Kinship and Society under Vietnam's Le Dynasty', *Journal of South Eastern Asian Studies* 15(1984): 307–14.

Haley, J.O., 'The Myth of the Reluctant Litigant', *Journal of Japanese Studies* 4(2)(1978): 359–90.

———, 'Relational Contracting: Does Community Count?', in H. Baum (ed.), *Japan: Economic Success and Legal System* (Berlin: de Gruyter, 1997), pp. 167–91.

Hall, P. and Soskice, D., *Varieties of Capitalism: The Changes Facing Contemporary Political Economics* (Cambridge: Cambridge University Press, 2000).

Hannah, J., 'Civil-Society Actors and Action in Vietnam: Preliminary Empirical Results and Sketches from an Evolving Debate', in Heinrich Böll Foundation (ed.), *Towards Good Society: Civil Society Actors, The State, and The Business Class in Southeast Asia – Facilitators of or Impediments to a Strong, Democratic, and Fair Society?* (Berlin: Heinrich Böll Stiftung, 2005), pp. 101–10.

Hansmann, H. and Kraakman, R., 'The End of History for Corporate Law', *Georgetown Law Journal* 89(2)(2001): 439–78.

Harding, A., 'Comparative Law and Legal Transplantation in South East Asia: Making Sense of the "Nomic Din"', in J. Feest and D. Nelken (eds), *Adapting Legal Cultures* (Oxford: Hart Publishing, 2001), pp. 199–220.

Hart, H.L.A., *The Concept of Law* (Oxford: Clarendon Press, 1961).

Hayek, F.A., *The Road to Serfdom* (Chicago: University of Chicago Press, 1944).

Hazard, J.N., 'The Evolution of the Soviet Constitution' in D. Barry (ed.), *Towards the Rule of Law in Russia?* (New York: M.E. Sharpe, 1992), pp. 103–21.

Hegel, G.W., *The Philosophy of History*, trans. J. Sibree (London: Dover Publications, 1956).

Heim, S.J., 'Predicting Legal Transplants: The Case of Servitudes in the Russian

Federation', *Transnational Law and Contemporary Problems* 6(1996): 187–223.

Held, D., 'Democracy: From City-States to a Cosmopolitan Order?', in D. Held (ed.), *Prospects for Democracy: North, East, South, West* (Oxford: Polity Press, Blackwell, 1993), pp. 13–52.

Heydebrand, W., 'From Globalisation of Law to Law under Globalisation', in J. Feest and D. Nelken (eds), *Adapting Legal Cultures* (Oxford: Hart Publishing, 2001), pp. 117–40.

Higham, C., *The Archaeology of Mainland Southeast Asia: from 10,000 B.C. to the fall of Angkor* (Cambridge: Cambridge University Press, 1989).

Himawan, C., 'Indonesia', in Pho-Ling Tan (ed.), *Asian Legal Systems* (Sydney: Butterworths, 1997), pp. 223–33.

Ho Chi Minh, 'On Justice' in *Selected Works Volume II* (Hanoi: Foreign Languages Publishing House 1990), pp. 96–102.

———, 'Report to the 6th Plenum of the Viet Nam Workers' Party Central Committee', 15 July 1954, *Selected Writings of Ho Chi Minh (1920-1969)* (Hanoi: Gioi Publishers, 1994), pp. 172–83.

———, 'Report on the Draft Amended Constitution', 18 December 1959, reproduced in *Selected Writings of Ho Chi Minh (1920-1969)* (Hanoi: Gioi Publishers, 1994), pp. 209–30.

———, 'Political Report at the Second National Congress of the Vietnam Workers Party', in *Selected Writings of Ho Chi Minh* (Hanoi: Gioi Publishers, 1994), pp. 101–29.

———, *Complete Works*, Vol. 5 (Hanoi: The National Political Publishing House, 1995), reproduced in Nguyen Duy Quy, 'Ho Chi Minh's Viewpoint on Socialism and the Path to Socialism in Vietnam', *Vietnam Social Sciences* (5)(1997): 15–26.

———, *Ho Chi Minh's Collected Works* (Hanoi: National Politics Publishing House, 2000).

Hoang Hai Van, 'Ky 2: Dan "Tien" Nha Nuoc "Lui"' (Number 2: People 'Marching Forward' State 'Stepping Backwards'), *Tuoi Tre* 6 August 2001: 3.

———, 'Nha Nuoc Co Chay Theo Thi Truong?' (Is the State Running After the Market?), *Tuoi Tre* 6 August 2001: 3.

———, 'Bo Tu Phap, UBND TPHCM de Nghi: Giu Nguyen Muc Thue Thu Nhap Doanh Nghiep 10% Cho Lien Doanh Phu My Hung' (Ministry of Justice and Ho Chi Minh City People's Committee Propose that Corporate Income Tax Rate Remain at 10% for Phu My Hung Joint Venture), *Thanh Nien-Online* 17 February 2004: 3.

Hoang Kim Giao and Nguyen Dac Thang, 'A Profile of Vietnamese Owners of Private Enterprise', *Vietnam Economic Review* (4)(1995): 29–30.

Hoang Quoc Viet, 'Viec Xay Dung Phap Che Xa Hoi Chu Nghia va Giao Duc Moi Nguoi Ton Trong Phap Luat' (Building-Up Socialist Legality and Educating People to Respect Laws) *Hoc Tap* (6)(1962): 14–16.

———, 'Can Dam Bao Cho Phap Luat Duoc Ton Trong Trong Cong Tac Quan Ly Linh Te Cua Nha Nuoc' (We Must Ensure the Enforcement of Law in State

Economic Management) in *Nghien cuu Nha Nuoc va phap quyen* (Studies about State and Law) (Hanoi: Truth Publishing 1964), pp. 31–41.

———, *Tang Cuong Phap Che Xa Hoi Chu Nghia Trong Cong Tac Quan Ly Xi Nghiep* (Strengthening Socialist Legality in Management Enterprises) (Hanoi: Nha Xuat Ban Su That, 1973).

Hoang The Lien, 'On the Model of an Economic Court in Vietnam', *Nha Nuoc va Phap Luat* (2)(1993): 19–25.

———, 'On the Legal System of Vietnam', *Vietnam Law and Legal Forum* 1(1994): 33–35.

———, 'Subject System in Vietnam's Civil Code', *Vietnam Law and Legal Forum* 2(18)(1996): 22–25.

———, 'Xac Dinh Doi Tuong va Pham Vi Dieu Chinh Cua Phap Lenh Hop Dong Kinh Te (Amendment)' (Identification of Governing Objectives and Governing Scope of the Ordinance on Economic Contracts (Amendment)) Kien Nghi Ve Xay Dung Phap Luat Hop Dong Kinh Te Tai Viet Nam, (Recommendations in Building up the Economic Contract Legislation in Vietnam), VIE/95/017 (Hanoi: Ministry of Justice-UNDP, 2000), pp. 21–30.

Hoang Trung, 'Pham Tru Trung—Hieu Trong Triet Ly Phuong Dong va Tu Tuong Ho Chi Minh Voi Van De Giao Duc Dao Duc Cach Mang Hien Nay' (The Notion of Loyalty—Piety in the Oriental Philosophy and Ho Chi Minh's Ideas about the Current Problem of Morality Education) *Tap Chi Cong San* (9)(2002): 18–23.

Hoang Van Minh, 'Giai Phong Mat Bang, Di Doi Dan o Da Nang – Mot Cach Lam Dang De Tham Khao' (Site-Clearance and Population Relocation in Da Nang – A Worthy Measure to be Consulted), *Lao Dong* (Labourer), 15 August 2001: 3.

Hoc Vien Hanh Chinh Quoc Gia (The National Administrative Institute), Ve *Cai Cach Bo May Nha Nuoc* (On the Reform of the State Apparatus) (Hanoi: The Truth Publishing House, 1991).

Honey, P.J., 'The Position of the DRV Leadership and the Succession to Ho Chi Minh', *The China Quarterly* 9(1962): 24–36.

Hooker, M.B., *Legal Pluralism: An Introduction to Colonial and Neo-Colonial Law* (Oxford: Clarendon Press, 1975).

———, *A Concise Legal History of South East Asia* (Oxford: Clarendon Press, 1979).

———, *The Laws of South East Asia*, Volume II (Singapore: Butterworths, 1986).

Horn, N., 'The Lawful German Revolution: Privatization and Market Economy in a Re-Unified Germany', *American Journal of Comparative Law* 39(4)(1991): 725–47.

Hsun-tzn, *Basic Writings of Mo Tzu, Hsun Tzu and Han Fie Tzu*, trans. and ed. B. Watson (New York: Columbia University Press, 1967).

Human Rights Watch, 'Vietnam 2001', *Human Rights Watch World Report* (New York: Human Rights Watch, 2001). Available online at <www.hrw.org/wr2k1/asia/vietnam.html>.

Hunt, A., 'The Ideology of Law: Advances and Problems in Recent Applications of

Ideology to the Analysis of Law', *Law and Society Review* 19(1)(1985): 11–38.

Huy Duc, 'Bi An Minh Phung' (Minh Phung Mystery), *Thoi Bao Kinh Te Sai Gon* (Saigon Economic Times), 24 April 1997: 36, 38.

Huynh Kim Khanh, *Vietnamese Communism, 1925-1945* (Ithaca: Cornell University Press, 1982).

Hy Van Luong, 'Vietnamese Kinship: Structural Principles and the Socialist Transformation in Northern Vietnam', *Journal of Asian Studies* 48(4)(1989): 741–56.

———, *Discursive Practices and Linguistic Meanings: The Vietnamese System of Person Reference* (Amsterdam: John Benjamins Publishing Company, 1990).

———, *Revolution in the Village* (Honolulu: University of Hawaii Press, 1992).

———, 'Capitalism and Non-Capitalist Ideologies in the Structure of Northern Vietnamese Ceramics Enterprises', in T. Brook and Hy V. Luong (eds), *Culture and Economy: The Shaping of Capitalism in Eastern Asia* (Ann Arbor: The University of Michigan Press, 1997), pp. 187–206.

——— and Diep Dinh Hoa, 'Culture and Capitalism in the Pottery Enterprises of Bien Hoa, South Vietnam (1878–1975)', *Journal of Southeast Asian Studies* 22(1991): 16–32.

Indochinese Communist Party, 'Political Thesis of Indochinese Communist Party', October 1930. Partially reproduced in *Vietnam Documents and Research Notes* 103(1970): 58–91.

Institute of State and Law, *Giao Trinh Ly Luan Nha Nuoc va Phap Luat* (Text Book on State and Law), (Hanoi: Nha Xuat Ban Cong An Nhan Dan, 1998).

Insun Yu, *Law and Society in 17th and 18th Century Vietnam* (Seoul: Asiatic Research Center, Korea University, 1990).

Ioffe, O.S., *Soviet Law and Soviet Reality* (Dordrecht: Martinus Nijhoff Publishers, 1985).

Jackson, B., *Law, Fact and Narrative Coherence* (Merseyside, England: Deborah Charles, Roby, 1988).

Jacobson, A.J., 'Autopoietic Law: The New Science of Niklas Luhmann', *Michigan Law Review*, 87(6)(1989): 1647–89.

Jamieson, N.L. , *Understanding Vietnam* (Berkeley: University of California Press, 1993).

Jayasuriya, K., 'The Rule of Law and Governance in the East Asian State', *The Australian Journal of Asian Law* 1(2)(1999): 107–23.

Jenkins, A., 'Just-in-Time "Regimes" and Reductionism', *Sociology* 28(1)(1994): 21–30.

Jensen, P. and Mecklin, C., 'Theory of the Firm: Managerial Behavior, Agency Costs and Ownership Structure', *Journal of Financial Economics* 4(1996): 305–27.

Jianfu Chen, 'Market Economy and the Internationalisation of Civil and Commercial Law in the People's Republic of China', in K. Jayasuriya (ed.), *Law, Capitalism and Power in Asia* (London: Routledge, 1999), pp. 69–86.

———, *Towards an Understanding of Chinese Law, Its Nature and Development*

(The Hague: Kluwer Law International, 1999).

Jones, C., 'Capitalism, Globalisation and Rule of Law: an Alternative Trajectory of Legal Change in China', *Social and Legal Studies* 3(2)(1994): 195–222.

Jowell, J., 'The Rule of Law Today', in J. Jowell (ed.), *The Changing Constitution* (London: Clarendon Press, 1994), pp. 57–78.

Kahn-Freund, O., 'Legislation Through Adjudication', *Modern Law Review* 11(3)(1948): 269–89.

———, 'On Uses and Misuses of Comparative Law', *Modern Law Review* 37(1)(1974): 1–27.

———, 'On the Uses and Misuses of Comparative Law' in Otto Kahn-Freund (ed.), *Selected Writings* (London: Stevens, 1978), pp. 298–319.

———, 'Common Law and Civil Law-Imaginary and Real Obstacles to Assimilation', in M. Cappelletti (ed.), *New Perspectives for a Common Law of Europe* (Leyden: Sijhoff, 1978), pp. 137–70.

Kairys, D. (ed.), *The Politics of Law: A Progressive Critique* (New York: Pantheon Books, 1982).

Kammen, M., *A Machine that Would Go of Itself: The Constitution in American Culture* (New York: Knoft, 1986).

Kamuwanga, M., 'The Teaching of International Trade and Investment Law in a "Law and Development" Context: A View from Zambia', *Third World Legal Studies* 5(1987): 131–50.

Kanda, H. and Milhaupt, C., 'Re-Examing Legal Transplants: The Director's Fiduciary Duty in Japanese Corporate Law', *American Journal of Comparative Law* 51(4)(2003): 887–902.

Kauffman Winn, J., 'Relational Practices and Marginalization of Law: Informal Financial Practices of Small Business in Taiwan', *Law and Society Review* 28(2)(1994): 193–232.

Kerkvliet, B.J.T., 'Dialogical Law Making and Implementation in Vietnam' in Alice Tay (ed.), *East Asia – Human Rights, Nation-Building, Trade* (Baden-Baden: Nomos, 1999), pp. 372-400.

———, 'An Approach for Analyzing State-Society Relations in Vietnam', *Sojourn* 16(2)(2001): 238–78.

———, *The Power of Everyday Politics: How Vietnamese Peasants Transformed National Policy* (Ithaca: Cornell University Press, 2005).

———, Heng, R.H.H., and Koh, D.W.H. (eds), *Getting Organised in Vietnam: Moving in and Around the Socialist State* (Singapore: Institute of Southeast Asian Studies, 2003).

Khanh Van, 'Cai Cach Tu Phap: Nhin Tu Nhieu Goc Do' (Judicial Reform: From Different Angles), *Tap Chi Nghien Cuu Lap Phap* (4)(2003): 3–8.

Khng, R.H.H., 'Leadership in Vietnam: Pressure for Reform and Their Limits', *Contemporary Southeast Asia* 15(1)(1993): 98–110.

———, Of the State, For the State, Yet Against the State, unpublished PhD thesis (Canberra: The Australian National University, 2000).

———, 'Media Negotiating the State: In the Name of the Law in Anticipation',

Sojourn 16(2)(2001): 213–37.

Khoo Boo Teik, 'Between Law and Politics: the Malaysian Judiciary since Independence', in K. Jayasuriya (ed.), *Law, Capitalism and Power in Asia* (London: Routledge, 1999), pp. 205–32.

Kim Chi, 'Potential Quicksand', *Vietnam Economic News* (33)(1998): 18–19.

Kim, A., 'A Market Without the "Right" Property Rights: Ho Chi Minh City, Vietnam's Newly Emerged Private Real Estate Market', *Economics of Transition* 12(2)(2004): 275–305.

King, M. 'The Truth about Autopoiesis', *Journal of Law and Society* 20(2)(1993): 218–36.

Koh, D., Wards of Hanoi and State-Society Relations in the Socialist Republic of Vietnam, unpublished PhD (Canberra: The Australian National University, 2000), chapter five.

Koperdraar, A., Hanoi's Colonial Villas in Transition, unpublished thesis (Amsterdam: University of Amsterdam 1998).

Kraakman, R., 'Comments on the Draft General Report: Law of Enterprises of Different Forms in Vietnam', unpublished paper, VIE/94/003 (Hanoi: United Nations Development Programme, 1997).

Krygier, M., 'Transitional Questions About the Rule of Law: Why, What and How?', *East Central Europe* 28(2001): 1–34.

KT-PL, 'Hinh Su Hoa De Lam Gi?' (What is Criminalisation For?), *Thoi Bao Kinh Te Viet Nam*, 16 April 2001: 12.

Kutchinsky, B., 'The Legal Consciousness: A Survey of Research and Opinion about Law', in A Podgorecki *et al.* (eds), *Knowledge and Opinion About Law* (London: M. Robertson, 1973), pp. 101–38.

Lam Nguyen, 'Procedures-Observations from a National Assembly Session', *Legislative Studies Journal* (8)(2002): 12–13.

Lan Phuong Nguyen, 'Local News', *Reuters*, Hanoi, 1 November (2000): pp. 1–2.

Landa, J., 'A Theory of the Ethnically Homogeneous Middleman Group: An Institutional Alternative to Contract Law', *Journal of Legal Studies* 10(2)(1981): 349–62.

Landes, E. and Posner, R.A., 'The Economics of the Baby Shortage', *Journal of Legal Studies* 7(1)(1978): 323–48.

Law Committee of the National Assembly, Draft Report Synthesising People's Opinions on the Draft Civil Procedure Code, unpublished report (Hanoi: National Assembly, 2004).

Lawson, F.H., Anton, A.E., Brown, L.N., *Introduction to French Law*, 3rd edn (Oxford: Clarendon Press, 1967).

Lawton, P., 'Berle and Means, Corporate Governance and the Chinese Firm', *Australian Journal of Corporate Law* 16(3)(1996): 348–80.

Le Cam, 'Cai Cach He Thong Toa An Trong Giai Doan Xay Dung Nha Nuoc Phap Quyen Viet Nam' (Reform the Court System to Build Up a Law Based State in Vietnam), *Tap Chi Nghien Cuu Lap Phap* (4)(2002): 21–27.

Le Dang Doanh, 'Foreign Investment and the Macro-Economy in Vietnam' in V.H. Tran (ed.), *Economic Development and Prospects in the ASEAN – Foreign Investment and Growth in Vietnam, Thailand, Indonesia and Malaysia* (Basingstoke: Macmillan, 1997), pp. 44–86.

———, 'Enterprise Law – A Must for Further Development of Multi-Sectorial Economy', *Vietnam Law and Legal Forum* (56)(1999): 11–13.

———, 'The Enterprise Law and the Development of the Domestic Private Business Sector in Vietnam', *Vietnam's Socio-Economic Development* (38)(2004): 6–12.

Le Duan, 'Political Report to the Fourth VWP Congress 1976', FBIS East Asia Daily Service, 29 June 1976: K1–K28.

———, *Le Duan: Selected Writings* (Hanoi: The Gioi Publishers, 1994).

Le Duc Tho, 'Report Summarizing Party Building Work and the Amended Party Statues', *Nhan Dan*, 20–23 December 1976: 2–3. Trans. FBIS East Asia Daily Report, 14 January 1976.

Le Duy Vau, 'The Nao La Phat Huy Tap The va Dan Chu Dung Muc?' (How to Satisfactory Expand Collectivism and Democracy?', *Hoc Tap* (2)(1956): 70–72.

Le Hong Hanh, *Giao Trinh Ly Luan Nha Nuoc va Phap Luat* (Text Book on State and Law) (Hanoi: Nha Xuat Ban Cong An Nhan Dan (People's Police Publishing), Hanoi 1998).

Le Hong Son, 'Village Conventions and their Role in Rural Management in Vietnam', *Vietnam Law and Legal Forum* 1(11)(1995): 21–24.

Le Kha Phieu, 'Party Leader Addresses Cultural Officials', *Nhan Dan*, 9 October 1998: 1, 5. Trans. FBIS East Asia Daily Reports 98-289 (October 1988).

Le Minh Tam, 'Phap Che Xa Hoi Chu Nghia' (Socialist Legality), in *Giao Trinh Ly Luan Nha Nuoc va Phap Luat* (Text Book on State and Law) (Hanoi: Nha Xuat Ban Cong An Nhan Dan, 1998), pp. 497–512.

Le Minh Thong, 'Mot So Van De Phap Ly Cua Qua Trinh Toan Cau Hoa' (Some Legal Issues on Globalisation), *Tap Chi Nghien Cuu Lap* (1)(2003): 65–75.

Le Thanh Nghi, *Mot So Van De Co Ban Trong Quan Ly Kinh Te Xa Hoi Chu Nhgia* (Several Basic Matters on Socialist Economic Management) (Hanoi: Nhan Xuat Su That, 1975).

Le Thi, 'Create a Correct Relationship between the Collective and the Individual in the Socialist System', *Tap Chi Cong San* (8)(1977): 54–61.

———, *The Role of the Family in the Formation of the Vietnamese Personality* (Hanoi, The Gioi Publishers, 1999), pp. 140–46.

Le Tho Binh and Vu Thuong, 'Fighting Corruption: In Addition to Energy, Courage is Needed', *Tuoi Tre* 8 April 1997: 3.

Le Trung Ha, 'Chuyen Huong To Chuc Cua Cac Toa An Nhan Dan Dia Phuong De Dap Ung Voi Tinh Hinh va Nhiem Vu Moi' (Changes in Local Court to Meet the Requirements of the New Conditions and Requirements), *Tap San Tu Phap* (8)(1965): 1–2.

Le Truyen, 'Ho Chi Minh's Thoughts on Unity', *Nhan Dan* August 2003, reproduced in *Vietnam Law and Legal Forum* 9(108)(2003): 10–11.

Le Van Luong, 'Tang Cuong Che Do Tap Trung Dan Chu Trong Dang Ta' (Strengthening the Democratic Centralism in Our Party), *Hoc Tap* (6)(1960):

27–33.

Lee, T.V., 'Risky Business: Courts Culture, and the Market Place', *University of Miami Law Review* 47(5)(1993): 1335–414.

Legal Research Institute, *Mot So Van Ve Phap Luat Dan Su Viet Nam Tu The Ky 15 Den Thoi Phap Thuoc* (Some Issues about Civil Vietnamese Law Since the 15th Century until French Colonization) (Hanoi: Vien Khoa Phap Ly, 1999).

Le Gall, J-P. and Morel, P., *French Company Law*, 2nd edn (London: Longman, 1992).

Legis, 'The National Assembly in a Nutshell', *Tap Chi Nghien Cuu Lap Phap*, English edition (1)(2001): 57–65.

Legrand, P., 'Comparative Legal Studies and Commitment to Theory', *Modern Law Review* 58(2)(1995): 262–73.

———, 'European Legal Systems are Not Converging', *International Comparative Law Quarterly* 45(1996): 52–81.

———, 'The Impossibility of Legal Transplants', *Maastricht Journal of European Comparative Law* 4(1997): 111–19.

———, 'Against a European Civil Code', *Modern Law Review* 60(1)(1997): 44–63.

———, 'What "Legal Transplants"?', in D. Nelken and J. Feest (eds), *Adapting Legal Culture* (Oxford: Hart Publishing 2001), pp. 55–69.

Lehman, E.W., *The Viable Polity* (Philadelphia: Temple University Press, 1992).

Lesnoi, V., 'Nen Tu Phap Cua Nuoc Viet Nam Dan Chu Cong Hoa' (The Judiciary of the Democratic Republic of Vietnam), *Tap San Tu Phap* (11)(1963): 26–28.

———, 'Phap Che Xa Hoi Chu Nghia Xo Viet', (Soviet Socialist Legality) *Tap San Tu Phap* (4)(1961): 30–34.

———, 'Viec Bao Dam Phap Che Xa Hoi Chu Nghia', (Implementing Socialist Legality) *Tap San Tu Phap* (12)(1961): 32–38.

Lets Noi B.M. [V.M. Lesnoi], 'Phap Che Xa Hoi Chu Nghia Xo Viet: Tinh Lich Su va Tinh Giai Cap Cua Phap Che' (Socialist Legality: Historical and Class Features), *Tap San Tu Phap* (6)(1961): 36–41.

Lindsey, T., 'Paradigms, Paradoxes and Possibilities: Towards an Understandings of Indonesia's Legal System', in V. Taylor (ed.), *Asian Laws Through Australian Eyes* (Sydney: Law Book Company, 1997).

Luhmann, N., *The Differentiation of Society* (New York: Columbia University Press, 1982).

———, *A Sociological Theory of Law* (London: Routledge, 1985).

———, 'The Unity of the Legal System' in G. Teubner (ed.), *Autopoietic Law: A New Approach to Law* and Society (New York: W. de Gruyter, 1987), pp. 1–28.

———, A Sociological Theory of Law, trans., Elizabeth King and Martin Albrow (London: Routledge, 1987).

———, 'The Unity of Legal System' in G. Teubner (ed.), Autop*oietic Law: A New Approach to Law and Society* (Berlin: W. de Gruyter, 1988), pp. 21–35.

Luu Quang Dinh 'Dung Do Loi Cho Luat Doanh Nghiep' (Do Not Blame the

Enterprise Law), *Lao Dong* 30 July 2001: 3.

Macaulay, S., 'Non-Contractual Relations in Business: A Preliminary Study', *American Sociological Review* 28(1963): 55–67.

———, 'Relational Contract Theory: Unanswered Questions – A Symposium in Honor of Ian R. MacNeil: Relational Contracts Floating on a Sea of Custom? Thoughts about the Ideas of Ian MacNeil and Lisa Berstein', *Northwestern University Law Review* 94(3)(2000): 775–804.

Macey, J.R., 'Public Choice: The Theory of the Firm and the Theory of Market Exchange', *Cornell Law Review* 74(1)(1988): 43–61.

Macneil, I.R., 'Contracts: Adjustment of Long-Term Economic Relations Under Classical, Neoclassical and Relational Contract Law', *Northwestern University Law Review* 72(6)(1978): 854–905.

MacPherson, C.B., 'Capitalism and the Changing Concept of Property', in E. Kamenka and R.S. Neale (eds), *Feudalism, Capitalism and Beyond* (Canberra: Australian National University Press, 1975), pp. 105–221.

Mai Huu Thuc, 'Characteristics of Market Economy with Socialist Orientation in Vietnam', *Vietnam Social Sciences* (1)(2001): 20–24.

Maine, H., *Ancient Law* (London: J.M. Dent, 1917).

Mallon, R., 'Approaches to Support the Development of an Enabling Environment for Small Enterprises: Viet Nam Case Study', GTZ Report to the Committee of Donor Agencies for Small Enterprise (Turin: Committee of Donor Agencies for Small Enterprise, 2002).

Manh Quan, 'Doan Truong Hau Dang Ky Kinh Doanh' (The Painful Process of Post-Registration), *Thanh Nien* 7 August 2003: 5.

Manyin, M., 'The Vietnam-US Bilateral Trade Agreement, CRS Report for Congress' (Washington DC: 2001); available online at <www.usitc.gov>.

March, J. and Olsen, J., *Rediscovering Institutions: The Organizational Basis of Politics* (New York: Macmillan, 1989).

Marr, D., *Vietnamese Anticolonialism* (Berkeley: University of California Press, 1971).

———, *Vietnamese Tradition on Trial 1920–1945* (Berkeley: University of California Press, 1981).

———, *Vietnam 1945: The Quest for Power* (Berkeley: University of California Press, 1995).

———, 'History and Memory in Vietnam Today: The Journal Xua & Nay', *Journal of Southeast Asian Studies* 31(1)(2000): 1–25.

———, 'A Brief History of Local Government in Vietnam', in B.J.T. Kerkvliet and D. Marr (eds), *Beyond Hanoi: Local Government in Vietnam* (Singapore: Institute of Southeast Asian Studies, 2004), pp. 28–53.

Marx, K., 'Otechestvenniye Zapiski' 1877, reproduced in *Karl Marx on Colonialism and Modernization*, ed. Shlomo Avineri (New York: Doubleday, 1969).

Mattei, U., 'Efficiency in Legal Transplants: An Essay in Comparative Law and Economics', *International Review of Law and Economics* 14(1)(1994): 3–19.

———, 'Three Patterns of Law: Taxonomy and Change in the World's Legal

Systems', *American Journal of Comparative Law* 45(1)(1997): 5–44.

———, 'A Theory of Imperial Law: A Study on U.S. Hegemony and the Latin Resistance', *Global Jurist Frontier* 3(1)(2003): pp. 1–61. Available at <www.bepress.com/gj/frontiers>.

Maturana, H. and Varela, F., *Autopoiesis and Cognition: The Realization of the Living* (D. Reidel, Dordrecht 1980).

McAdams, R., 'The Origin, Development and Regulation of Norms', *Michigan Law Review* 96(2)(1997): 338–433.

McAuslan, P., 'Law, Governance and the Development of the Market: Practical Problems and Possible Solutions' in J. Faundez (ed.), *Good Government and Law* (New York: St Martin's Press, 1997), pp. 25–44.

McCormick, B., 'Political Change in China and Vietnam: Coping with the Consequences of Economic Reform', in A. Chan, B. Kerkvliet and J. Unger (eds), *Transforming Asian Socialism: China and Vietnam Compared* (Sydney: Allen and Unwin, 1999), pp. 151–75.

McCoubrey, H., *The Development of Naturalist Legal Theory* (London: Croom Helm, 1987).

McDonough, L., 'The Transferability of Labor Law: Can an American Transplant Take Root in British Soil?' *Comparative Labour Law Journal* 13(1992): 504–30.

McDowell, J., 'Towards Rehabilitating Objectivity', in R.B. Brandom (ed.), Rorty and His Critics (Malden, Massachusetts: Blackwell, 2000).

McMillan, J. and Woodruff, C., 'Interfirm Relationships and Informal Credit in Vietnam', *Quarterly Journal of Economics* 114(4)(1999): 1285–320.

———, 'Private Order under Dysfunctional Public Order', *Michigan Law Review* 98(8)(2000): 2421–58.

Mead, G.H., *Mind, Self, and Society* (Chicago: University of Chicago Press, 1934).

Meek, R.L., *Social Science and the Ignoble Savage* (Cambridge: Cambridge University Press, 1976).

Meidinger, E., 'Regulatory Culture: Theoretical Outline', *Law and Policy* 9(4)(1987): 355–86.

Mekong Project Development Facility, *Private Companies in Vietnam: A Survey of Public Perceptions*, Private Sector Discussion No. 9 (Hanoi: Mekong Project Development Facility, 1999).

Mensch, E., 'The History of Mainstream Legal Thought' in D. Kairys (ed.), *The Politics of Law* (New York: Pantheon Books, 1982), 18–37.

Merryman, J., 'Comparative Law and Social Change: On the Origins, Style, Decline and Revival of the Law and Development Movement', *American Journal of Comparative Law* 25(3)(1977): 457–91.

——— and Clark, D. (eds), *Comparative Law: Western European and Latin American Legal Systems: Cases and Materials* (Indianapolis: Bobbs Merrill, 1978).

Mid Term National Party Conference, 'Sixth Installment of "Basic Contents" of the Hanoi 20–25 Mid Term National Party Conference Resolution' *Saigon Giai Phong*, 20 March 1994: 2. Trans. FBIS East Asia Daily Report 94-070 (April

1994).

Milhaupt, C.J., 'A Relational Theory of Japanese Corporate Governance: Contract Culture and Rule of Law', *Harvard International Law Journal* 37(1)(1996): 3–64.

Minh Chi, 'Buddhism's Entry into Vietnam and Its Practice During Chinese Control', in Nguyen Tai Thu (ed.), *History of Buddhism in Vietnam* (Hanoi: Social Sciences Publishing House, 1992), 1–15.

Minh Duc, 'Tieng Noi Doanh Nhan Trong Quoc Hoi' (Entrepreneurs' Voice in the National Assembly), *Tap Chi Nghien Cuu Lap Phap* (12)(2002): 14–15.

Ministry of Justice, 'General Report: Law of Enterprises of Different Forms in Vietnam', VIE/94/003 (Hanoi: United Nations Development Programme, 1997).

———, *Final Report Legal Needs Assessment* (Hanoi: Ministry of Justice, 2002).

———, *Program on Reforms of Drafting, Promulgating and Enhancing the Quality of Legal Normative Documents* (Hanoi: Ministry of Justice, 2002), 1.

———, Summary Matrix in Order of Priority: The Action Plan for Implementing Vietnam's Strategy for Development of its Legal System until 2010, unpublished paper (Hanoi: Ministry of Justice, 2002).

———, Action Plan for Implementing Vietnam's Strategy for Development of Its Legal System Until 2010, unpublished paper (Hanoi: Ministry of Justice, 2002).

———, *Report on the Comprehensive Needs of Developing Law Making Bodies, Law Implementation and Enforcement, International Treaty Reception and Dispute Resolution* (Hanoi: Ministry of Justice, 2002).

Moise, E., 'Land Reform and Land Reform Errors in North Vietnam', *Pacific Affairs* 49(1)(1976): 70–92.

Montesquieu, C. De Secondat, *The Political Theory of Montesquieu*, selected and translated by Melvin Richter (New York: Cambridge University Press, 1977).

Moore, S, 'Law and Social Change in the Semi-Autonomous, Social Field as an Appropriate Subject of Study', *Law and Society Review* 7(4)(1973): 719–46.

Moran, M., 'Politics and Law in Financial Regulation', in C. Graham and T. Prosser (eds), Waiving the Rules (Milton Keys: Open University Press, 1988), pp. 68–89.

Mueller, D., *Public Choice II* (Cambridge: Cambridge University Press, 1989).

Murphy, T., 'Modernising Justice Inside "UK PLC": Minesis, De-differentiation and Colonisation', in J. Přibáň and D. Nelken (eds), *Law's New Boundaries: The Consequences of Legal Autopoiesis* (Aldershot: Ashgate, 2001), pp. 218–48.

Myrdal, G., *Asian Drama: An Inquiry into the Poverty of Nations* (New York: Pantheon, 1968).

Nelken, D., 'Law as Communication: Constituting the Field' in D. Nelken (ed.), *Law as Communication* (Aldershot: Dartmouth, 1996), pp. 3–30.

———, 'Beyond the Metaphor of Legal Transplants? Consequences of Autopoietic Theory for the Study of Cross-Cultural Legal Adaptation' in J. Přibáň and D. Nelken (eds), *Law's New Boundaries: The Consequences of Legal Autopoiesis* (Aldershot: Ashgate, 2001), pp. 265–302.

Nelken, D., 'Towards a Sociology of Legal Adaptation', in D. Nelken and J. Feest (eds), *Adapting Legal Cultures* (Oxford: Hart Publishing, 2001), pp. 7–51.

Ngo Duc Manh, 'Some Thoughts on the Legislation by the National Assembly', *Nha Nuoc va Phap Luat* (4)(1994): 8–14.

———, 'Legislative Work for Implementation of Vietnam-US Bilateral Trade Agreement', *Vietnam Law and Legal Forum* 10(110)(2003): 21–22.

Ngo Huy Cuong, 'Luat Hien Phap va Van Hoa Chinh Tri' (Constitutional Law and Political Culture) *Tap Chi Nghien Cuu Lap Phap* (1)(2001): 29–34.

Ngo Phuong Lan, 'The Changing Face of Vietnamese Cinema During Ten Years of Renovation', in D. Marr (ed.), *The Mass Media in Vietnam*, Political and Social Change Monograph 25 (Canberra, Australian National University, 1998), pp. 91–96.

Ngo Quang Xuan, 'Vietnam: Potential Market and New Opportunities', *Fordham International Law Journal* 19(1)(1995): 32–39.

Nguyen Dang Dung, 'Phap Luat Khong Chi La Cong Cu Cua Nha Nuoc' (Law is Not Only the Instrument of the State), *Tap Chi Nghien Cuu Lap Phap* (11)(2001): 53–57.

Nguyen Dang Quang, 'What is Socialism?', *Tap Chi Cong San* (1)(1989): 3–5 Trans. FIBIS East Asia Daily Report, 12 May 1989: 54.

Nguyen Dinh Loc, 'Bo Luat Dan Su Co Vai Tro To Lon Trong Viec To Chuc Cuoc Song Cong Dong' (The Civil Code Plays an Important Role in Organising Community Life), *Nhan Dan* 13 February 1995: 1.

Nguyen Dinh Tai, 'Entrepreneurship in Vietnam and Promotion of the Private Sector: Some Judgements from a Survey', *Vietnam Socio-Economic Development* (29)(2002): 25–30.

Nguyen Duc Lam, 'De Tien Toi Chuyen Nghiep' (Towards Professionalism in the National Assembly), *Nghien Cuu Lap Phap* (6)(2002): 23–30.

———, 'Suy Nghi Hau Ky Hop Cung Lo' (Some Thoughts on a National Assembly Session), *Tap Chi Nghien Cuu Lap Phap* (9)(2002): 8–12.

Nguyen Duc Nghinh, 'Markets and Villages', in Phan Huy Le *et al.* (eds), *The Traditional Village in Vietnam* (Hanoi: The Gioi Publishers, 1993), pp. 315–68.

Nguyen Duy Quy, 'On the Problem of Building a Juridical State in Our Country', *Vietnam Social Science* 3(10)(1993): 10–11.

———, 'The Question of Building a State of Law in Vietnam', *Vietnam Law and Legal Forum* 1(2)(1994): 32–33.

Nguyen Duy Trinh, 'Phat Trien Che Do Dan Chu Nhan Dan va Bao Dam Quyen Tu Do Dan Chu Cua Nhan Dan' (Developing the People's Democratic Regime and Ensuring People's Liberties and Democratic Rights), *Hoc Tap* (3)(1956): 23–32.

Nguyen Hong, 'Policies Given Modest Thumbs up at Forum', *Vietnam Investment Review* 27 May 2002: 4.

Nguyen Hung Quang, 'Provincial Case Study: Ha Tay', unpublished paper (Hanoi: UNDP Private Sector Study, 2003).

Nguyen Huu Dang, 'It is Necessary to Have a More Regularised Society', *Nhan Van* 5 November 1956. Trans. and reproduced in G. Boudarel, 'Intellectual Dissidence in the 1950s: The Nhan-Van Giai-Pham Affair', *Vietnam Forum*

13(1990): 154–66.

Nguyen Huu Tho, 'The Eighth National Assembly: Some Problems of Renovation', *Tap Chi Cong San* March 1987: 4–6. Trans. FBIS East Asia Daily Report, 18 May 1987, K/6–7.

———, 'Phan Dinh Chuc Nang Giua To Chuc Dang va Nha Nuoc-Dieu Kien Dau Tien Thuc Hien Phap Luat' (Assignment of Functions between Party Organisations and the State-the Pre-Conditions for Observance of Laws), *Tap Chi Cong San* (5)(1988): 7–9.

Nguyen Khac Vien, *Tradition and Revolution in Vietnam* (Berkeley: Indochina Resource Centre, 1974).

———, 'Confucianism and Marxism', *Vietnam Studies* (1)(1994): 45–55.

Nguyen Manh Cuong, 'Yeu Cau Cua Viec Xay Dung Nha Nuoc Phap Quyen Doi Voi Doi Moi To Chuc va Hoat Dong Cua Cac Co Quan Tu Phap' (How to Reform Judicial Authorities to Build up a Law-Based-State), *Tap Chi Nghien Cuu Lap Phap* (10)(2002): 30–35.

Nguyen Minh Hoan 'The Trend of Globalisation and Vietnam's Integration and Protection of National Interests', *Vietnam Social Sciences* (6)(1999): 88–91.

Nguyen Minh Tu, 'Integration of Vietnam's Economy into the Regional and World Economy at Present', *Vietnam Social Sciences* (6)(1999): 91–96.

Nguyen Ngoc Huy and Ta Van Tai, 'The Vietnamese Texts' in M.B. Hooker (ed.), *The Laws of Southeast Asia: The Pre-Modern Texts* (Singapore: Butterworths, 1986), pp. 435–94.

———, *The Le Code: Law in Traditional Vietnam* (Athens, Ohio: Ohio University Press, 1987).

Nguyen Ngoc Tuan, 'Renovating the Enterprise Model in Our Country', *Tap Chi Cong San* (12)(1993): 29–33.

Nguyen Nhu Phat, 'Conceptions on the Legal Status of Entrepreneurs in the Market Economy', *Nha Nuoc va Phap Luat* (2)(1993): 25–27.

———, 'Minh Bach Hoa Phap Luat va Yeu Cau Dat Ru Doi Voi He Thong Phap Luat Trong Qua Trinh Hoi Nhap Kinh Te Quoc Te' (Transparent Laws and their Requirement for the Legal System During International Economic Integration), *Nha Nuoc va Phap Luat* (4) (2005): 16–20.

———, Our Country's Economic Laws During the Transition to the Market Economy', *Nha Nuoc va Phap Luat* (2)(1993): 4–7.

———, 'The Role of Law During the Formation of a Market-Driven Mechanism in Vietnam' in J. Gillespie (ed.), *Commercial Legal Development in Vietnam: Vietnamese and Foreign Commentaries* (Singapore: Butterworths, 1997), 397–412.

Nguyen Nhu Phong and Vu Cao, 'Minh Phung Lam Giau va Sup Do The Noa' (Minh Phung – How did It Get Rich? How did It Collapse?), *Anh Ninh The Gioi* (World Security Magazine) 13 February 1998: 1–3.

Nguyen Nien, 'Several Legal Problems in the Leadership and Management of Industry Under the Conditions of the Present Improvement of Economic Management in Our Country', *Luat Hoc* (Jurisprudence) (14)(1976): 33–35. Trans. JPRS, 30

September 1976: 34–36.

———, 'Several Legal Matters Concerning Planning in Our Country' *Luat Hoc* (2)(1977): 22–28. Trans. JPRS 70119, (1977): 24–26.

Nguyen Phu Son, 'Bo Luat To Tung Dan Su Can The Hien Thin Than Cai Cach Tu Phap' (Civil Procedure Code Should Express the Spirit of Judicial Reform), *Tap Chi Nghien Cuu Lap Phap* (4)(2004): 24–31.

Nguyen Phu Trong, 'In Vietnam Does the Market Economy Require the Party's Leadership?', *Tap Chi Cong San* (1)(1994): 29–33.

Nguyen Phuong Quynh Trang, *Doing Business Under the New Enterprise Law: A Survey of Newly Registered Companies*, Private Sector Discussions 12 (Hanoi: Mekong Project Development Facility, 2001).

——— and Stromseth, J., *Business Associations in Vietnam: Status, Roles and Performance*, Private Sector Discussions 13 (Hanoi: Mekong Project Development Facility, 2002).

Nguyen Quang Minh, Nhan Dan Voi Viec Tham Gia Y Kien Xay Dung Phap Luat (People and their Participation in the Law Making Process), Paper presented to the Workshop on Perfecting the System to Facilitate People's Participation in Forming and Implementing Law, Hanoi, August 2002.

Nguyen Tan Dung, 'Building a Socialist-Oriented Independent and Sovereign Economy', *Quan Doi Nhan Dan* 13 September 2002: 3–5. Reprinted in *Vietnam Law and Legal Forum* 9(98): 18–20.

Nguyen The Anh, 'The Vietnamese Monarchy Under the French Colonial Rule 1884-1945', *Modern Asian Studies* 19(1)(1985): 147–62.

Nguyen The Phung, *Nguyen Tac Tap Trung Dan Chu: Dam Bao Thuc Hien Tot Nhiem Vu Cach Mang Truoc Mat* (The Principle of Democratic Centralism: A Justification for Implementing the Revolutionary Task Before Us) (Hanoi: Nha Xuat Ban Su That, 1960).

Nguyen Thi Doan and Do Minh Cuong, *Triet Ly Kinh Doanh: Voi Quan Ly Doanh Nghiep* (The Business Philosophy of the Management of Enterprises) (Hanoi: Nha Xuat Ban Chinh Tri Quoc Gia, 1999).

Nguyen Thi Khe, 'Cac Bien Phap Bao Dam Thuc Hien Hop Dong Kinh Te Trong Nen Kinh Te Thi Truong O Vietnam' (Measures to Ensure the Implementation of Economic Contracts in the Market Economy in Vietnam), *Nha Nuoc va Phap Luat* (9)(1996): 17–24.

Nguyen Thi Thu Ha, 'Weak Commercial Law Gets Extra Muscle', *Vietnam Investment Review*, 24 May 2004: np. Available at <www.asia.proquestrefercne.info/pqrasia>.

Nguyen Thua Hy, *Economic History of Hanoi in the 17th, 18th and 19th Centuries* (Hanoi: National Political Publishing House, 2002).

Nguyen Trinh Binh, 'It is Time to Amend the Law on Companies', *Saigon Giai Phong* 3 July 1995: 3.

Nguyen Van Cam, 'Business Beat', *Vietnam News* 2 February 2000: 2.

Nguyen Van Huyen, *The Ancient Civilization of Vietnam*, reprint edition (Hanoi: The

Gioi Publishers, 1995).

Nguyen Van Tai, 'On the State Ruled by Law and a Multipartisan Regime', *Vietnam Social Sciences* (1)(1996): 3, 7.

Nguyen Viet Huong, '*Quoc Trieu Hinh Luat* and the Personal and Property Relations in Feudal Families' *Vietnam Law and Legal Forum* 3(25)(1996): 22–25.

Nguyen Vinh, 'Building the System of Socialist Collective Ownership' *Tap Chi Cong San* (4)(1977): 55–56; trans. JPRS 69283, 20 June 1977: 28.

Nicholas, B., *An Introduction to Roman Law* (Oxford: Clarendon Press, 1962).

Nichols, P.M., 'The Viability of Transplanted Law: Kazakhstani Reception of a Transplanted Foreign Investment Code', *University of Pennsylvania Journal of International Economic Law* 18(4)(1997): 1235–80.

Nicholson, P., 'Borrowing Court Systems: The Experience of the Democratic Republic of Vietnam, 1945–1976', unpublished PhD Thesis (Melbourne: University of Melbourne, 2000).

———, and Nguyen Hung Quang, 'The Vietnamese Judiciary: The Politics of Appointment and Promotion', *Pacific Rim Law and Policy Journal* 14(1)(2005): 1–35.

Norland, I., Tran Ngoc and Nguyen Dinh Tuyen, *Dealing with Donors: The Politics of Vietnam's Comprehensive Poverty Reduction and Growth Strategy*, Policy Paper 4 (Helsinki: Institute of Development Studies, University of Helsinki, 2003).

North, D., *Institutions, Institutional Change and Economic Performance* (Cambridge: Cambridge University Press, 1990).

———, *The New Institutional Economics and Third World Development* (London: Routledge, 1995).

Office of Government, Study Report to Improve the Quality of Law and Ordinances Drafted by the Government to be Submitted to the NA and NA Standing Committee, unpublished report, Working Delegation No. 804 (Hanoi: Office of Government, 2003).

Office of National Assembly, Viec To Chuc Tap Hop, Tong Hop Y Kien, Viec Tiep Thu, Chinh Ly Du An Luat (On the Collection and Synthesis of Public Comments and Revisions of Draft Bills), unpublished paper presented at the Workshop on Perfecting the System to Facilitate People's Participation in Forming and Implementing Law, Hanoi, November 2002.

Oquendo, A.R., 'Deliberative Democracy in Habermas and Nino', *Oxford Journal of Legal Studies* 22(2)(2002): 189–226.

Osborne, M., *The French Presence in Cochin China and Cambodia: Rule and Response (1859-1905)* (Ithaca, New York: Cornell University Press, 1969).

Pachakop, 'Van De Xay Dung Bo Luat Dan Su O Lien Xo' (Drafting the Civil Code in the Soviet Union), *Tap San Tu Phap* (2)(1964): 20–24.

Parker, C., 'Compliance Professionalism and Regulatory Community: The Australian Trade Practices Regime', *Journal of Law and Society* 26(2)(1999): 215–39.

Party Central Committee, 'The Party on Further Development of Private Economy', *Vietnam Law and Legal Forum* 8(93)(2002): 20–27.

Paterson, J. and Teubner, G., 'Changing Maps: Empirical Legal Autopoiesis', *Social and Legal Studies* 7(1998): 451–86.

Pech, L., 'Rule of Law in France', in R. Peerenboom (ed.), *Asian Discourses of Rule of Law* (London: Routledge, 2004), 79–112.

Peerenboom, R., 'Confucian Harmony and Freedom of Thought' in W.T. de Barry and Tu Weiming (eds), *Confucianism and Human Rights* (New York: Columbia University Press, 1998), 234–60.

———, 'Globalization, Path Dependency and the Limits of Law: Administrative Law Reform and Rule of Law in the People's Republic of China', *Berkeley Journal of International Law* 19(2)(2001): 161–264.

———, *China's Long March Toward Rule of Law* (Cambridge: Cambridge University Press, 2002).

Pennington, K., 'The Spirit of Legal History', *University of Chicago Law Review* 64(3)(1997):1097–116.

Pennisi, C., 'Sociological Uses of the Concept of Legal Culture', in D. Nelken (ed.), *Comparing Legal Cultures* (Aldershot: Dartmouth, 1997), pp. 105–18.

Pham Diem, 'A Brief Look at the Rule by Feudal China (from 179 BC to the Xth Century)', *Vietnam Law and Legal Forum* 1(10)(1995): 28–29.

———, 'The State Structure in French-Ruled Vietnam (1858-1945)', *Vietnam Law and Legal Forum* 3(33)(1997): 25–27.

———, 'Criminal Offences Under Ancient Laws of Vietnam', *Vietnam Law and Legal Forum* 5(58)(1999): 27–29.

———, 'Vietnamese Court System Under the French', *Vietnam Law and Legal Forum* 5(54)(1999): 27–30.

———, 'Judiciary Offences under Vietnam's Ancient Laws' *Vietnam Law and Legal Forum* 7(82)(2001): 20–32.

———, 'Civil Law Making in Vietnam During the 1945-1995 Period', *Vietnam Law and Legal Forum* 11(122)(2004): 20–21.

Pham Duy Nghia, 'Hinh Su Hoa Cac Giao Dich Dan Su Kinh Te: Quan Niem Bieu Hien va Mot So Giai Phap Khac Phuc' (The Process of Criminalisation of Civil and Economic Transactions: Ideas, Manifestations and Some Solutions), *Tap Chi Nghien Cuu Lap Phap* (6)(2000): 30–36.

———, 'Mot So Anh Huong Truc Tiep Cua Qua Trinh Hoi Nhap Kinh Te Khu Vuc va The Gioi Doi Voi Phap Luat Viet Nam' (Some Direct Influences of the World's and Regional Economic Integration into Vietnamese Law), *Tap Chi Nghien cuu Lap Phap*(2)(2001): 2–7.

———, 'Tiep Nhan Phap Luat Nuoc Ngoai – Thoi Co va Thach Thuc Moi Cho Nghien Cu Lap Phap' (Transplantation of Foreign Law-Chances and Challenges for Legislative Studies in Vietnam) *Tap Chi Nghien cuu Lap Phap* (Legislative Studies) (5)(2002): 50–56.

———, 'Noi Doanh Nhan Tim Den Cong Ly' (Where do Entrepreneurs Go for Justice?), *Tap Chi Nghien Cuu Lap Phap* (3)(2003): 45–54.

———, 'Confucianism and the Conception of the Law in Vietnam' in J. Gillespie and P. Nicholson (eds), *Asian Socialisms and Legal Change: The Dynamics of*

Vietnamese and Chinese Reforms (Canberra: Asia Pacific Press, 2005): 76–88.

Pham Hong Hai, 'Vai Tro Cua Luat Su Trong Hoat Dong To Tung – Thuc Trang va Phuong Huong Doi Moi' (The Role of Lawyers in Procedures – A Look at Reality and Recommendations for Change), *Tap Chi Hghien Cuu Lap* (4)(2002): 110–16.

Pham Thanh Vinh, 'Tinh Chat Phap Lenh Trong Ke Hoach 5 Nam Lan Thu Nhat (1961–1965)' (Command Nature of the First Five Year Plan – 1961–1965), in *Nghien Cuu Nha Nuoc va Phap Quyen* (Studies about State and Legality) (Hanoi: Nha Xuat Ban Su Hoc, 1964), pp. 120–34.

———, 'The Obligatory Nature of Planning Targets', *Review of Contemporary Law* 12(1966): 89–97.

Pham Tuan Khai, 'Nang Cao Chat Luong Xay Dung Cac Du An Luat Phap Lenh Do Chinh Phu Soan Thao' (The Quality of Laws Drafted by Government Bodies), *Tap Chi Nghien Cuu Lap Phap* (3)(2004): 20–28.

Pham Van Bach, 'Le Nin Voi Van De Phap Che Xa Hoi Chu Nghia' (Lenin and Socialist Legality), *Tap San Tu Phap* (3)(1970): 9–16.

Pham Van Chuc, 'Dang Co Chang Mot Toan Cau Hoa Cho Moi Nguoi' (Is There Now a Globalisation for all People?), *Tap Chi Cong San* (12)(2002): 33–37.

Pham Van Dong, *May Van De Cot Yeu cua Chinh Quyen Dan Chu Nhan Dan Viet Nam*, (Some Crucial Aspects of the People's Democratic Regime in Viet Nam) (Hanoi: Ban Chap Hanh Trung Uong (Party Central Committee Publishing), 1952).

———, 'Ho Chi Minh: His Theory and Action', *Vietnam Social Sciences* (2)(1990): 3–11.

Pham Van Hung, 'Tu Tuong Ho Chi Minh Ve Viec To Chuc va Xay Dung Quoc Hoi Thuc Hien Quyen Luc Cua Nhan Dan' (Ho Chi Minh's thoughts on the National Assembly as an Institution to Perform People's Power), *Tap Chi Nghien Cuu Luat Phap* (4)(2001): 65–69.

Pham Xuan Nam, 'Some Preliminary Ideas on the Change of Social Structure and Classes in Viet Nam During the Transition to a Socialist-Oriented Market Economy', *Vietnam Social Sciences* 6(92)(2002): 31–42.

Phan Huu Chi, Explanation on the Civil Code Sixth Draft, unpublished paper (Hanoi: Ministry of Justice, 1994).

Phan Huy Le, 'The Vietnamese Traditional Village: Historical Evolution and Socio-Economic Structure', *Vietnam Social Sciences* (1)(1991): 39–43.

———, 'The Problem of Democracy in Vietnam's Traditions', *Vietnam Social Sciences* (4)(1994): 3–10.

Phan Van Khai, 'Pho Thu Tuong Phan Van Khai: Chinh Phu Thong Qua Phong Thuong Mai va Cong Nghiep Viet Nam De Cac Doanh Nghiep Hop Tac Voi Chinh Phu Nham Day Nhanh Tien Trinh Doi Moi' (Deputy Prime Minister Phan Van Khai: The Government Approves the Chamber of Commerce and Industry of Vietnam to Cooperate with the Government to Speed up the Process of Renovation), *Dien Dan Doanh Nghiep*, 4 April 1997: 2.

Phan Van Tan, 'Laws Should Predict New Economic Forms', *Kinh Doanh va Phap*

Luat (Law and Enterprises), 27 May 1998: 3.

Phung Long, 'The High Quality Vietnamese Product Club', *Vietnam Economic News* (29)(2004): 34–35.

Phung Minh, *40 Nam Quan Ly Nha Cua O Ha Noi* (40 Years of Housing Management in Hanoi), unpublished monograph (Hanoi: Self-published, 1998).

Phuong-Khanh T. Nguyen, 'The Criminal Code of the Socialist Republic of Vietnam', *Review of Socialist Law* 13(2)(1987): 103–20.

Pistor, K., Keinan, Y., Kleinheisterkamp, J. and West, M.D., 'The Evolution of Corporate Law: A Cross-Country Comparison', *University of Pennsylvania Journal of International Economic Law* 23(4)(2002): 791–872.

Pistor, K. and Wellons, P., *The Role of Law and Legal Institutions in Asian Economic Development 1960–1995* (Hong Kong: Oxford University Press, 1999).

Poggi, G., *The Development of the Modern State: A Sociological Introduction* (Stanford: Stanford University Press 1978).

Poivre, P., 'Journey to Cochinchina' in L. Tana and A. Reid (eds), *Southern Vietnam under the Nguyen*, Data Paper Series (Singapore: Institute of Southeast Asian Studies, 1993), pp. 60–97.

Political Bureau, 'Conclusions on Ideological Work', Hanoi Domestic Service, 8 December 1989. Trans. FBIS East Asia Daily Report, 9 December 1989: 63.

Posner, R., *The Economic Analysis of Law* (Boston: Little and Brown, 1986).

———, 'Creating a Legal Framework for Economic Development' *World Bank Research Observer* 13(1)(1998): 1–11.

Post, R., 'The Relatively Autonomous Discourse of Law', in R. Post (ed.), *Law and the Order of Culture* (Berkeley: University of California Press, 1991), pp. i–ix.

Potter, J. and Wetherell, M., *Discourse and Social Psychology: Beyond Attitudes and Behavior* (London: Sage Publications, 1987).

Potter, P., 'The Chinese Legal System: Continuing Commitment to the Primacy of State Power', *The China Quarterly* 159(1999): 673–83.

Poulantzas, N., *Political Power and Social Classes*, trans. T. O'Hagan (London: NLB Sheed and Ward, 1973).

Quan Xuan Dinh, 'The Political Economy of Vietnam's Transformation Process', *Contemporary Southeast Asia* 22(2)(2000): 360–88.

Quigley, J., 'Vietnam's Legal Regulation of Foreign Trade and Investment', *International Trade Law* 6(1980–81): 24–38.

Quy Hoa, 'Dung Lam Kho Doanh Nghiep: Nhin Lai Mot Nam Thi Hanh Luat' (Do Not Make it Difficult for Business: Reviewing a Year's Enforcement of the Enterprise Law), *Hoi Khoa Hoc Kinh Te Viet Nam* (43)(2001): 2.

Radetzki, M., 'From Communism to Capitalism in Laos: The Legal Dimension', *Asian Survey* 34(9)(1994): 799–806.

Ramseyer, M., 'Doctrine of Rents in Japan: A Comment on Professors Osaka and Nakamuru', *Law and Contemporary Problems* 53(2)(1990): 29–34.

Raz, J., *The Authority of Law: Essays in Law and Morality* (Oxford: Clarendon

Press, 1979).
———, *Ethics and the Public Domain* (Oxford: Clarendon Press, 1994).
Reid, A., *Southeast Asia in the Age of Commerce 1450–1680*, vol. II (Changmai: Silkworm Press, 1993).
Reuschemeyer, D. and Evens, P., 'The State and Economic Transformation', in P. Evens, D. Reuschemeyer and T. Evens (eds), *Bring the State Back In* (New York: Cambridge University Press, 1985), pp. 44–77.
Roberts, S.H., *The History of French Colonial Policy 1870-1925* (new impression 1963) (London: Frank Cass, 1929).
Ronnas, P., 'The Transformation of the Private Manufacturing Sector in Vietnam in the 1990s', unpublished paper (Stockholm: Stockholm Institute for Economics, University of Stockholm 1998).
Rorty, R., *Philosophy and the Mirror of Nature* (Princeton: Princeton University Press, 1979).
Rose, C., 'Propter Honoris Respectum: Property As the Keystone Right?', *Notre Dame Law Review* 71(3)(1996): 329–70.
———, 'The "New" Law and Development Movement in the Post-Cold War Era: A Vietnam Case Study', *Law and Society Review* 32(1)(1998): 93–140.
Ross, R.J., 'The Commoning of the Common Law: The Renaissance Debate over Printing English Law, 1520–1640', *University of Pennsylvania Law Review* 146(2)(1998): 323–462.
Rostow, W.W., *Stages of Economic Growth: A Non-Communist Manifesto* (New York: Cambridge University Press, 1990).
Rubin, E., 'Law and Legislation in the Administrative State', *Columbia Law Review* 89(3)(1989): 369–426.
Samuels, W.J., 'A Critique of Capitalism, Socialism and Democracy', in R.D. Coe and C.K. Wilber (eds), *Capitalism and Democracy: Schumpeter Revisited* (Chicago: University of Notre Dame Press, 1985).
Sarat, A., 'Support for the Legal System: An Analysis of Knowledge, Attitudes, and Behavior', *American Politics Quarterly* 3(1975): 5–15.
——— and Kearns, T.R., 'The Cultural Lives of Law', in A. Sarat and T.R. Kearns (eds), *Law in the Domains of Culture* (Ann Arbor: University of Michigan Press, 2001), pp. 1–20.
Sarogoratisk, 'Vai Tro va Quan He Giua Cuong Che va Thuyet Phuc Cua Phap Luat Trong Thoi Ky Xay Dung Chu Nghia Cong San Tren Quy Mo Rong Lon', (Roles and Relations between Enforcement and Legal Education in the Communist Period) *Tap San Tu Phap* (11)(1961): 41–57.
Schachter, O., 'The Decline of the Nation–State and its Implications for International Law', *Columbia Journal of Transnational Law*, 36(1)(1997): 7–24.
Scheuerman, W., *Between the Norm and the Exception: The Frankfurt School and the Rule of Law* (Cambridge: MIT Press, 1994), 96.
———, 'Globalisation and the Fate of Law', in D. Dyzenhaus (ed.), *Recrafting the Rule of Law* (Oxford: Hart Publishing, 1999), 243–66.
Schutz, A., *The Problem of Social Reality*, Collected Papers vol. II (The Hague:

Martinus Nijhoff, 1962).

———, *The Problem of Social Reality*, Collected Papers vol. I (The Hague: Martinus Nijhoff, 1973).

Selznick, P., 'Legal Cultures and the Rule of Law', in M. Krygier and A. Czarnota (eds), *The Rule of Law after Communism* (Aldershot: Ashgate Dartmouth, 1999), pp. 21–38.

Shapiro, M., 'Toward a Theory of *Stare Decisis*', *Journal of Legal Studies* 1(1972): 125–34.

Sharlet, R., *Soviet Constitutional Crisis from De Stalinistion to Disintegration* (New York: M.E. Sharpe, 1992).

Shetreet, S. and Deschenes, J., *Judicial Independence: The Contemporary Debate* (Boston: Martinus Nijhof, 1985).

Sidel, M., 'Law Reform in Vietnam: The Complex Transition from Socialism and Soviet Models in Legal Scholarship and Training', *UCLA Pacific Basin Law Journal* 11(2)(1993): 221–25.

———, 'The Re-emergence of China Studies in Vietnam', *The China Quarterly*, 142(1995): 521–40.

———, Some Preliminary Thoughts in Contending Approaches to Law in Vietnam, 1954–1975, unpublished paper, Association for Asian Studies, March 1997.

———, 'Analytical Models for Understanding Constitutions and Constitutional Dialogue in Socialist Transitional States: Re-Interpreting Constitutional Dialogue in Vietnam', *Singapore Journal of International and Comparative Law* 6(2002): 42–89.

Simon, H.A., *Administrative Behavior* (New York: Free Press, 1976).

Smith, R.B., 'The Cycle of Confucianization in Vietnam', in W.F. Vella (ed.), *Aspects of Vietnamese History* (Honolulu: University Press of Hawaii, 1973), pp. 6–24.

———, 'The Work of the Provisional Government of Vietnam', August-December 1945', *Modern Asian Studies* 12(4)(1978): 571–609.

———, The Matrifocal Family: Power, Pluralism, and Politics (New York: Routledge, 1995).

Song Thanh, 'President Ho Chi Minh Laid the Foundation for a Law-Governed State', *Vietnam Law and Legal Forum* 1(9)(1995): 3, 6.

Steart, J.H., *A Documentary Survey of the French Revolution* (New York: Free Press, 1951).

Steer, L., The Private Sector in Vietnam, unpublished paper (Hanoi: Centre of International Economics, 2000).

Stein, P., *Legal Evolution: The Story of an Idea* (Cambridge: Cambridge University Press, 1980).

Stern, L., 'The Political Report to the 8th Congress of the Vietnamese Communist Party: An Anatomy of the Writing Process', *Journal of Third World Studies* 16(1)(1999): 49–66.

Stiglitz, J., Whither Reform? Ten Years of the Transition, unpublished paper presented at the Annual World Bank Conference on Development Economics, Washington,

DC, 28–30 April 1999.

Stone, A., 'The Birth and Development of Abstract Review: Constitutional Courts and Policymaking in Western Europe', *Policy Studies Journal* 19(1)(1990): 81–95.

Stromseth, J., 'Reform and Response in Vietnam: State-Society Relations and the Changing Political Economy', unpublished PhD thesis (New York: Columbia University, 1998).

———, 'Business Associations and Policy-Making in Vietnam' in B.J.T. Kerkvliet, R. Heng and D. Koh (eds), *Getting Organized in Vietnam: Moving In and Around the Socialsit State* (Singapore: Institute of Southeast Asian Studies, 2003), pp. 62–109.

Sugarman, D., 'Law, Economy and The State in England, 1750–1914: Some Major Issues', in D. Sugarman (ed.), *Legality, Ideology and the State* (London: Academic Press, 1983), pp. 213–66.

Summers, R., 'A Formal Theory of Rule of Law', *Ratio Juris* 6(2)(1993): 127–42.

Sumner, C., *Reading Ideologies: An Investigation into the Marxist Theory of Ideology and Law* (London: Academic Press, 1979).

Sunstein, C., 'On the Expressive Function of Law', *University of Pennsylvania Law Review* 144(5)(1996): 2021–54.

Supreme Court, 'Bao Cao Cong Tac Nganh Toa An Nam 2000 va Phuong Huong Nhiem Vu Cong Tac Toa An Nam 2001', (Report on Court Sector in 2000 and Operational Direction in 2001), 9 February (Hanoi: Supreme Court of Vietnam, 2001).

Suzuki, H., Vietnam Private Promotion and Business Environment, unpublished paper (Hanoi: Vietnam Business Forum, 2002).

Ta Thu Khue, 'Can Than Trong Trong Viec Ap Dung Kinh Nghiem Lien-Xo Vao Trinh Tu Phuc Tham' (We Need to be Cautious in Applying Soviet Experience in Appellate Procures), *Tap San Tu Phap* (2)(1963): 12–14.

Ta Van Tai, 'Vietnam's Code of the Le Dynasty (1428-1788)', *American Journal of Comparative Law* 30(3)(1982): 523–54.

———, *The Vietnamese Tradition on Human Rights* (Berkeley: Institute of East Asian Studies, 1988).

———, 'The Rule of Law in the Traditional Law of Traditional China and Vietnam: Traditional East Asian Legal Practice in the Light of the Standards of the Modern Rule of Law', *Vietnamese Studies* (4)(2001): 128–35.

Tamanaha, B., 'An Analytical Map of Social Scientific Approaches to the Concept of Law', *Oxford Journal of Legal Studies* 15(3)(1995): 501–36.

———, 'The Lessons of Law-and-Development Studies', *American Journal of International Law* 89(1995): 470–86.

———, *Realistic Socio-Legal Theory* (Oxford: Clarendon Press, 1998).

———, 'A Non-Essentialist Version of Legal Pluralism', *Journal of Law and Society* 27(2)(2000): 296–321.

Tan Duc, 'Bo Dieu 164 Cho Doanh Nhan Yen Tam Lam An' (Revoke Article 164 to Make Businessman Feel Assured in Doing Their Business), *Thoi Bao Kinh Te Sai*

Gon (Saigon Economic Times), 20 May 1999: 10–11.

Tang Thi Thanh and Trai Le, 'The Foreign Investment Code of the Socialist Republic of Vietnam', *International Lawyer* 13(2)(1979): 329–43.

Taussig, M. and Pham Thi Thu Hang, 'Private Enterprise Formality and the Role of Local Government', unpublished paper (Hanoi: Asian Development Bank, 2004).

Taylor, K.W., 'Authority and Legitimacy in Eleventh-Century Vietnam', *Vietnam Forum* 12(1988): 20–59.

———, 'An Evaluation of the Chinese Period in Vietnamese History', *Journal of Asiatic Studies* 23(1)(1980): 131–49.

———, *The Birth of Vietnam* (Berkeley: University of California Press, 1983).

———, 'Preface' in K.W. Taylor and J.K. Whitmore (eds), *Essays Into Vietnamese Pasts* (Ithaca: Southeast Asia Program, Cornell University, 1995), pp. 1–14.

———, 'Surface Orientations in Vietnam: Beyond Histories of Nations and Regions', *Journal of Asian Studies* 57(4)(1998): 949–78.

Taylor, P., 'Apocalypse Now? Hoa Hao Buddhism Emerging from the Shadows of War', *Australian Journal of Anthropology* 12(3)(2001): 339–54.

———, *Goddess on the Rise: Pilgrimage and Popular Religion in Vietnam* (Honolulu: University of Hawaii Press, 2004).

Taylor, V.L., 'Continuing Transactions and Persistent Myths: Contracts in Contemporary Japan', *Melbourne University Law Review* 19(2)(1993): 352–98.

Taysheng Wang, 'Taiwan', in Pho-Ling Tan (ed.), *Asian Legal Systems* (Sydney: Butterworths, 1997), pp. 124–61.

Tenev, S. Carlieer, A., Chaudry O., Nguyen, Quynh-Trang, *Informality and the Playing Field in Vietnam's Business Sector* (Washington, DC: IFC, 2003).

Teubner, G., *Autopoietic Law: A New Approach to Law and Society* (Berlin and New York: W. de Gruyter, 1988).

———, 'How the Law Thinks: Towards a Constructivist Epistemology of Law', *Law and Society Review* 23(5)(1989): 727–58.

———, 'The Two Faces of Janus: Rethinking Legal Pluralism', *Cardozo Law Review* 13(5)(1992): 1443–62.

———, *Law as an Autopoietic System* (Oxford: Blackwell, 1993).

———, '"Global Bukowina": Legal Pluralism in the World Society' in G. Teubner (ed.), *Global Law Without States* (Aldershot: Dartmouth, 1997), 3–38.

———, 'Legal Irritants: Good Faith in British Law or How Unifying Law Ends up in New Divergences', *Modern Law Review* 61(1)(1998): 11–32.

———, 'Alienating Justice: On the Surplus Value of the Twelfth Camel', in J. Pribán and D. Nelken (eds), *Law's New Boundaries: The Consequences of Legal Autopoiesis* (Dartmouth: Ashgate, 2001), pp. 21–44.

Thanh Duy, 1997, 'Co So Khoa Hoc va Van Hoa Trong Tu Tuong Ho Chi Minh Ve Nha Nuoc va Phap Luat' (Scientific and Cultural Basis of Ho Chi Minh's Ideas of State and Law), *Tap Chi Cong San* (1) 26, 27–28.

Thayer, C.A., 'Mono-Organizational Socialism and the State', in B.J.T. Kerkvliet and D.J. Porter (eds), *Vietnam's Rural Transformation* (Boulder: Westview Press,

1995), pp. 39–64.

Theo Duong Day Nong, 'Day Dut Lon Tu Vu An Nho' (Deep Concern Over a Small Case), *Dau Tu* 18 September 2001: 6.

Therborn, G., *The Ideology of Power and the Power of Ideology* (London: New Left Books, 1980).

Tingmei Fu, 'Legal Person in China: Essence and Limits', *American Journal of Comparative Law* 41(2)(1993) 261–98.

Toa An Nhan Dan Toi Cao, *Bao Cao Tong Ket Cong Tac Nganh Toa An Nam 2001 va Phuong Huong Nhiem Vu Cong Tac Toa An Nam 2001* (Report on 2000 and the Plan for 2001 Supreme People's Court) (Hanoi: Supreme People's Court of Vietnam, 2000).

———, *Giai Dap Mot So Van De Ve Hinh Su, Dan Su, Kinh Te, Lao Dong, Hanh Chinh va To Tung* (Annual Report on Criminal, Civil, Economic, Labour, Administrative and Procedural Laws) (Hanoi: Supreme People's Court, 2000).

———, *Bao Cao Tong Ket Cong Tac Nganh Toa An Nam 2001 va Phuong Huong Nhiem Vu Cong Tac Toa An Nam 2005* (Report on 2004 and the Plan for 2005 Supreme People's Court) (Hanoi: Supreme People's Court 2004).

Tomasic, R. and Jian Fu, 'Company Law in China', in R. Tomasic (ed.), *Company Law in East Asia* (Aldershot: Dartmouth 1999), pp. 135–81.

Tran Dai Hung, 'Improving Party Leadership over Judicial Work', *Vietnam Law and Legal Forum* 11(126)(2005): 2–5, 20.

Tran Dinh Huynh, 'Moi Quan He Giua Tri Luc—Dao Duc—Phap Luat Trong Quan Ly Dat Nuoc Cua Chu Tich Ho Chi Minh' (Relationship between Intelligence—Morality-Law in Ho Chi Minh Thoughts on Administration), *To Chuc Nha Nuoc* (5)(1999): 3–5.

Tran Hieu, *25 Nam Xay Dung Nen Phap Che Viet Nam* (25 Years of Building Vietnamese Legality), (Hanoi: Nha Xuat Ban Lao Dong, 1971), p. 108.

Tran Huu Hiep, 'Thuat Ngu Phap Ly Trong Cac Van Ban Phap Luat Kinh Te' (Legal Terminology in Economic Legal Instruments), *Tap Chi Toa An Nhan Dan* (2)(1996): 7–11.

Tran Huu Huynh, Roles Played by the Chamber of Commerce and Industry of Vietnam on the Participation in the Formulation and Implementation of the Legal Normative Documents on the Economy, unpublished paper, Workshop on Amending, Supplementing the 1996 Law on the Promulgation of Legal Normative Documents, 22–24 August (Hanoi: Ministry of Justice, 2002).

Tran Ngoc Duong, 'Noi Dung va Phuong Thuc Lanh Dao Cua Dang Doi Voi Quoc Hoi O Nuoc Ta Hien Nay' (Leadership of the Communist Party Over the National Assembly in Vietnam – Content and Method), *Tap Chi Nghien Cuu Lap Phap* (2)(2005): 17–23.

Tran Quang Huy, *Giao Trinh Luat Dat Dai* (Land Law Text Book) (Hanoi: Nha Xuat Ban Cong An Nhan Dan, 2001).

Tran Thi Thu Trang, 'Local Politics and Democracy in a Muong Ethnic Community', in B.J.T. Kerkvliet and D. Marr (eds), *Beyond Hanoi: Local Government in*

Vietnam (Singapore: Institute of Southeast Asian Studies, 2004), pp. 137–66.

Tran Thi Tuyet, 'The State and the Law of the Tran Dynasty', *Vietnam Law and Legal Forum* 2(18)(1996): 28–29.

———, 'The Nguyen Dynasty and its Legislation in the First Half of the 19th Century', *Vietnam Law and Legal Forum* 3(32)(1997): 24–25.

———, 'The Young State Prepares for the Anti-French Colonialist War of Resistance (1946–1954)', *Vietnam Law and Legal Forum* 4(38)(1997): 25–26.

———, 'Vietnam's Feudal Laws and the Protection of Women's Interests', *Vietnam Law and Legal Forum* 6(65)(2000): 28–30

Tran Thu Hang, 'Vietnam's Trade in the Course of International Integration', *Vietnamese Studies* (2)(1999): 111–23.

Tran Tu Binh, *The Red Earth: A Vietnamese Memoir of Life on a Colonial Rubber Plantation*, trans. and ed. J. Spragens and D.G. Marr (Athens, Ohio: Ohio University Press 1985).

Tran Van Su, 'Nhung Vuong Mac Trong Che Do Hop Dong Kinh Te Hien Hanh' (Problems in the Current Economic Contract Regime), *Kien Nghi Ve Xay Dung Phap Luat Hop Dong Kinh Te Tai Viet Nam* (Recommendations in Building up the Economic Contract Legislation in Vietnam), VIE/95/017 (Hanoi: Ministry of Justice-UNDP, 2000).

Trubek, D.M., 'Max Weber on Law and the Rise of Capitalism', *Wisconsin Law Review* 3(1972): 720–53.

———, 'Toward a Social Theory of Law: An Essay on the Study of Law and Development', *Yale Law Journal* 82(1)(1972): 1–50.

———, 'Reconstructing Max Weber's Sociology of Law', *Stanford Law Review* 37(3)(1985): 919–36.

——— and Galanter, M., 'Scholars in Self-Estrangement: Some Reflections on the Crisis in Law and Development Studies in the United States', *Wisconsin Law Review* (4)(1974): 1062–1103.

Trubek, D., Dezalay, Y., Buchanan, R. and Davis, J., *Global Restructuring and the Law: The Internationalisation of Legal Fields and the Creation of Transnational Arenas*, Working Paper on the Political Economy of Legal Change No. 1 (Madison: University of Wisconsin, Madison, 1993).

Truong Chinh, 'Marxism and Vietnamese Culture' report delivered at the Second National Cultural Conference, July 1948, reproduced in *Truong Chinh Selected Writings* (Hanoi: The Gioi Publishers, 1994), pp. 203–78.

———, *Thuc Hien Cai Cach Ruong Dat* (Report to First Party Congress), (Hanoi: Dang Lao Dong Viet Nam Xuat Ban (Vietnam Workers Party Publishers), Hanoi 1954).

———, 'Forward Along the Path Charted by Karl Marx', in *Truong Chinh Selected Writings* (Hanoi: The Gioi Publishers, 1994), 527–640.

———, 'Introduction to the Political Report', *Vietnam News Agency* 15 December 1986: Part 4.

Truong Thanh Duc, 'Nhung Bat Cap Trong Viec Xay Dung va Ban Hanh Van Ban Quy Pham Phap Luat' (Defects in Building and Promulgating Legal Instruments),

Nha Nuoc va Phap Luat (2)(1999): 22–29.

Tshuma, L., 'The Political Economy of the World Bank's Legal Framework for Economic Development', *Social and Legal Studies* 8(1)(1999): 75–96.

Tu Giang, 'The Nation's Corporate Spirit' *Vietnam Investment Review* 12 September 2003. Available online at <www.vietnam.investmentreview.com.vn>.

Tu Tuan Anh, *Vietnam's Economic Reform: Results and Problems* (Hanoi: Social Science Publishing House, 1994).

Turner, R.F., *Vietnamese Communism: Its Origins and Development* (Stanford: Hoover Institution Press, Stanford University, 1975).

Twining, W., *Globalisation and Legal Theory* (London: Butterworths, 2000).

United Nations Development Programme, *Completion of Viet Nam's Legal Framework for Economic Development*, UNDP Discussion Paper No. 2 (Hanoi: United Nations Development Programme, 1999).

———, 'Legal System Development, Past Ongoing, and Planned Donor Programmes', unpublished paper (Hanoi: United Nations Development Programme, 2002). Available online at <www.undp.org.vn/themes/governance/matrix.html>.

———, 'Access to Justice: Survey from the People's Perspective', unpublished paper (Hanoi: United Nations Development Programme, Hanoi 2004).

Ungar, E., 'From Myth to History: Imagined Polities in 14th Century Vietnam', in D. Marr and A.C. Milner (eds), *Southeast Asia in the 9th and 14th Centuries* (Singapore: Institute of Southeast Asian Studies, 1986), pp. 177–86.

Unger, R., *Law in Modern Society* (New York: Free Press, 1976).

Van Arkadie, B. and Mallon, R., *Viet Nam: A Transition Tiger?* (Canberra: Asia Pacific Press, 2003).

van Dijk, T.A., 'The Study of Discourse' in T.A. van Dijk (ed.), *Discourse as Structure and Process* (Thousand Oaks, California: Sage Publications 1997), pp. 1–20.

Van Hoecke, M. and Warrington, M., 'Legal Cultures, Legal Paradigms and Legal Doctrine: Towards a New Model for Comparative Law', *International and Comparative Law Quarterly* 47(3)(1998): 495–536.

Vasavakul, T., 'Vietnam: The Changing Models of Legitimization', in M. Alagappa (ed.), *Political Legitimacy in Southeast Asia: The Quest for Moral Economy* (Stanford: Stanford University Press, 1995), pp. 257–89.

———, 'Reform of State Institutions in the Post-Socialist Era', in Suiwah Leung (ed.), *Vietnam Assessment: Creating a Sound Investment Climate* (Singapore: Institute of Southeast Asian Eastern Studies, 1996), pp. 42–68.

VCCI, 'Strengthening the Organization and Activities of the Chamber of Commerce', unpublished paper 11 (Hanoi: VCCI, 1993).

Vien Nghien Cuu Quan Ly Kinh Te Trung Uong (Central Institute of Economic Management (CIEM)), *Danh Gia Tong Ket: Luat Cong Ty va Kien Nghi Nhung Dinh Huong Sua Doi Chu Yeu* (Review of the Current Company Law and Key Recommendations for Its Revision), (Hanoi: CIEM, 1998).

Viet Xuan, 'Market Economy: Which Orientation?', *Vietnam Social Sciences*

(4)(1998): 15–29.

Vo Chi Cong, 'Thay Gi Ve Cong Tac To Chuc va Quan Ly Can Bo Qua Vu An Truong Van Cam' (What Can be Seen About Organising and Managing Cadres Through the Truong Van Cam Affair?), *Tap Chi Cong San* (9)(2002). Available online at <www.tapchicongsan.org.vn>.

Vo Dai Luoc, *Vietnam's Industralisation and Modernisation and Resources* (Hanoi: Social Sciences Publishing House, 1996).

Vo Khanh Vinh, Ve Cac Dac Diem va Dieu Kien Cua Su Hinh Thanh Nha Nuoc Phap Quyen O Viet Nam (The Characteristics and Conditions for the Establishment of a Law-Based State in Vietnam), unpublished paper presented at the 'Rule of Law and its Acceptance in Vietnam' Conference, Hanoi, 11 September 2000.

Vo Tri and Vo Vi, 'Ve Bai Dan Chu va Viec Thuc Hien Quyen Dan Chu' (Democracy and Improving Democratic Rights), *Tap Chi Nghien Cuu Luat Phap* (3)(2003): 21–24.

Vo Van Kiet, 'Report to the National Assembly on the 1987 Socio-Economic Development Plan', Hanoi Domestic Service, 26 December 1986. Trans. FBIS Asia and Pacific Daily Report, 30 December: 9.

———, 'A Look Back at the Guidance and Operation of the Government', *Vietnam Social Sciences* (5)(1997): 3–6.

Vu Khac Trai, 'Legislative Framework for Intellectual Property Rights in Vietnam' in M. Blakeney and P. Sinden (eds), *Proceedings of the National Symposium on the Role of Intellectual Property Rights in International Trade and Business* (Hanoi: Asia Pacific Intellectual Property Law Institute, 1996), pp. 23–37.

Vu Mao, 'The Civil Code – A Great Achievement in the 5-Year History of Legislation of the National Assembly of Vietnam', *Vietnam Law and Legal Forum* 2(17)(1996): 17–22.

Vu Ngoc Nhung, 'Role of the State in Market Economy with Socialist Orientation', *Vietnam Social Sciences* (6)(1999): 19–23.

Vu Oanh, 'Phong Thuong Mai da Tro Thanh Mot To Chuc Tin Cay de Tap Hop, Van Dong, Giup Do Ho Tro va Bao Ve Loi Ich cac Doanh Nghiep Trong Su Nghiep Kinh Doanh: Bai Phat Bieu cua Dong Chi Vu Oanh Uy Vien Bo Chinh Tri Ban Chap Hanh Trung Uong Dang Cong San Viet Nam tai Hoi Nghi Hoi Dong Quan Tri Phong Thuong Mai va Cong Nghiep Viet Nam Lan Thu VI' (The Chamber of Commerce has Become a Reliable Organisiation for Gathering, Mobilising, Assisting and Protecting the Interests of Enterprises in Business Affairs: Speech by Vu Oanh, Meeting of the Politburo of the Communist Party of Vietnam at the Sixth Meeting of the Executive Committee of the Chamber of Commerce and Industry of Vietnam), *Dien Dan Doanh Nghiep*, 22 September 1995: 7–15.

Vu Quoc Huy, 'Trade Liberalisation and Poverty in Vietnam', *Vietnam's Socio-Economic Development* (29)(2002): 37–49.

Vu Son Thuy, 'Interview With Politburo Standing Board Member Nguyen Tan Dung, Head of the CPV Central Committee Economic Department: New Year Discussion on Economic Issues', *Hanoi Tuan Quoc Te* 16 February 1997: 1–2.

Vu Tuan Anh (ed.), *The Role of the State in Economic Development: Experiences of the Asian Countries* (Hanoi: Social Sciences Publishing House, 1994).

Vu Van Vinh, 'Development of Confucianism in the Tran Dynasty and the Struggle of Confucian Scholars against Buddhism at the End of the XIV Century', *Vietnam Social Science* (2)(1999): 55–60.

Walker, G., *The Rule of Law* (Melbourne: Melbourne University Press, 1988).

Walzer, M., 'The Civil Society Argument', in C. Mouffe (ed.), *Dimensions of Radical Democracy: Pluralism, Citizenship, Community* (London: Verso, 1992), pp. 89–107.

Watson, A., *The Law of the Ancient Romans* (Dallas: Southern Methodist University Press, 1970).

———, 'Comparative Law and Legal Change', *Cambridge Law Journal*, 37(2)(1978): 313–36.

———, *The Evolution of Law* (Baltimore: John Hopkins University Press, 1985).

———, *Legal Transplants: An Approach to Comparative Law*, 2nd edn (Athens, Georgia: University of Georgia Press, 1993).

———, 'Aspects of the Reception of Law' *American Journal of Comparative Law* 44(2)(1996): 335–352.

Weber, M., *Economy and Society* (New York: Bedminster Press, 1968).

———, *Economy and Society*, ed. G. Roth and R. Wittich (Berkeley: University of California Press, 1978).

Webster, L., *SMEs in Vietnam: On the Road to Prosperity*, MPDF Private Sector Discussions No. 10 (Hanoi: Mekong Project Development Facility, 1999).

Weggel, O., 'The Vietnamese Communist Party and Its Status Under Law', in D. Loeber (ed.), *Ruling Communist Parties and their Status Under Law* (The Hague: Martinus Nijhoff, 1986), pp. 401–19.

Wetherell, M., 'Introduction', in M. Wetherell, S. Taylor and S. Yates (eds), *Discourse Theory and Practice: A Reader* (London: Sage, 2001), pp. 1–8.

Whitmore, J.K., 'Note: The Vietnamese Confucian Scholar's View of His County's Early History', in J.K. Whitmore and K. Hall (eds), *Explorations of Early Southeast Asian History*, vol. 1 (Ithaca: Cornell University Press, 1972), pp. 193–223.

———, 'Chiao-chih and Neo-Confucianism', *Ming Studies* 4(1977): 51–91.

———, 'Social Organization and Confucian Thought in Vietnam', *Journal of Southeast Asian Studies* 15(1984): 296–306.

———, 'Foreign Influences and the Vietnamese Cultural Core: A Discussion of the Pre-modern Period', in Truong Buu Lam (ed.), *Borrowings and Adaptations in Vietnamese Culture*, Southeast Asia Paper No. 25 (Honolulu: Center for Asian and Pacific Studies, University of Hawaii, 1987), pp. 1–21.

———, 'Chung-hsing and Cheng-t'-ung in Texts of and on Sixteenth-Century Viet Nam', in K.W. Taylor and J.K. Whitmore (eds), *Essays Into Vietnamese Pasts*, Studies on Southeast Asia No. 19 (Ithaca: Cornell University Press, 1995), pp. 116–36.

Williams, H., 'Property Reform and Legitimacy', *Journal of Contemporary Asia* 28(2)(1998): 159–74.

Williamson, O., *The Economic Institutions of Capitalism: Firms, Markets, Relational*

Contracting (New York: Free Press, 1985).

Wolters, O., 'Assertions of Cultural Well-being in Vietnam', *Journal of Southeast Asian Studies* 10(1979): 435–50.

Woodside, A., *A Comparative Study of Nguyen and Ch'ing Civil Government in the First Half of the Nineteenth Century* (Cambridge, Massachusetts: Harvard University Press, 1971).

———, *Vietnam and the Chinese Model* (Cambridge, Massachusetts: Harvard University Press, 1971).

———, 'Exalting the Latecomer State', in A. Chan, B. Kerkvliet and J. Unger (eds), *Transforming Asian Socialism: China and Vietnam Compared* (Sydney: Allen and Unwin, 1999), pp. 15–42.

World Bank, *Entering the 21st Century: World Development Report 1999/2000* (New York: Oxford University Press, 1999).

———, *World Development Indicators* (Washington, DC: World Bank, 2005). Available online at <www.devdata.worldbank.org/wdi2005/Table5 3.htm>.

Young, S., 'Unpopular Socialism in United Vietnam', *Orbis* 22(2)(1977): 227–28.

———, 'Vietnamese Marxism: Transition in Elite Ideology', *Asian Survey*, 19(8)(1979): 770–79.

Index

www.ingramcontent.com/pod-product-compliance
Ingram Content Group UK Ltd.
Pitfield, Milton Keynes, MK11 3LW, UK
UKHW022008180926
475701UK00003B/264
* 9 7 8 0 3 6 7 6 0 3 8 9 2 *